HOLT

Biology

Interactive Reader

HOLT, RINEHART AND WINSTON
A Harcourt Education Company
Orlando • Austin • New York • San Diego • London

Printed in the United States of America

ISBN-13: 978-0-03-096006-2

12 13 14 15 0304 18 17 16 15
4500569674

Contents

UNIT 1: INTRODUCTION

UNIT 2: ECOLOGY

UNIT 3: CELLS

UNIT 4: HEREDITY

Name ______________________ Class ______________ Date ______________

CHAPTER 1 Biology and You

SECTION 1

The Nature of Science

KEY IDEAS

As you read this section, keep these questions in mind:
- What does it mean to practice scientific thought?
- What are universal laws in science?
- How do ethics apply to science?
- Why should someone who is not planning to become a scientist study science?

What Is Scientific Thought?

The goal of science is to help us understand the natural world and make people's lives better. Thinking like a scientist can help you solve problems and think critically about your world.

Scientists carefully examine, or *observe*, the natural world. Then, they ask questions about what they observe. Often, the questions that they ask lead to even more questions. This process of making observations and asking questions is the basis of scientific thought.

Scientific thought also requires **skepticism**—a questioning and often doubtful attitude. Scientists question everything. They require evidence, not opinions, to support ideas. As scientists challenge old claims and make new discoveries, they change the way that people view the world. ☑

In summary, scientific thought involves:
- making observations
- being skeptical about ideas
- using evidence to draw conclusions
- being open to change when new discoveries are made

READING TOOLBOX

Apply Concepts After you read this section, think about how you can apply scientific thought to the decisions you make in your everyday life. List five of your ideas in your notebook.

1. Describe What do scientists use to support ideas?

____

What Are Universal Laws?

Certain truths are valid everywhere in the universe. These truths are called *universal laws*. Universal laws apply to all branches of science and to every person. For example, all objects in the universe are affected by gravity. Whether scientists are studying birds, stars, or landscapes, they must all understand the law of gravity. Other universal laws include the law of conservation of energy and the law of planetary motion.

Talk About It

Identify In a small group, try to identify some other universal scientific laws. Discuss how each law may affect scientists studying many different subjects.

Why Are Ethics Important in Science?

Science has many important effects on our everyday lives. For example, health scientists work to develop medicines, vaccines, and surgery methods. Agricultural scientists produce fertilizers and pesticides for our food crops. Scientists also work to provide people with better electrical power, computers, and automobiles. Because people depend so heavily on science, it is important for scientists to practice ethical behavior. ☑

2. Explain Why is it important for scientists to behave ethically?

Ethics are a system of moral principles and values. Scientists must behave ethically when they carry out investigations. This means they must allow other scientists to review their work. They must also report only correct and accurate data. All scientists depend upon the work of other scientists. If one scientist reports false data, other scientists may waste resources conducting investigations based on that unethical and incorrect work. ☑

3. Identify Relationships If one scientist reports false data, what may happen to other scientists?

Scientists must also obey laws and behave ethically when people or other organisms are involved in scientific investigations. For example, scientists may test new medications on people. A scientist carrying out such a study must follow ethical rules, such as those given below.

- The scientist must get a person's permission before involving the person in an investigation.
- The scientist must tell the person about all the risks of being involved in the investigation.
- The scientist must not try to force the person to participate in the investigation if the person does not want to. ☑

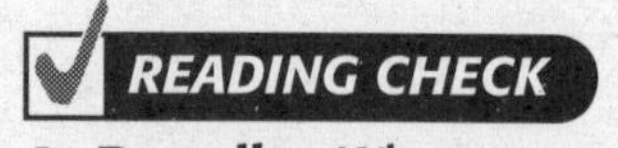

4. Describe What must an ethical scientist do before involving a person in a scientific investigation?

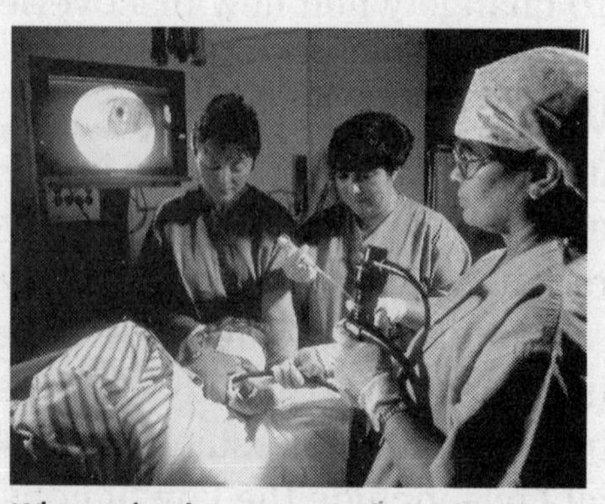

When scientists carry out investigations, they must behave ethically.

Why Study Science?

Scientific thinking is not just for people who make a living working as scientists. You can use the same critical-thinking process that scientists use as a tool in your everyday life.

An understanding of science can help you take better care of your health. For example, suppose you read an advertisement for a pill. The advertisement states that the pill can make you grow taller. Should you take the pill?

To think scientifically, you should be skeptical of the claim in the advertisement. You should learn more about the ingredients in the pill. You may learn that some of the ingredients in the pill can be harmful. By thinking scientifically, you can reduce the chances that you will take a pill that could make you sick.

Scientific thinking can help you decide whether the claims of a product are accurate.

LOOKING CLOSER

5. Identify The student in the figure wants to decide whether or not to use the product in the bottle. What are two questions he could ask to help decide?

____

____

____

Thinking like a scientist can also help you make good decisions about how to spend your money. For example, suppose you are looking for an acne medication. One type claims to be more effective than another, less expensive type. Before buying the more expensive medication, you should look for evidence that it is more effective than the less expensive type. By learning more about each product, you can decide which one will be best for you to purchase.

You can also use scientific thinking to improve the world around you. You may see a problem in your town, such as dangerous crosswalks or litter being left in parks. You can investigate these problems with skepticism and creativity to discover helpful solutions. By applying scientific thinking to these problems, you can help your whole community.

Critical Thinking

6. Infer It is especially important to be skeptical of claims made by people who are trying to sell you something. What do you think is the reason for this?

____

____

____

____

____

____

Name ______________ Class ______________ Date ______________

Section 1 Review

SECTION VOCABULARY

skepticism a habit of mind in which a person questions the validity of accepted ideas	

1. Explain Why is skepticism important in science?

2. List Describe four ways to practice scientific thought.

3. Define What is a universal law?

4. List Identify two universal laws.

5. Identify Give three examples of ethical scientific behavior.

6. Apply Concepts Think about some decisions you make every day. Give two examples of how you can use scientific thought to help you make good decisions.

Name ______________________ Class ____________ Date ____________

CHAPTER 1 | Biology and You

SECTION 2

Scientific Methods

KEY IDEAS

As you read this section, keep these questions in mind:

- How do scientists know how to begin an investigation?
- What are two types of experiments that scientists can use to test hypotheses?
- What is the difference between a theory and a hypothesis?

How Do Scientific Investigations Begin?

Most scientific investigations begin with observations that lead to questions. **Observation** is the act of studying objects or events using your senses. Tools, such as microscopes, can also help you make observations. Many observations lead to questions. Scientists formulate hypotheses to answer these questions. A **hypothesis** is a possible explanation that can be tested. ☑

READING TOOLBOX

Compare After you read this section, make a table comparing how the words *hypothesis* and *theory* are used in science and in everyday speech.

1. Define What is a hypothesis?

____

____

____

What Is a Scientific Experiment?

An **experiment** is a set of planned steps used to test a hypothesis. Scientists conduct controlled experiments or perform studies in order to test a hypothesis.

A controlled experiment tests one factor at a time and uses a control group and an experimental group. A control group gets no experimental treatment. Experimental groups are the same as the control group except for one factor, called the *independent variable.* Factors that may change because of the independent variable are called *dependent variables.* Scientists study changes to the dependent variables to understand how the independent variable affects the system.

There are often cases in which experiments are not possible or not ethical. In these cases, researchers perform a study. They gather information from many sources and look for trends in the data. Researchers try to limit the number of variables that may affect their data.

CONTROL AND EXPERIMENTAL GROUPS

Many scientific experiments use control groups and experimental groups. A **control group** is a group in an experiment that receives no experimental treatment. ☑

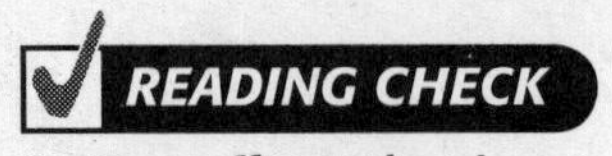

2. Describe What is a control group?

____

____

____

Scientists try to make everything about the control and experimental groups the same except for one factor, or *variable*. This variable, which scientists change during the experiment, is called the *independent variable*. Variables that change as a result of changes in the independent variable are called *dependent variables*. In many experiments, scientists try to learn how changes in the independent variable affect the dependent variables.

What Is a Scientific Theory?

In everyday speech, people often use the word *theory* to mean "a guess." However, in science, a theory is much more than just a guess. A scientific **theory** is a generally accepted explanation for a large amount of data and observations. The quantum theory, the cell theory, and the theory of evolution are examples of scientific theories. ☑

3. Identify Give two examples of scientific theories.

____

____

The figure below shows how questions, hypotheses, experiments, and observations can lead to the formation of a scientific theory.

Questions → Predictions and hypotheses → Experimentation and observation → Hypotheses are supported. / Hypotheses are rejected. → Many other experiments support the hypotheses. → Theory

Scientists make predictions and hypotheses, which are possible answers to questions.

Scientists test their predictions and hypotheses using experiments and observations.

Scientists share the results of their experiments with other scientists. The results may support or disprove a particular hypothesis or prediction.

Scientists continue to test hypotheses. If many different experiments support a hypothesis, more scientists accept the hypothesis as a correct explanation.

When many different experiments and observations support a hypothesis or set of hypotheses, scientists may accept it as a theory. If new data are discovered that conflict with the theory, scientists may revise or replace the theory.

LOOKING CLOSER

4. Explain What can happen if new data conflict with an accepted theory?

____

____

Name ______________________ Class ______________ Date ______________

Section 2 Review

SECTION VOCABULARY

control group in an experiment, a group that serves as a standard of comparison with another group to which the control group is identical except for one factor

experiment a procedure that is carried out under controlled conditions to discover, demonstrate, or test a fact, theory, or general truth

hypothesis a testable idea or explanation that leads to scientific investigation

observation the process of obtaining information by using the senses; the information obtained by using the senses

theory a system of ideas that explains many related observations and is supported by a large body of evidence acquired through scientific investigation

1. Describe How do most scientific investigations begin?

____

____

2. Compare What is the difference between a dependent variable and an independent variable?

____

____

____

3. Explain How is a theory different from a hypothesis?

____

____

____

Name ______________________ Class ______________ Date ____________

CHAPTER 1 Biology and You

SECTION 3

Tools and Techniques

KEY IDEAS

As you read this section, keep these questions in mind:
- Why do scientist use the SI sytem of measurement?
- What are some tools and techniques that scientists use in the laboratory?
- What can you do to stay safe during an investigation?

Compare After you read about the SI system of measurement, make a table comparing the English and SI units for everyday measurements such as your height, weight, and distance from your home to school.

What Is SI?

Scientists from all around the world share data. However, different units of measurement are commonly used in different countries. Therefore, scientists use a common measurement system called the International System of Units (**SI**). By using SI units, scientists can easily understand and test the results of other scientists.

Scientists also use SI because each SI unit can be organized into smaller or larger units based on powers of 10. This makes it easy for scientists to convert between large and small measurements.

Most SI units have a prefix that indicates the relationship between the unit and a base unit. For example, the base unit for length is the meter. The prefix *kilo-* means 1,000. Therefore, a kilometer is equal to 1,000 meters. The table below shows common SI base units and prefixes. ☑

READING CHECK

1. Describe What does a prefix in an SI unit indicate?

____

____

____

Math Skills

2. Convert How many liters equal 2,450 mL?

____

Common SI units

Prefix	none	*kilo-*	*centi-*	*milli-*
Factor	1 (base unit)	1,000	0.01	0.001
Units used to describe volume	1 liter (L)	1 kiloliter (kL) = 1,000 L	1 centiliter (cL)= 0.01L	1 milliliter (mL) = 0.001 L
Units used to describe length	1 meter (m)	1 kilometer (km) = 1,000 m	1 centimeter (cm) = 0.01 m	1 millimeter (mm) = 0.001 m
Units used to describe mass	1 gram (g)	1 kilogram (kg) = 1,000 g	1 centigram (cg) = 0.01 g	1 milligram (mg) = 0.001 g

What Tools and Techniques Do Scientists Use?

When conducting investigations, scientists always make precise measurements and keep detailed notes. Many scientists also use special tools to boost their senses. For example, scientists use microscopes to observe objects that are too small to see with the unaided eye. Scientists also use special procedures in the lab. For example, they may use a technique called *sterile technique* to prevent samples from being contaminated.

Critical Thinking

3. Identify Give three examples of tools that scientists may use when conducting an investigation.

____

____

____

How Can You Stay Safe in the Lab?

Studying science can be exciting, but it can also be dangerous. Here are some guidelines for working safely in the lab:

- Follow the instructions your teacher gives you.
- Read your lab procedure carefully before beginning.
- Do not skip any steps in your lab procedure.
- Always wear safety equipment in the lab.
- Measure chemicals carefully and precisely.
- Ask your teacher how to get rid of any extra chemicals or materials at the end of a procedure.
- Never taste or smell any materials or chemicals in lab unless your teacher instructs you to do so.
- Do not use any damaged or broken equipment.
- Keep your lab area clean and organized.
- Be careful when you place something on the lab bench. Make sure that the object will not fall or tip over.
- Walk carefully in the lab.
- If you are working outside, be aware of your surroundings. Avoid poisonous plants and dangerous animals that live in the area. Wear sunscreen and a hat that shades your neck and ears. ☑

4. Describe Name one thing you should do before you begin a lab activity.

____

____

____

5. Compare Name one thing you should do when conducting an investigation outside that you do not need to do inside.

____

____

____

Before a lab begins, be sure you know where the safety equipment is located and how to use it. If an accident occurs in the lab, stay calm. Make sure that you are safe and that no one else is in danger. Then, inform your teacher right away. Follow all the instructions your teacher gives you.

Name ______________________ Class ______________ Date ______________

Section 3 Review

SECTION VOCABULARY

SI Le Système International d'Unités, or the International System of Units, which is the measurement system that is accepted worldwide	

1. List Describe two benefits of using the SI system of measurement.

____

____

2. Understand Relationships How many centimeters are in 1 m?

____

3. Explain Why might a scientist use a microscope in a laboratory?

____

____

4. Describe What is the purpose of using the sterile technique in the laboratory?

____

____

5. Apply Concepts Why is it important to keep your lab area clean and organized? Give two reasons.

____

____

____

6. Summarize What should you do before a lab to be prepared for an accident?

____

____

7. Describe What should you do if an accident occurs in the lab?

____

____

____

____

What Is Biology?

KEY IDEAS

As you read this section, keep these questions in mind:

- What do biologists study?
- What are seven characteristics that all living things share?

What Is Biology?

Biology is the study of life. Biologists study the characteristics of *organisms*, or living things. They also study how organisms interact with their environment. Living things share seven characteristics, shown below, that separate them from nonliving things.

READING TOOLBOX

Summarize After you read this section, create flashcards to help you remember the seven characteristics of living things.

Characteristic	Description
Cells	Organisms are made of one or more cells. A **cell** is a tiny, organized structure that is surrounded by a thin covering called a membrane. A cell is the smallest unit that can perform all life functions.
Homeostasis	Organisms maintain **homeostasis**, or constant conditions inside their bodies, even when conditions outside their bodies change.
Metabolism	Organisms carry out many chemical reactions to obtain energy. Organisms use energy to grow, to move, and to process information. **Metabolism** is the sum of all the chemical reactions carried out in an organism.
Responsiveness	In addition to maintaining a stable internal environment, living organisms also respond to their external environment.
Reproduction	Most organisms can reproduce. **Reproduction** is the process by which organisms make more of their own kind.
Heredity	When an organism reproduces, it passes on its own characteristics, or *traits,* to its offspring. This is called **heredity**. Inherited characteristics change over generations. This process is called **evolution**.
Growth	All living organisms grow. As organisms grow, many change. This process is called development. Development differs from evolution because development refers to change in a single individual during that individual's life.

Critical Thinking

1. Infer Give one example of an internal condition in your body that remains fairly constant over time.

____

____

____

LOOKING CLOSER

2. Explain Why do helpful traits tend to become more common in a species over time?

____

____

____

Name ______________________ Class ______________ Date ____________

Section 4 Review

SECTION VOCABULARY

biology the scientific study of living organisms and their interactions with the environment

cell in biology, the smallest unit that can perform all life processes; cells are covered by a membrane and contain DNA and cytoplasm

evolution generally, in biology, the process of change by which new species develop from preexisting species over time; at the genetic level, the process in which inherited characteristics within populations change over time; the process defined by Darwin as "descent with modification"

heredity the passing of genetic traits from parent to offspring

homeostasis the maintenance of a constant internal state in a changing environment; a constant internal state that is maintained in a changing environment by continually making adjustments to the internal and external environment

metabolism the sum of all chemical processes that occur in an organism

reproduction the process of producing offspring

1. **Apply Concepts** Give an example of a topic a biologist might study.

____

____

2. **Identify** What is the smallest unit that can perform all life functions?

____

3. **Explain** Why must all organisms carry out metabolism?

____

____

____

____

4. **Apply Concepts** How might you help your body maintain homeostasis on a cold day?

____

____

5. **Understand Relationships** How are reproduction and heredity related?

____

____

____

Name ______________________ Class ______________ Date ______________

CHAPTER 2 Applications of Biology

SECTION 1

Health in the 21st Century

KEY IDEAS

As you read this section, keep these questions in mind:

- How are biologists working to reduce the spread of major diseases that affect humans?
- How has our understanding of the biological nature of disease changed over time?
- How will medical advances improve and extend human lives?

How Do Biologists Study Diseases?

The study of how diseases spread is called **epidemiology**. Biologists combine information from different fields of science to help reduce the spread of disease.

Viruses, bacteria, and other agents that cause disease are called *pathogens*. Biologists study pathogens to learn how they cause disease. They may use computer models and satellite data to predict and track the spread of pathogens. Biologists may also study human behavior to find ways to reduce the spread of pathogens. ☑

READING TOOLBOX

Define As you read this section, underline words you don't know. When you figure out what the words mean, write the words and their definitions in your notebook.

READING CHECK

1. Describe Give two ways that biologists can learn how to reduce the spread of pathogens.

____

____

____

____

What Causes Disease?

Until about 100 years ago, many people thought diseases were caused by supernatural forces. As we have learned more about the biological nature of disease, our ability to prevent and treat diseases has improved. Today, we know that all diseases are either infectious or noninfectious.

Type of disease	Causes
Infectious	pathogens, such as bacteria and viruses
Noninfectious	• inherited characteristics, which are passed from parents to offspring • environmental factors, such as eating habits or pollution

Vaccination can prevent many infectious diseases. During **vaccination**, a dead or weakened pathogen is put into a person's body. The person's immune system learns to fight that pathogen. This makes it less likely that the live pathogen will be able to infect the person later.

Talk About It

Brainstorm In a small group, talk about different environmental factors that may cause noninfectious disease. Discuss ways that scientists can reduce the spread of these diseases.

PREVENTING NONINFECTIOUS DISEASES

Inherited characteristics contribute to most noninfections diseases. By studying genetics, scientists have found ways to prevent or treat many of these diseases. **Genetics** is the study of how traits are passed from parents to offspring.

In 2003, scientists finished recording the entire human genome. A **genome** is the complete set of genetic information for an organism or species. Scientists can use the information in the genome to learn about genes that can cause disease. This can help them discover ways to prevent and treat these diseases. ☑

2. Define What is a genome?

____

____

____

How Can Advances in Science Help People Live Longer and Healthier Lives?

In many parts of the world, the average person's life span has greatly increased over the last century. This is mainly because of advances in the treatment of diseases. As our understanding of biology and other areas of science increases, humans will live longer and healthier lives.

For example, *assistive technologies* are products or devices that help people with injuries, diseases, or disabilities perform everyday tasks. Examples of assistive technologies are given in the table below.

Critical Thinking

3. Infer What do you think is one way that researchers develop ideas for assistive technologies?

____

____

____

____

____

____

____

Assistive technology	Description
Prosthetic limbs	replace missing arms, legs, hands, or feet
Hearing aids	help hearing-impaired or deaf people hear speech or other sounds
Computer-generated speech programs	translate text into speech to help blind people read or to help speech-impaired people communicate

Sometimes, technology that is developed for a small group of people can benefit many people. For example, researchers have developed a special kind of bandage for soldiers injured in battle. This bandage can help prevent the injured soldiers from losing a great deal of blood. Although it was developed for soldiers, it may one day be used in hospitals to help people with serious injuries.

Name ______________________ Class ______________ Date ______________

Section 1 Review

SECTION VOCABULARY

epidemiology the study of the distribution of diseases in populations and the study of factors that influence the occurrence and spread of disease

genetics the science of heredity and of the mechanisms by which traits are passed from parents to offspring

genome the complete genetic material contained in an individual or species

vaccination the administration of treated microorganisms into humans or animals to induce an immune response

1. List Describe three ways that biologists work to get rid of diseases that affect humans.

____

____

____

2. Infer How can scientists reduce the spread of noninfectious diseases that are caused mainly by environmental factors?

____

____

____

3. Compare How is our understanding of the causes of disease today different from our understanding several hundred years ago?

____

____

____

____

4. Identify Give two examples of assistive technologies.

____

____

5. Explain Why can it be important for researchers to study things that benefit only a small group of people?

____

____

____

Name ______________________ Class ______________ Date ______________

CHAPTER 2 Applications of Biology

SECTION 2

Biology, Technology, and Society

KEY IDEAS

As you read this section, keep these questions in mind:

- How does biotechnology affect our lives?
- How has biotechnology provided new tools for scientists to understand biological processes?
- How are biological factors used to determine an individual's identity and to increase public safety?
- What ethical issues are raised by the use of biotechnology?

READING TOOLBOX

Apply Concepts After you read this section, make a list of five to ten ways that biotechnology affects your life. Share your ideas with a partner or a small group.

What Are Some Examples of Biotechnology?

Technology that is based on living systems is called *biotechnology*. Genetic engineering is one of the most common examples of biotechnology. **Genetic engineering** is a technology in which the genetic material of a living cell is changed.

Biotechnology affects many parts of our lives, such as agriculture. In one case, genes from bacteria were added to corn. The bacterial genes cause the corn to make a chemical that kills certain harmful insects. Farmers can use less pesticide on this genetically engineered corn. ☑

1. Explain How could growing genetically engineered corn be helpful for a farmer?

____

____

____

____

____

Scientists also use biotechnology to make medicines and to create new materials. For example, scientists use genetic engineering to make vaccines and other medical products.

Biological research has also benefited from advances in nanotechnology. *Nanotechnology* is the science of creating products by changing individual atoms or molecules. It may one day be used to help fix damaged body tissues or to control how drugs act in the body.

Talk About It

Identify In a small group, talk about other words you may have heard that include the prefix *nano-*. Together, try to figure out what that prefix means.

This tiny robot was created using nanotechnology. One day, such robots might build or repair tiny electronics or other devices.

How Can Biotechnology Help Scientists?

Many scientists use biotechnology to study biological processes. For example, a biologist may genetically engineer laboratory animals to discover how certain genes work. Scientists and engineers may also use biotechnology to develop new products. ☑

2. Describe How can scientists use biotechnology?

____

____

Many organisms produce compounds with remarkable properties. For example, the material that spiders use to make their webs can hold a great deal of weight for its thickness. However, many of these compounds are difficult to obtain from the organisms that produce them.

Using biotechnology, scientists and engineers can create materials that have the same useful properties as compounds made by living things. These materials, called *biomolecular materials*, are based on these chemical compounds.

Sometimes, scientists and engineers get ideas for new products by studying the structures and functions of living things. These products are called *biomimetic* products. The table below gives examples of some biomolecular materials and biomimetic products.

Talk About It

Infer Relationships Look up the word *mimetic* in a dictionary. In a small group, talk about why *biomimetic* describes products based on structures and processes in living things.

Biomolecular materials	Biomimetic products
• drugs based on chemicals produced by plants, animals, and other organisms	• hook-and-loop fasteners, such as Velcro®, modeled after how prickly plant pieces attach to animal fur
• glue based on the molecules that bacteria use to stick to rocks	• telescopes based on how animal eyes collect and focus light
• fabric based on the structure of the material in spider webs	• hearing aids based on how insect eardrums respond to sounds
• materials based on bird feathers that can keep people warm and dry in cold weather	• robots based on how insects and other organisms move

Critical Thinking

3. Compare How is a biomolecular material different from a biomimetic product?

____

____

____

____

____

____

____

____

ADAPTING TOOLS AND METHODS

Scientists often adapt tools and methods developed for one purpose for a different use. For example, CAT scanning technology was first developed to help doctors make three-dimensional images of organs inside the body. Biologists now use CAT scans to create models of fossils and of living organisms. In this way, scientists can study specimens without dissecting them.

How Can Biotechnology Keep People Safe?

Biological traits, such as fingerprints, iris patterns, and genetic material, are slightly different in each person. Therefore, these biological traits can be used to identify people. For example, materials such as hair and skin cells can be matched to a person using DNA fingerprinting. A *DNA fingerprint* represents a person's unique genetic material. The use of biological traits to determine a person's identity is called **biometrics**. ☑

4. Define What is biometrics?

____

____

____

Police can search for criminals by using information gathered from an iris scan. Other software programs can tell the difference between human faces or can analyze brain waves and speech patterns.

LOOKING CLOSER

5. Describe Identify two things that are different between the irises shown in the figure.

____

____

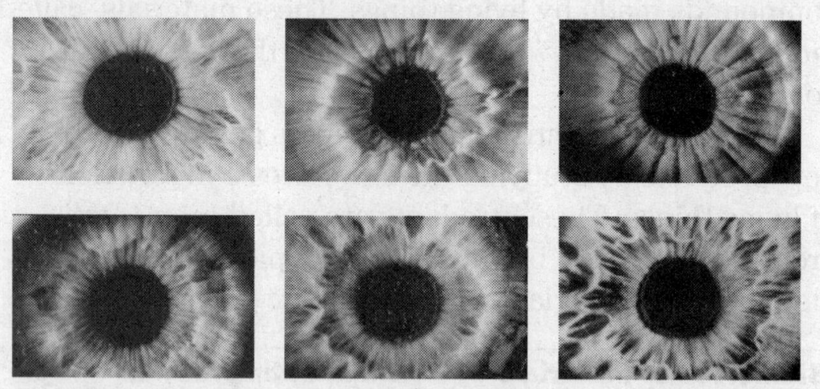

The iris is the colored part of the eye. Every person's iris is different. Therefore, iris patterns can be used to identify people.

What Ethical Concerns Relate to Biotechnology?

Although biotechnology can be very helpful, it also raises ethical concerns for many people. For example, some people worry that genetically engineered organisms could harm ecosystems. Others worry that eating food made from genetically engineered crops might be harmful to their health. ☑

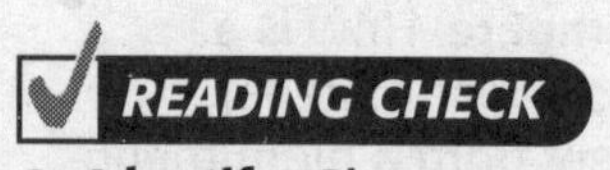

6. Identify Give one reason some people are concerned about genetically engineered organisms.

____

____

____

____

Some people think that some research methods, such as research on animals, are unethical. At the same time, others feel that limiting research that might save lives is unethical.

Using biometric identification methods can also raise ethical concerns. To use biometrics for identification, there must be databases of personal information. Many people feel that such databases are an invasion of privacy. Some fear that the information could be used improperly.

Name ______________________ Class ______________ Date ____________

Section 2 Review

SECTION VOCABULARY

biometrics the statistical analysis of biological data; especially the measurement and analysis of unique physical or behavioral characteristics to verify the identity of a person	**genetic engineering** a technology in which the genome of a living cell is modified for medical or industrial use

1. Identify Give three examples of characteristics that can be used for biometric identification.

____

____

____

2. Describe Fill in the blank spaces in the table below.

Type of biotechnology	Description	Examples or uses
Nanotechnology		can be used to help fix damaged body tissues or to control the actions of drugs in the body
	changing the genome of a living cell	
Biomolecular materials		fabric based on the material in spider webs; glue based on molecules bacteria use to stick to rocks; drugs based on compounds in living things
Biomimetic products		

3. Explain Why do some people object to biometric identification methods? Give two reasons.

____

____

4. Describe Give an example of how genetic engineering can be helpful.

____

____

Name ______________________ Class ______________ Date ____________

CHAPTER 2 Applications of Biology

SECTION 3

Biology and the Environment

KEY IDEAS

As you read this section, keep these questions in mind:
- How does biological research help protect the environment?
- How do new technologies help us study the environment?
- How do biologists rely on the help of community members to solve environmental problems?

READING TOOLBOX

Summarize As you read this section, underline the main ideas. When you are finished reading, write a one- or two-paragraph summary of the section.

What Is Environmental Science?

The environment provides natural resources that are important to all organisms, including humans. Biological research helps us understand how to protect the environment. The study of how living organisms interact with one another and with their physical environment is called **ecology**. The study of how humans affect the environment is called **environmental science**.

Critical Thinking

1. Compare How is ecology different from environmental science?

____

____

____

____

____

____

How Do Biologists Use Technology to Study the Environment?

Biologists use many different technologies to study and protect the environment. Examples of these technologies include satellite tagging, geographic information systems, and DNA fingerprinting.

SATELLITE TAGGING

Researchers may use special tiny radios to track the movements of different organisms, such as the one shown below.

Scientists like this one attach special radio transmitters to molas. They can use the radio transmitters to track the movements of the fish. They can use this information to learn about the fish's behavior.

This fish is called a mola. Molas are some of the largest fish in the world.

LOOKING CLOSER

2. Describe Why do scientists attach radio transmitters to animals?

____

____

GIS AND DNA FINGERPRINTING

Data from satellite tagging can be used in computer modeling programs called geographic information systems (GIS). These systems allow biologists to compare different types of data on a map. For example, biologists may use a GIS to compare weather conditions, locations of food sources, and movements of animals. ☑

3. Describe What can scientists use a GIS for?

____

____

____

Biologists can also use genetics to study and protect the environment. For example, many endangered animals are killed illegally, or *poached*, for their body parts. Biologists can use DNA fingerprinting to identify the people who killed the animals. Biologists also collect the DNA of endangered animals so that the species can still be studied if it becomes extinct.

How Can Communities Help Biologists?

Biologists rely on the help of individuals and communities to find solutions for environmental problems. These "citizen scientists" can contribute to biological research and environmental conservation. For example, many high schools have clubs that involve students in environmental research and conservation.

These students are part of the Raptor Rehabilitation Center in Kentucky. The students help care for injured birds of prey, such as eagles, hawks, and owls.

LOOKING CLOSER

4. Identify How do the students at the Raptor Rehabilitation Center help protect and preserve the environment?

____

____

If your school does not have an environmental club, find a teacher who can help you start one. Begin by working with other students to create a list of local environmental issues. Then, discuss some ways that your science class can learn more about these issues.

Name ______________________ Class ______________ Date ______________

Section 3 Review

SECTION VOCABULARY

ecology the study of the interactions of living organisms with one another and with their environment	**environmental science** the study of the air, water, and land surrounding an organism or a community, which ranges from a small area to Earth's entire biosphere; it includes the study of the impact of humans on the environment

1. Evaluate Why is it important for biologists to study the environment?

____

____

2. List Name three tools that biologists use to study the environment.

____

____

____

3. Infer How could attaching a radio transmitter to an animal help biologists protect that species?

____

____

____

____

4. Describe How do biologists use genetic tools to protect endangered animals?

____

____

____

5. Apply Concepts How can you and other community members help to protect and preserve the environment? Describe three ways.

____

____

____

____

____

____

Name ______________________ Class ______________ Date ______________

CHAPTER 3 Chemistry of Life

SECTION 1

Matter and Substances

KEY IDEAS

As you read this section, keep these questions in mind:

- What makes matter?
- Why do atoms form bonds?
- What are some important interactions between substances in living things?

What Does All Matter Have in Common?

Everything in the universe is made of matter. *Matter* is anything that has mass and takes up space. All matter is made up of atoms.

READING TOOLBOX

Discuss Read this section quietly to yourself. As you read, write down questions that you have about the material. Then, go over the material with a partner or a small group. Together, try to figure out any parts you didn't understand.

ATOMS

An **atom** is the smallest unit of matter that cannot be broken down by chemical reactions. An atom has a core called a nucleus. The nucleus contains two types of particles: protons and neutrons. Protons and neutrons both have about the same mass. However, a *proton* has a positive charge. A *neutron* has no charge. ☑

READING CHECK

1. Compare Give one similarity and one difference between protons and neutrons.

An atom also contains *electrons*. An electron has a negative charge and moves around the nucleus in a region called the *electron cloud*. The mass of an electron is much smaller than the mass of a proton or a neutron.

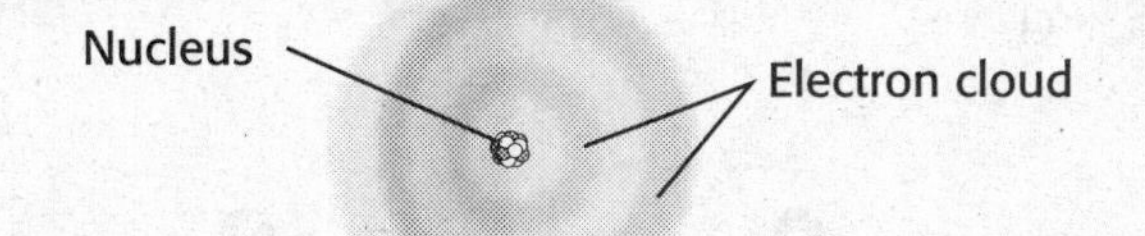

The nucleus of an atom contains protons and neutrons. Electrons move around the nucleus in the electron cloud.

ELEMENTS

An **element** is a substance that is made up of atoms that all have the same number of protons. For example, all atoms of the element carbon contain six protons. Also, all atoms that contain six protons are atoms of the element carbon. An atom is the smallest unit that has all the chemical properties of an element.

Atoms of the same element can have different numbers of neutrons. Atoms of the same element with different numbers of neutrons are called *isotopes*.

Critical Thinking

2. Apply Concepts An atom has five protons and six neutrons. Is the atom an atom of carbon? Explain your answer.

What Are Chemical Bonds?

Electrons occupy only specific levels within the electron cloud. Up to two electrons can occupy the first level. Other levels can hold more electrons. Electrons in the outermost level are called **valence electrons**. ☑

3. Define What is a valence electron?

____

____

____

Atoms are most stable when their outermost electron levels are filled. Therefore, most atoms combine, or *bond*, with each other so that each atom has a full outermost electron level. A **compound** forms when a chemical bond joins atoms of two or more different elements.

One way that atoms can form a chemical bond is by sharing electrons. This is called a *covalent bond*. Atoms held together by covalent bonds form a **molecule**. ☑

4. Define What is a molecule?

____

____

Atoms generally do not share the electrons in a covalent bond equally. As a result, one end, or *pole*, of a molecule has a slight negative charge. The other pole of the molecule has a slight positive charge. The result is a *polar molecule*. Water is an example of a polar molecule.

Another way that atoms can form chemical bonds is by losing or gaining electrons. When atoms gain or lose electrons, they form charged particles called **ions**.

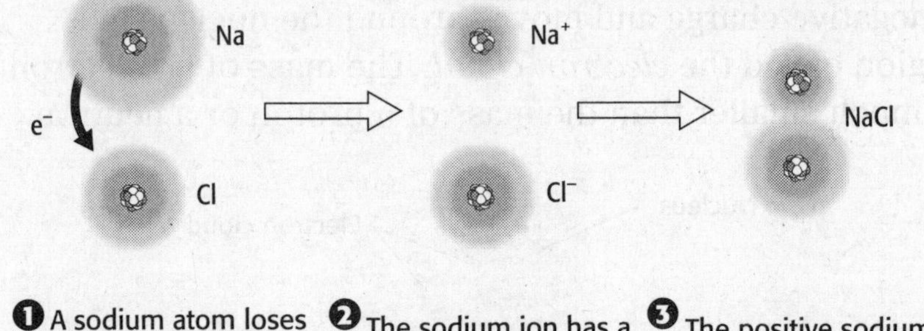

❶ A sodium atom loses an electron. The electron moves to a chlorine atom.

❷ The sodium ion has a positive charge. The chloride ion has a negative charge.

❸ The positive sodium ion and the negative chloride ion attract each other. This forms an *ionic bond*.

LOOKING CLOSER

5. Explain Why does the sodium ion have a positive charge?

____

____

What Are Hydrogen Bonds?

When a hydrogen atom is bonded to an oxygen, nitrogen, or fluorine atom, the hydrogen atom has a relatively strong positive charge. It can attract the negative pole of other nearby molecules. This attraction is called a *hydrogen bond*, even though it is not a true chemical bond.

Hydrogen bonds are very important in many compounds in living things. For example, they help form the structures of DNA and of proteins.

Name ______________________ Class ______________ Date ______________

Section 1 Review

SECTION VOCABULARY

atom the smallest unit of an element that maintains the chemical properties of that element

compound a substance made up of atoms of two or more different elements joined by chemical bonds

element a substance that cannot be separated or broken down into simpler substances by chemical means; all atoms of an element have the same atomic number

ion an atom, radical, or molecule that has gained or lost one or more electrons and has a negative or positive charge

molecule a group of atoms that are held together by chemical forces; a molecule is the smallest unit of matter that can exist by itself and retain all of a substance's chemical properties

valence electron an electron that is found in the outermost shell of an atom and that determines the atom's chemical properties

1. **Describe Relationships** How are atoms and elements related?

____

____

2. **Compare** Fill in the blank spaces in the table below.

Type of particle	Location within an atom	Charge
	outside the nucleus	
Proton		
	in the nucleus	0

3. **Explain** Why do atoms form chemical bonds?

____

____

4. **Compare** How is a covalent bond different from an ionic bond?

____

____

____

5. **Define** What is a hydrogen bond?

____

____

6. **Explain** Give one reason that hydrogen bonds are important in living things.

____

Name ______________________ Class ______________ Date ______________

CHAPTER 3 Chemistry of Life

SECTION 2

Water and Solutions

KEY IDEAS

As you read this section, keep these questions in mind:
- What makes water such a unique substance?
- How does the presence of substances dissolved in water affect water's properties?

READING TOOLBOX

Summarize After you read this section, make a Concept Map using the terms *solution*, *water*, *pH*, *base*, and *acid*.

How Is Water Unique?

The properties of water make it a unique substance. These properties are the result of the hydrogen bonds that form between water molecules.

Property	Description
Density	Hydrogen bonds cause the water molecules in ice to be farther apart than those in liquid water. As a result, ice is less dense than liquid water. This is why ice floats.
Heat absorption	Hydrogen bonds in liquid water are constantly breaking and reforming. This allows water to absorb a great deal of heat without its temperature changing very much.
Cohesion	Hydrogen bonds cause water molecules to stick to one another. This allows water to form droplets.
Adhesion	Hydrogen bonds cause water molecules to stick to other substances. This allows water to move within organisms.

LOOKING CLOSER

1. Identify What property of water allows it to form droplets?

____

What Is a Solution?

A **solution** forms when molecules or ions of one substance mix evenly with, or *dissolve* in, another substance. Solutions of substances in water are very important for living things.

Some substances dissolve in water to form acids. An **acid** is a compound that forms extra hydronium ions, H_3O^+, when dissolved in water. Some substances dissolve in water to form bases. A **base** is a substance that forms extra hydroxide ions, OH^-, when dissolved in water.

A solution's **pH** is a measure of how acidic or basic it is. A solution with a pH below 7 is acidic. A solution with a pH above 7 is basic. A solution with a pH of 7 is *neutral*.

Living things contain many solutions. Living things can survive only if the solutions within them have stable pH values. Therefore, the solutions in living things contain **buffers**. These substances help prevent changes in pH.

Critical Thinking

2. Apply Concepts A solution contains the same number of hydronium ions as hydroxide ions. Is the solution acidic, basic, or neutral? What is the pH of the solution?

____

____

Name ______________________ Class ______________ Date ____________

Section 2 Review

SECTION VOCABULARY

acid any compound that increases the number of hydronium ions when dissolved in water; acids turn blue litmus paper red and react with bases and some metals to form salts

adhesion the attractive force between two bodies of different substances that are in contact with each other

base any compound that increases the number of hydroxide ions when dissolved in water; bases turn red litmus paper blue and react with acids to form salts

buffer a solution made from a weak acid and its conjugate base that neutralizes small amounts of acids or bases added to it

cohesion the force that holds molecules of a single material together

pH a value that is used to express the acidity or alkalinity (basicity) of a system; each whole number on the scale indicates a tenfold change in acidity; a pH of 7 is neutral, a pH of less than 7 is acidic, and a pH of greater than 7 is basic

solution a homogeneous mixture throughout which two or more substances are uniformly dispersed

1. **Identify** A student empties the water out of a glass. The student observes that small droplets of water remain stuck to the glass. Which two properties of water explain the student's observation?

2. **Explain** Oceans and other bodies of water warm up more slowly than air or land. Describe how the hydrogen bonds between water molecules cause this effect.

3. **Apply Concepts** When carbon dioxide, CO_2, dissolves in water, some of the CO_2 molecules react with water. This forms carbonate ions and hydronium ions. Will a solution of CO_2 in water be acidic, basic, or neutral? Explain your answer.

4. **Explain** Why do the solutions in living things contain buffers?

Name ______________________ Class ______________ Date ______________

CHAPTER 3 Chemistry of Life

SECTION 3

Carbon Compounds

KEY IDEAS

As you read this section, keep these questions in mind:

- What are the chemicals of life made from?
- What is the role of carbohydrates in cells?
- What do lipids do?
- What allows proteins to have such diverse functions?
- What do nucleic acids do?

READING TOOLBOX

Compare After you read this section, make a table comparing the structure and functions of carbohydrates, lipids, proteins, and nucleic acids.

What Are the Chemicals of Life?

Remember that cells are the building blocks of living things. The building blocks of cells are compounds called *biomolecules*. Most biomolecules are large and complex. They are made of many smaller, simpler molecules that are bonded together. There are four kinds of biomolecules: carbohydrates, lipids, proteins, and nucleic acids. ☑

The most common element in biomolecules is carbon. Carbon atoms can bond with one another and with other atoms easily. Therefore, they can form many different compounds.

1. Identify What are the four kinds of biomolecules?

____

____

____

____

What Are Carbohydrates?

A **carbohydrate** is a biomolecule that is made of sugars. A *sugar* is a compound that contains carbon, hydrogen, and oxygen in a ratio of 1:2:1. Glucose, $C_6H_{12}O_6$, is an example of a sugar.

There are different kinds of carbohydrates. Glucose is a *monosaccharide*, or single sugar. Two monosaccharides can bond to form a type of carbohydrate called a *disaccharide*. Examples of disaccharides include sucrose, or table sugar, and lactose, which is found in milk. Many sugars can bond to each other to form a *polysaccharide*. Starch and glycogen are examples of polysaccharides.

Critical Thinking

2. Apply Concepts Is the compound C_6H_6 a sugar? Explain your answer.

____

____

____

____

Functions of Carbohydrates

Function	Description
Energy supply	Most organisms get energy by breaking down carbohydrates.
Structure and support	Many organisms use complex carbohydrates to form hard shells and cell walls.
Cell recognition	Carbohydrates on the outsides of cells allow other cells to recognize them.

What Are Lipids?

A **lipid** is a biomolecule that consists of chains of carbon atoms bonded to each other and to hydrogen atoms. Fats, steroids, waxes, and hormones are lipids.

Functions of Lipids	
Function	**Description**
Energy storage	Lipids can store more energy in fewer molecules than can carbohydrates. Many organisms store energy in lipids to be used later.
Water barriers	Lipids cannot dissolve in water. Therefore, lipids prevent the movement of water. For example, waxes on plant leaves prevent the plant from losing water.

Talk About It

Research and Share Find out more about one type of lipid. What is its structure? What are its functions? Share what you learn with a small group.

What Are Proteins?

A **protein** is a biomolecule that is formed by linking smaller molecules called amino acids into chains. An **amino acid** has an amino group (-NH_2) on one end and a carboxyl group (-COOH) on the other end. There are about 20 different amino acids.

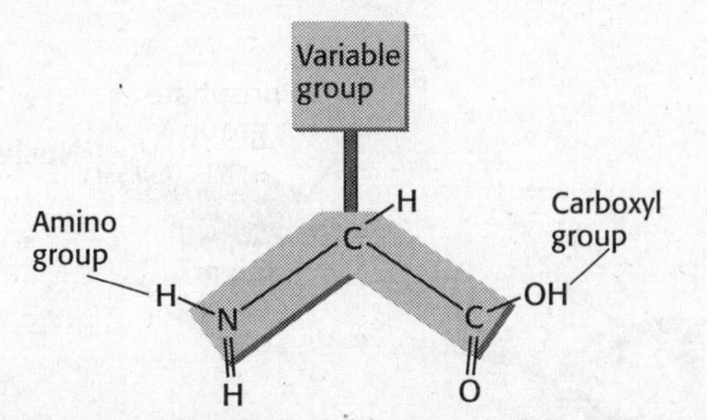

Each amino acid has a different variable group. The amino group of one amino acid can bond with the carboxyl group of another amino acid. This bond is called a *peptide bond*. Many amino acids that are joined by peptide bonds form a protein.

LOOKING CLOSER

3. Describe What do all amino acids have in common?

____

LEVELS OF PROTEIN STRUCTURE

The order of amino acids in a protein is the protein's *primary structure*. The amino acids can interact to form coils and bends in the chain. This is the protein's *secondary structure*. The bent and coiled chain can further fold to form the protein's *tertiary structure*. ☑

Most proteins contain several chains of amino acids. The combination of different amino acid chains in a protein makes up its *quaternary structure*.

The structure of a protein affects its function. Because amino acids can be joined in any order, proteins can have many different structures. This variety in structure allows proteins to perform many different functions.

4. Describe What is the primary structure of a protein?

____

LOOKING CLOSER

5. Describe How are proteins related to chemical reactions in living things?

____

____

____

Functions of Proteins	
Function	**Description**
Structure and support	Proteins form many of the materials that maintain a cell's structure.
Movement	Interactions between proteins in cells produce movement in many organisms.
Communication	Proteins can carry signals from one part of an organism to another.
Chemical reactions	Proteins help make many chemical reactions in living things possible.

What Are Nucleic Acids?

A **nucleic acid** is a biomolecule that is made of smaller units called nucleotides. A **nucleotide** contains three parts: a sugar, a base, and a phosphate group. If the sugar is deoxyribose, then the nucleic acid is called *deoxyribonucleic acid*, or **DNA**. If the sugar is ribose, then the nucleic acid is called *ribonucleic acid*, or **RNA**.

Critical Thinking

6. Compare Give one difference between DNA and RNA.

____

____

____

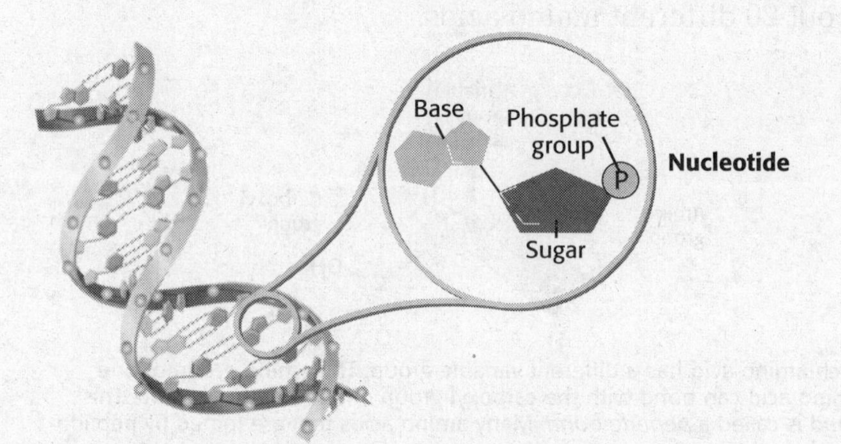

A molecule of DNA is a long chain of nucleotides. Each nucleotide contains a phosphate group, a sugar, and a base.

LOOKING CLOSER

7. Identify What are the three parts of a nucleotide?

____

____

____

Functions of Nucleic Acids and Nucleotides	
Function	**Description**
Heredity	DNA stores and transmits genetic information between organisms. A DNA molecule contains the *genetic code*, or instructions, for producing all of the proteins in an organism.
Energy transfer	The main molecule that cells use to transfer energy is *adenosine triphosphate*, or **ATP**. ATP consists of a single nucleotide connected to two additional phosphate groups. Some other important energy-transferring molecules also contain nucleotides.

LOOKING CLOSER

8. List Give two functions of nucleic acids and nucleotides.

____

____

Name ______________________ Class ______________ Date ______________

Section 3 Review

SECTION VOCABULARY

amino acid a compound of a class of simple organic compounds that contain a carboxyl group and an amino group and that combine to form proteins

ATP adenosine triphosphate, an organic molecule that acts as the main energy source for cell processes; composed of a nitrogenous base, a sugar, and three phosphate groups

carbohydrate a class of molecules that includes sugars, starches, and fiber; contains carbon, hydrogen, and oxygen

DNA deoxyribonucleic acid, the material that contains the information that determines inherited characteristics

lipid a fat molecule or a molecule that has similar properties; examples include oils, waxes, and steroids

nucleic acid an organic compound, either RNA or DNA, whose molecules are made up of one or two chains of nucleotides and carry genetic information

nucleotide an organic compound that consists of a sugar, a phosphate, and a nitrogenous base; the basic building block of a nucleic-acid chain

protein an organic compound that is made of one or more chains of amino acids and that is a principal component of all cells

RNA ribonucleic acid, a natural polymer that is present in all living cells and that plays a role in protein synthesis

1. Define What are biomolecules?

____

____

2. Describe Fill in the spaces in the table below.

Type of biomolecule	What are the building blocks of this type of biomolecule?	What is one main function of this type of biomolecule?
Carbohydrate		
	chains of carbon and hydrogen atoms	
Protein		
	nucleotides	

3. Explain Why can proteins perform so many different functions?

____

4. Compare What is the difference between a nucleic acid and a nucleotide?

____

____

Name ______________________ Class ______________ Date ______________

CHAPTER 3 Chemistry of Life

SECTION 4

Energy and Metabolism

KEY IDEAS

As you read this section, keep these questions in mind:

- Where do living things get energy?
- How do chemical reactions occur?
- Why are enzymes important to living things?

READING TOOLBOX

Outline As you read, underline the main ideas. After you have read this section, make a short outline using the information you underlined.

What Happens When Matter Changes?

You know that matter can change. You may have seen wood burning to ash in a fire, or watched salt dissolve in water before cooking pasta. All changes in matter require energy. **Energy** is the ability to move or change matter. Matter can change in two main ways.

Type of change	Description	Examples
Chemical change	a substance changes into another substance	burning wood; cooking food
Physical change	only the form of a substance changes	melting ice; dissolving salt in water

Critical Thinking

1. Infer Give one example of a chemical change and one example of a physical change, other than the ones shown in the table.

____

____

What Is a Chemical Reaction?

A chemical change is also called a *chemical reaction.* During a chemical reaction, bonds between atoms are broken and new bonds form. However, the total amount of energy and matter does not change. Scientists represent chemical reactions using equations like the one below: ☑

$$\text{Reactants} \rightarrow \text{Products}$$

2. Describe What happens to the total amount of matter and energy during a chemical reaction?

____

____

A **reactant** is a substance that is changed in a chemical reaction. A **product** is a new substance that is formed. The arrow in a chemical equation means "changes to" or "forms." The arrow may point in one direction or in both directions. An arrow that points in both directions indicates that the products can react with each other to re-form the reactants.

Critical Thinking

3. Apply Concepts Sugar and oxygen can react to form carbon dioxide and water. What are the products in this reaction?

____

____

Chemical reactions release the energy that organisms need to survive. Remember that *metabolism* is the total of all chemical reactions that occur in an organism. Organisms get energy through the chemical reactions that make up metabolism.

REACTION CONDITIONS

Chemical reactions can occur only if two conditions are met. First, the reactants must have enough energy for the reaction to occur. This amount of energy is known as the **activation energy**. Second, the reactant molecules must collide with the proper alignment. If the reactants do not line up correctly, a reaction will not take place. ☑

4. Define What is activation energy?

____

____

What Is an Enzyme?

Most chemical reactions that occur in living things have large activation energies. They also generally involve the collisions of very large biomolecules. This makes it difficult for these reactions to occur. Therefore, most chemical reactions in living things can proceed only in the presence of an enzyme. An **enzyme** is a biomolecule that makes a chemical reaction happen more easily. ☑

5. Explain Why is it difficult for most chemical reactions in living things to occur without an enzyme?

____

____

____

____

____

Enzymes make chemical reactions more likely in two main ways. One way is by reducing the activation energy required for a reaction to occur. The other way is by binding to reactants and forcing them to align correctly.

The place on an enzyme where a reactant can bind is called the **active site**. Only specific substances can bind to the active site in a given enzyme. The substances that can bind to a specific enzyme are called **substrates**.

How an Enzyme Works

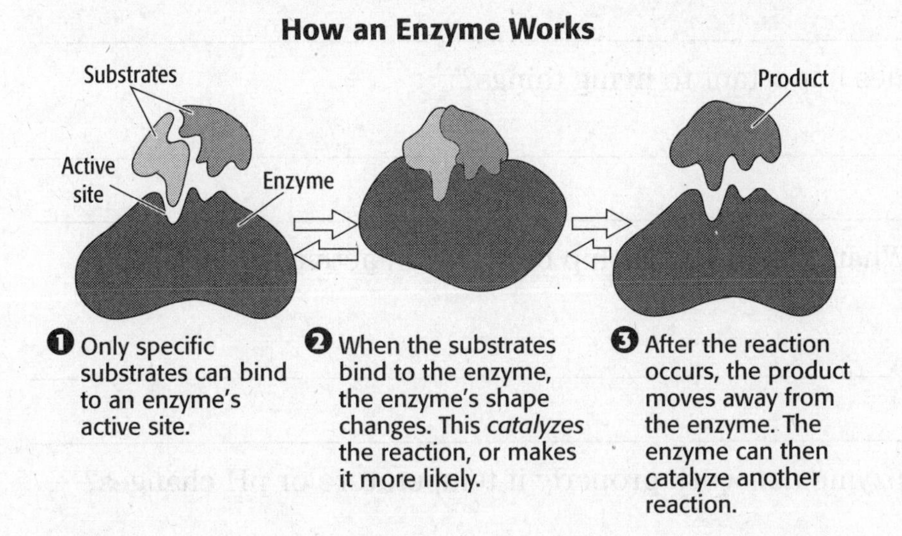

❶ Only specific substrates can bind to an enzyme's active site.

❷ When the substrates bind to the enzyme, the enzyme's shape changes. This *catalyzes* the reaction, or makes it more likely.

❸ After the reaction occurs, the product moves away from the enzyme. The enzyme can then catalyze another reaction.

LOOKING CLOSER

6. Describe What happens when substrates bind to the active site of an enzyme?

____

____

____

Most enzymes are proteins, which change shape if temperature or pH changes. Therefore, each enzyme generally works best within a certain temperature and pH range.

Name ______________________ Class ______________ Date ____________

Section 4 Review

SECTION VOCABULARY

activation energy the minimum amount of energy required to start a chemical reaction **active site** on an enzyme, the site that attaches to a substrate **energy** the capacity to do work **enzyme** a molecule, either protein or RNA, that acts as a catalyst in biochemical reactions	**product** a substance that forms in a chemical reaction **reactant** a substance or molecule that participates in a chemical reaction **substrate** a part, substance, or element that lies beneath and supports another part, substance, or element; the reactant in reactions catalyzed by enzymes

1. Identify Where do living things get the energy they need?

____

2. Compare How is a physical change different from a chemical change?

____

____

3. Describe Give two conditions that must be met for a chemical reaction to occur.

____

____

4. Apply Concepts Identify the products and the reactants in the chemical reaction shown below. Write only the chemical formulas for the products and reactants.

$$CO_2 + H_2O \rightarrow C_6H_{12}O_6 + O_2$$

____

____

5. Explain Why are enzymes important to living things?

____

____

6. Identify Relationships What is the relationship between an active site and a substrate?

____

____

7. Explain Why may an enzyme not work properly if temperature or pH changes?

____

____

Name ______________________ Class ______________ Date ______________

CHAPTER 4 Ecosystems

SECTION 1

What Is an Ecosystem?

KEY IDEAS

As you read this section, keep these questions in mind:
- What are the parts of an ecosystem?
- How does an ecosystem respond to change?
- What two key factors of climate determine a biome?
- What are the three major groups of terrestrial biomes?
- What are the four kinds of aquatic ecosystems?

What Makes Up an Ecosystem?

Every living thing is part of a community. A **community** is a group of species that live in the same area and interact with each other. For example, a community in a forest may include trees, birds, and other organisms.

A community and its nonliving environment make up an **ecosystem**. Ecosystems contain both *biotic factors*, or living things, and *abiotic factors*, or nonliving things. ☑

Biotic factors include both living things and once-living things, such as dead organisms. Abiotic factors include nonliving things, such as air, water, rocks, sunlight, temperature, and climate.

READING TOOLBOX

Organize As you read this section, create a Concept Map using the following vocabulary terms: ecosystem, community, succession, biome.

1. Identify Relationships How is a community related to an ecosystem?

____

____

Ecosystems, such as the one shown here, have both living and nonliving factors.

LOOKING CLOSER

2. List Name three biotic and three abiotic factors in the ecosystem in this picture.

____

____

____

____

____

____

BIODIVERSITY

Ecosystems contain different organisms. The variety of organisms in a given area is called **biodiversity**. Some ecosystems have greater biodiversity than others. For example, a tropical rain forest has a greater variety of organisms than a desert.

Talk About It

Discuss What can cause an ecosystem to change? In groups of two or three, discuss different factors or events that can change an ecosystem.

How Do Ecosystems Respond to Change?

All ecosystems change. As an ecosystem changes, the community of organisms that lives in it changes. **Succession** is the replacement of one kind of community by another at a single place over a period of time.

An ecosystem responds to change by restoring equilibrium. When a major change happens in an ecosystem, many organisms may die. However, this creates an opportunity for new organisms to replace them.

A place where an organism lives is called its **habitat**. Changes in ecosystems create new habitats. The first organisms to appear in a new habitat are called *pioneer species*. Pioneer species are often small, fast-growing plants. Pioneer species may change a habitat and make it possible for other organisms to live there.

For example, after a forest fire, grasses and weeds may appear first. They enrich the soil, which allows shrubs and bushes to grow. Eventually, these shrubs and bushes replace the grasses and weeds. As succession proceeds, other species replace the shrubs and bushes. Eventually, the forest may be restored. The flow chart below shows an example of succession after a forest fire.

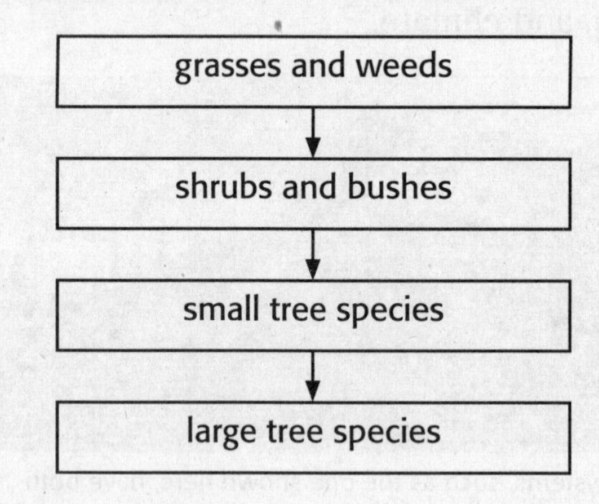

LOOKING CLOSER

3. Identify Which types of organisms in the diagram are the pioneer species?

____

____

What Is a Biome?

Every ecosystem is part of a biome. A **biome** is a large region that has certain weather conditions and certain kinds of organisms. The weather conditions in an area over a long period of time make up its **climate**. Scientists define biomes based on the average temperature and precipitation of their climate. ☑

4. Describe How are biomes defined?

____

____

TERRESTRIAL BIOMES

The latitude of a *terrestrial*, or land, biome affects how much energy it receives from the sun. Therefore, latitude affects a biome's average temperature.

Scientists classify Earth's terrestrial biomes into three major groups based on latitude: tropical, high-latitude, and temperate. *Tropical* biomes are near the equator. *High-latitude* biomes are near the polar regions. *Temperate* biomes are at latitudes between tropical biomes and high-latitude biomes.

Each biome group contains several biomes. The chart below lists the climates that are characteristic of these terrestrial biomes.

Biome Group	Biome	Climate
Tropical	tropical rain forest	warm; rainy
	savanna	warm; dry and wet seasons
	tropical desert	warm; dry
Temperate	temperate grassland	cool; moderate precipitation
	temperate forest	mild; rainy
	temperate desert	wide temperature range; dry
High-latitude	taiga	cold; wet
	tundra	very cold; dry

Background
Recall that *latitude* describes how far north or south of the equator a place on Earth is.

Critical Thinking
5. Infer Which major biome group is most of the United States part of?

______

LOOKING CLOSER
6. Compare How do the climates of a tropical desert and a temperate desert differ?

______

______

______

What Is an Aquatic Ecosystem?

The communities found in Earth's bodies of water belong to aquatic ecosystems. There are four types of aquatic ecosystems:

- *Freshwater ecosystems* include lakes, ponds, and rivers. They are habitats for a variety of plants, animals, and other organisms.
- *Wetlands* are the areas that link land and aquatic habitats. They support many species of birds, fish, plants, and other organisms. They also help control flooding.
- *Estuaries* are areas where fresh water from a river mixes with salty water from an ocean. They are productive ecosystems because they contain many nutrients.
- *Marine ecosystems* are made up of the salty water of the oceans. They stretch from the open ocean waters to the shore and support a variety of organisms. ☑

READING CHECK
7. Identify What are two aquatic ecosystems that contain salt water?

______

______

Name ______________________ Class ______________ Date ______________

Section 1 Review

SECTION VOCABULARY

biodiversity the variety of organisms in a given area, the genetic variation within a population, the variety of species in a community, or the variety of communities in an ecosystem

biome a large region characterized by a specific type of climate and certain types of plant and animal communities

climate the average weather conditions in an area over a long period of time

community a group of various species that live in the same habitat and interact with each other

ecosystem a community of organisms and their abiotic environment

habitat the place where an organism usually lives

succession the replacement of one type of community by another at a single location over a period of time

1. Identify What two types of factors make up an ecosystem?

____

____

2. Describe How does an ecosystem restore equilibrium after a major change?

____

____

____

____

3. Compare Explain how the location and temperature of a high-latitude biome is different from the location and temperature of a tropical biome.

____

____

____

____

4. Identify What are the two major components of climate?

____

____

5. Predict Suppose you relocate a fish from a freshwater ecosystem to a marine ecosystem. What abiotic factor in the marine ecosystem will most likely make it hard for the fish to survive?

____

____

Name ______________ Class ______________ Date ______________

CHAPTER 4 Ecosystems

SECTION 2

Energy Flow in Ecosystems

KEY IDEAS

As you read this section, keep these questions in mind:

- How does energy flow through an ecosystem?
- How is energy transferred between trophic levels in a community?

How Does Energy Flow Through an Ecosystem?

Every living thing needs energy to survive. The primary source of energy in an ecosystem is the sun. Plants and algae use energy from sunlight to carry out photosynthesis. During *photosynthesis*, light energy from the sun is changed into chemical energy. Organisms that carry out photosynthesis are called **producers**. Producers are the basic food source for an ecosystem.

Organisms that eat other organisms instead of making their own food are called **consumers**. A consumer that eats mostly producers is a *herbivore*. Cows are herbivores because they eat grasses. A consumer that eats mostly animals is a *carnivore*. Hawks are carnivores because they eat small animals. A consumer that eats both plants and animals is an *omnivore*. Bears are omnivores because they eat animal meat and plant berries.

Organisms that break down the remains of plants and animals are called **decomposers**. Bacteria and fungi are examples of decomposers. In an ecosystem, energy flows from the sun to producers to consumers to decomposers. Each step in this flow of energy is called a **trophic level**.

READING TOOLBOX

Apply Concepts After you read this section, construct a food chain with three or four trophic levels. Include yourself at the end of the food chain.

Talk About It

Discuss With a partner, identify as many consumers as you can. Discuss whether the consumers are herbivores, carnivores, or omnivores.

FOOD CHAINS AND FOOD WEBS

The flow of energy from one trophic level to the next is called a *food chain*. The following diagram is an example of a food chain.

plants → caterpillars → blue jays

A food chain does not usually show all the feeding relationships in an ecosystem. This is because most organisms eat different types of food. Different organisms may also eat the same type of food. As a result, in most ecosystems, several food chains join to form a *food web*.

LOOKING CLOSER

1. Identify Which type of organism in this food chain uses energy from the sun to make food?

____

What Is an Energy Pyramid?

Organisms get energy from the food they eat. However, most of this energy does not stay in the organism. When a zebra eats grass, it uses most of the energy from the grass to grow, run, and even sleep. The energy the zebra uses changes into heat. Heat energy is released into the environment. The zebra's body stores some energy from the grass in compounds such as fat. ☑

2. Describe What happens to the energy not stored in an organism's body?

____

____

An organism uses up approximately 90% of the energy it gets from a lower trophic level. About 10% of the energy an organism gets from a lower trophic level is stored in its body. That means only 10% of the energy from one trophic level is available to the next.

This loss of usable energy through trophic levels is often shown as an **energy pyramid** like the one below. Each layer in an energy pyramid represents one trophic level. The bottom layer represents the first trophic level, the producers. This level contains the most energy in the pyramid. The top of the pyramid represents the highest trophic level, consumers. The organisms in the highest trophic level contain the least energy in the pyramid.

3. Calculate A blue jay obtains 100 energy units from eating caterpillars. About how much of this energy will it store in its body?

____

Third trophic level: (10%) × (1,000 energy units) = 100 energy units

Second trophic level: (10%) × (10,000 energy units) = 1,000 energy units

First trophic level: 10,000 energy units

LOOKING CLOSER

4. Explain Why is the base of the energy pyramid wider than the top?

____

____

____

____

In an ecosystem, there are fewer organisms at the top of an energy pyramid than at the bottom. This is because usable energy is lost at each trophic level. In addition, those at the top usually require more energy to function.

Name ______________________ Class ______________ Date ______________

Section 2 Review

SECTION VOCABULARY

consumer an organism that eats other organisms or organic matter instead of producing its own nutrients or obtaining nutrients from inorganic sources

decomposer an organism that feeds by breaking down organic matter from dead organisms; examples include bacteria and fungi

energy pyramid a triangular diagram that shows an ecosystem's loss of energy, which results as energy passes through the ecosystem's food chain; each row in the pyramid represents a trophic (feeding) level in an ecosystem, and the area of a row represents the energy stored in that trophic level

producer an organism that can make organic molecules from inorganic molecules; a photosynthetic or chemosynthetic autotroph that serves as the basic food source in an ecosystem

trophic level one of the steps in a food chain or food pyramid; examples include producers and primary, secondary, and tertiary consumers

1. Summarize Fill in the generalized food chain to show how energy flows through an ecosystem. Use words from the vocabulary list above.

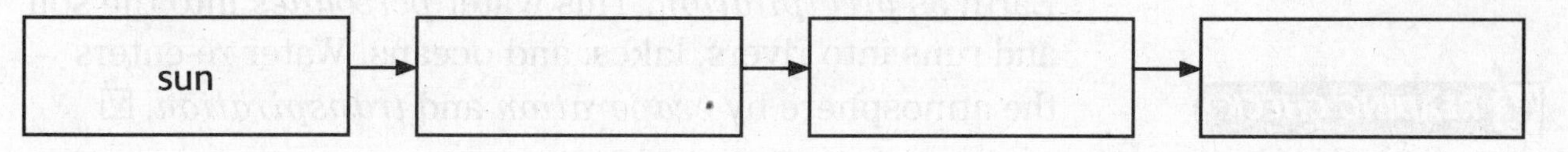

2. Compare What is the difference between an omnivore and a herbivore?

____

____

____

3. Explain Why is there more energy in the bottom trophic level of an energy pyramid than in the next highest trophic level?

____

____

____

4. Identify Name two types of organisms that are decomposers.

____

____

5. Calculate A lion stores 100 energy units after eating zebra meat from the trophic level below it. How many energy units did the zebra meat have?

____

____

Name ______________________ Class ______________ Date ______________

CHAPTER 4 Ecosystems

SECTION 3

Cycling of Matter

KEY IDEAS

As you read this section, keep these questions in mind:

- What is the water cycle?
- Why are plants and animals important for carbon and oxygen in an ecosystem?
- Why must nitrogen cycle through an ecosystem?
- Why must phosphorus cycle through an ecosystem?

READING TOOLBOX

Diagram As you read about each cycle, create your own diagram to summarize what happens. Include all the processes of the cycle.

How Does Water Cycle in Nature?

All living things need water to survive. Water is continuously cycled on Earth between the atmosphere, the land, and the oceans. This is known as the *water cycle.*

Water vapor in the atmosphere *condenses* and falls to Earth as *precipitation.* This water *percolates* into the soil and runs into rivers, lakes, and oceans. Water re-enters the atmosphere by *evaporation* and *transpiration.* ☑

READING CHECK

1. Describe What happens when water vapor in the atmosphere condenses?

____

____

LOOKING CLOSER

2. Examine What happens to water that falls to Earth as precipitation and does not percolate into the soil?

____

____

____

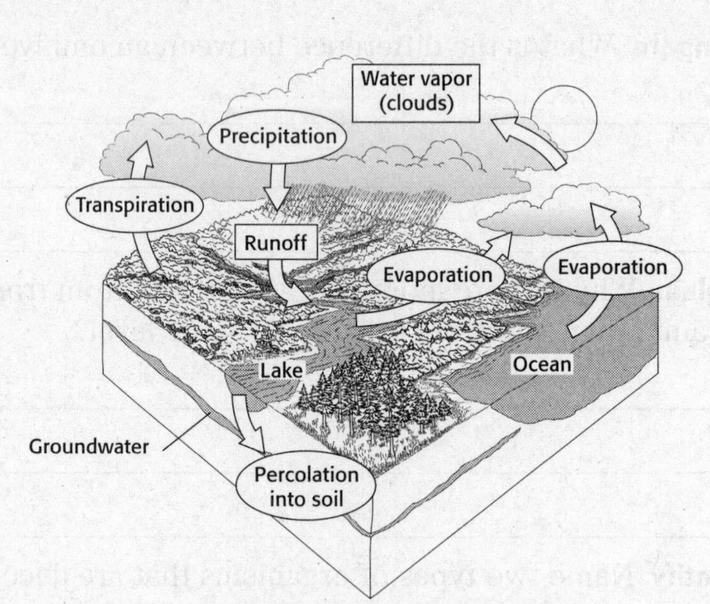

Water cycles through an ecosystem.

Processes that Are Part of the Water Cycle	
Process	**Description**
Condensation	Water vapor in the air cools and becomes liquid.
Precipitation	Water falls to Earth as rain, snow, hail, or sleet.
Percolation	Water enters the soil and becomes groundwater.
Evaporation	Liquid water warms and forms water vapor.
Transpiration	Water vapor evaporates from plants.

How Do Carbon and Oxygen Cycle in Nature?

The movement of carbon in nature is called the **carbon cycle**. Carbon can be cycled in the form of carbon dioxide, CO_2. Oxygen, O_2, is moved through ecosystems in the *oxygen cycle*. The carbon cycle and the oxygen cycle are closely linked.

Plants and animals play an important role in cycling carbon and oxygen through an ecosystem. Plants use CO_2 to make food during photosynthesis. They also release O_2 into the atmosphere during photosynthesis. ☑

Both plants and animals carry out respiration. **Respiration** is the exchange of O_2 and CO_2 between organisms and their environment. During respiration, plants and animals use O_2 to obtain the energy stored in food. Respiration releases CO_2 into the atmosphere.

Combustion is the burning of a substance, such as a fossil fuel. Burning coal or oil uses O_2 and releases CO_2. *Decomposition* also releases CO_2 into the atmosphere. Recall that decomposers break down dead organisms. Decomposition of organic matter releases CO_2.

READING CHECK

3. Explain How do plants contribute to the carbon and oxygen cycles?

____

____

____

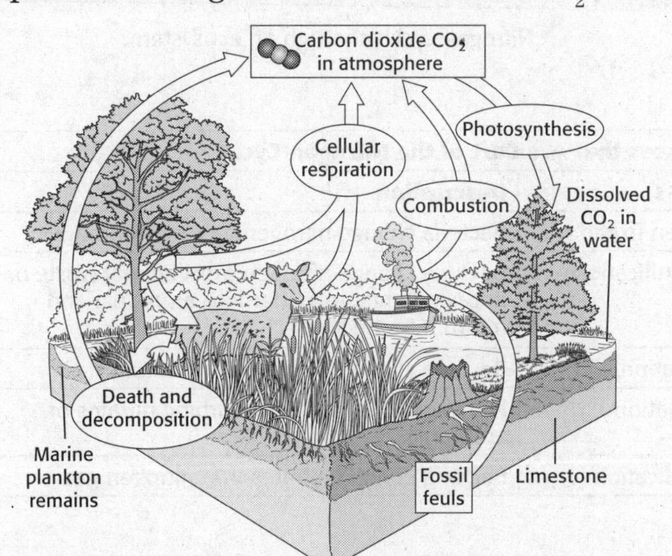

Carbon and oxygen cycle through an ecosystem.

LOOKING CLOSER

4. List Name three processes that release carbon dioxide into the atmosphere.

____

____

____

Processes that Are Part of the Carbon and Oxygen Cycles

Process	Description
Photosynthesis	uses _______ and releases _______
Respiration	uses _______ and releases _______
Combustion	uses _______ and releases _______
Decomposition	releases _______

LOOKING CLOSER

5. Identify Fill in the blanks in the table using CO_2 (for carbon dioxide) and O_2 (for oxygen).

How Does Nitrogen Cycle in Nature?

All organisms need nitrogen to live, because they use it to build proteins. The **nitrogen cycle** is the movement of nitrogen between organisms and their environment.

Organisms cannot use the nitrogen gas in the atmosphere directly. They need the help of bacteria. Bacteria convert nitrogen gas into usable forms, such as ammonia and nitrates. The table below describes the processes of the nitrogen cycle. ☑

6. Identify Relationships How do bacteria help organisms use nitrogen?

____

____

____

____

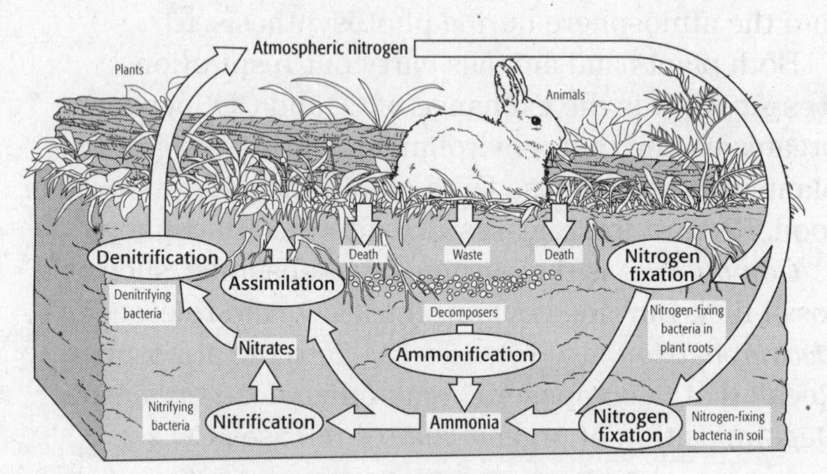

Nitrogen cycles through an ecosystem.

Critical Thinking

7. Infer How do animals get nitrogen?

____

____

____

____

Processes that Are Part of the Nitrogen Cycle	
Process	**Description**
Nitrogen fixation	Bacteria change nitrogen gas into ammonia.
Ammonification	Bacteria change nitrogen from animal waste or decaying organic matter into ammonia and return it to the soil.
Nitrification	Bacteria change ammonia into nitrates.
Assimilation	Plants get nitrogen by absorbing nitrates or ammonia.
Denitrification	Bacteria convert nitrates into nitrogen gas.

LOOKING CLOSER

8. Identify What process recycles nitrogen to the atmosphere as nitrogen gas?

____

How Does Phosphorus Cycle in Nature?

The **phosphorus cycle** is the movement of phosphorus between organisms and their environment. Plants absorb and use phosphorus from the soil as phosphate. Animals that eat plants reuse phosphorus. When plants and animals die, decomposers return phosphorus to the soil.

Name ____________________ Class ____________ Date ____________

Section 3 Review

SECTION VOCABULARY

carbon cycle the movement of carbon from the nonliving environment into living things and back **nitrogen cycle** the cycling of nitrogen between organisms, soil, water, and the atmosphere	**phosphorus cycle** the cyclic movement of phosphorus in different chemical forms from the environment to organisms and then back to the environment **respiration** in biology, the exchange of oxygen and carbon dioxide between living cells and their environment; includes breathing and cellular respiration

1. Describe What role does precipitation play in the water cycle?

____

____

2. Predict How might an increase in the burning of fossil fuels affect the carbon cycle?

____

____

3. Explain What role do decomposers play in the phosphorus cycle?

____

____

4. Compare How are the processes of nitrogen fixation and denitrification different?

____

____

____

5. Predict If nitrogen-fixing bacteria did not exist in an ecosystem, what would organisms be unable to make?

____

6. Compare How are photosynthesis and respiration different?

____

7. Compare In the water cycle, what do the processes of transpiration and evaporation have in common?

____

____

Name ______________________ Class ______________ Date ____________

CHAPTER 5 Populations and Communities

SECTION 1 Populations

KEY IDEAS

As you read this section, keep these questions in mind:

- Why is it important to study populations?
- What is the difference between exponential growth and logistic growth?
- What factors affect population size?
- How have science and technology affected human population growth?

READING TOOLBOX

Summarize As you read, underline the main ideas. When you finish reading, make an outline of this section using the underlined ideas.

Why Do We Study Populations?

Some biologists study groups of organisms and how the groups change over time. A group of organisms of the same species that live in the same place at the same time is called a **population**.

LOOKING CLOSER

1. **Define** What is a population?

____

____

____

These zebras are part of a population that lives in Kenya, Africa.

In an ecosystem, populations of different species, including humans, interact. These interactions can have many effects. Therefore, biologists study populations to learn how they interact and the effects of the interactions. This can help them better understand how changes in one population may affect the whole ecosystem.

Background

Recall that an *ecosystem* is made up of many groups of organisms, together with their environment.

The size of a population can change over time. If a population increases too quickly, it may use up all the resources in an area. This can harm the population, as well as populations of other species.

For example, in the 1850s, people brought about 24 rabbits from Europe to Australia. In Australia, the rabbits had plenty of food, but there were few predators. As a result, the rabbit population increased to about 600 million by the 1950s. These rabbits ate so much vegetation that populations of native organisms began to decrease.

Talk About It

Discuss In a small group, talk about different ways that populations can interact with one another and with ecosystems. Try to come up with ten examples of different interactions.

How Do Populations Grow?

Biologists may use graphs of population size versus time to show how populations grow. Populations can grow exponentially or logistically.

EXPONENTIAL GROWTH

Exponential growth occurs when a population increases by a certain factor in a given time period. For example, a population that doubles in size every year is growing exponentially.

Math Skills

2. Calculate A population of bacteria is growing exponentially. It doubles in size every 3 hours. If the population starts out with 10 bacteria, how many bacteria will there be after 12 hours?

____

Exponential Growth

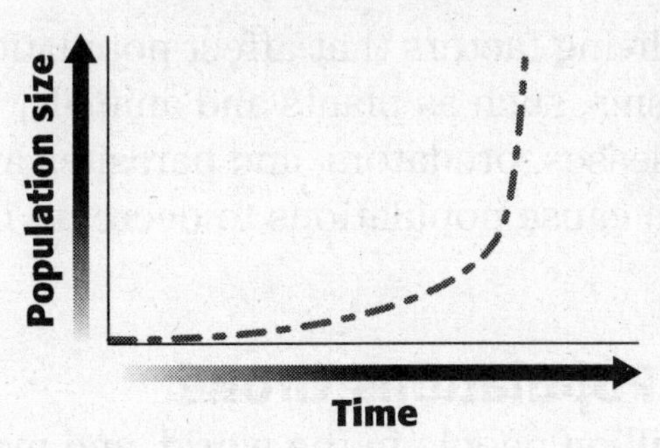

On a graph of population size versus time, a J-shaped curve represents a population that is growing exponentially.

LOGISTIC GROWTH

No population can grow forever. When a population reaches a certain size, its environment can no longer support it. The largest population that an environment can support at a given time is its **carrying capacity**. The carrying capacity of a particular environment can vary over time. ☑

3. Explain Why can't a population grow forever?

____

____

____

____

Logistic growth occurs when a population increases until it reaches the carrying capacity. Then, it stops growing. Most populations grow logistically.

Logistic Growth

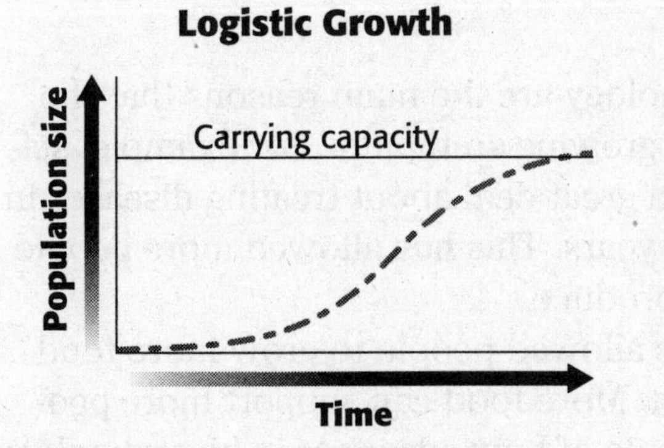

On a graph of population size versus time, an S-shaped curve represents a population that is growing logistically. The population grows until it reaches the carrying capacity.

What Factors Affect Population Growth?

There are two main factors that affect population growth: abiotic factors and biotic factors.

ABIOTIC FACTORS

Abiotic factors are nonliving factors that affect population size. Weather and climate are two of the most important abiotic factors. For example, if the summer in an area is hotter and drier than usual, populations in the area may shrink.

BIOTIC FACTORS

Biotic factors are living factors that affect population size. All living organisms, such as plants and animals, are biotic factors. Diseases, predators, and parasites are biotic factors that can cause populations to decrease in size.

Critical Thinking

4. Infer How could biotic factors cause a population to increase? Give one example.

____

____

____

How Do Human Populations Grow?

There are over 6 billion people in the world, and many more are born than die every day. Right now, the human population is growing exponentially. If the human population continues to grow exponentially, there may be more than 9 billion people on Earth by the year 2050.

LOOKING CLOSER

5. Explain How does the shape of this curve show that the human population is growing exponentially?

____

____

____

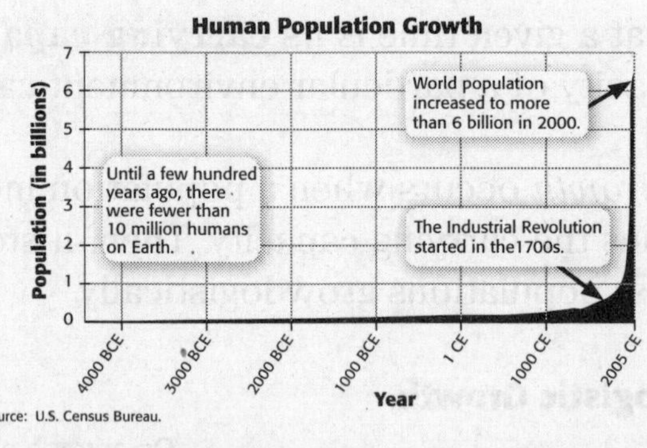

Source: U.S. Census Bureau.

Science and technology are the main reasons that the human population is growing so rapidly. For example, scientists have learned a great deal about treating diseases in the last few hundred years. This has allowed more people to live longer and reproduce.

Biotechnology has allowed people to grow more food today than in the past. More food can support more people. This is one example of how advances in biotechnology have allowed the human population to grow rapidly.

Talk About It

Identify With a partner, try to think of four other ways that advances in science and technology have allowed the human population to grow exponentially.

Name ______________________ Class ______________ Date ____________

Section 1 Review

SECTION VOCABULARY

carrying capacity the largest population that an environment can support at any given time	**population** a group of organisms of the same species that live in a specific geographical area

1. Explain Why do biologists study populations?

____

____

2. Apply Concepts One group of rabbits lives in a forest in New York. Another group of rabbits of the same species lives in a forest in Connecticut. Are these two groups of rabbits part of the same population? Explain your answer

____

____

3. Compare Describe how a graph showing exponential growth is different from a graph showing logistic growth.

____

4. Identify Give two examples of abiotic factors that can affect population size.

____

____

5. Describe Give an example of how a biotic factor can affect a population.

____

____

6. Explain Give one example of how advances in science and technology have allowed the human population to increase rapidly.

____

____

7. Infer Give one example of a biotic factor that could affect the size of the human population. Describe how a change in this biotic factor could affect the human population.

____

____

Name ______________________ Class ______________ Date __________

CHAPTER 5 Populations and Communities

SECTION 2

Interactions in Communities

KEY IDEAS

As you read this section, keep these questions in mind:

- How do predator-prey interactions influence both predators and prey?
- What are two other types of interactions in a community?

READING TOOLBOX

Summarize After you read this section, make a Concept Map using the highlighted vocabulary words. Also include the words *populations* and *interact.*

How Do Populations Affect One Another?

Populations of many different species may live in the same area. The different populations can interact in many different ways. The most common type of interaction is predation. In **predation**, one organism—the *predator*—kills another organism—the *prey*—for food. For example, lions are predators that kill zebras and other animals.

In some kinds of interactions, two organisms live very closely together. This type of relationship is called **symbiosis**. There are three main kinds of symbiosis: parasitism, mutualism, and commensalism.

Critical Thinking

1. Compare How is parasitism different from predation?

____

____

____

____

Type of symbiosis	Description	Example
Parasitism	One organism (the *parasite*) feeds on another organism (the *host*). The parasite harms the host, but generally does not kill it.	tapeworms (parasites) that live in the intestines of humans (hosts)
Mutualism	Both organisms are helped by their interaction.	fish that eat parasites from the mouths of larger fish
Commensalism	One organism is helped, and the other is neither helped nor harmed.	fish that live in the tentacles of anemones for protection

LOOKING CLOSER

2. Identify What are three types of symbiosis?

____

____

____

Populations that interact by predation or parasitism may develop adaptations in response to one another. For example, a parasite may infect a host. The host species may develop an adaptation, such as thicker skin, that prevents the parasite from infecting it. Then, the parasite species may develop new ways of infecting the host. This back-and-forth cycle of evolution is called **coevolution**.

Name ______________________ Class ______________ Date ______________

Section 2 Review

SECTION VOCABULARY

coevolution the evolution of two or more species that is due to mutual influence, often in a way that makes the relationship more mutually beneficial

commensalism a relationship between two organisms in which one organism benefits and the other is unaffected

mutualism a relationship between two species in which both species benefit

parasitism a relationship between two species in which one species, the parasite, benefits from the other species, the host, which is harmed

predation an interaction between two organisms in which one organism, the predator, kills and feeds on the other organism, the prey

symbiosis a relationship in which two different organisms live in close association with each other

1. Compare Give one difference and one similarity between mutualism and commensalism.

____

____

____

2. Apply Concepts Fill in the blank spaces in the table below.

Description of relationship	What type of relationship is this?
Bears kill and eat salmon.	
Shrimp in coral reefs eat parasites off of large fish. The shrimp and the fish are both helped.	
Leeches suck blood from mammals. The leech is helped, and the mammals are harmed.	
Rabbits eat plants.	
Orchids grow along the trunks of trees to get more sunlight. The trees are not harmed.	

3. Describe How might two species in a predator-prey relationship coevolve?

____

____

____

4. Apply Concepts Some plants produce chemicals that can kill organisms that eat them. Is this an example of predation? Explain your answer.

____

____

____

Name ______________ Class ______________ Date ______________

SECTION 3

Shaping Communities

KEY IDEAS

As you read this section, keep these questions in mind:

- How does a species' niche affect other organisms?
- How does competition for resources affect species in a community?
- What factors influence the stability of an ecosystem?

READING TOOLBOX

Define After you read this section, write your own definitions for the highlighted vocabulary words.

What Is a Niche?

Imagine a shark living in the ocean. The shark can survive only in water of a certain temperature, with a certain amount of salt. In addition, the shark must eat other organisms to survive. If the shark were placed in a different kind of environment, it would not survive.

Like the shark, every species has a specific environment in which it can survive. In addition, every species plays a particular role within its ecosystem. The environment in which a species lives and the roles it plays in its community make up its **niche**. ☑

1. Define What is a niche?

____

A niche is not the same thing as a habitat. A *habitat* is the place where an organism lives. A niche includes both an organism's habitat and the organism's functions in the community. The roles a species plays affect the other organisms in the community.

How Does Competition Affect a Community?

Many species can survive in a wide range of conditions. The entire range of conditions in which a species can survive is called its **fundamental niche**. However, many species have similar niches. Species with similar fundamental niches may compete for resources. Therefore, most species do not occupy their entire fundamental niches. The niche that a species actually occupies is called its **realized niche**.

Critical Thinking

2. Infer Which do you think is generally larger, a fundamental niche or a realized niche?

____

Type of niche	Description
Fundamental niche	the entire range of conditions in which a species can survive
Realized niche	the actual niche an organism occupies in a community

COMPETITIVE EXCLUSION

In general, two species cannot occupy the exact same niche. If two species do occupy the same niche, they compete with each other for resources. In most cases, one of the species ends up eliminating the other one through competition. This is called **competitive exclusion**. ☑

READING CHECK

3. Explain Why can't two species occupy the exact same niche?

____

____

____

____

____

DIVIDING RESOURCES

Species with similar fundamental niches can coexist by having slightly different realized niches. Different realized niches let them share the resources in their environment. For example, the three warblers shown below are all potential competitors. They all have the same fundamental niche. However, each species of warbler has a slightly different realized niche. Because they use slightly different parts of the tree, the species can coexist.

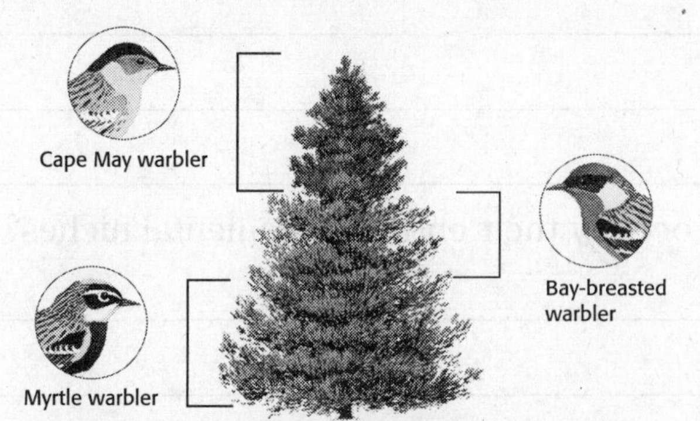

Each of these warbler species uses a different part of the tree. Therefore, the species can coexist.

LOOKING CLOSER

4. Explain Why doesn't one of these species eliminate the others through competitive exclusion?

____

____

____

____

What Factors Help Make an Ecosystem Stable?

Severe weather, human actions, and other events can damage or destroy ecosystems. However, all ecosystems do not respond the same way to disturbances. Some ecosystems are more stable and resilient than others.

The number of species in an ecosystem can affect how stable and resilient the ecosystem is. In general, the more species in an ecosystem, the more stable and resilient the ecosystem is.

In many ecosystems, a single species with a relatively small population affects the survival of many other species. These species are called **keystone species**. If a keystone species disappears, the ecosystem may become unstable.

Talk About It

Research Find out about a certain keystone species, such as sea otters. What roles does it play in its community? Why is it considered a keystone species? What could happen to the community if the species disappeared? Share your findings with your class.

Name ______________________ Class ______________ Date ______________

Section 3 Review

SECTION VOCABULARY

competitive exclusion the exclusion of one species by another due to competition

fundamental niche the largest ecological niche where an organism or species can live without competition

keystone species a species that is critical to the functioning of the ecosystem in which it lives because it affects the survival and abundance of many other species in its community

niche the unique position occupied by a species, both in terms of its physical use of its habitat and its function within an ecological community

realized niche the range of resources that a species uses, the conditions that the species can tolerate, and the functional roles that the species plays as a result of competition in the species' fundamental niche

1. **Compare** How is a niche different from a habitat?

____

____

____

2. **Describe** How is a fundamental niche different from a realized niche?

____

____

____

3. **Explain** Why don't most species occupy their entire fundamental niches?

____

____

____

4. **Explain** How can species with similar fundamental niches coexist?

____

____

5. **Describe Relationships** In general, how does the number of species in an ecosystem affect the stability of the ecosystem?

____

6. **Identify** Give two examples of factors that can damage or destroy an ecosystem.

____

____

Name ______________________ Class ______________ Date ______________

CHAPTER 6 The Environment

SECTION 1

An Interconnected Planet

KEY IDEAS

As you read this section, keep these questions in mind:

- How are humans and the environment connected?
- What is the difference between renewable resources and nonrenewable resources?
- How can the state of the environment affect a person's health and quality of life?

How Are Humans and the Environment Connected?

Humans are a part of the environment. We depend on the environment for food, water, air, shelter, fuel, and many other resources. However, human actions can affect the quality and availability of these important resources. The study of the impact of humans on the environment is called *environmental science*. ☑

All parts of Earth are connected. The environment provides us with resources, and it is affected by our actions. As the human population increases, our impact on the environment increases. We need to learn about our connection with Earth so that we can care for the environment. With this knowledge, we can be sure we do not use up or damage the resources we all need to survive.

READING TOOLBOX

Compare As you read this section, make a Venn diagram to compare renewable and nonrenewable resources. In your Venn diagram, be sure to include examples of each.

1. Define What is environmental science?

____

____

____

What Are Earth's Resources?

Humans live in almost every ecosystem on Earth. As the human population grows, we use more and more resources. Humans today consume far more resources than our ancestors did. What are these resources?

We can classify Earth's resources into two groups: renewable and nonrenewable. Some examples of these two groups of resources are listed in the table below. ☑

Renewable resources	Nonrenewable resources
wind energy	oil
solar energy	coal
fresh water	natural gas
trees and other living things	precious metals and minerals

2. Identify What are the two main groups of natural resources?

____

____

Critical Thinking

3. Infer Is water always a renewable resource? Explain your answer.

____

____

____

____

____

LOOKING CLOSER

4. Identify What is the function of these windmills?

____

____

____

5. Explain Where did the fossil fuels that we use today come from?

____

____

____

RENEWABLE RESOURCES

Renewable resources are natural resources that can be replaced at the same rate at which we use, or consume, them. Water is an example of a renewable resource. However, many renewable resources are being used up or damaged faster than they can be replaced. In these cases, such resources become nonrenewable.

Windmills such as these use energy from the wind to produce electricity. Wind energy is a renewable resource.

NONRENEWABLE RESOURCES

Nonrenewable resources are natural resources that form much more slowly than we consume them. In other words, we use them up, or deplete them, more quickly than they can be replaced.

Most of our energy today comes from fossil fuels. **Fossil fuels** formed from the remains of organisms that lived millions of years ago. We are using fossil fuels much faster than they form. Thus, Earth's supply of fossil fuels is decreasing and will be gone one day. Coal, oil, and natural gas are examples of fossil fuels. ☑

How Does the Environment Affect Our Health?

Damaging the environment can harm or destroy resources, such as air, water, and food, that we need to survive. The table below describes some effects of a damaged environment on human health.

Human action	Effect
Cutting down trees	increased number of landslides and floods which can cause injuries and deaths
Polluting air	headaches, nausea, respiratory infections; may cause lung cancer and heart disease
Polluting water	birth defects, cancer, and the spread of infectious diseases such as cholera

Name ______________________ Class ______________ Date ______________

Section 1 Review

SECTION VOCABULARY

fossil fuel a nonrenewable energy resource formed from the remains of organisms that lived long ago; examples include oil, coal, and natural gas	

1. Explain How does a growing human population affect resources?

____

____

2. Apply Concepts Complete the table below to identify each resource as renewable or nonrenewable. For renewable resources, indicate if the resource could become nonrenewable.

Resource	Renewable or nonrenewable?
Trees	Renewable; could become nonrenewable
Gold	
Sunlight	
Fish	
Clean air	
Steel	

3. List What are three examples of fossil fuels?

____

4. Explain Why is natural gas a nonrenewable resource?

____

____

5. Apply Concepts Identify one nonrenewable resource that you used today.

____

6. Identify Name two environmental disturbances that can affect our health.

____

____

SECTION 2 Environmental Issues

KEY IDEAS

As you read this section, keep these questions in mind:

- What are the effects of air pollution?
- How might burning fossil fuels lead to climate change?
- What are some sources of water pollution?
- Why is soil erosion a problem?
- How does ecosystem disruption affect humans?

READING TOOLBOX

Outline As you read this section, make an outline to summarize the information. Use the header questions to help you organize your outline.

1. List Identify three pollutants that are released when fossil fuels are burned.

____

____

____

What Are the Effects of Air Pollution?

Natural processes, such as volcanic activity, can affect air quality. However, human activities cause most air pollution. For example, when power plants and vehicles burn fossil fuels for energy, they release pollutants. These include carbon dioxide (CO_2), sulfur dioxide (SO_2), and nitrogen oxides (NO_2 and NO_3). ☑

Some problems caused by air pollution are listed below:

- causes acid rain
- causes respiratory problems in humans
- damages the ozone layer
- leads to changes in global temperatures

ACID RAIN

Acid rain is precipitation that has an unusually high concentration of sulfuric or nitric acids. Acid rain damages forests and lakes and the organisms that live in these habitats.

OZONE LAYER

The ozone layer protects life on Earth from some of the sun's damaging ultraviolet (UV) rays. Chemicals called chlorofluorocarbons (CFCs) have damaged the ozone layer. *CFCs* are human-made chemicals that are used as coolants in refrigerators and air conditioners. They are also used in spray cans. Today, many countries limit or forbid the use of CFCs. ☑

2. Explain Why do many countries limit or forbid the use of CFCs?

____

____

How Can Air Pollution Cause Climate Change?

Air pollutants may be a cause of global warming. **Global warming** is the gradual increase in the average global temperature.

GREENHOUSE EFFECT

Why does the inside of a car become so hot on a bright sunny day? As sunlight passes through the windows, the seats and other objects send out, or *radiate*, energy back toward the glass. However, the radiated energy is in a different form (heat) than the sunlight energy. Heat energy becomes trapped because it cannot pass through the windows as easily as light energy. ☑

READING CHECK

3. Explain Why does sunlight energy pass through car windows, but the energy radiated from objects inside the car does not?

____

Earth's atmosphere acts much like the windows of a car. In this process, known as the **greenhouse effect**, gases in the atmosphere trap heat energy that is radiated from Earth's surface. The gases that trap energy radiating from Earth are called *greenhouse gases*. CO_2 and water vapor are two examples of greenhouse gases.

❷ Heat radiates from Earth. Some of this heat escapes into space.

❸ Greenhouse gases absorb some of the heat and radiate it back to Earth.

❶ Radiation from the sun passes through the atmosphere and warms Earth's surface.

LOOKING CLOSER

4. Explain Do greenhouse gases trap all the energy radiated from Earth? Explain your answer.

____

GLOBAL WARMING

Without the greenhouse effect, Earth would be too cold to support life. However, Earth's average global temperatures have been rising rapidly for many decades.

Burning fossil fuels increases the amount of CO_2 in the atmosphere. Larger amounts of CO_2 and other greenhouse gases in the atmosphere trap more heat, which can lead to global warming. The effects of such climate change include changing sea levels, powerful storms, and droughts. ☑

READING CHECK

5. List Identify three effects that climate change may cause.

____

What Causes Water Pollution?

Every person needs 20–70 L of clean water each day for drinking, washing, and other needs. Unfortunately, many sources of water are polluted. Water pollution can come from fertilizers and pesticides, livestock farms, industrial wastes, septic tanks, landfills, and runoff from roads.

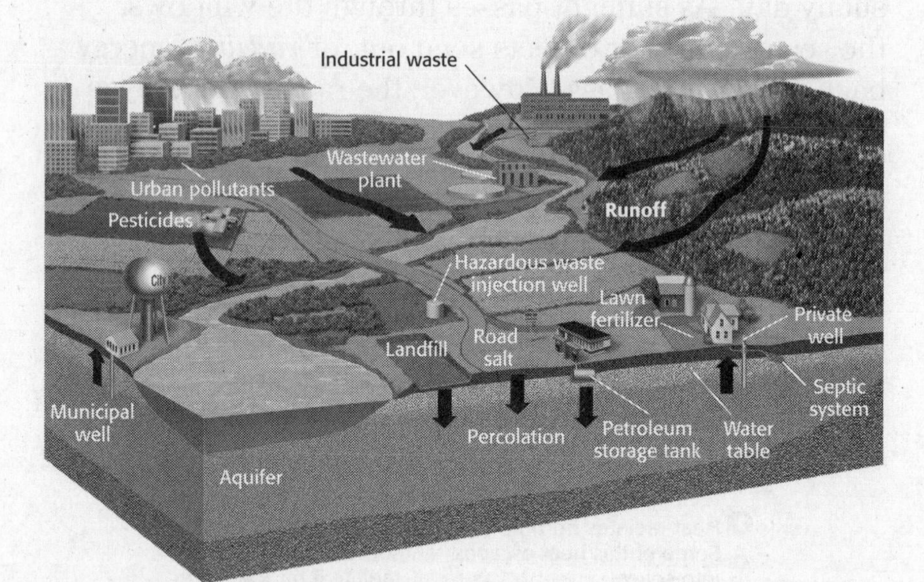

Pollutants on Earth's surface run off the land and into groundwater and other water systems.

LOOKING CLOSER

6. Identify On the figure, circle all the possible sources of water pollution shown.

7. Infer Why can the water in a well far from a source of pollution be polluted?

____

____

____

____

What Is Soil Erosion?

Without fertile soil, we cannot grow crops to feed ourselves or the livestock we depend on. The processes that form just a few centimeters of fertile soil can take thousands of years. However, this important resource can be depleted or harmed much more rapidly. The greatest threat to soil is soil erosion. **Erosion** is the process in which wind, water, or gravity carries materials such as rocks or soil from one place to another.

Roots of trees and other plants help hold soil together and protect it from erosion. If these plants are removed, the soil may erode easily. Many farming methods can also lead to soil erosion. For example, plowing loosens the topsoil and removes plants that hold the soil in place. As a result, wind and rain can wash away or blow away the topsoil. Farmers and scientists are working to develop farming methods that help conserve fertile soil.

Critical Thinking

8. Apply Concepts Is fertile soil a renewable or a nonrenewable resource? Explain your answer.

____

____

____

____

How Does Ecosystem Disruption Affect Us?

As the human population has grown, we have disrupted or damaged many ecosystems. Ecosystem disruption can affect humans and other organisms. Some of the effects on humans are listed below:

- loss of biodiversity
- decrease in food supplies
- loss of potential cures for diseases
- disruption of the balance of ecosystems that supports all life

LOSS OF BIODIVERSITY AND EXTINCTION

Biodiversity is the variety of organisms in a given area. Ecosystem disruption can decrease biodiversity. How does this decrease in biodiversity affect the function of an ecosystem? Every species plays a role in the cycling of nutrients and the flow of energy in an ecosystem. Species depend on one another. One lost species may lead to the loss of others.

Extinction is the death of every member of a species. When a species becomes extinct, an important link in a food web disappears. We also lose the benefits and the knowledge we might have gained from studying the species.

Talk About It

Debate Many zoos try to breed endangered species, or species that may soon become extinct. They hope to increase the number of individuals of each species. With a partner, debate how effective this plan may be. Will increasing the number of individuals solve the problem of extinction?

HABITAT DESTRUCTION

People have cleared many forests for farmland, pastureland, or timber. The process of clearing forests is called **deforestation**. As forests disappear, the organisms that live there also disappear. Today, habitat destruction causes more extinctions than any other human activity.

INVASIVE SPECIES

Humans have disrupted ecosystems by bringing in, or introducing, nonnative species. Some introduced species become very successful in their new habitats. Their success may cause some native species to leave an area or become extinct. Many invasive species can also cause damage that costs the public millions of dollars each year. For example, zebra mussels in the Great Lakes clog the pipes of water-treatment facilities. ☑

9. Describe What effect can invasive species have on native species?

____

____

____

____

Name ______________________ Class ______________ Date ______________

Section 2 Review

SECTION VOCABULARY

acid rain precipitation that has a pH below normal and has an unusually high concentration of sulfuric or nitric acids, often as a result of chemical pollution of the air from sources such as automobile exhausts and the burning of fossil fuels

biodiversity the variety of organisms in a given area, the genetic variation within a population, the variety of species in a community, or the variety of communities in an ecosystem

deforestation the process of clearing forests

erosion a process in which the materials of Earth's surface are loosened, dissolved, or worn away and transported from one place to another by a natural agent, such as wind, water, ice, or gravity

extinction the death of every member of a species

global warming a gradual increase in average global temperature

greenhouse effect the warming of the surface and lower atmosphere of Earth that occurs when carbon dioxide, water vapor, and other gases in the air absorb and reradiate infrared radiation

1. List Identify three effects of air pollution.

____

____

____

2. Explain How do increased CO_2 levels in the atmosphere lead to climate change?

____

____

3. Explain Why is soil erosion a problem for humans?

____

____

4. Describe How does deforestation affect biodiversity?

____

____

____

5. Explain Why can the loss of one species lead to the loss of other species?

____

____

____

Name ______________________ Class ______________ Date ______________

CHAPTER 6 The Environment

SECTION 3

Environmental Solutions

KEY IDEAS

As you read this section, keep these questions in mind:

- How do conservation and restoration solve environmental issues?
- What are three ways that people can reduce the use of environmental resources?
- How can research and technology affect the environment?
- How do education and advocacy play a part in preserving the environment?
- Why is it important for societies to consider environmental impact when planning for the future?

Why Are Conservation and Restoration Important for the Environment?

Two major techniques for solving environmental problems are conservation and restoration. *Conservation* involves protecting natural habitats. *Restoration* involves cleaning up and restoring damaged habitats.

Conservation is the best way to solve environmental problems because it prevents them from happening. For example, parks, nature preserves, and wildlife refuges protect areas where many species live.

Restoration reverses damage to ecosystems. A recent project to clean Boston's harbor is an example of restoration. For more than 200 years, the city dumped sewage directly into the harbor. The wastes caused disease, and most of the marine life disappeared. To solve the problem, the city built a sewage-treatment facility. Since then, the harbor waters have become cleaner, and plants and fish have returned.

How Can We Conserve Resources?

Our impact on the environment depends on how many resources we use. We can conserve resources in three main ways:

- *reduce* the amount of resources, such as water and fossil fuels, that we use
- *reuse* products rather than throw them away
- *recycle* wastes rather than make products from raw materials ☑

READING TOOLBOX

Underline As you read this section, underline the main idea of each paragraph or subsection. Review these main ideas after you read. With a partner, compare what you underlined.

Talk About It

Discuss Consider the case of sewage in Boston's harbor. In a small group, discuss how a conservation approach would have differed from a restoration approach. Was a conservation approach possible in this case? In the future, can the city of Boston use conservation instead of restoration?

1. List What are the three main ways we can conserve resources?

____

____

____

REDUCE

You can help conserve resources by reducing the amount of a resource you use and the amount of waste you produce. For example, low-flow toilets and shower heads can help reduce the amount of water you use. You can use ceramic plates instead of paper ones to reduce the amount of wastes you produce. ☑

2. Identify What two things can you reduce to conserve resources?

____

____

____

____

REUSE

Many people throw items away even though they are still useful. Reusing items saves both money and resources. For example, you can use plastic bags and utensils several times instead of just once. You can reuse plastic shopping bags to carry groceries or your lunch.

RECYCLE

The process of using old, used materials to make new products is called **recycling**. Recycling provides the following benefits:

- Using old materials to make new products generally costs less than making products from raw materials.
- Recycling uses less energy than making an item from raw materials.
- Because recycled materials are not put into landfills, recycling can also help prevent pollution.

Critical Thinking

3. Identify Relationships How are reducing resource use and recycling related?

____

____

____

____

When we recycle, we send fewer items to landfills.

How Can Technology and Research Help the Environment?

Advances in technology have lead to the production of cars and the development of industry. Both of these processes have contributed to the problem of pollution. However, technology can be part of many environmental solutions. Technology and research can help protect the environment by providing:

- cleaner sources of energy
- better ways to deal with waste
- improved methods for cleaning up pollution

ADVANCES IN TECHNOLOGY

Solar panels, hybrid cars, and scrubbers are three examples of technologies that can help limit pollution. Solar panels use energy from the sun to generate electricity. Solar panels generate electricity without producing pollution. Using solar energy also helps conserve fossil fuel resources. ☑

4. Identify What are two benefits of using solar energy to generate electricity?

____

____

____

____

Using solar panels to generate electricity helps us use fewer fossil fuels.

Hybrid cars use a combination of batteries and gasoline as energy sources. A hybrid car uses less fuel and releases less pollution than a typical car. ☑

5. Explain How do hybrid cars help us conserve resources?

____

____

____

Scrubbers are devices that reduce harmful sulfur emissions from factory smokestacks. Scrubbers have decreased emissions of sulfur dioxide, carbon monoxide, and soot from factories by more than 30%.

RESEARCHING SOLUTIONS

Scientists and engineers must determine the cause of an environmental problem before they can propose a solution. Research is necessary to develop technologies that can help solve these problems. Researchers use scientific methods to study an environmental problem. After they analyze a problem, they propose a solution. Their proposals must consider the costs, risks, and benefits of a particular solution. ☑

6. List What are three factors a proposal for an environmental solution must consider?

____

____

____

How Do Education and Advocacy Help the Environment?

Conservation groups, individuals, and governments must cooperate to solve environmental problems. Education and advocacy help more individuals play a role in this process.

EDUCATION

Education helps make people more aware of environmental problems and how they can help solve them. Some environmental education happens in schools. However, people can learn about the environment in other ways, too. For example, some people travel to coral reefs or rain forests to learn about those ecosystems. When people travel to learn about an environment or to help conserve an environment, it is known as **ecotourism**.

Talk About It

Debate Ideas Many people think ecotourism is a good way to educate people about the environment. However, some people think ecotourism can cause problems. In a small group, discuss possible ways ecotourism might both help and harm an environment.

ADVOCACY

Giving support, or *advocating*, for efforts to protect the environment can help more people become involved. Conservation groups work to help educate people, protect land, and influence laws. Some groups advocate for the environment internationally. Others advocate for the environment close to home. ☑

7. Identify What are three roles conservation groups may play in advocating for efforts to protect the environment?

____

____

____

How Should We Plan for the Future?

What will our planet look like in 50 years? Will we still have the resources we need to live? If we plan carefully, we can avoid damaging the environment, and we can solve environmental problems. For example, people in Staten Island, N.Y., are planning to turn a landfill into a park. We need to study the effects of certain activities, such as development, to protect our resources for years to come.

Name ______________________ Class ______________ Date ____________

Section 3 Review

SECTION VOCABULARY

ecotourism a form of tourism that supports the conservation and sustainable development of ecologically unique areas	**recycling** the process of recovering valuable or useful materials from waste or scrap; the process of reusing some items

1. Compare Why is conservation of a habitat better than restoration?

2. Apply Concepts Complete the table below to identify each example as a way to reduce, reuse, or recycle. You may have more than one answer for each example.

Example	Reduce, reuse, or recycle?
Using low-flow shower heads	
Using ceramic plates instead of paper ones	
Walking to school instead of riding in a car	
Making new aluminum cans from old ones	
Giving old clothes to a charity	
Carrying groceries in a cloth bag instead of a paper or plastic one	

3. List Identify three technologies that can help reduce air pollution.

4. Identify Relationships How are education and advocacy related?

5. Apply Concepts How does planning for the future relate to conservation?

Name ______________________ Class ______________ Date ______________

CHAPTER 7 Cell Structure

SECTION 1

Introduction to Cells

KEY IDEAS

As you read this section, keep these questions in mind:
- How were cells discovered?
- What defines cell shape and size?
- Why can eukaryotes perform more specialized functions than prokaryotes can?

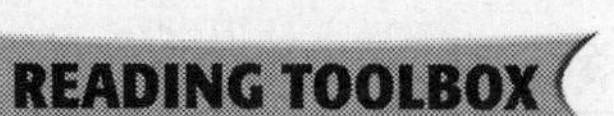

Outline As you read, make an outline of this section. Use the header questions to help you organize the main ideas in your outline.

1. Explain Why didn't scientists know about cells before the microscope was invented?

____

____

How Were Cells Discovered?

Most cells are too small to see with the eye alone. Before the microscope was invented, no one knew about cells. In 1665, an English scientist named Robert Hooke used a crude microscope to look at a thin slice of cork. The microscope made the image 30 times larger. He saw many little boxes in the cork, which he called *cells*. ☑

As different scientists used better microscopes to look at more objects, they realized three major points. Together, these points are known as the *cell theory*.

- All living things are made up of one or more cells.
- Cells are the basic units of structure and function in organisms.
- All cells come from existing cells.

What Defines the Size and Shape of a Cell?

Cells vary in size and shape. Human body cells range from 5 to 20 µm in diameter. Bacteria cells are even tinier. Why are cells so small?

Anything that enters or leaves a cell must pass through the cell's surface. Therefore, a cell's size is limited by the cell's *surface area-to-volume ratio*.

2. Calculate What are the volume and surface area of the large cube?

____

____

3. Calculate What are the total volume and surface area of the small cubes?

____

____

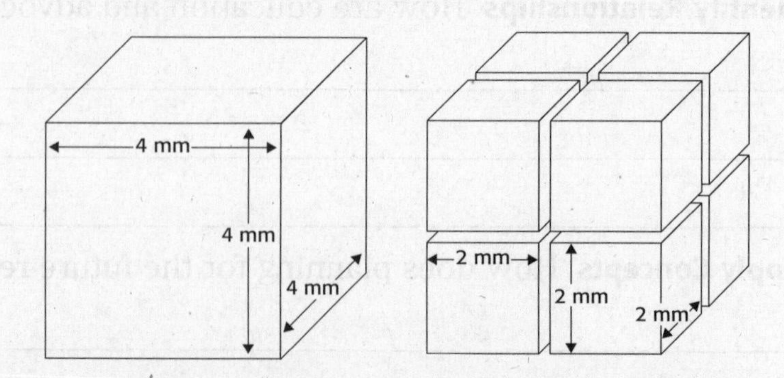

As a cell gets larger, its surface area-to-volume ratio gets smaller even though it must take up more nutrients and remove more wastes.

CELL SHAPE

The shape of a large cell generally helps increase the cell's surface area. For example, some skin cells are broad and flat. Some nerve cells are very long and thin. With both of these cell shapes, the surface area is larger than it would be if the cells were spheres.

What Features Do All Cells Have?

All cells have the following features:

- **cell membrane**, the layer that covers the cell, separates the cell from its environment, and controls what moves into and out of the cell ☑
- **cytoplasm**, the area of the cell inside the cell membrane
- **ribosomes**, organelles where proteins are made
- DNA, a cell's genetic material

4. Identify What is one function of the cell membrane?

____

____

PROKARYOTIC CELLS

A **prokaryote** is an organism that is made up of a single prokaryotic cell. Prokaryotic cells generally have very simple organization.

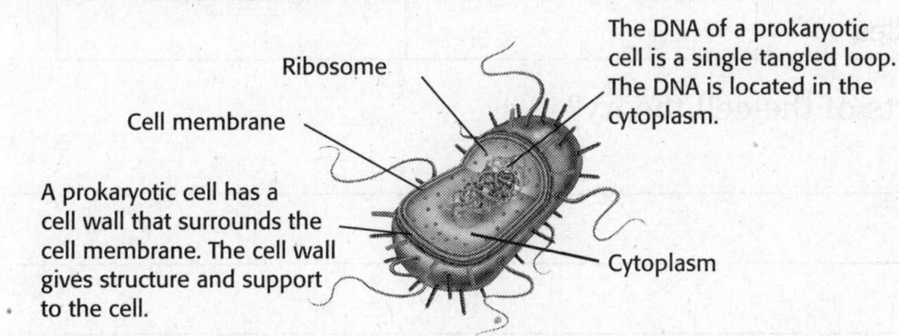

LOOKING CLOSER

5. Describe What is the structure of a prokaryotic cell's DNA?

____

____

EUKARYOTIC CELLS

A **eukaryote** is an organism that is made up of one or more eukaryotic cells. Eukaryotic cells have a more complex organization than prokaryotic cells. Because of this, eukaryotic cells can carry out more specialized functions than prokaryotic cells.

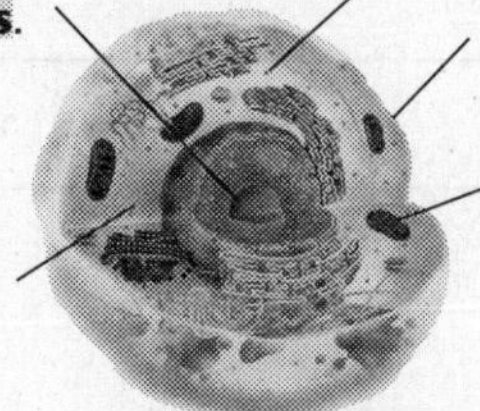

Critical Thinking

6. Infer Are humans prokaryotes or eukaryotes? Explain your answer.

____

____

____

____

Name ______________________ Class ______________ Date ______________

Section 1 Review

SECTION VOCABULARY

cell membrane a phospholipid layer that covers a cell's surface and acts as a barrier between the inside of a cell and the cell's environment

cytoplasm the region of the cell within the membrane

eukaryote an organism made up of cells that have a nucleus and membrane-bound organelles

nucleus in a eukaryotic cell, a membrane-bound organelle that contains the cell's DNA

organelle one of the small bodies that are found in the cytoplasm of a cell and that are specialized to perform a specific function

prokaryote a single-celled organism that does not have a nucleus or membrane-bound organelles

ribosome a cell organelle where protein synthesis occurs

1. Summarize Indicate whether each structure or feature below is found in a prokaryotic cell, a eukaryotic cell, or both.

Cell structure or feature	Prokaryotic cell	Eukaryotic cell
Nucleus	no	yes
Cell membrane		
Cytoplasm		
DNA		
Ribosomes		
Membrane-bound organelles		

2. List What are the three parts of the cell theory?

____

____

____

3. Infer Could a cell be the size of an elephant? Explain your answer.

____

____

____

4. Compare How does the location of DNA differ in prokaryotic and eukaryotic cells?

____

____

____

Name ______________________ Class ______________ Date ____________

CHAPTER 7 Cell Structure

SECTION 2

Inside the Eukaryotic Cell

KEY IDEAS

As you read this section, keep these questions in mind:

- What does the cytoskeleton do?
- How does DNA direct activity in the cytoplasm?
- Which organelles play a role in protein production?
- What is the role of vesicles in cells?
- How do cells get energy?

What Gives a Cell Structure and Support?

A cell has a web of protein fibers called a *cytoskeleton*. The cytoskeleton has three main functions:

- to help the cell move
- to support the cell and help it keep its shape
- to organize the parts of the cell and keep some structures in place

READING TOOLBOX

Organize As you read, make a chart that lists the major features of a eukaryotic cell and their functions.

How Are Activities of the Cell Directed?

Almost all of a cell's activities depend on proteins that the cell makes. The instructions for making these proteins are stored in the cell's DNA. RNA carries a copy of the instructions from the DNA in the nucleus to the ribosomes in the cytoplasm.

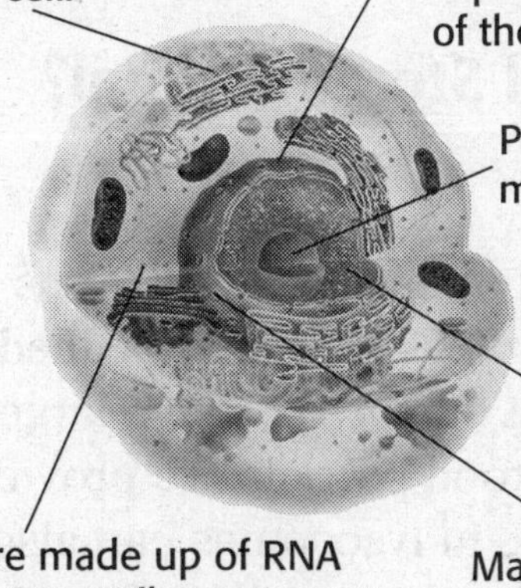

LOOKING CLOSER

1. Compare How does the function of free ribosomes differ from the function of ribosomes attached to other organelles?

____

____

____

____

2. Explain How do materials leave the nucleus?

____

____

____

How Do Proteins Move Out of a Cell?

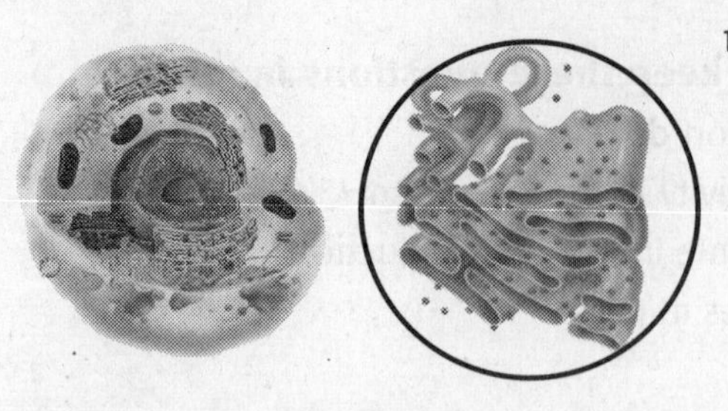

1. The **endoplasmic reticulum** is a system of membranes that prepares proteins to leave the cell. Ribosomes on the rough endoplasmic reticulum (ER) make proteins. The ER packages the proteins in parts of its membrane that pinch off to form vesicles. A **vesicle** is a small membrane sac that moves materials throughout a cell. Vesicles carrying proteins from the ER move to the Golgi apparatus.

A vesicle carries newly made proteins through the cytoplasm to the Golgi apparatus.

2. The **Golgi apparatus** is a set of flat, membrane-bound sacs. Like the ER, the Golgi apparatus also helps prepare proteins to leave the cell. A vesicle empties the proteins from the ER into one side of the Golgi apparatus. The proteins move through the membranes. The Golgi apparatus changes the proteins and repackages them in new vesicles.

Another vesicle carries the modified proteins from the Golgi apparatus to the cell membrane.

3. The vesicle moves to the cell membrane and releases the proteins outside of the cell. The vesicle membrane becomes part of the cell membrane.

How Does a Cell Store Material?

VESICLES

Vesicles store and release substances as the cell needs them. Special types of vesicles called *lysosomes* contain enzymes that can break down large molecules. The enzymes digest food particles to provide nutrients to the cell. The enzymes in lysosomes can also break down old, damaged, or unused organelles. This helps recycle materials in the cell. ☑

LOOKING CLOSER

3. Identify Relationships How do ribosomes and the endoplasmic reticulum work together?

____

____

____

4. Compare How are the functions of the endoplasmic reticulum and the Golgi apparatus similar?

____

____

____

5. Identify What are two functions of the enzymes in lysosomes?

____

____

____

VACUOLES

A **vacuole** is a fluid-filled vesicle found in plant cells and in unicellular, or single-celled, protists. Many plant cells have a large structure called the *central vacuole.* The central vacuole stores water, ions, nutrients, and wastes. Water in the central vacuole can make the cell rigid, or stiff, which allows a plant to stand upright. Some protists have *contractile vacuoles* that pump excess water out of the cell.

Critical Thinking

6. Infer What do you think happens when a central vacuole loses water?

____

____

____

How Does a Cell Get Energy?

A cell needs a large supply of energy to carry out its life processes. Chemical reactions in mitochondria and chloroplasts supply the energy that cells need.

A **chloroplast** is an organelle that uses light energy, carbon dioxide, and water to make sugars. This process is called *photosynthesis.* Plant cells generally have several chloroplasts.

LOOKING CLOSER

7. Identify In what organelle does photosynthesis take place?

____

8. Identify What molecule carries energy to where it is needed in the cell?

____

9. Describe What is the function of mitochondria?

____

____

____

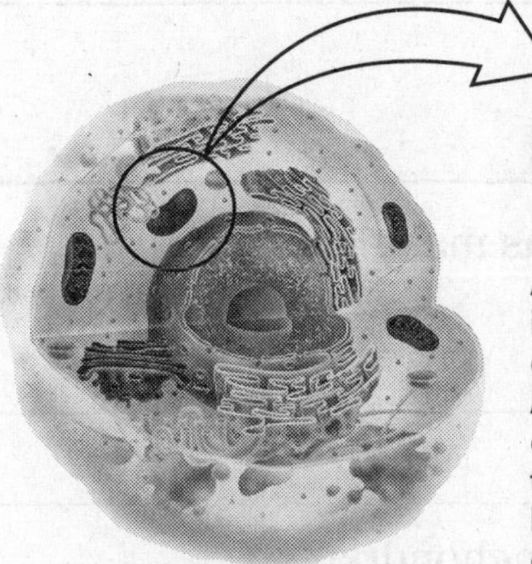

A **mitochondrion** (plural, *mitochondria*) is an organelle that breaks down organic compounds, such as sugars, to make ATP. ATP is a molecule that stores energy in its chemical bonds and carries energy to where the cell needs it. When the bonds in ATP break, energy is released. The cell uses this energy for its life processes.

The cells of plants and plantlike protists have chloroplasts. Almost all eukaryotic cells, including plant and animal cells, have mitochondria.

Name ______________________ Class ______________ Date ______________

Section 2 Review

SECTION VOCABULARY

chloroplast an organelle found in plant and algae cells where photosynthesis occurs

endoplasmic reticulum a system of membranes that is found in a cell's cytoplasm and that assists in the production, processing, and transport of proteins and in the production of lipids

Golgi apparatus a cell organelle that helps make and package materials to be transported out of the cell

mitochondrion in eukaryotic cells, the cell organelle that is surrounded by two membranes and that is the site of cellular respiration

vacuole a fluid-filled vesicle found in the cytoplasm of plant cells or protozoans

vesicle a small cavity or sac that contains materials in a eukaryotic cell

1. Summarize Complete the process chart to describe how proteins are made and moved out of the cell.

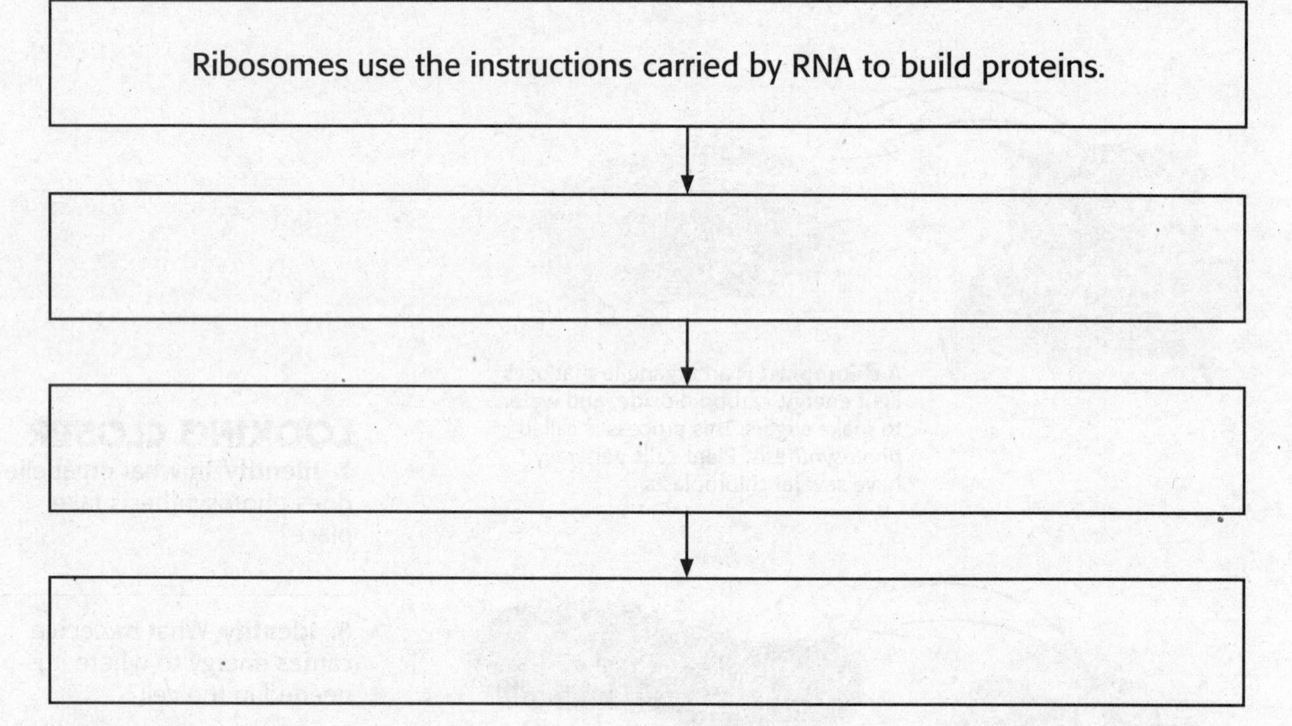

2. Explain How does DNA direct the cell's activities, such as making proteins, if DNA stays inside the nucleus?

____

____

3. Infer Why do plant cells need both chloroplasts and mitochondria?

____

____

____

Name ______________________ Class ______________ Date ______________

CHAPTER 7 Cell Structure

SECTION 3

From Cell to Organism

KEY IDEAS

As you read this section, keep these questions in mind:

- What makes cells and organisms different?
- How are cells organized in complex multicellular organisms?
- What makes an organism multicellular?

What Makes Cells and Organisms Different?

Both prokaryotic and eukaryotic cells can have a variety of shapes and structures. The different organelles and features of cells help the organism function in unique ways in different environments.

Prokaryotes can have different shapes. They also differ in how they get and use energy, what their cell walls are made of, and how they move.

A **flagellum** is a long, threadlike structure that helps the organism move.

Pili are short, thick structures that grow out of the cell's surface. They help a prokaryote attach to surfaces or to other cells.

Like prokaryotic cells, eukaryotic cells may have different structures for different functions. Also, certain organelles are more numerous in some types of eukaryotic cells than in others. For example, muscle cells use large amounts of energy, so they have many mitochondria.

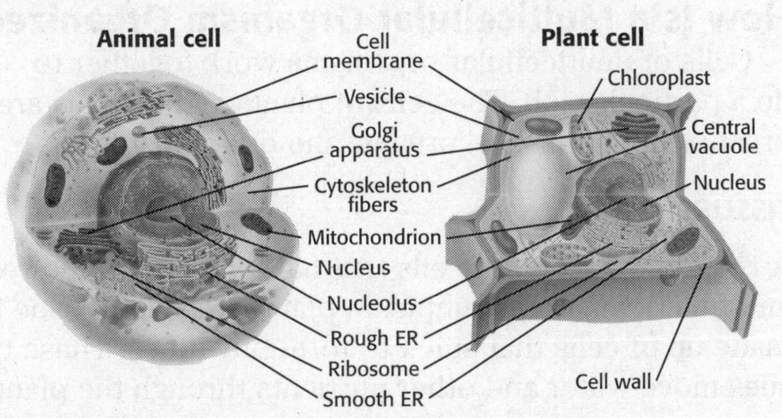

READING TOOLBOX

Organize After you read this section, make a Concept Map that shows the relationships among the following: multicellular, unicellular, prokaryotes, eukaryotes, colonial organisms, cells, tissues, organs, organ systems.

LOOKING CLOSER

1. Describe What is the function of pili?

____

____

____

LOOKING CLOSER

2. List What three structures are found in a plant cell but not in an animal cell?

____

____

____

What Body Types Can Organisms Have?

UNICELLULAR

In a unicellular organism, one cell must carry out all the organism's activities. Some unicellular organisms live independently, but others live in groups. Cells that live in connected groups but do not depend on one another to survive are called **colonial organisms**. For example, some bacteria stay attached to one another after dividing. However, the cells will survive if they are separated.

MULTICELLULAR

A multicellular organism is made up of many individual cells that coordinate their activities. Multicellular organisms, such as plants and animals, are made up of thousands, millions, or even trillions of cells. In most cases, their cells are *specialized*. This means they have different structures that let them carry out particular functions for the organism. Specialized cells form during the process of *differentiation*. ☑

Talk About It

Discuss With a partner, identify as many multicellular organisms and unicellular organisms as you can. Compare the lists and talk about why one list may be longer than the other.

3. Describe What happens during the process of differentiation?

How Is a Multicellular Organism Organized?

Cells of multicellular organisms work together to do a particular job. The cells of plants and animals are organized into tissues, organs, and organ systems.

TISSUES

A **tissue** is a group of cells that have similar structures and functions. For example, in plants, vascular tissue is made up of cells that stack to form tiny tubes. These tissues move water and other nutrients through the plant.

Critical Thinking

4. Apply Concepts Could a prokaryote have tissues, organs, and organ systems? Explain your answer.

ORGANS

An **organ** is a structure made up of two or more tissues that has a specialized function. For example, in animals, the heart is an organ made of muscle, nerve, and other tissues. These tissues work together to pump blood. In plants, a leaf is an organ made of vascular and other tissues. These tissues work together to collect sunlight and make sugars. ☑

READING CHECK

5. Explain What is the relationship between tissues and organs?

____

____

ORGAN SYSTEMS

An **organ system** is a group of organs that work together to carry out a major body function. For example, many animals have a circulatory system that is made up of a heart, blood vessels, and blood. In plants, the shoot system is made up of stems, leaves, and vascular tissues.

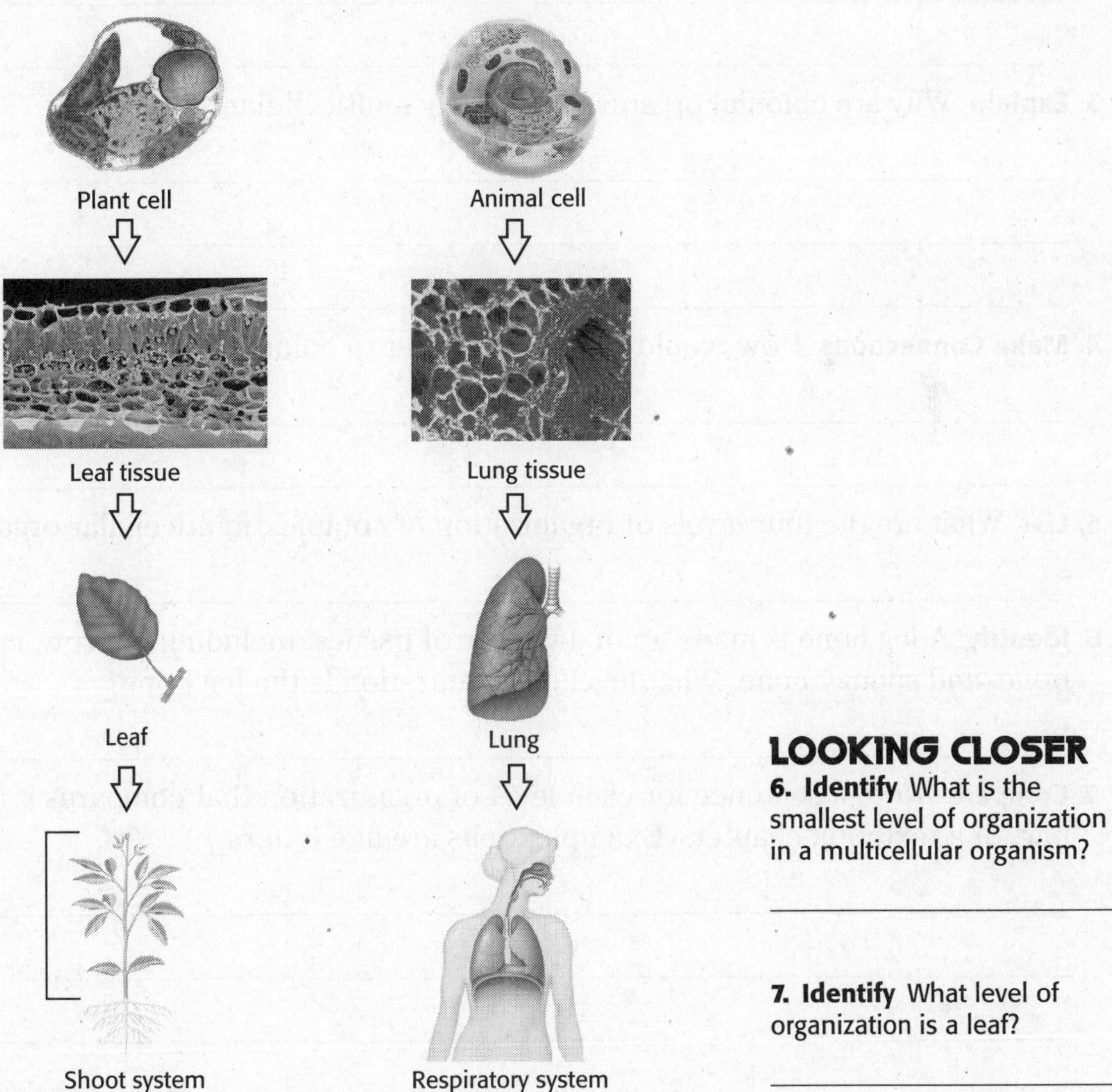

LOOKING CLOSER

6. Identify What is the smallest level of organization in a multicellular organism?

____

7. Identify What level of organization is a leaf?

____

Name ______________________ Class ______________ Date ____________

Section 3 Review

SECTION VOCABULARY

colonial organism a collection of genetically identical cells that are permanently associated but in which little or no integration of cell activities occurs **flagellum** a long, hairlike structure that grows out of a cell and enables the cell to move	**organ** a collection of tissues that carry out a specialized function of the body **organ system** a group of organs that work together to perform body functions **tissue** a group of similar cells that perform a common function

1. Explain Why are specialized cells found only in multicellular organisms?

____

____

____

2. List Identify four ways that prokaryotes can differ from one another

____

____

3. Explain Why are colonial organisms not truly multicellular?

____

____

____

4. Make Connections How would pili be important to colonial bacteria?

____

____

5. List What are the four levels of organization of complex multicellular organisms?

____

6. Identify A leg bone is made up of a variety of tissues, including marrow, compact bone, and spongy bone. What level of organization is the leg bone?

____

7. Compare Write a sentence for each level of organization that compares it to a part of a textbook chapter. (Example: Cells are like letters.)

____

____

____

Name ______________________ Class ______________ Date ______________

CHAPTER 8 Cells and Their Environment

SECTION 1

Cell Membrane

KEY IDEAS

As you read this section, keep these questions in mind:
- How does the cell membrane help a cell maintain homeostasis?
- How does the cell membrane restrict the exchange of substances?
- What are some functions of membrane proteins?

How Does a Cell Maintain Homeostasis?

Like organisms, individual cells must maintain homoeostasis to live. The cell membrane performs many functions that help a cell maintain homeostasis. Some of these functions are listed below:

- control which substances pass into the cell
- help the cell keep its shape
- recognize substances that might harm the cell
- communicate with other cells

The cell membrane acts like a gatekeeper. It allows some materials to enter the cell, but not others. The structure of the cell membrane allows it to perform its function.

READING TOOLBOX

Underline As you read this section, underline the answers to the Key Ideas questions.

Background

Recall that *homeostasis* is the maintenance of stable internal conditions in a changing environment.

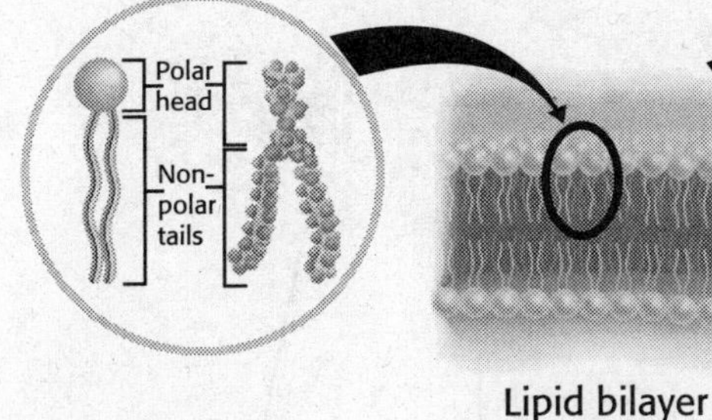

Lipid bilayer

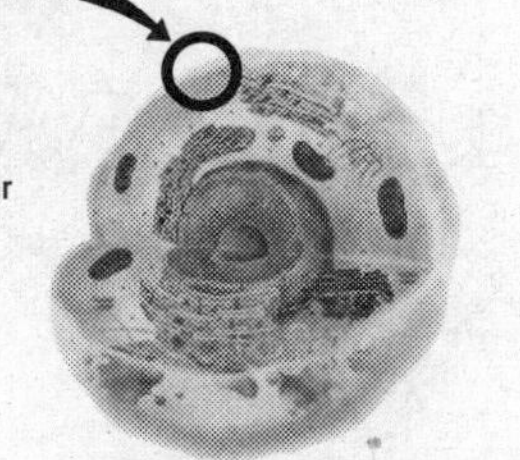

A **phospholipid** is a specialized lipid made of a phosphate "head" and two fatty acid "tails." Water attracts the polar end. Water repels the nonpolar end.

The **lipid bilayer** is two layers of phospholipids. One of the two layers of the lipid bilayer faces the cytoplasm of the cell. The other layer faces the cell's surroundings.

The cell membrane is made of a lipid bilayer.

Critical Thinking

1. Infer Why do you think the nonpolar tails of phospholipids face away from the cell cytoplasm and the cell's surroundings?

____

____

____

____

____

MEMBRANE STRUCTURE AND FUNCTION

The arrangement of phospholipids in the lipid bilayer makes the cell membrane *selectively permeable.* That is, the lipid bilayer allows only certain substances, such as small nonpolar molecules, to pass through. For example, the nonpolar area between the two layers of lipids repels ions and most polar molecules. Thus, such substances cannot pass easily through the membrane. ☑

2. Define What does *selectively permeable* mean?

____

____

____

What Do Membrane Proteins Do?

The lipid bilayer has many different kinds of proteins in it. Membrane proteins perform important functions for the cell.

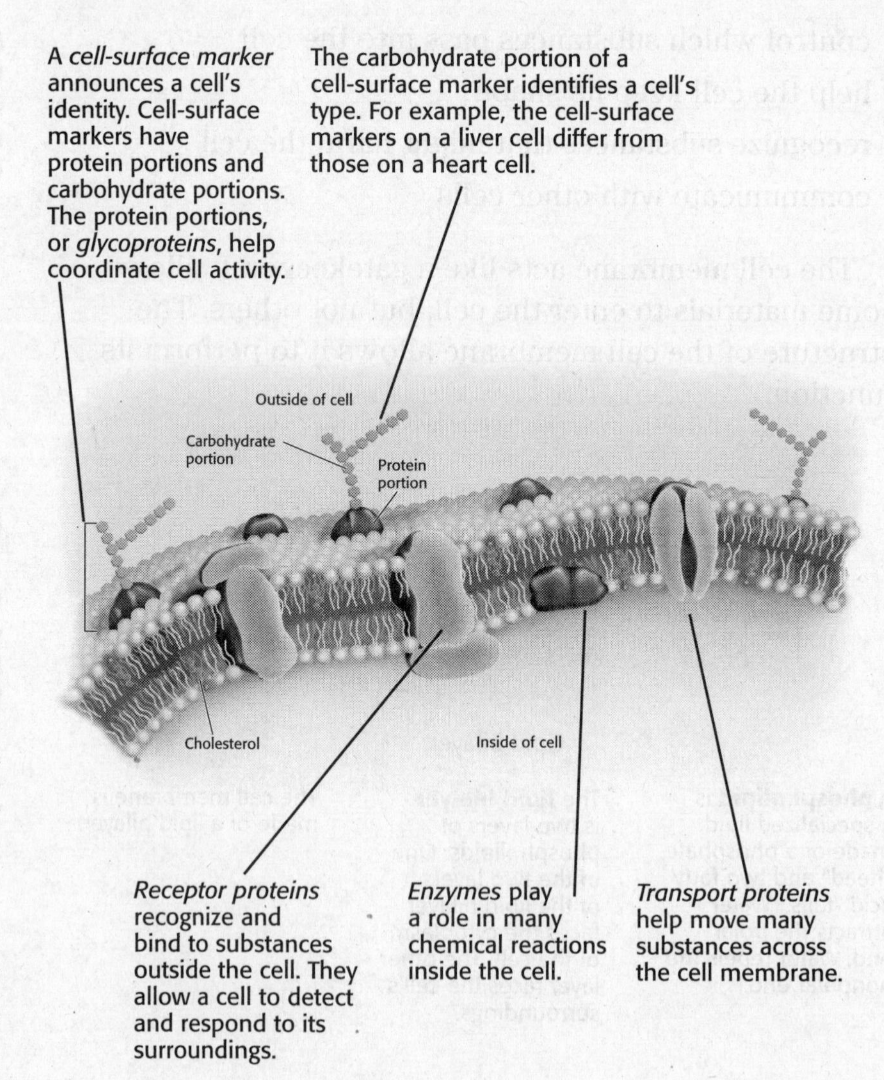

LOOKING CLOSER

3. Identify What kinds of membrane proteins allow a cell to detect its surroundings?

____

____

4. Identify What is the function of transport proteins?

____

____

____

Name ______________________ Class ______________ Date ______________

Section 1 Review

SECTION VOCABULARY

lipid bilayer the basic structure of a biological membrane, composed of two layers of phospholipids	**phospholipid** a lipid that contains phosphorous and that is a structural component in cell membranes

1. List What are four functions of the cell membrane that help a cell maintain homeostasis?

____

____

____

____

2. Identify Label the two main parts of the structure below. Which of these parts faces the area between the two layers of the lipid bilayer?

____

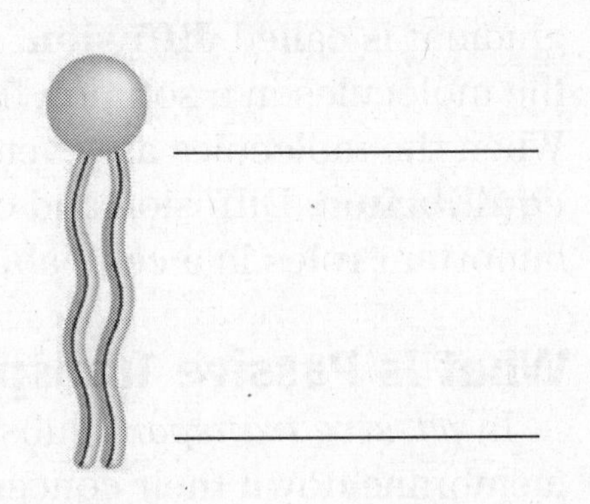

3. Explain Why are ions and polar molecules unable to pass easily though the lipid bilayer?

____

____

4. Identify What are two functions of cell-surface markers?

____

____

5. Predict Suppose a cell were exposed to a drug that caused transport proteins in the cell membrane to stop working. What would happen to the cell?

____

____

____

Name ______________________ Class ______________ Date ______________

CHAPTER 8 Cells and Their Environment

SECTION 2

Cell Transport

KEY IDEAS

As you read this section, keep these questions in mind:

- What determines the direction in which passive transport occurs?
- What is osmosis?
- How do substances move against their concentration gradients?

What Is a Concentration Gradient?

The *concentration* of a substance is the amount of that substance in a given volume. Substances in a solution tend to move from an area of higher concentration to an area of lower concentration. When one area has a higher concentration than another area, a **concentration gradient** exists.

Movement of a substance down its concentration gradient is called **diffusion**. Diffusion continues until the molecules in a solution fill up the space evenly. When the molecules are evenly spaced, the solution is in **equilibrium**. Diffusion and concentration gradients play important roles in a cell's ability to function and survive.

READING TOOLBOX

Summarize After you read this section, make a Concept Map to show the relationships among the vocabulary terms. In your Concept Map, also include the following: active transport, passive transport, vesicles, simple diffusion, and facilitated diffusion.

Critical Thinking

1. Compare How does simple diffusion differ from facilitated diffusion?

____

____

____

____

____

____

What Is Passive Transport?

In *passive transport*, substances cross the cell membrane down their concentration gradients. Passive transport does not require energy from the cell.

A cell uses two main types of passive transport: simple diffusion and facilitated diffusion. In *simple diffusion*, small, nonpolar molecules can pass directly through the lipid bilayer. In *facilitated diffusion*, transport proteins help ions and polar molecules diffuse into the cell.

LOOKING CLOSER

2. Infer What are two likely reasons a Cl^- ion cannot pass through a sodium ion channel?

____

____

____

____

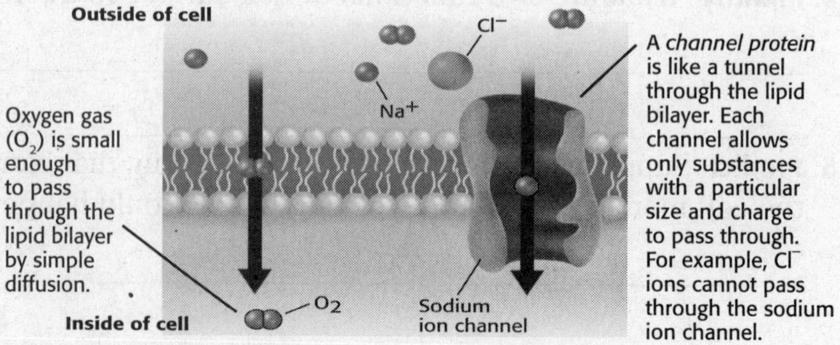

CARRIER PROTEINS

Carrier proteins are another type of transport protein. They move substances through the lipid bilayer by binding to them. A carrier protein transports only substances that fit its binding site.

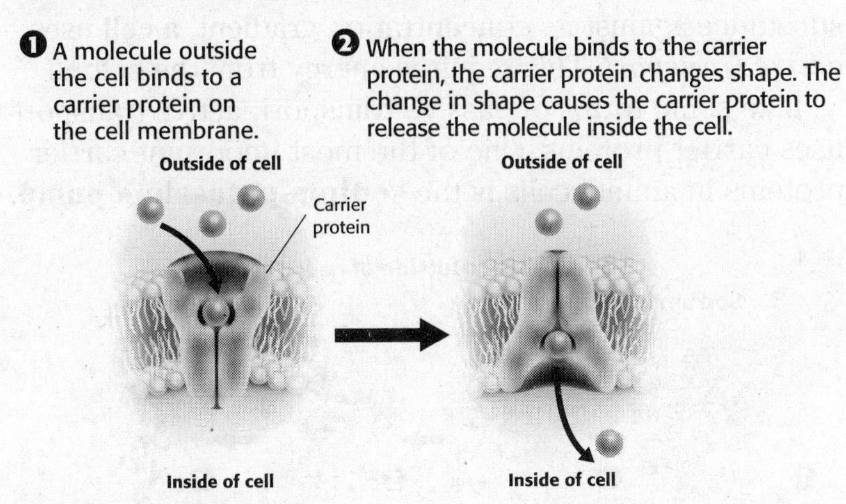

LOOKING CLOSER

3. Identify What happens to a carrier protien when a molecule outside the cell binds to it?

____

____

What Is Osmosis?

Water diffuses across the cell membrane in a process called **osmosis**. Osmosis is a form of passive transport.

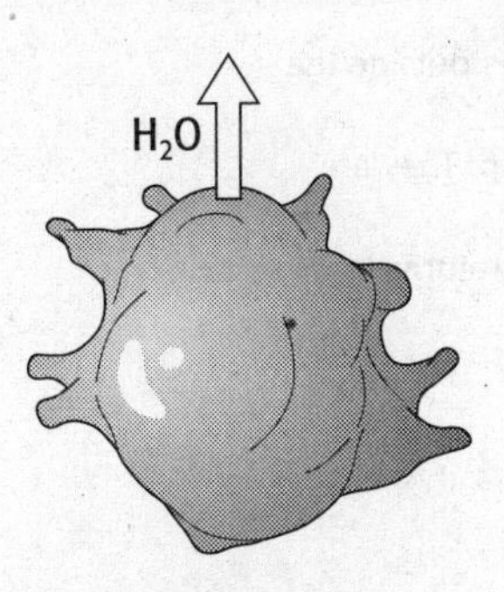

A cell in a hypertonic solution will shrink.

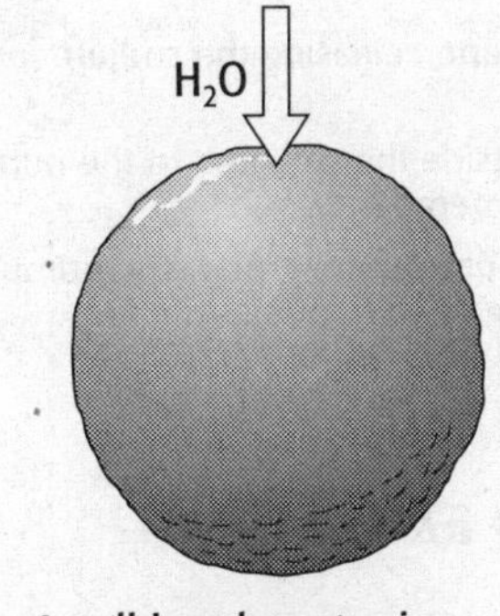

A cell in a hypotonic solution will swell and may burst.

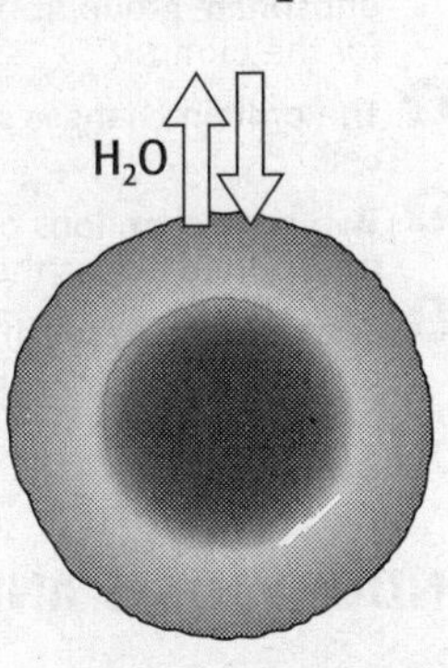

A cell in an isotonic solution stays the same size.

Type of solution	Description
Hypertonic	The solution has a higher concentration of solutes than the cell cytoplasm has. Thus, the solution has a lower concentration of water. Water flows out of the cell down its concentration gradient.
Hypotonic	The solution has a lower concentration of solutes and a higher concentration of water than the cell cytoplasm has. Water flows into the cell down its concentration gradient.
Isotonic	The concentrations of solutes and water in the solution are equal to those in the cell cytoplasm. Water diffuses into and out of the cell at equal rates.

LOOKING CLOSER

4. Describe In which direction does water move when a cell is placed into a hypotonic solution?

____

____

LOOKING CLOSER

5. Compare A cell is placed into a hypertonic solution. How does the concentration of water differ in the solution and the cell cytoplasm?

____

____

____

____

What Is Active Transport?

Often, a cell must move substances from an area where they are less concentrated to an area where they are more concentrated. That is, the cell must move substances against their concentration gradients. To move a substance against its concentration gradient, a cell uses *active transport*. This requires energy from the cell. ☑

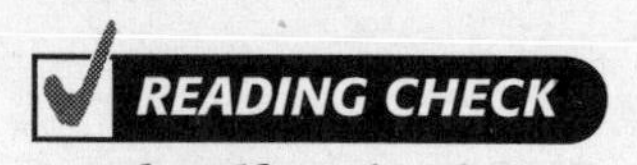

READING CHECK

6. Identify Why do cells need active transport?

____

____

____

Like some forms of passive transport, active transport uses carrier proteins. One of the most important carrier proteins in animal cells is the **sodium-potassium pump**.

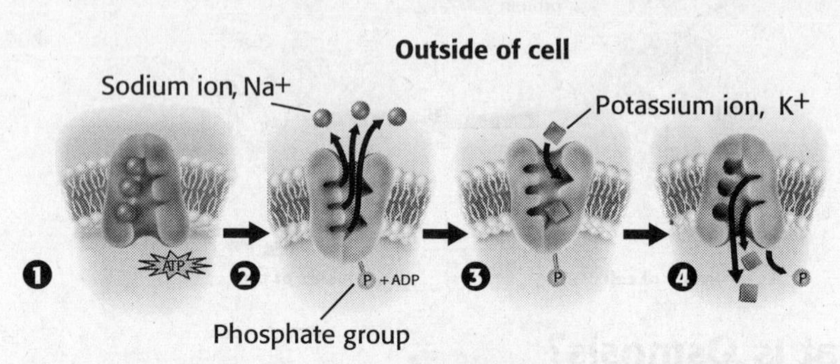

1. Three sodium ions from inside the cell bind to the protein pump. A phosphate group from ATP also binds. ATP is the source of energy for the pump.
2. The protein changes shape, releasing the sodium ions outside the cell.
3. Two potassium ions outside the cell bind to the pump. They are transported across the membrane.
4. The pump releases the phosphate group. The pump returns to its original shape, releasing the two potassium ions.

LOOKING CLOSER

7. Describe What is the role of ATP in the sodium-potassium pump?

____

____

____

ENDOCYTOSIS AND EXOCYTOSIS

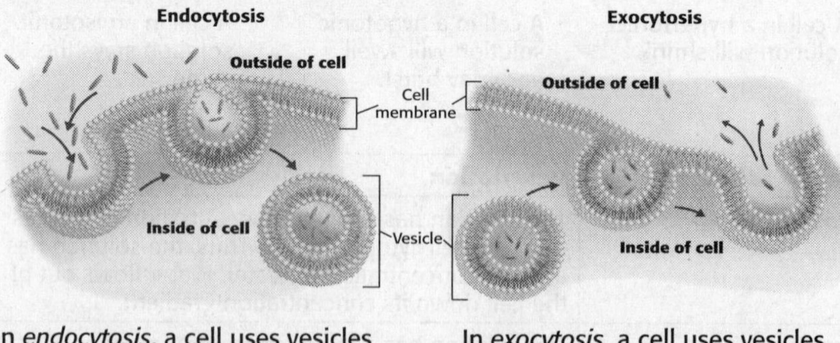

In *endocytosis*, a cell uses vesicles to move materials, such as nutrients, into the cell.

In *exocytosis*, a cell uses vesicles to move materials, such as wastes, pathogens, or proteins, out of the cell.

LOOKING CLOSER

8. Describe What is the role of vesicles in endocytosis and exocytosis?

____

____

____

Name ______________________ Class ______________ Date ______________

Section 2 Review

SECTION VOCABULARY

carrier protein a protein that transports substances across a cell membrane **concentration gradient** a difference in the concentration of a substance across a distance **diffusion** the movement of particles from regions of higher density to regions of lower density **equilibrium** in biology, a state that exists when the concentration of a substance is the same throughout a space	**osmosis** the diffusion of water or another solvent from a more dilute solution (of a solute) to a more concentrated solution (of the solute) through a membrane that is permeable to the solvent **sodium-potassium pump** a carrier protein that uses ATP to actively transport sodium ions out of a cell and potassium ions into the cell

1. Explain Why does diffusion of water happen when there are dissolved particles on one side of a membrane but not on the other?

____

____

____

____

2. Compare Complete the Venn diagram to compare passive transport and active transport. In the diagram, include at least one example of each.

3. Predict If a cell were unable to make ATP, how would the cell's transport processes be affected?

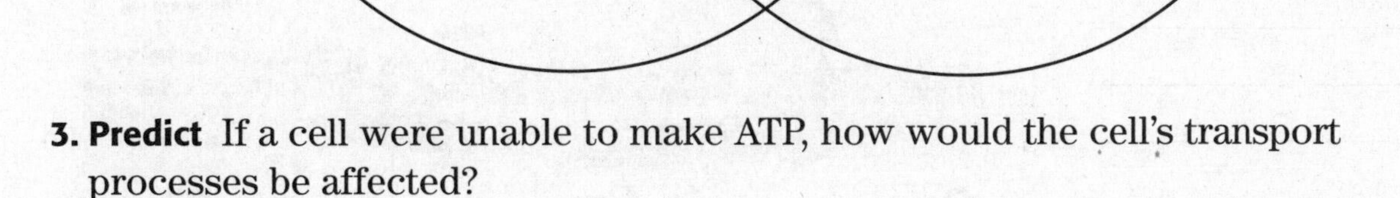

____

____

____

Name ______________________ Class ______________ Date ____________

SECTION 3

Cell Communication

KEY IDEAS

As you read this section, keep these questions in mind:

- How do cells use signal molecules?
- What are receptor proteins?
- How do cells respond to signals?

READING TOOLBOX

Draw Sometimes drawings can help you explain and remember what you have read. After you read this section, draw a picture to represent the answers to each Key Ideas question.

Talk About It

Brainstorm In a small group, discuss some reasons cells need to communicate. Why is communication important among cells in a multicellular organism? Why do you think unicellular organisms need to communicate with one another?

How Do Cells Communicate?

To coordinate their activities, cells must communicate. Cells use signal molecules to communicate with one another. A **signal** is something that directs, guides, or warns an organism. A cell can use hormones and electrical signals to communicate with other cells over long distances. It can use receptor proteins to communicate with cells nearby.

Receptor proteins on a cell's membrane receive, and sometimes respond to, signals. A receptor protein has a very specific shape that allows it to bind to signal molecules from other cells. When a receptor protein binds to a signal molecule, the protein changes shape. The shape change passes information to the cytoplasm of the cell.

How Do Cells Respond to Signals?

A cell may respond to signals in three main ways:

- change how permeable its membrane is
- activate enzymes, which trigger chemical reactions
- form a **second messenger**, which acts as a signal molecule within the cell ☑

READING CHECK

1. Identify What is the role of a second messenger?

____

____

____

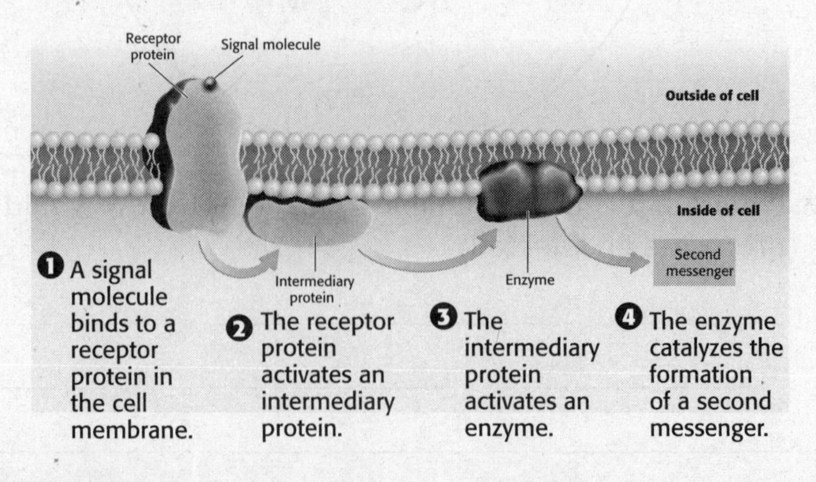

❶ A signal molecule binds to a receptor protein in the cell membrane. ❷ The receptor protein activates an intermediary protein. ❸ The intermediary protein activates an enzyme. ❹ The enzyme catalyzes the formation of a second messenger.

Name ________________ Class ________ Date ________

Section 3 Review

SECTION VOCABULARY

receptor protein a protein that binds specific signal molecules, which causes the cell to respond **second messenger** a molecule that is generated when a specific substance attaches to a receptor on the outside of a cell membrane, which produces a change in cellular function	**signal** anything that serves to direct, guide, or warn

1. **Identify** What are two ways cells can communicate over long distances? What is one way cells can communicate with cells that are nearby?

2. **Identify** What is the function of receptor proteins?

3. **Describe** What happens when a receptor protein binds to a signal molecule?

4. **List** What are three ways a cell may respond when a signal molecule binds to a receptor protein?

5. **Infer** Why is it important that each receptor protein binds to only one signal molecule?

Name ______________________ Class ______________ Date ______________

CHAPTER 9 Photosynthesis and Cellular Respiration

SECTION 1

Energy in Living Systems

KEY IDEAS

As you read this section, keep these questions in mind:

- What type of energy is used in cells?
- How is an organism's metabolism related to the carbon cycle?
- How is energy released in a cell?

READING TOOLBOX

Ask Questions Read this section quietly to yourself. As you read, write down any questions you have. When you finish reading, work in a small group to figure out the answers to your questions.

Where Do Organisms Get Energy?

Why do you shiver when you are cold? Your body is trying to maintain homeostasis. When you shiver, your muscles produce heat to help warm you up. You and all other organisms need chemical energy to maintain homeostasis. This chemical energy comes from carbon compounds in food.

Background

Recall that *homeostasis* is the process of maintaining consistent internal conditions, even if the outside environment changes.

Almost all of the energy in carbon compounds comes from the sun. Plants, algae, and some prokaryotes use energy from sunlight to change carbon dioxide and water into carbon compounds. This process is called **photosynthesis**. During photosynthesis, the energy in sunlight is stored in chemical bonds in carbon compounds. Organisms that carry out photosynthesis are called *autotrophs*.

Critical Thinking

1. Predict What would happen to life on Earth if all the autotrophs disappeared?

____

____

____

____

Other organisms, including all animals and fungi, cannot perform photosynthesis. They get energy by absorbing carbon compounds from other organisms or by eating other organisms.

Watermelon plants, like other autotrophs, produce their own food through photosynthesis. Humans, like many other animals, get energy by eating autotrophs.

LOOKING CLOSER

2. Identify Where do autotrophs get food?

____

____

____

How Is Metabolism Part of the Carbon Cycle?

Metabolism involves either using energy to build carbon compounds or breaking down carbon compounds to release the energy in them. Therefore, metabolism is part of Earth's carbon cycle. The processes of the carbon cycle move carbon compounds between and within ecosystems. Because organisms obtain energy from carbon compounds, the carbon cycle also delivers chemical energy to organisms. ☑

Background

Recall that *metabolism* is all of the chemical reactions that occur within an organism.

3. Explain How is metabolism part of the carbon cycle?

____

____

____

____

How Do Cells Use the Energy from Food?

The main organic compound that cells use is glucose. Glucose is produced during photosynthesis. The overall chemical reaction that occurs during photosynthesis is shown below.

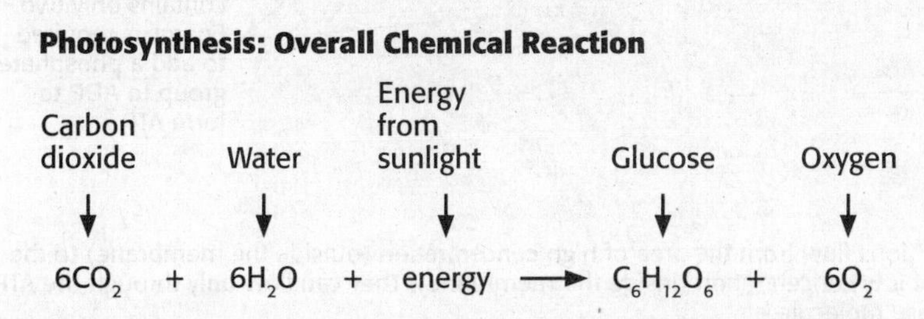

In order to get energy from glucose molecules, most organisms use cellular respiration. During **cellular respiration**, glucose combines with oxygen to produce carbon dioxide, water, and energy, as shown below.

Cellular Respiration: Overall Chemical Reaction

Glucose		Oxygen		Carbon dioxide		Water		Energy for metabolism
↓		↓		↓		↓		↓
$C_6H_{12}O_6$	+	$6O_2$	→	$6CO_2$	+	$6H_2O$	+	energy

LOOKING CLOSER

4. Compare How is the overall chemical reaction for cellular respiration related to the overall chemical reaction for photosynthesis?

____

____

If glucose and oxygen combined in a single step, all of the energy would be released as heat. Therefore, within a cell, the reaction between glucose and oxygen is broken up into several steps. The energy that is released at each step is stored as chemical energy in a molecule called adenosine triphosphate, or **ATP**.

ATP is the main energy source for cell processes. The figure at the top of the next page shows how ATP is produced. ☑

5. Identify What molecule is the main energy source for cell processes?

____

Talk About It

Summarize Review this figure by yourself. Then, describe what is shown in the figure to a partner.

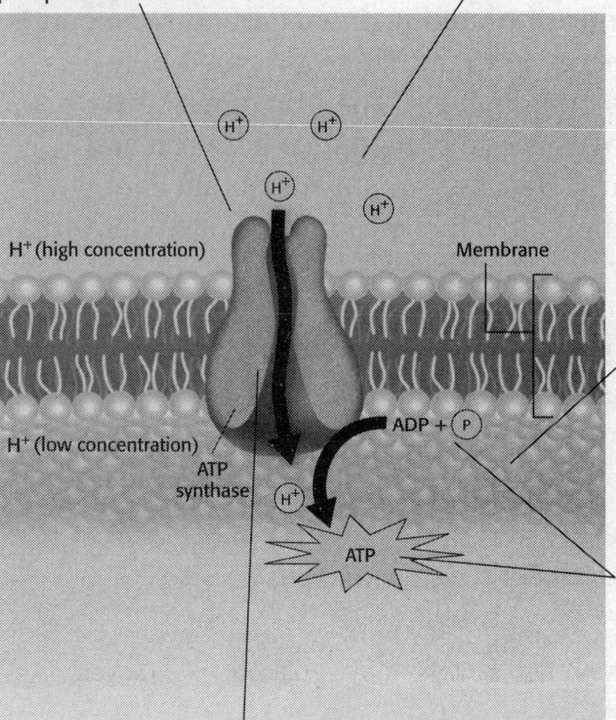

The H^+ ions flow from the area of high concentration (outside the membrane) to the area of low concentration (inside the membrane). They can flow only through the ATP synthase molecule.

LOOKING CLOSER

6. Identify What two molecules combine to form ATP?

____

____

The diagram above shows that the concentration of H^+ ions outside the membrane is higher than that inside the membrane. Remember that ions flow from areas of high concentration to low concentration. How, then, is the area of high concentration outside the membrane produced? The cell must use energy to move the hydrogen ions from inside the membrane to outside. This energy comes from an electron transport chain.

In an **electron transport chain**, energy is released as electrons move between different molecules. This released energy is used to move hydrogen ions from areas of low concentration to areas of high concentration. ☑

There are three main molecules that are part of electron transport chains: NADH, $FADH_2$, and NADPH. Each of these molecules can release energy by losing electrons. The energy can then be used to move hydrogen ions across the membrane.

7. Describe How is energy released in an electron transport chain?

____

____

____

Name ______________________ Class ______________ Date ______________

Section 1 Review

SECTION VOCABULARY

ATP adenosine triphosphate, an organic molecule that acts as the main energy source for cell processes; composed of a nitrogenous base, a sugar, and three phosphate groups

ATP synthase an enzyme that catalyzes the synthesis of ATP

cellular respiration the process by which cells produce energy from carbohydrates; atmospheric oxygen combines with glucose to form water and carbon dioxide

electron transport chain a series of molecules, found in the inner membranes of mitochondria and chloroplasts, through which electrons pass in a process that causes protons to build up on one side of the membrane

photosynthesis the process by which plants, algae, and some bacteria use sunlight, carbon dioxide, and water to produce carbohydrates and oxygen

1. Describe How does ATP synthase produce ATP?

____

____

2. Explain How does the carbon cycle deliver energy to organisms?

____

____

3. Identify How do organisms that are not autotrophs get energy?

____

____

4. Explain In cells, glucose is combined with oxygen in a series of steps instead of all at once. What is the reason for this?

____

____

____

5. Describe What happens in an electron transport chain?

____

____

____

6. Identify Name two molecules that can release energy as part of the electron transport chain.

____

____

Name ______________________ Class ______________ Date ______________

SECTION 2

Photosynthesis

KEY IDEAS

As you read this section, keep these questions in mind:

- Where does photosynthesis occur?
- What is the role of pigments in photosynthesis?
- What are the roles of the electron transport chains?
- How do plants make sugars and store extra unused energy?
- What are three environmental factors that affect photosynthesis?

Where Does Photosynthesis Occur?

Most photosynthetic organisms have special organelles called *chloroplasts* that allow them to carry out photosynthesis. The diagram below shows the cellular structures that are used to perform photosynthesis.

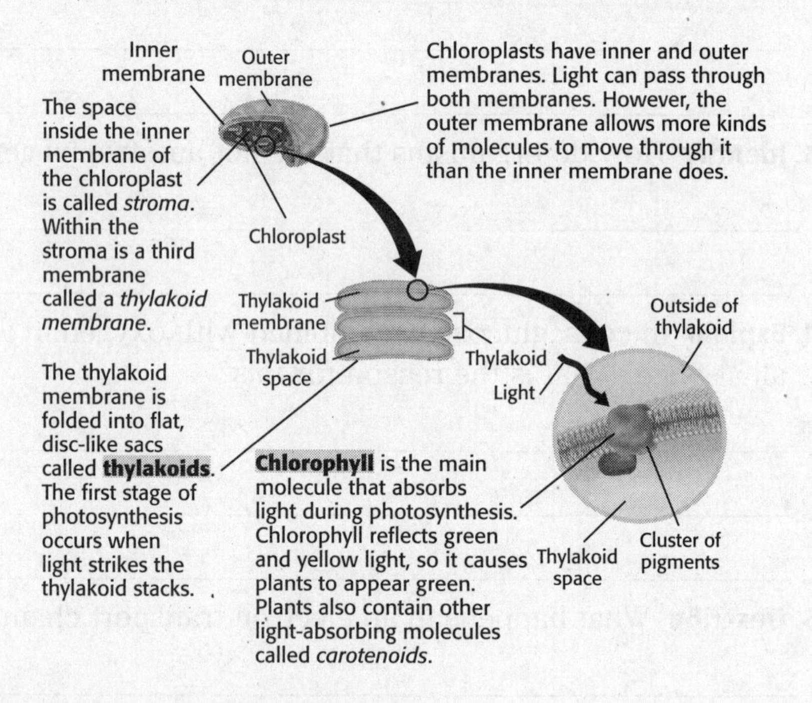

What Are Pigments?

Some of the molecules that are part of the thylakoid membrane are pigments. A **pigment** is a substance that absorbs certain colors of light. When light strikes a thylakoid, pigment molecules absorb energy. The energy is transferred to a special chlorophyll molecule. There, electrons absorb the energy and become excited. The excited electrons have more energy. They can transfer this energy to other molecules.

READING TOOLBOX

Summarize After you read this section, make flowcharts showing what happens during the electron transport chains and during the Calvin cycle.

Background

Recall that during *photosynthesis*, energy from sunlight is used to convert carbon dioxide and water into glucose and oxygen.

LOOKING CLOSER

1. Compare How is the inner membrane of a chloroplast different from the outer membrane?

____

____

____

____

How Is Light Energy Converted into Chemical Energy?

Molecules called *electron carriers* transfer the excited electrons to two electron transport chains. The first chain uses the energy in the excited electrons to make ATP. The second chain uses the energy in the excited electrons to make NADPH. ☑

READING CHECK

2. Identify What are two compounds that are produced by the electron transport chains in photosynthesis?

____

Electron Transport Chains in Photosynthesis

❶ Light excites electrons in pigments such as chlorophyll. The excited electrons leave the pigments. Electrons from water replace the electrons lost by the chlorophyll. The water breaks down to produce hydrogen ions, H^+, and oxygen gas, O_2. The O_2 is released into the atmosphere.

❷ A protein in the thylakoid membrane uses the energy in the excited electrons to pump hydrogen ions into the thylakoid.

❸ The hydrogen ions move through ATP synthase molecules to the outside of the thylakoid, producing ATP. The ATP is used in later stages of photosynthesis.

❹ Light excites electrons in another chlorophyll molecule. The excited electrons then move on to the second chain. The electrons from the first chain replace these excited electrons.

❺ The excited electrons combine with H^+ ions and $NADP^+$ to form NADPH. Like ATP, NADPH provides energy for the final stage of photosynthesis.

First electron transport chain

Second electron transport chain

Light

Light

Pigments

$NADP^+$

NADPH

Path of electrons

e^-

4 H^+

O_2

2 H_2O

ATP synthase

ADP + Ⓟ

ATP

LOOKING CLOSER

3. Describe Where does the oxygen that is produced during photosynthesis come from?

____

How Does Photosynthesis Produce Sugar?

In the final stage of photosynthesis, ATP and NADPH are used to produce sugar molecules from carbon dioxide, CO_2. Unlike the electron transport chains, these reactions do not require light.

Different autotrophs use different processes to change carbon dioxide into sugar. The most common process is the **Calvin cycle**, which is shown on the next page. ☑

4. Define What is the Calvin cycle?

____

____

____

The Calvin Cycle

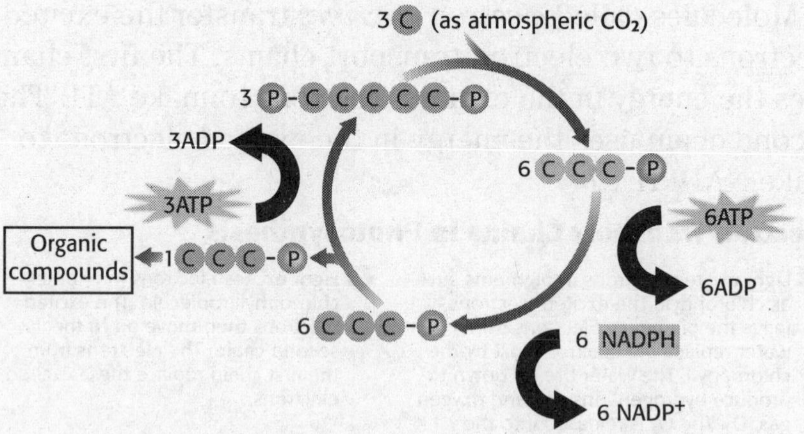

During the Calvin cycle, three molecules of CO_2 combine with three molecules of another compound in a series of steps. Proteins use energy from ATP and NADPH to combine the CO_2 with other molecules. The Calvin cycle produces molecules of a three-carbon sugar that can be used to produce other carbon compounds, including glucose.

LOOKING CLOSER

5. Describe Where do proteins get the energy to combine CO_2 and other compounds in the Calvin cycle?

____

____

What Factors Affect Photosynthesis?

Photosynthesis does not happen at the same rate under all conditions. Temperature, amount of light, and amount of carbon dioxide are three factors that can affect how fast photosynthesis occurs. The table below shows how each factor affects the rate of photosynthesis.

Factor	Effect
Amount of light	In general, as the amount of light increases, the rate of photosynthesis increases.
Amount of carbon dioxide	In general, as the amount of carbon dioxide increases, the rate of photosynthesis increases.
Temperature	Photosynthesis occurs most quickly within a certain range of temperatures. Temperatures that are too high or too low can make the proteins involved in photosynthesis stop working.

Critical Thinking

6. Explain What do you think is the reason that an increase in carbon dioxide generally increases the rate of photosynthesis?

____

____

____

____

____

Name ______________________ Class ______________ Date ______________

Section 2 Review

SECTION VOCABULARY

Calvin cycle a biochemical pathway of photosynthesis in which carbon dioxide is converted into glucose using ATP

chlorophyll a green pigment that is present in most plant and algae cells and some bacteria, that gives plants their characteristic green color, and that absorbs light to provide energy for photosynthesis

pigment a substance that gives another substance or a mixture its color

thylakoid a membrane system found within chloroplasts that contains the components for photosynthesis

1. Identify Name two pigments that are found in chloroplasts.

____

____

2. Describe What is the role of pigments in photosynthesis?

____

____

3. Compare Fill in the blanks in the table below.

Process in photosynthesis	Purpose of this process	Does this process require light?
	convert light energy into chemical energy in ATP and NADPH	
	produce organic compounds, such as glucose, from carbon dioxide	

4. Identify Where does the energy to move hydrogen ions across the thylakoid membrane come from?

____

____

5. Explain Why does the amount of light present affect the rate of photosynthesis?

____

____

____

6. Infer A student places a plant in a dark room that contains a great deal of carbon dioxide. Will the plant be able to carry out photosynthesis?

____

Name ______________________ Class ______________ Date ______________

CHAPTER 9 Photosynthesis and Cellular Respiration

SECTION 3

Cellular Respiration

KEY IDEAS

As you read this section, keep these questions in mind:

- How does glycolysis produce ATP?
- How is ATP produced in aerobic respiration?
- Why is fermentation important?

READING TOOLBOX

Summarize As you read, underline the important ideas in this section. When you are finished reading, write a one- or two-paragraph summary of the section, using the underlined ideas.

What Is Glycolysis?

There are three main parts of cellular respiration: glycolysis, the Krebs cycle, and the electron transport chain. During **glycolysis**, glucose is broken down into two molecules of a three-carbon compound called *pyruvate*. The figure below shows how this occurs.

Background

Recall that *cellular respiration* is the process by which organisms get energy from organic compounds.

Glycolysis

1. Enzymes add two phosphate molecules from ATP to a glucose molecule and break the glucose apart. This forms two three-carbon molecules, each of which contains a phosphate group.
2. Each three-carbon molecule reacts with another phosphate group. During this reaction, two hydrogen atoms are transferred to two molecules of NAD^+. This forms two molecules of NADH, an electron carrier.
3. Each three-carbon molecule is then converted into a molecule of pyruvate. This process produces 4 ATP molecules. Because the first part of glycolysis requires two ATP molecules, the overall process produces two molecules of ATP.

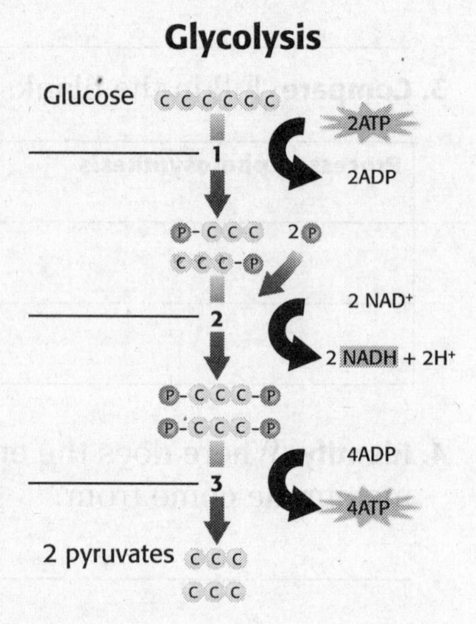

LOOKING CLOSER

1. Identify How many molecules of ATP does the overall process of glycolysis produce?

____

What Happens During Aerobic Respiration?

Glycolysis is an **anaerobic** process. That means it does not require oxygen. Most organisms use oxygen to release even more energy from glucose. This process is called **aerobic** respiration, because it requires oxygen. ☑

2. Define What does *aerobic* mean?

____

____

The Krebs cycle and the electron transport chain are the two parts of aerobic respiration. They occur within mitochondria. During the **Krebs cycle**, pyruvate is broken down to produce energy. This energy is stored in the molecules NADH, $FADH_2$, and ATP. During the electron transport chain, ATP and water are produced.

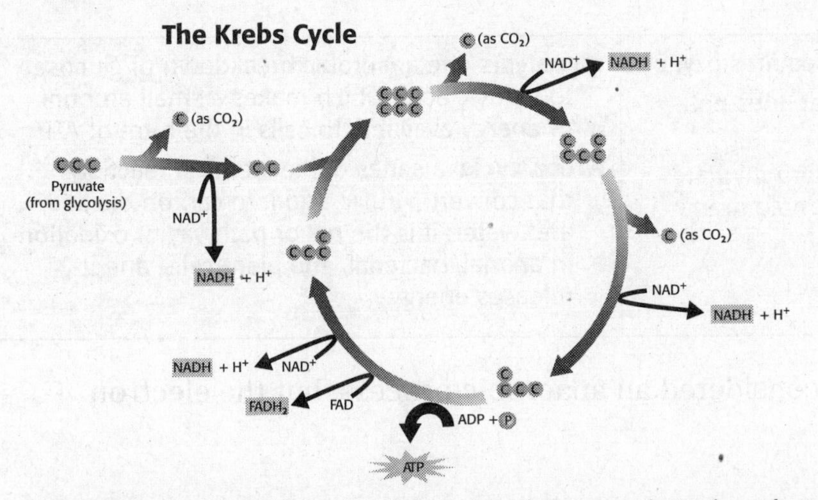

A pyruvate molecule that is produced during glycolysis enters the Krebs cycle. It reacts with other compounds through a series of steps. At each step, energy is released. This energy is then stored in the compounds ATP, NADH, and $FADH_2$. For each molecule of pyruvate that enters the Krebs cycle, one molecule of ATP, three molecules of NADH, and one molecule of $FADH_2$ are produced.

The Electron Transport Chain in Cellular Respiration

❶ Electrons from NADH and $FADH_2$ move through the electron transport chain. Proteins use the energy from the electrons to move hydrogen ions across the membrane of the mitochondrion.

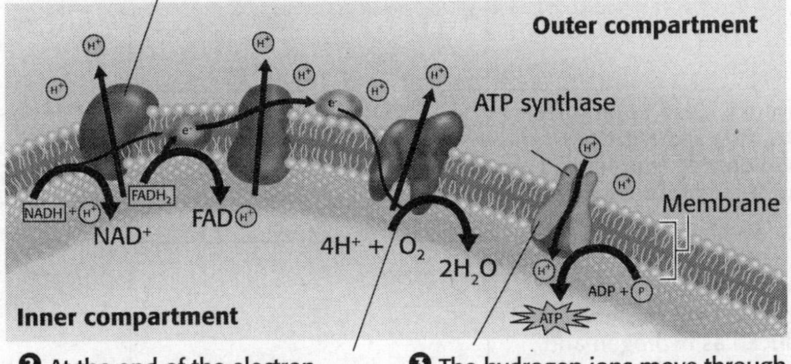

❷ At the end of the electron transport chain, the electrons have lost most of their energy. They combine with oxygen atoms and hydrogen ions to form water.

❸ The hydrogen ions move through ATP synthase molecules, producing ATP molecules. The electron transport chain can produce up to 32 molecules of ATP for each molecule of glucose that enters glycolysis.

FERMENTATION

Some organisms get all of their energy from glycolysis. They use a process called **fermentation** to produce the NAD^+ that accepts electrons during glycolysis. During fermentation, electrons move from NADH to pyruvate. ☑

Fermentation allows cells in aerobic organisms to continue to carry out glycolysis when there is no oxygen around. For example, your muscles can use fermentation to produce energy when you exercise too hard.

Talk About It

Summarize After you read this page, describe what happens during the Krebs cycle and the electron transport chain to a partner. Put the information into your own words.

Critical Thinking

3. Apply Concepts How many molecules of ATP, NADH, and $FADH_2$ are produced by the Krebs cycle for every molecule of glucose that enters glycolysis? (Hint: How many molecules of pyruvate are produced by each molecule of glucose?)

____

____

____

LOOKING CLOSER

4. Identify How many molecules of ATP can be produced by the electron transport chain for every molecule of glucose?

____

5. Explain How is NAD^+ generated during fermentation?

____

____

Name ______________________ Class ______________ Date __________

Section 3 Review

SECTION VOCABULARY

aerobic describes a process that requires oxygen

anaerobic describes a process that does not require oxygen

fermentation the breakdown of carbohydrates by enzymes, bacteria, yeasts, or mold in the absence of oxygen

glycolysis the anaerobic breakdown of glucose to pyruvic acid, which makes a small amount of energy available to cells in the form of ATP

Krebs cycle a series of biochemical reactions that convert pyruvic acid into carbon dioxide and water; it is the major pathway of oxidation in animal, bacterial, and plant cells, and it releases energy

1. Explain Why is glycolysis considered an anaerobic process, but the electron transport chain is not?

____

____

2. Describe Fill in the blank spaces in the table below.

Process	Description	Overall number of ATP molecules produced per molecule of glucose
	Glucose is broken down into two pyruvate molecules.	
	Pyruvate is used to produce NADH, ATP, and $FADH_2$; carbon dioxide is produced as pyruvate breaks down.	
	Energy from electrons in NADH and $FADH_2$ is used to produce ATP; water is produced as hydrogen and oxygen accept electrons.	

3. Compare Organism A can carry out cellular respiration. Organism B can carry out only glycolysis. Which organism will be able to use more of the energy in a molecule of glucose? Explain your answer. (Hint: Remember that ATP is the main source of energy for cellular processes.)

____

____

____

4. Describe Why is fermentation important?

____

____

Name _______________ Class _______________ Date _______________

SECTION 1

Cell Reproduction

KEY IDEAS

As you read this section, keep these questions in mind:

- Why do cells divide?
- How is DNA packaged into the nucleus?
- How do cells prepare for division?

Why Do Cells Divide?

Multicellular organisms, such as humans, grow and develop by making more cells. The new cells help organs and tissues grow and stay healthy. They also help repair injuries.

Larger cells are harder to maintain. Therefore, organisms grow by producing more cells instead of larger cells. The table below describes two reasons that large cells are harder to maintain.

Reason	Explanation
A larger cell requires more nutrients and produces more wastes.	As the cell gets larger, it becomes harder for enough materials to move into and out of the cell. If the cell gets too large, it cannot take in nutrients or get rid of wastes quickly enough.
A larger cell requires more proteins to function.	DNA must be copied in order to produce proteins. If a cell gets too large, DNA cannot be copied quickly enough to produce all the proteins the cell needs.

READING TOOLBOX

Summarize After you read this section, write a summary of the information in each figure. If you have trouble, work with a partner or a small group.

LOOKING CLOSER

1. Identify Give two reasons that a larger cell is harder to maintain.

____

____

____

What Are Chromosomes?

DNA is organized into units called genes. A **gene** is a segment of DNA that codes for RNA and protein. A human cell contains about 25,000 genes.

If the DNA in all these genes were stretched out, it would be about two meters long. To fit inside the nucleus of a cell, the DNA is organized and packaged into structures called **chromosomes**. Prokaryotic cells, such as bacteria, generally have only one circular chromosome. Eukaryotic cells contain many linear chromosomes. The figures on the next page show how DNA forms chromosomes in eukaryotic cells.

Critical Thinking

2. Compare What is the difference between genes, DNA, and chromosomes?

____

____

____

____

____

Proteins called **histones** help to organize DNA into chromosomes. The DNA wraps around groups of histones.

The DNA and the histone it is wrapped around make up a **nucleosome**. The nucleosomes and the DNA between them make up the **chromatin**.

A DNA molecule consists of two strands that are twisted in a double helix. In a chromosome, DNA is combined with proteins to form a material called chromatin.

The nucleosomes coil up and form a fiber. The fiber is about 30 nm in diameter, so it is called the *30-nm fiber*.

LOOKING CLOSER

3. Compare How is a histone different from a nucleosome?

____

____

____

____

What Happens As a Cell Prepares to Divide?

As a cell gets ready to divide, the DNA in each chromosome duplicates. The chromosomes also change form, as shown below.

Talk About It

Describe Relationships With a partner or in a small group, come up with some memory tricks to help you remember the difference between chromatin, chromosomes, and chromatids.

After the DNA has duplicated, the chromatin condenses even further. It forms loops around other proteins.

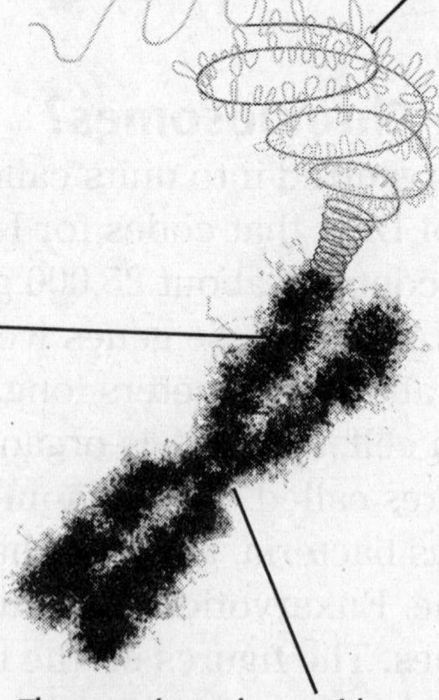

Each of the duplicated DNA strands coils up tightly. Each strand is called a **chromatid**. Each chromatid is made of a single strand of DNA. The two strands are called *sister chromatids* because they are identical.

The two sister chromatids are held together at a region called the **centromere**.

LOOKING CLOSER

4. Define What is a centromere?

____

____

____

Name ______________________ Class ______________ Date ______________

Section 1 Review

SECTION VOCABULARY

centromere the region of the chromosome that holds the two sister chromatids together during mitosis

chromatid one of the two strands of a chromosome that become visible during meiosis or mitosis

chromatin the substance that composes eukaryotic chromosomes; it consists of specific proteins, DNA, and small amounts of RNA

chromosome in a eukaryotic cell, one of the structures in the nucleus that are made up of DNA and protein; in a prokaryotic cell, the main ring of DNA

gene the most basic physical unit of heredity; a segment of nucleic acids that codes for a functional unit of RNA and/or a protein

histone a type of protein molecule found in the chromosomes of eukaryotic cells but not prokaryotic cells

nucleosome a eukaryotic structural unit of chromatin that consists of DNA wound around a core of histone proteins

1. Describe Relationships How is a cell's size related to its need for nutrients? How does this relationship make larger cells harder to maintain?

____

____

____

2. Summarize Fill in the blanks in the Concept Map below using the terms *chromatin*, *nucleosomes*, *histones*, and *DNA*.

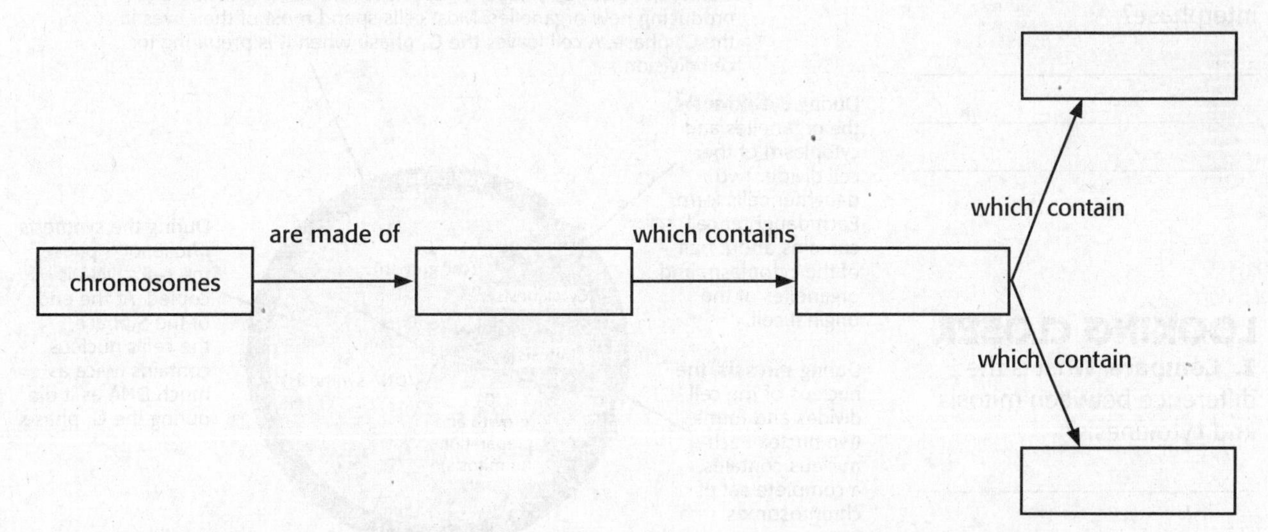

3. Describe Name two things that happen when a cell prepares to divide.

____

____

Name ______________________ Class ______________ Date ______________

CHAPTER 10 Cell Growth and Division

SECTION 2

Mitosis

KEY IDEAS

As you read this section, keep these questions in mind:

- What are the phases of the eukaryotic cell cycle?
- What are the four stages of mitosis?
- How does cytokinesis occur?

READING TOOLBOX

Summarize After you finish reading this section, make a flowchart describing the phases of the eukaryotic cell cycle. Make a second flowchart describing the stages of mitosis.

What Is the Eukaryotic Cell Cycle?

As a cell grows, it gets larger. Eventually, it divides to form two *daughter cells*. Each daughter cell then grows, gets larger, and eventually divides. This repeating sequence of cellular growth and division is called the **cell cycle**.

The eukaryotic cell cycle is made up of five phases, as shown in the figure below. During three of the phases, the cell is growing. Together, these three phases are known as **interphase**. During the other two phases, the cell is dividing. These two phases together are known as *cell division*. ☑

1. Define What is interphase?

____

____

____

During the *first gap phase*, or G_1 phase, the cell is growing and producing new organelles. Most cells spend most of their lives in the G_1 phase. A cell leaves the G_1 phase when it is preparing for cell division.

During **cytokinesis**, the organelles and cytoplasm of the cell divide. Two daughter cells form. Each daughter cell contains about half of the cytoplasm and organelles of the original cell.

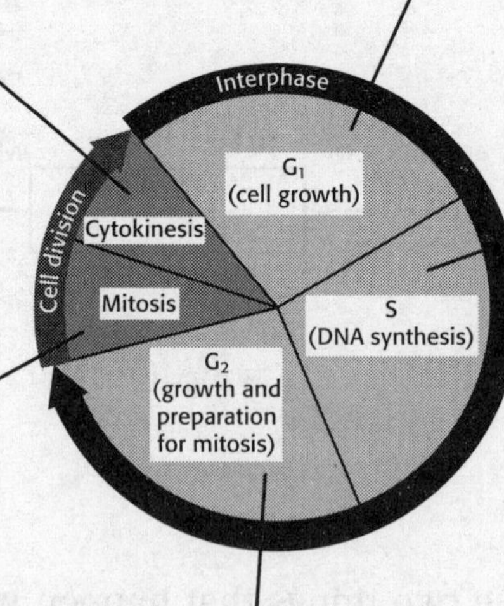

During the *synthesis phase*, or S phase, the cell's DNA is copied. At the end of the S phase, the cell's nucleus contains twice as much DNA as it did during the G_1 phase.

During **mitosis**, the nucleus of the cell divides and forms two nuclei. Each nucleus contains a complete set of chromosomes.

During the *second gap phase*, or G_2 phase, the cell continues to grow and prepares to divide. Special structures form within the cell that will help it to divide.

LOOKING CLOSER

2. Compare What is the difference between mitosis and cytokinesis?

____

____

____

____

____

____

THE STAGES OF MITOSIS

There are four main stages of mitosis, as shown in the figure below.

The first stage of mitosis is *prophase*. During this stage, the chromosomes begin to condense. The nuclear membrane breaks down.

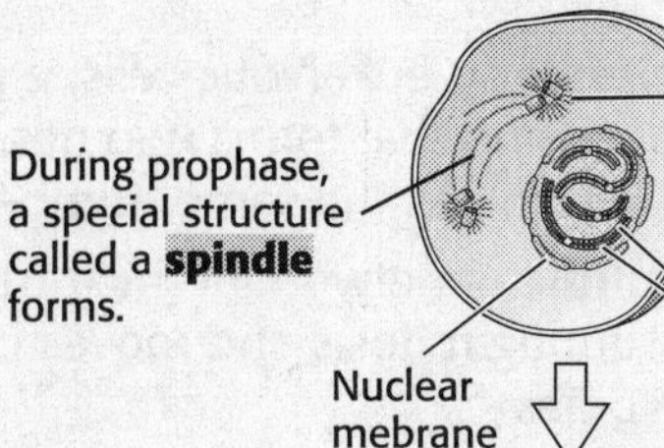

The second stage of mitosis is *metaphase*. During this stage, the chromosomes line up along the equator of the cell.

The spindle fibers connect the centromere of each pair of chromatids to opposite poles of the cell.

Equator

The third stage of mitosis is *anaphase*. During this stage, the spindle fibers shorten. The chromatids are pulled to opposite sides of the cell.

The final stage of mitosis is *telophase*. During this stage, a new nuclear envelope forms at each pole. The spindle fibers break down and disappear.

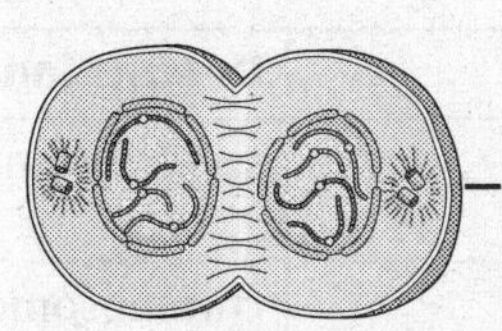

HOW CYTOKINESIS OCCURS

During cytokinesis, the cell membrane grows into the center of the cell. The membrane divides the cell into two daughter cells that are about the same size. In animal cells and other cells without cell walls, protein threads pull the cellular membrane in. This causes the cell to split in half.

Plant cells undergo cytokinesis in a different way because of their rigid cell wall. Vesicles containing cell wall materials line up across the middle of the cell. These vesicles fuse to form a *cell plate*. The cell plate eventually divides the plant cell into two daughter cells.

Talk About It

Create a Mnemonic To help you remember the order of the stages of mitosis, create a sentence in which the first letter of each word is the first letter of one of the stages of mitosis. (For example, **P**olly **M**akes **A**mazing **T**ortellini.) Share your sentence with a partner or a small group.

LOOKING CLOSER

3. Describe What happens during metaphase?

____

____

____

Critical Thinking

4. Infer Compared to the size of the original cell, about how large is a daughter cell formed during mitosis?

____

Background

Recall that *vesicles* are small organelles that contain different materials.

Name ______________________ Class ______________ Date ______________

Section 2 Review

SECTION VOCABULARY

cell cycle the life cycle of a cell; in eukaryotes, it consists of a cell-growth period in which DNA is synthesized and a cell-division period in which mitosis takes place

centrosome an organelle that contains the centrioles and is the center of dynamic activity in mitosis

cytokinesis the division of the cytoplasm of a cell; cytokinesis follows the division of the cell's nucleus by mitosis or meiosis

interphase the period of the cell cycle during which activities such as cell growth and protein synthesis occur without visible signs of cell division

mitosis in eukaryotic cells, a process of cell division that forms two new nuclei, each of which has the same number of chromosomes

spindle a network of microtubules that forms during mitosis and moves chromatids to the poles

1. Describe What happens during the G_1 phase of the cell cycle?

____

____

2. Identify What two processes make up cell division?

____

____

3. Explain What role do spindles play in mitosis?

____

____

4. Describe Fill in the blank spaces in the table below.

Stage	Description
	sister chromatids move to opposite sides of the cell
	chromosomes condense; nuclear membrane breaks down
	new nuclear envelopes form around each set of chromosomes; chromosomes uncoil
	chromosomes line up along the equator of the cell

5. Compare How is cytokinesis in plant cells different from cytokinesis in animal cells?

____

____

____

Name ______________________ Class ______________ Date ______________

CHAPTER 10 Cell Growth and Division

SECTION 3

Regulation

KEY IDEAS

As you read this section, keep these questions in mind:
- What are some factors that control cell growth and division?
- How do feedback signals affect the cell cycle?
- How does cancer relate to the cell cycle?

What Controls Cell Growth and Division?

If you get a cut, the wound will heal as new skin cells are produced. These skin cells will stop dividing once the cut has been healed. If they continued to divide, they would start piling up at the site of the cut. Signals from within the cell, from other cells, or from the environment cause cells to grow, divide, or stop growing.

Summarize As you read this section, underline the main ideas. When you finish reading, write a short summary of the section using the underlined ideas.

What Signals Affect the Cell Cycle?

Remember that there are different phases of the cell cycle. Cells move from one phase to the next. However, cells cannot move between phases at just any time. The cell must not move on to the next phase until conditions are right. The environment must also be favorable for the cell to move on.

To ensure that cells move on only when they are ready, there are several *checkpoints* in the cell cycle. At each checkpoint, feedback signals tell the cell whether or not to move to the next phase. There are three main checkpoints in the eukaryotic cell cycle, as shown below.

Critical Thinking

1. Infer What do you think is one condition that a cell must meet before it can move from the G_1 phase to the S phase?

____

____

The *metaphase checkpoint* ensures that genetic material is evenly split between the daughter cells. At this point, the cell checks to make sure that the chromosomes are properly attached to the spindle fibers.

The *G_1 checkpoint* determines whether a cell's DNA is replicated. Before a cell copies its DNA, it checks its surroundings. If conditions are right and the cell is healthy and large enough to divide, the S phase begins.

The *G_2 checkpoint* determines whether mitosis can begin. Before mitosis begins, the copied DNA is checked for errors. Enzymes correct any mistakes. In addition, proteins double-check that the cell is large enough to divide.

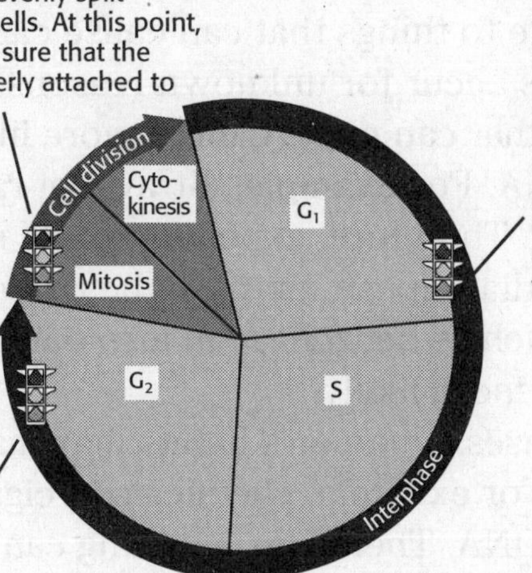

LOOKING CLOSER

2. Describe What happens at the metaphase checkpoint?

____

____

____

____

____

____

What Is Cancer?

Normally, the signals and controls in the cell cycle determine when a cell divides or grows. However, damage to a cell's DNA can cause the cell to stop responding properly to signals. If this happens, the cell may start to divide in an uncontrolled way. The result can be cancer. **Cancer** is a disease that is caused by uncontrolled cell growth and division. There are many kinds of cancer. ☑

3. Identify What can cause a cell to stop responding to signals?

Cells that continue dividing in an uncontrolled way may form a mass called a **tumor**. Tumors can invade and destroy healthy tissue. There are two main kinds of tumors: benign and malignant.

LOOKING CLOSER

4. Describe What is metastasis?

Type of tumor	Description
Benign	• does not spread to other parts of the body • most can be removed through surgery
Malignant	• invades nearby healthy tissue • pieces of tumor may break off and travel to other parts of the body (metastasis) • can be more difficult to treat than benign tumors

TREATMENT AND PREVENTION OF CANCER

The treatment for cancer depends on which type of cancer a person has. Many cancers are treated by *chemotherapy*, which involves using drugs to kill cancer cells. In some cases, doctors can use radiation to kill cancer cells. Surgery can also be used to treat cancers. In many cases, a combination of treatments is used.

Talk About It

Discuss In a small group, talk about any habits or conditions in your life that might increase your risk of cancer. How can you reduce your risk?

The best way to reduce the risk of cancer is to reduce your exposure to things that can cause cancer. Although many cancers occur for unknown reasons, there are some things that can make cancer more likely by damaging DNA. For example, ultraviolet radiation can damage DNA. Therefore, exposure to too much ultraviolet radiation can increase the risk of cancer. Some chemicals, such as benzene, can also damage DNA and make cancer more likely.

In some cases, a person's habits may make cancer more likely. For example, chemicals in cigarette smoke can damage DNA. Therefore, smoking can increase the risk of cancer.

Name ______________________ Class ______________ Date ______________

Section 3 Review

SECTION VOCABULARY

cancer a type of disorder of cell growth that results in invasion and destruction of surrounding healthy tissue by abnormal cells	**tumor** a growth that arises from normal tissue but that grows abnormally in rate and structure and lacks a function

1. Describe How is cancer related to the cell cycle?

2. Identify Where can signals that regulate the cell cycle come from? Name three sources.

3. Describe Explain what happens at each of the three checkpoints in the eukaryotic cell cycle.

4. Explain How do feedback signals affect the cell cycle?

5. Compare Give two differences between benign tumors and malignant tumors.

6. Identify Give two examples of things that can make cancer more likely.

Name ______________________ Class ______________________ Date ______________________

CHAPTER 11 Meiosis and Sexual Reproduction

SECTION 1

Reproduction

KEY IDEAS

As you read this section, keep these questions in mind:

- How does an individual produced by asexual reproduction compare to its parent?
- How does an individual produced by sexual reproduction compare to its parents?
- Why are chromosomes important to an organism?

READING TOOLBOX

Describe As you read this section, make a chart that describes the differences between asexual and sexual reproduction.

Background

Recall that *reproduction* is the process in which organisms produce offspring.

What Is Asexual Reproduction?

In order for a species to survive, its members must reproduce. There are two kinds of reproduction: asexual reproduction and sexual reproduction. In *asexual reproduction*, a single parent produces offspring. Because only one parent produces the offspring, the offspring has the same genetic information as the parent. There are many types of asexual reproduction, as shown below.

Type of asexual reproduction	Description	Example of an organism that can reproduce this way
Binary fission	An organism splits in half.	prokaryotes, such as bacteria
Fragmentation	An organism breaks into several pieces, each of which may grow into a complete organism.	starfish
Parthenogenesis	An unfertilized female sex cell grows into an adult.	water flea
Budding	An individual splits off from an existing organism.	potato

LOOKING CLOSER

1. List What are four types of asexual reproduction?

____

____

____

____

Some kinds of organisms, such as bacteria, can reproduce only asexually. Some kinds of organisms, such as starfish, can reproduce both asexually and sexually. Other kinds of organisms, such as humans, can reproduce only sexually.

2. Describe In terms of genetic information, how do offspring produced by sexual reproduction compare to their parents?

____

What Is Sexual Reproduction?

In *sexual reproduction*, two parents contribute genetic material to the offspring. Because it inherits genetic information from both parents, the offspring is not genetically identical to either parent. Each offspring is genetically unique. ☑

HOW SEXUAL REPRODUCTION HAPPENS

In organisms that reproduce sexually, each parent produces reproductive cells called **gametes**. Gametes are *germ cells*, which participate only in reproduction. Other body cells are somatic cells. *Somatic cells* do not participate in reproduction.

When a female gamete joins with a male gamete, they produce a single cell called a **zygote**. This process is called *fertilization*. Because a zygote has a complete set of genetic information, it can develop into an adult organism.

Critical Thinking

3. Infer Why can't a single gamete grow into an adult organism?

______

______

______

Why Are Chromosomes Important?

Each chromosome has thousands of genes, which determine the characteristics of an organism. In sexually reproducing organisms, each somatic cell contains two sets of chromosomes. Cells that have two sets of chromosomes, such as somatic cells, are **diploid**. Cells that have only one set of chromosomes, such as gametes, are **haploid**. During fertilization, two haploid gametes combine to form a diploid zygote. ☑

4. Explain Why are chromosomes important?

______

______

______

Scientists use the symbol n to represent the number of chromosomes in a haploid cell. Therefore, the number of chromosomes in a diploid cell is $2n$. Different organisms have different numbers of chromosomes, as shown below.

Organism	$2n$
Mosquito	6
Housefly	12
Fern	480–1,020

Organism	$2n$
Frog	26
Human	46
Dog	78

There are two kinds of chromosomes: autosomes and sex chromosomes. An *autosome* does not have genes that determine the sex of an individual. A *sex chromosome* has genes that determine the sex of an individual.

Humans, like many other sexually reproducing organisms, have two kinds of sex chromosomes: X and Y. Females have two X chromosomes. Males have one X and one Y chromosome. ☑

5. Explain What is the difference between an autosome and a sex chromosome?

______

______

______

______

Each chromosome in a diploid cell is part of a pair of homologous chromosomes. **Homologous chromosomes** are similar in shape, size, and kinds of genes they contain. One chromosome from each pair comes from each parent.

Name ____________________ Class ____________ Date ____________

Section 1 Review

SECTION VOCABULARY

diploid a cell that contains two haploid sets of chromosomes **gamete** a haploid reproductive cell that unites with another haploid reproductive cell to form a zygote **haploid** describes a cell, nucleus, or organism that has only one set of unpaired chromosomes	**homologous chromosomes** chromosomes that have the same sequence of genes, that have the same structure, and that pair during meiosis **zygote** the cell that results from the fusion of gametes; a fertilized egg

1. Describe How are gametes and zygotes related?

____

____

2. Identify What is one thing that all types of asexual reproduction have in common?

____

____

3. Apply Concepts What would happen if the gametes of sexually reproducing organisms were diploid instead of haploid? Explain your answer.

____

____

____

____

4. Describe How many chromosomes does a gamete of a dog have? Explain your answer.

____

____

5. Compare Give two differences between sexual reproduction and asexual reproduction.

____

____

____

____

Name ____________________ Class ______________ Date ____________

CHAPTER 11 Meiosis and Sexual Reproduction

SECTION 2

Meiosis

KEY IDEAS

As you read this section, keep these questions in mind:

- What occurs during the stages of meiosis?
- How does the function of mitosis differ from the function of meiosis?
- What are three mechanisms of genetic variation?

How Do Gametes Form?

Recall that gametes are haploid cells. Haploid gametes form from diploid cells through the process of meiosis. **Meiosis** is a form of cell division that produces daughter cells with half as many chromosomes as the parent cell.

During meiosis, a diploid cell goes through two divisions to form four haploid cells. There are two main parts of meiosis: meiosis I and meiosis II. Each part is, in turn, made up of several stages. The figures below and on the next page show the stages of meiosis. ☑

Meiosis I

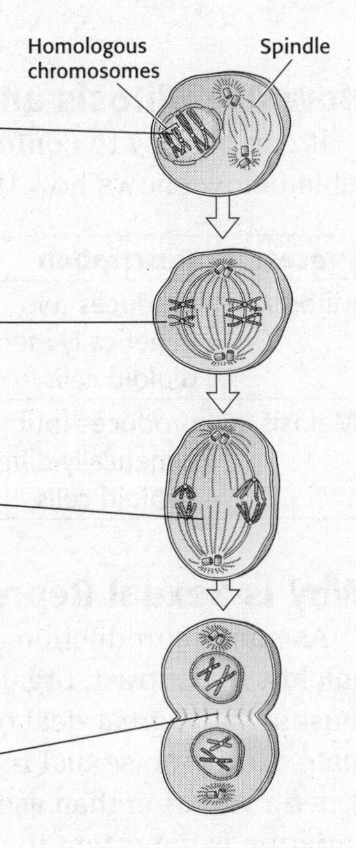

Meiosis I begins with a cell that has copied its chromosomes. The first stage of meiosis I is prophase I. During prophase I, the chromosomes condense. Homologous chromosomes pair up. The membrane around the nucleus breaks down.

The second stage of meiosis I is metaphase I. During metaphase I, the pairs of homologous chromosomes move to the equator of the cell.

The third stage of meiosis I is anaphase I. During anaphase I, the homologous chromosomes separate. The spindle fibers pull one chromosome from each pair to each pole of the cell.

The fourth stage of meiosis I is telophase I. During telophase I, the cytoplasm divides (cytokinesis). Two new cells form. Each cell contains one chromosome from each pair of homologous chromosomes.

READING TOOLBOX

Summarize After you read this section, draw a flowchart showing what happens during each stage of meiosis.

READING CHECK

1. Identify How many times does a diploid cell divide during meiosis?

____

Critical Thinking

2. Apply Concepts Does meiosis produce germ cells or somatic cells?

____

LOOKING CLOSER

3. Describe What happens during metaphase I?

____

____

____

____

Talk About It

Compare In a small group, compare the stages of meiosis I, meiosis II, and mitosis. What happens during each stage? How are the stages similar? How are they different?

Background

Recall that a *chromatid* is one of a pair of duplicated chromosomes that are joined in the middle at a *centromere*.

LOOKING CLOSER

4. Describe What happens during prophase II?

____

____

____

____

Meiosis II

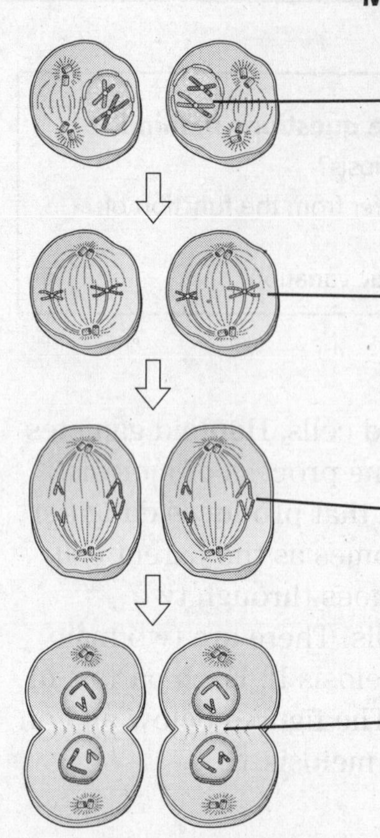

Meiosis II begins with the two cells formed at the end of meiosis I. The chromosomes are not copied at the end of meiosis I. The first stage of meiosis II is prophase II. During prophase II, a new spindle forms.

The second stage of meiosis II is metaphase II. During metaphase II, the chromosomes move to the equators of the cells.

The third stage of meiosis II is anaphase II. During anaphase II, the centromeres divide and the chromatids in each chromosome separate. The spindle fibers pull one chromatid from each pair to the pole of each cell.

The fourth stage of meiosis II is telophase II. During telophase II, the cytoplasm in each cell divides (cytokinesis). Four new haploid cells form. Each cell contains one chromatid from each pair of homologous chromosomes.

How Are Mitosis and Meiosis Different?

It can be easy to confuse mitosis and meiosis. The table below shows how they are different.

Process	Description	Function
Mitosis	produces two genetically identical diploid cells	makes new cells for growth, development, repair, and asexual reproduction
Meiosis	produces four genetically different haploid cells	makes sex cells (gametes) for sexual reproduction

LOOKING CLOSER

5. Identify What is the function of meiosis?

____

____

Why Is Sexual Reproduction Helpful?

Asexual reproduction allows organisms to reproduce quickly. In contrast, organisms that reproduce sexually must spend a great deal of time and energy looking for a mate. However, sexual reproduction produces much more genetic variation than asexual reproduction. Genetic variation is important to a species. It can allow members of the species to survive changes in their environment.

Talk About It

Infer With a partner, talk about ways that genetic variation might help a species survive changes in the environment. Remember that an organism's genes affect its traits.

CROSSING-OVER

Three processes that contribute to genetic variation during sexual reproduction are crossing-over, independent assortment, and random fertilization. **Crossing-over** occurs during prophase I, when homologous chromosomes form pairs. ☑

During crossing-over, an arm of one chromatid crosses over the same arm on another chromatid. The chromatids break at the point of the crossover. The chromatid pieces are exchanged. When each chromatid re-forms, it contains a piece of the other chromatid.

6. Identify During which stage of meiosis does crossing-over occur?

____

INDEPENDENT ASSORTMENT

During metaphase I, chromosomes line up randomly along the equator. This random distribution of homologous chromosomes during meiosis is called **independent assortment**. This process produces gametes with different genetic information, as shown below.

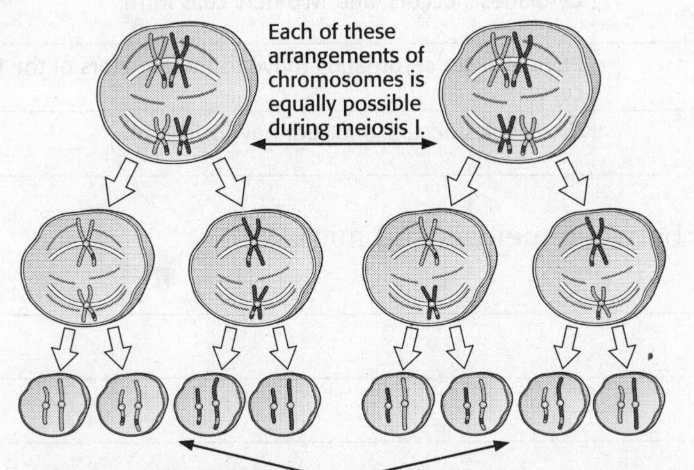

The alleles that each gamete contains depend on how the chromosomes were arranged at the beginning of meiosis. Different arrangements of chromosomes produce gametes with different alleles.

LOOKING CLOSER

7. Infer If the diploid cell in the figure had four pairs of homologous chromosomes instead of two, would there be more or fewer possible gene combinations in the gametes?

____

RANDOM FERTILIZATION

Fertilization is a random process. It can increase genetic variation. For example, because of independent assortment, there are more than 8 million possible chromosome combinations for a human female gamete. There are also more than 8 million possible chromosome combinations for a human male gamete. Therefore, there are more than $(8 \text{ million})^2 = 64$ trillion possible chromosome combinations in each human zygote.

Name ______________________ Class ______________ Date ________

Section 2 Review

SECTION VOCABULARY

crossing-over the exchange of genetic material between homologous chromosomes during meiosis; can result in genetic recombination

independent assortment the random distribution of the pairs of genes on different chromosomes to the gametes

meiosis a process in cell division during which the number of chromosomes decreases to half the original number by two divisions of the nucleus, which results in the production of sex cells (gametes or spores)

1. Compare Describe the difference between what happens during anaphase I and what happens during anaphase II.

____

____

____

2. Identify Fill in the blank spaces in the table below.

Stage of meiosis	Description
	Chromosomes condense, homologous chromosomes pair up, and crossing-over occurs.
	Cytokinesis occurs, and two new cells form.
	Pairs of sister chromatids move to the equators of the two cells.
	Cytokinesis occurs, and four new cells form.

3. Describe Give two differences between meiosis and mitosis.

____

____

____

____

4. Identify What are three processes that contribute to genetic variation during sexual reproduction?

____

____

____

5. Explain Why is sexual reproduction helpful to a species?

____

____

Name ______________________ Class ______________ Date ______________

CHAPTER 11 Meiosis and Sexual Reproduction

SECTION 3

Multicellular Life Cycles

KEY IDEAS

As you read this section, keep these questions in mind:

- What is a diploid life cycle?
- What is a haploid life cycle?
- What is alternation of generations?

What Is a Life Cycle?

The **life cycle** of an organism is all the events in its growth and development until it reaches sexual maturity. There are three types of life cycles.

READING TOOLBOX

Compare After you read this section, make a chart comparing the three types of life cycles.

DIPLOID LIFE CYCLE

Most animals have a diploid life cycle. This means that most of the cells in the animal's body are diploid. Only the gametes produced by meiosis are haploid. In males, the gametes are called **sperm**. In females, the gametes are called ova (singular, **ovum**). ☑

In males, meiosis produces four haploid sperm cells. In females, meiosis also produces four haploid cells. However, only one of the cells is an ovum. The other three cells are much smaller *polar bodies*, which die.

1. Describe What does it mean to have a diploid life cycle?

____

____

HAPLOID LIFE CYCLE

Most fungi and some protists have a haploid life cycle. This means that most of the cells in the organism's body are haploid. The only diploid cell is the zygote, which immediately produces haploid cells through meiosis.

Critical Thinking

2. Apply Concepts The diploid number of chromosomes in a certain fungus is 26. The fungus has a haploid life cycle. How many chromosomes are in most of the cells in the fungus? Explain your answer.

____

____

____

____

____

____

ALTERNATION OF GENERATIONS

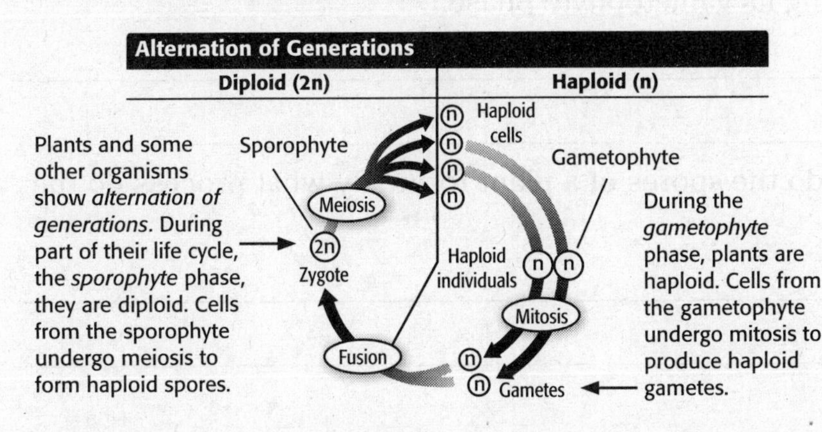

Name ______________________ Class ______________ Date ______________

Section 3 Review

SECTION VOCABULARY

life cycle all of the events in the growth and development of an organism until the organism reaches sexual maturity	**ovum** a mature egg cell **sperm** the male gamete (sex cell)

1. Identify Label the haploid and diploid cells in the figure below.

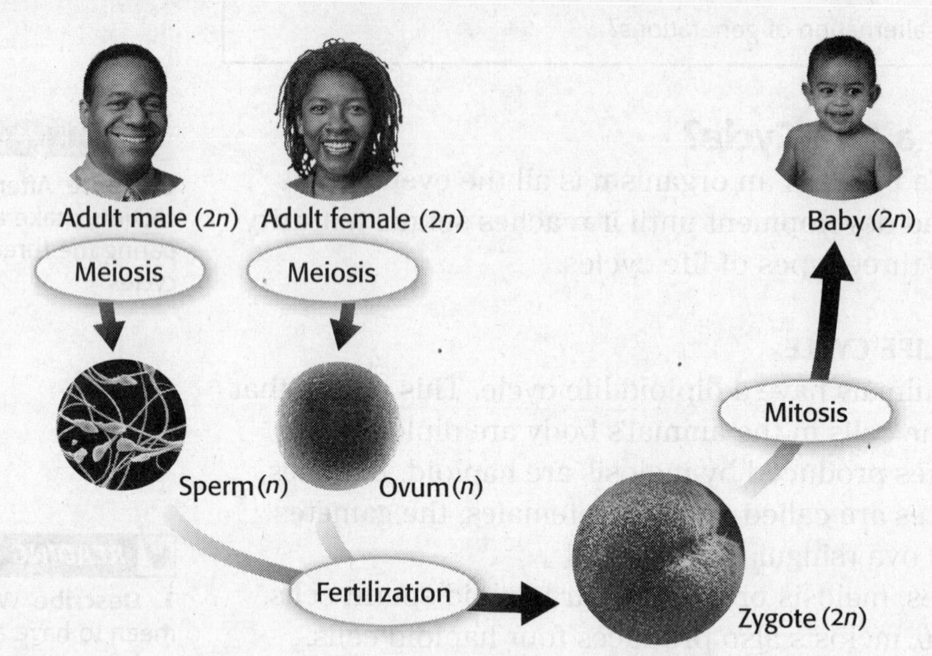

2. Describe What type of life cycle does the figure above show? Explain your answer.

____

____

____

3. Apply Concepts A particular plant's diploid number of chromosomes is 50. Describe the number of chromosomes in one of the plant's cells during its sporophyte phase and during its gametophyte phase.

____

____

4. Describe By what process do the spores of a plant form? By what process do the gametes form?

____

____

SECTION 1

Origins of Hereditary Science

KEY IDEAS

As you read this section, keep these questions in mind:

- Why was Gregor Mendel important for modern genetics?
- Why did Mendel conduct experiments with garden peas?
- What were the important steps in Mendel's first experiments?
- What were the important results of Mendel's first experiments?

Who Was Gregor Mendel?

In the 1800s, Gregor Mendel did breeding experiments with the garden pea plant, *Pisum sativum*. Mendel was the first to develop rules to predict patterns of heredity. Modern genetics is based on his explanations for patterns of heredity.

READING TOOLBOX

List Science Terms Many science terms will appear over and over throughout the book. As you read, list on a piece of paper or in a notebook any science terms and definitions. Add to this list as you read other sections. Refer to this list whenever you need to remind yourself of the meaning of a word.

Why Did Mendel Use Garden Peas?

In his experiments, Mendel bred, or *crossed*, different types of garden peas. Mendel used garden peas for several reasons:

- They are easy to grow.
- One cross produces many offspring.
- Every flower has both male and female reproductive structures. Thus, a pea plant can *self-pollinate*, or fertilize itself. It can also *cross-pollinate*, or fertilize another plant. ☑

READING CHECK

1. Explain Why can a pea plant self-pollinate and cross-pollinate?

______

In some of his experiments, Mendel crossed plants that had purple flowers with those that had white flowers. The plants were *true-breeding*. That is, each produced offspring with all the same traits when it self-pollinated.

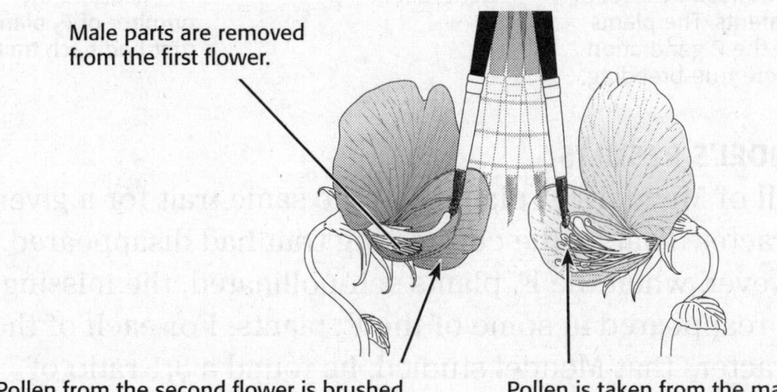

Critical Thinking

2. Infer Why did Mendel remove the male parts from the first flower?

______

MENDEL'S FIRST EXPERIMENTS

Physical features that are inherited are called **characters**. In pea plants, flower color is a character. A form of a character is called a **trait**. Purple flowers and white flowers are two traits. Mendel studied seven characters of pea plants, each with two traits. ☑

3. Identify Relationships What is the relationship between a character and a trait?

Mendel carried out monohybrid crosses in his first experiments. A *monohybrid cross* studies one pair of contrasting traits. The offspring of true-breeding parents with a contrasting trait are called **hybrids**.

Seven Characters with Contrasting Traits Studied by Mendel

Flower color	Seed color	Seed shape	Pod color	Pod shape	Flower position	Plant height
purple	yellow	round	green	smooth	mid-stem	tall
white	green	wrinkled	yellow	bumpy	end of stem	short

Three Steps of Mendel's First Experiments

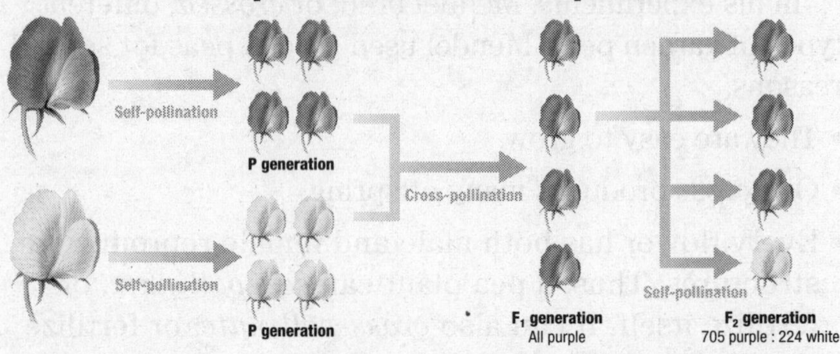

❶ The first generation that Mendel crossed was called the *parent*, or *P, generation*. A **generation** is all the offspring produced by a set of parents. The plants of the P generation were true-breeding.

❷ Mendel crossed two P generation plants that had contrasting traits. The offspring of the P generation is called the *first filial*, or *F_1, generation*.

❸ Mendel let the F_1 generation self-pollinate. He called the new generation of offspring the *second filial*, or *F_2, generation*. He recorded the number of F_2 plants that had each trait.

LOOKING CLOSER

4. Compare How did the F_2 generation differ from the F_1 generation?

MENDEL'S RESULTS

All of Mendel's F_1 plants had the same trait for a given character. That is, the contrasting trait had disappeared. However, when the F_1 plants self-pollinated, the missing trait reappeared in some of the F_2 plants. For each of the characters that Mendel studied, he found a 3:1 ratio of contrasting traits in the F_2 generation.

Name _______________ Class _______________ Date _______________

Section 1 Review

SECTION VOCABULARY

character a recognizable inherited feature or characteristic of an organism; in Mendelian herdity, a feature that exists in one of two or more possible variations called traits

generation the entire group of offspring produced by a given group of parents

hybrid in biology, the offspring of a cross between parents that have differing traits; a cross between individuals of different species, subspecies, or varieties

trait a genetically determined characteristic

1. Identify What was Mendel's main contribution to hereditary science?

____

2. Summarize Complete the process chart below to describe the major steps of Mendel's first experiment.

Mendel let plants that had each type of trait self-pollinate for several generations. This produced plants that were true-breeding for each trait.

↓

↓

3. List Identify three reasons Mendel chose to use garden peas in his experiments.

____

____

____

4. Identify What was the typical ratio of traits in the F_2 generation in Mendel's first experiments?

____

5. Analyze Methods Mendel examined thousands of pea plants in his experiments. Why do you think he used so many?

____

____

Name ______________________ Class ______________ Date ______________

CHAPTER 12 Mendel and Heredity

SECTION 2

Mendel's Theory

KEY IDEAS

As you read this section, keep these questions in mind:

- What patterns of heredity were explained by Mendel's hypotheses?
- What is the law of segregation?
- How does genotype relate to phenotype?
- What is the law of independent assortment?

What Is the Mendelian Theory of Heredity?

Mendel developed several hypotheses to explain the results of his experiments. Together, these hypotheses form the *Mendelian theory of heredity*, a foundation of modern genetics. This theory explains simple patterns of inheritance. In these patterns, two of several versions of a gene combine and result in one of several possible traits.

Mendel proposed that each character in pea plants, such as flower color, was controlled by two factors. Today, scientists call these factors alleles. An **allele** is one form, or version, of a gene. ☑

READING TOOLBOX

Define As you read, identify pairs of words, such as *genotype* and *phenotype*, that are used to describe aspects of heredity. On a sheet of paper, list and define these pairs of words. How do the words differ? What is the relationship between them?

READING CHECK

1. Identify What is the relationship between genes and alleles?

____

____

____

ONE ALLELE FROM EACH PARENT

Mendel noticed that traits can come from either parent. Each parent has two alleles for a character. When gametes form, pairs of alleles are separated. Each parent passes only one allele for a character to its offspring.

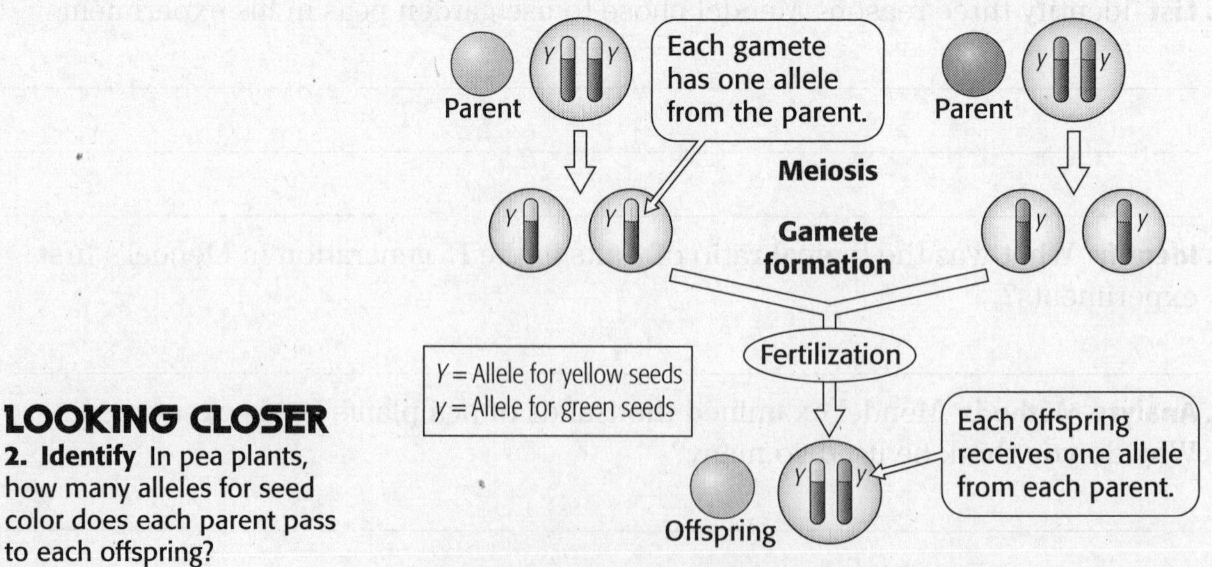

Each individual has two alleles for a particular character. A single gamete carries only one of the two alleles.

LOOKING CLOSER

2. Identify In pea plants, how many alleles for seed color does each parent pass to each offspring?

____

DOMINANT AND RECESSIVE

For every pair of traits that Mendel studied, one trait always seemed to "win" over the other. That is, whenever both alleles were present, only one was fully expressed as a trait. The allele that is expressed is **dominant**. A **recessive** allele is shown, or expressed, only when the dominant allele is not present.

A dominant allele is generally written as a capital letter. A recessive allele is generally written as a lowercase letter. For example, a pea plant that has one dominant and one recessive allele for flower color has *P* and *p* alleles.

Critical Thinking

3. Infer Under what condition could a recessive allele be expressed in an individual?

What Is Mendel's Law of Segregation?

Mendel found that a parent allele remains unchanged, even if it is not expressed in the parent. The allele can be passed on to the offspring. Mendel explained this observation in his law of segregation of alleles. The law of segregation has two main ideas.

The Law of Segregation of Alleles

1. When an organism produces gametes, each pair of alleles is separated.
2. Each gamete has an equal chance of receiving either one of the alleles.

GENOTYPE AND PHENOTYPE

Mendel realized that offspring do not express a trait for every allele that they receive. Instead, combinations of alleles determine an individual's traits. The set of alleles that an individual has for a character is called the **genotype**. The trait that results from a set of alleles is called the **phenotype**. Genotype determines phenotype. ☑

READING CHECK

4. Identify What is the relationship between genotype and phenotype?

This plant's alleles for flower color may be *PP* or *Pp*. Because the allele for purple flowers is dominant (*P*), both genotypes produce the same phenotype.

Because this plant produces white flowers, it does not carry the dominant allele for purple flowers. Its genotype is *pp*.

LOOKING CLOSER

5. Explain Why do *PP* and *Pp* genotypes produce the same phenotype?

HOMOZYGOUS AND HETEROZYGOUS

An individual that has two of the same alleles for a character is **homozygous** for that character. For example, a pea plant that produces white flowers is homozygous for flower color. Its genotype is *pp*.

An individual that has two different alleles for a character is **heterozygous** for that character. For example, a pea plant with the genotype *Pp* is heterozygous for flower color. Its alleles for flower color are different.

Critical Thinking

6. Apply Concepts For a particular character, an organism has alleles *Rr*. Is the organism homozygous or heterozygous for that character? Explain your answer.

____

____

____

____

What Is the Law of Independent Assortment?

In his second experiments, Mendel used dihybrid crosses. A *dihybrid cross* involves two characters. Mendel found that the inheritance of one trait did not affect the inheritance of another. For example, the round-seed trait did not always appear in a plant with the yellow-seed trait. It seemed that alleles for one character could "mix and match" with alleles for another character. This result is explained by the law of independent assortment. ☑

7. Define What is a dihybrid cross?

____

____

____

The Law of Independent Assortment

During gamete formation, the alleles of each gene segregate independently.

Each gamete that a parent produces will receive one allele for each character. For seed color and shape, this parent can produce the gametes with the following combinations of alleles: YR, Yr, yR, and yr.

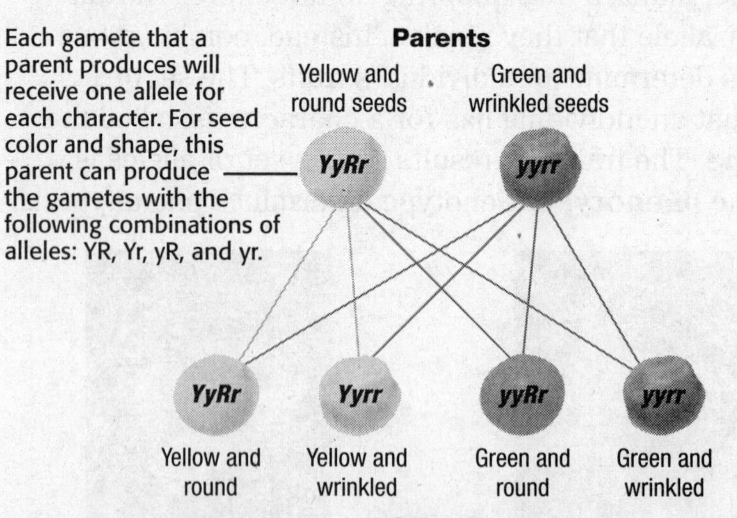

Seed shape and seed color are two different characters in pea plants. Mendel found that the inheritance of alleles for seed color did not affect the inheritance of alleles for seed shape. Thus, an individual may have a combination of traits that neither parent had.

LOOKING CLOSER

8. Infer What allele combinations could a plant with green and wrinkled seeds produce in a gamete?

____

Name ______________________ Class ______________ Date ______________

Section 2 Review

SECTION VOCABULARY

allele one of the alternative forms of a gene that governs a characteristic, such as hair color

dominant in genetics, describes an allele that is fully expressed whenever the allele is present in an individual

genotype a specific combination of alleles in an individual

heterozygous describes an individual that carries two different alleles of a gene

homozygous describes an individual that has identical alleles for a trait on both homologous chromosomes

phenotype an organism's appearance or other detectable characteristic that results from the organism's genotype and the environment

recessive in genetics, describes an allele that is expressed only when there is no dominant allele present in an individual

1. Identify Relationships Complete the Concept Map to show the relationships between the vocabulary terms in the box above.

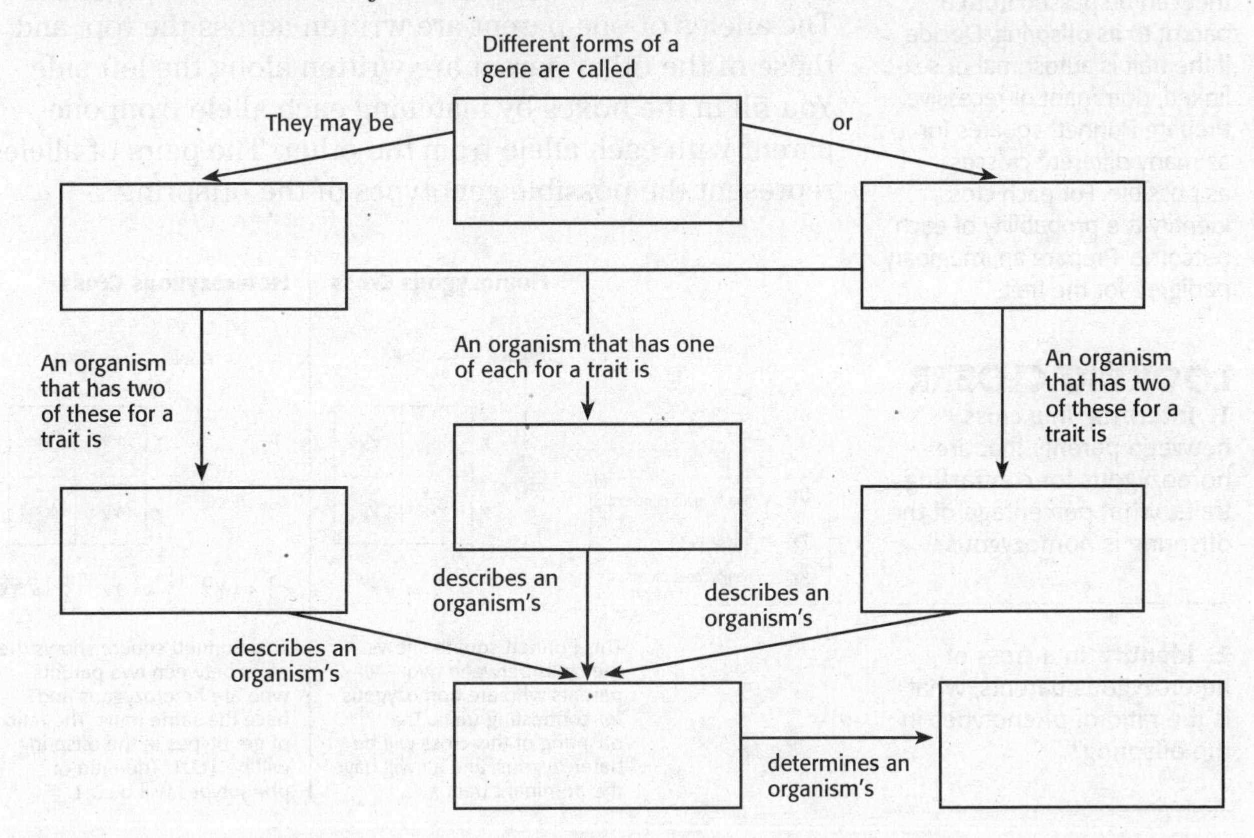

2. Analyze Is it possible for two individuals to have the same phenotype and different genotypes? Explain your answer.

____

____

3. Predict According to the law of independent assortment, what gametes can an individual with the genotype *AaBb* produce?

____

Name ______________________ Class ______________ Date ______________

CHAPTER 12 Mendel and Heredity

SECTION 3

Modeling Mendel's Laws

KEY IDEAS

As you read this section, keep these questions in mind:

- How can a Punnett square be used in genetics?
- How can mathematical probability be used in genetics?
- What information does a pedigree show?

READING TOOLBOX

Apply Concepts After you read this section, invent a trait that can be passed from a parent to its offspring. Decide if the trait is autosomal or sex-linked, dominant or recessive. Prepare Punnett squares for as many different crosses as possible. For each cross, identify the probability of each outcome. Prepare an imaginary pedigree for the trait.

What Is a Punnett Square?

A **Punnett square** is a model that shows all the genotypes that could result from a particular cross. The alleles of one parent are written across the top, and those of the other parent are written along the left side. You fill in the boxes by matching each allele from one parent with each allele from the other. The pairs of alleles represent the possible genotypes of the offspring.

LOOKING CLOSER

1. Interpret In a cross between parents that are homozygous for contrasting traits, what percentage of the offspring is homozygous?

____

2. Identify In a cross of heterozygous parents, what is the ratio of phenotypes in the offspring?

____

YY = homozygous dominant
Yy = heterozygous
yy = homozygous recessive

Homozygous Cross

Parents → YY; yy

	Y	Y
y	Yy	Yy
y	Yy	Yy

$\frac{4}{4}$ are Yy

This Punnett square shows the cross between two parents who are homozygous for contrasting traits. The offspring of this cross will be heterozygous, and all will have the dominant trait.

Heterozygous Cross

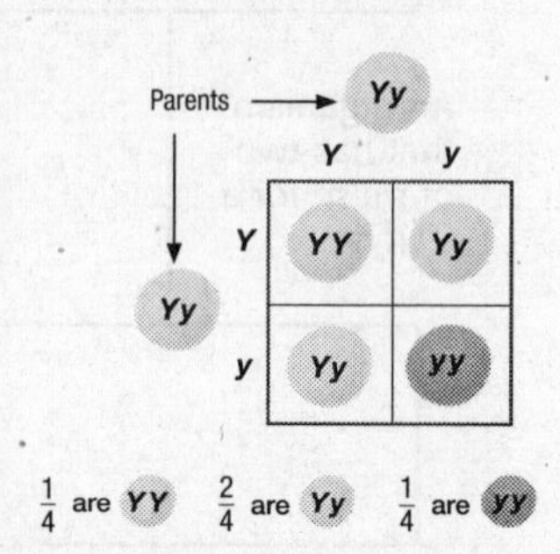

This Punnett square shows the cross between two parents who are heterozygous and have the same traits. The ratio of genotypes in the offspring will be 1:2:1. The ratio of phenotypes will be 3:1.

What Is Probability?

You can also use a Punnett square to calculate the probability of each outcome of a genetic cross. **Probability** is the likelihood that a specific event will occur.

$$\text{probability} = \frac{\text{number of one kind of possible outcomes}}{\text{total number of all possible outcomes}}$$

PROBABILITY OF A SPECIFIC ALLELE IN A GAMETE

Recall that each gamete has an equal chance of receiving either allele of a pair. Thus, if a pea plant has two alleles for seed color, only one of the two alleles can end up in a particular gamete. For example, the probability that a gamete will carry the allele for green seeds is 1/2.

PROBABILITY IN A HETEROZYGOUS CROSS

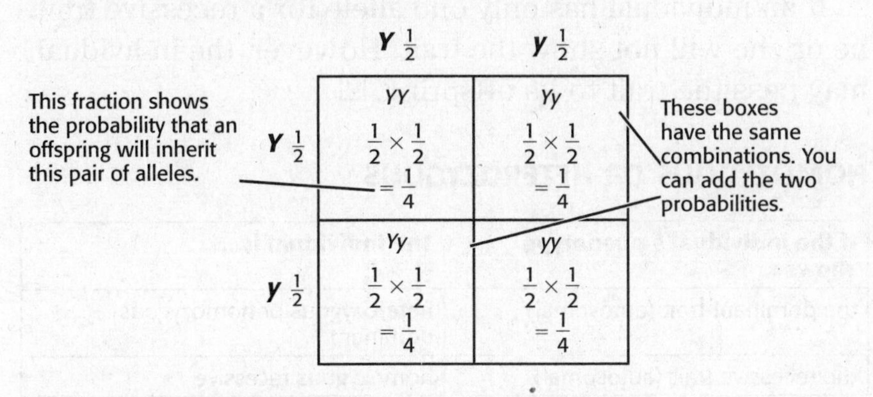

LOOKING CLOSER

3. Identify What is the probability that a cross between heterozygous parents will produce heterozygous offspring?

____

What Is a Pedigree?

A **pedigree** is a family history that shows how a trait is inherited over several generations.

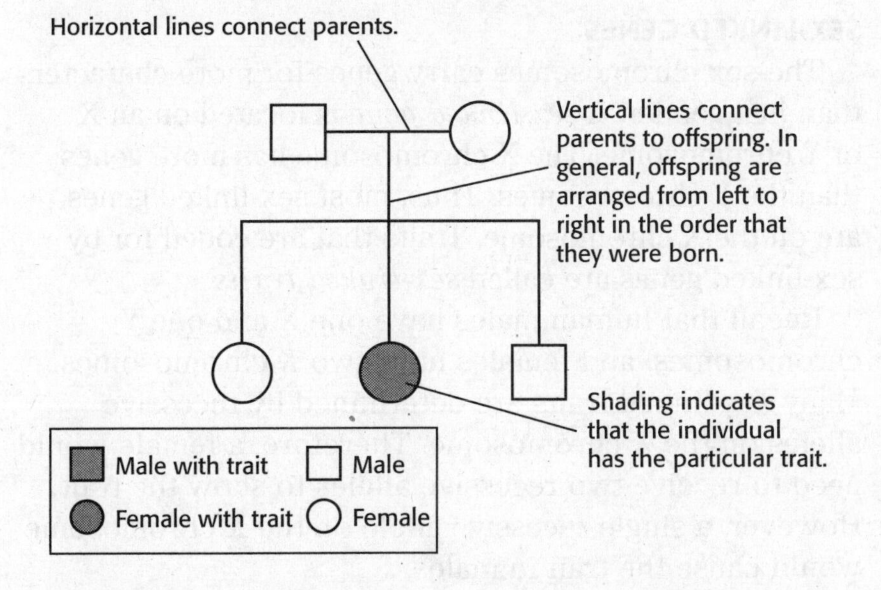

LOOKING CLOSER

4. Identify How many offspring are represented in this pedigree?

____

5. Identify How many individuals in this family have the particular trait?

____

Healthcare workers can use pedigrees to help a family understand a genetic disorder. A **genetic disorder** is a disease or disorder that can be inherited. Some individuals may be carriers of a disorder. *Carriers* have alleles for a disorder, but do not have symptoms.

What Can a Pedigree Tell You?

DOMINANT OR RECESSIVE

If the individual's phenotype shows ...	The individual has...
the dominant trait (autosomal)	at least one dominant allele
the recessive trait (autosomal)	two recessive alleles

If an individual has only one allele for a recessive trait, he or she will not show the trait. However, the individual may pass the trait to its offspring. ☑

READING CHECK

6. Identify For an autosomal gene, how many recessive alleles does an individual need to have the trait?

____

HOMOZYGOUS OR HETEROZYGOUS

If the individual's phenotype shows ...	The individual is...
the dominant trait (autosomal)	heterozygous or homozygous dominant
the recessive trait (autosomal)	homozygous recessive

Heterozygous parents can have a child that is homozygous recessive. Thus, if a child shows a recessive trait but the parents do not, both parents are heterozygous.

Critical Thinking

7. Apply Concepts An individual is homozygous recessive for a particular character. Can one of its parents be homozygous dominant? Explain your answer.

____

____

____

____

____

____

SEX-LINKED GENES

The sex chromosomes carry genes for more characters than just gender. A *sex-linked gene* is located on an X or Y chromosome. The X chromosome has more genes than the Y chromosomes. Thus, most sex-linked genes are on the X chromosome. Traits that are coded for by sex-linked genes are called *sex-linked traits*.

Recall that human males have one X and one Y chromosomes, and females have two X chromosomes. Many sex-linked traits are determined by recessive alleles on the X chromosome. Therefore, a female would need to receive two recessive alleles to show the trait. However, a single recessive allele on the X chromosome would cause the trait in males.

Traits that are not expressed equally in both sexes are commonly sex linked. For example, the gene for color-blindness is on the X chromosome. More males than females have colorblindness.

Talk About It

Predict A man who has colorblindness and a woman who is a carrier for colorblindness have a son. With a partner, talk about the possible genotypes and phenotypes that the son may have.

Name ______________________ Class ______________ Date ______________

Section 3 Review

SECTION VOCABULARY

genetic disorder an inherited disease or disorder that is caused by a mutation in a gene or by a chromosomal defect

pedigree a diagram that shows the occurrence of a genetic trait in several generations of a family

probability the likelihood that a possible future event will occur in any given instance of the event; the mathematical ratio of the number of times one outcome of any event is likely to occur to the number of possible outcomes of the event

Punnett square a graphic used to predict the results of a genetic cross

1. Describe What are two ways a Punnett square can be used in genetics?

____

____

2. Predict What is the probability that a cross between two heterozygous individuals will produce homozygous offspring?

____

3. Explain When you analyze a pedigree, how can you determine whether an individual is a carrier for the trait?

____

____

Use the pedigree to answer the questions that follow. The pedigree shows the presence of albinism in a family. The gene for albinism is found on an autosome.

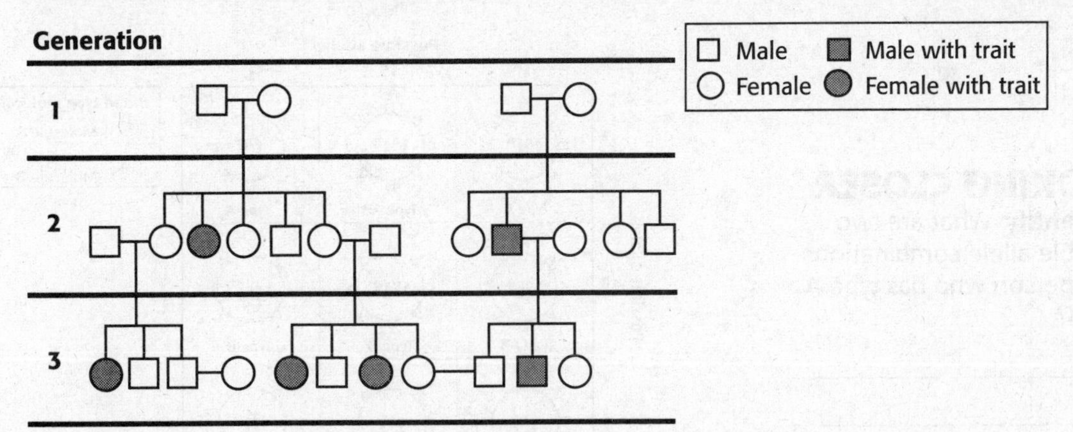

4. Analyze Is the allele for albinism recessive or dominant? How can you tell?

____

____

____

5. Identify On the pedigree above, circle all the individuals who are definitely carriers for albinism.

Name ______________________ Class ______________ Date ______________

CHAPTER 12 Mendel and Heredity

SECTION 4

Beyond Mendelian Heredity

KEY IDEAS

As you read this section, keep these questions in mind:

- Are there exceptions to the simple Mendelian pattern of inheritance?
- How do the heredity and the environment interact to influence phenotype?
- How do linked genes affect chromosome assortment and crossing over during meiosis?

READING TOOLBOX

Summarize As you read, write paragraphs to summarize each of the exceptions to patterns of Mendelian inheritance. In your paragraphs, describe how each exception differs from the patterns Mendel saw in pea plants.

What Are Some Exceptions to Mendelian Inheritance?

Mendel's work formed the foundation of hereditary science. However, scientists have discovered that traits are not always inherited according to the patterns Mendel described. In fact, the inheritance of most traits do not follow Mendel's rules.

MULTIPLE ALLELES

An individual can have only two alleles for a gene. However, some genes have *multiple alleles*. That is, they have more than two possible alleles. For example, three alleles determine human blood types: I^A, I^B, and i.

LOOKING CLOSER

1. Identify What are two possible allele combinations for a person who has type A blood?

____

____

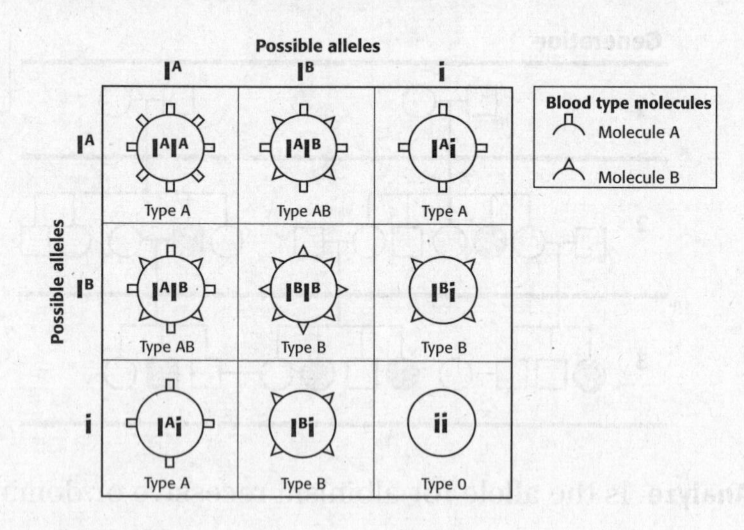

READING CHECK

2. Explain What is codominance?

____

____

____

CODOMINANCE

The human AB blood types show a condition called codominance. In **codominance**, both alleles for the same gene are expressed fully. That is, two traits can appear at the same time. ☑

INCOMPLETE DOMINANCE

For some characters, the offspring's trait is intermediate between the traits of its parents. This pattern is called *incomplete dominance.* For example, in snapdragons, neither allele for color is dominant or recessive. If you cross a snapdragon that has red flowers with one that has white flowers, the offspring will have pink flowers. ☑

3. Describe In incomplete dominance, how does the offspring's trait compare to the traits of the parents?

POLYGENIC INHERITANCE

Some traits, such as human eye color, are determined by more than one gene. When several genes affect a character, it is called a **polygenic character**. The genes for a polygenic trait may be on the same chromosome or a different chromosome. Height and skin color are two other polygenic characters in humans.

How Can the Environment Affect a Character?

A character is not always determined entirely by genes. An organism's phenotype can be affected by its environment. For example, temperature affects the fur color of Arctic foxes. During summer, genes cause production of pigments that result in dark fur. During winter, the genes stop causing production of pigment.

Critical Thinking

4. Infer How is the effect of the environment on the fur color of Arctic foxes an advantage for the foxes?

What Are Linked Genes?

Recall that during meiosis, genes on different chromosomes can be sorted independently. Some genes are close together on the same chromosome. During meiosis, these genes are less likely to be separated than genes that are far apart. Genes that are close together and the traits they determine are **linked**. Linked genes tend to be inherited together. ☑

5. Explain Why do linked genes tend to be inherited together?

Name ______________________ Class ______________ Date ______________

Section 4 Review

SECTION VOCABULARY

codominance a condition in which both alleles for a gene are fully expressed **linked** in genetics, describes two or more genes that tend to be inherited together	**polygenic character** describes a character or pattern of inheritance that is influenced by more than one gene

1. **List** What are three exceptions to the Mendelian pattern of one character controlled by two alleles?

2. **Compare** How does codominance differ from incomplete dominance?

3. **Predict** What are the possible genotypes and phenotypes for blood type of an individual whose father is I^AI^B and whose mother is *ii*? Use a Punnett square to show these possibilities.

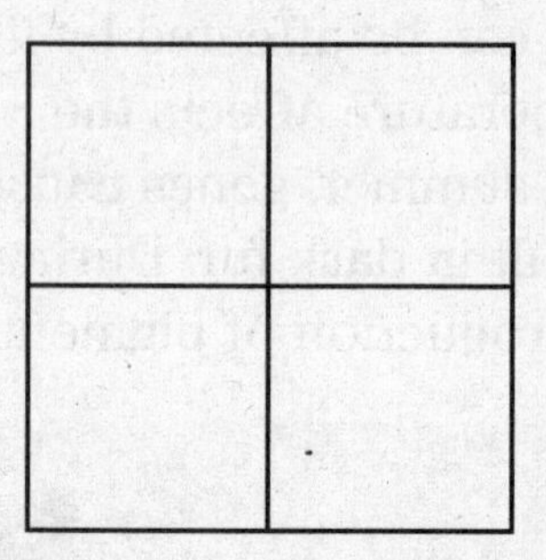

4. **Analyze** In humans, height may be affected by both heredity and the environment. If an individual has tall parents, what kind of environmental, or outside, factors may cause the individual to be short?

5. **Explain** If two genes are known to be linked, what would you expect to happen to these genes during meiosis?

Name ______________ Class ______________ Date ______________

SECTION 1

The Structure of DNA

KEY IDEAS

As you read this section, keep these questions in mind:

- What makes up genetic material?
- What experiments helped identify the role of DNA?
- What is the shape of a DNA molecule?
- How is information organized in a DNA molecule?
- What scientific investigations led to the discovery of DNA's structure?

What Is DNA?

In the 1800s, Austrian monk Gregor Mendel showed that parents can pass traits to their children. Scientists later discovered that **genes** carry the instructions for inherited traits. However, scientists did not learn what genes consist of until the 1950s.

We now know that genes consist of small segments of deoxyribonucleic acid, or **DNA**. DNA is the genetic material in cells.☑

READING TOOLBOX

Summarize After you read this section, make a chart summarizing the main results of the experiments of Griffith, Avery, and Hershey and Chase.

READING CHECK

1. Identify What are genes made of?

____

SHOWING THAT DNA IS GENETIC MATERIAL

DNA consists of only four subunits. At first, many scientists did not think that it was complex enough to be genetic material. Three important experiments helped to show that DNA is genetic material.

In 1928, Frederick Griffith found that harmless live bacteria (R bacteria) became harmful when mixed with dead harmful bacteria (S bacteria), as shown below. The experiment proved that genetic material, which caused the bacteria to be harmful, can be transferred between cells.

❶ Live S bacteria kill the mouse.

❷ Live R bacteria do not kill the mouse.

❸ Dead S bacteria do not kill the mouse.

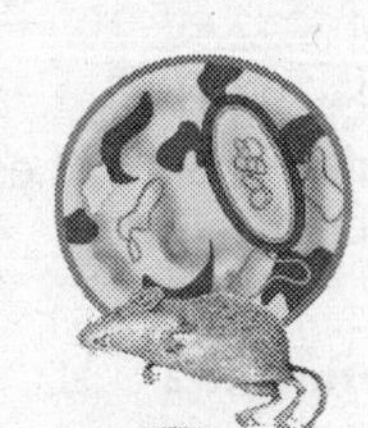

❹ A mixture of live R bacteria and dead S bacteria kills the mouse.

LOOKING CLOSER

2. Infer The mouse that received dead S bacteria and live R bacteria died. What would have happened to the mouse if genetic information could not be transferred between cells?

____

____

How Did Scientists Link DNA and Genes?

Griffith's experiment showed that genetic material can be transferred. However, it did not show whether genetic material is protein, ribonucleic acid (RNA), or DNA.

In the 1940s, Oswald Avery and his team followed up on Griffith's experiment. They found that dead bacteria that were missing protein or RNA could still change harmless cells into harmful cells. However, dead bacteria that were missing DNA did not transform the harmless cells. They concluded that DNA is the genetic material. ☑

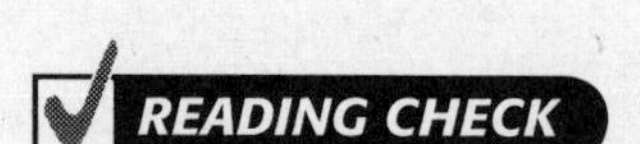

3. Explain How did Avery's experiments show that DNA is the genetic material?

____

____

____

____

____

In 1952, Alfred Hershey and Martha Chase provided support for Avery's results by studying bacteriophages. *Bacteriophages* are viruses that contain both proteins and DNA. They infect bacterial cells, causing the bacteria to produce more viruses.

Hershey and Chase used radioactive atoms of sulfur and phosphorus to learn whether proteins or DNA entered cells. Proteins contain sulfur, but not phosphorus. DNA contains phosphorus, but not sulfur. The results of their experiment supported Avery's conclusion that DNA is the genetic material.

LOOKING CLOSER

4. Identify Which radioactive atom was found in the infected bacteria?

____

____

____

Hershey-Chase Experiment

1. First, the scientists grew two batches of bacteriophages. One batch grew in an environment rich in ^{32}P. The DNA in these viruses therefore contained a great deal of ^{32}P. The second batch grew in an environment rich in ^{35}S. The protein in those viruses contained a great deal of ^{35}S. Each batch of viruses was allowed to infect a separate batch of bacteria.
2. Then, the bacteria and viruses were broken apart in a blender. The scientists spun the mixture in a tool called a centrifuge. This separated the heavier bacteria from the lighter bacteriophage proteins.
3. Finally, the scientists used machines to detect radioactivity from the ^{32}P and ^{35}S. They found radioactivity from ^{32}P, but not from ^{35}S, in the bacteria. This showed that the DNA of the virus, but not the protein, was transferred to the bacteria.

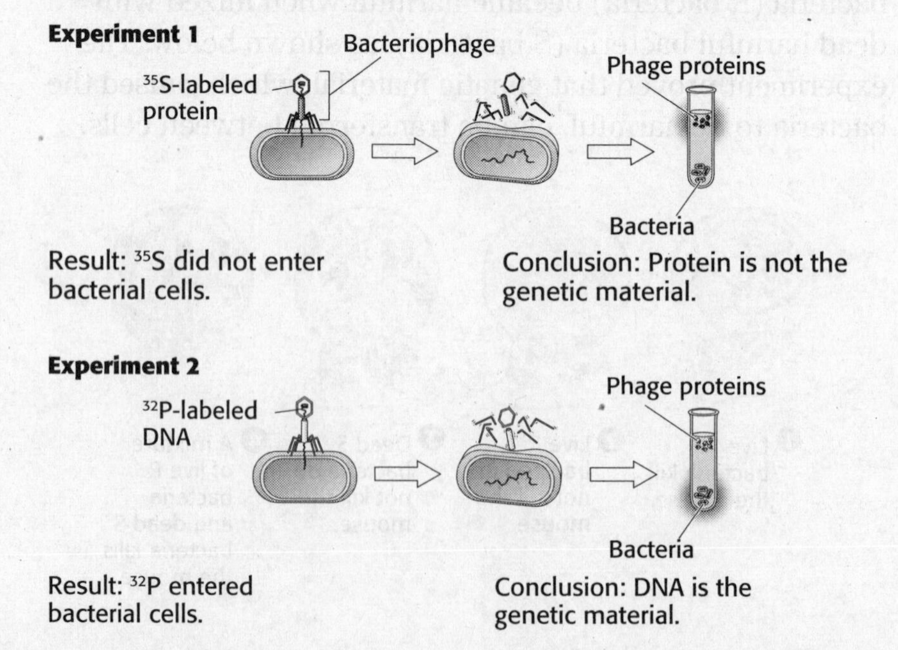

Critical Thinking

5. Infer Describe how the results of the Hershey-Chase experiment would have been different if proteins were the genetic material.

____

____

____

____

What Does DNA Look Like?

By the late 1950s, scientists accepted that genes consisted of DNA. However, they still knew nothing about the DNA's structure. Several groups set out to discover this structure and the role of DNA in the transfer of genetic information. The research of many scientists helped James Watson and Francis Crick to determine the structure of DNA. ☑

The structure of DNA is a *double helix*. It looks like a spiral staircase made of two parallel, winding strands of linked subunits called nucleotides. Each **nucleotide** consists of three chemical groups: a phosphate group, a five-carbon sugar, and a nitrogen-containing, or *nitrogenous*, base. The five-carbon sugar, called deoxyribose, gives DNA its name.

Phosphate and sugar groups link together to form the "backbone" of a DNA strand. Bases link up to connect the two strands. The figure below shows the structure of DNA. ☑

6. Identify Which two scientists determined the structure of DNA?

____

____

7. Describe What are the two chemical groups that form the backbone of a DNA strand?

____

____

Nucleotides are the subunits of nucleic acid. Each nucleotide consists of a sugar, a phosphate, and a nitrogenous base.

Phosphate group

Nitrogen base

Sugar (deoxyribose)

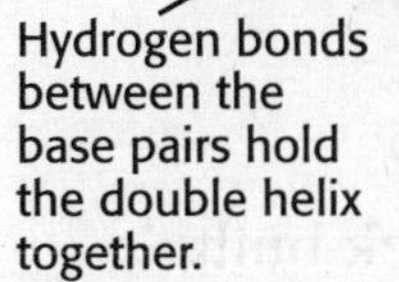

Hydrogen bonds between the base pairs hold the double helix together.

Sugar-phosphate bonds make up the backbone of each DNA strand.

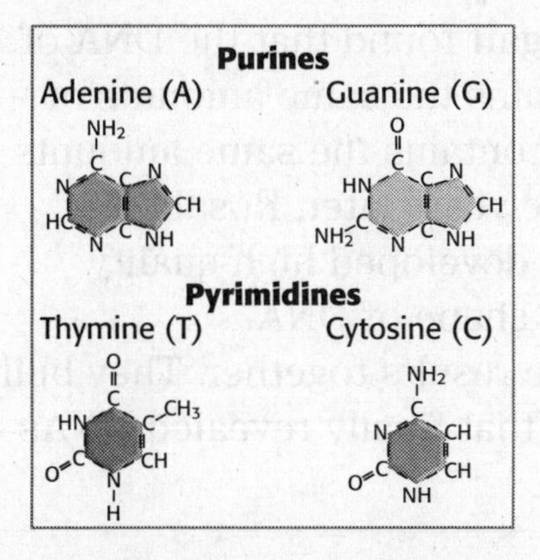

Purines contain two rings of carbon and nitrogen atoms. Adenine (represented by the letter A) and guanine (G) are purines.

Pyrimidines contain one ring of carbon and nitrogen atoms. Thymine (T) and cytosine (C) are pyrimidines.

LOOKING CLOSER

8. Identify Give one difference between purines and pyrimidines.

____

____

____

How Do Bases in DNA Link Together?

A purine on a DNA strand always pairs with a pyrimidine on the other strand, as shown below. Weak hydrogen bonds keep those base pairs close to each other. They also hold the two strands of DNA together.

You know that letters placed in a certain order can carry information in the form of words. In a similar way, the order of bases in a DNA strand carries information. Because the bases in DNA pair only in specific ways, each strand of a DNA molecule contains the same information. However, the bases on one strand are in the opposite order from those on the other strand, as shown below.

Background
Recall that a *hydrogen bond* is a weak attraction between a hydrogen atom and an oxygen, nitrogen, or fluorine atom.

Talk About It
Explain In a small group, discuss how you could determine the order of bases on one DNA strand if you knew the order of bases on the other strand.

Hydrogen bonds link complementary bases and hold the two strands of DNA together.

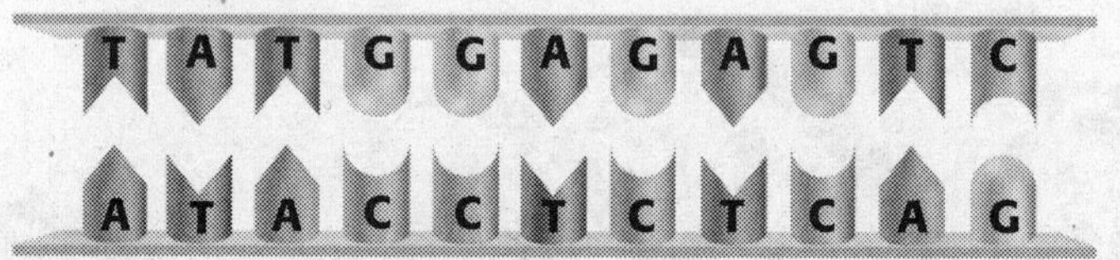

This diagram shows how complementary base pairs join together. Note that adenine (A) always pairs with thymine (T), and cytosine (C) always pairs with guanine (G). In other words, the bases are *complementary*.

LOOKING CLOSER
9. Identify Which base always pairs with cytosine?

____

DETERMINING THE STRUCTURE OF DNA

As is common in science, Watson and Crick built on information gathered by many other scientists. For example, in 1949, Erwin Chargaff found that the DNA of all organisms he studied contains the same amounts of cytosine and guanine. It also contains the same amounts of adenine and thymine. Three years later, Rosalind Franklin and Maurice Wilkins developed high-quality X-ray images that showed the shape of DNA.

Watson and Crick put those results together. They built models based on the findings that finally revealed DNA's unique structure.

Critical Thinking
10. Explain Why must an organism have the same amount of adenine as thymine?

____

Name ______________________ Class ______________ Date ______________

Section 1 Review

SECTION VOCABULARY

DNA deoxyribonucleic acid, the material that contains the information that determines inherited characteristics

gene the most basic physical unit of heredity; a segment of nucleic acids that codes for a functional unit of RNA and/or a protein

nucleotide an organic compound that consists of a sugar, a phosphate, and a nitrogenous base; the basic building-block of a nucleic-acid chain

purine a nitrogenous base that has a double-ring structure; one of the two general categories of nitrogenous bases found in DNA and RNA; either adenine or guanine

pyrimidine a nitrogenous base that has a single-ring structure; one of the two general categories of nitrogenous bases found in DNA and RNA; thymine, cytosine, or uracil

1. **List** Describe the results of three experiments that helped to show that DNA is the genetic material.

____

____

____

____

2. **Describe** What is the shape of a DNA molecule?

____

____

____

3. **Apply Concepts** Give the sequence of bases that is complementary to the sequence AATGCCGTATAG.

____

4. **Explain** How does the complementary pairing of bases allow both strands of a DNA molecule to contain the same information?

____

____

____

5. **Describe** Explain how the results of Chargaff's experiment may have helped Watson and Crick determine the structure of DNA.

____

____

____

Name ______________________ Class ______________ Date ______________

CHAPTER 13 DNA, RNA, and Proteins

SECTION 2

Replication of DNA

KEY IDEAS

As you read this section, keep these questions in mind:

- How does DNA replicate, or make a copy of itself?
- What are the roles of proteins in DNA replication?
- How is DNA replication different in prokaryotes and eukaryotes?

READING TOOLBOX

Summarize As you read this section, underline the main ideas. When you finish reading, write an outline of the section using the underlined ideas.

How Is DNA Copied?

When cells divide, each new cell contains an exact copy of the DNA in the original cell. That happens because DNA consists of two strands of complementary base pairs. If the two strands are separated, each strand serves as a pattern to make a new complementary strand. So, a single DNA molecule can be used as a *template*, or pattern, to produce two identical DNA molecules. This process of **DNA replication** involves three steps.

First, the DNA double helix unwinds and forms the Y shapes shown below. These Y shapes are called *replication forks*. At the replication forks, the complementary DNA strands separate from each other.

Critical Thinking

1. Apply Concepts A particular DNA molecule contains 10,000 base pairs. How many base pairs will be in each of the two new strands formed during DNA replication?

____

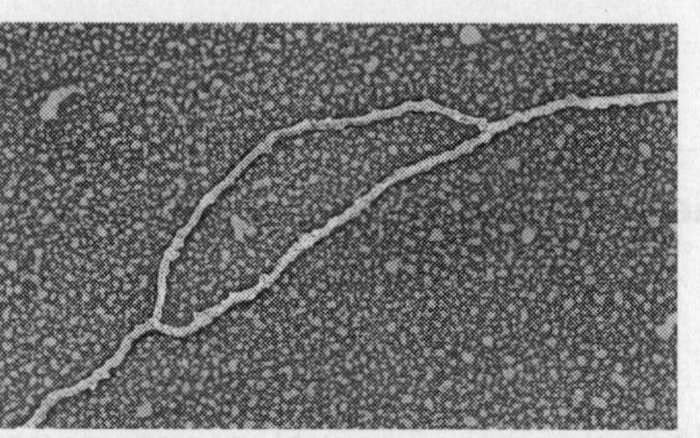

Y-shaped replication forks form where two strands of DNA separate.

LOOKING CLOSER

2. Identify Label the two replication forks on the figure.

____

____

Next, new nucleotides are added at each fork. The nucleotides form new base pairs according to the base-pairing rules. For example, adenine on an original strand will pair with thymine on a new strand. In this way, the original two strands act as templates for two new strands. Two new double helixes form as more nucleotides are added.

Finally, the two new DNA molecules split apart. Each molecule consists of one strand of the original DNA and one new strand. The nucleotide sequences in both new DNA molecules are identical to each other and to the original DNA molecule.

How Do Proteins Help to Copy DNA?

DNA cannot copy itself. Instead, many different proteins help to copy a DNA molecule. Each protein has a different set of functions.

Proteins called **DNA helicases** unwind the DNA double helix during replication. These proteins wedge themselves between the two DNA strands and break the hydrogen bonds that hold the strands together. That causes the helix to unwind and form a replication fork. Other proteins keep the two strands separated so that they can be copied. ☑

Proteins called **DNA polymerases** help to form the new DNA molecules. Starting at the replication fork, DNA polymerases move along each single strand. They add nucleotides that form pairs with each base on the single strands to form two new double helixes.

DNA polymerases also have another job: they act as proofreaders. Sometimes, the wrong nucleotide attaches to the DNA strand. However, DNA polymerases cannot add another nucleotide to the strand if the previous one is paired to the wrong base. If an error occurs, the DNA polymerase removes the incorrectly paired nucleotide and replaces it with the correct one.

READING CHECK

3. Describe What is the function of DNA helicase in DNA replication?

____

____

Critical Thinking

4. Apply Concepts Give an example of an incorrect base pairing.

____

DNA Replication

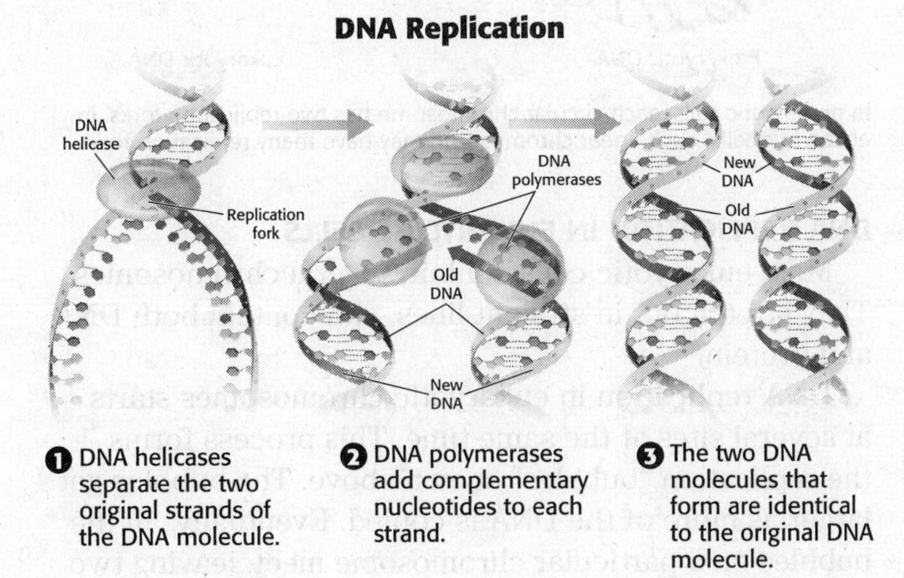

❶ DNA helicases separate the two original strands of the DNA molecule.

❷ DNA polymerases add complementary nucleotides to each strand.

❸ The two DNA molecules that form are identical to the original DNA molecule.

LOOKING CLOSER

5. Identify Name two proteins that are important in DNA replication.

____

____

DNA REPLICATION IN PROKARYOTIC CELLS

Remember that the DNA in cells is packaged in the form of *chromosomes*. All cells have chromosomes, but prokaryotes and eukaryotes replicate their chromosomes in different ways.

Prokaryotic cells usually have a single, circular chromosome. It is a closed loop attached to the inner cell membrane. Replication starts at one place along the chromosome. Two replication forks begin at that point. Replication proceeds in opposite directions until the two replication forks meet on the opposite side of the chromosome. At that point, the entire DNA molecule has been copied, as shown in the figure below. ☑

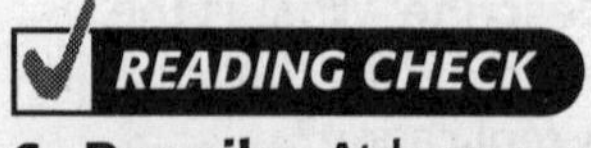

6. Describe At how many points on a prokaryotic chromosome does DNA replication begin?

____

LOOKING CLOSER

7. Compare How does the shape of a prokaryotic chromosome compare to the shape of a eukaryotic chromosome?

____

____

____

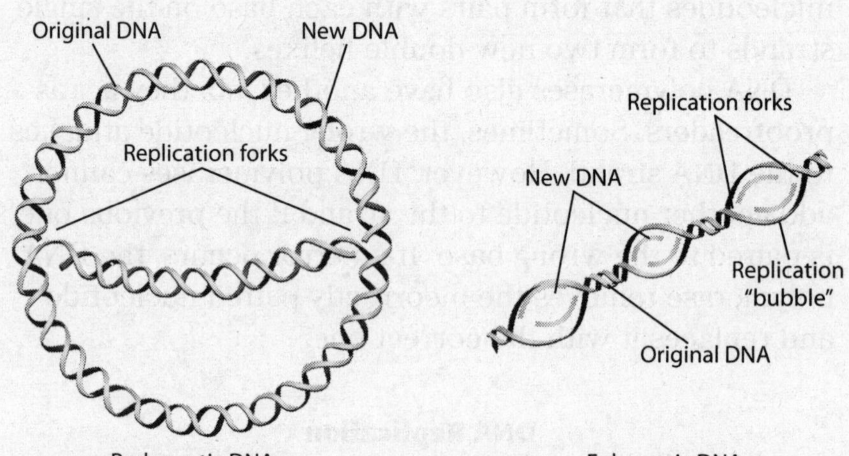

In prokaryotic cells, each circular chromosome has two replication forks. In eukaryotic cells, each linear chromosome may have many replication forks.

DNA REPLICATION IN EUKARYOTIC CELLS

Most eukaryotic cells contain several chromosomes. They stretch out in straight lines, and contain both DNA and protein.

DNA replication in eukaryotic chromosomes starts at several sites at the same time. This process forms the replication "bubbles" shown above. The bubbles get larger as more of the DNA is copied. Eventually, all the bubbles on a particular chromosome meet, leaving two identical DNA molecules.

Name ______________________ Class ______________ Date ______________

Section 2 Review

SECTION VOCABULARY

DNA helicase an enzyme that unwinds the DNA double helix during DNA replication	**DNA polymerase** an enzyme that catalyzes the formation of the DNA molecule **DNA replication** the process of making a copy of DNA

1. Identify Give two functions of DNA polymerase in DNA replication.

____

____

2. Describe Fill in the blanks in the flowchart below to show how DNA replication occurs.

______________ separate the two complementary strands of DNA, forming ______________.

↓

At the ______________, DNA polymerases add ______________ bases to each strand, forming two new DNA molecules.

↓

______________ bases continue to be added until the entire DNA strand has been copied.

↓

Two new DNA molecules form. Each is ______________ to the other and to the original DNA molecule.

3. Compare Give one difference and one similarity between DNA replication in eukaryotic cells and DNA replication in prokaryotic cells.

____

____

____

____

Name ______________________ Class ______________ Date ______________

CHAPTER 13 DNA, RNA, and Proteins

SECTION 3

RNA and Gene Expression

KEY IDEAS

As you read this section, keep these questions in mind:

- What is the process of gene expression?
- What role does RNA play in gene expression?
- What happens during transcription?
- How do codons determine the sequence of amino acids that results after translation?
- What are the major steps of translation?
- Do traits result from the expression of a single gene?

READING TOOLBOX

Summarize After you read this section, make a flowchart showing the sequence of steps involved in the production of a protein from a DNA molecule.

What Is Gene Expression?

Gene expression is the process by which genes control the traits of an organism. The process of gene expression results in the production of proteins, as shown below.

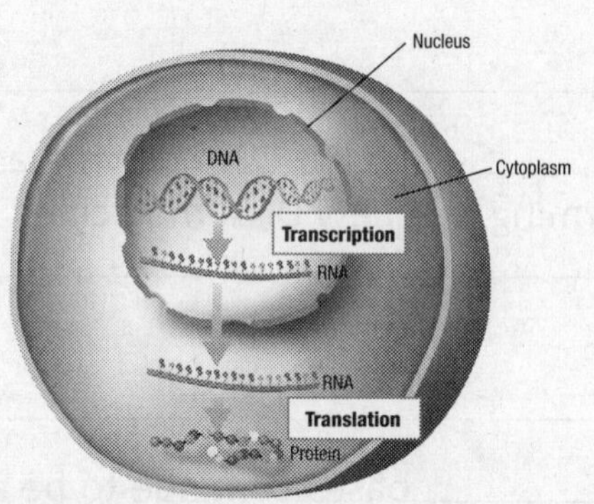

Gene expression consists of two main steps: transcription and translation. In eukaryotic cells, like the one shown here, transcription occurs in the nucleus, and translation occurs in the cytoplasm.

LOOKING CLOSER

1. Identify What are the two main steps in gene expression?

____

____

Both transcription and translation involve **RNA**, or ribonucleic acid. Like DNA, RNA consists of nucleotide subunits linked together. RNA also has four bases and carries information. However, RNA differs from DNA in three ways:

- RNA generally consists of a single strand of nucleotides.
- RNA nucleotides contain the five-carbon sugar *ribose* instead of the sugar deoxyribose.
- RNA nucleotides contain a base called uracil (U) instead of thymine. Like thymine, uracil is complementary to adenine.

There are three main kinds of RNA. Each kind is described in the table on the next page.

Critical Thinking

2. Apply Concepts A DNA strand has the base sequence GCCATATTG. What is the complementary RNA sequence?

____

Type of RNA	Description
Messenger RNA (mRNA)	produced during transcription; is complementary to a DNA strand
Transfer RNA (tRNA)	used during translation; attaches to an amino acid; contains a sequence of bases that are complementary to part of an mRNA strand
Ribosomal RNA (rRNA)	found in ribosomes; helps to bind amino acids together during translation

LOOKING CLOSER

3. Identify Which type of RNA is produced during transcription?

____

What Is Transcription?

The first stage of gene expression is **transcription**. During transcription, information in a particular region of DNA is copied into mRNA. A protein called *RNA polymerase* carries out transcription in three stages.

Talk About It

Find Word Roots Look up the word *polymer* in a dictionary. In a small group, talk about the most likely reason that proteins that produce DNA and RNA from free nucleotides are called *polymerases*.

Transcription

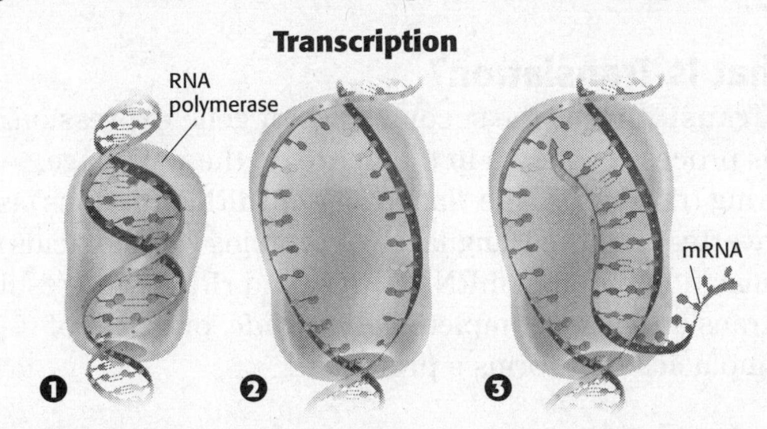

1 RNA polymerase binds to a specific part of the gene called the promoter region.

2 The two DNA strands unwind and separate.

3 The RNA polymerase moves along the DNA strand. It adds complementary mRNA nucleotides to a growing mRNA strand as it moves. At the end of transcription, the RNA polymerase has produced an mRNA strand that is complementary to the DNA in the gene.

LOOKING CLOSER

4. Summarize What happens during transcription?

____

____

____

You can think of a gene as a "sentence." Each "word" in the sentence consists of a group of three bases called a **codon**. During transcription, the sentence of DNA codons is translated into a complementary sentence of mRNA codons. After transcription, the mRNA sentence moves from the cell nucleus to ribosomes in the cytoplasm. There, it is translated into proteins. ☑

Each mRNA codon either matches one amino acid or acts as a signal to start or stop translation. This system of paired codons and amino acids is called the *genetic code*. The figure at the top of the next page shows how to determine which amino acid a certain codon codes for.

5. Define What is a codon?

____

____

LOOKING CLOSER

6. Identify Which amino acid does the codon ACU code for?

____

7. Identify Give two examples of a stop codon.

____

____

Find the first base of the mRNA codon in this column. | Follow that row to the column that matches the second base of the codon. | Move up or down in that box until you match the third base of the codon with this column.

First base	Codons in mRNA — Second base: U	C	A	G	Third base
U	UUU, UUC — Phenylalanine; UUA, UUG — Leucine	UCU, UCC, UCA, UCG — Serine	UAU, UAC — Tyrosine; UAA, UAG — Stop	UGU, UGC — Cysteine; UGA–Stop; UGG–Tryptophan	U C A G
C	CUU, CUC, CUA, CUG — Leucine	CCU, CCC, CCA, CCG — Proline	CAU, CAC — Histidine; CAA, CAG — Glutamine	CGU, CGC, CGA, CGG — Arginine	U C A G
A	AUU, AUC, AUA — Isoleucine; AUG–Start/Methionine	ACU, ACC, ACA, ACG — Threonine	AAU, AAC — Asparagine; AAA, AAG — Lysine	AGU, AGC — Serine; AGA, AGG — Arginine	U C A G
G	GUU, GUC, GUA, GUG — Valine	GCU, GCC, GCA, GCG — Alanine	GAU, GAC — Aspartic acid; GAA, GAG — Glutamic acid	GGU, GGC, GGA, GGG — Glycine	U C A G

What Is Translation?

Translation is the second stage of gene expression. This process is shown in the figure on the next page. During translation, the "language" of mRNA (codons) is converted into the "language" of proteins (amino acids). Translation requires mRNA, tRNA, and rRNA. The result of translation is a complete *polypeptide*, or group of amino acids that forms a protein. ☑

8. Describe What is the end result of translation?

____

____

____

How Are Genes Linked to Traits?

Genes contain the information to produce proteins. Proteins, in turn, produce almost all the traits of an organism. However, the relationship between genes and the traits they affect is complex. Variations, mistakes, and other complex interactions can occur at each stage of DNA replication and gene expression. These interactions can cause the effects of a gene to change.

A particular gene does not necessarily cause only one effect. Some genes are expressed only at certain times or under particular conditions. The protein a gene codes for may have many effects on an organism. In addition, a particular trait is not necessarily the result of only one gene. Some traits result from the expression of several genes. ☑

9. Explain Does a particular trait result from the expression of a single gene?

____

Several factors determine the final outcome of gene expression. They include the cell's environment, the presence of other cells, and the timing of gene expression.

Name ______________________ Class ______________ Date ____________

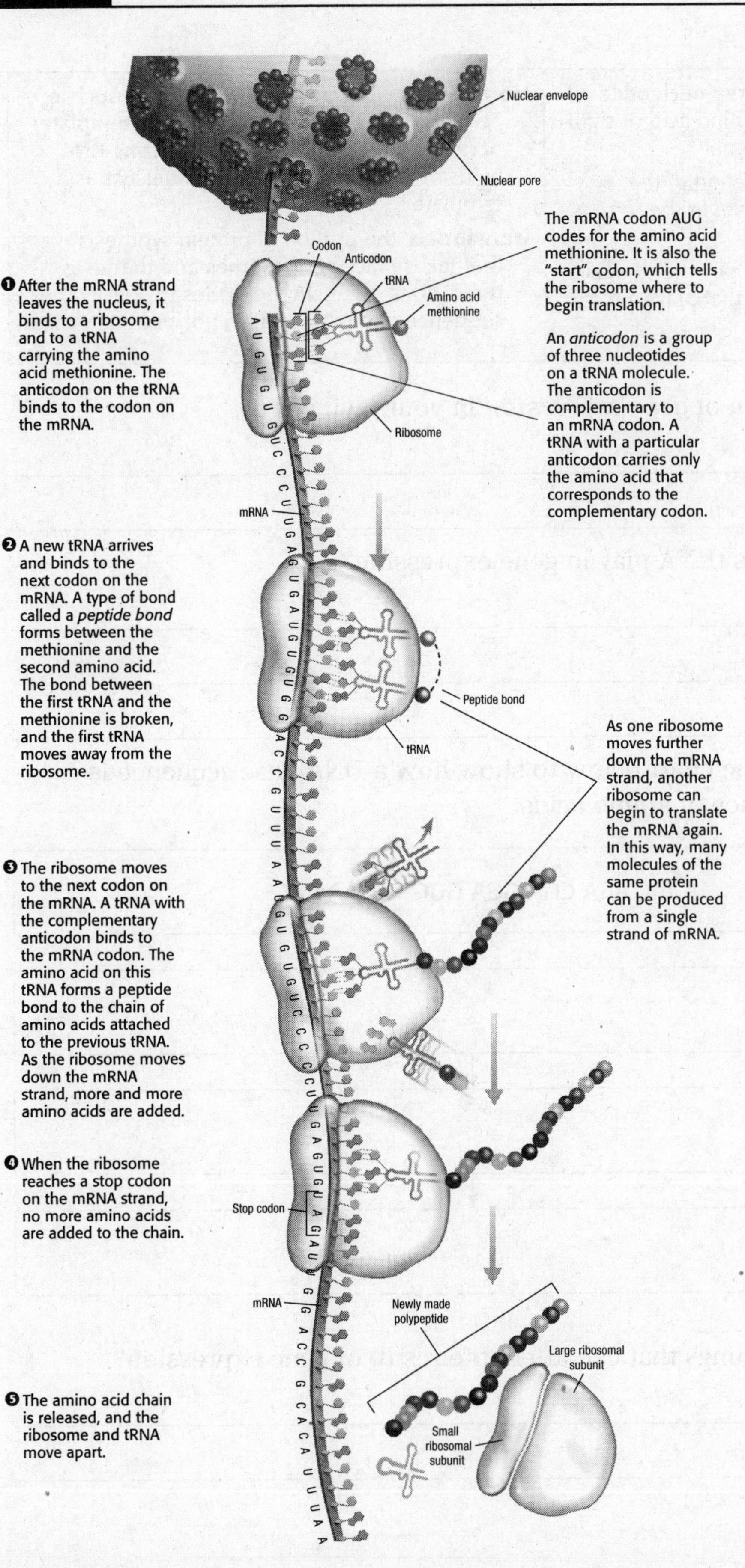

LOOKING CLOSER

10. Explain The first amino acid in most polypeptides is methionine. What is the reason for this?

____

____

____

11. Describe What causes translation to end?

____

12. Identify Where is the rRNA in the figure?

____

13. Explain How can the same mRNA strand be used to produce more than one polypeptide at the same time?

____

____

____

____

____

Name ______________________ Class ______________ Date ______________

Section 3 Review

SECTION VOCABULARY

codon in DNA and mRNA, a three-nucleotide sequence that encodes an amino acid or signifies a start signal or a stop signal

gene expression the manifestation of the genetic material of an organism in the form of specific traits

RNA ribonucleic acid, a natural polymer that is present in all living cells and that plays a role in protein synthesis

transcription the process of forming a nucleic acid by using another molecule as a template; particularly the process of synthesizing RNA by using one strand of a DNA molecule as a template

translation the portion of protein synthesis that takes place at ribosomes and that uses the codons in mRNA molecules to specify the sequence of amino acids in polypeptide chains

1. Define Write a definition of *gene expression* in your own words.

____

____

2. Describe What role does tRNA play in gene expression?

____

____

____

3. Apply Concepts Fill in the chart below to show how a DNA base sequence is converted into a sequence of amino acids.

DNA codons	TAC ACA CGA GGA GGG TCT AAA ATT
mRNA codons	
tRNA anticodons	
Amino acids	

4. Identify What are two things that can affect the result of gene expression?

____

____

Name ______________________ Class ______________ Date ______________

CHAPTER 14 Genes in Action

SECTION 1

Mutation and Genetic Change

KEY IDEAS

As you read this section, keep these questions in mind:

- What is the origin of genetic differences among organisms?
- What kinds of mutations are possible?
- What are the possible effects of mutations?
- How can genetic change occur on a larger scale?

What Are Mutations?

In genetics, a **mutation** is a change in the structure or amount of genetic material in an organism. Most genetic differences between organisms began with a mutation. Most mutations occur when DNA or chromosomes are damaged. *Mutagens*, such as radiation and some chemicals, can make mutations more likely. ☑

READING TOOLBOX

Summarize After you read this section, write a short summary of the information in each figure. If you have trouble, work with a partner or a small group.

1. Define What is a mutagen?

____

____

What Kinds of Mutation Are Possible?

There are three main ways that DNA can change. In a *point mutation*, a single nucleotide in a DNA molecule changes. In an *insertion mutation*, extra nucleotides are added to a DNA molecule. In a *deletion mutation*, nucleotides are removed from a DNA molecule.

EFFECTS OF POINT MUTATIONS

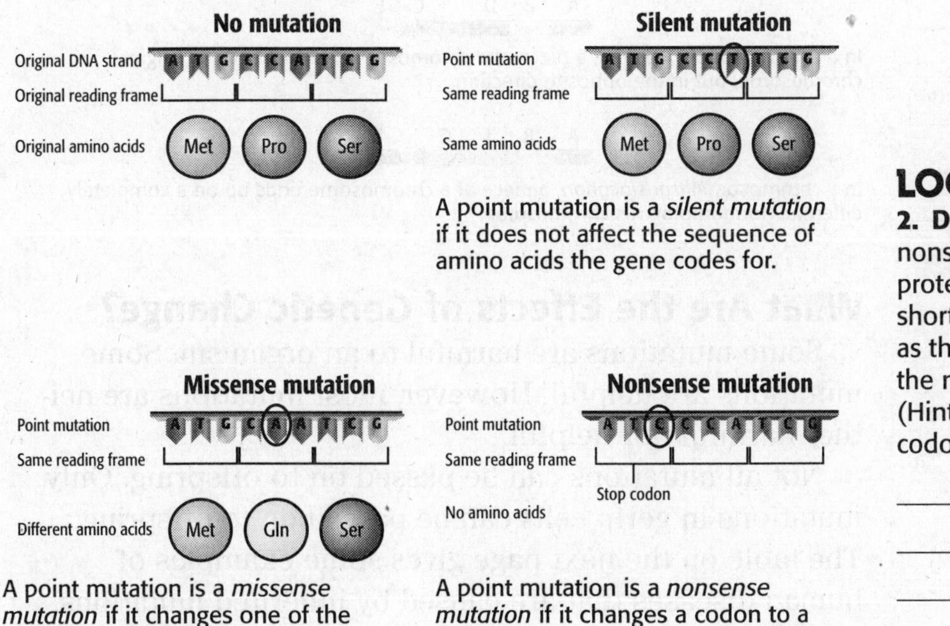

A point mutation is a *silent mutation* if it does not affect the sequence of amino acids the gene codes for.

A point mutation is a *missense mutation* if it changes one of the amino acids in the sequence.

A point mutation is a *nonsense mutation* if it changes a codon to a stop codon.

LOOKING CLOSER

2. Describe A gene has a nonsense mutation. Will the protein it produces be longer, shorter, or the same length as the protein produced by the normal gene? (Hint: What does a stop codon do?)

____

____

____

____

EFFECTS OF INSERTIONS AND DELETIONS

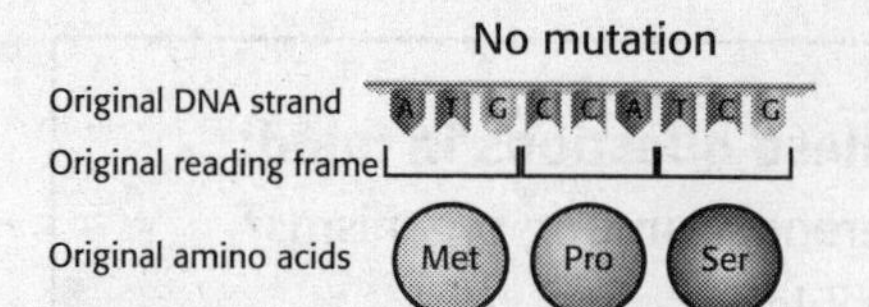

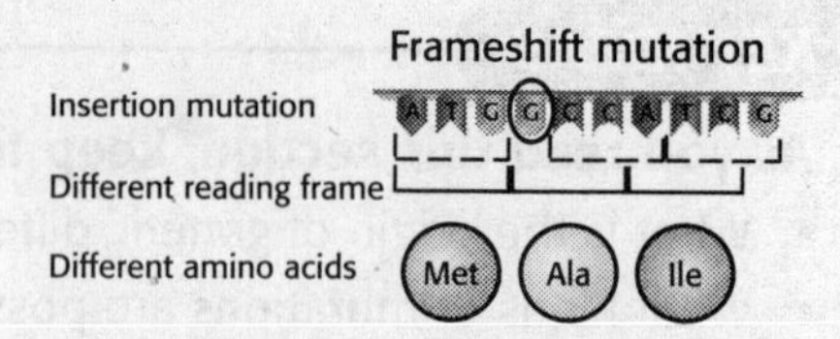

Remember that the genetic code is "read" in "words" of three letters each (codons). Insertions or deletions can change the *reading frame* by changing the groupings of nucleotides that are read during translation.

This insertion mutation has caused a *frameshift mutation*. It has changed the reading frame of the DNA sequence. As a result, the DNA codes for a different set of amino acids.

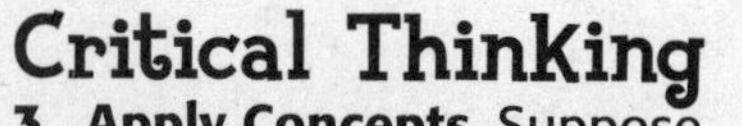

Critical Thinking

3. Apply Concepts Suppose three nucleotides are inserted into a gene. Will this insertion mutation cause a frameshift mutation? Explain your answer.

____

____

____

____

____

____

____

What Are Chromosomal Mutations?

In some cases, mutations can affect an entire chromosome. Most of these *chromosomal mutations* occur during crossing-over in meiosis.

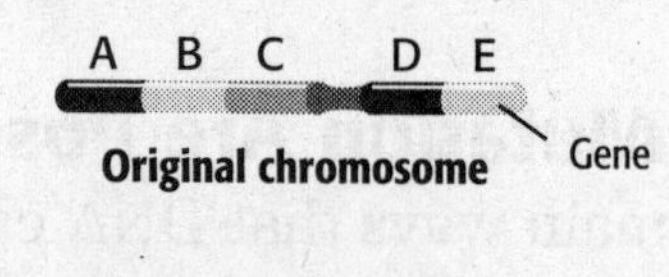

A B D E

In a chromosomal *deletion*, a piece of a chromosome is lost.

A B A B C D E

In a chromosomal *duplication*, a piece of a chromosome remains attached to its homologous chromosome after meiosis. The chromosome then carries both alleles for all the genes on that piece.

In a chromosomal *inversion*, a piece of a chromosome reattaches to its original chromosome, but in the opposite direction.

In a chromosomal *translocation*, a piece of a chromosome ends up on a completely different, nonhomologous chromosome.

LOOKING CLOSER

4. Compare How is a chromosomal duplication different from a chromosomal translocation?

____

____

____

____

____

What Are the Effects of Genetic Change?

Some mutations are harmful to an organism. Some mutations are helpful. However, most mutations are neither harmful nor helpful.

Not all mutations can be passed on to offspring. Only mutations in germ cells can be passed on to offspring. The table on the next page gives some examples of human diseases that are caused by inherited mutations.

Disorder	Dominant or recessive?	Effect of mutant allele	Physical symptoms
Sickle cell anemia	recessive	The protein that carries oxygen in the blood is defective.	poor blood circulation; organ damage
Tay-Sachs disease	recessive in most cases	An enzyme in nerve cells is defective.	nervous system damage; early death
Cystic fibrosis	recessive	An enzyme in cells that secrete proteins is defective.	mucus buildup in certain organs; shortened life span
Hemophilia A	recessive (sex-linked)	A protein that helps blood clot is defective.	lack of formation of blood clots; can cause severe bleeding from minor injuries
Huntington disease	dominant	A protein in brain cells is abnormal.	brain damage; shortened life span

LOOKING CLOSER

5. Identify Give two examples of recessive genetic disorders and one example of a dominant genetic disorder.

____

CANCER-CAUSING MUTATIONS

Mutations in somatic cells may change the cells' functions. Mutations in genes that control the normal growth or division of cells can cause cancer. This occurs when mutations cause normal somatic cells to start growing and dividing abnormally.

What Is Large-Scale Genetic Change?

Large-scale genetic change can occur when entire chromosomes or sets of chromosomes are copied or sorted incorrectly during meiosis.

Normally, during meiosis, pairs of chromosomes separate in a process called *disjunction*. As a result, each gamete contains one copy of each chromosome. During **nondisjunction**, a pair of chromosomes does not separate properly. As a result, a gamete can have more than one copy of a chromosome. If the gamete fertilizes another gamete, the resulting zygote will have an extra chromosome. ☑

Another kind of large-scale genetic change happens through nondisjunction of all chromosomes. This produces a cell with multiple sets of chromosomes. This condition of **polyploidy** is common in plants.

6. Define What is nondisjunction?

____

____

____

____

Name ______________________ Class ______________ Date ______________

Section 1 Review

SECTION VOCABULARY

mutation a change in the structure or amount of the genetic material of an organism **nondisjunction** the failure of homologous chromosomes to separate during meiosis I or the failure of sister chromatids to separate during mitosis or meiosis II	**polyploidy** an abnormal condition of having more than two sets of chromosomes

1. **Describe** How are nondisjunction and polyploidy related?

____

____

2. **Identify** What is the origin of almost all genetic differences between organisms?

____

3. **Describe** Explain the difference between point mutations, insertion mutations, and deletion mutations.

____

____

____

4. **Compare** How is a missense mutation different from a nonsense mutation? How are they similar?

____

____

____

5. **Apply Concepts** Skin cancer can occur if the DNA in skin cells is mutated by ultraviolet radiation in sunlight. Can the mutation that causes skin cancer be passed on to offspring? Explain your answer.

____

____

6. **List** Describe three types of chromosomal mutations.

____

____

____

Name ______ Class ______ Date ______

SECTION 2

Regulating Gene Expression

KEY IDEAS

As you read this section, keep these questions in mind:

- Can the process of gene expression be controlled?
- What is a common form of gene regulation in prokaryotes?
- How does gene regulation in eukaryotes differ from gene regulation in prokaryotes?
- Why are proteins so important and versatile?

What Is Gene Regulation?

Every somatic cell in your body has the same chromosomes and, therefore, the same genes. However, your somatic cells are not all the same because not all genes are expressed in all cells all the time.

Cells have complex systems that *regulate*, or determine, which genes are expressed in a given cell at a given time. The particular genes that are expressed in a cell determine the proteins that the cell produces. This affects the cell's structure and function.

READING TOOLBOX

Define As you read this section, underline words you don't understand. When you figure out what they mean, write the words and their definitions in your notebook.

How Are Genes Regulated in Prokaryotes?

Most gene regulation in prokaryotes depends on operons. An example of such regulation is shown below.

An Example of Gene Regulation in Prokaryotes: The *lac* Operon

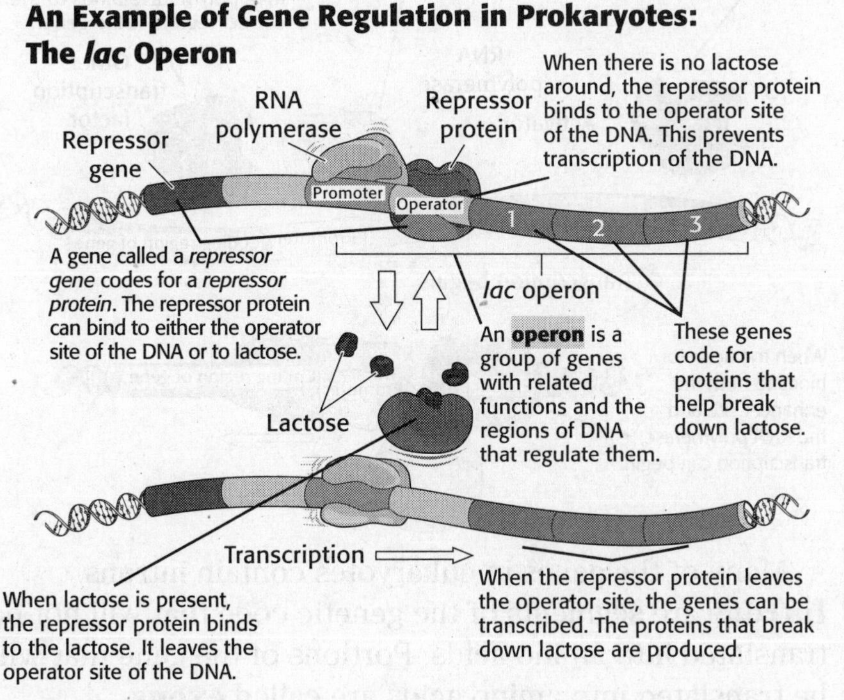

LOOKING CLOSER

1. Define What is an operon?

______

______

2. Infer Would the *lac* operon work if the repressor protein could not bind to lactose? Explain your answer.

______

______

______

______

How Are Genes Regulated in Eukaryotes?

There are several differences between gene regulation in prokaryotic cells and eukaryotic cells:

- More proteins are involved in gene regulation in eukaryotic cells than in prokaryotic cells.
- Transcription and translation in eukaryotic cells can be regulated separately, because they are separated by the nuclear membrane.
- Operons are very rare in eukaryotic cells.
- Much of the DNA in a eukaryotic cell will never be transcribed or translated into proteins.

Gene regulation in eukaryotic cells can happen before transcription, after transcription, or after translation.

Background
Recall that *transcription* is the process in which the information in a gene is translated into an mRNA molecule. *Translation* is the process in which the information in an mRNA molecule is converted into a polypeptide.

GENE REGULATION BEFORE TRANSCRIPTION

Most gene regulation in eukaryotes happens before transcription. The proteins that are involved in this kind of regulation are called **transcription factors**. The figure below shows an example of gene regulation by transcription factors. ☑

3. Define What is a transcription factor?

____

____

____

____

An Example of Gene Regulation in Eukaryotes

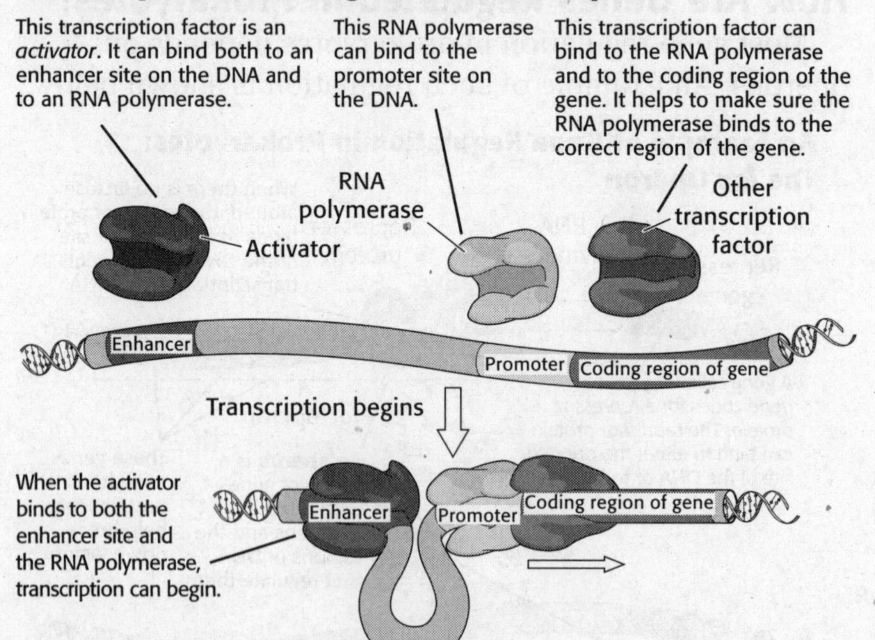

LOOKING CLOSER
4. Describe In the figure, what allows transcription to begin?

____

____

____

____

Many of the genes in eukaryotes contain introns. **Introns** are segments of the genetic code that will not be translated into amino acids. Portions of the gene that will be translated into amino acids are called **exons**.

GENE REGULATION AFTER TRANSCRIPTION

The mRNA that forms during transcription contains both introns and exons. During a process called *RNA splicing*, the introns are removed from the mRNA strand. The remaining exons are *spliced*, or joined, together to form the mRNA strand that will be translated into a protein.

RNA Splicing

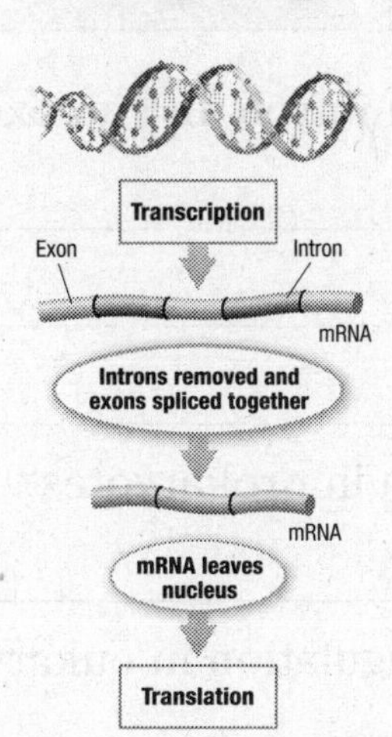

GENE REGULATION AFTER TRANSLATION

Proteins do not always go straight into action after they are formed. Some undergo chemical changes that alter their shape, stability, and reactions with other molecules. During the process of *protein sorting*, specific proteins are directed to places in the cell where they are needed. ☑

What Roles Do Proteins Have in Cells?

A protein's sequence of amino acids determines its structure. The structure, in turn, determines the protein's function. Parts of a protein that have specific chemical structures and functions are called **domains**.

Proteins play key roles in gene expression. Some help to make mRNA, tRNA, and rRNA. Others serve as *regulatory proteins*, such as transcription factors.

Proteins are also important in other ways. They help to control the shape and activity of a cell. In fact, proteins do most of the work that keeps a cell functioning. Because proteins have so many different functions, they have a huge variety of structures.

Critical Thinking

5. Explain Why is RNA splicing necessary?

____

____

____

____

LOOKING CLOSER

6. Describe Where does RNA splicing occur?

____

7. Define What is protein sorting?

____

____

____

____

Name ______________________ Class ______________ Date ______________

Section 2 Review

SECTION VOCABULARY

domain in a protein, a functional unit that has a distinctive pattern of structural folding

exon one of several nonadjacent nucleotide sequences that are part of one gene and that are transcribed, joined together, and then translated

intron a nucleotide sequence that is part of a gene and that is transcribed from DNA into mRNA but not translated into amino acids

operon a unit of adjacent genes that consists of functionally related structural genes and their associated regulatory genes; common in prokaryotes and phages

transcription factor an enzyme that is needed to begin and/or continue genetic transcription

1. Compare What is the difference between an intron and an exon?

____

____

____

2. Identify What controls most gene regulation in prokaryotes?

____

3. List Give three differences between gene regulation in eukaryotes and gene regulation in prokaryotes.

____

____

____

4. Identify Fill in the blank spaces in the table to describe ways that genes are regulated in eukaryotic cells.

When regulation occurs	Example and description
	transcription factors determine when a gene is transcribed
After transcription, but before translation	
After translation	

5. Describe Give two ways that proteins are important to cells.

____

____

Name ______________ Class ______________ Date ______________

SECTION 3

Genome Interactions

KEY IDEAS

As you read this section, keep these questions in mind:
- What can we learn by comparing genomes?
- Can genetic material be stored and transferred by mechanisms other than chromosomes?
- What are the roles of genes in the development of multicellular organisms?

What Can We Learn from Genomes?

Remember that a **genome** is all the DNA that an organism or species has in one set of its chromosomes. Genomes can vary in size from about 400 genes in some microbes to more than 100,000 genes in some plants. Human genomes contain about 30,000 genes.

By comparing the genomes of different organisms, scientists can learn how different species are related to one another. For example, scientists have learned that humans have about 81% of our genes in common with dogs, but only about 16% in common with slime molds. This indicates that humans and dogs are more closely related than humans and slime molds.

READING TOOLBOX

Summarize As you read this section, underline the main ideas. When you finish reading, write an outline of the section using the underlined ideas.

Talk About It

Describe Which species do you think humans share the most genes with? Which species do you think we share the fewest genes with? Talk about your ideas with a small group. Then, use the resources in your library or on the World Wide Web to find out if you are correct.

Is All DNA Found in Chromosomes?

Not all DNA in a cell is part of a gene, or even part of a chromosome. For example, mitochondria and chloroplasts contain DNA.

Mobile genetic elements (MGEs) are units of DNA or RNA that can move among locations in a genome. They exist outside chromosomes. MGEs can transfer genetic material between individuals and species. The table below describes some examples of MGEs.

Type of MGE	Description
Plasmid	small, circular piece of DNA; can be transferred between bacterial cells
Transposon	set of genes that move randomly between chromosomes; also called "jumping genes"
Virus	small, nonliving particle consisting of DNA or RNA inside a protein coating

LOOKING CLOSER

1. Compare What is the difference between a plasmid and a transposon?

____

____

____

How Do Genes Affect Growth and Aging?

In multicellular eukaryotes, different cells in different parts of the body have different functions. As the organism develops from a zygote, different genes are expressed in different cells. The genes that are expressed in a cell affect the structure and function of the cell. ☑

READING CHECK

2. Describe What produces the different structures and functions of different cells in multicellular eukaryotes?

During the process of **cell differentiation**, new cells are modified and specialized as they multiply to form an organism. *Homeotic* genes regulate cell differentiation. Mutations in these genes can cause physical deformities.

Genetic regulation of development is similar in all animals. For example, a set of homeotic genes called *hox* occurs in all animals with a head and a tail end.

LOOKING CLOSER

3. Describe What do *hox* genes control?

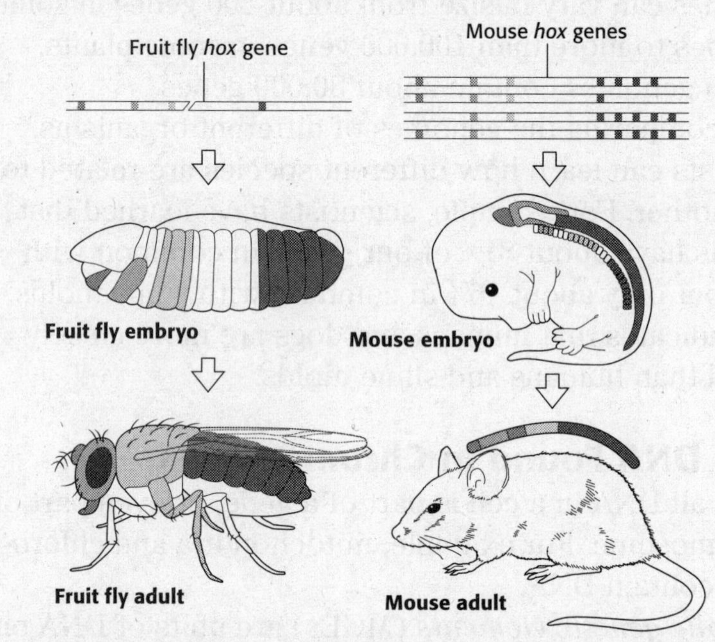

Hox genes are found in most animals that have a head and a tail end. These genes control the locations at which different body parts develop. Mutations in *hox* genes can cause physical deformities, such as a leg developing in place of an antenna.

In multicellular organisms, two kinds of proteins regulate the cell cycle: *CDK* and *cyclin*. Without one or both of these proteins, cells may develop too slowly or too quickly. For example, errors in CDK or cyclin proteins can cause cancer.

Most cells in multicellular organisms are genetically "programmed" to stop functioning and fall apart if they are damaged or get too old. This process of "programmed cell death" is called **apoptosis**.

Name ______________________ Class ______________ Date ______________

Section 3 Review

SECTION VOCABULARY

apoptosis in multicellular organisms, a genetically controlled process that leads to the death of a cell; programmed cell death **cell differentiation** the process by which a cell becomes specialized for a specific structure or function during multicellular development **genome** the complete genetic material contained in an individual or species	**plasmid** a genetic structure that can replicate independently of the main chromosome(s) of a cell; usually, a circular DNA molecule in bacteria (prokaryotes) **transposon** a genetic sequence that is randomly moved, in a functional unit, to new places in a genome

1. Compare What is the difference between a genome and a gene?

____

____

2. Infer A scientist is studying three different species. The scientist concludes that species A is more closely related to species B than to species C. How might the scientist have come to this conclusion?

____

____

3. Identify Give three examples of MGEs.

____

____

____

4. Describe What can happen to an organism if its *hox* genes are mutated?

____

____

5. Apply Concepts Most cells undergo apoptosis if their DNA is damaged. How can this be beneficial to an organism?

____

____

____

6. Identify Give two groups of proteins that help to regulate the cell cycle.

____

____

Name ______________________ Class ______________ Date ____________

CHAPTER 15 Gene Technologies and Human Applications

SECTION 1

The Human Genome

KEY IDEAS

As you read this section, keep these questions in mind:

- Why is the Human Genome Project so important?
- How do genomics and gene technologies affect our lives?
- What questions about the human genome remain to be studied?

READING TOOLBOX

Organize As you read this section, make a chart describing the findings, applications, and questions of human genomics.

What Is the Human Genome Project?

Recall that a *genome* is the complete set of genetic material (DNA) in an organism or species. **Genomics** is the study of genomes. Genomics often involves comparing genes within and between species. To do this, scientists *sequence* genomes. Sequencing a genome means identifying every DNA base pair that makes up the genome. This collection of DNA base pairs is called a sequence. ☑

1. Explain What does sequencing a genome mean?

____

____

____

The human genome has billions of DNA base pairs. *The Human Genome Project* was an international effort to sequence the human genome. A draft of the sequence was completed in 2003. Scientists were surprised and excited by what the sequence showed:

- Humans have only about 25,000 genes. Scientists had expected to find around 120,000 genes.
- Less than 2% of human DNA codes for proteins. The rest of the DNA consists of introns or is unexplained.
- Humans have many of the same genes as other species.
- The DNA sequence of all humans is very similar. The genome of any two people is 99.9% identical.

Background

Recall that *introns* are regions of DNA that do not code for amino acids or proteins.

How Do Scientists Use Genomic Information?

The human genome includes much information. Scientists use gene technologies to obtain and apply this information. *Gene technologies* allow scientists to find genes, copy genes, and turn the expression of genes on and off. They also enable scientists to do *genetic engineering* that moves genes between organisms. ☑

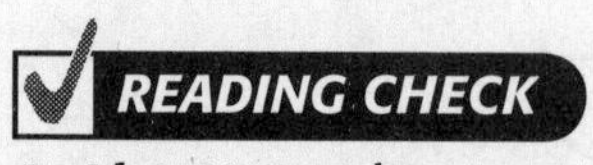

2. List Name three uses of gene technologies.

____

____

____

Genomic information and gene technologies have many applications in human healthcare and society. They can be used to diagnose, prevent, and treat diseases, and to identify people.

DIAGNOSING AND PREVENTING DISEASE

A **microarray** is a gene technology that can show when genes in a genome are active. Certain patterns of gene activity displayed by a microarray can indicate diseases.

Vaccines are often used to prevent diseases. Genomic information enables new and safer vaccines to be produced through genetic engineering. ☑

READING CHECK

3. Describe How can a microarray be used to diagnose a disease?

____

____

____

TREATING DISEASE

When a mutated gene cannot make a specific protein, it can cause a genetic disorder. This type of disorder can be treated by supplying the missing protein. Some drug companies genetically engineer organisms to produce human proteins for treatment use.

Gene therapy is a treatment that supplies a functional gene to replace a mutated one. *Pharmacogenomics* is a new field in which scientists make drugs based on genomic information. Scientists in this field may eventually develop drugs for a person's genetic profile.

IDENTIFYING INDIVIDUALS

Although the DNA sequence of all humans is very similar, each person (except identical twins) has some sequence that is completely unique. The unique regions of a person's genome can be used to make a pattern of DNA bands called a **DNA fingerprint**. DNA fingerprints are often used to identify criminals and dead bodies.

Critical Thinking

4. Infer What individuals would have the same DNA fingerprint?

____

What Are the Remaining Questions About the Human Genome?

The table below summarizes remaining questions about the human genome and how scientists are answering them.

Question	How scientists are answering the question
How do our genes interact?	Scientists are studying how the proteins made from one gene affect other genes.
How unique are we?	Scientists are comparing the human genome with genomes of other organisms.
Can genetics help us live longer?	Scientists are learning about how genes are involved in diseases.
How do we deal with ethical issues?	Scientists are discussing who should own genetic information and how it should be used.

Talk About It

Discuss With a partner or in a small group, discuss what each question about the human genome means and how scientists are addressing these questions.

Name ________________ Class ________ Date ________

Section 1 Review

SECTION VOCABULARY

DNA fingerprint a pattern of DNA characteristics that is unique, or nearly so, to an individual organism

genomics the study of entire genomes, especially by using technology to compare genes within and between species

microarray a device that contains, in microscopic scale, an orderly arrangement of biomolecules; a device that is used to rapidly test for the presence of a range of similar substances, such as specific DNA sequences

1. **Explain** What was the goal of the Human Genome Project?

____

____

2. **Identify** What percentage of DNA in the human genome does not code for proteins?

____

3. **Explain** How can a genome be used to identify a person if the DNA sequence of any two people is 99.9% identical?

____

____

____

4. **Describe** How are scientists studying how the genes in the human genome interact?

____

____

5. **Identify** Name three general ways that human genomics can be applied to healthcare.

____

____

6. **Infer** Genes code for proteins. Humans have many of the same genes as other species. What does this imply about the proteins in humans and other species?

____

____

7. **Calculate** About how many fewer genes do humans have than scientists expected?

____

Name ______________________ Class ______________ Date ______________

CHAPTER 15 | Gene Technologies and Human Applications

SECTION 2

Gene Technologies in Our Lives

KEY IDEAS

As you read this section, keep these questions in mind:

- For what purposes are genes and proteins manipulated?
- How are cloning and stem cell research related?
- What ethical issues arise with the uses of gene technologies?

Why Do Scientists Manipulate Genes?

Scientists use *gene technologies* to analyze and manipulate genes from organisms. The use of gene technologies to create a change in an organism's DNA is called **genetic engineering**. Genetic engineering often involves the transfer of genes between organisms.

DNA that combines genetic material from different organisms is **recombinant DNA**. Organisms with recombinant DNA are called *genetically modified organisms* (GMOs). Scientists often create GMOs to study organisms in new ways and to improve human lives. The table below shows the uses of GMOs in different fields. ☑

Field	How GMOs are used in the field
Food crops	Many corn and soybean crops in the U.S. are GMOs that contain a gene from bacteria. The gene makes a protein that protects the plants from insects. Scientists also genetically engineer crops to be easier to grow and to be more nutritious.
Livestock	Scientists genetically engineer livestock to grow faster, have more muscle, have less fat, and produce more nutritious milk.
Medicine	Scientists genetically engineer bacteria to rapidly produce human proteins. These human proteins can be used to treat people with genetic disorders, such as diabetes and hemophilia.
Basic research	Scientists can link a gene that glows to a gene they are studying. When they insert these genes into an organism, proteins from the gene they are studying will glow. This makes them easy to locate.

MANIPULATING PROTEINS

Scientists can also use gene technologies to control when genes make proteins and where these proteins act. The study of how proteins interact within cells is called *proteomics*. Scientists can use gene technologies to produce specific proteins at specific times. They manipulate proteins for medical treatment and research.

READING TOOLBOX

Ask Questions As you read this section, write down any questions you have. When you finish reading, talk about your questions with a partner or a small group. Together, try to figure out the answers to your questions.

1. Identify Name two reasons why scientists create GMOs.

____

____

2. Describe What are two possible advantages of GMO crops to farmers?

____

____

Why Do Scientists Manipulate Development?

A **clone** is a genetically identical copy of an organism or piece of genetic material. Organisms that reproduce asexually clone themselves. Scientists can clone large animals, such as the sheep shown below, using a process called *somatic-cell nuclear transfer* (SCNT). However, most cloned animals do not develop normally or live long.

Background
Recall that a *somatic* cell is a body cell, and not a reproductive cell.

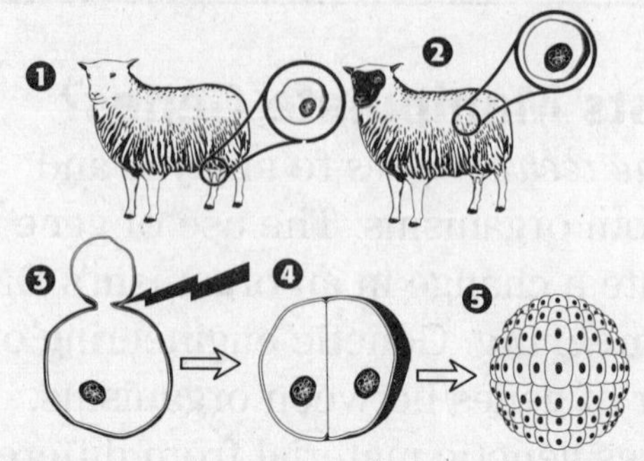

1. Scientists extracted somatic cells from the adult sheep being cloned.
2. Scientists also extracted egg cells from another sheep. They removed the nucleus from these cells.
3. Scientists placed a somatic cell and an "empty" egg cell near each other. They applied an electric shock that caused the two cells to fuse.
4. Scientists then triggered the cell to divide and begin to form an embryo.
5. Scientists implanted the embryo into a surrogate mother where it developed into a baby sheep. This sheep had the same genetic information as the sheep in step 1.

LOOKING CLOSER
3. Analyze Why can't the baby sheep be a clone of the sheep in step 2?

____
____
____
____

A **stem cell** is a cell that can develop into various cell types. *Totipotent* stem cells can give rise to any cell type. *Pluripotent* stem cells can give rise to all cell types except reproductive cells. *Multipotent* stem cells can give rise to just a few cell types. Cells of new embryos are totipotent.

Scientists use cloning and stem cell techniques to study animal development. These techniques help scientists learn how multicellular organisms develop from single cells. They also have potential for treating certain diseases. Scientists can use embryonic stem cells to create cell types to treat people with missing or damaged tissue.

Critical Thinking
4. Infer Why are the cells of new embryos totipotent?

____
____
____

What Issues Arise From Gene Technologies?

Human embryos are a major source of stem cells. However, there is controversy over whether stem cells from potential human babies should be used for research. Ethical concerns also surround the cloning of organisms and the use of GMOs. In some cases, the modified genes in GMOs have entered non-GMO organisms. In addition, proteins made by GMO crops can kill harmless insects.

Name ______________________ Class ______________ Date ______________

Section 2 Review

SECTION VOCABULARY

clone an organism, cell, or piece of genetic material that is genetically identical to one from which it was derived; to make a genetic duplicate

genetic engineering a technology in which the genome of a living cell is modified for medical or industrial use

recombinant DNA DNA molecules that are artificially created by combining DNA from different sources

stem cell a cell that can divide repeatedly and can differentiate into specialized cell types

1. **Describe** What kind of DNA do genetically modified organisms have?

____

2. **Apply Concepts** How can genetically modified bacteria with human genes be used to treat human diseases?

____

____

3. **Explain** What can a stem cell do that most body cells cannot do?

____

4. **Compare** Complete the following table to illustrate the advantages and disadvantages of GMOs, cloning, and stem cell research.

Technology	Advantage	Disadvantage
GMOs	GMOs improve the yield and nutrition of food crops and livestock.	
Cloning		Most cloned animals do not develop normally or live long.
Stem cell research	Stem cells enable scientists to create cell types for treating individuals with missing or damaged tissue.	

Name ______________________ Class ______________ Date ______________

CHAPTER 15 Gene Technologies and Human Applications

SECTION 3

Gene Technologies in Detail

KEY IDEAS

As you read this section, keep these questions in mind:

- What are the basic tools of genetic manipulation?
- How are these tools used in the major processes of modern gene technologies?
- How do scientists study entire genomes?

READING TOOLBOX

Define As you read this section, underline words you don't understand. When you learn what they mean, write the words and their definitions in your notebook. If you have trouble, work with a partner or in a small group.

What Tools Are Used in Genetic Manipulation?

Scientists use a set of basic tools to manipulate genetic material. These tools are adapted from natural processes in cells, and they rely on the chemical nature of DNA. The table describes the basic tools of genetic manipulation.

Basic tool	Description
Restriction enzymes	Bacteria make **restriction enzymes** to cut DNA from invading viruses. Restriction enzymes cut DNA at specific places called *restriction sites*. Scientists use these restriction enzymes to cut DNA samples in specific ways.
DNA polymorphisms	Differences between the DNA sequences of individuals are called **DNA polymorphisms**. A difference of just one nucleotide is a single *nucleotide polymorphism*. Scientists use polymorphisms to create DNA fingerprints and to compare individuals and species.
Gel Electrophoresis	DNA carries an electric charge. The process of **electrophoresis** uses an electric current to pull DNA fragments through a partly solid material called a *gel*. Shorter fragments move faster through a gel than longer fragments. Scientists use gel electrophoresis to separate DNA fragments by size.
Denaturation	DNA is usually double-stranded. Scientists can use heat or strong chemicals to *denature* DNA. Denaturing splits DNA into two single strands.
Hybridization	Scientists can *hybridize*, or bind, complementary single strands of DNA. Short single strands of DNA, called *primers*, hybridize to denatured DNA to start replication.

Critical Thinking

1. Apply Concepts Would you expect there to be more DNA polymorphisms between two different people or between a person and a dog?

____

Critical Thinking

2. Make Connections If a sample of double-stranded DNA is denatured by heat, what can cause the single strands of DNA to hybridize?

____

____

What Are Gene Technology Processes?

Gene technology processes are methods for manipulating genes. They combine the basic tools of genetic manipulation and cellular functions. The major gene technology processes are blotting, DNA sequencing, gene recombination, and polymerase chain reaction.

BASIC TOOLS AND GENE TECHNOLOGY PROCESSES

After DNA fragments have been separated by gel electrophoresis, scientists often use *blotting* processes. Blotting transfers fragments of DNA or RNA to a special surface. Scientists can then analyze the fragments.

DNA sequencing is a process that determines the exact order of every nucleotide in a region of DNA. The process uses almost all of the basic tools of genetic manipulation.

Gene recombination involves cutting out a gene with restriction enzymes and putting it into a vector, such as a plasmid. The vector is then put into a host organism where the gene is copied, or cloned. **Polymerase chain reaction** (PCR), shown below, also makes DNA clones.

Talk About It

Discuss With a partner or a small group, discuss the basic tools of genetic manipulation used in blotting processes.

Background

Recall that a *plasmid* is a genetic structure separate from a chromosome.

Polymerase Chain Reaction (PCR)

❶ Add DNA polymerase, nucleotides, and primers. Heat to denature, or separate, the DNA strands.

❷ Cool to allow the primers to bind, or hybridize, to complementary regions on the original strands.

❸ DNA polymerase will then add nucleotides to complete a copy of the original strands.

❹ Repeat the process by heating and cooling the DNA.

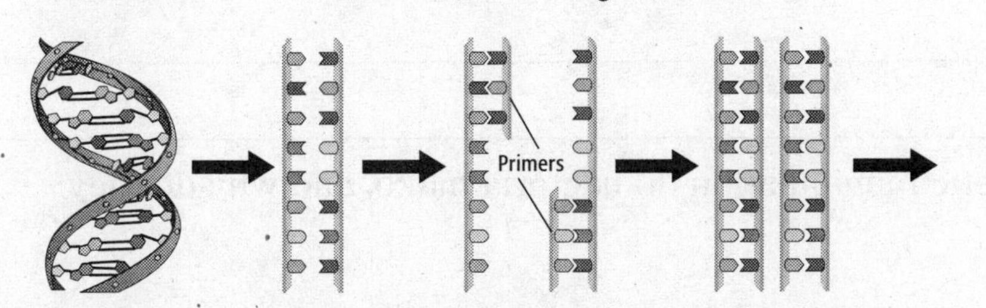

LOOKING CLOSER

3. Identify Name two basic tools of genetic manipulation used in PCR.

____

____

How Can Scientists Explore Genomes?

Scientists can explore a genome at the level of species, individual, chromosome, gene, or nucleotide. The following techniques help scientists explore genomes:

- Scientists use bioinformatics to manage all the data in a genome. **Bioinformatics** is the use of computer technology in biology. It can be used to store, map, classify, and analyze genomic information. ☑
- **Genome mapping** determines the relative positions of all the genes in an organism's genome. It determines where on a chromosome a gene is.
- A **genetic library** is a collection of many small fragments of DNA that represent all the genes in a genome. Scientists sequence genetic libraries to determine their DNA base pairs. They then sort and assemble the data.

4. Explain What does bioinformatics add to biology?

____

Name ______________________ Class ______________ Date ______________

Section 3 Review

SECTION VOCABULARY

bioinformatics the application of information technologies in biology, especially in genetics

DNA polymorphisms variations in DNA sequences; can be used as a basis for comparing genomes

DNA sequencing the process of determining the order of every nucleotide in a gene or genetic fragment; also referred to as gene sequencing

electrophoresis the process by which electrically charged particles suspended in a liquid move through the liquid because of the influence of an electric field

genetic library a collection of genetic sequence clones that represent all of the genes in a given genome

genome mapping the process of determining the relative position of genes in a genome

polymerase chain reaction a technique that is used to make many copies of selected segments of DNA (abbreviation, PCR)

restriction enzyme an enzyme that cuts double-stranded DNA into fragments by recognizing specific nucleotide sequences and cutting the DNA at those sequences

1. List What basic tools do scientists use to manipulate genetic material?

____

____

2. Describe How are denaturation and hybridization used in PCR?

____

____

____

3. Explain What tool of genetic manipulation do bacteria make, and why do they make it?

____

____

4. Predict A scientist is separating three fragments of DNA by gel electrophoresis. The first fragment is 500 base pairs long, the second is 5,000 base pairs long, and the third is 1,500 base pairs long. Which fragment will move the fastest through the gel?

____

5. Identfiy Name three ways that bioinformatics helps scientists explore genomes.

____

____

6. Identify How can scientists determine the location of genes on a chromosome?

____

SECTION 1

Developing a Theory

KEY IDEAS

As you read this section, keep these questions in mind:

- Why is evolutionary theory associated with Charles Darwin?
- How was Darwin influenced by his personal experiences?
- How was Darwin influenced by the ideas of others?

How Did Darwin's Experiences Influence His Ideas About Evolution?

Evolution is the process by which species change over time. Modern evolutionary theory began when Charles Darwin presented evidence that evolution happens and gave an explanation of how it happens.

THE VOYAGE OF THE *BEAGLE*

In the 1830s, Darwin took a global voyage on a ship called the *Beagle*. This voyage inspired many of his ideas. During the voyage, Darwin collected many natural objects, including nine species of finches in the Galápagos Islands. The birds were very similar, but their beaks differed in size and shape. He also noted that many of the islands' plant and animal species were similar to species in South America.

Each finch has a beak that is suited to the food it eats.

Darwin proposed that the finch species descended from a single South American species. The descendants became modified, or changed, over time to survive on different foods. Darwin called such a change *descent with modification*. This idea was a key part of his theory. ☑

After he returned from his voyage, Darwin studied his data for years. He did not report his ideas about evolution right away. Instead, he took time to gather more data and to form a good explanation for how evolution happens.

READING TOOLBOX

Underline As you read, underline the descriptions of experiences and ideas that influenced Darwin.

Background

Recall that in science, a *theory* is a broad explanation that has been scientifically tested and supported repeatedly.

Talk About It

Hypothesize How do you think the foods eaten by the small-beaked finch and the large-beaked finch differ? What kinds of foods do you think the different finches eat? With a partner, discuss how the beaks of the different finch species help them eat different foods.

READING CHECK

1. Explain According to Darwin, why did the different populations of finches become modified over time?

____

____

____

ARTIFICIAL SELECTION

Later in his life, Darwin became interested in breeding exotic pigeons. He noted that breeders take advantage of natural variation within a species. Breeders identify traits in each generation that they prefer. For example, a dog breeder may prefer a dog with thicker fur or longer legs. If these traits can be inherited, breeders can simply select individuals that have the traits. Darwin called this process **artificial selection**.

Critical Thinking

2. Infer Why is it important for breeders to select traits that are inherited?

____

____

____

____

How Did the Ideas of Others Influence Darwin?

Most people in Darwin's time thought that species stayed the same forever. However, some scientists proposed ways that species may change over time. Darwin was influenced by ideas from the fields of natural history, economics, and geology.

LOOKING CLOSER

3. List Identify three fields of study that influenced Darwin's ideas.

____

____

____

4. Identify How was the work of Hutton and Lyell important to Darwin's theory?

____

____

____

____

____

Individuals and Ideas that Influenced Darwin

Individual(s) and field	Major ideas	Importance to Darwin's theory
Jean Baptiste Lamarck (natural history)	• proposed that organisms change over time as they adapt to changing environments • thought (incorrectly) that changes due to use or disuse of a trait would be passed on to offspring	suggested that inheritance plays a role in evolution
Thomas Malthus (economics)	• noted that the human population was growing faster than the food supply • predicted that limited resources would cause deaths from disease, war, or famine	Darwin proposed that all populations, not just human populations, are limited by their environments.
Georges Cuvier (geology)	argued that fossils in rock layers showed: • differences in species over time • that species from the past differed from those of the present	showed that species change over time
James Hutton and Charles Lyell (geology)	thought that geologic processes, such as those that form rocks and fossils, work gradually and constantly	showed that Earth's history was long enough for species to have evolved gradually

Name _______________ Class _______________ Date _______________

Section 1 Review

SECTION VOCABULARY

artificial selection the human practice of breeding animals or plants that have certain desired traits	**evolution** generally, in biology, the process of change by which new species develop from preexisting species over time; at the genetic level, the process in which inherited characteristics within populations change over time; the process defined by Darwin as "descent with modification"

1. Describe What were Darwin's two major contributions to modern evolutionary theory?

____

____

2. Identify How did Darwin explain the similarities among finches in the Galápagos Islands and in South America?

____

____

3. Define What is *descent with modification?*

____

____

4. Infer How does artificial selection provide evidence that species can change over time?

____

____

____

5. Identify What idea did Lamarck and Darwin share?

____

____

6. Describe What evidence from fossils and rock layers influenced Darwin's ideas?

____

____

____

7. Identify What idea of Malthus did Darwin extend to all populations?

____

Name ______________________ Class ______________ Date ____________

CHAPTER 16 Evolutionary Theory

SECTION 2

Applying Darwin's Ideas

KEY IDEAS

As you read this section, keep these questions in mind:

- What does Darwin's theory predict?
- Why are Darwin's ideas now widely accepted?
- What were the strengths and weaknesses of Darwin's ideas?

What Is Natural Selection?

Darwin noted that individuals with particular traits are more likely to survive in their environments. He also noted that individuals with these traits tend to produce more offspring than those without the traits do. A trait that helps individuals survive and reproduce in a given environment is called an **adaptation**. Differences in ability to survive and reproduce are part of the process of **natural selection**. ☑

Darwin proposed that natural selection is a cause of evolution. Evolution is a change in inherited characteristics in a population from one generation to the next. Darwin's explanation is commonly called *the theory of evolution by natural selection*. His theory predicts that, over time, the number of individuals with beneficial traits will increase in a population. ☑

READING TOOLBOX

Underline As you read this section, underline the answers to the Key Ideas questions.

READING CHECK

1. Define What is an adaptation?

____

____

____

____

READING CHECK

2. Identify What mechanism for evolution did Darwin propose?

____

____

The Theory of Evolution by Natural Selection

LOOKING CLOSER

3. Explain What happens to traits that help individuals survive and reproduce in their environment?

____

____

____

What Does Darwin's Theory Explain?

In his book *On the Origin of Species by Means of Natural Selection*, Darwin presented evidence that evolution happens. He also presented a logical explanation for how evolution happens. Darwin's ideas are widely accepted today because large amounts of evidence continue to support them. ☑

READING CHECK

4. Explain Why are Darwin's ideas widely accepted today?

____

____

____

THE FOSSIL RECORD

Fossils are traces of organisms that have lived in the past. The *fossil record* is made up of all the fossils known to science. Darwin noticed patterns in the fossil record that suggested that species change over time. However, he also knew that the pattern had gaps. The conditions that create fossils are rare. Thus, we will never find fossils of every species that ever lived. The fossil record will grow but will never be complete. ☑

READING CHECK

5. Identify For Darwin, what evidence for evolution does the fossil record provide?

____

____

ANATOMY

Scientists can compare the internal structures, or *anatomy*, of different species to see the results of evolution. Evolution explains the similarities in internal structures. Similar internal structures are evidence of how species are related. Structures that are similar in two or more species and were inherited from a common ancestor are called **homologous** structures.

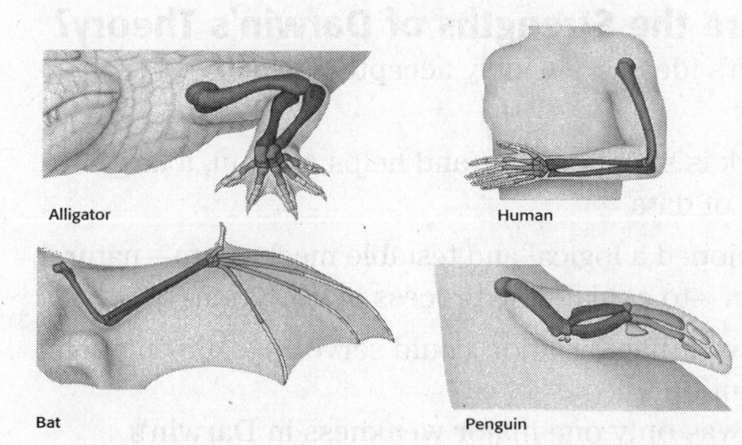

Although they look very different from one another on the outside, the forelimbs of these four vertebrates have very similar groups of bones. This suggests that all vertebrates descended from a common ancestor.

LOOKING CLOSER

6. Identify What do the similarities in the forelimb structures of these vertebrates suggest?

____

____

____

Critical Thinking

7. Apply Concepts Why is Darwin's explanation of evolution a *theory* and not a *hypothesis*?

____
____
____
____
____
____

BIOGEOGRAPHY

Biogeography is the study of the locations of organisms around the world. Darwin noticed similarities in three species of large birds: the rhea in South America, the ostrich in Africa, and the emu in Australia. These species are similar in size, shape, eating habits, and habitats. Darwin's observation was evidence that similar environments shape the evolution of organisms in similar ways.

Sometimes geography separates populations. For example, a population may split into two groups that live on two different islands. Over time, the two groups may evolve in different ways.

DEVELOPMENTAL BIOLOGY

Scientists may compare the development of embryos of different species to look for similar patterns and structures. For example, scientists have found that all vertebrate embryos have tails at some time in their development. This similarity most likely comes from an ancestor that vertebrate species share.

BIOCHEMISTRY

A comparison of DNA or amino-acid sequences shows that some species are more genetically similar than others. Organisms with similar sequences are more closely related than are organisms with more differences in their sequences.

Critical Thinking

8. Apply Concepts Horses share a larger percentage of their genes with dogs than with earthworms. What does this suggest?

____
____
____
____

What Are the Strengths of Darwin's Theory?

Darwin's ideas are widely accepted because of their strengths:

- His work is supported by, and helps explain, a large amount of data.
- He developed a logical and testable mechanism—natural selection—to explain the process of evolution.
- He showed that variation could serve as a starting point for evolution.

There was only one major weakness in Darwin's theory. Inherited variation was important to the theory of natural selection. However, because he knew little about genetics, Darwin could not propose a clear mechanism for inheritance.

Name ______________________ Class ______________ Date ______________

Section 2 Review

SECTION VOCABULARY

adaptation the process of becoming adapted to an environment; an anatomical, physiological, or behavioral change that improves a population's ability to survive

fossil the trace or remains of an organism that lived long ago, most commonly preserved in sedimentary rock

homologous describes a character that is shared by a group of species because it is inherited from a common ancestor

natural selection the process by which individuals that are better adapted to their environment survive and reproduce more successfully than less well adapted individuals do; a theory to explain the mechanism of evolution

1. **Identify** What does Darwin's theory of evolution by natural selection predict?

____

____

2. **List** What are the four steps of Darwin's theory of evolution?

____

3. **Summarize** Complete the table below to summarize how evidence supports Darwin's theory of evolution.

Source of evidence	What the evidence indicates
Fossil record	
Anatomy	
Biogeography	
Developmental biology	Species with embryos that show similar patterns of development probably share a common ancestor.
Biochemistry	

4. **Identify** What are three major strengths of Darwin's theory of evolution by natural selection?

____

____

____

____

Name _______________ Class _______________ Date _______________

SECTION 3

Beyond Darwinian Theory

KEY IDEAS

As you read this section, keep these questions in mind:
- How has Darwin's theory been updated?
- At what scales can evolution be studied?

READING TOOLBOX

Make Flashcards After you read this section, make flashcards that identify the processes of microevolution and macroevolution. Write the name of the process on one side of the card. Describe the process in your own words on the other side of the card. Be sure to identify whether each process is an example of microevolution or macroevolution.

How Has Darwin's Theory Been Updated?

Since Darwin's time, new discoveries, particularly in the field of genetics, have helped explain the evolution of species. Scientists have modified parts of Darwin's theory and added to it. However, most recent discoveries support his theory.

What Are Microevolution and Macroevolution?

Microevolution refers to changes in the genes of populations.

LOOKING CLOSER

1. Identify Which microevolutionary process involves individuals moving into or out of a population?

____

Processes of Microevolution

Process	Description
Natural selection	Individuals with a particular trait are more likely to survive and reproduce than those without the trait.
Migration	Individuals with different alleles may move into or out of a population.
Mate choice	Parents that are limited or selective in their choice of mates pass a limited set of traits to the next generation.
Mutation	Mutations are the source of completely new alleles.
Genetic drift	Random effects of everyday life can cause differences in survival and reproduction of individuals.

Background

Recall that a *species* is a group of organisms that are closely related and that can mate to produce fertile offspring.

Macroevolution refers to the appearance of new species over time. The formation of a new species is called **speciation**.

Patterns of Macroevolution

Pattern	Description
Convergent evolution	Species living in similar environments may evolve similar adaptations.
Coevolution	Two or more species that live in close contact may affect how each species evolves.
Adaptive radiation	A species may give rise to many new species after it enters an environment that contains few other species.
Extinction	All members of a lineage die off or fail to reproduce.
Gradualism	The formation of some new species requires many small changes to build up gradually over time.
Punctuated equilibrium	Many species remain stable, or unchanged, for a long time. If environmental changes create new pressures, many new species evolve rapidly.

Talk About It

Brainstorm With a partner, brainstorm examples of species that show convergent evolution. What adaptations do they have that are similar?

Name _______________ Class _______________ Date _______________

Section 3 Review

SECTION VOCABULARY

speciation the formation of a new species as a result of evolution	

1. **Identify** Name one field of study that has contributed discoveries that support Darwin's theory of evolution.

2. **Compare** How does microevolution differ from macroevolution?

3. **Infer** How does migration cause a change in the genes in a population?

4. **Compare** How does genetic drift differ from natural selection?

5. **Identify** According to the punctuated equilibrium model of speciation, what causes many new species to evolve rapidly?

6. **Analyze Relationships** How do you think adaptive radiation and extinction are related?

7. **Make Conclusions** A scientist observes that a particular species of butterfly has a very long tongue. The butterfly feeds on a flower that has nectar at the bottom of a long tube. What pattern of macroevolution best explains the traits that the scientist observed? Explain your answer.

Name ______________________ Class ______________ Date ______________

CHAPTER 17 Population Genetics and Speciation

SECTION 1

Genetic Variation

KEY IDEAS

As you read this section, keep these questions in mind:
- How is microevolution studied?
- How is phenotypic variation measured?
- How are genetic variation and change measured?
- What is the source of genetic variation?

READING TOOLBOX

Review Before you read this section, review the following terms: allele, gene, phenotype, genotype, population, dominant, recessive, homozygous, and heterozygous. Make a Concept Map to show how these terms are related.

What Is Population Genetics?

Recall that microevolution is evolution at the level of genetic change in a population. **Population genetics** studies changes in the numbers and types of alleles in a population.

MEASURING PHENOTYPIC VARIATION

Phenotypic variation refers to differences in the phenotypes of individuals in a population. In some cases, describing the phenotypes in a population is simple. For example, Mendel studied pea plants, which have only two different traits for each character. However, genetics is rarely so simple.

Background

Recall that a *polygenic character* is influenced by several genes. Height and eye color in humans are two examples of polygenic characters.

Polygenic characters tend to have a larger variety of possible traits than characters that are not polygenic. To study polygenic phenotypes, scientists describe the phenotype of each individual in a population. Then, they analyze the distribution of phenotypes. A *distribution* shows the range of phenotypes for a character and how common each phenotype is.

Height Distribution

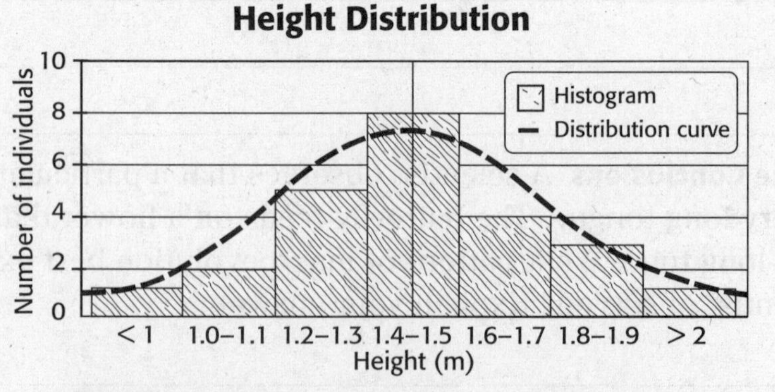

This histogram shows the distribution of heights in a population. A distribution that forms a bell-shaped curve is a **normal distribution**. In a normal distribution, the values for the mean, median, and mode are similar to one another.

Graphing Skills

1. Identify What is the most common height value in this population?

____

2. Identify What are the least common height values in this population?

____

____

MEASURING GENETIC VARIATION

The set of all of the alleles that exist in a population is the population's *gene pool*. A population that has only one possible allele for a given character has no genetic variation. A population that has many possible alleles for a given character has a lot of genetic variation. Scientists measure how much genetic variation a population has by calculating allele frequencies. The *frequency* of an allele describes how common the allele is.

Critical Thinking

3. Compare How do populations with a lot of genetic variation for a given character differ from those with no genetic variation?

How Can You Calculate Genotype and Allele Frequencies?

Consider the example shown in the figure below.

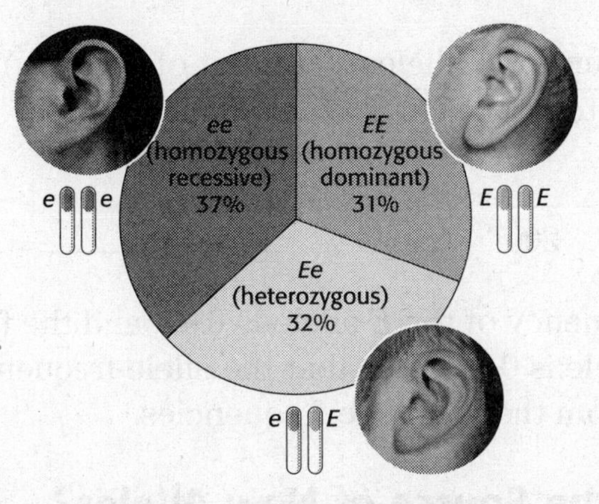

In humans, the allele for unattached earlobes is dominant (*E*) and the allele for attached earlobes is recessive (*e*).

Background

Recall that you can represent *alleles* as letters. Typically, a capital letter represents a dominant allele, and a lowercase letter represents a recessive allele.

LOOKING CLOSER

4. Identify How many genotypes for earlobes are possible in this population? How many phenotypes?

CALCULATING GENOTYPE FREQUENCIES

A genotype's frequency describes how common the genotype is in a population. Frequencies are expressed as decimals or percentages. The sum of genotype frequencies in a population equals 1, or 100%. In the human population, three earlobe genotypes are possible: *EE*, *Ee*, and *ee*.

(Frequency of *EE*) + (Frequency of *Ee*) + (Frequency of *ee*)

$$0.31 + 0.32 + 0.37 = 1$$

Talk About It

Collect Data The allele for right handedness is usually dominant. As a class, identify how many people in the class are left handed and how many are right handed. What are the possible genotypes for each phenotype?

CALCULATING ALLELE FREQUENCIES

Suppose the population represented on the last page has 100 people. Each person has two alleles for the earlobe character, so the total number of alleles is 200.

Condition	Number of people	Total number of each allele	
Homozygous recessive	37	*E*: 0	*e*: 37 × 2 = 74
Homozygous dominant	31	*E*: 31 × 2 = 62	*e*: 0
Heterozygous	32	*E*: 32 × 1 = 32	*e*: 32 × 1 = 32

READING CHECK

5. Identify What is the sum of all allele frequencies for a gene?

____

Allele frequencies must add up to 1, or 100%. Thus: ☑

$$(\text{Frequency of } E) + (\text{Frequency of } e) = 1$$

$$\frac{(\text{count of } E \text{ alleles})}{(\text{total alleles})} + \frac{(\text{count of } e \text{ alleles})}{(\text{total alleles})} = 1$$

Math Skills

6. Complete Complete the equation to show the allele frequencies for earlobe type in this population.

$$\frac{\_\_\_\_}{200} + \frac{\_\_\_\_}{200} = \_\_\_\_\_\_ + \_\_\_\_\_\_ = 1$$

The frequency of the *E* allele is 0.47, and the frequency of the *e* allele is 0.53. Note that the allele frequencies are different from the genotype frequencies.

What Is the Source of New Alleles?

Evolution cannot happen if a population has no genetic variation. Adding new alleles to a population increases genetic variation. Where do new alleles come from?

The major source of new alleles in a population is mutation, or changes to DNA, in germ cells. However, mutations do not happen frequently. If a germ cell with a mutation forms offspring, a new allele is added to the gene pool. Mutations can happen in nongerm cells (called somatic cells), but individuals do not pass these to offspring. ☑

7. Explain Why are mutations in germ cells passed to offspring but mutations in somatic cells are not?

____

____

____

____

Name ______________________ Class ______________ Date ______________

Section 1 Review

SECTION VOCABULARY

normal distribution a distribution of numerical data whose graph forms a bell-shaped curve that is symmetrical about the mean	**population genetics** the study of the frequency and interaction of alleles and genes in populations

1. **Explain** How do scientists study microevolution?

2. **Identify Relationships** How does the number of genes that affect a phenotype relate to the variation in traits?

3. **Describe** How do scientists measure phenotypic variation?

4. **Describe** How do scientists measure genetic variation?

5. **Calculate** A population consists of 100 individuals. In this population, 61 people have unattached earlobes. Of these individuals, 33 are homozygous dominant and 28 are heterozygous. The remaining individuals have attached earlobes. What is the frequency of each genotype? What is the frequency of each allele?

6. **Identify** What is the major source of variation in a population?

Name ______________________ Class ______________ Date ______________

CHAPTER 17 Population Genetics and Speciation

SECTION 2

Genetic Change

KEY IDEAS

As you read this section, keep these questions in mind:

- What does the Hardy-Weinberg principle predict?
- How does sexual reproduction influence evolution?
- Why does population size matter?
- What are the limits of the force of natural selection?
- What patterns can result from natural selection?

READING TOOLBOX

Underline As you read, underline the answers to the Key Ideas questions.

What Is Genetic Equilibrium?

In 1908, English mathematician G. H. Hardy and German physician Wilhelm Weinberg began to use algebra to model population genetics. Their work showed that the frequency of alleles in a population should not change from one generation to the next. They also showed that genotype frequencies should not change. When no genetic change is happening in a population, the population is in **genetic equilibrium**. ☑

READING CHECK

1. Describe When is a population in genetic equilibrium?

____

____

____

Scientists can measure genetic changes as a change in genotype frequency or allele frequency. However, a change in one does not necessarily mean a change in the other. Consider the snapdragon population described below. Recall that the alleles for flower color in snapdragons show incomplete dominance.

Allele Frequencies in Two Generations

Genotype frequency	Allele frequency	
$RR = 0.5$ $Rr = 0.5$ $rr = 0$	$R = 0.75$ $r = 0.25$	RR RR Rr Rr RR Rr Rr RR
$RR = 0.625$ $Rr = 0.25$ $rr = 0.125$	$R = 0.75$ $r = 0.25$	RR Rr rr RR RR Rr RR RR

LOOKING CLOSER

2. Identify What happened to allele frequencies from the first generation to the second generation?

____

____

Notice that the genotype frequencies changed, but the allele frequencies did not. A population is in genetic equilibrium if allele frequencies stay the same.

HARDY-WEINBERG PRINCIPLE

The Hardy Weinberg principle describes the conditions that must be met for a population to be in genetic equilibrium.

Hardy-Weinberg principle

Frequencies of alleles and genotypes in a population will not change unless at least one of five forces acts on the population.

Forces that Can Change Allele Frequencies

Force	Description
Gene flow	Individuals that join a population might bring in new alleles. Individuals that leave a population might remove alleles from the population.
Nonrandom mating	In nonrandom mating, individuals may have a limited choice of mates, or they may prefer mates with certain traits. Thus, certain alleles may get passed to more offspring than other alleles.
Genetic drift	Chance events, such as fire or flood, can cause rare alleles to be lost from a population.
Mutation	Mutations can create new alleles.
Natural selection	Natural selection can remove individuals with certain traits from a population. The alleles for those traits may become less common in the population.

LOOKING CLOSER

3. Compare How does genetic drift differ from natural selection?

____

____

____

____

If one or more of the forces described above acts on a population, the population will no longer be in genetic equilibrium. Instead, the population will be evolving.

The Hardy-Weinberg principle can be expressed by the equation below. You can use the equation to predict genotype frequencies in a population that is in genetic equilibrium.

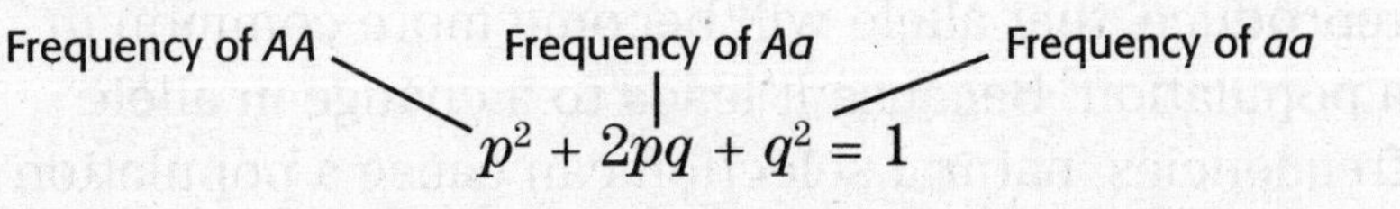

$$p^2 + 2pq + q^2 = 1$$

Math Skills

4. Calculate In a population, 80% of individuals are homozygous dominant for a particular character, and 5% are homozygous recessive. What is the frequency of heterozygotes in the population?

____

How Does Population Size Affect Evolution?

Allele frequencies are more likely to stay the same in large populations than in small ones. In a small population, a chance event, such as a fire or flood, may reduce an allele's frequency quickly. The allele may even disappear. This kind of change in allele frequencies is called *genetic drift*.

LOOKING CLOSER

5. Describe After 100 years, how did the small population differ from the larger one?

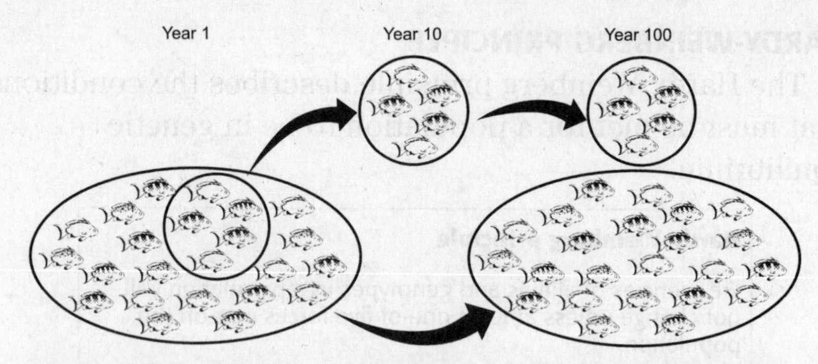

Genetic drift is caused by random events that may cause some alleles to disappear completely. Thus, small populations tend to have less variation than large populations do.

How Does Sexual Reproduction Affect Evolution?

Recall that sexual reproduction allows alleles from parents to combine in different ways in offspring. Thus, any mating pattern or behavior can play a role in which alleles are passed to offspring. For example, some female animals choose mates based on the male's size, color, ability to gather food, or other characteristic. This kind of nonrandom mating behavior is called *sexual selection*.

Another example of nonrandom mating is inbreeding. In *inbreeding*, individuals either self-fertilize or mate with closely related individuals. Inbreeding tends to result in more homozygous offspring. For example, most of the individuals in a population of self-fertilizing plants are homozygous. Inbreeding is more common in small populations than in large ones.

Critical Thinking

6. Infer Female peacocks, or peahens, prefer males with long tails. How do you think this preference affects alleles for tail length in a peacock population?

How Does Natural Selection Affect Evolution?

If a particular allele helps individuals survive and reproduce, that allele will become more common in a population. Because it leads to a change in allele frequencies, natural selection can cause a population to evolve. However, two factors limit natural selection: ☑

1. Natural selection can change the frequencies of alleles, but it cannot create new ones.
2. Natural selection acts directly on phenotype, not genotype. Thus, natural selection can act only on traits that are expressed.

7. Explain How does natural selection cause a population to evolve?

What Are Three Patterns of Natural Selection?

Recall that many traits have a bell-shaped distribution in natural populations. When natural selection acts on polygenic traits, the shape of the distribution curve changes.

In *directional selection*, phenotypes at one extreme are eliminated. Thus, alleles for phenotypes at one extreme become less common.

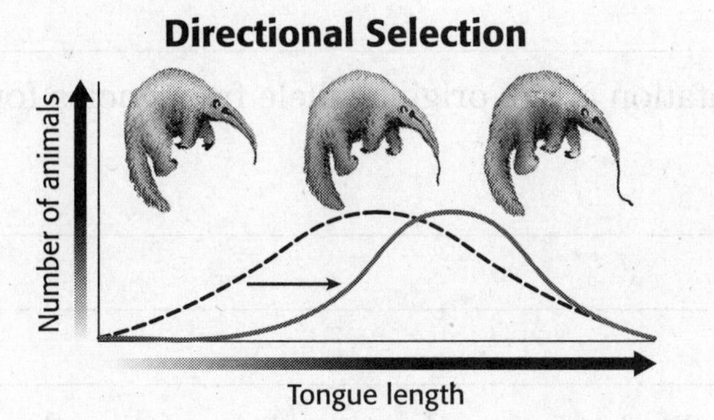

LOOKING CLOSER

8. Analyze Which trait allows the anteaters in this population to survive and reproduce most successfully?

____

In *stabilizing selection*, phenotypes at both extremes are eliminated. Thus, alleles for phenotypes at both extremes become less common.

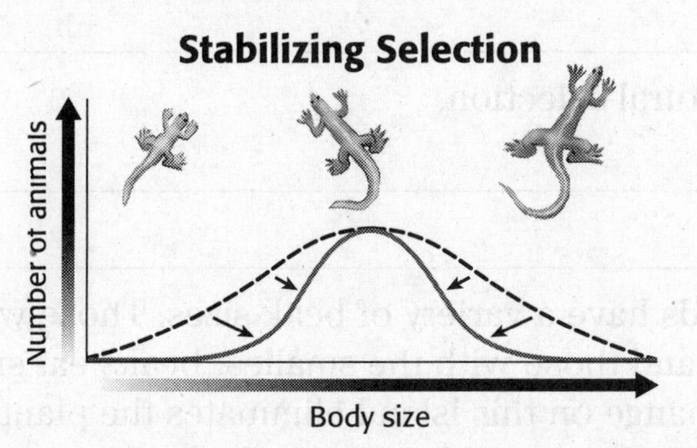

LOOKING CLOSER

9. Identify Does stabilizing selection tend to increase variation of phenotypes or decrease variation?

____

In *disruptive selection*, average phenotypes are eliminated. Thus, alleles for average phenotypes become less common.

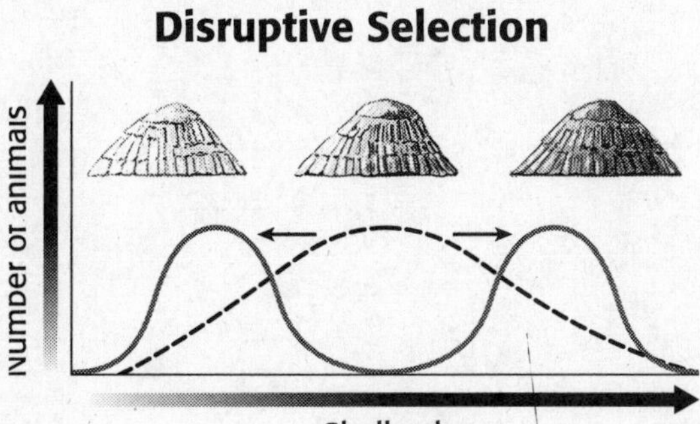

LOOKING CLOSER

10. Identify What happens to average phenotypes in a population that shows disruptive selection?

____

____

Name ______________________ Class ______________ Date ____________

Section 2 Review

SECTION VOCABULARY

genetic equilibrium a state in which the allele frequencies of a population remain in the same ratios from one generation to the next	

1. List What five forces can cause allele frequencies in a population to change?

____

____

2. Infer How would a beneficial mutation affect original allele frequencies for a particular character?

____

____

____

3. Explain Why is genetic drift more likely to occur in a small population than in a large population?

____

____

4. Identify List two limitations of natural selection.

____

____

5. Predict On a particular island, birds have a variety of beak sizes. Those with the largest beaks can eat hard seeds, and those with the smallest beaks eat smaller, softer seeds. An environmental change on this island eliminates the plants that produce small, soft seeds. Over time, what will happen to the beak sizes of the birds? Draw a graph to show the pattern of natural selection that is likely to happen on the island. Be sure to label the axes of your graph.

Name ______________________ Class ______________ Date ______________

CHAPTER 17 Population Genetics and Speciation

SECTION 3

Speciation

KEY IDEAS

As you read this section, keep these questions in mind:

- How can a species be defined?
- How do we know when new species have formed?
- Why is studying extinction important to understanding evolution?

What Is a Species?

Two people can look very different, but they are members of the same species. In contrast, a monarch butterfly looks similar to a viceroy butterfly, but they are members of different species. Physical appearance cannot always tell you whether individuals are members of the same species.

The traditional definition of *species* is based on the *biological species concept*. However, we cannot apply this concept to organisms that reproduce asexually or to organisms that we know only from fossils. Today, scientists use more than one definition for *species*. The definition they use depends on the organism and the field of science. Scientists may define a species based on:

- physical features
- ecological roles
- genetic similarities

READING TOOLBOX

Outline As you read this section, make an outline to summarize the answers to the Key Ideas questions. Use the Key Ideas and the header questions to help you organize your outline.

Background

Recall that the traditional definition of *species* is a group of natural populations that can interbreed and produce fertile offspring.

How Do New Species Arise?

Different populations of a single species live in different places. Natural selection acts on the different populations and tends to result in offspring that are better adapted to their environments. If the environments differ, the adaptations may differ. Over time, the populations differ more and more. An increasing number of differences between populations is called *divergence*. Divergence can lead to speciation.

Recall that the biological species concept defines a species as an interbreeding group. If two groups stop interbreeding for any reason, they take a step toward speciation. Over time, the two groups may no longer be able to produce offspring. When this happens, the populations are in a state of **reproductive isolation**. ☑

Background

Recall that *speciation* is the process in which new species form by evolution from existing species.

READING CHECK

1. Identify What happens when populations become reproductively isolated?

How Do We Know When New Species Have Formed?

Speciation rarely happens quickly. Typically, speciation happens in stages over many generations. Thus, we cannot be sure speciation is happening until the process is complete. We know a new species has formed when

- the population has unique traits
- the population is reproductively isolated

SUBSPECIES

A **subspecies** is a population that has diverged in some way from other populations of the same species. Subspecies can eventually become separate species if they become unable to interbreed and produce fertile offspring.

Critical Thinking

2. Infer Can two individuals from different subspecies interbreed? Explain your answer.

____

____

____

____

____

How Do Populations Become Reproductively Isolated?

Divergence and speciation can happen in many ways. Any of the mechanisms described in the table below can lead to the reproductive isolation of populations.

Mechanisms of Reproductive Isolation	
Mechanism	**Description**
Geography	A physical barrier may form that separates populations. The barrier prevents the populations from interbreeding. Over time, if the populations diverge enough, they will not be able to interbreed, even if the barrier is removed.
Ecological niche	Divergence can happen when populations use different niches.
Mating behavior and timing	Many species that reproduce sexually use specific behaviors to attract mates. These behaviors may include sounds or actions. The individuals of some species mate at particular times. If two populations develop different mating behaviors or mate at different times, they may no longer interbreed.
Polyploidy	A polyploid individual may not be able to mate with others in the population because it cannot pair gametes. However, it may be able to reproduce with other polyploid individuals or self-fertilize. The offspring would form a new population.
Hybridization	In hybridization, two closely related species mate and produce offspring. In many cases, the offspring are not fertile or are not adapted to survive in their environment. However, some hybrids may be able to survive and produce fertile offspring. These hybrids may form a new species.

Background

Recall that the *niche* of a species is the role it plays in its environment.

LOOKING CLOSER

3. Apply Concepts The members of a particular population of insects live and feed high up in the trunks of trees. As time passes, some members of the population begin to feed on different parts of the trees. Eventually, the two groups diverge and no longer interbreed. What mechanism of reproductive isolation does this show?

____

The bluehead wrasse lives on the eastern side of the Isthmus of Panama.

The rainbow wrasse lives on the western side of the Isthmus of Panama.

These two fish species probably once belonged to the same species. When the isthmus rose from the ocean about 3 million years ago, the separated populations began to diverge.

LOOKING CLOSER

4. Apply Concepts What mechanism of reproductive isolation caused the original fish population to diverge?

____

What Is the Role of Extinction in Evolution?

Extinction happens when a species does not produce any new individuals. Environmental changes can cause the extinction of many species. For example, a combination of volcanic eruptions, an asteroid impact, and climate change caused most dinosaurs to become extinct. Scientists estimate that more than 99% of all the plant and animal species that ever lived have become extinct. ☑

When an environment changes, a species that was well adapted may be poorly adapted to the new conditions. If an environment changes too rapidly, new adaptations do not have time to arise. If individuals cannot adapt, the species will become extinct.

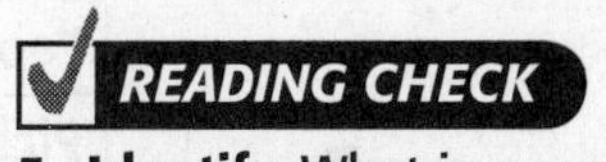

5. Identify What is a major cause of extinctions?

____

____

Name ____________________ Class ____________ Date ____________

Section 3 Review

SECTION VOCABULARY

reproductive isolation a state in which two populations can no longer interbreed to produce future generations of offspring	**subspecies** a taxonomic classification below species that groups organisms that live in different geographical areas, differ morphologically from other populations of the species, but can interbreed with other populations of the species

1. **Explain** Why do scientists use more than one definition for *species*?

2. **List** What are the five mechanisms that can cause reproductive isolation of a population?

3. **Analyze** Scientists studied the mating activity of four closely related species of frogs and recorded the peak mating times of each species. Which two species show the greatest amount of divergence in mating activity? Explain your answer.

Frog species	Peak mating time
Leopard frog	first week of April
Pickerel frog	third week of April
Tree frog	first week of June
Bullfrog	first week of July

4. **Identify** What two forms of evidence show that a new species has formed?

5. **Make Analogies** If you represented evolution with a diagram of a tree, what part of the tree would represent speciation? How would you represent extinction?

Name ______________________ Class ______________ Date ______________

CHAPTER 18 Classification

SECTION 1

The Importance of Classification

KEY IDEAS

As you read this section, keep these questions in mind:

- Why do biologists have classification systems?
- What makes up a scientific name for a species?
- What is the structure of the modern system of classification?

Why Do Biologists Classify Organisms?

Scientists have named and described about 1.7 million species, and they think millions more have not yet been discovered. Much like a library uses a system to organize books, scientists use systems to organize information about living things. Scientists use classification systems to name and group organisms. The branch of biology that involves naming and classifying organisms is called **taxonomy**.

Create a Mnemonic A mnemonic is a sentence or phrase that can help you remember information. In general, the first letter of each word in the mnemonic represents the information you want to remember. Create a mnemonic to help you remember the eight levels of classification. For example, "Did King Phillip Come Over For Green Spinach?"

SCIENTIFIC NAMES

A species' common name is the one most people use every day. People may have different common names for the same species. For example, a cougar and a puma are the same animal. Sometimes, two different species may have the same common name. For example, the bird called a "robin" in North America is very different from the bird called a "robin" in Great Britain.

When scientists talk about a species, they need to be sure that they are all talking about the same one. Thus, scientists give each species a scientific name. Every organism has only one scientific name. Typically, the scientific name is different from the common name.

Critical Thinking

1. Explain Why are scientific names more useful to scientists than common names?

____

____

____

____

____

In the 1750s, Swedish biologist Carl Linnaeus developed a system for naming organisms that scientists use today. In his system, called **binomial nomenclature**, each species has a two-part scientific name. The characteristics of a scientific name are listed below: ☑

- Both words are Latin and italicized or underlined.
- The first word is the genus name, and it is capitalized. A **genus** is a category that includes very similar species.
- The second word often describes the species. It is not capitalized.

2. Define What is binomial nomenclature?

____

____

____

____

LEVELS OF CLASSIFICATION

To catalog all the species known at the time, Linnaeus developed a classification system. This system groups organisms into levels of a hierarchy based on how similar they are. Since Linnaeus's time, scientists have added new groups and levels. Today, the Linnaean classification system has eight levels. ☑

READING CHECK

3. Describe How do scientists classify organisms in the Linnaean system?

____

____

____

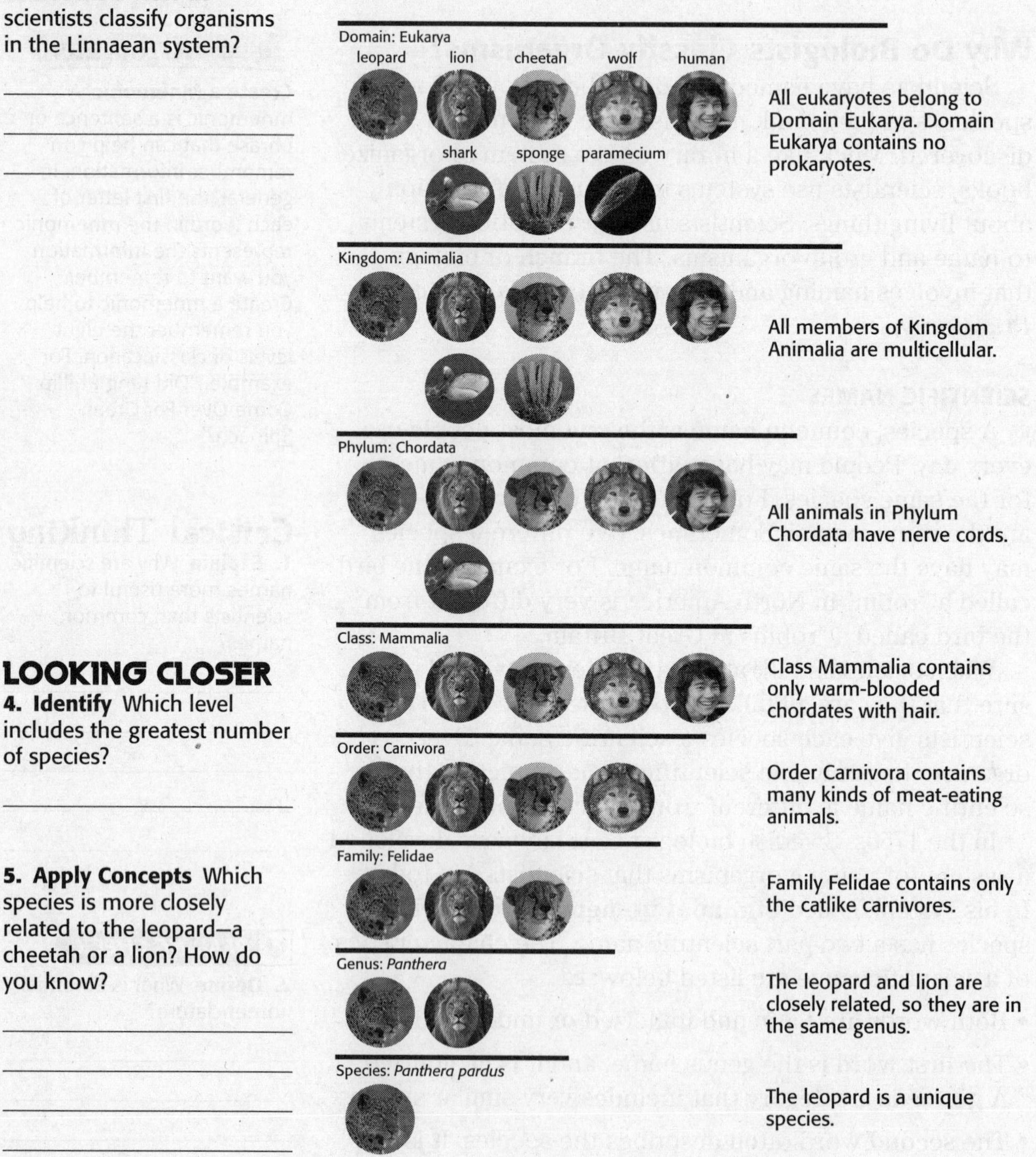

LOOKING CLOSER

4. Identify Which level includes the greatest number of species?

____

5. Apply Concepts Which species is more closely related to the leopard—a cheetah or a lion? How do you know?

____

____

____

____

Name ______________________ Class ______________ Date ____________

Section 1 Review

SECTION VOCABULARY

binomial nomenclature a system for giving each organism a two-word scientific name that consists of the genus name followed by the species name

genus the level of classification that comes after family and that contains similar species

taxonomy the science of describing, naming, and classifying organisms

1. Identify What are two reasons common names for species can be confusing?

____

____

2. Organize Complete the hierarchy below to show the eight levels of classification in the Linnaean system. Start at the top with the most general level.

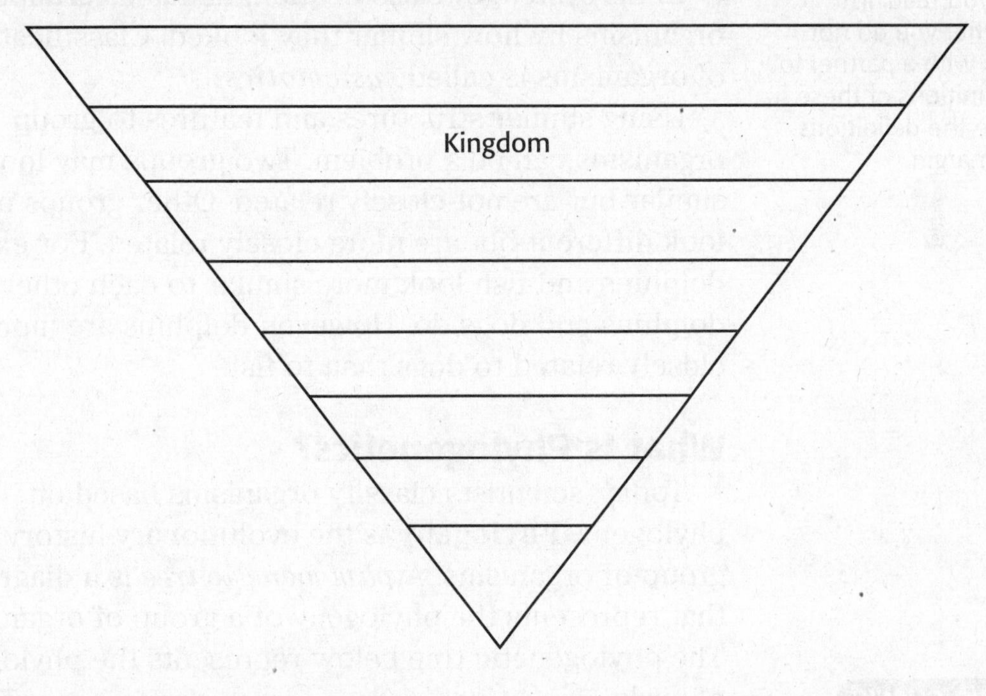

3. Apply Concepts Circle the cheetah's correctly written scientific name.

Acinonyx jubatus   *Acinonyx jubatus*

Acinonyx Jubatus   *acinonyx jubatus*

4. Infer If two organisms are classified in the same order, what other levels of classification do they share?

____

5. Explain Are there more phyla or genera on Earth? Explain your answer.

____

____

Name ______________________ Class ______________ Date ______________

CHAPTER 18 Classification

SECTION 2

Modern Systematics

KEY IDEAS

As you read this section, keep these questions in mind:
- What problems arise when trying to group organisms by apparent similarities?
- Is the evolutionary past reflected in modern systematics?
- How is cladistics used to construct evolutionary relationships?
- What evidence do scientists use to analyze these relationships?

READING TOOLBOX

Define As you read, list any words that you do not know. Work with a partner to find the definitions of these words. Write the definitions in the text margin.

What Is Systematics?

In his system of classification, Linnaeus grouped organisms by how similar they looked. Classification of organisms is called *systematics*.

Using similar structures and features to group organisms can be a problem. Two groups may look similar but are not closely related. Other groups may look different but are more closely related. For example, dolphins and fish look more similar to each other than dolphins and dogs do. However, dolphins are more closely related to dogs than to fish.

What Is Phylogenetics?

Today, scientists classify organisms based on phylogeny. **Phylogeny** is the evolutionary history of a group of organisms. A *phylogenetic tree* is a diagram that represents the phylogeny of a group of organisms. The phylogenetic tree below represents the phylogeny of birds. ☑

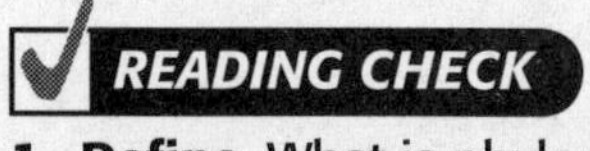

1. Define What is phylogeny?

____

____

____

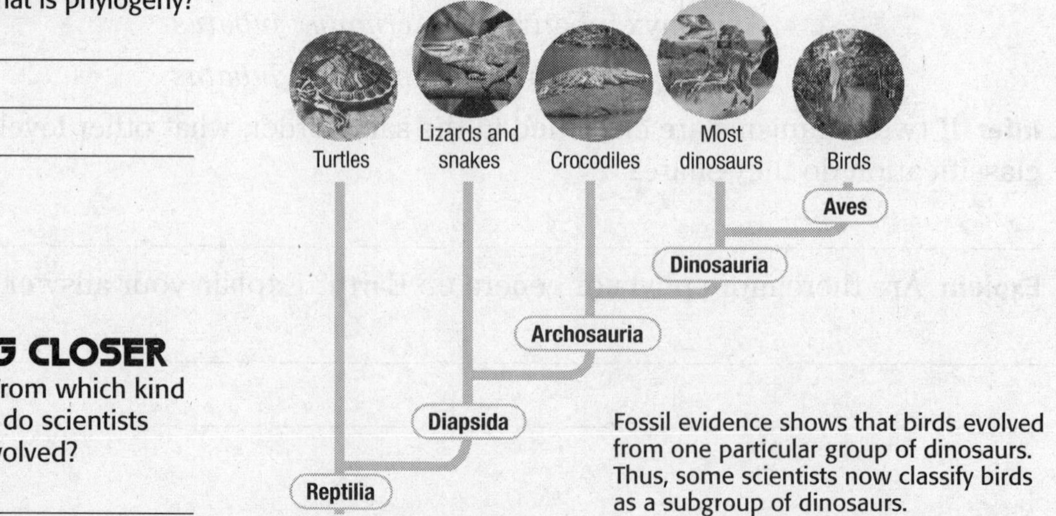

Fossil evidence shows that birds evolved from one particular group of dinosaurs. Thus, some scientists now classify birds as a subgroup of dinosaurs.

LOOKING CLOSER

2. Identify From which kind of organisms do scientists think birds evolved?

____

ANALOGOUS CHARACTERS

In many cases, scientists infer that organisms with similar features evolved from a common ancestor. However, as we have seen, similar structures and features can be misleading.

Consider the wings of birds and insects. Birds and insects share this structural feature, but they did not inherit the structures from a common ancestor. In fact, insects evolved long before birds. The wings of birds and insects are examples of *analogous characters*. Analogous characters result from convergent evolution.

Background

Recall that in *convergent evolution,* different populations that live in similar environments may evolve in similar ways.

JUDGING THE IMPORTANCE OF A FEATURE

Choosing which features of an organism are most important is another problem of classifying organisms by their similarities. Are all characters equally important, or are some more important than others? Scientists do not always agree on the answers to these questions.

Critical Thinking

3. Explain Why do scientists avoid using analogous characters when they study phylogeny?

____

____

____

____

____

What Is Cladistics?

Cladistics is a method to determine the phylogeny of groups of organisms by comparing shared characters. A *shared character* is one that scientists think evolved in a common ancestor. In contrast, a *derived character* is a character that evolved in one group but not another. Consider three characters and four types of plants. ☑

Type of plant	Vascular tissue	Seeds	Flowers
Mosses	no	no	no
Ferns	yes	no	no
Conifers	yes	yes	no
Flowering plants	yes	yes	yes

4. Define What is a derived character?

____

____

____

Members of the conifers and flowering plants all have vascular tissue and seeds. Thus, scientists think these characters evolved in a common ancestor. Flowering plants evolved flowers but conifers did not. Scientists have concluded that the ancestor of both groups did not have flowers. That is, flowers are a derived character.

CLADOGRAMS

You can use shared characters to construct a cladogram. A *cladogram* is a phylogenetic tree based on shared ancestral and derived characters.

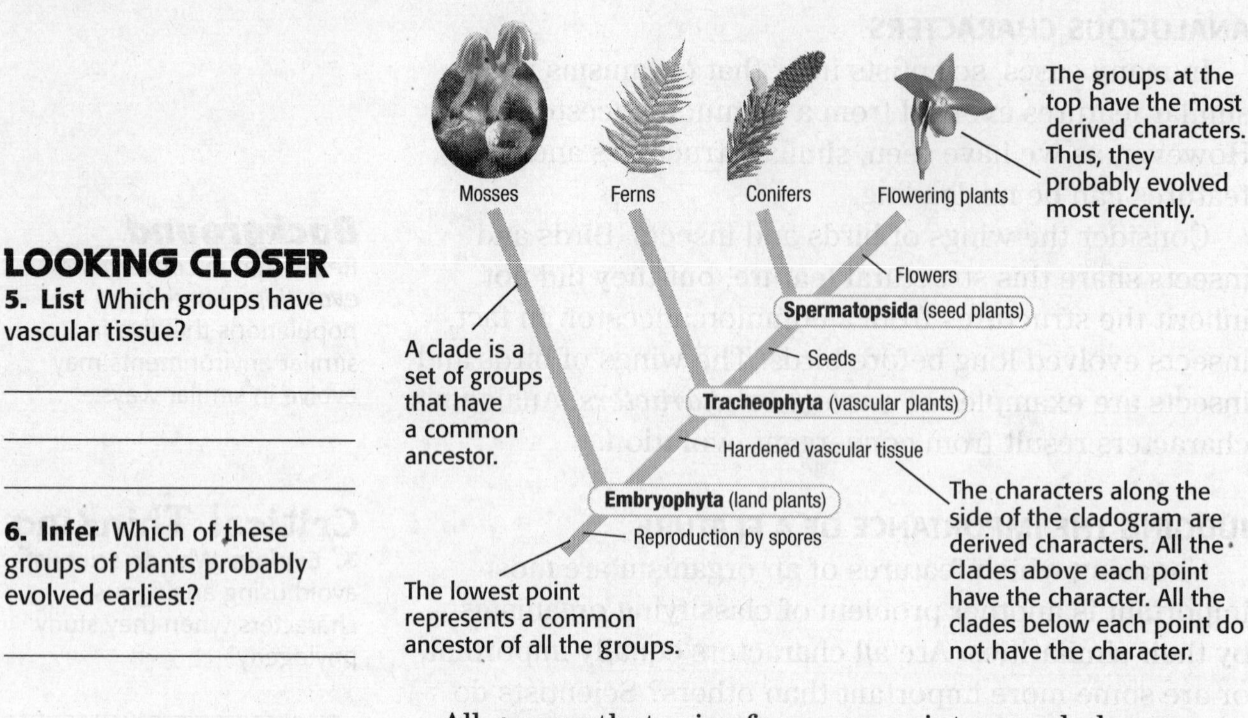

LOOKING CLOSER

5. List Which groups have vascular tissue?

____

6. Infer Which of these groups of plants probably evolved earliest?

____

All groups that arise from one point on a cladogram belong to a *clade*. Each clade in a phylogenetic tree is typically compared with an outgroup. An *outgroup* is a group that does not have many of the shared characters. Mosses do not have many of the characters being considered. Thus, mosses are an outgroup.

TYPES OF PHYLOGENETIC EVIDENCE

As we have seen, using structural similarities to infer phylogeny is not always possible. Thus, biologists compare different kinds of evidence and use careful logic to infer phylogenies. The table below describes some of these types of evidence.

LOOKING CLOSER

7. Infer How can scientists use DNA to determine how closely two groups of organisms are related?

____

Type of Evidence	Description
Morphological	*Morphology* refers to the anatomy or physical structures of organisms. Morphology also includes the patterns of development shown by embryos. Organisms that share a more recent common ancestor tend to show similar patterns of development.
Molecular	Recall that mutations in DNA can be passed from one generation to another. Some mutations may be passed on to all species that descend from a common ancestor.
Fossil record	In many cases, the fossil record helps scientists identify when a group may have branched off, or diverged.

Name ______________________ Class ______________ Date ____________

Section 2 Review

SECTION VOCABULARY

cladistics a phylogenetic classification system that uses shared derived characters and ancestry as the sole criterion for grouping taxa	**phylogeny** the evolutionary history of a species or taxonomic group

1. Describe What are two reasons grouping organisms by similar structures and features can be a problem?

____

____

2. Identify List three sources of evidence that scientists use to construct cladograms.

____

3. Explain Reasoning Many scientists who study dinosaurs have stated that dinosaurs are not extinct. Explain this view.

____

____

4. Apply Concepts Use the information in the table to draw a cladogram that represents a possible phylogeny for a house cat. In your cladogram, be sure to include the derived characters.

Animal	Four legs	Internal fertilization	Hair
Salmon	no	no	no
Frog	yes	no	no
Lizard	yes	yes	no
House cat	yes	yes	yes

Name ______________________ Class ______________ Date ____________

CHAPTER 18 Classification

SECTION 3

Kingdoms and Domains

KEY IDEAS

As you read this section, keep these questions in mind:

- Have biologists always recognized the same kingdoms?
- What are the domains and kingdoms of the three-domain system of classification?

READING TOOLBOX

Organize After you read, make a Venn diagram to compare the three domains of life.

Why Do Systems of Classification Change?

If you read very old books, you might read about plants and animals, but probably not about bacteria and fungi. For many years after Linnaeus, scientists grouped all known organisms into two kingdoms: Plantae (plants) and Animalia (animals).

As scientists discovered more organisms, they modified the classification system that Linnaeus had created. By the 1950s, scientists grouped organisms into five kingdoms. In the 1990s, they added another kingdom.

Today, most scientists group organisms into six kingdoms. They organize the six kingdoms into three larger groups called *domains*. As scientists discover more organisms and learn how groups of organisms are related, the system of classification may change again.

Critical Thinking

1. Infer Why do you think Linnaeus did not describe and classify bacteria?

____

____

____

____

LOOKING CLOSER

2. Identify What are the three domains of life?

____

____

____

3. Infer Based on the diagram, which kingdom's members are more closely related to organisms in Kingdom Plantae—Kingdom Archaebacteria or Kingdom Animalia? Explain your answer.

____

____

____

____

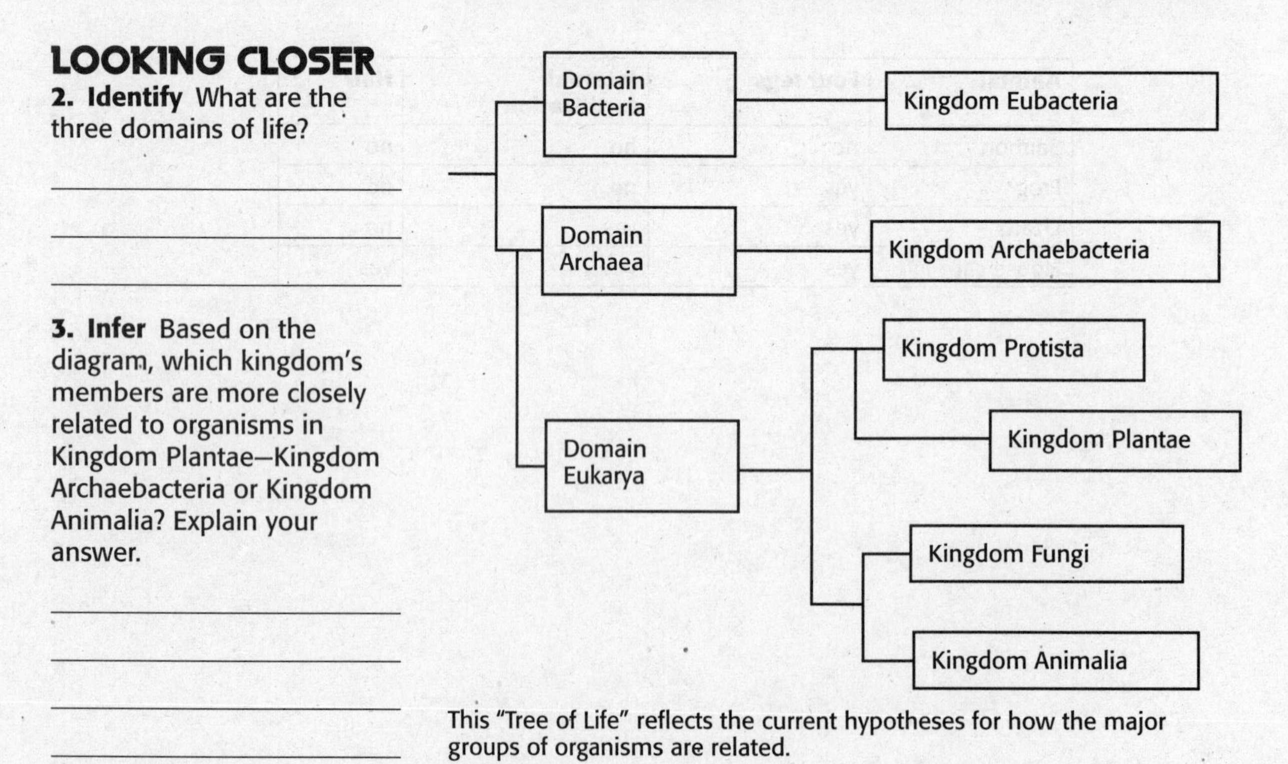

This "Tree of Life" reflects the current hypotheses for how the major groups of organisms are related.

How Do Scientists Define Domains and Kingdoms?

Scientists use genetic similarities to group organisms. They also use the following characteristics to define domains and kingdoms:

- cell type (prokaryotic or eukaryotic)
- cell walls (have cell walls or lack cell walls)
- body type (unicellular or multicellular)
- mode of nutrition (autotrophic or heterotrophic)

Background

Recall that *autotrophs* make their own food. *Heterotrophs* consume other organisms.

DOMAIN BACTERIA

Bacteria are prokaryotes that have strong cell walls and unique genetic systems. Bacteria are the most abundant organisms on Earth and are found in almost every environment.

Cell type	Cell walls	Body type	Mode of nutrition
prokaryotic	cell walls with peptidoglycan	unicellular	autotrophic or heterotrophic

Talk About It

Discuss Scientists once classified members of Domains Bacteria and Archaea into one kingdom. With a partner, discuss why they might have grouped these organisms together. Why do you think scientists now classify them in separate domains?

DOMAIN ARCHAEA

Archaea are prokaryotes with chemically unique cell walls and membranes and unique genetic systems. Many archaea are extremophiles. *Extremophiles* live in extreme environments, such as hot springs, where other organisms cannot survive.

Cell type	Cell walls	Body type	Mode of nutrition
prokaryotic	cell walls with unique lipids	unicellular	autotrophic or heterotrophic

DOMAIN EUKARYA

Eukaryotes are made up of cells that have a nucleus and multiple chromosomes. Most eukaryotes have life cycles that include sexual reproduction.

Kingdom	Cell walls	Body type	Mode of nutrition
Protista	some species with cell walls	unicellular or multicellular	autotrophic or heterotrophic
Fungi	cell walls with chitin	mostly multicellular	heterotrophic
Plantae	cell walls with cellulose	mostly multicellular	autotrophic
Animalia	no cell walls	multicellular	heterotrophic

LOOKING CLOSER

4. Identify Which kingdom's members do not have cell walls?

____

Name ______________________ Class ______________ Date ______________

Section 3 Review

SECTION VOCABULARY

archaea prokaryotes (most of which are known to live in extreme environments) that are distinguished from other prokaryotes by differences in their genetics and in the makeup of their cell wall; members of the domain Archaea (singular, *archaeon*)

bacteria extremely small, single-celled organisms that usually have a cell wall and that usually reproduce by cell division (singular, *bacterium*)

eukaryote an organism made up of cells that have a nucleus enclosed by a membrane, multiple chromosomes, and a mitotic cycle; eukaryotes include protists, animals, plants, and fungi but not archaea or bacteria

1. List What are the six kingdoms scientists use today to classify all organisms?

____

____

2. Identify Which two domains are made up of prokaryotes?

____

3. Identify Which domain contains multicellular organisms?

____

4. Define What is an *extremophile*? Which domain contains extremophiles?

____

____

____

5. Explain Why do systems of classification change?

____

____

____

6. Apply Concepts Into which kingdom would you classify a unicellular organism that has a nucleus but no cell wall? Explain your answer.

____

____

____

____

Name ______________________ Class ______________ Date ______________

CHAPTER 19 History of Life on Earth

SECTION 1

How Did Life Begin?

KEY IDEAS

As you read this section, keep these questions in mind:

- What did the Miller-Urey experiment show about the formation of the basic molecules of life?
- What are two theories that propose where the building blocks of life originated on early Earth?
- How could molecules have become packaged into cells that contain heritable cellular instructions?

How Did the First Organic Molecules Form?

All living things are made of complex organic molecules. However, scientists think there were not many of these molecules on early Earth. They think that the first complex organic molecules formed when energy caused simpler organic and inorganic molecules to react.

In the 1950s, Harold Urey and Stanley Miller mixed some simple chemicals in a device like the one shown below.

The Miller-Urey Experiment

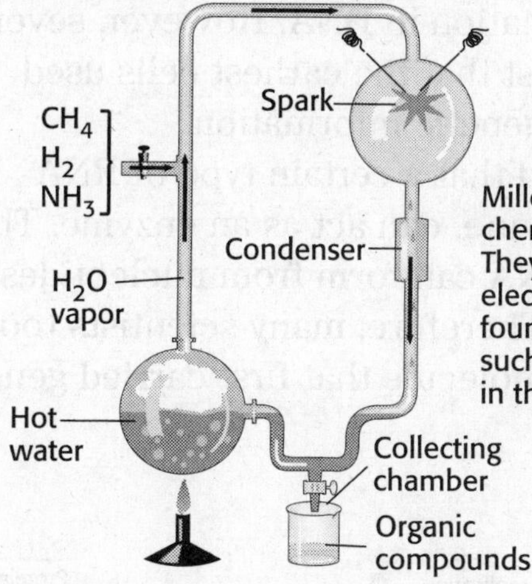

Miller and Urey combined simple chemicals in a device like this one. They added energy in the form of an electric spark. After a few days, they found complex organic molecules, such as amino acids and fatty acids, in the mixture.

Today, we know that the chemicals in the Miller-Urey experiment probably were not very common on early Earth. However, the experiment did show that organic compounds can form from simpler molecules under certain conditions.

Scientists are still not sure exactly where the organic compounds on early Earth came from. Some scientists think that they formed at hot vents deep below the oceans. Other scientists think meteorites could have carried the compounds to Earth.

READING TOOLBOX

Ask Questions Read this section silently to yourself. As you read, write down any questions you have. When you finish reading, discuss the section with a partner. Together, try to figure out the answers to your questions.

LOOKING CLOSER

1. List Name three molecules that Miller and Urey used in their experiment.

____

____

____

Talk About It

Research Learn more about the Miller-Urey experiment and other experiments on the origin of organic compounds. Share what you learn with a small group.

Critical Thinking

2. Infer How do you think scientists learn about how life began, if no one was around to see it?

3. Define What is a microsphere?

Background

Recall that an *enzyme* is a protein that can make chemical reactions in living things happen more easily.

4. Define What is a ribozyme?

How Did the First Cells Form?

Scientists are still trying to learn how organic molecules first began to group together and form cells. They are also trying to learn how heredity developed.

FORMING CELLS

Remember that cell membranes are made of lipids. If some kinds of lipids are placed in water, they group together. Under some conditions, they can form droplets with surfaces similar to cell membranes.

Scientists have learned that lipids can also form tiny, round structures called **microspheres** in water. Many scientists think that microspheres may have been the first steps in the formation of cells. However, these structures could not be considered cells until they had all the characteristics of life, including heredity. ☑

HEREDITY

Remember that *heredity* is the process of passing on genetic information to offspring. Modern organisms store their genetic information in DNA. However, several pieces of evidence suggest that the earliest cells used RNA, not DNA, to carry genetic information.

Scientists have learned that a certain type of RNA molecule, called a **ribozyme**, can act as an enzyme. They have also learned that RNA can form from nucleotides in water, but DNA cannot. Therefore, many scientists today think that RNA was the molecule that first carried genetic information. ☑

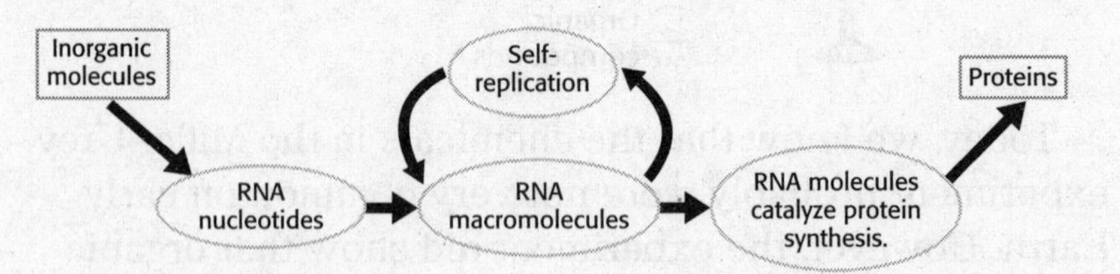

In the earliest cells, RNA may have catalyzed the formation of proteins and replicated itself.

Name ______________________ Class ______________ Date ______________

Section 1 Review

SECTION VOCABULARY

microsphere a hollow microscopic spherical structure that is usually composed of proteins or a synthetic polymer	**ribozyme** a type of RNA that can act as an enzyme

1. **Identify** Why do scientists think that RNA may have been the molecule that first carried genetic information?

____

____

2. **Describe** How do scientists think the first organic compounds formed?

____

____

3. **Identify** How did Miller and Urey add energy to the mixture of chemicals in their device?

____

4. **Identify** What were two kinds of complex organic molecules that formed during the Miller-Urey experiment?

____

____

5. **Explain** The compounds that Miller and Urey used in their experiment were probably not found on early Earth. Why are the results of their experiment still useful today?

____

____

6. **Identify** What are two possible places that the organic molecules on Earth could have come from?

____

____

7. **List** According to scientists, what two types of structures may have been the first steps toward the formation of cells?

____

____

Name ____________ Class ____________ Date ____________

CHAPTER 19 History of Life on Earth

SECTION 2

The Age of Earth

KEY IDEAS

As you read this section, keep these questions in mind:

- How is the fossil record used to learn about the history of life?
- How do paleontologists date fossils?
- What evidence was used to make the geologic time scale?

READING TOOLBOX

Compare After you read this section, make a chart comparing and contrasting relative dating and radiometric dating.

How Do Scientists Study Past Life?

How do scientists know what Earth was like in the past? One way is by studying *fossils*, or the traces of organisms that are preserved in rock or other materials. The figure below shows one way that a fossil can form.

Some fossils form when an organism dies and is buried in sediment before it decays. Over time, the organism's body dissolves and leaves an impression in the sediment. More sediment can fill the impression and solidify to form a fossil.

LOOKING CLOSER

1. Infer What do you think is the reason that most organisms do not become fossils?

____

____

____

The **fossil record** is the history of life on Earth that is shown by fossils. By studying the fossil record, scientists can learn both where and when different organisms lived. Although the fossil record is not complete, it presents strong evidence that evolution has taken place. For example, fossils provide evidence of forms of life that suggest how living and extinct organisms are related. ☑

READING CHECK

2. Identify What are two things that a scientist can learn about organisms by studying the fossil record?

____

____

How Do Scientists Learn the Ages of Fossils?

To use a fossil to learn about Earth's history, scientists must know how old the fossil is. One way to learn the age of a fossil is by using relative dating. **Relative dating** involves determining whether one rock or fossil is older or younger than another.

In many cases, a scientist can determine the relative age of a fossil by examining the rock in which it is found. In general, older rocks lie below younger rocks. Therefore, older fossils generally lie below younger fossils.

ABSOLUTE DATING

Relative dating can be used only to learn whether one fossil is older or younger than another. To determine the actual age of a fossil in years, scientists often use radiometric dating. In **radiometric dating**, scientists use isotopes to determine the actual age of a rock or fossil.

Some isotopes are unstable, or *radioactive*. These *parent isotopes* can break down into other isotopes called *daughter isotopes*. Each parent isotope breaks down at a specific rate that does not change. The time it takes for one-half of a sample of the parent isotope to break down is called its **half-life**.

As the parent isotope breaks down, it forms the daughter isotope at a constant rate. Therefore, scientists can compare amounts of parent and daughter isotopes in a material as one method of learning its age.

Background

Recall that *isotopes* are atoms of the same element that have different numbers of neutrons.

Critical Thinking

3. Infer If parent isotopes decayed randomly instead of at a constant rate, could they be used to determine the ages of rocks and fossils? Explain your answer.

____

____

____

____

____

____

How Do Scientists Describe Geologic Time?

Earth is more than 4.5 billion years old. To describe Earth's history, scientists use the **geologic time scale**. It is based on evidence from the fossil record and from rock layers around the world.

In the geologic time scale, Earth's history is divided into different segments of time. The divisions between many of these segments are based on **mass extinctions**, or times when many different species became extinct.

The Geologic Time Scale

Era	Period	When the period began (millions of years ago)
Cenozoic	Quaternary	1.8
	Tertiary	65.5
Mass extinction		
Mesozoic	Cretaceous	146
	Jurassic	200
	Triassic	251
Mass extinction		
Paleozoic	Permian	299
	Carboniferous	359
	Devonian	416
	Silurian	444
	Ordovician	488
	Cambrian	542
Mass extinction		
Precambrian time (not an era)		more than 4,500

LOOKING CLOSER

4. Identify Name the three eras in the geologic time scale.

____

____

____

Name ______________________ Class ______________ Date ____________

Section 2 Review

SECTION VOCABULARY

fossil record the history of life in the geologic past as indicated by the traces or remains of living things

geologic time scale the standard method used to divide Earth's long natural history into manageable parts

half-life the time required for half of a sample of a radioactive isotope to break down by radioactive decay to form a daughter isotope

mass extinction an episode during which large numbers of species become extinct

radiometric dating a method of determining the absolute age of an object, often by comparing the relative percentages of a radioactive (parent) isotope and a stable (daughter) isotope

relative dating a method of determining whether an event or object, such as a fossil, is older or younger than other events or objects without referring to the object's age in years

1. Describe How does the fossil record provide evidence that evolution has occurred?

____

____

2. Apply Concepts The diagram below shows several rock layers that contain fossils. Which fossil is probably the oldest? Which fossil is probably the youngest?

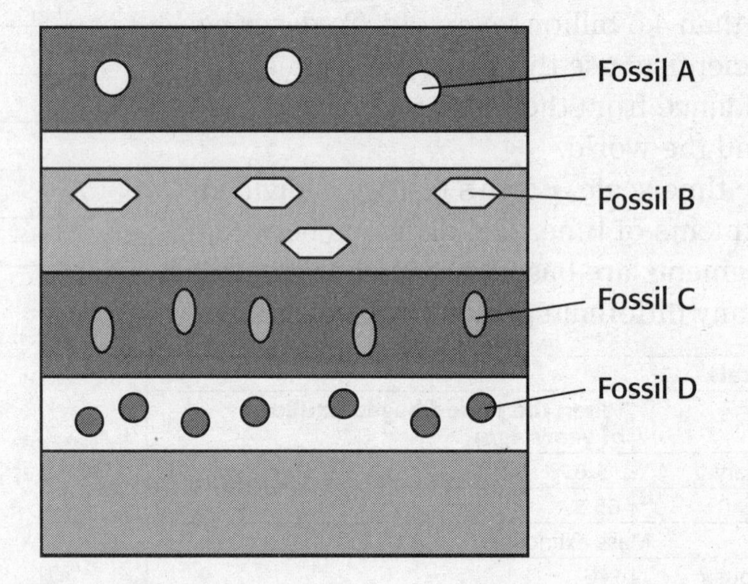

____

3. Identify Relationships How is the fossil record related to the geologic time scale?

____

____

____

Name ______________________ Class ______________ Date ______________

CHAPTER 19 History of Life on Earth

SECTION 3

Evolution of Life

KEY IDEAS

As you read this section, keep these questions in mind:

- What major evolutionary developments occurred during Precambrian time?
- What dominant organisms evolved during the Paleozoic Era?
- What dominant organisms evolved during the Mesozoic Era and the Cenozoic Era?

What Happened in Precambrian Time?

Precambrian time lasted from the time Earth formed, about 4.5 billion years ago, until about 542 million years ago. During this long span of time, many important events occurred, as shown below.

Event	Description
Evolution of prokaryotes	The oldest known fossils are of prokaryotes. They are more than 3.5 billion years old. Scientists think that some of the first prokaryotes were marine cyanobacteria (singular, **cyanobacterium**), which could carry out photosynthesis.
Formation of oxygen	Oxygen gas was rare in Earth's early atmosphere. By about 2.4 billion years ago, cyanobacteria had begun to add oxygen to the atmosphere by carrying out photosynthesis.
Formation of the ozone layer	As the amount of oxygen in Earth's atmosphere increased, the ozone layer began to form. The ozone layer protected early organisms from ultraviolet rays in sunlight. As a result, organisms were eventually able to survive on land.

EVOLUTION OF EUKARYOTES

Remember that eukaryotic cells contain mitochondria, and some contain chloroplasts. Mitochondria and chloroplasts have their own DNA, and these organelles are about the same size as some prokaryotes. Therefore, many scientists think that mitochondria and chloroplasts evolved through endosymbiosis.

In **endosymbiosis**, one organism lives inside another, and both organisms benefit. According to the *endosymbiotic theory*, mitochondria and chloroplasts began as small prokaryotes that were absorbed by larger prokaryotes. The smaller cells lived and reproduced inside the larger cells. Eventually, they formed a symbiotic relationship. ☑

READING TOOLBOX

Summarize After you read this section, make a flowchart that shows when prokaryotes, eukaryotes, fishes, amphibians, reptiles, birds, and mammals first evolved.

Critical Thinking

1. Apply Concepts Which two domains of life were the first organisms probably part of? Explain your answer.

____

____

____

____

____

2. Identify Which two types of organelles may have evolved through endosymbiosis?

____

____

EVOLUTION OF MULTICELLULAR ORGANISMS

The first multicellular organisms evolved during Precambrian time. Scientists think that multicellular organisms evolved from groups of single-celled protists, such as the ones shown below. Eventually, the different cells began to take on different functions. ☑

3. Identify What organisms did multicellular organisms probably evolve from?

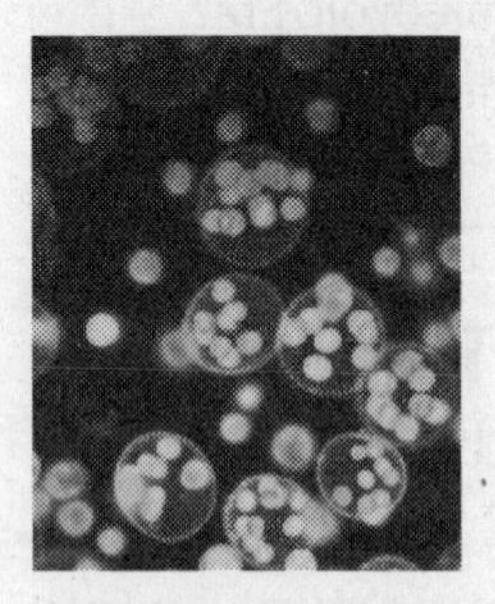

Scientists think the earliest multicellular organisms were groups of protists, such as these. Protists are eukaryotic organisms that belong to the kingdom Protista and share some characteristics with plants, animals, or fungi.

What Life Forms Evolved in Later Eras?

During the Paleozoic Era, most of the major groups of plants and animals evolved. The first organisms to live on land were probably plants and fungi. By the middle of the Paleozoic Era, huge forests existed on many of the continents. ☑

4. Identify What types of organisms were probably the first to live on land?

The first animals to live on land were probably *arthropods*, which have jointed legs and hard outer shells. For example, insects evolved during the Paleozoic Era.

Vertebrates, or animals with backbones, also evolved during the Paleozoic Era. The first vertebrates were fishes. The first land vertebrates, amphibians, evolved about 370 million years ago. The first reptiles evolved about 340 million years ago.

The largest mass extinction in Earth's history marks the end of the Paleozoic Era. More than 96% of the animal species on Earth at the time became extinct. ☑

5. Identify What happened at the end of the Paleozoic Era?

During the Mesozoic Era, dinosaurs and other reptiles were the dominant animals. Early birds and mammals evolved during this era. Flowering plants also evolved during the Mesozoic Era.

A mass extinction marks the end of the Mesozoic Era. About two-thirds of all land species, including most dinosaur species, became extinct at this time.

The Cenozoic Era began about 65 million years ago. The Cenozoic Era is still going on. The dominant animals in the Cenozoic Era are mammals, including humans. Birds have also become more dominant in this era.

Name ______________________ Class ______________ Date ______________

Section 3 Review

SECTION VOCABULARY

cyanobacterium a bacterium that carries out photosynthesis; a blue-green alga	**endosymbiosis** a mutually beneficial relationship in which one organism lives within another

1. Identify What type of organism was probably one of the first prokaryotes to evolve?

____

2. Describe Where did most of the oxygen in Earth's atmosphere probably come from?

____

____

3. Explain How did the increasing amounts of oxygen in Earth's atmosphere allow organisms to live on land?

____

____

____

4. Identify Why do scientists think that mitochondria and chloroplasts evolved through endosymbiosis? Give two reasons.

____

____

5. List Name three kinds of organisms that evolved during the Paleozoic Era.

____

____

____

6. List Name three kinds of organisms that evolved during the Mesozoic Era.

____

____

____

7. List Name two kinds of organisms that are dominant in the Cenozoic Era.

____

____

Name ______________________ Class ______________ Date ______________

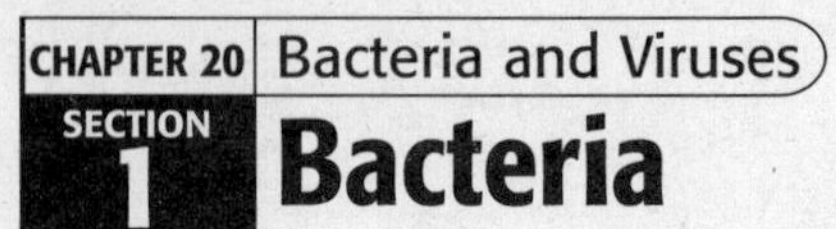
CHAPTER 20 Bacteria and Viruses

SECTION 1

Bacteria

KEY IDEAS

As you read this section, keep these questions in mind:
- What are the two major groups of prokaryotes?
- How are Gram-positive and Gram-negative bacteria different?
- How can bacteria be grouped by energy source?
- How do bacteria reproduce and adapt?

READING TOOLBOX

Learn New Words As you read this section, underline words you don't understand. When you figure out what they mean, write the words and their definitions in your notebook.

How Do Scientists Group Prokaryotes?

Prokaryotes are single-celled organisms that do not have nuclei or other membrane-bound organelles. Scientists divide prokaryotes into two major groups: the domain Archaea and the domain Bacteria.

Although members of the domain Archaea are prokaryotes, some of their molecules are similar to those of eukaryotes. Many archaea live in harsh environments, such as hot springs. Most prokaryotes belong to the domain Bacteria. Organisms in both prokaryote domains are generally referred to as *bacteria*. ☑

READING CHECK

1. Identify Which domain do most prokaryotes belong to?

____

What Is the Structure of Bacteria?

Bacteria have a single chromosome made up of DNA. This chromosome is a large loop gathered into a mass called a *nucleoid*. In addition, bacteria often have small extra loops of DNA called **plasmids**. ☑

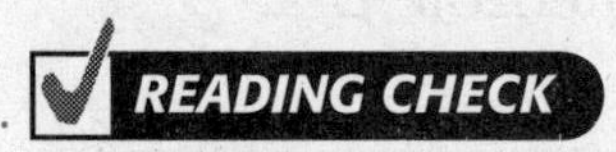
READING CHECK

2. Identify How many chromosomes does a bacterium have?

____

The bacterial cell membrane is made up of two lipid layers. A cell wall surrounds the cell membrane. The cell wall is made of a protein-carbohydrate compound called **peptidoglycan**. In some bacteria, such as *E. coli* shown below, an outer membrane covers the cell wall.

Critical Thinking

3. Apply Concepts Are the ribosomes of *E. coli* surrounded by a membrane? Explain your answer.

____

____

____

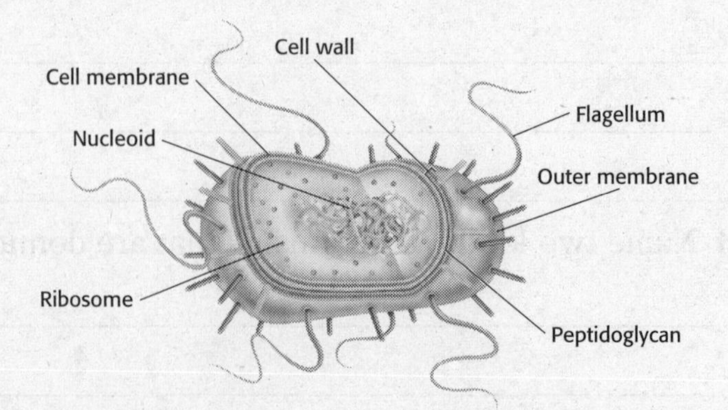

E. coli is a common bacterium that lives in the intestines of humans.

GRAM-POSITIVE AND GRAM-NEGATIVE BACTERIA

Scientists classify bacteria based on their structure using a technique called *Gram staining*. Gram staining involves colored dyes. As shown below, **Gram-positive** bacteria have a thick layer of peptidoglycan in their cell wall and no outer membrane. They stain darkly with Gram staining dyes because their peptidoglycan layer is very thick.

As shown below, **Gram-negative** bacteria have a thin layer of peptidoglycan in their cell walls covered by an outer membrane. The thin peptidoglycan layer does not trap the dark dye, but does absorb the pink dye. Their outer membrane makes them more resistant to medicines and the body's defenses than Gram-positive bacteria.

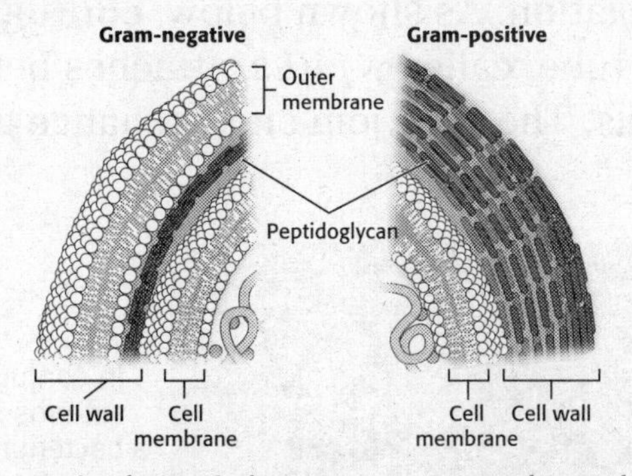

Gram-negative bacteria have an outer membrane but Gram-positive bacteria do not.

Critical Thinking

4. Apply Concepts Why can an infection by Gram-negative bacteria be more dangerous than an infection by Gram-positive bacteria?

____

____

____

____

LOOKING CLOSER

5. Compare How does the layer of peptidoglycan compare in Gram-negative and Gram-positive bacteria?

____

____

How Do Bacteria Obtain Energy and Nutrients?

Bacteria can be divided into three groups based on their energy sources. These groups are photoautotrophs, chemoautotrophs, and heterotrophs.

Bacteria that use energy from sunlight to make their own food are *photoautotrophs*. Recall that this process of making food is called photosynthesis.

Bacteria that use energy from inorganic molecules, such as sulfur and ammonia, to make their own food are *chemoautotrophs*. These bacteria are the only organisms that can obtain energy from inorganic sources.

Bacteria that use other organisms for food are called *heterotrophs*. These bacteria cannot make their own food. Most heterotrophic bacteria absorb nutrients from dead organisms. However, some heterotrophic bacteria obtain nutrients from living organisms. ☑

6. Identify What type of bacteria cannot make their own food?

____

How Do Bacteria Reproduce and Adapt?

Bacteria reproduce by binary fission. They can form new genetic combinations by conjugation, transformation, and transduction. They can also survive harsh conditions by forming endospores.

BINARY FISSION

Bacteria reproduce asexually by binary fission. In this process, a single cell divides to produce two genetically identical cells. Mutations often occur during binary fission that can produce new genetic forms of bacteria. ☑

7. Describe How do cells that result from binary fission compare to each other genetically?

____

____

NEW GENETIC COMBINATIONS

Bacteria can transfer genetic material in a process called conjugation. As shown below, **conjugation** occurs when a thin tube, called a *pilus*, attaches between two bacterial cells. The cells join and exchange genetic information.

LOOKING CLOSER

8. Describe What is a pilus?

____

____

____

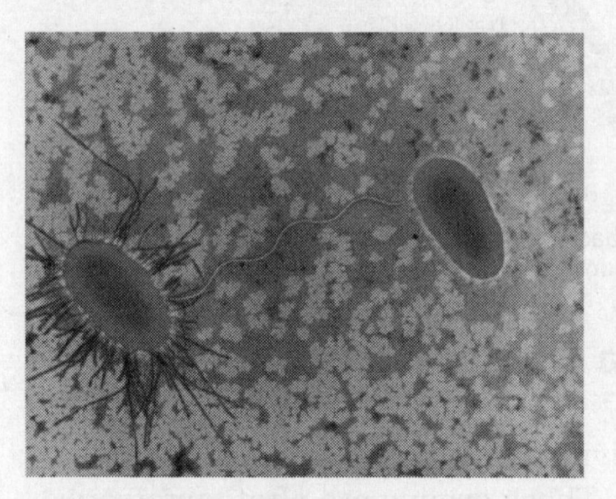

In conjugation, a pilus extends from one bacterium and attaches to a second bacterium. Genetic material is then transferred through the pilus from the first bacterium to the second bacterium.

Bacteria can also form new genetic combinations by transformation and transduction. In **transformation**, bacteria take up small pieces of DNA around them. In **transduction**, viruses transfer DNA between bacteria. ☑

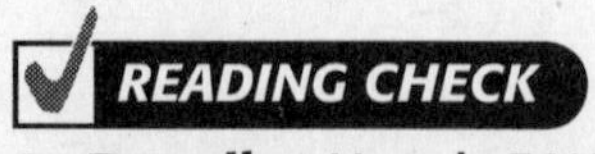

9. Describe How is DNA transferred between two bacterial cells in tranduction?

____

ENDOSPORES

Some bacteria survive harsh conditions by forming thick-walled structures called **endospores**. Endospores form inside bacteria. They contain a copy of the bacteria's DNA and a small bit of cytoplasm.

Endospores can survive conditions that kill most bacteria, such as heat, radiation, and acids. When conditions improve, endospores form new bacteria.

Name ______________________ Class ______________ Date ____________

Section 1 Review

SECTION VOCABULARY

conjugation in prokaryotes, algae, and fungi, a type of sexual reproduction in which two cells join temporarily to recombine nuclear material

endospore a thick-walled protective spore that forms inside a bacterial cell and resists harsh conditions

Gram-negative describes a type of prokaryote (eubacteria) that has a small amount of peptidoglycan in its cell wall, has an outer membrane, and is stained pink by a counterstain during Gram staining

Gram-positive describes a type of prokaryote (eubacterium) that has a large amount of peptidoglycan in its cell wall and is stained violet during Gram staining

peptidoglycan a protein-carbohydrate compound that makes the cell walls of bacteria rigid

plasmid a genetic structure that can replicate independently of the main chromosome(s) of a cell; usually, a circular DNA molecule in bacteria (prokaryotes)

transduction the transfer of a bacterial gene from one bacterium to another through a bacteriophage

transformation the transfer of genetic material in the form of DNA fragments from one cell to another or from one organism to another

1. **Identify** What are the two major domains of prokaryotes?

____

2. **Compare** Describe two ways in which the structure of Gram-positive bacteria is different from that of Gram-negative bacteria.

____

____

____

____

3. **Define** What are chemoautotrophs?

____

____

4. **Calculate** If eight bacterial cells each undergo binary fission, how many bacterial cells will result?

____

5. **Explain** How do endospores help bacteria survive harsh conditions?

____

____

____

Name ______________________ Class ______________ Date ______________

CHAPTER 20 Bacteria and Viruses

SECTION 2

Viruses

KEY IDEAS

As you read this section, keep these questions in mind:
- Why is a virus not considered a living organism?
- What two structures are characteristic of viruses?
- What are two ways that a virus can reproduce?
- What are viroids and prions?

READING TOOLBOX

Summarize As you read this section, underline the main ideas. When you finish reading, write a summary of the section using the underlined ideas.

Is a Virus Alive?

All living things are made of cells, are able to grow and reproduce, and have DNA that dictates their traits. Viruses are not considered living because they do not share all the characteristics of living things. Viruses have the following properties:

Critical Thinking

1. Apply Concepts Do viruses have mitochondria? Explain your answer.

____

____

- Viruses are not made of cells. They have genetic material, but they do not have any cytoplasm or organelles.
- Viruses cannot reproduce on their own. They reproduce by infecting host cells and using the cell's ribosomes, enzymes, and other molecules to make more viruses.
- Viruses do not grow. They become full size within the host cells where they are reproduced.
- Viruses do not carry out metabolic activities, and do not maintain internal balance or homeostasis.

Background

Recall that *metabolism* is the sum of all chemical processes that occur in an organism.

What Is the Structure of a Virus?

All viruses have nucleic acid and a protein coat called a **capsid**. In addition, viruses may have tail fibers or a covering called an envelope.

NUCLEIC ACIDS

Viral nucleic acid can be either DNA or RNA. Both DNA and RNA viruses insert their genetic material into a host cell. They use the host cell's enzymes and nucleotides to make more copies of their genetic material. ☑

READING CHECK

2. Identify Where do viruses make copies of their genetic information?

____

The genetic material of viruses codes for the structural parts of a virus. Viruses also use the host cell to make new viral proteins. In RNA viruses called *retroviruses*, viral DNA is first transcribed into DNA before it can be used to make viral proteins.

CAPSID AND TAIL FIBERS

The protein coat, or capsid, of a virus surrounds its genetic material. Viruses can enter a host cell only if the proteins in their capsid match the proteins on the surface of the host cell. Capsids have a variety of shapes.

In some viruses, such as bacteriophages, the capsid is attached to a helical tail with tail fibers. **Bacteriophages**, shown below left, are viruses that infect bacteria. Their tail and tail fibers help inject the viral DNA into a bacterium. ☑

READING CHECK

3. Define What is a bacteriophage?

____

____

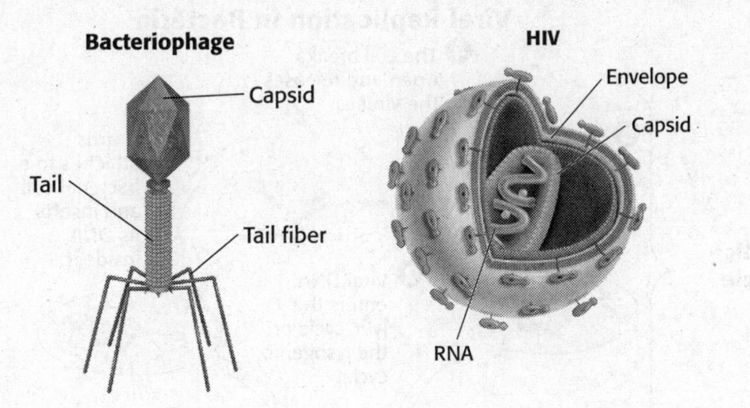

LOOKING CLOSER

4. Identify What is the genetic material in HIV?

____

ENVELOPE

Many viruses have a membrane, called an **envelope**, which surrounds the capsid. The envelope is covered with molecules that help the virus attach to its host cell. HIV, shown above right, is a retrovirus that has an envelope. The envelope of HIV covers an oval-shaped capsid. ☑

READING CHECK

5. Identify What viral structure does an envelope cover?

____

How Do Viruses Reproduce?

A viral infection begins when the genetic material of a virus enters a host cell. Once inside a host cell, a virus can reproduce by a lysogenic cycle and/or a lytic cycle.

LYSOGENIC CYCLE

In the **lysogenic** cycle, a virus inserts its DNA into the host cell's chromosome. The infecting virus is then called a provirus or *prophage*. When the host cell replicates its own DNA, it also replicates the viral DNA. When the host cell divides, each new cell receives a copy of the viral DNA along with a copy of its own DNA. In the lysogenic cycle, viral DNA is replicated but no new viruses are made. In addition, the host cell is not destroyed. ☑

6. Explain When does a prophage form?

____

____

____

LYTIC CYCLE

After a period of time, a prophage may leave the host cell's DNA and enter the lytic cycle. In the **lytic** cycle, viral DNA remains separate from the host cell's DNA. The virus uses the host cell to replicate its genetic material and make proteins to build new viruses. The host cell then breaks open and dies, releasing the newly made viruses. Some viruses reproduce only by the lytic cycle. ☑

7. Describe What happens to the host cell at the end of the lytic cycle?

____

____

____

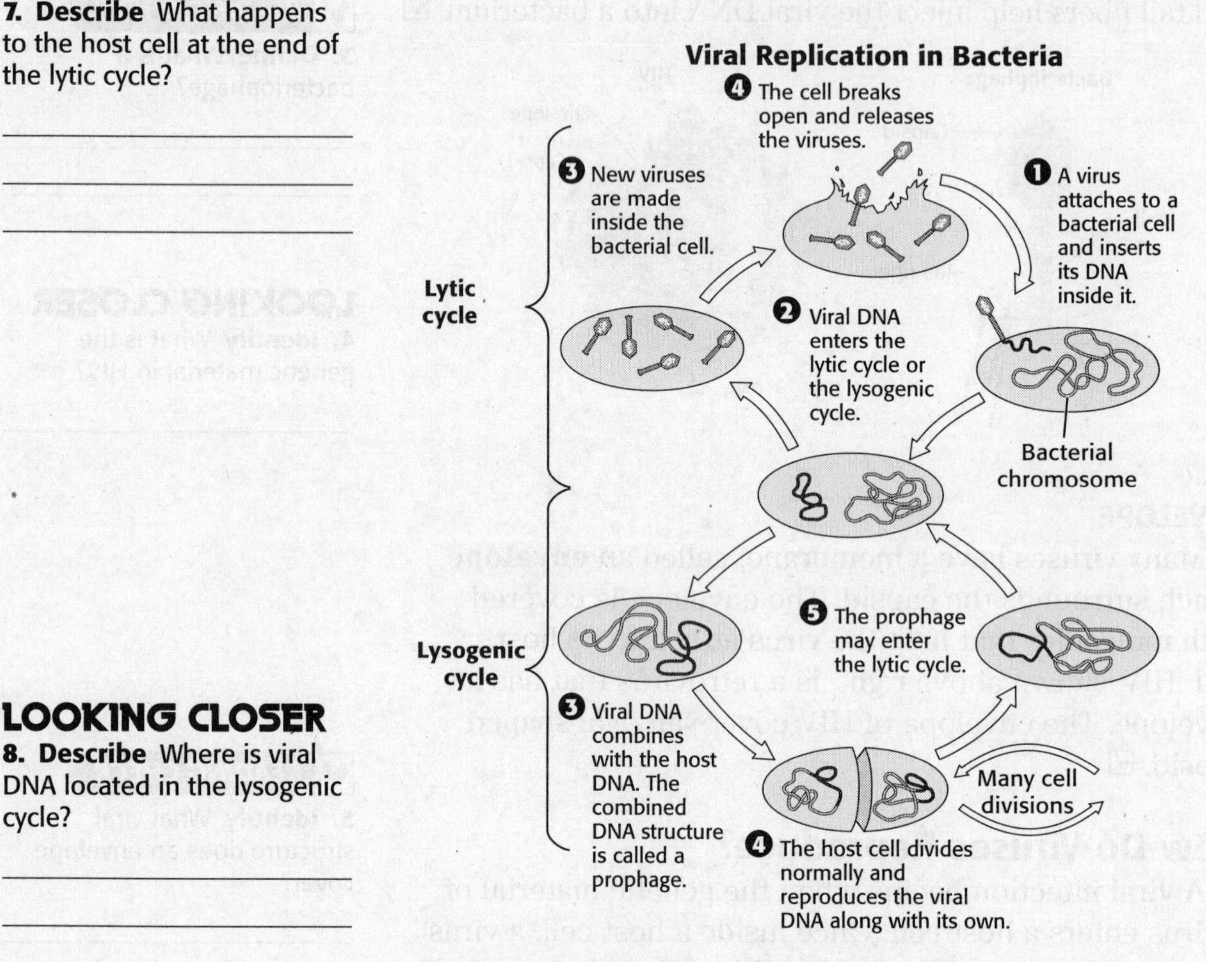

LOOKING CLOSER

8. Describe Where is viral DNA located in the lysogenic cycle?

____

____

What Are Viroids and Prions?

Viroids and prions are nonliving particles that can cause disease. A *viroid* is a single strand of RNA that has no capsid. Inside a host cell, this RNA can make new viroids that interfere with the host cell's growth. ☑

A *prion* is a protein with an abnormal shape that attaches to normal proteins in the brain. The prion causes the normal proteins to stop functioning. As a result, brain tissue is destroyed. Prions cause mad cow disease in cattle and Creutzfeldt-Jakob disease in humans.

READING CHECK

9. Compare How is the structure of a viroid different from the structure of a virus?

____

____

Name ______________________ Class ______________ Date ____________

Section 2 Review

SECTION VOCABULARY

bacteriophage a virus that infects bacteria

capsid a protein sheath that surrounds the nucleic acid core in a virus

envelope a membranelike layer that covers the capsids of some viruses

lysogenic describes viral replication in which a viral genome is replicated as a provirus without destroying the host cell

lytic describes viral replication that results in the destruction of a host cell and the release of many new virus particles

1. Summarize Use the words "yes" and "no" to indicate whether each property listed below describes living things, viruses, or both.

Property	Living Things	Viruses
Made of cells		
Have genetic material		
Can grow		
Can reproduce on their own		
Can only replicate DNA inside host cells		

2. Identify What two structures do all viruses have?

____

3. Identify What structures help a bacteriophage inject its DNA into a bacterium?

____

4. Compare Describe three ways in which the lysogenic cycle and lytic cycle are different.

____

____

____

5. Describe When a host cell divides in the lysogenic cycle, what genetic material does each new cell receive?

____

____

6. Describe What is a prion and how does it cause disease?

____

____

____

Name ______________________ Class ______________ Date ____________

CHAPTER 20 Bacteria and Viruses

SECTION 3

Bacteria, Viruses, and Humans

KEY IDEAS

As you read this section, keep these questions in mind:
- What are the benefits of bacteria and viruses?
- What are the steps described in Koch's Postulates?
- What are two ways that bacteria cause disease?
- How does antibiotic resistance develop?
- Why are viral diseases difficult to cure?
- How can a disease emerge?

READING TOOLBOX

Outline As you read, make an outline of this section. Use the header questions to help you organize the main ideas in your outline.

How Can Bacteria and Viruses Be Beneficial?

Although bacteria and viruses can cause diseases, they can also be beneficial. The table below describes the benefits of bacteria and viruses.

Benefit To	Description
Ecosystems and other organisms	• Bacteria produce oxygen, make nitrogen available to plants, and decompose dead organisms. • Many bacteria form relationships that benefit other organisms. For example, bacteria inside the large intestines of humans produce vitamin K.
Industry	• Bacteria are used to make foods such as pickles, soy sauce, and sourdough bread. • Bacteria are used to produce certain chemicals. • Mining companies use bacteria to extract valuable minerals, such as copper. • Bacteria are used to clean up oil spills and to clean the water in sewage treatment plants.
Scientific research	• Bacteria and viruses are used in genetic research. They provide information about DNA replication, transcription, and translation. • Viruses are used to deliver genetic material directly to target cells.

LOOKING CLOSER

1. Explain How do bacteria in the large intestine benefit humans?

____

____

How Are Diseases Caused by Viruses and Bacteria Transmitted?

Some bacteria and viruses can infect people and animals and cause diseases. Diseases that can spread from person to person are called contagious diseases. ☑

Some diseases must be transmitted directly from one host to another by contact, such as kissing or animal bites. Other diseases can survive outside a host for a period of time. These diseases can be passed through the air, in food or water, or on objects.

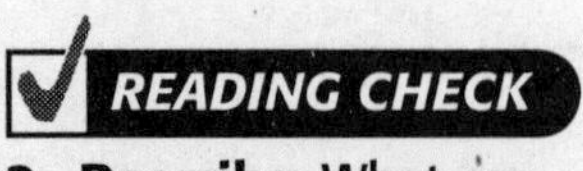

2. Describe What are contagious diseases?

____

____

____

How Is the Cause of an Infection Diagnosed?

The German physician Robert Koch developed a technique for identifying disease-causing agents, or **pathogens**. His technique involves four steps called **Koch's Postulates**. These steps are still used today to identify a pathogen that causes a certain disease. The four main steps in Koch's Postulates are shown below. ☑

3. Identify What do Koch's Postulates help identify?

___

Koch's Postulates

❶ Finding the Pathogen
The pathogen must be found in an animal that has the disease. It must not be present in healthy animals.

❷ Growing the Pathogen
The pathogen must be taken from an animal that has the disease and grown in a laboratory culture.

❸ Infecting a Healthy Animal
The pathogen from the laboratory culture is injected into a second animal that is healthy. The second animal must develop the same disease as the first animal.

❹ Finding the Same Pathogen
The pathogen must be taken from the second animal and grown in a laboratory culture. This pathogen culture must be the same as the pathogen culture from the first animal.

Critical Thinking

4. Infer Suppose that the pathogens injected into a healthy animal in Step 3 of Koch's Postulates do not cause the same disease. What can you conclude about the pathogens?

___

How Do Bacteria Cause Disease?

Bacteria can cause a variety of diseases such as food poisoning, tooth decay, tetanus, stomach ulcers, and bacterial meningitis. Bacteria can cause diseases by producing toxins or by destroying body tissues.

Poisonous chemicals produced by bacteria are called **toxins**. Bacteria may release toxins or store them in their cells. The bacterium *C. botulinum* produces a toxin that damages nerve cells. When these bacteria are consumed in food, their toxins cause a disease called botulism. ☑

5. Identify What chemicals produced by bacteria can cause diseases?

___

Bacteria can also produce enzymes that break down a host's tissues. The bacteria obtain nutrients from the host's tissues. *M. tuberculosis* is a bacterium that destroys human tissues and causes a disease called tuberculosis.

What Is Antibiotic Resistance?

Bacterial diseases can be treated with antibiotics. An **antibiotic** is a chemical that stops the growth of bacteria or kills bacteria. However, bacteria can develop resistance to antibiotics. Antibiotic **resistance** is the evolution of bacteria that antibiotics are unable to kill. ☑

6. Define What is an antibiotic?

____

____

____

DEVELOPMENT OF RESISTANCE

Mutations that cause antibiotic resistance occur naturally in bacteria. When an antibiotic is present in a bacterial population, it kills bacteria that are not resistant. However, antibiotic-resistant bacteria survive.

Antibiotic-resistant bacteria divide by binary fission to produce more antibiotic-resistant bacteria. As a result, a whole population of antibiotic-resistant bacteria can be produced in a short time. The figure below shows how a population of antibiotic-resistant bacteria develops. Bacteria can also pass an antibiotic-resistant gene to other bacteria during conjugation.

LOOKING CLOSER

7. Explain How does a bacterium become resistant to antibiotics?

____

____

LOOKING CLOSER

8. Explain What happened to the antibiotic-resistant bacteria when an antibiotic was not present?

____

____

____

Antibiotic Resistance

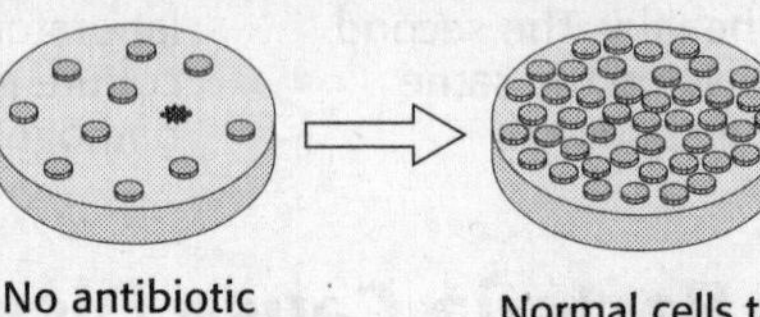

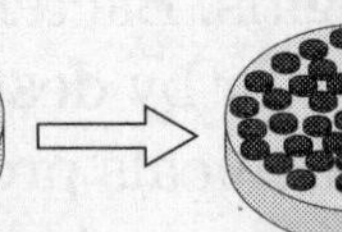

CONSEQUENCES OF RESISTANCE

Diseases that were once easy to treat with antibiotics are now more difficult to treat because of antibiotic resistance. As bacteria become resistant to antibiotics, new antibiotic drugs are being used. Over time, bacteria may develop resistance to these antibiotics as well.

How Do Viruses Cause Disease?

Viruses cause a variety of diseases in humans, as shown in the table below. A virus usually infects only certain cells. For example, the virus that causes colds infects only cells of the upper respiratory tract. Any action that brings viruses in contact with host cells can cause a viral disease. For this reason, certain diseases can be transmitted only by exchange of body fluids, whereas others can be transmitted through the air.

Symptoms of a viral illness can be caused by several factors. Some viruses have toxic parts, such as envelope proteins. Other viruses cause the host cell to produce toxins that destroy its own tissues. However, many of the symptoms of a viral infection, such as aches and fever, result from the body's own response to infection. ☑

Talk About It

Discuss With a partner or in a small group, talk about different ways in which colds can be transmitted between people. What can you do to prevent the spread of colds?

9. Explain How do aches and fever result from a viral infection?

____

____

____

Virus	Disease	Symptoms
Influenza virus	flu	fever, headache, tiredness, muscle aches, cough
Varicella zoster virus	chickenpox, shingles	fever, tiredness, itchy or painful blisters
Measles virus	measles	fever, cough, runny nose, pink-eye, a rash that covers the body
Mumps virus	mumps	fever, headache, muscle aches, tiredness, loss of appetite, swelling of salivary glands
HIV virus	HIV infection/AIDS	early symptoms: fever, tiredness, swollen lymph nodes; later symptoms: weight loss, infections, death
Human papillloma virus	HPV infection, cervical cancer	usually no symptoms; occasionally genital warts; can cause cervical cancer
Hepatitis B virus	hepatitis, liver cancer	jaundice, tiredness, abdominal pain, nausea, joint pain, liver disease, liver cancer, death
West Nile virus	West Nile virus infection	fever, headache, bodyache; in rare cases coma, numbness, and paralysis

LOOKING CLOSER

10. Identify What pathogen causes HPV infection?

____

____

TREATMENT

Since viruses enter host cells to reproduce, it is difficult to develop a drug that kills the virus without harming the host. Antibiotics do not work against viruses.

Many viral diseases can be prevented by vaccination. A vaccine contains a harmless form of a pathogen. It prepares the immune system to recognize and destroy a pathogen before it causes a disease.

How Do Diseases Emerge?

Diseases can appear, or emerge, in a population in several ways. New forms of bacteria and viruses can cause new diseases to emerge. Some known diseases can emerge in new areas or in new hosts. Known diseases that have been controlled can also reappear, or reemerge in a population.

NEW DISEASES

In 2004, a new form of bird flu appeared in Asia. The bird flu is deadly to birds. The virus that causes the bird flu is transmitted between birds. In some cases, the virus has been transmitted from birds to people. However, the virus has not been transmitted from person to person. If the virus mutates so that it can be passed between people, the result could be a global spread of the bird flu. ☑

READING CHECK

11. Explain What could result if the virus that causes bird flu mutates so it can be transmitted between people?

____

____

The graph below shows the number of human cases of bird flu between January and April of 2006.

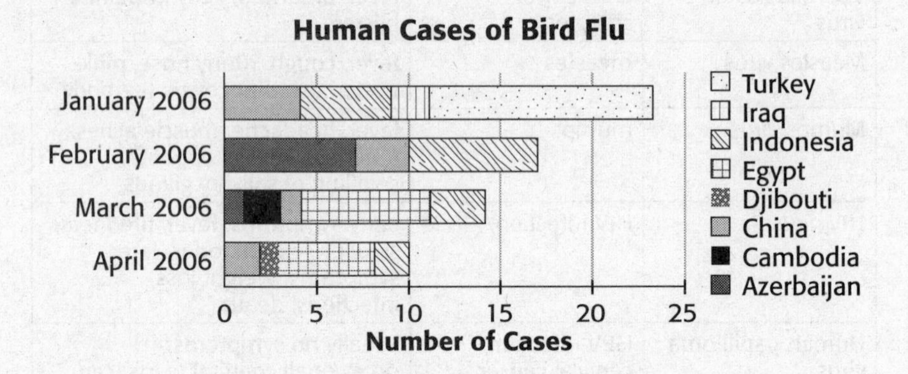

Graphing Skills

12. Identify Which two countries had more human bird flu cases in February 2006 than in January 2006?

____

____

NEW AREAS AND NEW HOSTS

Diseases can spread to new areas or a new host when people come in contact with a pathogen in a new way. For example, eating meat from new animal sources in China resulted in the transmission of a respiratory syndrome to humans. The ease of global travel has also made it possible for diseases to spread worldwide.

Talk About It

Discuss With a partner or in a small group, talk about how travel can contribute to the emergence of diseases.

REEMERGENCE

Sometimes diseases that have been controlled can reemerge in a population. A decrease in the use of certain vaccinations has allowed diseases such as whooping cough, measles, and diptheria to reemerge.

Section 3 Review

SECTION VOCABULARY

antibiotic a substance that can inhibit the growth of or kill some microorganisms

Koch's Postulates a four-stage procedure that Robert Koch formulated for identifying specific pathogens and determining the cause of a given disease

pathogen a microorganism, another organism, a virus, or a protein that causes disease; an infectious agent

resistance in biology, the ability of an organism to tolerate a chemical or disease-causing agent

toxin a substance that is produced by one organism and that is poisonous to other organisms

1. **Describe** What are three ways in which bacteria benefit ecosystems?

2. **Describe** What is the second step in Koch's Postulates?

3. **Explain** What are two ways that bacteria cause disease?

4. **Explain** Why are some diseases that were once easy to treat with antibiotics now more difficult to treat?

5. **Explain** Why are viral diseases difficult to cure?

6. **Identify** What has caused diseases such as whooping cough, measles, and diptheria to reemerge?

Name ______________________ Class ______________ Date ______________

CHAPTER 21 Protists

SECTION 1

Characteristics of Protists

KEY IDEAS

As you read this section, keep these questions in mind:
- What types of organisms are classified as protists?
- What methods of reproduction do protists use?
- Why is the classification of protists likely to change in the future?

READING TOOLBOX

Identify Patterns
The terms for many structures can remind you of the structure's function. For example, the *gametophyte* generation produces *gametes*. As you read, underline other terms that can remind you of an object or structure's function.

What Are Protists?

The kingdom Protista is made up of organisms that do not belong in any other kingdom. As a result, the members of this kingdom are very different from one another. However, all protists have one thing in common: they are eukaryotic.

Many important characteristics arose among protists, such as membrane-bound organelles, complex cillia and flagella, sexual reproduction with gametes, and multicellularity. Many protists share some characteristics with plants, animals, or fungi. Scientists use genetic studies to show how closely protists are related to one another and to organisms in other kingdoms. Thus, scientists may classify protists into several different kingdoms.

Background
Recall that a *eukaryotic* cell has a nucleus and other membrane-bound organelles.

How Do Protists Reproduce?

Different kinds of protists have different ways, or methods, of reproducing. Protists can reproduce asexually or sexually. Asexual reproduction results in offspring that are genetically identical to the parent. Sexual reproduction results in offspring that are genetically different from either parent.

How Do Protists Reproduce Asexually?

Method	Description
Binary fission	A unicellular organism reproduces by binary fission. In binary fission, the organism splits in half after replicating its DNA. In eukaryotic cells, this process is called *mitosis*.
Budding	Part of the parent organism pinches off and forms a new organism.
Fragmentation	Part of a multicellular organism breaks off and grows into a new organism.

LOOKING CLOSER

1. Compare How does binary fission differ from mitosis?

____

____

____

____

How Do Protists Reproduce Sexually?

During sexual reproduction, haploid reproductive cells, called **gametes**, join. When gametes join, they form a diploid **zygote**. Many protists reproduce sexually in response to environmental stress.

2. Identify Relationships What is the relationship between gametes and a zygote?

____

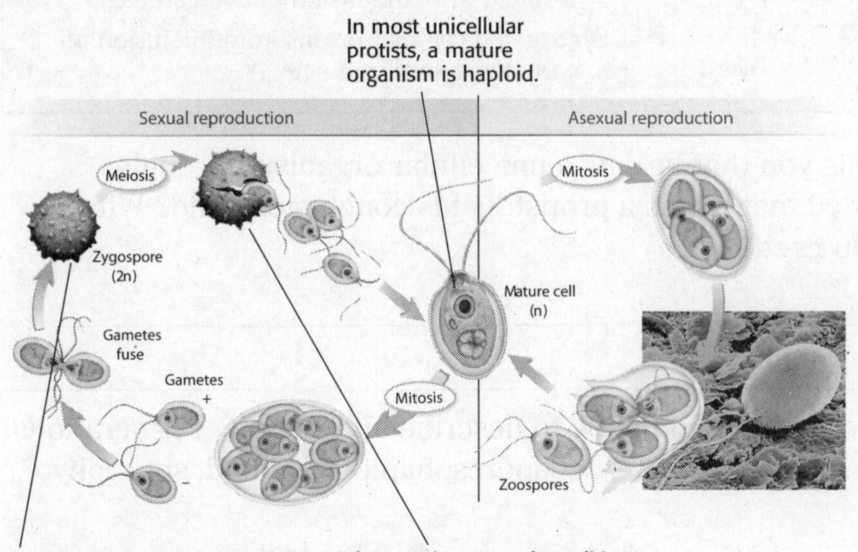

LOOKING CLOSER

3. Identify Is a zygospore haploid or diploid?

____

Many multicellular protists can reproduce both sexually and asexually in a process called **alternation of generations**. The diploid, spore-producing phase is called the *sporophyte generation*. The haploid, gamete-producing phase is called the *gametophyte generation*.

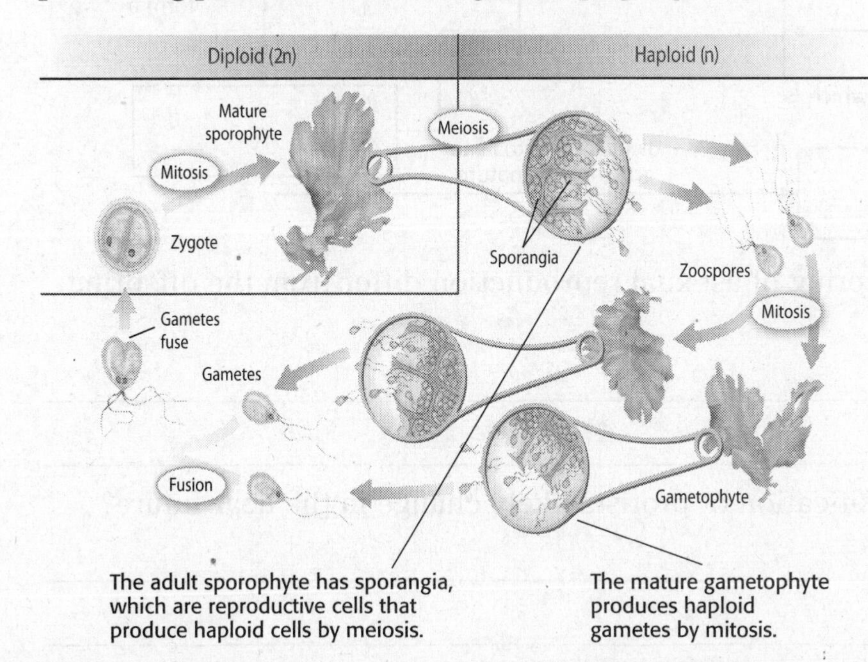

LOOKING CLOSER

4. Identify By what process does the gametophyte produce gametes?

____

5. Identify By what process does a sporophyte produce zoospores?

____

Name ______________________ Class ______________ Date ______________

Section 1 Review

SECTION VOCABULARY

alternation of generations within the life cycle of an organism, the occurrence of two or more distinct forms (generations), which differ from each other in method of reproduction; usually, one generation is haploid and reproduces sexually, and the other generation diploid and reproduces asexually

gamete a haploid reproductive cell that unites with another haploid reproductive cell to form a zygote

zygospore in some algae, a thick-walled protective structure that contains a zygote that resulted from the fusion of two gametes

zygote the cell that results from the fusion of gametes; a fertilized egg

1. Evaluate A classmate tells you that he saw a unicellular organism through a microscope and concluded that it was a protist. Is his conclusion valid? What other information do you need?

____

____

2. Organize Complete the concept map below to describe alternation of generations. Use the following terms: gamete, zygote, zoospores, haploid, diploid, sporophyte, and gametophyte.

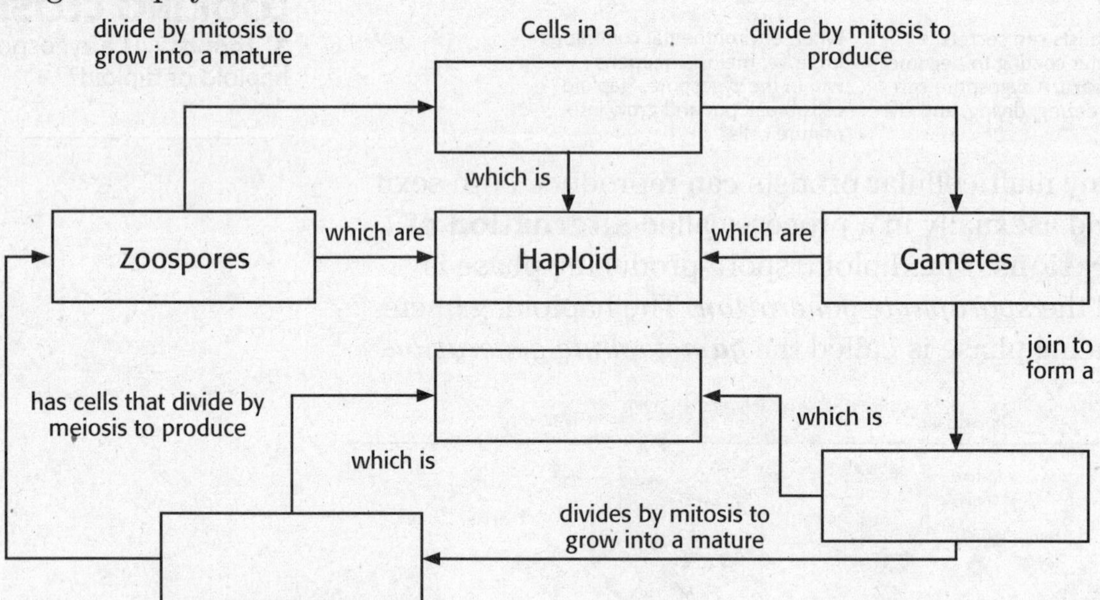

3. Compare How do the offspring of asexual reproduction differ from the offspring of sexual reproduction?

____

____

4. Explain Why will the classification of protists likely change in the near future?

____

____

SECTION 2

Groups of Protists

KEY IDEAS

As you read this section, keep these questions in mind:

- Why is it useful to group protists based on their methods of getting nutrition?
- What characteristic do animal-like protists share?
- What key characteristic do plant-like protists share?
- What characteristic makes fungus-like protists similar to fungi?

How Are Protists Grouped?

One common way to group protists is by their methods of feeding. Grouping protists in this way helps us understand their ecological roles. Protists can be divided into three groups based on how they feed.

READING TOOLBOX

Summarize In your notebook, create a three-column table to organize the main ideas in this section about animal-like protists, plant-like protists, and fungus-like protists.

Fungus-like protists, such as the slime mold *Physarum*, absorb nutrients from their environment.

Plant-like protists, such as the green algae *Acetebularia*, use energy from the sun to produce food through photosynthesis.

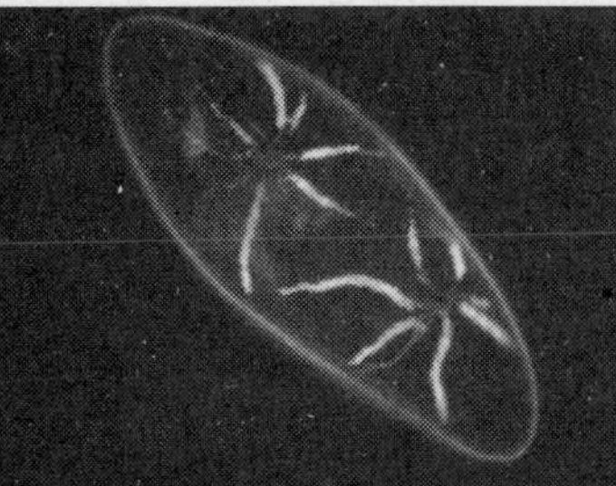

Animal-like protists, such as *Paramecium*, get energy by eating other protists and bacteria.

LOOKING CLOSER

1. Compare How do plant-like and fungus-like protists differ in their methods of feeding?

What Are Some Characteristics of Animal-like Protists?

Animal-like protists are sometimes called *protozoans*, which means "first animals." Like animals, these protists are heterotrophs. They must eat other organisms to get energy. All animal-like protists are unicellular, most can move, and most reproduce asexually. Many use extensions of the cell membrane called pseudopodia (singular, **pseudopodium**) to move and to capture prey. ☑

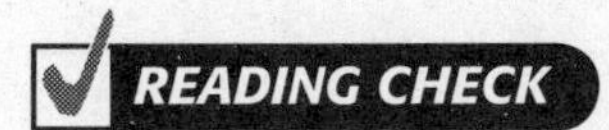

READING CHECK

2. Identify What are two functions of pseudopodia in animal-like protists?

____

____

Some Groups of Animal-like Protists		
Group and example	**Major structures**	**Other characteristics**
Amoeboids (*Amoeba proteus*)	• pseudopodia to move and capture prey	• found in fresh water, salt water, and soils • most free-living; some parasitic
Ciliates (*Paramecium*)	• short, hair-like structures called *cilia* for movement and hunting for food • tough, flexible outer covering for protection	• typically free-living • found in fresh water and salt water
Flagellates (*Leishmania*)	• flagella (one or many) for movement • cilia for movement in some • pseudopodia for movement and catching prey in some	• many free-living; some parasitic • free-living species typically found in fresh water
Sporozoans (*Plasmodium*)	• spore-like cells for reproduction	• parasitic • cause disease • do not move

LOOKING CLOSER

3. List Identify three groups of animal-like protists that have parasitic members.

____

____

____

4. Identify What are two functions of cilia in animal-like protists?

____

____

What Are Some Characteristics of Plant-like Protists?

Plant-like protists include phytoplankton and algae. These protists are the major producers in aquatic ecosystems. Most plant-like protists can get energy through photosynthesis. However, different kinds of plant-like protists use different pigments for photosynthesis.

Diatoms

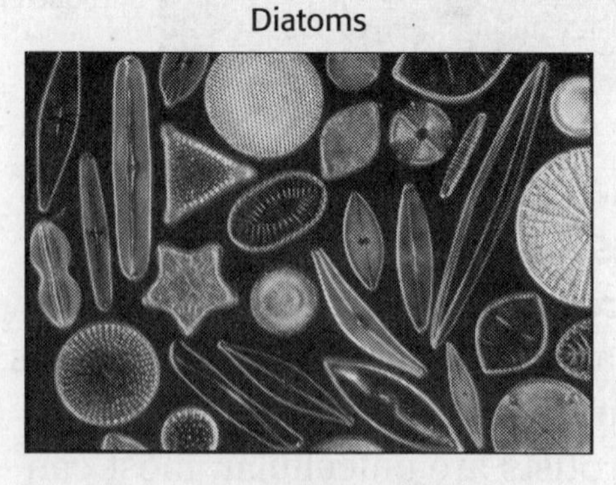

Dinoflagellates

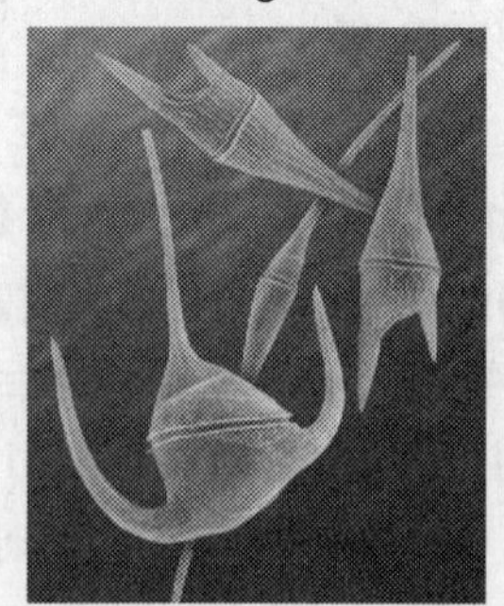

Critical Thinking

5. Predict What would happen to aquatic ecosystems if all plant-like protists were removed?

____

____

____

____

____

____

Some Groups of Plant-like Protists		
Group and example	**Major structures**	**Other characteristics**
Diatoms (*Cyclotella*)	• glassy double shells made of silica or calcium carbonate	• unicellular • found in salt water and fresh water
Euglenoids (*Euglena*)	• flagella for movement • in some, an eyespot that detects light	• unicellular • found in fresh water • some heterotrophic
Dinoflagellates (*Ceratium*)	• typically two flagella for movement • cellulose coats for protection	• unicellular • many found in salt water • some heterotrophic
Red algae (*Corillina*)	• pigments that can absorb blue light in deep water	• mostly multicellular • typically found in warm ocean environments • in some, calcium carbonate in cell walls
Brown algae (*Macrocystis*)	• a root-like *holdfast* • a stem-like *stipe* • leaf-like *blades*	• multicellular • found in cool ocean environments • the only algae that have differentiated tissues
Green algae (*Ulva*)	• cell walls contain cellulose	• some unicellular; some multicellular • use same photosynthetic pigments that plants do

LOOKING CLOSER

6. Identify What two groups of unicellular plant-like protists have flagella?

____

____

____

7. List What are three groups of multicellular plant-like protists?

____

____

____

What Are Some Characteristics of Fungus-like Protists?

Like fungi, fungus-like protists absorb nutrients from their environment and reproduce by releasing spores. Scientists once classified fungus-like protists as fungi. However, genetic studies show that they are not closely related. Fungus-like protists include slime molds, water molds, and downy mildews. Many water molds and downy mildews break down, or decompose, dead organisms. Others are parasites.

Cellular slime molds usually live as separate cells. Under dry conditions or when there is little food, the cells form colonies and release spores. The colony is a **plasmodium**, a mass of cytoplasm that has many nuclei. If the plasmodium begins to dry out or starve, it divides into many small mounds and releases spores. ☑

8. Identify Under what conditions do cellular slime molds join together to form a plasmodium?

____

____

____

Name ______________________ Class ______________ Date ______________

Section 2 Review

SECTION VOCABULARY

plasmodium the multinucleate cytoplasm of a slime mold that is surrounded by a membrane and that moves as a mass	**pseudopodium** a retractable, temporary cytoplasmic extension that functions in food ingestion and movement in certain amoeboid cells

1. **List** What are three feeding methods that scientists use to classify protists?

2. **Infer** Why is it useful to classify protists by feeding method?

3. **Analyze Methods** What might be a major drawback of grouping protists based on how they get food?

4. **Identify** What characteristic do animal-like protists share with animals?

5. **Identify** Which group of animal-like protists has only parasitic members?

6. **Explain** What is the general difference between flagellates and dinoflagellates?

7. **Identify** What are two ways that fungi and fungus-like protists are similar?

8. **Compare** How does a plasmodium differ from a typical single cell?

Name ______________________ Class ______________ Date ______________

CHAPTER 21 Protists

SECTION 3

Protists and Humans

KEY IDEAS

As you read this section, keep these questions in mind:

- What are seven diseases that protists cause?
- How do protists affect the environment?
- What are five examples of the ways that humans use protists in industry?

What Are Some Diseases Caused by Protists?

Many human diseases are caused by protists. Protist parasites are a major cause of illness and death, especially in the developing world. Some of these diseases are described in the table below.

Disease and parasite	How it is spread	Symptoms
Giardiasis (*Giardia*)	drinking water contaminated with animal (including human) feces	severe diarrhea and cramps
Amoebic dysentery (*Entamoeba histolytica*)	by contaminated water; in raw fruits and vegetables washed with contaminated water	pain, bloody diarrhea, fever; liver, lungs, or brain damage, death (rarely)
Toxoplasmosis (*Toxoplasma gondii*)	through feces of an infected cat; eating undercooked meat	flu-like symptoms; nerve, brain, or eye damage (rarely); can cause birth defects
Trichomoniasis (*Trichomonas vaginalis*)	sexually transmitted	colored discharge, itching, urge to urinate
Cryptosporidiosis (*Cryptosporidium*)	by contaminated water or objects; in uncooked food	severe cramps and diarrhea
Chagas' disease (*Trypanosoma cruzi*)	through the feces of kissing bugs	can damage the heart, esophagus, and large intestine
Malaria (*Plasmodium*)	by the bite of an infected mosquito	anemia and cycles of fever; can lead to ruptured spleen, kidney failure, coma, brain damage, and death

Reorganize On a sheet of paper, rearrange the table of diseases caused by parasites to present the information in a different way. For example, you could group the diseases by how they are spread or their symptoms.

Talk About It

Discuss In a small group, talk about some ways people may be able to prevent he spread of each of these diseases.

LOOKING CLOSER

1. List Which of these diseases can be spread by contaminated water?

____

____

2. Identify Which of these diseases is spread by mosquitoes?

____

What Roles Do Protists Play?

Protists make up a large percentage of the plankton in the oceans. They form the base of almost all freshwater and ocean food chains. Other protists are important decomposers. They break down the bodies of once-living things. Decomposition releases nutrients, such as carbon, nitrogen, and other minerals, back into the environment. These nutrients can then be used by other organisms. ☑

3. Explain What is the function of decomposition in an ecosystem?

____

____

____

Sometimes, protists can harm the environment by producing deadly blooms. An **algal bloom** is a rapid increase in the population of algae in an aquatic ecosystem. Algal blooms typically happen during warm seasons, when nutrients in ocean water are plentiful.

A *red tide* is caused by blooms of dinoflagellates. Dinoflagellates produce toxins. Humans can become ill if they eat fish or shellfish from the location of a red tide. When the protists in the bloom die, bacteria decompose them. Decomposition uses up oxygen in the water. Low oxygen levels can kill large numbers of fish and other marine animals.

Background

Recall that in *symbiosis*, two species live closely together. The relationship may benefit both species, benefit one and harm the other, or benefit one and have no effect on the other.

Symbiotic protists make up about 15% of the species on Earth. Some photosynthetic protists live with corals. The protists supply the coral with nutrients. The coral provides the protists with a stable environment and some minerals. Many protists live in the digestive tracts of animals, including cattle, termites, and humans. The animals could not digest their food without the help of these protists.

Critical Thinking

4. Infer A lichen is an association between a protist (an alga) and a fungus. What benefit do you think the alga provides to the fungus?

____

____

____

____

How Do Humans Use Protists?

Protists and their products are used in many foods, consumer products, and in scientific research.

Protist or protist product	Uses
Carrageenan, agar, and alginate	thickener in foods such as ice cream, salad dressings, and gelatin desserts
Agar	gelatin capsules for medication
Carrageenan	paints, fire-fighting foam, and cosmetics
Empty shells of diatoms	abrasives in cleaning agents and toothpastes, reflective roadway paint, natural insect control
Slime molds	studied as models of cell movement and cell signaling

Name ______________________ Class ______________ Date ______________

Section 3 Review

SECTION VOCABULARY

algal bloom a rapid increase in the population of algae in an aquatic ecosystem	

1. List Identify seven diseases that protists can cause in humans.

____

____

2. Identify What are three ways that disease-causing protists can infect humans?

____

____

____

3. Identify What are two major roles that protists play in aquatic food chains?

____

____

4. Describe Describe two ways red tides can harm fish and other marine animals.

____

____

____

5. Explain Why do algal blooms cause a decrease in oxygen levels in seawater?

____

____

6. Describe Describe the relationship between some photosynthetic protists and corals.

____

____

____

7. List Identify five common products that are made using protists.

____

____

____

Name ______________________ Class ______________ Date ______________

CHAPTER 22 Fungi

SECTION 1

Characteristics of Fungi

KEY IDEAS

As you read this section, keep these questions in mind:

- What are three characteristics that all fungi share?
- How is the structure of a fungus related to the way in which a fungus takes in nutrients?
- What is the difference between sexual and asexual production of spores in fungi?

READING TOOLBOX

Learn New Words As you read this section, underline words that you don't know. When you figure out what the words mean, write the words and their definitions in your notebook.

What Are Fungi?

Fungi are a diverse group of organisms, but all fungi share characteristics in common. The three common characteristics of fungi are described in the table below.

Characteristic	Description
Threadlike bodies	Fungi are made of long, thin filaments called **hyphae** (singular, *hypha*). The main body of a fungus is made up of loosely tangled hyphae. Reproductive structures, such as mushrooms, are made up of tightly arranged hyphae.
Cell walls made of chitin	The cells of fungi have cell walls made of chitin. **Chitin** is a tough carbohydrate that is also found in the hard outer covering of insects.
Absorb nutrients from the environment	Fungi are heterotrophic. They cannot make their own food or move to capture food. Instead, they get energy by breaking down materials in the environment and absorbing their nutrients.

LOOKING CLOSER

1. Describe How do fungi get energy?

____

____

____

How Does the Structure of a Fungus Help It Absorb Nutrients?

Fungi release enzymes to break down living and nonliving materials into nutrients. They absorb these nutrients through their many hyphae. The long and thin structure of hyphae gives fungi a large surface area to absorb nutrients through. Fungi that absorb nutrients from dead organisms are called **saprobes**. These fungi help to recycle the nutrients in an ecosystem. Fungi that absorb nutrients from living organisms are called *parasites*. ☑

2. Identify What structures enable fungi to absorb nutrients?

____

The main body of a fungus is a tangled mass of hyphae called a **mycelium**. In fungi that produce mushrooms, shown on the next page, the mycelium is hidden in the ground. In some fungi, hyphae can also form rootlike structures, called **rhizoids**, that hold the fungi in place.

STRUCTURE OF HYPHAE

Hyphae contain many cells with haploid nuclei. In some fungi, these cells do not have cell walls between them. In other fungi, the cells of hyphae are separated by partial cell walls, called *septa*. Septa, shown below, contain large gaps. These gaps allow cytoplasm, nutrients, and some organelles to flow easily through the hyphae.

Background
Recall that *haploid* nuclei contain one set of an organism's chromosomes.

Critical Thinking
3. Apply Concepts What material are septa made of?

____

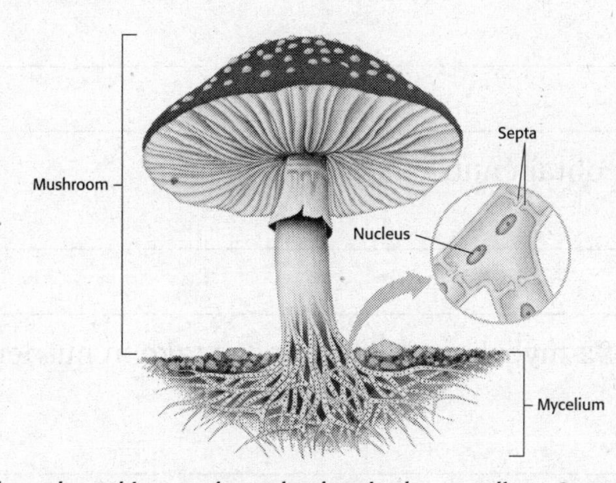

The enlarged image shows hyphae in the mycelium. Septa separate the cells in these hyphae. Gaps in the septa allow nutrients to flow through the hyphae.

LOOKING CLOSER
4. Explain How can nutrients move from the ground to the mushroom?

____
____
____

How Do Fungi Reproduce?

Most fungi reproduce both sexually and asexually. Fungi that do not have an observed sexual stage are called *imperfect fungi*. In asexual reproduction, specialized hyphae form long stalks. Haploid spores are produced by mitosis in the tips of the stalks. Fungi that grow from these spores are genetically identical to their parent. ☑

5. Describe How do fungi that grow from spores produced by asexual reproduction compare to their parent?

____
____
____

In sexual reproduction, hyphae from one fungus join, or fuse, with hyphae from a fungus with the opposite mating type. The fused hyphae form a reproductive structure. Haploid nuclei from the two mating types fuse inside the structure to form diploid nuclei. These nuclei undergo meiosis to produce haploid spores. Fungi that grow from these spores are genetically different from their parents.

Some types of fungi usually exist in a unicellular state called a yeast. Yeasts usually reproduce asexually by budding. In budding, a part of a parent cell pinches off to form a new identical cell.

Name ______________ Class ______________ Date ______________

Section 1 Review

SECTION VOCABULARY

chitin a carbohydrate that forms part of the cell walls of fungi and part of the exoskeleton of arthropods, such as insects and crustaceans

hypha a nonreproductive filament of a fungus

mycelium the mass of fungal filaments, or hyphae, that forms the body of a fungus

rhizoid in fungi and nonvascular plants, a rootlike structure that holds the organism in place and aids in absorption

saprobe an organism that absorbs nutrients from dead or decaying organic matter

1. List What are three characteristics that all fungi share?

____

____

2. Describe How do fungal parasites obtain nutrients?

____

____

3. Explain How does the structure of a mycelium help a fungus take in nutrients from the soil?

____

____

____

4. Explain How does the structure of septa help a fungus move nutrients from one cell to another in hyphae?

____

____

5. Identify What type of reproduction takes place in a mushroom?

____

6. Compare What is different about the division of nuclei to produce haploid spores in asexual reproduction and in sexual reproduction?

____

____

____

7. Describe How does sexual reproduction in fungi begin?

____

____

Name ______________________ Class ______________ Date ______________

CHAPTER 22 Fungi

SECTION 2

Groups of Fungi

KEY IDEAS

As you read this section, keep these questions in mind:

- Which group of fungi gives us clues about how fungi evolved?
- Which reproductive structure characterizes the zygote fungi?
- Which reproductive structure characterizes the sac fungi?
- What structure makes spores in club fungi?
- What are two symbiotic partnerships that fungi form?

How Do Scientists Classify Fungi?

Scientists classify fungi into four phyla, shown below, based on the type of sexual reproductive structures they form. Most fungi reproduce both asexually and sexually. Sexual reproduction in fungi involves two mating types. These mating types are not referred to as male and female. Instead, they are called "+" and "–." ☑

Phylum	Type of fungi	Reproductive characteristics
Chytridiomycota	chytrids	produce spores or gametes that have flagella
Zygomycota	zygote fungi	sexual reproductive structures contain zygotes in a tough capsule
Ascomycota	sac fungi	saclike sexual reproductive structures produce spores
Basidiomycota	club fungi	clublike sexual reproductive structures produce spores

READING TOOLBOX

Compare After you read about zygote fungi, sac fungi, and club fungi, make a chart that shows the similarities and differences in their methods of reproduction.

READING CHECK

1. Explain How do scientists classify different types of fungi?

____

____

____

How Do Chytrids Provide Clues About the Evolution of Fungi?

Chytrids are a group of fungi that live mostly in the water. They produce gametes or spores with flagella. Chytrids were once classified with protists because they share characteristics with them. Protists also live in the water, and many protists have flagella to help them swim. In addition, many protists and chytrids are unicellular. ☑

However, chytrids also share characteristics with fungi. Like all fungi, they have chitin in their cell walls, digest food outside their bodies, and have hyphae.

The similarities between chytrids and protists suggest that fungi may have evolved in the water from protists that have flagella. Fossils of the earliest fungi show that they produced spores and gametes with flagella.

Background

Recall that *flagella* are long, hairlike structures that grow out of cells and enable the cells to move.

2. List Name three ways in which chytrid fungi are like protists.

____

____

____

What Are the Characteristics of Zygote Fungi?

During sexual reproduction in zygote fungi, hyphae from different mating types join, or fuse. Fused hyphae form a reproductive structure called a zygosporangium. A **zygosporangium** is a tough capsule that contains and protects zygotes. It grows to produce a *sporangium* (plural *sporangia*) that releases spores produced by meiosis.

However, zygote fungi usually reproduce asexually. During asexual reproduction, specialized hyphae produce sporangia. Haploid spores form within these sporangia by mitosis. The spores are genetically identical to the parent.

Background
Recall that a *zygote* is a cell that results from the fusion of nuclei from two parents.

Background
Recall that *spores* are reproductive cells that can develop into an adult without fusion with another cell.

Critical Thinking
3. Explain Can a zygote fungus reproduce if there are no fungi of the opposite mating type nearby? Explain your answer.

____

____

Critical Thinking
4. Apply Concepts How do zygote fungi that grow from spores produced by sexual reproduction compare to their parents?

____

____

____

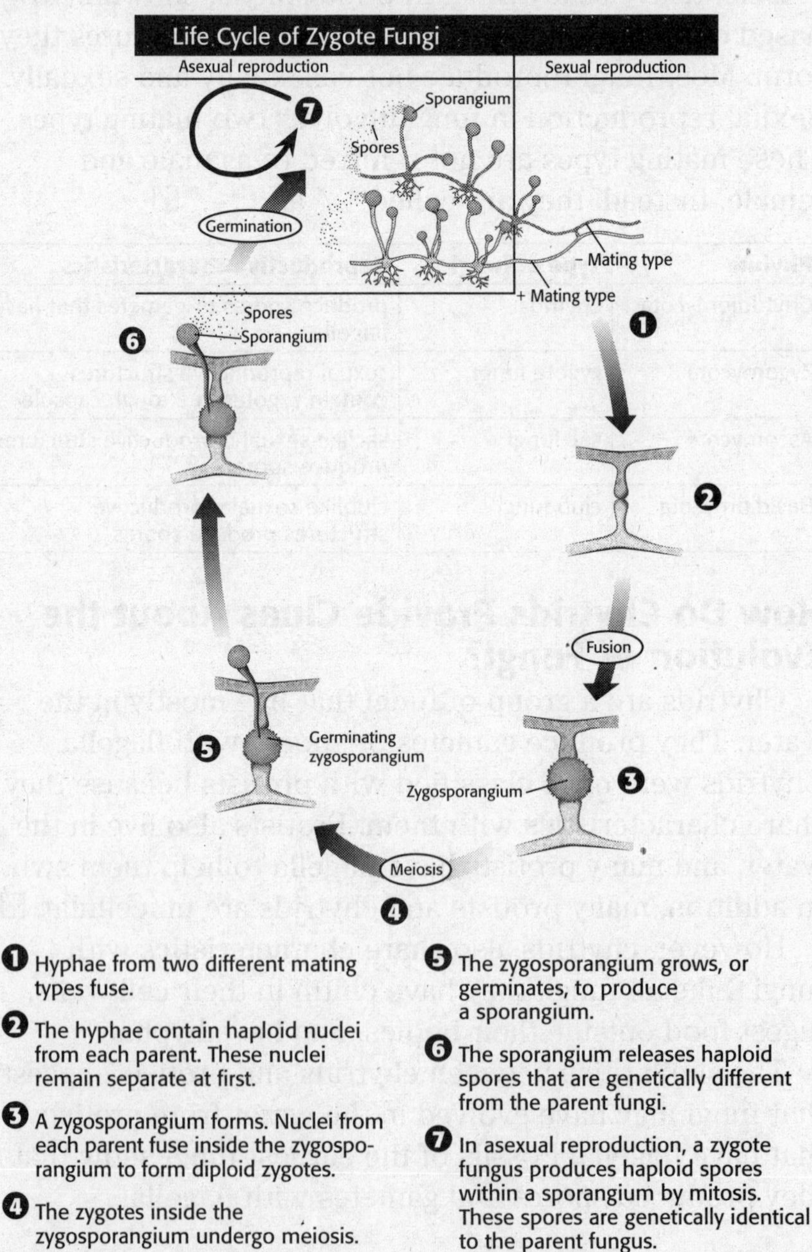

1. Hyphae from two different mating types fuse.
2. The hyphae contain haploid nuclei from each parent. These nuclei remain separate at first.
3. A zygosporangium forms. Nuclei from each parent fuse inside the zygosporangium to form diploid zygotes.
4. The zygotes inside the zygosporangium undergo meiosis.
5. The zygosporangium grows, or germinates, to produce a sporangium.
6. The sporangium releases haploid spores that are genetically different from the parent fungi.
7. In asexual reproduction, a zygote fungus produces haploid spores within a sporangium by mitosis. These spores are genetically identical to the parent fungus.

LOOKING CLOSER
5. Identify In what structure do nuclei from two different mating types fuse?

____

What Are the Characteristics of Sac Fungi?

In sexual reproduction in sac fungi, hyphae from different mating types fuse. Nuclei from one hypha move into the other. Hyphae form that have nuclei from both parents. Cells with two nuclei, called *dikaryotic* cells, form a structure called an *ascocarp*. Nuclei within the cells fuse and produce spores by meiosis. The spores are contained in a saclike structure called an **ascus** (plural, *asci*). ☑

However, sac fungi usually reproduce asexually. They produce spores, called *conidia*, by mitosis. Conidia form in chains on specialized hyphae called *conidiophores*.

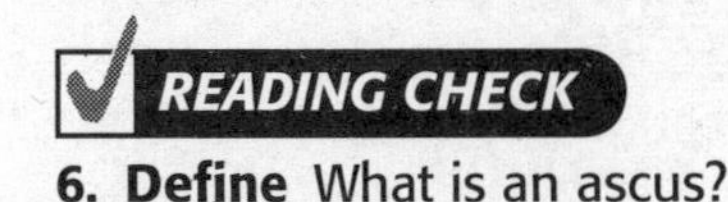

6. Define What is an ascus?

____

____

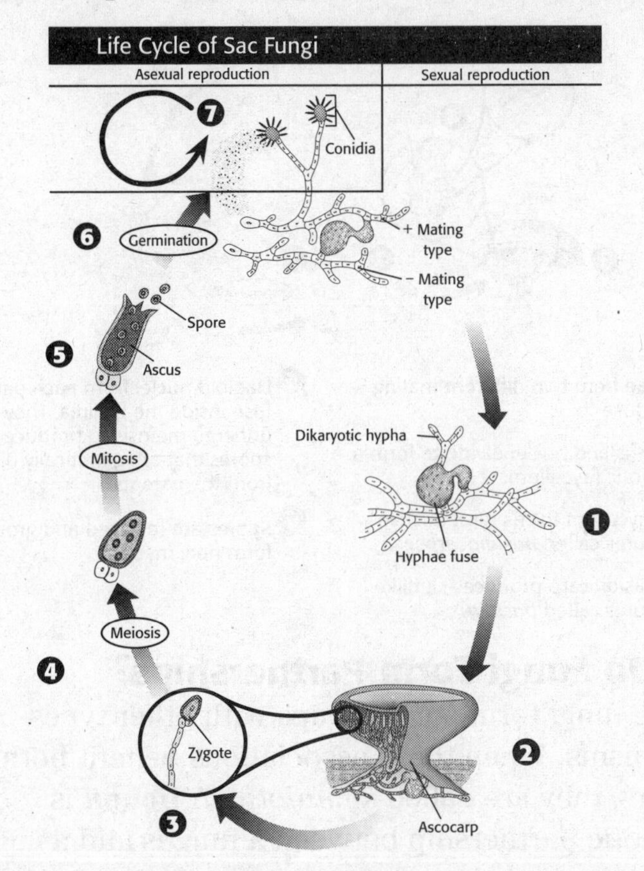

1. Hyphae from two different mating types fuse. Nuclei from one mating type move into hyphae from the other. This creates dikaryotic hyphae, or hyphae with two nuclei in each cell.
2. A structure called an ascocarp forms. The cells of the ascocarp are dikaryotic.
3. Asci form within the ascocarp. Haploid nuclei from each parent in the asci fuse to form diploid zygotes.
4. The zygotes inside the asci undergo meiosis. This produces four haploid cells that are genetically different from the parents.
5. These cells undergo mitosis to produce eight spores within an ascus. The spores are released from the ascus.
6. The spores grow to form new fungi that are genetically different from the parent fungi.
7. In asexual reproduction, a sac fungus produces haploid spores, called conidia, on conidiophores by mitosis. Conidia are genetically identical to the parent fungus.

Talk About It

Discuss With a partner or in a small group, discuss how asexual reproduction is the same and how it is different in zygote fungi and sac fungi.

LOOKING CLOSER

7. Describe What do the dikaryotic cells in an ascocarp contain?

____

____

LOOKING CLOSER

8. Identify Where does meiosis take place in sac fungi?

____

What Are the Characteristics of Club Fungi?

Asexual reproduction is not common in club fungi. During sexual reproduction, club fungi form a reproductive structure, called a *basidiocarp*, when hyphae from opposite mating types fuse. A mushroom is one example of a basidiocarp. Club-shaped structures, called basidia (singular, **basidium**), form on a basidiocarp. Spores are produced by meiosis inside these basidia.

Critical Thinking

9. Infer Why do you think mushrooms grow above the ground?

____

____

____

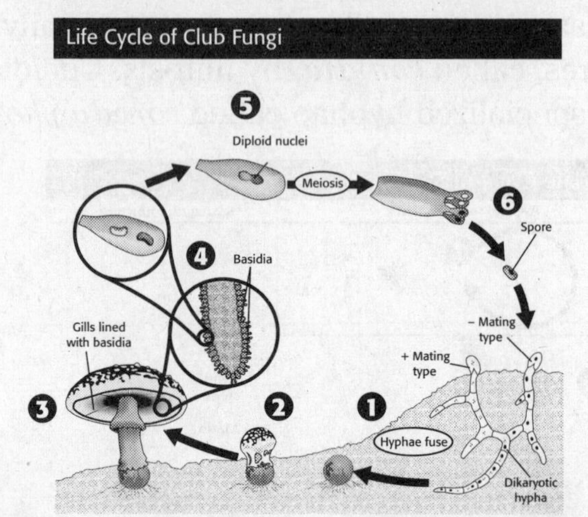

1. Hyphae from two different mating types fuse.
2. The cells and nuclei divide to form a dikaryotic mycelium.
3. The mycelium forms reproductive structures called *basidiocarps*.
4. The basidiocarp produces clublike structures called *basidia*.
5. Haploid nuclei from each parent fuse inside the basidia. They then undergo meiosis to produce haploid spores that are genetically different from the parents.
6. Spores are released and grow to form new mycelia.

LOOKING CLOSER

10. Identify Where do nuclei from each parent fuse?

____

How Do Fungi Form Partnerships?

Some fungi form partnerships with other types of organisms. When these associations benefit both members, they are called *symbiotic*. A **lichen** is a symbiotic partnership between a fungus and a photosynthetic organism, such as a cyanobacterium or a green alga. The fungus provides protection, vitamins, and minerals to the photosynthetic partner. The photosynthetic partner supplies carbohydrates to the fungus. ☑

A **mycorrhiza** is a symbiotic partnership between fungi and the roots of nearly all plants. The fungal hyphae grow inside or around the plant roots and into the soil. The hyphae bring minerals from the soil to the roots of the plant. The plant supplies carbohydrates to the fungus.

11. Describe How do the fungi in lichen benefit their photosynthetic partners?

____

____

____

Name ______________________ Class ______________ Date ______________

Section 2 Review

SECTION VOCABULARY

ascus the spore sac where ascomycetes produce ascospores

basidium a structure that produces asexual spores in basidiomycetes

lichen a mass of fungal and algal cells that grow together in a symbiotic relationship and that are usually found on rocks or trees

mycorrhiza a symbiotic association between fungi and plant roots

zygosporangium in members of the phylum Zygomycota, a sexual structure that is formed by the fusion of two gametangia and that contains one or more zygotes that resulted from the fusion of gametes produced by the gametangia

1. **Explain** What do the similarities between chytrids and protists suggest?

____

____

2. **Summarize** Fill in the blank spaces in the diagrams below to show the characteristic sexual reproductive structures of each type of fungi.

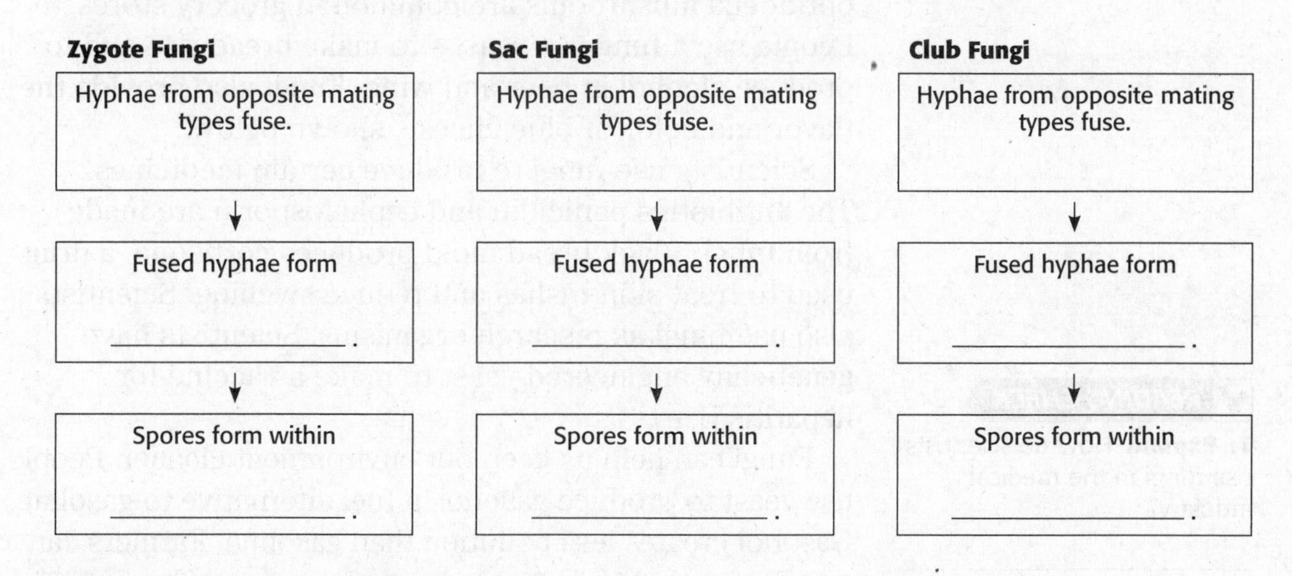

3. **Describe** What feature of a zygosporangium allows it to protect zygotes?

____

4. **Describe** What type of structure are mushrooms, and in what types of fungi do they appear?

____

5. **Understand Relationships** How do both organisms in a mycorrhiza benefit from their symbiotic relationship?

____

____

____

Name ______________________ Class ______________ Date ______________

CHAPTER 22 Fungi

SECTION 3

Fungi and Humans

KEY IDEAS

As you read this section, keep these questions in mind:

- What are some common ways in which humans use fungi?
- How are fungi ecologically important?
- What are some diseases that fungi cause in humans?

READING TOOLBOX

Make A List As you read this section, make a list of the different ways in which fungi affect humans. Be sure to include both positive and negative effects.

How Do Humans Use Fungi?

Fungi have a great impact on industry. Different types of fungi are commonly used for food, medicines, research, alternative fuels, and pest control.

Fungi can often be eaten as food. Many different mushrooms are safe to eat. White button, shiitake, and portabella mushrooms are common in grocery stores. People use a fungus—yeast—to make bread rise and to produce alcohol in beer and wine. Fungi also provide the flavor and color of blue cheese, shown below.

Scientists use fungi to produce certain medicines. The antibiotics penicillin and cephalosporin are made from fungi. Black bread mold produces cortisone, a drug used to treat skin rashes and reduce swelling. Scientists also use fungi as research organisms. Scientists have genetically engineered yeast to make a vaccine for hepatitis B. ☑

Fungi can help us keep our environment cleaner. People use yeast to produce gasohol, a fuel alternative to gasoline. Gasohol creates less pollution than gasoline. Farmers can use fungi to kill insects that harm their crops. This use of fungi reduces use of harsh pesticides. ☑

READING CHECK

1. Explain How do scientists use fungi in the medical industry?

____

____

READING CHECK

2. Define What is gasohol?

____

____

The dark lines in blue cheese (left) are fungi. The fungi give blue cheese its color and flavor. Bakers use yeast to make bread (right) rise.

Talk About It

Discuss With a partner or in a small group, talk about different uses of fungi.

What Is the Role of Fungi in Ecosystems?

Fungi play many important roles in an ecosystem. The main role of fungi in ecosystems is as decomposers. Fungi help decompose, or break down, dead organisms. They are one of the few types of organisms that can break down wood from dead trees. As decomposers, fungi release nutrients from dead organisms into the environment. Other organisms can use these nutrients to live and grow.

As part of lichens, fungi slowly break down rocks. They release minerals from the rocks that other organisms in the environment can use. As part of mycorrhizae, fungi absorb minerals from the soil and bring them into plant roots. Almost all plants have mycorrhizae. Some plants, such as orchids, could not survive without them.

Critical Thinking

3. Predict Without fungi, what would happen to the nutrients in dead organisms?

____

____

____

____

What Diseases Do Fungi Cause in Humans?

Fungi cause diseases in humans by absorbing nutrients from their tissues, and by making toxins. **Dermatophytes** are fungi that infect the skin, hair, and nails. Some diseases caused by fungi are described in the table below. ☑

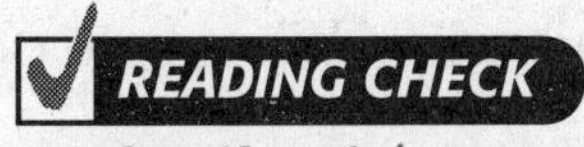

4. Identify What type of infections do dermatophytes cause?

____

____

Disease	Description
Toenail fungus	Dermatophytes that infect the nails cause toenail fungus.
Ringworm and athlete's foot	Dermatophytes that infect the skin can cause ringworm and athlete's foot. These fungi absorb nutrients from the skin and release metabolic wastes that irritate the skin.
Yeast infections	Yeast normally lives inside the body. However, antibiotics, hormones, or illness may enable the yeast to grow too much. This results in a yeast infection. Yeast infections occur on tissues of the reproductive organs and in the mouth.
Histoplasmosis	Histoplasmosis is a lung infection caused by a fungus that grows in bat and bird feces. When its spores are breathed in, this fungus can cause serious respiratory illness.

LOOKING CLOSER

5. Explain How can a yeast infection occur?

____

____

____

____

Many fungi make toxins that can be dangerous to humans. Toxins in certain mushrooms can cause vomiting, diarrhea, liver damage, and even death. A type of fungus that grows on corn, peanuts, and cottonseed makes *aflatoxins*, which can cause liver cancer. Molds that grow in houses and buildings can cause allergic reactions.

Name ______________________ Class ______________ Date ______________

Section 3 Review

SECTION VOCABULARY

dermatophyte a fungus that infects the skin, hair, or nails	

1. List Name four foods that are made using fungi.

____

____

2. Describe How have scientists used yeast in the medical industry?

____

____

3. Identify What two antibiotics are made using fungi?

____

4. Describe What is the main role of fungi in ecosystems?

____

____

5. Describe What role do fungi play in mycorrhizae?

____

____

6. Describe How do fungi make the minerals in rocks available to other organisms?

____

____

7. List Name four diseases that fungi can cause in humans.

____

____

8. Explain What are aflatoxins, and how can they be harmful to humans?

____

____

9. Apply Concepts Why can it be dangerous to eat mushrooms in the wild?

____

____

Name ______________ Class ______________ Date ______________

SECTION 1

Introduction to Plants

KEY IDEAS

As you read this section, keep these questions in mind:

- What are the key characteristics of plants?
- What adaptations helped plants live successfully on land?
- Why is a plant's life cycle called "alternation of generations"?

What Are Characteristics of Plants?

The plant kingdom is a diverse group of species. However, all plants are multicellular eukaryotes. The cells of plants have cell walls, as shown below. Most plants are *autotrophs* that produce their own food by photosynthesis.

Recall that photosynthesis is a process in which plants use the energy from sunlight to make food from water and carbon dioxide. Photosynthesis takes place in organelles called *chloroplasts*. To survive, plants need sunlight, water, air, and minerals. ☑

READING TOOLBOX

Summarize in Pairs Read this section quietly to yourself. Then, talk about the material with a partner. Together, try to figure out the parts that you didn't understand.

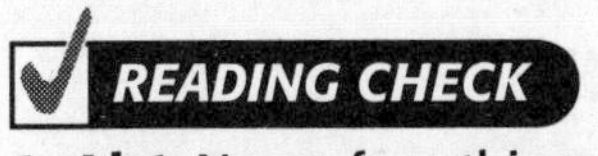

READING CHECK

1. List Name four things that plants need to survive.

____

____

____

____

Plant cell

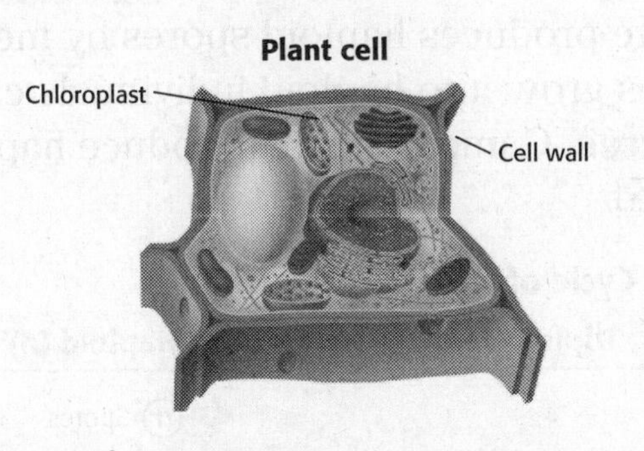

How Are Plants Adapted to Live on Land?

Plants probably evolved from green algae that lived in the water. To live on land, plants had to be able to absorb nutrients from their surroundings and prevent water loss. They also had to scatter, or disperse, their offspring.

Scientists divide plants into two main groups: vascular and nonvascular. *Vascular plants* have *vascular tissues*, which move nutrients throughout a plant. Vascular plants can photosynthesize when the soil surface is dry, because they have roots that can reach water below the surface.

Nonvascular plants do not have vascular tissues. Nonvascular plants cannot photosynthesize when the soil surface is dry, because they grow close to the soil surface and do not have roots.

Critical Thinking

2. Make Connections How does the way green algae obtain food suggest that plants evolved from them?

____

____

____

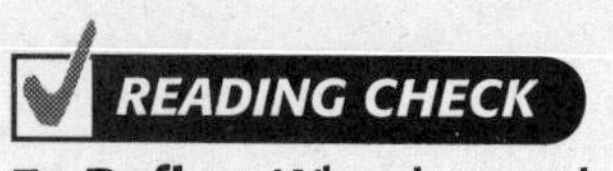

3. Define What is a cuticle?

____

____

____

4. Identify What do haploid spores produced by sporophytes become?

____

LOOKING CLOSER

5. Identify What is the diploid generation of a plant life cycle called?

____

____

ABSORBING NUTRIENTS AND SAVING WATER

On land, most vascular plants absorb nutrients through their roots. Symbiotic relationships, called *mycorrhizae*, between fungi and plant roots help plants obtain minerals from the soil. Most aboveground plant parts are covered by a waxy layer called a **cuticle**. The cuticle reduces water loss so that plants can live in dry habitats. ☑

DISPERSING OFFSPRING

Some plants produce reproductive cells called **spores** that can be dispersed by wind. Spores grow into adult plants without fertilization.

Other plants produce *pollen* grains. Pollen is scattered by wind and animals and brings sperm cells to eggs. After pollen fertilizes an egg, a zygote forms. The zygote becomes an embryo that is dispersed in a seed.

What Is the Basic Life Cycle of Plants?

After fertilization, the diploid zygote divides by mitosis to produce diploid individuals called **sporophytes**. A sporophyte produces haploid spores by meiosis. These spores grow into haploid individuals called **gametophytes**. Gametoyphytes produce haploid gametes by mitosis. ☑

Basic Life Cycle of a Plant

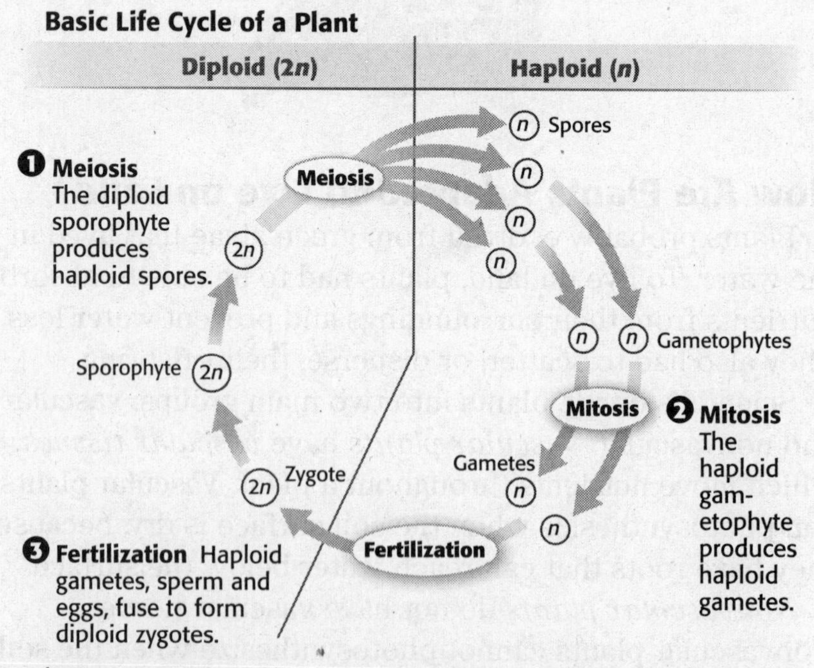

In plants, a generation of haploid gametophytes switches, or alternates, with a generation of diploid sporophytes. This type of life cycle is called *alternation of generations*.

Name ______________________ Class ______________ Date ______________

Section 1 Review

SECTION VOCABULARY

cuticle a waxy or fatty and watertight layer on the external wall of epidermal cells

gametophyte in alternation of generations, the phase in which gametes are formed; a haploid individual that produces gametes

spore a reproductive cell or multicellular structure that is resistant to environmental conditions and that can develop into an adult without fusion with another cell

sporophyte in plants and algae that have alternation of generations, the diploid individual or generation that produces haploid spores

1. List What are four key characteristics of plants?

2. Identify Where in plant cells does photosynthesis take place?

3. Explain How can fungi benefit plants?

4. Explain How do roots help vascular plants survive on land?

5. Define What is alternation of generations?

6. Describe What are gametophytes, and what is their role in plant reproduction?

7. Describe In the life cycle of a plant, how do sporophytes form?

Name ______________________ Class ______________ Date ______________

SECTION 2

Seedless Plants

KEY IDEAS

As you read this section, keep these questions in mind:
- What are the characteristics of nonvascular plants?
- What characterizes reproduction in nonvascular plants?
- How do seedless vascular plants differ from nonvascular plants?
- How does reproduction in a seedless vascular plant compare with reproduction in a nonvascular plant?

READING TOOLBOX

Compare As you read this section, make a chart comparing nonvascular plants and seedless vascular plants.

What Are the Characteristics of Nonvascular Plants?

There are two types of plants that do not have seeds: nonvascular plants and seedless vascular plants. Nonvascular plants reproduce by spores. They do not have true roots, stems, or leaves, which contain vascular tissues. As such, water and nutrients move between cells of nonvascular plants by osmosis and diffusion.

Osmosis and diffusion move materials slowly over short distances. Therefore, nonvascular plants must be small so that all their cells can get water and nutrients. ☑

1. Describe How do water and nutrients move through nonvascular plants?

____

____

Group	Description
Mosses	Mosses grow in moist places. They have green mats of gametophytes. Their sporophytes are stalks with a spore capsule that grow from gametophytes.
Liverworts	Liverworts have mats of gametophytes that look like stems and leaves. Their sporophytes are small stalks.
Hornworts	Hornworts have green horn-like sporophytes that grow upward from short, flat gametophytes.

How Do Nonvascular Plants Reproduce?

Like all plants, nonvascular plants have an alternation of generations. In nonvascular plants, the gametophyte is the main generation. That is, the gametophyte is usually larger than the sporophyte. The life cycle of a nonvascular plant is shown on the next page.

Sporophytes produce spores in a spore capsule called a **sporangium**. The gametophytes produce gametes in two different structures. The structure that produces eggs is called an **archegonium**. The structure that produces sperm is called an **antheridium**. The gametophytes of nonvascular plants must be covered by water for fertilization to occur. ☑

Background

Recall that *fertilization* is the joining of a male and female gamete (sperm and egg) to form a zygote.

2. Identify What does an antheridium produce?

____

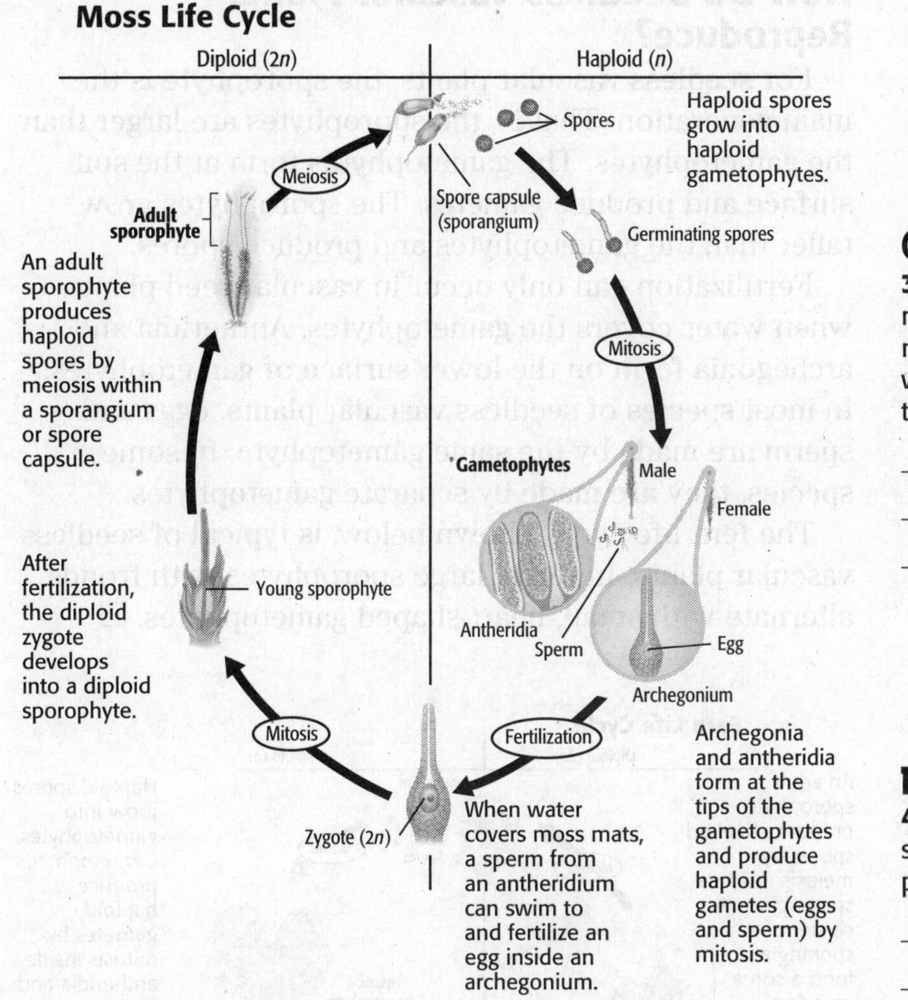

Critical Thinking

3. Make Connections Why must the gametophytes of nonvascular plants be covered with water for fertilization to occur?

____

____

____

What Are Seedless Vascular Plants?

Plants that have vascular tissues but do not produce seeds are *seedless vascular plants*. Seedless vascular plants have true roots, stems, and leaves. Their vascular tissues allow them to grow much larger than nonvascular plants. However, like nonvascular plants, seedless vascular plants need water for fertilization to occur. ☑

Club mosses are one group of seedless vascular plants. Unlike true mosses, club mosses have stems that branch from a flat, underground stem called a **rhizome**. Spores develop in sporangia on specialized leaves of club mosses.

The second group of seedless vascular plants includes ferns and similar species. Most fern sporophytes have leaves called **fronds** and rhizomes that are anchored by roots. A **sorus** (plural *sori*) is a brownish dot on a frond made of a cluster of sporangia.

LOOKING CLOSER

4. Identify Where on a sporophyte are spores produced?

____

____

5. Describe What is a seedless vascular plant?

____

____

____

Name ______________________ Class ______________ Date ____________

How Do Seedless Vascular Plants Reproduce?

For seedless vascular plants, the sporophyte is the main generation. That is, the sporophytes are larger than the gametophytes. The gametophytes form at the soil surface and produce gametes. The sporophytes grow taller than the gametophytes and produce spores.

Fertilization can only occur in vascular seed plants when water covers the gametophytes. Antheridia and archegonia form on the lower surface of gametophytes. In most species of seedless vascular plants, eggs and sperm are made by the same gametophyte. In some species, they are made by separate gametophytes.

The fern life cycle, shown below, is typical of seedless vascular plants. In ferns, large sporophytes with fronds alternate with small, heart-shaped gametophytes. ☑

Talk About It

Discuss With a partner or in a small group, talk about how reproduction in seedless vascular plants and nonvascular plants is the same and how it is different.

READING CHECK

6. Identify Does the life cycle of seedless vascular plants have an alternation of generations?

____

LOOKING CLOSER

7. Identify What are the brownish dots on fronds called, and what do they contain?

____

____

LOOKING CLOSER

8. Explain How does an adult sporophyte stay in the ground?

____

____

____

Fern Life Cycle

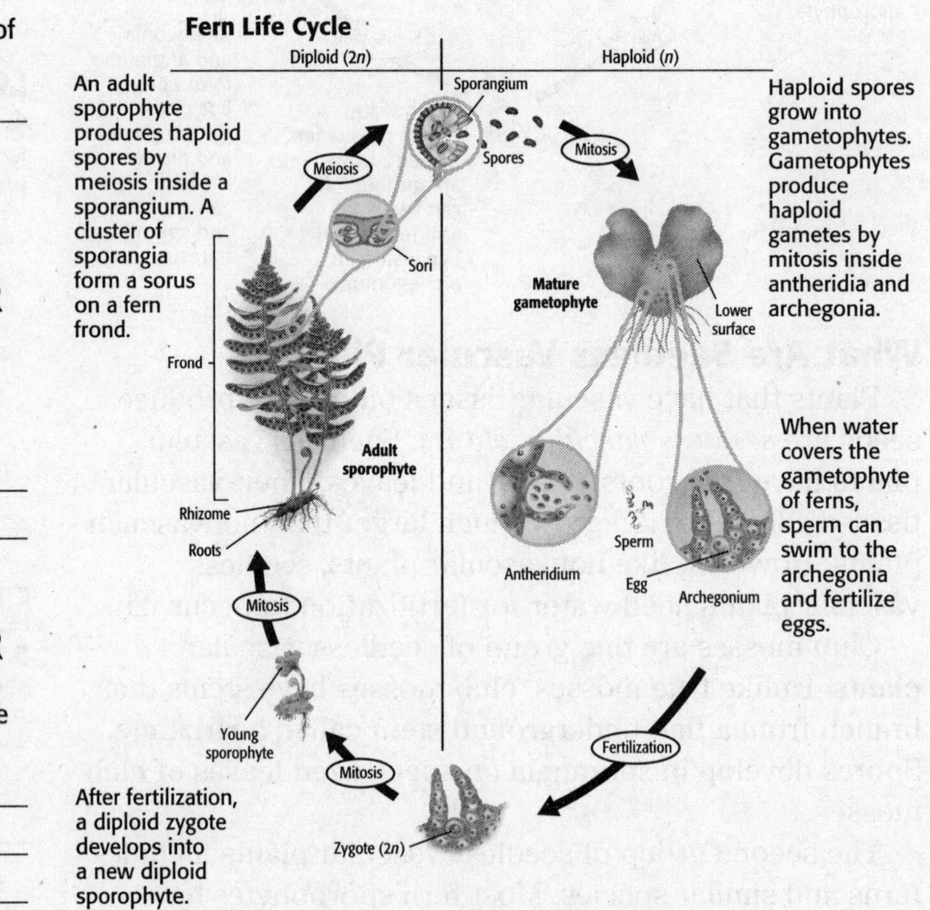

Name ____________________ Class ____________ Date ____________

Section 2 Review

SECTION VOCABULARY

antheridium a reproductive structure that produces male sex cells in flowerless and seedless plants

archegonium a female reproductive structure of small, nonvascular plants that produces a single egg and in which fertilization and development take place

frond the leaf of a fern or palm

rhizome a horizontal, underground stem that provides a mechanism for asexual reproduction

sorus a cluster of spores or sporangia

sporangium a specialized sac, case, capsule, or other structure that produces spores

1. **Explain** Why are nonvascular plants small?

____

____

____

2. **List** Identify three groups of nonvascular plants.

____

3. **Identify** What is the main generation in the life cycle of a nonvascular plant?

____

4. **Compare** Describe two ways in which seedless vascular plants are different from nonvascular plants.

____

____

____

____

5. **Identify** In addition to gametes, what is needed for fertilization to occur in both nonvascular plants and seedless vascular plants?

____

6. **Describe** What is the role of spores in the reproduction of nonvascular plants and seedless vascular plants?

____

____

7. **Identify** What two structures on the gametophytes of nonvascular plants and seedless vascular plants produce eggs and sperm?

____

Name ______________________ Class ______________ Date ______________

SECTION 3

Seed Plants

KEY IDEAS

As you read this section, keep these questions in mind:

- What are the two groups of seed plants?
- What characterizes reproduction in seed plants?
- What are the four major groups of living gymnosperms?
- What characterizes reproduction in a conifer?

READING TOOLBOX

Learn New Words As you read this section, underline words you don't understand. When you figure out what they mean, write the words and their definitions in your notebook.

What Is a Seed Plant?

Most plants living today are seed plants. Seeds plants have vascular tissues and produce seeds. Scientists classify seed plants into gymnosperms and angiosperms, described in the table below.

Type of seed plant	Description
Gymnosperm	The seeds of **gymnosperms** typically develop inside a cone, such as a pinecone.
Angiosperm	The seeds of **angiosperms** develop inside a fruit. Fruits develop from a plant structure called a flower. Therefore, angiosperms are flowering plants.

LOOKING CLOSER

1. Identify What develops inside the cones of gymnosperms?

____

How Do Seed Plants Reproduce?

Recall that seedless plants need water for fertilization to occur. Seed plants do not. Seed plants have a very tiny gametophyte and a much larger sporophyte. The sporophyte is the main generation in seed plants.

Sporophytes of seed plants produce two kinds of spores that develop into male or female gametophytes. Female gametophytes produce eggs, and male gametophytes produce sperm. The female gametophyte develops inside an **ovule**, which is part of the sporophyte. The male gametophyte develops inside a **pollen grain**. ☑

2. Describe Where does the male gametophyte of a seed plant develop, and what does it produce?

____

____

____

POLLINATION AND FERTILIZATION

The transfer of pollen grains from male structures to female structures is called **pollination**. Wind and animals help carry pollen grains to female structures.

Once on a female reproductive structure, a *pollen tube* grows from the pollen grain to the ovule. The pollen tube allows sperm to pass directly to an egg. The joining of an egg and sperm is called *fertilization*.

SEED FORMATION

After fertilization in seed plants, the ovule develops into a **seed**. The outer cell layers of an ovule harden to form a tough seed coat. The seed coat protects the *embryo* within the seed from harsh environmental conditions. ☑

Seeds also contain tissues that provide nutrients to the developing plant embryo. The seeds of some angiosperms contain a tissue called *endosperm* that nourishes the embryo.

3. Describe What is the function of a seed coat?

____

____

____

SEED DISPERSAL

Seeds are dispersed so that the new sporophytes can grow far away from the parent plant. This may prevent competition between parents and offspring for living space, water, nutrients, and light.

Many seeds have special structures that help carry them away from their parent plant. For example, dandelions have structures that act like parachutes and allow the seeds to drift long distances on the wind.

Fruits are important for seed dispersal by animals. Some fruits have hooks that stick to an animal's fur. They stay on the animal's fur while it moves and eventually fall off in new locations. Other fruits provide food for animals. The seeds within these fruits are spread to new areas when they pass through an animal's body.

Critical Thinking

4. Make Connections How can birds and holly berry trees benefit each other?

____

____

____

____

What Are the Major Groups of Gymnosperms?

Gymnosperms include four main groups: conifers, cycads, ginkgoes, and gnetophytes.

Group	Description
Conifers (examples: pines, firs)	• The leaves look like needles or are tiny scales. • Seeds and pollen are produced in cones. • Pollen grains are usually dispersed by wind.
Cycads (example: sago palm)	• They have short stems and palm-like leaves. • Pollen and seeds develop in cones. • Pollen grains are usually dispersed by insects.
Ginkgoes (example: maidenhair tree)	• They have fan-shaped leaves. • Male and female gametophytes develop on separate trees. • Seeds do not develop in cones. • Pollen grains are spread by wind.
Gnetophytes (example: *Welwitschia*)	• It is a diverse group of trees, shrubs, and vines. • Pollen and seeds are produced in cones.

LOOKING CLOSER

5. Identify Which gymnosperms do not produce seeds in cones?

____

How Do Conifers Reproduce?

Most gymnosperms are conifers. Reproduction in conifers includes a main sporophyte generation. The sporophytes produce female *seed cones* and male *pollen cones*. The cones are made up of hard *scales*. ☑

READING CHECK

6. Identify What is the main generation of a conifer?

Pollen grains, which contain male gametophytes, develop on the scales of pollen cones. Wind disperses the pollen grains. Sperm in pollen grains fertilize eggs within female gametophytes on the scales of seed cones.

After fertilization, the zygote develops into an embryo. The embryo and the tissues around it form a seed. When the seeds are mature, they fall out of the seed cone. Seeds of some conifers have a wing that helps the wind disperse them. Seeds grow into new sporophytes. ☑

READING CHECK

7. Explain What happens to conifer seeds once they are mature?

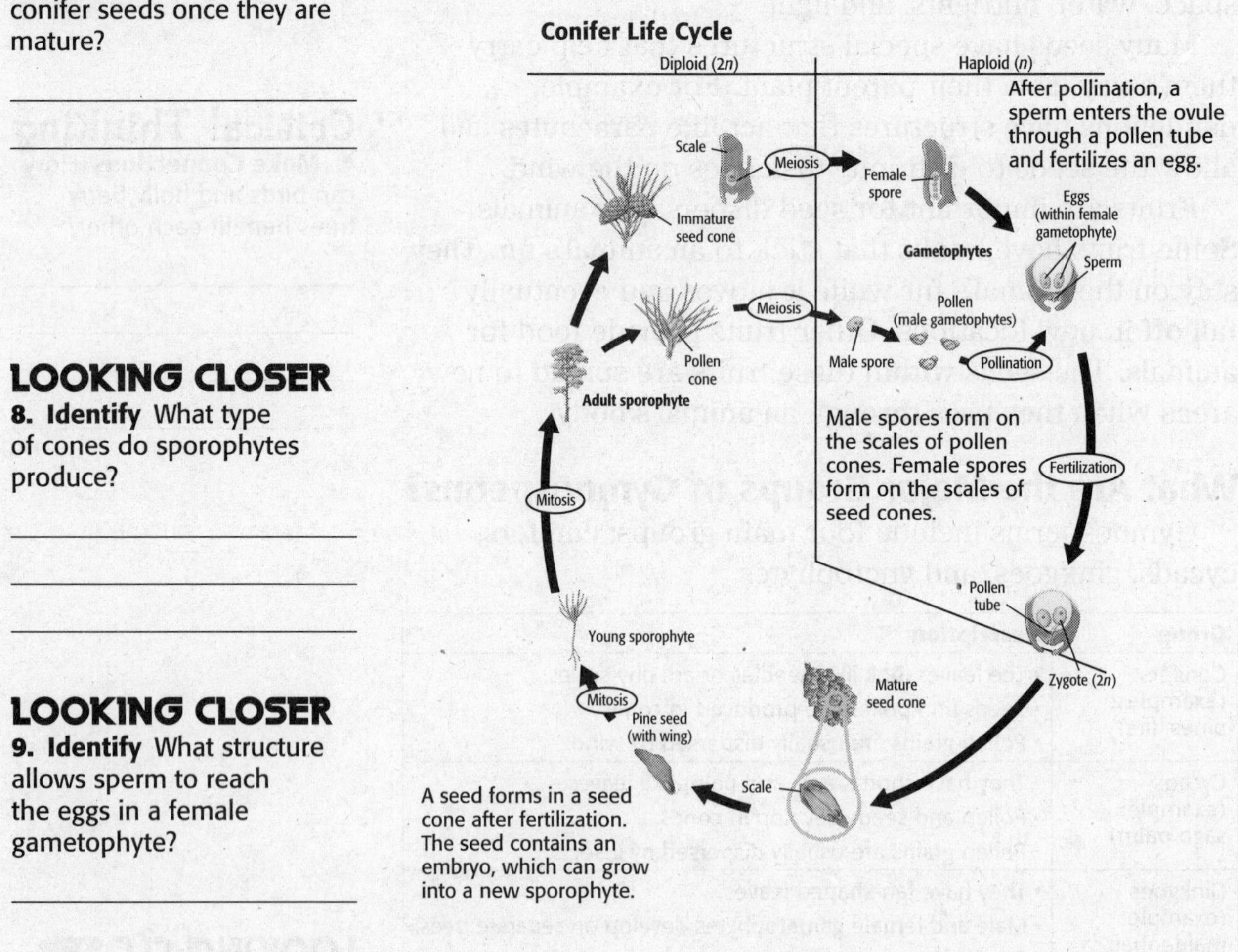

LOOKING CLOSER

8. Identify What type of cones do sporophytes produce?

LOOKING CLOSER

9. Identify What structure allows sperm to reach the eggs in a female gametophyte?

Name ______________________ Class ______________ Date ______________

Section 3 Review

SECTION VOCABULARY

angiosperm a flowering plant that produces seeds within a fruit **gymnosperm** a woody, vascular seed plant whose seeds are not enclosed by an ovary or fruit **ovule** a structure in the ovary of a seed plant that contains an embryo sac and that develops into a seed after fertilization	**pollen grain** the structure that contains the male gametophyte of seed plants **pollination** the transfer of pollen from the male reproductive structures (the anthers) to the tip of a female reproductive structure (the pistil) of a flower in angiosperms or to the ovule in gymnosperms **seed** a plant embryo that is enclosed in a protective coat

1. Summarize Fill in the Concept Map below to show the two main groups of seed plants and where their seeds develop.

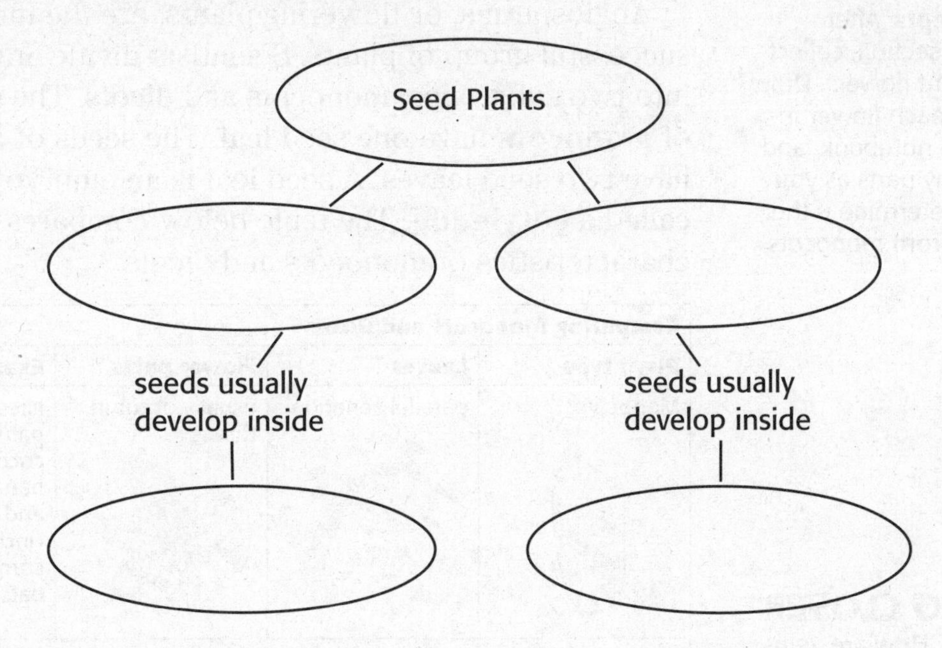

2. Compare In seed plants, how does the size of the gametophyte compare with the size of the sporophyte?

____

____

3. Explain How does seed dispersal benefit both parent plants and their offspring?

____

____

4. List Name the four major groups of gymnosperms.

____

5. Describe In conifers, how are pollen grains typically carried to seed cones?

____

Name ______________________ Class ______________ Date ______________

CHAPTER 23 Plant Diversity and Life Cycles

SECTION 4

Flowering Plants

KEY IDEAS

As you read this section, keep these questions in mind:

- What are the names of the two subgroups of angiosperms?
- What is a flower, and how does it function in reproduction?
- How does a flower's structure relate to pollination?
- What is the main function of a fruit?
- How do plants reproduce vegetatively?

READING TOOLBOX

Apply Concepts After reading this section, collect three different flowers. Draw a picture of each flower in your science notebook, and label as many parts as you can. Try to determine if the flowers are from monocots or dicots.

What Are the Subgroups of Angiosperms?

Angiosperms, or flowering plants, are the most successful group of plants. Scientists divide angiosperms into two subgroups: monocots and dicots. The seeds of **monocots** have one seed leaf. The seeds of **dicots** have two seed leaves. A seed leaf is an embryonic leaf called a **cotyledon**. The table below compares other characteristics of monocots and dicots.

LOOKING CLOSER

1. Describe How are veins arranged in monocot and dicot leaves?

____

____

____

Comparing Monocots and Dicots

Plant type	Leaves	Flower parts	Examples
Monocots	parallel venation	usually occur in threes	lilies, irises, palms, orchids, coconuts, onions, bananas, tulips, and grasses (including wheat, corn, rice, and oats)
Dicots	net venation	usually occur in fours or fives	beans, lettuce, oaks, maples, roses, carnations, elms, cactuses, and most broad-leaved forest trees

How Do Angiosperms Reproduce?

Angiosperms have a specialized reproductive structure called a flower. The male and female gametophytes of angiosperms develop within flowers. Flowers help pollination and fertilization occur. The female part of a flower provides a path for sperm to reach and fertilize an egg. The sperm do not need to swim through water. ☑

2. Define What is a flower?

____

____

____

STRUCTURE OF A TYPICAL FLOWER

The outermost portion of most flowers consists of sepals and petals. The *sepals* protect a flower bud from damage. The *petals* attract pollinators to the flower.

The inside of a flower has male structures, called **stamens**. Each stamen is made of a thin *filament* with an anther on top. An **anther** is a sac that produces pollen. ☑

The center of a flower has the female parts, or pistils. **Pistils** produce ovules. Ovules develop within the large, lower part of the pistil called the *ovary*. A stalk called the *style* usually rises from the ovary. The style has a sticky tip called a *stigma*, where pollen usually lands.

READING CHECK

3. Identify What two structures make up a stamen?

____

____

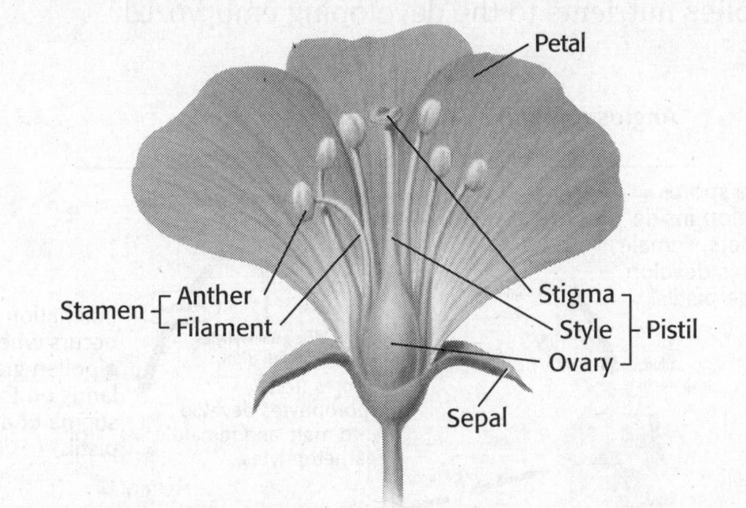

A typical flower contains sepals, petals, stamens, and one or more pistils.

LOOKING CLOSER

4. Identify What three structures make up a pistil?

____

____

____

POLLINATION

The flowers of angiosperms are adapted for pollination by wind or animals. Many flowers have sugary nectar that is a source of food for animals, such as insects, bats, and birds. When an animal enters a flower to collect nectar, it becomes coated with sticky pollen. As the animal travels from flower to flower, pollen from one flower can land on the stigma of another flower and pollinate it.

Flowers have different features to attract pollinators. For example, the petals of flowers that are pollinated by bees are typically blue or yellow. Flowers that are pollinated by moths typically have strong scents. Moths feed at night and can find these flowers in the dark.

Some flowers, such as those of grasses and oaks, are pollinated by wind. Wind-pollinated flowers are typically small and do not have odors, nectar, or bright colors.

Critical Thinking

5. Make Connections Do animal pollinators pollinate flowers on purpose? Explain your answer.

____

____

____

____

____

Name ______________________ Class ______________ Date ______________

LIFE CYCLE OF AN ANGIOSPERM

In the life cycle of an angiosperm, large sporophytes produce spores that grow into tiny gametophytes inside flowers. Female gametophytes grow inside ovules in the ovary of a pistil. Male gametophytes, or pollen grains, are produced in the anther of a stamen.

Pollination occurs when a pollen grain lands on the stigma of a pistil. The pollen grain forms a pollen tube that grows down the style to the ovary. Two sperm enter the pollen tube and carry out *double fertilization*. One sperm fertilizes the egg to form a zygote. The other sperm fuses with haploid nuclei to form an endosperm. The endosperm supplies nutrients to the developing embryo. ☑

6. Describe What is the function of an endosperm?

____

____

____

Angiosperm Life Cycle

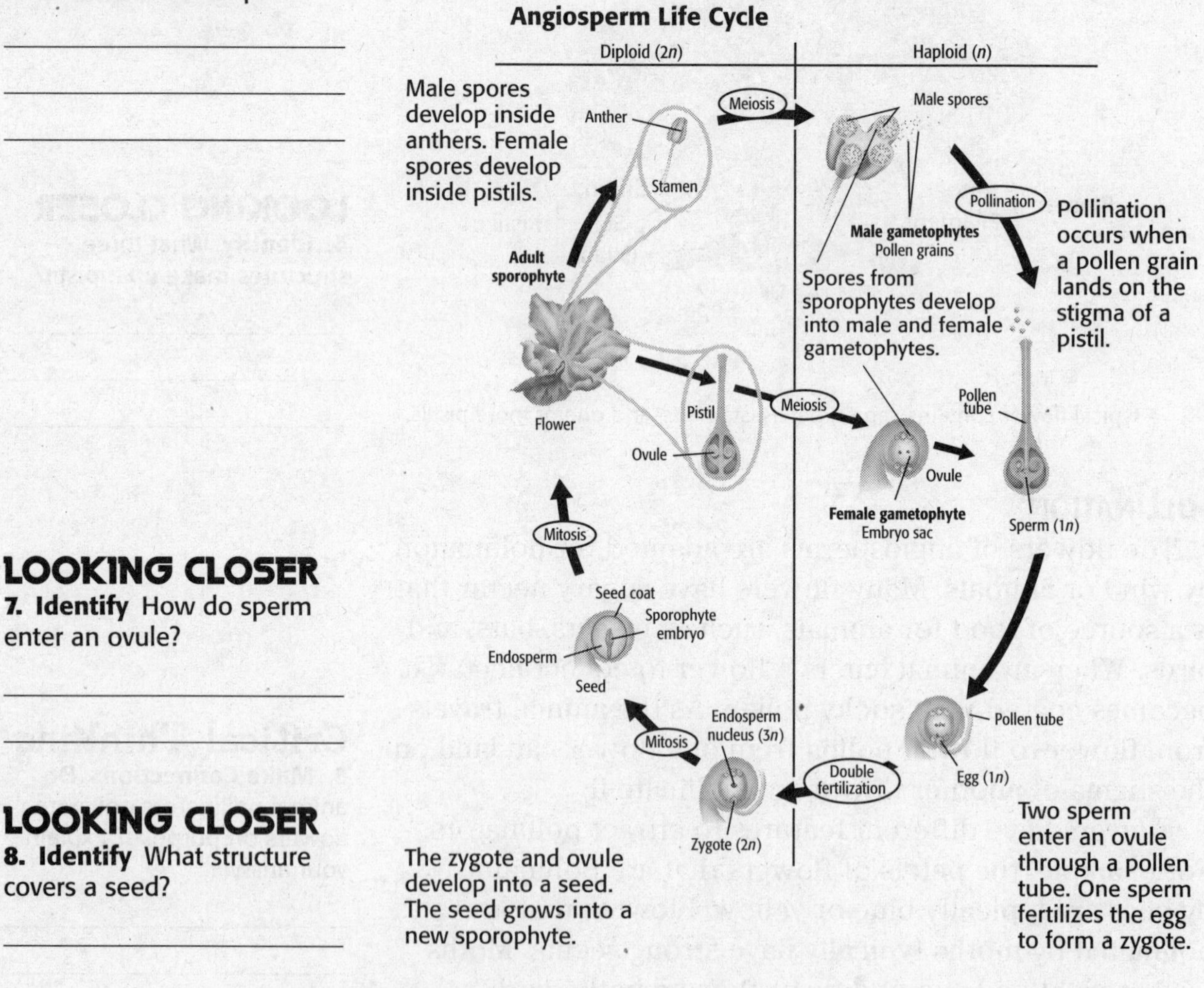

LOOKING CLOSER

7. Identify How do sperm enter an ovule?

____

____

LOOKING CLOSER

8. Identify What structure covers a seed?

____

What Is a Fruit?

The scientific definition of *fruit* is different from its everyday meaning. The ovary of a pistil is called a fruit after its ovules are fertilized. A **fruit** is a structure that develops from an ovary of a flower and contains seeds. In science, fruits include tomatoes, pumpkins, pea pods, and nuts. Although fruits provide some protection for seeds, their main function is to disperse seeds. ☑

Many fruits are eaten by animals. The seeds of fruits are dispersed as they pass undigested through an animal's body. Other fruits, such as those from maple trees, have structures that help them float on wind or water.

Discuss With a partner or in a small group, talk about different fruits. Describe the seeds they contain.

9. Identify From which part of a flower does a fruit develop?

____

What Is Vegetative Reproduction?

Many plants can reproduce asexually using stems, roots, and leaves. The reproduction of plants from these parts is called *vegetative reproduction*. Plants produced by vegetative reproduction are genetically the same as their parent. In most plants, vegetative reproduction is faster than sexual reproduction. By reproducing asexually, a single plant can spread quickly in a habitat. ☑

Vegetative reproduction is often caused by modified stems, such as bulbs and tubers, shown below. People often grow plants, such as potatoes, from vegetative parts. A single potato tuber can be broken into many pieces. Each piece with a growth bud can then develop into a new potato plant.

10. Explain What is one advantage of vegetative reproduction over sexual reproduction?

____

Many plants can reproduce asexually from nonreproductive, or vegetative, parts such as stems. Bulbs and tubers are modified stems.

LOOKING CLOSER

11. Describe What is a tuber?

____

Name ______________________ Class ______________ Date ____________

Section 4 Review

SECTION VOCABULARY

anther in flowering plants, the tip of a stamen, which contains the pollen sacs where grains form

cotyledon the embryonic leaf of a seed

dicot a dicotyledonous plant; an angiosperm that has two cotyledons, net venation, and flower parts in groups of four or five

fruit a mature plant ovary; the plant organ in which the seeds are enclosed

monocot a monocotyledonous plant; a plant that produces seeds that have only one cotyledon

pistil the female reproductive part of a flower that produces seeds and consists of an ovary, style, and stigma

stamen the male reproductive structure of a flower that produces pollen and consists of an anther at the tip of a filament

1. Identify What are the two subgroups of flowering plants?

____

2. Describe Where are pollen grains and ovules produced in a flower?

____

____

3. Describe How can an animal help in pollination?

____

____

____

4. Understand Relationships Why do many flowers have bright colors, strong smells, and sugary nectar?

____

____

5. Explain What are common characteristics of flowers that are pollinated by wind? Why do they have these characteristics?

____

____

____

6. Explain What is the main function of a fruit?

____

7. Explain How do offspring produced by vegetative reproduction compare with their parents?

____

Name ______________________ Class ______________ Date ______________

CHAPTER 24 Seed Plant Structure and Growth

SECTION 1

Plant Tissue Systems

KEY IDEAS

As you read this section, keep these questions in mind:

- What three types of tissue are found in vascular plants?
- What is the dermal tissue system?
- What are two types of vascular tissue?
- What is ground tissue?

How Is a Plant's Body Organized?

Like your body, a plant's body is made of cells, tissues, organs, and organ systems. However, in plants, tissues are also arranged into tissue systems. The three tissue systems of vascular plants are:

- the dermal tissue system
- the vascular tissue system
- the ground tissue system

READING TOOLBOX

Compare As you read, make a chart that compares the features and functions of the three tissue systems in vascular plants.

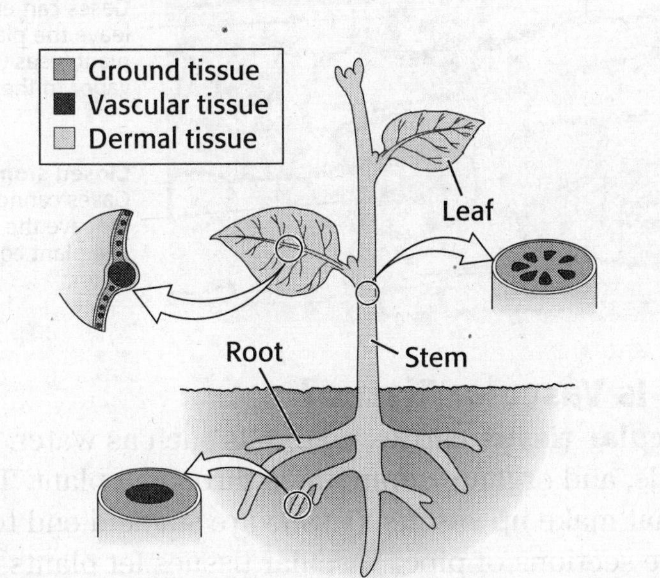

LOOKING CLOSER

1. Describe In general, where is ground tissue found in relation to vascular tissue?

____

____

What Is Dermal Tissue?

Dermal tissue covers and protects a plant. The functions of the dermal tissue system include:

- protection
- gas exchange
- absorption of minerals

Talk About It

Compare After you read this section, compare the different plant tissue systems with structures in the human body. What tissues or organs in the human body carry out functions similar to those in the three plant tissue systems?

Dermal System Features		
Feature	**Description**	**Function**
Epidermis	a single layer of flat cells covering the nonwoody parts of a plant	covers and protects the plant
Root hairs	hairlike extensions of epidermal cells covering root tips	help the plant absorb water
Cork	several layers of dead cells covering woody stems and roots	helps prevent water loss
Cuticle	coats the epidermis of leaves and nonwoody stems	helps protect the leaves and stem and prevents water loss
Stomata (singular, **stoma**)	tiny pores typically found on the surfaces of leaves	allow gases, such as carbon dioxide, oxygen, and water vapor, to enter and leave the plant
Guard cells	a pair of cells that borders each stoma	open and close the stoma

LOOKING CLOSER

2. Identify What kind of plants have cork?

____

3. Compare How are the functions of cork and a cuticle similar? How are these features different?

____

____

____

____

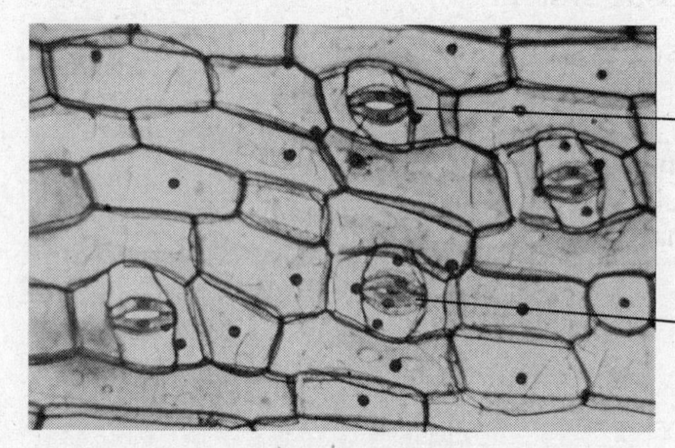

Open stomata Gases can enter and leave the plant. The plant loses water vapor to the air.

Closed stomata Gases cannot enter or leave the plant. The plant conserves water.

What Is Vascular Tissue?

Vascular tissue carries materials such as water, minerals, and organic compounds through a plant. The cells that make up vascular tissue are stacked end to end like sections of pipe. Vascular tissues let plants grow much taller than plants that do not have vascular tissues. The two kinds of vascular tissue are xylem and phloem.

Critical Thinking

4. Infer Why does photosynthesis slow down when stomata are closed?

____

____

____

____

XYLEM

Xylem carries water and minerals from the roots up to the leaves. Xylem is made up of cells called *tracheids* and *vessel elements*. These cells are dead, and only the cell walls remain. As a result, water can pass through these cells easily.

PHLOEM

Phloem carries organic compounds, such as sugars, from the leaves to the rest of the plant. Phloem is made up of sieve-tube members and companion cells. *Sieve-tube members* are specialized for moving materials from one cell to the next. *Companion cells* carry out cellular processes, such as respiration, for themselves and the sieve-tube members. Unlike the cells that make up xylem, the cells that make up phloem are living. ☑

READING CHECK

5. Describe What is the function of phloem?

____

____

____

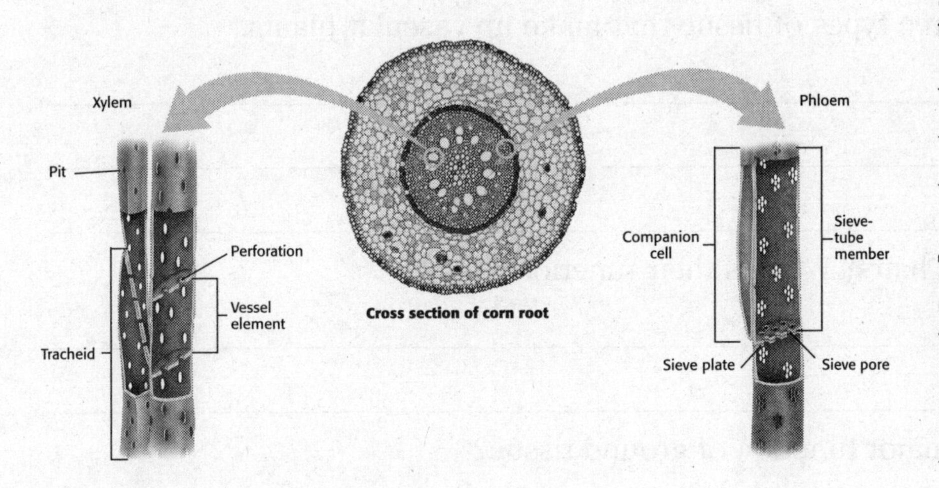

LOOKING CLOSER

6. Infer How do you think the functions of perforations in xylem and sieve pores in phloem are similar?

____

____

____

What Is Ground Tissue?

Much of the inside of the nonwoody parts of a plant is made up of **ground tissue**. Ground tissue surrounds and supports vascular tissue.

Ground tissue contains many different cell types. Each type has a particular function depending on where the cell is found in the plant. For example, the ground tissue in leaves is made up of cells that have many chloroplasts. These cells are specialized for photosynthesis. The ground tissue in stems and roots is specialized for support and storage of water and nutrients. The cells of these ground tissues typically have large vacuoles for storage. ☑

7. Explain Why does a plant have different kinds of ground tissue?

____

____

____

____

Name ______________________ Class ______________ Date ____________

Section 1 Review

SECTION VOCABULARY

dermal tissue the outer covering of a plant

ground tissue a type of plant tissue other than vascular tissue that makes up much of the inside of a plant

guard cell one of a pair of specialized cells that border a stoma and regulate gas exchange

phloem the tissue that conducts food (sugars, amino acids, and mineral nutrients) in vascular plants

stoma one of many openings in a leaf or a stem of a plant that enable gas exchange to occur (plural, stomata)

vascular tissue the specialized conducting tissue that is found in higher plants and that is made up mostly of xylem and phloem

xylem the type of tissue in vascular plants that provides support and conducts water and nutrients from the roots

1. Identify Name the three types of tissue that make up vascular plants.

____

____

____

2. Define What are root hairs? What is their function?

____

____

3. Identify What is the major function of ground tissue?

____

4. Compare Complete the table below to compare xylem and phloem.

Xylem	Phloem
	living cells
	made up of sieve-tube members and companion cells.
carries water and dissolved minerals from the roots to the rest of the plant	

5. Predict What would happen to a plant if its stomata were always open?

____

____

____

Name ______________________ Class ______________ Date ______________

SECTION 2

Roots, Stems, and Leaves

KEY IDEAS

As you read this section, keep these questions in mind:

- What are roots, and what is their function?
- What are stems, and what is their function?
- What are leaves, and what is their function?

What Are the Three Groups of Plant Organs?

Plants have three basic kinds of organs: stems, roots, and leaves. Each kind of organ contains all three tissue types. ☑

READING TOOLBOX

Color Code As you read, underline the functions and major features of roots, stems, and leaves. Use a different color for each group of plant organs.

What Are the Functions of Roots?

In most plants, roots have three main functions:

- to anchor the plant in the ground
- to absorb water and minerals
- to store organic nutrients, such as sugar and starch

READING CHECK

1. List What are the kinds of plant organs?

Most monocots, such as grasses, have highly branched root systems. This is a *fibrous root system*. There is not one main root.

Many dicots, such as these radishes, have a large central root called a *taproot*.

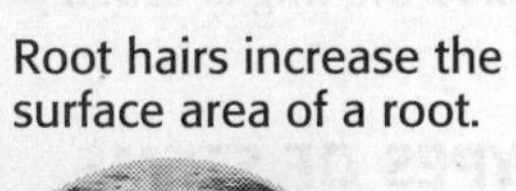

Root hairs increase the surface area of a root.

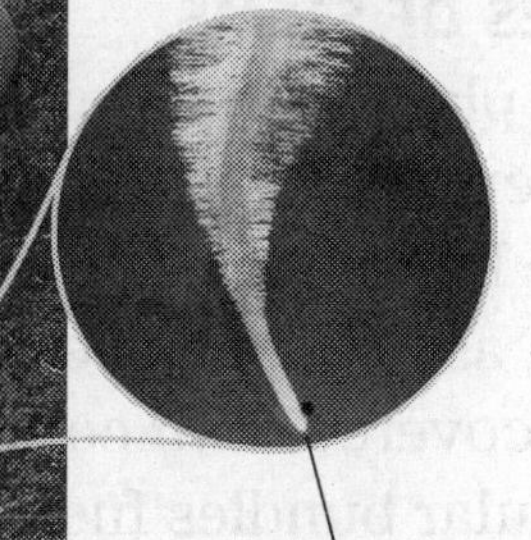

A *root cap* is a mass of cells that protects the growing root tip.

LOOKING CLOSER

2. Compare How does a taproot system differ from a fibrous root system?

3. Describe What is the function of the root cap?

What Are the Functions of Stems?

Stems have several functions:

- to support the leaves
- to carry, or *conduct*, water and materials

Stems of some plants are modified for particular functions. For example, potato stems are modified to store nutrients. Stems of cactuses are modified to store water.

Background

Recall that angiosperms, or flowering plants, are divided into two main groups: *monocots* and *dicots*.

VASCULAR BUNDLES

In a plant stem, the vascular tissues are found in bundles called **vascular bundles**. A vascular bundle contains both xylem and phloem. Monocots and dicots have different arrangements of vascular bundles.

In dicots, the vascular bundles are arranged in a ring. The ground tissue inside the ring is called **pith**.

In monocots, vascular bundles are scattered throughout the ground tissue.

Critical Thinking

4. Infer Do monocot stems have pith? Explain your answer.

____

____

____

____

TYPES OF STEMS

A plant with a flexible stem is *herbaceous*. An epidermis covers a herbaceous stem. Roses and corn have herbaceous stems. Trees, such as oaks, and shrubs, such as hollies, have woody stems. *Woody* stems are stiff and covered with cork. As a woody plant matures, the vascular bundles fuse together into a cylinder. Xylem is the major component of wood.

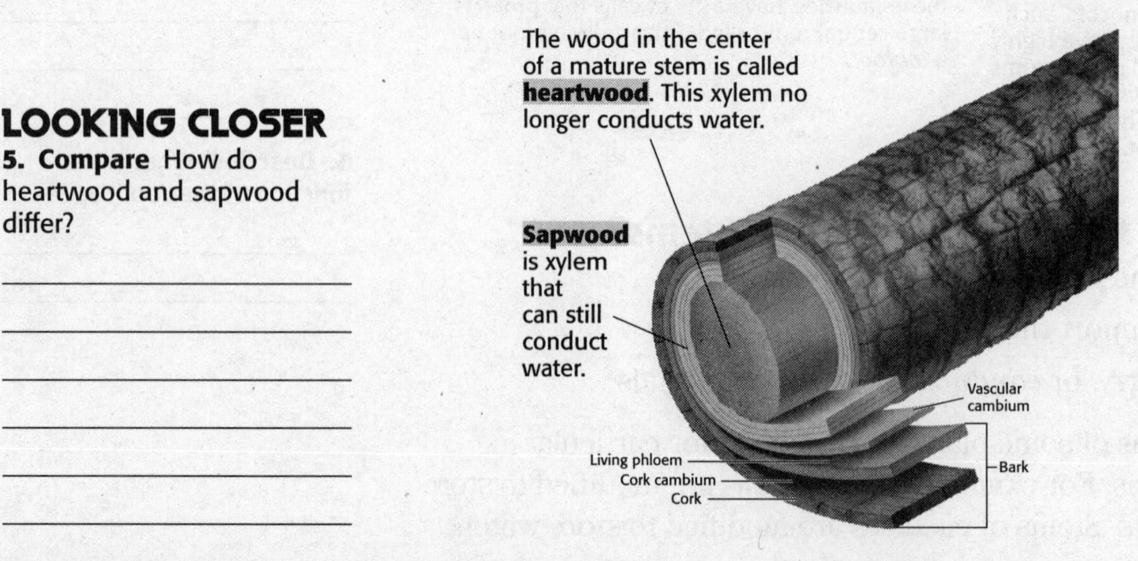

LOOKING CLOSER

5. Compare How do heartwood and sapwood differ?

____

____

____

____

____

____

What Are the Functions of Leaves?

The main function of a leaf is photosynthesis. The structure of a leaf helps it perform this function. ☑

6. Identify What is the main function of leaves?

____

____

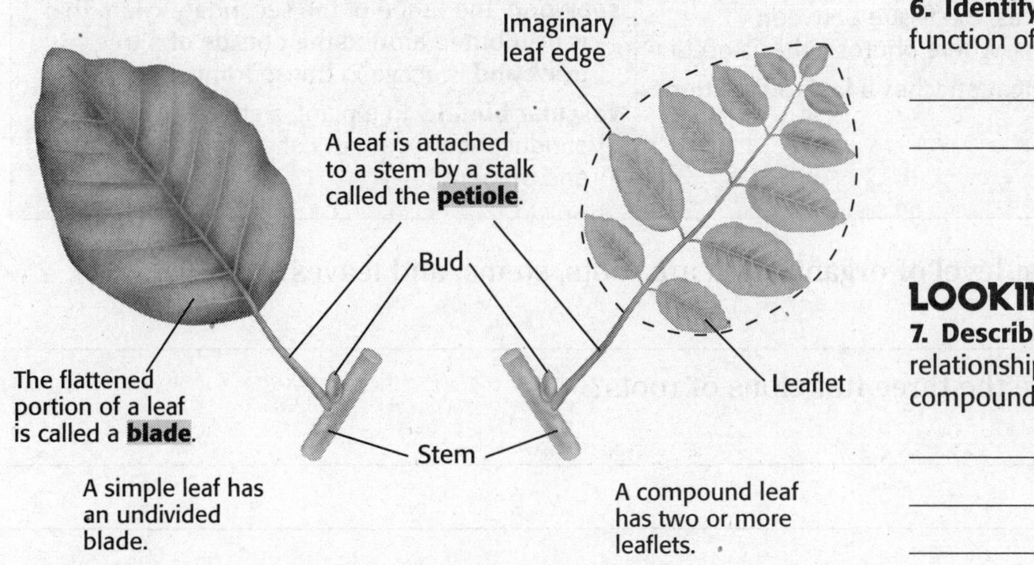

LOOKING CLOSER

7. Describe What is the relationship between a compound leaf and a leaflet?

____

____

____

A leaf is a mass of ground and vascular tissue covered by epidermis. The ground tissue in a leaf is called **mesophyll**. Cells in the mesophyll have many chloroplasts.

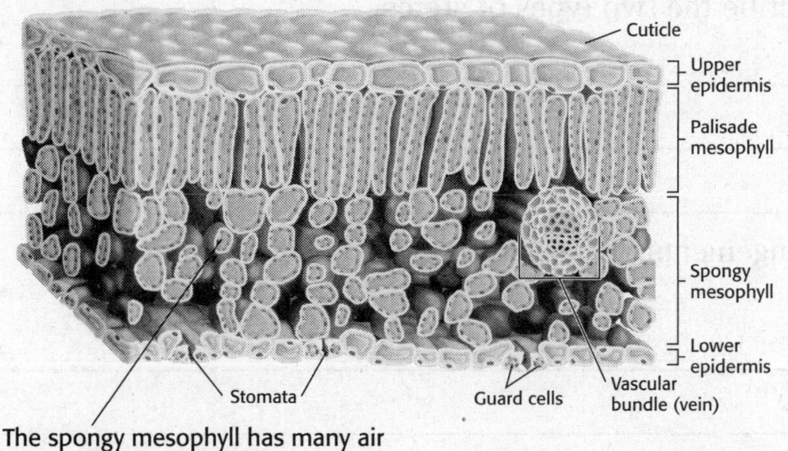

LOOKING CLOSER

8. Infer The cells of the palisades mesophyll generally have more chloroplasts than those in the spongy mesophyll. How does this explain the relative positions of these tissues in a leaf?

____

____

____

____

____

Many plants have modified leaves specialized for a particular function. For example, water lilies have leaves that help the plant float. The spines of a cactus are modified leaves that help protect the plant from herbivores. The leaves of garden peas have tendrils for climbing.

Name ______________________ Class ______________ Date ______________

Section 2 Review

SECTION VOCABULARY

blade the broad, flat portion of a typical leaf

heartwood the nonconducting older wood in the center of a tree trunk

mesophyll in leaves, the tissue between epidermal layers, where photosynthesis occurs

petiole the stalk that attaches a leaf to the stem of a plant

pith the tissue that is located in the center of the stem of most vascular plants and that is used for storage

sapwood the tissue of the secondary xylem that is distributed around the outside of a tree trunk and is active in transporting sap

vascular bundle in a plant, a strand of conducting tissue that contains both xylem and phloem

1. Identify What level of organization are roots, stems, and leaves?

____

2. List What are the three functions of roots?

____

____

____

3. Infer How would the lack of vascular tissue affect the function of stems?

____

4. Describe Identify and describe the two types of stems.

____

____

____

5. Compare How do the arrangements of vascular bundles differ in monocots and dicots?

____

____

6. Apply Concepts Identify and describe two features of the mesophyll that help a leaf perform its function.

____

____

____

Name ______________________ Class ______________ Date ____________

Plant Growth and Development

KEY IDEAS

As you read this section, keep these questions in mind:

- What are the characteristics of a seed plant embryo?
- How do meristems relate to plant growth?
- What is the result of primary growth on a plant?
- What is secondary growth, and what type of meristem is involved?

What Are the Characteristics of a Plant Embryo?

Recall that a seed develops from an ovule and contains a plant embryo. The plant embryo has two parts: an embryonic root and an embryonic shoot. Leaflike structures called *cotyledons*, or seed leaves, are attached to the embryonic shoot. The embryos of monocots, such as corn, have one cotyledon. The embryos of dicots, such as beans, have two cotyledons. ☑

READING TOOLBOX

Make Flashcards After you read this section, make flash cards for the vocabulary words. On one side of each card, write a vocabulary word. On the other side of the card, draw a picture that represents the term.

READING CHECK

1. Identify What are the two main parts of a plant embryo?

____

Corn grain **Bean seed**

Embryo
Seed coat
Embryonic leaves
Embryonic root
Cotyledons
Seed coat

Seeds contain the embryos of plants.

GERMINATION

The embryo within a seed is in a state of inactivity, or *dormancy*. The process in which a plant embryo comes out of dormancy and starts growing is called **germination**. You know a seed is germinating when the root pushes out of the seed. The embryonic shoot pushes out of the seed later. The roots and shoot continue to grow throughout the plant's life.

Critical Thinking

2. Define Use a dictionary to find the meanings of the roots *mono-* and *di-*. How can these roots help you remember a major difference between *monocots* and *dicots*?

____

____

____

____

What Are Meristems?

Plants grow by producing new cells in regions called meristems. A **meristem** is a region of cells that divide and can develop into specialized tissues.

PRIMARY GROWTH

To grow taller or longer, a plant adds cells to the tips of its body. The tips of roots and stems have small regions of undifferentiated cells called **apical meristems**. As cells in the apical meristems divide, the plant grows longer. Most of the new cells differentiate to become specialized for particular functions. Growth that makes a plant longer or taller is called **primary growth**. Primary growth produces *primary tissues.* ☑

READING CHECK

3. Identify What kind of meristem is responsible for primary growth?

____

____

To better understand primary growth, imagine a stack of dishes. As you add dishes to the top, the stack gets taller but does not get wider. Similarly, the cells in the apical meristems of most plants add cells to the tips of a plant's body. All types of plants can undergo primary growth.

LOOKING CLOSER

4. Predict What will happen to the width of this plant's stem as cells in the shoot meristem divide? Explain your answer.

____

____

____

____

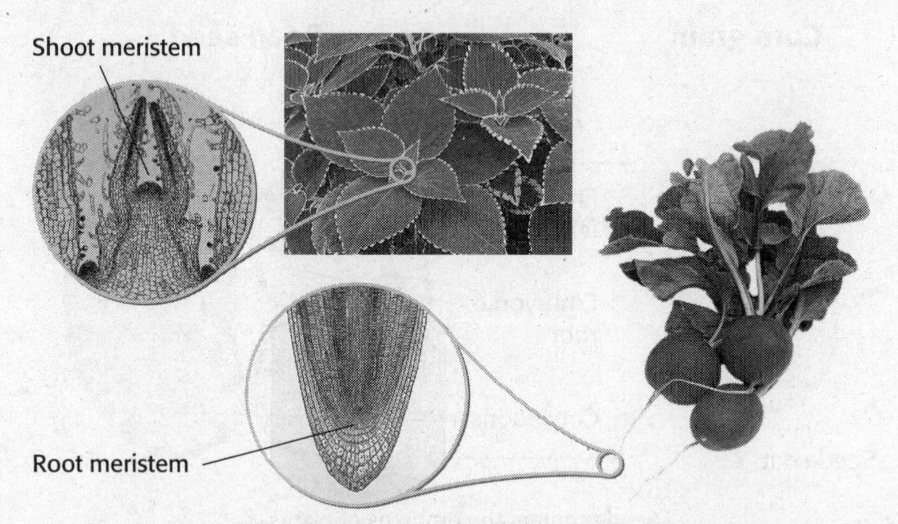

Growth happens in regions of undifferentiated cells called meristems.

Primary growth would stop if all the cells produced by an apical meristem differentiated. Some of the new undifferentiated cells replace, or replenish, the cells of the meristem. Others form new meristems as the stems and roots grow longer. When cells in these meristems start dividing, the stem or root begins to branch.

SECONDARY GROWTH

The stems and roots of most plants grow wider as they become longer. Cell division in regions of undifferentiated cells called **lateral meristems** causes roots and stems to grow wider. The stems and roots of many plant species become wider due to **secondary growth**. Secondary growth produces *secondary tissues.* ☑

A plant may have two types of lateral meristems: cork cambium and vascular cambium. *Cork cambium* produces cork cells. *Vascular cambium* produces secondary xylem and secondary phloem.

5. Describe How does secondary growth affect stems and roots?

____

____

____

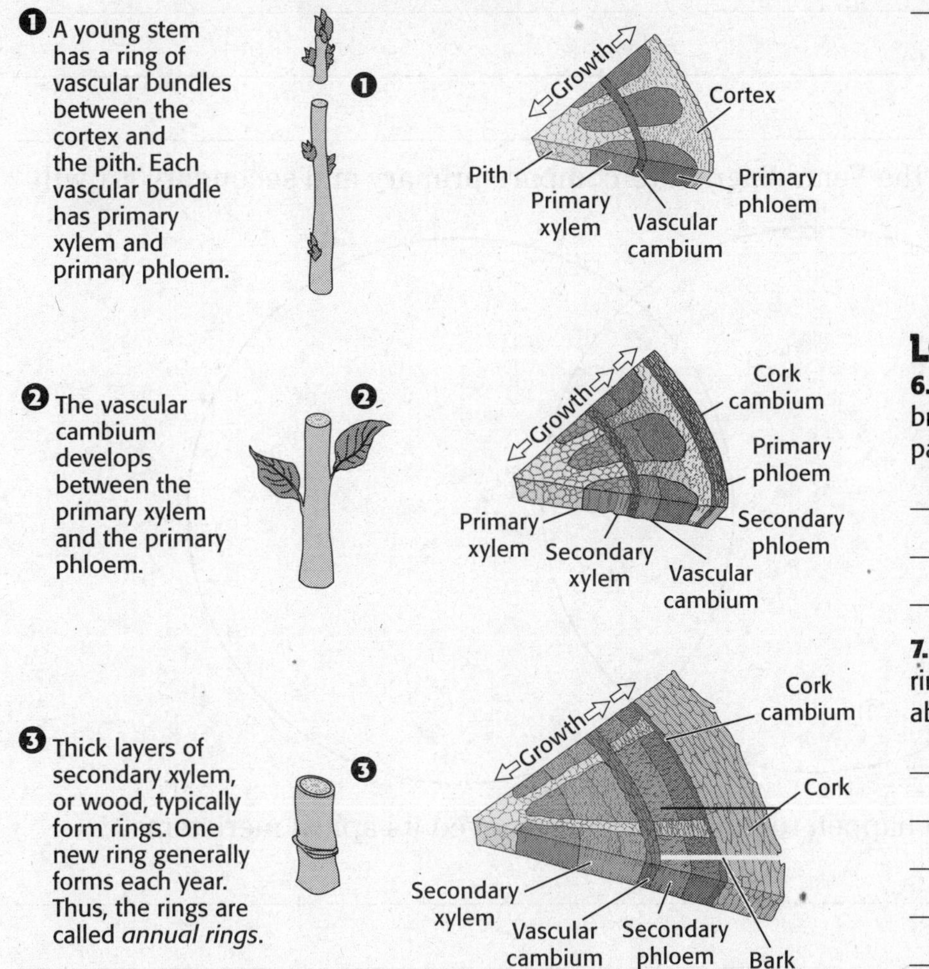

LOOKING CLOSER

6. Infer Which part of a branch is youngest? Which part is oldest?

____

____

____

7. Explain What can the rings in a tree stem tell you about the tree's age?

____

____

____

____

____

Gymnosperms and dicots have secondary growth. Some herbaceous plants, such as carrots, have secondary growth in their roots. However, secondary growth is most noticeable in woody plants such as trees. Monocots, such as corn, do not have secondary growth.

Name ______________________ Class ______________ Date ____________

Section 3 Review

SECTION VOCABULARY

apical meristem the growing region at the tips of stems and roots in plants **germination** the beginning of growth or development in a seed, spore, or zygote, especially after a period of inactivity **lateral meristem** dividing tissue that runs parallel to the long axis of a stem or a root	**meristem** a region of undifferentiated plant cells that are capable of dividing and developing into specialized plant tissues **primary growth** the growth that occurs as a result of cell division at the tips of stems and roots and that gives rise to primary tissue **secondary growth** the growth that results from cell division in the cambia, or lateral meristems, and that causes the stems and roots to thicken

1. List What are the three major characteristics of a seed plant embryo?

____

____

____

2. Compare Complete the Venn diagram to compare primary and secondary growth.

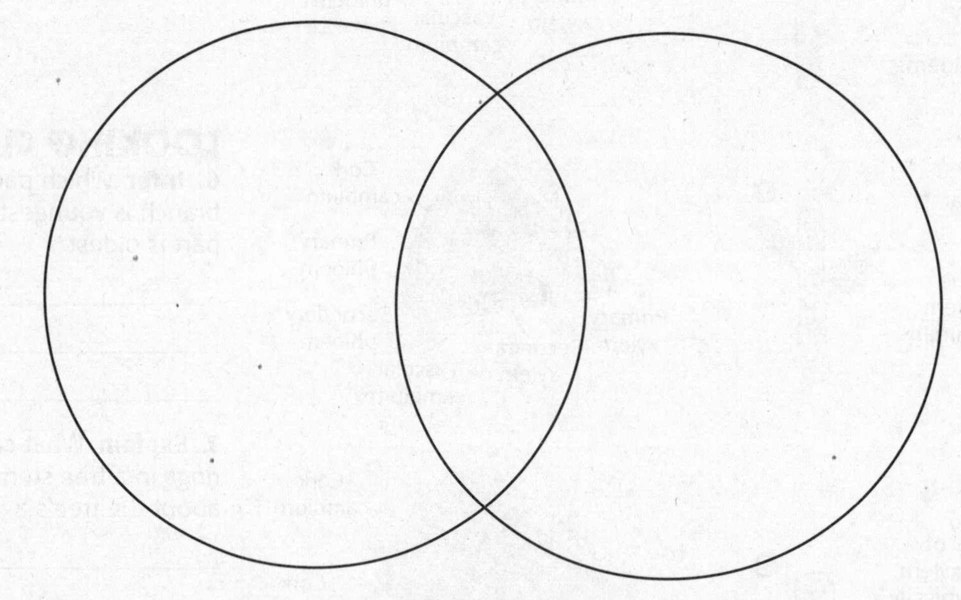

3. Predict What would happen to a plant if you removed its apical meristems?

____

____

4. Identify Name the two kinds of lateral meristems and the types of cells they produce.

____

____

Name ______________________ Class ______________ Date ______________

CHAPTER 25 Plant Processes

SECTION 1

Nutrients and Transport

KEY IDEAS

As you read this section, keep these questions in mind:
- What substances do plants need, other than water, carbon dioxide, and oxygen, to survive?
- How does water move through a vascular plant?
- How do organic compounds move through a vascular plant?

What Nutrients Do Plants Need?

Recall that plants need carbon dioxide, water, and light energy to perform photosynthesis. To perform respiration, plants need oxygen. Plants also need small amounts of at least 14 mineral nutrients. Some of these are listed below.

Mineral nutrient	Function
Nitrogen	part of proteins, nucleic acids, chlorophyll, ATP, and coenzymes; promotes growth
Phosphorus	part of ATP, ADP, nucleic acids, phospholipids of cell membranes, and some coenzymes
Potassium	needed for active transport, enzyme activation, water balance, and opening of stomata
Calcium	part of cell walls; needed for enzyme activity and membrane function
Magnesium	part of chlorophyll; needed for photosynthesis and activation of enzymes
Sulfur	part of some proteins and coenzyme A; needed for cellular respiration

READING TOOLBOX

Draw For many people, representing ideas in pictures can help them remember concepts more easily. As you read, draw pictures to illustrate the concepts described under each header.

LOOKING CLOSER

1. Identify Which two of these mineral nutrients does a plant need to produce chlorophyll?

____

____

What Is Transpiration?

Recall that the surfaces of leaves are covered with many tiny pores called stomata (singular, *stoma*). When stomata are open, water vapor diffuses out of a leaf. The loss of water vapor from a plant is called **transpiration**.

Background

Recall that gases such as carbon dioxide diffuse through *stomata*.

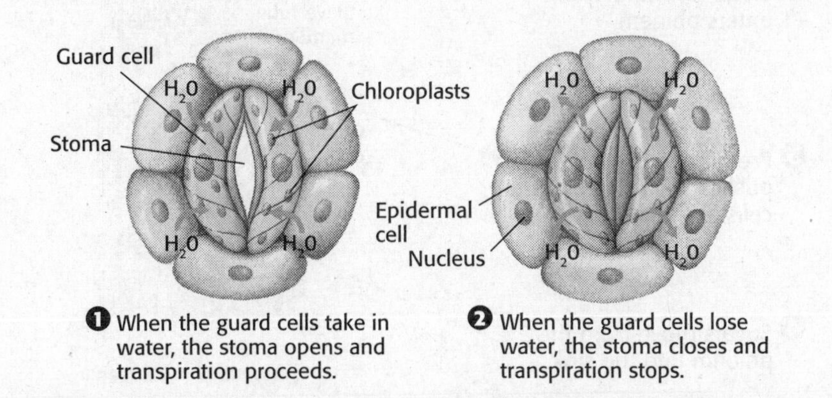

❶ When the guard cells take in water, the stoma opens and transpiration proceeds.

❷ When the guard cells lose water, the stoma closes and transpiration stops.

LOOKING CLOSER

2. Describe What is the relationship between guard cells and stomata?

____

____

How Does Water Move Through a Plant?

In a vascular plant, water and minerals move through xylem from the plant's roots to its leaves.

Critical Thinking

3. Infer If closed stomata help a plant decrease water loss, why does a plant not keep its stomata closed all the time?

____

____

____

____

____

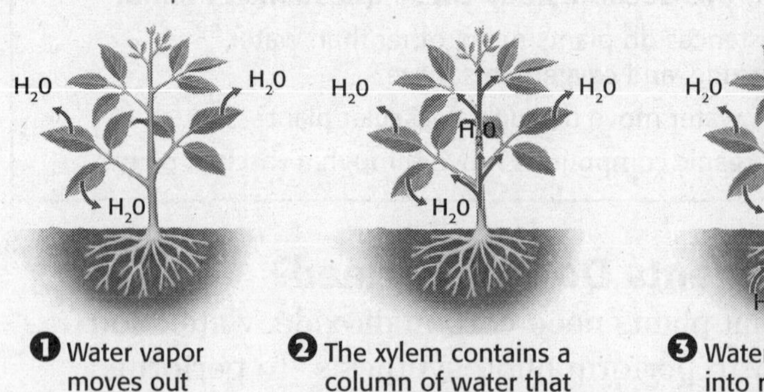

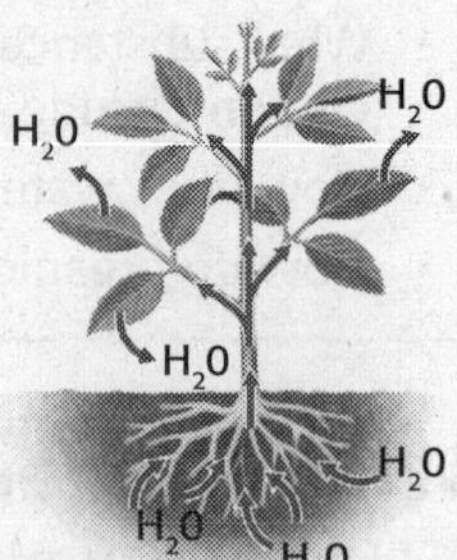

❶ Water vapor moves out of the leaves through stomata.

❷ The xylem contains a column of water that stretches from the root to the leaves. As water molecules move out of the plant through the stomata, they pull others up through the xylem.

❸ Water moves into roots by osmosis. The water molecules higher up in the xylem pull these water molecules from the roots up the stem.

How Do Organic Compounds Move Through a Plant?

Plants produce organic compounds, such as sugars, in their leaves. The plant must move these compounds from the leaves to other organs and tissues. In vascular plants, phloem moves organic compounds from a source to a sink. Examples of sinks include storage tissues, such as radish roots, and growing parts, such as developing fruits. ☑

4. Identify In general, what is the source of sugars in plants?

____

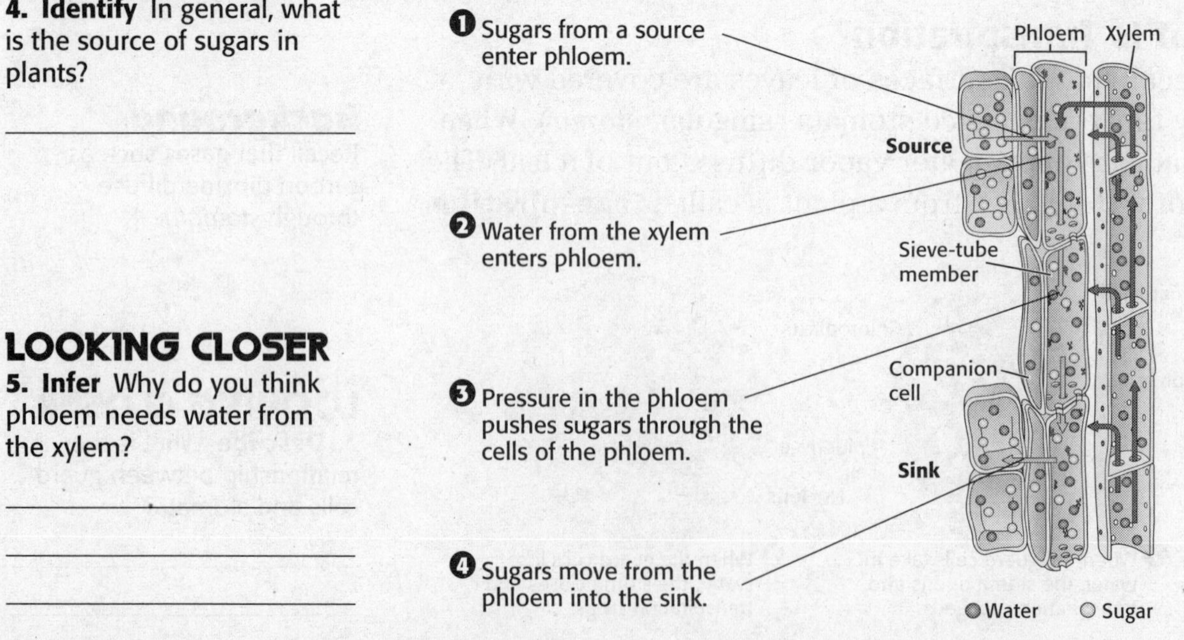

LOOKING CLOSER

5. Infer Why do you think phloem needs water from the xylem?

____

____

____

Name ______________________ Class ______________ Date ______________

Section 1 Review

SECTION VOCABULARY

transpiration the process by which plants release water vapor into the air through stomata	

1. List What are six major mineral nutrients plants need?

____

____

2. Describe What is the role of stomata in transpiration?

____

____

3. Explain What causes water molecules to move upward in xylem?

____

____

4. Identify What is the function of phloem?

____

____

5. Identify What process moves water from soil into roots?

____

6. Summarize Complete the Process Chart below to describe how organic compounds move through a plant from their source to a sink.

[ ]

↓

[Water from the xylem enters the phloem.]

↓

[ ]

↓

[ ]

Name ______________________ Class ______________ Date ______________

CHAPTER 25 Plant Processes

SECTION 2

Plant Responses

KEY IDEAS

As you read this section, keep these questions in mind:

- Why are hormones important for plant growth and development?
- How do tropisms affect plants?
- What triggers seasonal change in plants?
- How do nastic movements affect plants?

READING TOOLBOX

Make Flashcards After you read, make flashcards to describe the *–isms* in this section. On one side of each card, draw a picture that represents the response. On the other side of each card, write the name of the response and its cause.

How Do Hormones Affect Plants?

Like animals, plants sense changes in their environments and respond to these changes. Plant hormones play an important role in plant responses.

A *hormone* is a chemical made in one part of an organism that causes a response in another part of the organism. Plants produce only small amounts of each hormone. However, small amounts of hormones have large effects. Hormones can both stimulate a plant to grow or stop the plant from growing.

Hormone	Effect
Auxins	promote cell growth
Gibberellins	cause stems to grow longer, fruits to develop, and seeds to germinate
Cytokinins	stimulate cell division
Ethylene	causes fruits to ripen
Abscisic acid	keeps seeds dormant; slows growth

LOOKING CLOSER

1. Identify Which group of hormones causes seeds to germinate?

____

What Are Tropisms?

A plant cannot move away from unfavorable conditions. Instead, a plant responds to its environment by changing the rate and pattern of its growth. For example, if you place a plant near a window, the plant will bend toward the light. ☑

2. Describe How does a plant respond to its environment?

____

____

____

A response to a stimulus such as light is called a **tropism**. If a plant grows toward a stimulus, the response is a *positive tropism*. If the plant grows away from the stimulus, the response is a *negative tropism*.

PHOTOTROPISM

Phototropism is the movement or growth of a plant in response to light. Auxins accumulate on the shady side of a plant where they cause cells to grow. Cells in the stem on the shaded side of the plant become longer than cells on the sunny side. The different cell sizes cause the stem to bend toward the light. ☑

READING CHECK

3. Identify Which group of hormones is responsible for phototropism?

____

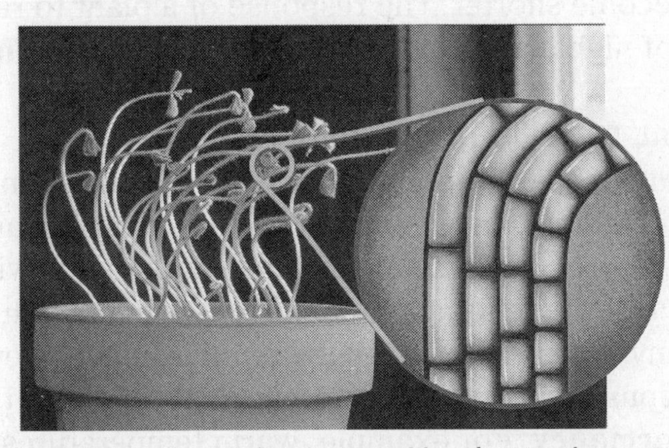

These shamrocks are showing a positive phototropism.

THIGMOTROPISM

Thigmotropism is the growth of a plant in response to touch. Tendrils and stems of climbing plants bend when they touch an object. Thigmotropism allows a climbing plant to grow tall without a thick stem to support its weight.

Critical Thinking

4. Hypothesize How does phototropism help a plant survive?

____

____

____

____

____

____

GRAVITROPISM

Gravitropism is the growth of a plant in response to gravity. Auxins cause stems to bend upward away from the pull of gravity. They cause roots to bend down toward the pull of gravity.

Thigmotropism Gravitropism

LOOKING CLOSER

5. Apply Concepts Does the photo on the right show a positive or a negative tropism? Explain your answer.

____

____

____

____

Name ____________ Class ____________ Date ____________

What Causes Seasonal Responses?

Many parts of the world have distinct seasons. In general, the lengths of days and nights in these areas are different depending on the season. Plants respond to the changes in amount of darkness each day. For example, in many regions, trees shed their leaves in autumn as nights become longer. They grow new leaves in spring as nights become shorter. The response of a plant to relative lengths of nights and days is called **photoperiodism**.

Talk About It

Hypothesize In some regions, temperatures do not change much throughout the year, but these regions may have distinct wet and dry seasons. Why do you think many trees shed their leaves in certain seasons? How does shedding their leaves help the trees survive? In a small group, create hypotheses to explain why trees in many regions shed their leaves when seasons change.

SEASONAL TEMPERATURE CHANGES

Although plants respond mainly to seasonal changes in length of nights, many also respond to seasonal changes in temperature. For example, most tomato plants will not produce fruit if nighttime temperatures are too high.

In many cases, a plant or seed remains inactive even if conditions are suitable for growth. This condition is called **dormancy**. For example, warm temperatures during a few winter days in cold regions may be favorable for a seed to germinate. However, if the weather becomes cold again, the young plant will not survive. Thus, many plants and seeds stay inactive, or dormant, until several weeks of low temperatures have passed.

What Are Nastic Movements?

Some plants responses are not influenced by the direction of the stimulus. Such a response is called a **nastic movement**. In general, sudden changes in the water content of certain cells cause nastic movements. ☑

6. Describe What causes nastic movements?

____

____

____

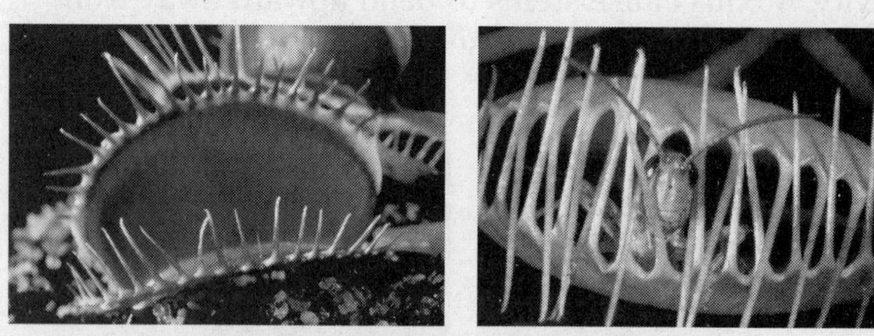

The leaf of a Venus flytrap snaps shut in response to a stimulus, such as this insect. The leaf will close no matter what direction the stimulus comes from.

Name ______________________ Class ______________ Date ______________

Section 2 Review

SECTION VOCABULARY

dormancy a state in which seeds, spores, bulbs, and other reproductive organs stop growth and development and reduce their metabolism, especially respiration

gravitropism the growth of a plant in a particular direction in response to gravity

nastic movement a type of plant response that is independent of the direction of a stimulus

photoperiodism the response of plants to seasonal changes in the relative length of nights and days

phototropism a plant growth movement that occurs in response to the direction of a source of light

thigmotropism a response of an organism or part of an organism to touch, such as the coiling of a vine around an object

tropism the movement of all or part of an organism in response to an external stimulus, such as light or heat; movement is either toward or away from the stimulus

1. **Describe** How do hormones affect the growth and development of a plant?

____

____

2. **Compare** What is the difference between a positive tropism and a negative tropism?

____

____

3. **Identify** What is the main factor that affects seasonal responses in plants?

____

4. **Compare** How is a tropism different from a nastic movement?

____

____

5. **Apply Concepts** Ripe fruits become damaged easily during shipment. Thus, fruit growers ship many fruits when they are unripe and later use a hormone to ripen them artificially. Which plant hormone do you think they use? Explain your answer.

____

____

6. **Infer** How do you think a stem growing upward due to gravitropism helps a plant survive?

____

____

Name ______________________ Class ______________ Date ______________

CHAPTER 26 Introduction to Animals

SECTION 1

Characteristics of Animals

KEY IDEAS

As you read this section, keep these questions in mind:
- What general features do all animals share?
- What are the two general groups of animals?

READING TOOLBOX

Identify Before you read this section, write the two Key Ideas questions in your notebook. After you read this section, write the answers to the questions in your own words.

What Are the General Characteristics of Animals?

When you hear the word *animal*, you may think of dogs, cats, whales, or birds. However, animals can be as simple as a sponge or as complex as a human being. No matter how different they are, all animals share four characteristics. The table below describes these characteristics.

LOOKING CLOSER

1. Define What is a heterotroph?

____

Characteristic	Description
Multicellular	All animals are made up of many cells. In most animals, these cells are specialized for different functions. For example, humans have more than 100 different kinds of cells in their bodies. Each kind of cell performs a specific function.
Heterotrophic	All animals are **heterotrophs**. This means that they cannot make their own food. Instead, they must eat other organisms to get the energy they need.
Cells without cell walls	Like plants, fungi, and protists, animals have eukaryotic cells. However, unlike plant cells and fungal cells, animal cells do not have cell walls.
Movement	All animals can move at some time during their lives. Some animals move slowly. Others move quickly. Some can move only during certain stages in their life cycles.

Critical Thinking

2. Apply Concepts Give two differences between animals and plants.

____

What Are the Two General Groups of Animals?

All animals are members of Kingdom Animalia. Kingdom Animalia contains about 35 major phyla. Animals in all but one of these phyla are **invertebrates**. In other words, they do not have backbones. In contrast, most animals in phylum Chordata are **vertebrates**. Vertebrates have backbones. They also have stiff internal skeletons and *crania* (singular, *cranium*), or hard cases that surround their brains.

Background

Recall that *kingdom* and *phylum* (plural, *phyla*) are levels of taxonomic classification. A kingdom contains one or more phyla.

Name ______________________ Class ______________ Date __________

Section 1 Review

SECTION VOCABULARY

heterotroph an organism that obtains organic food molecules by eating other organisms or their byproducts and that cannot synthesize organic compounds from inorganic materials	**invertebrate** an animal that does not have a backbone **vertebrate** an animal that has a backbone; includes mammals, birds, reptiles, amphibians, and fish

1. Describe What are three characteristics of vertebrates?

2. Compare What is the main difference between a vertebrate and an invertebrate?

3. Identify How do animals get food?

4. List What are four characteristics that all animals share?

5. Apply Concepts A scientist discovers a new organism. The organism consists of a single eukaryotic cell without a cell wall. The organism is heterotrophic and can move. Is this organism an animal? Explain your answer.

6. Infer Give three examples of vertebrates.

Name ______________________ Class ______________ Date ______________

SECTION 2

Animal Body Systems

KEY IDEAS

As you read this section, keep these questions in mind:

- Why is an animal's skeleton important?
- What are the functions of the digestive and excretory systems?
- What is the function of the nervous system?
- Why are the respiratory and circulatory systems important?
- What are two ways that animals reproduce?

READING TOOLBOX

Summarize After you read this section, make a chart comparing the characteristics and functions of different animal body systems. Be sure to include how the systems are different in simple and complex animals.

Why Do Animals Need Skeletons?

Remember that one of the characteristics of animals is the ability to move. For an animal to be able to move, its body must be flexible. Its body must also have support. In most animals, this flexibility and support come from the skeleton.

There are three main kinds of skeletons: hydrostatic skeletons, exoskeletons, and endoskeletons. The figure below shows examples of these skeleton types.

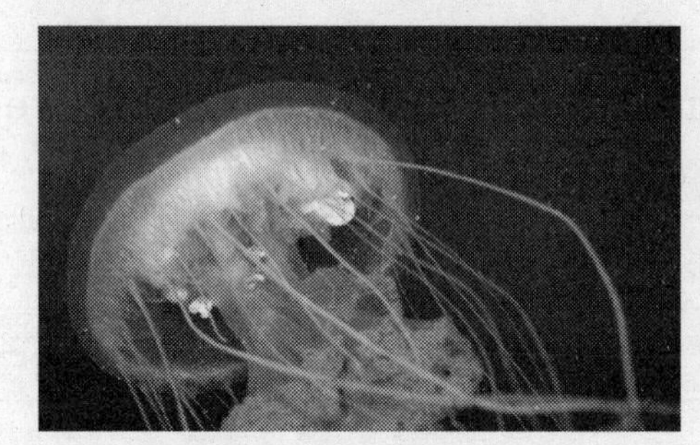

Many soft-bodied invertebrates, such as this jellyfish, have hydrostatic skeletons. A **hydrostatic skeleton** is a cavity within the animal's body that is filled with water. The pressure from the water provides support for the animal's body.

Many invertebrates, such as this beetle, have exoskeletons. An **exoskeleton** is a hard skeleton that grows on the outside of the animal. The animal's muscles attach to the inside of the skeleton.

Like all vertebrates, this salamander has an endoskeleton. Some invertebrates also have endoskeletons. An **endoskeleton** is a hard skeleton that grows within the animal. The animal's muscles attach to the outside of the skeleton.

Talk About It

Learn Word Roots Look up the prefixes *endo-* and *exo-* in a dictionary. With a partner, discuss why these prefixes are used to describe different kinds of skeletons.

Critical Thinking

1. Infer Where do you think most animals with hydrostatic skeletons live?

____

____

How Do Animals Break Down Food?

An animal's *digestive system* breaks down the food the animal eats. The digestive system allows the body to absorb nutrients from the food. It also allows the body to get rid of the parts of the food the animal can't use.

Different animals have different kinds of digestive systems. The figure below shows the digestive system of a simple animal, the hydra.

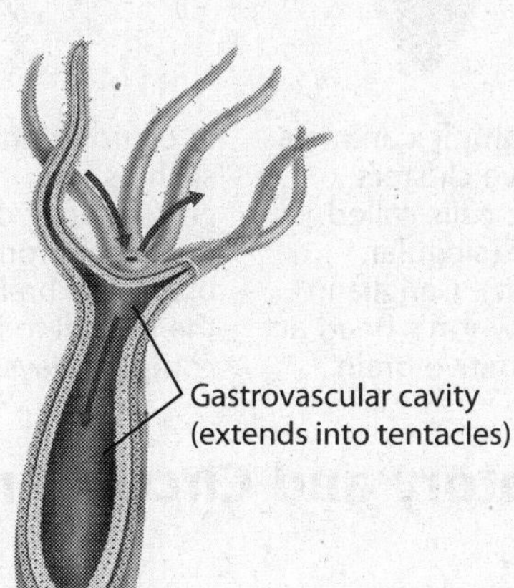

The digestive system of this hydra is a **gastrovascular cavity**. It has only one opening. Food and wastes both move through this opening.

In contrast, animals that are more complex—such as vertebrates—have a *digestive tract*, or gut, with two openings. Food enters through one opening, the mouth. Wastes leave through the other opening, the anus.

As the cells in an animal's body break down nutrient molecules, the cells produce wastes. An animal's *excretory system* removes these wastes from the body.

What Kinds of Nervous Systems Do Animals Have?

Most animals rely on their nervous systems to help them sense and respond to their environments. An animal's nervous system is made of specialized cells called *nerve cells*. These cells can carry messages in the form of electrical signals. ☑

The simplest animals—the sponges—do not have nervous systems. Other animals have different kinds of nervous systems. Some are very simple. Others are much more complex. The figure on the next page shows three examples of animal nervous systems.

Talk About It

Research and Share Learn more about the digestive systems of two different animals. One of the animals should be a vertebrate and one of them should be an invertebrate. What type of digestive system does each animal have? How is the structure of its digestive system related to the food it eats? Share what you learn with a small group.

LOOKING CLOSER

2. Describe How many openings does a hydra's digestive system have?

____

Critical Thinking

3. Apply Concepts How many openings does a bird's digestive system have?

____

4. Describe In what form do nerve cells carry messages?

____

____

____

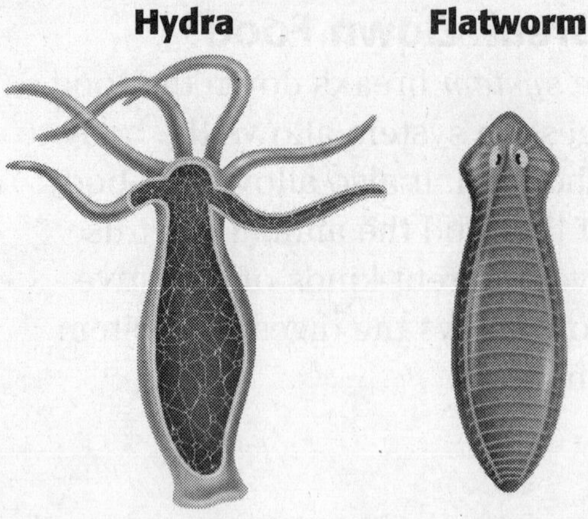

In simple animals, such as this hydra, the nerve cells are arranged into a *nerve net.*

More-complex animals may have clusters of nerve cells called *ganglia* (singular, *ganglion*). Ganglia in this flatworm's head act as a primitive brain.

In complex animals, such as this grasshopper, clusters of nerve cells form a true brain. The brain allows the animal to behave in complex ways.

LOOKING CLOSER

5. Identify How are nerve cells arranged in a hydra?

____

____

What Do the Respiratory and Circulatory Systems Do?

All animals carry out aerobic respiration. Therefore, their cells must take in oxygen and get rid of carbon dioxide. Most animals have specialized *respiratory systems* that help their body cells take in oxygen and get rid of carbon dioxide.

Many animals that live in water have *gills*. These feathery structures exchange oxygen and carbon dioxide with the water around the animal. In general, animals that live on land cannot use gills to exchange gases. They use other structures—such as lungs—to exchange gases with the air.

The cells in small, simple animals are very close to the outside environment. Therefore, they can take in oxygen and nutrients directly from the environment. However, the cells of larger animals may be far from sources of oxygen and nutrients. These animals have *circulatory systems* that carry oxygen and nutrients to all the cells in the animal's body. There are two kinds of circulatory systems. ☑

Critical Thinking

6. Compare What is the main difference between the nervous system of a flatworm and the nervous system of a grasshopper?

____

____

____

Background

Recall that during *aerobic respiration*, a cell uses oxygen and glucose to produce carbon dioxide, water, and energy.

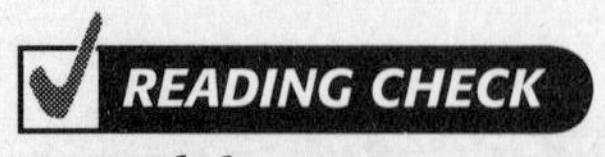

7. Explain How can small, simple animals survive without circulatory systems?

____

____

____

OPEN CIRCULATORY SYSTEM

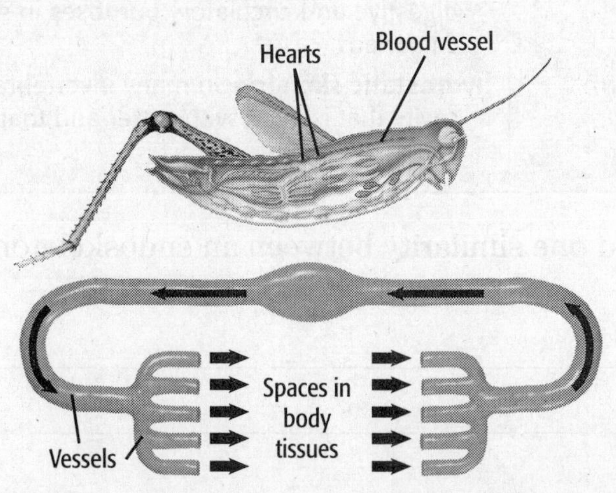

In an open circulatory system, a heart pumps blood into blood vessels. The blood leaves the blood vessels and washes over the body tissues. Then, the blood re-enters the blood vessels and flows back to the heart.

LOOKING CLOSER

8. Describe In an open circulatory system, what happens to blood that leaves the heart?

____

____

____

____

____

CLOSED CIRCULATORY SYSTEM

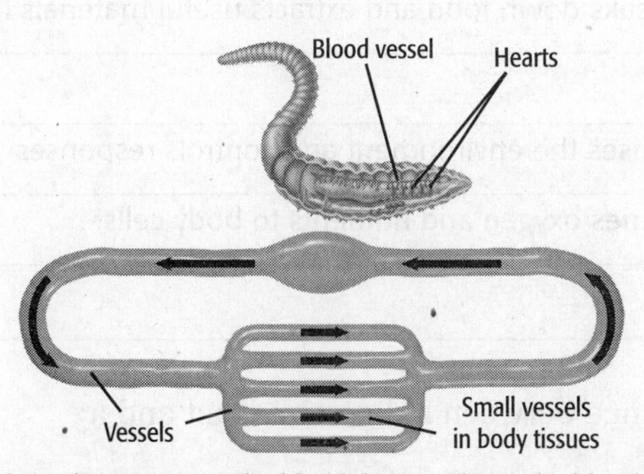

In a closed circulatory system, the blood does not leave the blood vessels. Gases and nutrients move between the blood and the body by moving through the walls of the blood vessels.

LOOKING CLOSER

9. Explain How do gases and nutrients move between the blood and the body in a closed circulatory system?

____

____

____

How Do Animals Reproduce?

Remember that there are two types of reproduction: asexual reproduction and sexual reproduction. Some animals, such as birds, reproduce using only sexual reproduction. Other animals, such as starfish, can reproduce using either sexual or asexual reproduction.

Name ______________________ Class ______________ Date ____________

Section 2 Review

SECTION VOCABULARY

endoskeleton an internal skeleton made of bone and cartilage **exoskeleton** a hard, external, supporting structure that develops from the ectoderm	**gastrovascular cavity** a cavity that serves both digestive and circulatory purposes in some cnidarians **hydrostatic skeleton** in many invertebrates, the cavity that is filled with water and that has a support function

1. Compare Give one difference and one similarity between an endoskeleton and an exoskeleton.

____

____

____

2. Describe Fill in the blank spaces in the table to describe the functions of different animal body systems.

System	Function
	breaks down food and extracts useful materials from it
Excretory system	
	senses the environment and controls responses
	carries oxygen and nutrients to body cells
Respiratory system	

3. Compare What is the main difference between a digestive tract and a gastrovascular cavity?

____

____

4. Explain What is the function of an animal's respiratory system?

____

____

5. Identify What are two ways that animals reproduce?

____

____

Name ______________________ Class ______________ Date __________

CHAPTER 26 Introduction to Animals

SECTION 3

Evolutionary Trends in Animals

KEY IDEAS

As you read this section, keep these questions in mind:

- What evolutionary trends in body structure do animals show?
- How do animal embryos develop?
- What types of internal body structures do animals with bilateral symmetry have?
- What two body characteristics give animals a greater ability to move and to be more flexible?

How Have Animals Evolved?

The first animals to evolve were small and simple. Over time, more-complex animals evolved. Two characteristics that have evolved in more-complex animals are true tissues and bilateral symmetry.

The earliest animals probably did not have tissues or organs. Today, all but the simplest animals have tissues, and many animals have organs. Tissues and organs help animals survive by allowing them to sense and interact with their environments. ☑

The earliest animals were probably asymmetrical, as many sponges are today. Over time, however, animals have evolved radial symmetry and bilateral symmetry.

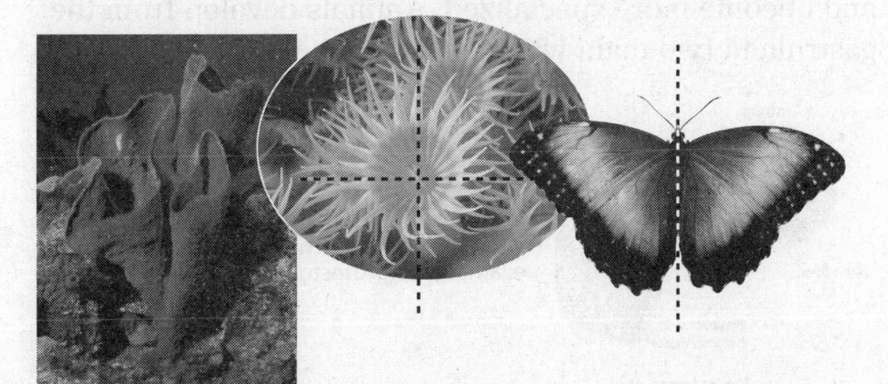

Early animals were probably *asymmetrical* like this sponge.

Animals with *radial symmetry*, such as this anemone, have repeating body parts. These parts are arranged around a central point.

Many complex animals show *bilateral symmetry*. Their bodies can be divided into mirror-image halves. Most animals with bilateral symmetry show **cephalization**. This means they have a head end that contains many sensory organs.

READING TOOLBOX

Learn New Words As you read this section, underline words you don't know. When you figure out what they mean, write the words and their definitions in your notebook.

1. Explain How do tissues and organs help animals survive?

____

____

____

____

Talk About It

Identify In a small group, try to identify the type of symmetry that various animals have. Can you think of any animals that have radial symmetry?

How Do Animal Embryos Develop?

Remember that most animals reproduce sexually. During sexual reproduction, a male gamete and a female gamete combine to form a *zygote*. The new organism develops as the zygote divides. Animal zygotes develop in a series of steps. These steps, shown below, are the same for all animals that reproduce sexually.

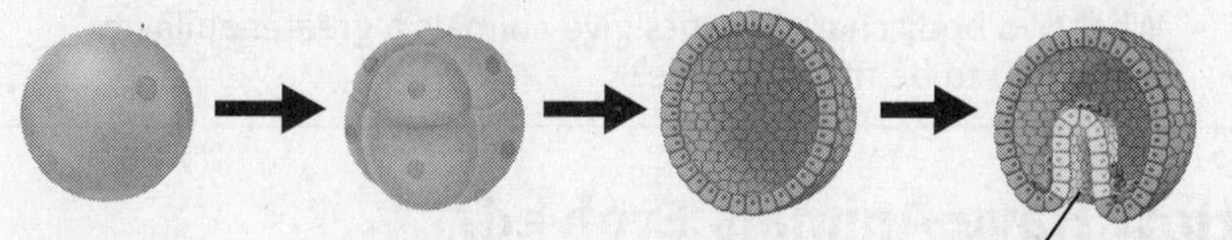

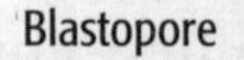

❶ The zygote is the first cell of the new organism. It will divide by mitosis. In a zygote, this process is called **cleavage**.

❷ Each cell division doubles the number of cells. However, the ball of cells stays about the same size. Therefore, the cells get smaller during cleavage.

❸ Eventually, cleavage produces a hollow ball of cells called a **blastula**.

❹ During **gastrulation**, one side of the blastula folds inward to form a pocket. The opening of the pocket is called a *blastopore*. The ball of cells is now called a *gastrula*.

LOOKING CLOSER

2. Compare How is a blastula different from a gastrula?

____

____

____

____

DIFFERENTIATION

During *differentiation*, the cells in the gastrula divide and become more specialized. Animals develop from the gastrula in two main ways, as shown below.

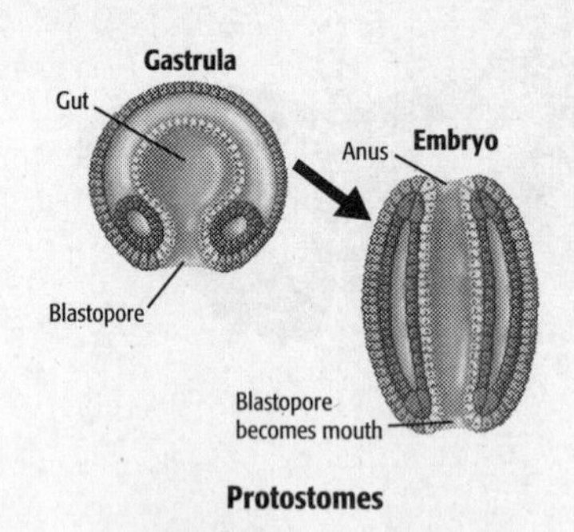

In **protostomes**, the blastopore develops into the mouth. Flatworms and insects are examples of protostomes.

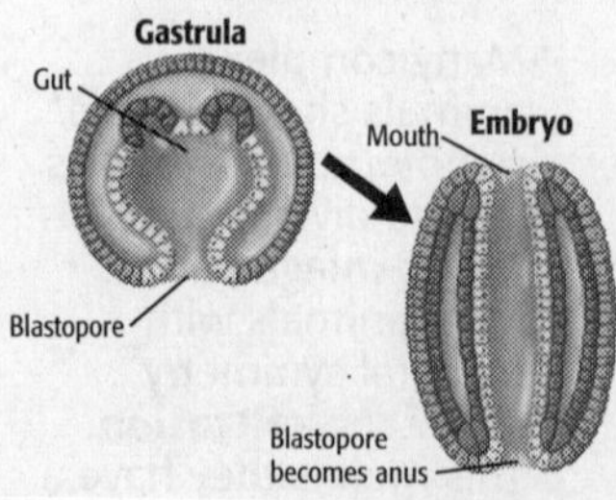

In **deuterostomes**, the blastopore develops into the anus. Vertebrates and starfish are examples of deuterostomes.

Critical Thinking

3. Apply Concepts Are humans protostomes or deuterostomes? Explain your answer.

____

____

____

____

What Internal Structures Do Animals with Bilateral Symmetry Have?

Remember that many animals show bilateral symmetry. Biologists classify these animals into three main groups based on their internal body structure. The three groups are acoelomates, pseudocoelomates, and coelomates. ☑

4. Identify What type of body symmetry do coelomates have?

____

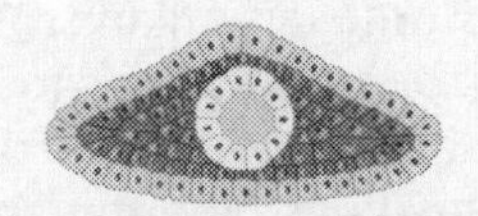

The space between an *acoelomate*'s body covering and its gut is completely filled with tissue. Flatworms are acoelomates.

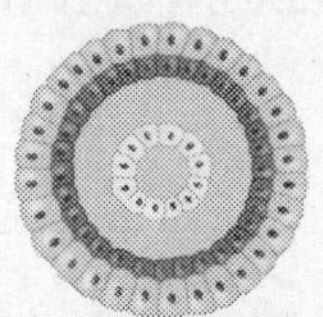

The space between a *pseudocoelomate*'s body covering and its gut is filled with liquid. However, there is no layer of tissue between the liquid and the gut. Roundworms are pseudocoelomates.

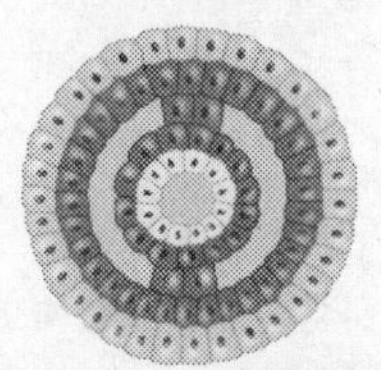

The space between a *coelomate*'s body covering and its gut is a coelom. A **coelom** is a fluid-filled space that is lined with tissue. Humans and other vertebrates are coelomates.

Talk About It

Learn Word Roots Look up the prefixes *a-* and *pseudo-* in a dictionary. With a partner, talk about why these prefixes are used to describe organisms without coeloms or with structures similar to coeloms.

LOOKING CLOSER

5. Define What is a coelom?

____

____

What Characteristics Allow Animals to Move?

Two body characteristics that help animals move are body segmentation and jointed legs. The bodies of many animals are made up of *segments*, or similar repeating units. In some animals, such as vertebrates, these segments are visible only in the embryo. Body segmentation allows animals to be flexible. For example, an earthworm's segments allow the earthworm to move in many different ways.

Arthropods, such as insects and crabs, were the first kinds of organisms to evolve jointed legs. Joints allow animals to move more easily. They also allow animals to carry out complex movements, such as flying or running. ☑

6. Explain How do joints help an animal?

____

____

____

____

Name ______________________ Class ____________ Date ____________

Section 3 Review

SECTION VOCABULARY

blastula in an animal, the stage of early embryonic development in which a hollow ball of cells forms; the stage before gastrulation

cephalization the concentration of nerve tissue and sensory organs at the anterior end of an organism

cleavage in biological development, a series of cell divisions that occur immediately after an egg is fertilized

coelom a body cavity that contains the internal organs

deuterostome an animal whose mouth does not derive from the blastopore and whose embryo has indeterminate cleavage

gastrulation the transformation of the blastula into the gastrula or the formation of the embryonic germ layers

protostome an organism whose embryonic blastopore develops into the mouth, whose coelom arises by schizocoely, and whose embryo has determinate cleavage

1. **Compare** Give one similarity and one difference between protostomes and deuterostomes.

____

____

____

2. **Identify** Is the animal shown below asymmetrical, radially symmetrical, or bilaterally symmetrical?

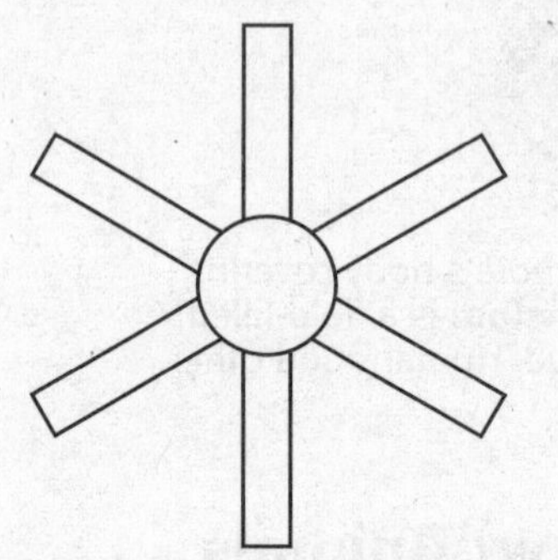

____

3. **Compare** Give one similarity and one difference between the internal body structure of a pseudocoelomate and the internal structure of a coelomate.

____

____

____

4. **Identify** What are two characteristics that help animals move?

____

____

Name ______________________ Class ______________ Date ______________

CHAPTER 26 Introduction to Animals

SECTION 4

Chordate Evolution

KEY IDEAS

As you read this section, keep these questions in mind:

- What are the key characteristics of chordates?
- What were the key evolutionary innovations in fish?
- What characteristics helped amphibians adapt to land?
- What major evolutionary innovations first appeared in reptiles?
- When did birds evolve, and what were the first birds like?
- When did mammals evolve, and from what group did they evolve?

What Are Chordates?

Most of the animals you see every day, including humans, are chordates. *Chordates* are members of phylum Chordata. Most chordates are vertebrates, but some are invertebrates. Although chordates can look very different from one another, they all share four characteristics. The diagram below shows what these characteristics are.

An Adult Lancet

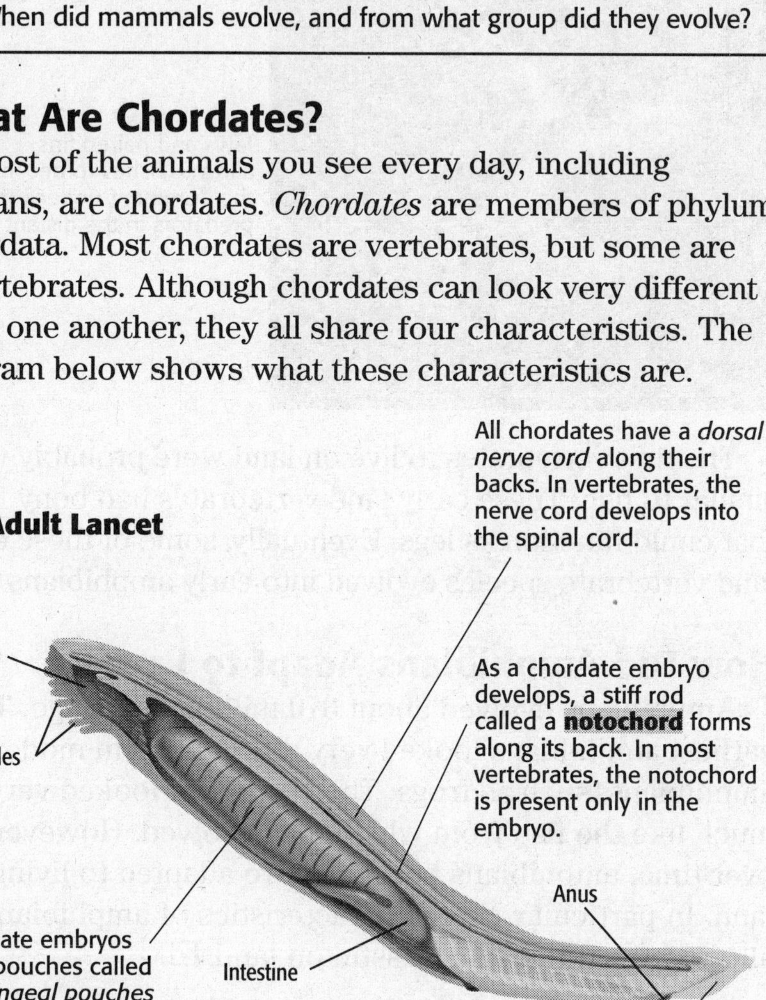

All chordates have a *dorsal nerve cord* along their backs. In vertebrates, the nerve cord develops into the spinal cord.

As a chordate embryo develops, a stiff rod called a **notochord** forms along its back. In most vertebrates, the notochord is present only in the embryo.

Chordate embryos have pouches called *pharyngeal pouches* on their throats. In chordates that live in water, these pouches develop into gills. In chordates that live on land, these pouches develop into structures in the head and neck.

All chordates have a *postanal tail*, which is a tail that extends beyond the anus. In some chordates, such as humans, the tail is present only in the embryo.

READING TOOLBOX

Describe Relationships When you finish reading this section, make a Concept Map using the terms *chordates, vertebrates, invertebrates, fishes, amphibians, land, water, reptiles, theropods, therapsids, birds*, and *mammals*.

Talk About It

Research and Share Learn more about invertebrate chordates. What kinds of animals are they? What are their characteristics? Where do they live? Share what you learn with a small group.

LOOKING CLOSER

1. Describe What happens to the dorsal nerve cord in vertebrates?

____

____

How Did Fishes Evolve?

The first vertebrates evolved about 500 million years ago. These early vertebrates were fish that did not have jaws. By about 430 million years ago, fish with jaws and paired fins had evolved. Their jaws and paired fins helped them catch and hold prey. Therefore, jawed fishes were better able to find food. This allowed them to become successful predators.

LOOKING CLOSER

2. Identify What are two characteristics that allowed fishes to become dominant?

____

____

Jaws and paired fins allowed fishes to become the dominant underwater predators in the distant past.

The first vertebrates to live on land were probably very similar to fish. These early land vertebrates had bony fins that could function as legs. Eventually, some of these early land vertebrate species evolved into early amphibians.

How Did Amphibians Adapt to Land?

Amphibians evolved about 370 million years ago. The earliest amphibians looked very different from modern amphibians, such as frogs. They probably looked very much like the fish from which they evolved. However, over time, amphibians became more adapted to living on land. In particular, three characteristics of amphibians allowed them to be successful on land: ☑

3. Describe What did the earliest amphibians probably look like?

____

____

____

- Amphibians have lungs that can exchange oxygen and carbon dioxide with the air. Fishes can exchange oxygen and carbon dioxide only with water.
- An amphibian's heart is more efficient than a fish's. Therefore, the amphibian's heart can deliver more oxygen to the amphibian's body.
- Amphibians have strong internal skeletons that can support their weight on land. In addition, they have limbs that allow them to move around on land.

What Characteristics Helped Reptiles Survive on Land?

Amphibians must keep their skin and eggs moist. Therefore, they must live near water or in wet areas. In contrast, reptiles lay **amniotic eggs** with tough, waterproof shells. In addition, reptiles have dry, scaly skin that prevents them from drying out. When reptiles evolved about 320 million years ago, these adaptations allowed them to live in places where amphibians could not.

Critical Thinking

4. Infer Which type of organism would you be more likely to find in a desert, an amphibian or a reptile? Explain your answer.

____

____

____

____

____

This turtle is hatching from an amniotic egg. Amniotic eggs and dry, scaly skin allowed reptiles to become the dominant land animals in the Mesozoic Era.

LOOKING CLOSER

5. Identify Is a turtle an amphibian or a reptile?

____

DINOSAURS

Reptiles dominated the land for hundreds of millions of years. One of the most well-known groups of reptiles is the dinosaurs. Dinosaurs evolved during the early Mesozoic Era, about 235 million years ago. They dominated the land for more than 150 million years.

There were many different kinds of dinosaurs. Huge, plant-eating *sauropods*, such as *Apatosaurus*, were some of the largest animals ever to live on land. Meat-eating *theropods*, such as *Tyrannosaurus rex*, were the main land predators on Earth until the end of the Mesozoic Era.

Scientists still do not know exactly what caused the dinosaurs to become extinct. Several factors probably contributed to their extinction. For example, geologic evidence indicates that there were large volcanic eruptions on Earth around the time the dinosaurs became extinct. A huge asteroid also hit Earth around this time. These events may have contributed to the extinction of the dinosaurs.

Critical Thinking

6. Describe Give two characteristics that dinosaurs probably had. Explain your answer.

____

____

____

____

____

____

How Did Birds Evolve?

Birds first evolved about 150 million years ago from small, meat-eating theropods. The earliest birds probably looked very similar to dinosaurs. For example, the figure below shows a fossil of an early species of bird known as *Archaeopteryx*. It shows characteristics of both modern birds and of the theropod dinosaurs from which it evolved.

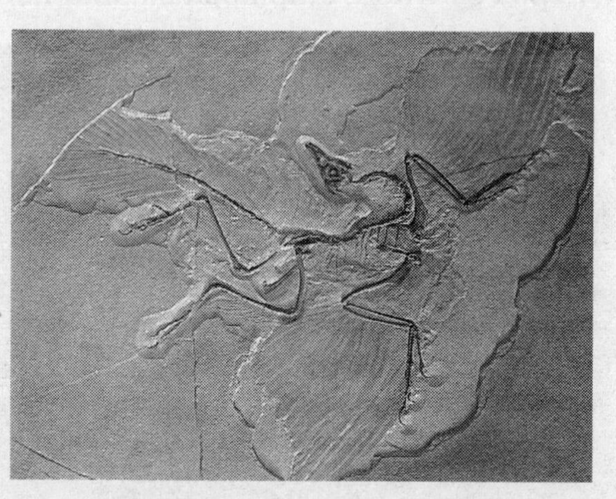

Like theropod dinosaurs, *Archaeopteryx* had a long tail, teeth, and arms with fingers and claws. It did not have a large breastbone, and it had solid bones. However, like modern birds, *Archaeopteryx* had feathers on its wings and tail. In addition, its collarbone was fused. These traits suggest that *Archaeopteryx* may have been an early species of bird. They also indicate that birds evolved from theropod dinosaurs.

LOOKING CLOSER

7. Identify Give two traits of birds that *Archaeopteryx* had.

____

____

8. Identify Give two traits of dinosaurs that *Archaeopteryx* had.

____

____

Some scientists think that birds' ability to fly began in theropod reptiles as an ability to glide through the air. This ability to glide gave the ancestors of birds a survival advantage. It allowed them to more easily avoid predators and find food. Over time, organisms that were better adapted for gliding or flying became more dominant. ☑

Through time, birds have evolved several characteristics that make flying easier. For example, birds have light, hollow bones. This makes their skeleton lighter. They also have large breastbones and chest muscles. The muscles attach to the breastbone. The large size of the chest muscles allows them to control a bird's wings.

9. Explain How might the ability to glide have helped the ancestors of modern birds survive?

____

____

____

Name ______________________ Class ______________ Date ______________

How Did Mammals Evolve?

The first mammals evolved about 220 million years ago. Mammals evolved from a group of mammal-like reptiles called **therapsids**. Therapsids are extinct, but their descendents—mammals—are now the dominant land animals on Earth. ☑

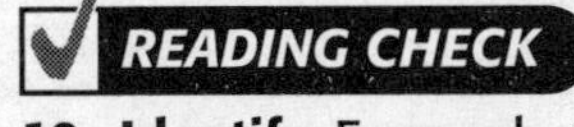

10. Identify From what group of animals did mammals evolve?

____

Early mammals were very small. They were probably not much larger than modern mice. They probably ate mainly insects and lived in trees. A few early mammal species may have lived mainly in the water, like modern beavers do. Some early mammals may have looked similar to the tree shrew in the figure below. ☑

11. Describe Give three characteristics of early mammals.

____

____

____

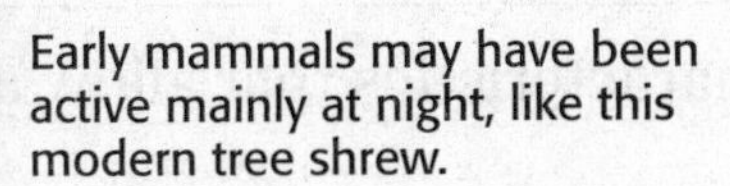

Early mammals may have been active mainly at night, like this modern tree shrew.

While the dinosaurs were alive, mammals were not very diverse. However, when the dinosaurs became extinct, mammals evolved and took over the niches that dinosaurs once filled. Many new groups of mammals appeared in the Tertiary Period.

Today, most large land animals are mammals. However, between about 2 million and 10,000 years ago, many more species of large land mammals existed. Many of these species became extinct due to climate change. However, hunting by early humans probably also contributed to their extinction. ☑

12. Explain Why are there fewer species of large land mammals alive today than there were in the past?

____

____

____

____

Name ________________ Class ________________ Date ________________

Section 4 Review

SECTION VOCABULARY

amniotic egg a type of egg that is produced by reptiles, birds, and egg-laying mammals and that contains a large amount of yolk; usually surrounded by a leathery or hard shell within which the embryo and its embryonic membranes develop	**notochord** the rod-shaped supporting axis found in the dorsal part of the embryos of all chordates, including vertebrates **therapsid** the extinct order of mammal-like reptiles that likely gave rise to mammals

1. Identify Give the four characteristics of all chordates.

____

____

____

____

2. Explain Why are humans classified as chordates, even though adult humans do not show all the characteristics of chordates?

____

____

3. Describe What are three characteristics that allow amphibians to live on land?

____

____

____

4. Explain What are two characteristics that helped reptiles become dominant on land? How did these characteristics help reptiles become dominant?

____

____

____

5. Identify What group of dinosaurs did birds probably evolve from?

____

6. Explain Early mammals were tiny and not very different from one another. How did mammals become the dominant land animals?

____

____

____

Name ______________________ Class ______________ Date ____________

CHAPTER 27 Simple Invertebrates

SECTION 1

Sponges

KEY IDEAS

As you read this section, keep these questions in mind:

- What are the key characteristics of sponges, and why are sponges considered to be animals?
- How do sponges reproduce?
- How are groups of sponges classified?

What Are Sponges?

A sponge is basically a mass of cells stuck together with a gel-like substance. However, sponges are considered animals because they have the following characteristics:

- are multicellular
- are heterotrophic
- have no cell walls
- have some specialized cells

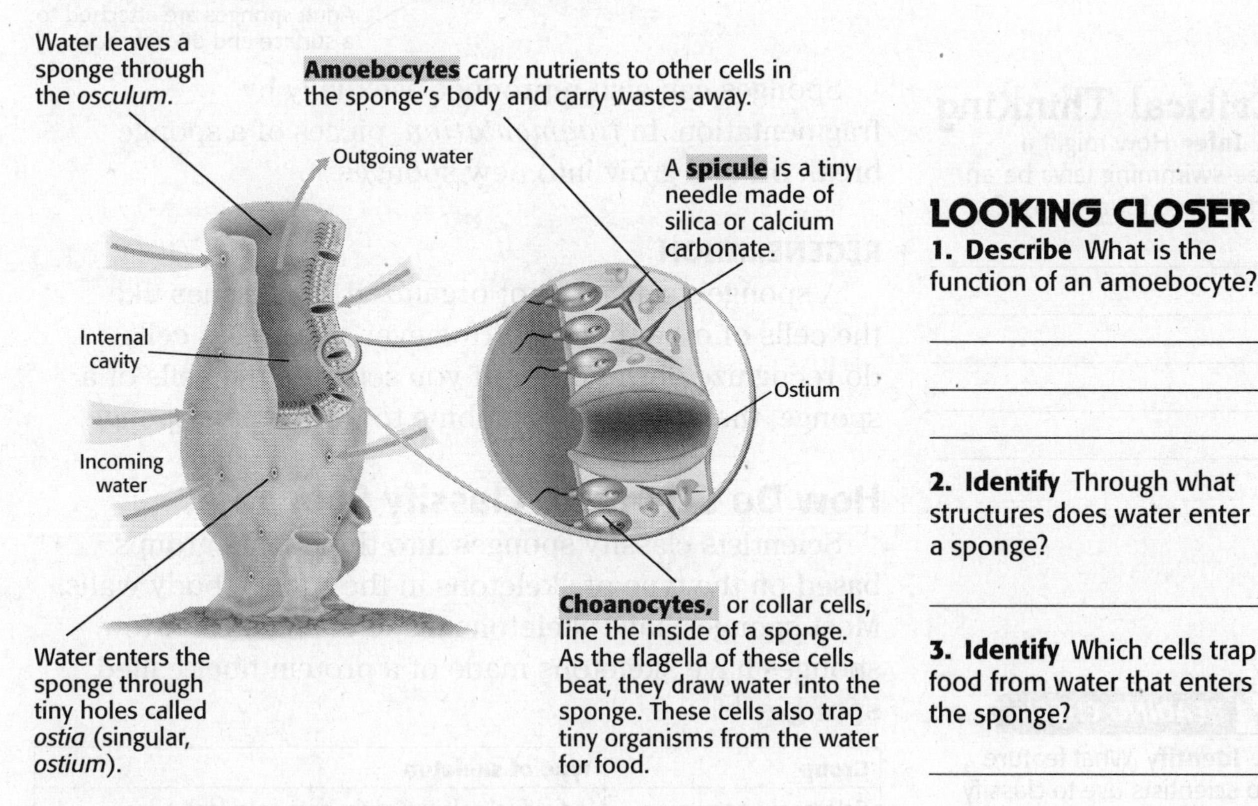

About 5,000 species of sponges are living today. Most sponges live in salt water. However, a few species of sponges can live in fresh water.

READING TOOLBOX

Summarize After you read this section, make a Process Chart that summarizes how a sponge reproduces sexually.

LOOKING CLOSER

1. Describe What is the function of an amoebocyte?

____

2. Identify Through what structures does water enter a sponge?

____

3. Identify Which cells trap food from water that enters the sponge?

____

How Do Sponges Reproduce?

Sponges reproduce both sexually and asexually. Most sponges are hermaphrodites. A *hermaphrodite* is an individual that produces both eggs and sperm. These sponges produce eggs and sperm at different times so that they do not self-fertilize. ☑

4. Define What is a hermaphrodite?

______

Sexual Reproduction in Sponges

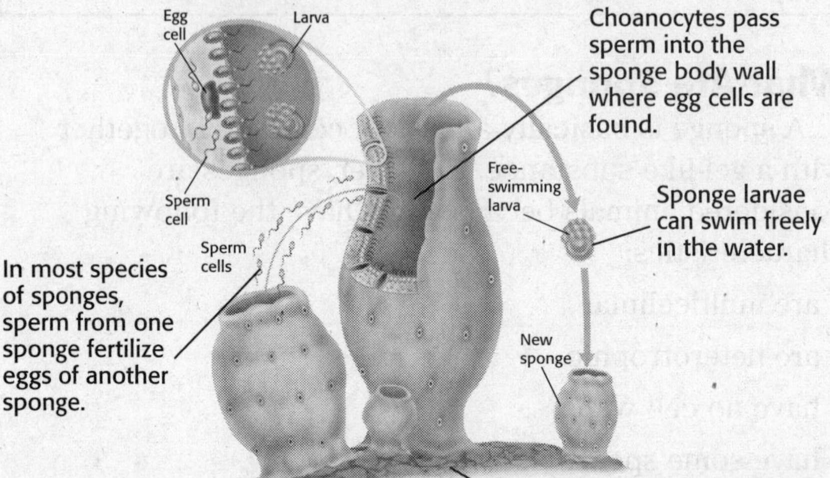

Sponges can also reproduce asexually by fragmentation. In *fragmentation*, pieces of a sponge break off and grow into new sponges.

Critical Thinking

5. Infer How might a free-swimming larva be an advantage for a sponge?

______

REGENERATION

A sponge's cells are not organized into tissues like the cells of other animals. However, a sponge's cells do recognize one another. If you separate the cells of a sponge, the cells can recombine to form a new sponge.

How Do Scientists Classify Sponges?

Scientists classify sponges into three main groups based on the type of skeletons in the sponge body walls. Most sponges have skeletons made of spicules. A few sponges have skeletons made of a protein fiber called **spongin**. ☑

6. Identify What feature do scientists use to classify sponges?

______

Group	Type of skeleton
Calcareous sponges	individual calcium carbonate spicules
Glass sponges	silica spicules
Demosponges	loose silica spicules, spongin fibers, both silica and spongin, or neither

Name ______________________ Class ______________ Date ____________

Section 1 Review

SECTION VOCABULARY

amoebocyte in sponges and other invertebrates, an amoeba-like cell that moves through the body fluids, removes wastes, and participates in other processes

choanocyte any of the flagellate cells that line the cavities of a sponge

spicule a needle of silica or calcium carbonate in the skeleton of some sponges

spongin a fibrous protein that contains sulfur and composes the fibers of the skeleton of some sponges

1. List What four characteristics do sponges share with other animals?

____

____

____

2. Identify What are three functions of choanocytes?

____

____

____

3. Compare How is a sponge larva different from an adult sponge?

____

____

4. Describe What happens in fragmentation?

____

____

5. List What are the three main groups of sponges?

____

____

____

6. Compare How are glass sponges different from calcareous sponges?

____

____

____

Name ______________________ Class ______________ Date ______________

SECTION 2

Cnidarians

KEY IDEAS

As you read this section, keep these questions in mind:

- What are the two body forms that are found in the cnidarian life cycle?
- What are the three main groups of modern cnidarians?

READING TOOLBOX

Ask Questions Read this section quietly to yourself. As you read, write down any questions you have. When you finish reading, work in a small group to figure out the answers to your questions.

What Are Cnidarians?

Hydras, corals, jellyfish, and sea anemones belong to the phylum Cnidaria. Most cnidarians live in the ocean.

Unlike the cells of a sponge, the cells of a cnidarian are arranged into tissues. The body of a cnidarian is radially symmetrical. In *radial symmetry*, an organism's body parts are arranged around a central axis, like the spokes of a wheel.

Cnidarians have two basic body forms: the medusa and the polyp. **Medusa** forms float freely in the water and are typically shaped like umbrellas. **Polyp** forms attach to rocks or other objects and are shaped like tubes. Many cnidarians live as medusas. Other cnidarians live only as polyps. ☑

1. Identify What are the two body forms of cnidarians?

____

____

LOOKING CLOSER

2. Describe How are the medusa and polyp body forms similar? How are they different?

____

____

____

____

____

A cnidarian does not have a central structure that functions as a brain. Instead, it has *nerve cells* arranged in a nerve net throughout its tissues.

Nematocyst (discharged)
Cnidocyte
Nematocyst (coiled)
Medusa
Polyp
Nematocyst (discharged)
Cnidocyte
Tentacles
Nerve cell
Nematocyst (coiled)
Gastrovascular cavity

The two body forms of cnidarians consist of the same body parts arranged differently.

REPRODUCTION

Some cnidarians exist as medusa and polyp forms during different parts of their life cycles. In these cnidarians, the medusa reproduces sexually by releasing sperm or eggs into the water. The gametes join to form a zygote, which grows into a free-swimming larva called a **planula** (plural, *planulae*). Planulae settle on the ocean floor and grow into polyps. The polyps reproduce asexually to produce male and female medusas.

FEEDING AND DEFENSE

Cnidarians have stinging cells called **cnidocytes** on their tentacles. Cnidocytes are the distinguishing characteristics of animals in the phylum Cnidaria. Inside each cnidocyte is a threadlike organelle called a **nematocyst**. Nematocysts typically contain toxins. A cnidarian can use nematocysts to defend itself and to capture prey.

Critical Thinking

3. Compare Consider a cnidarian that spends part of its life cycle as a medusa and part as a polyp. How do the methods of reproduction of the medusa and polyp stages differ?

____

____

____

____

What Are the Main Groups of Cnidarians?

Group	Description
Hydrozoans	• includes hydra and *Physalia*, or Portuguese man-of-war (a colonial organism) • Some live in fresh water (hydra); most live in the ocean. • Most go through polyp and medusa stages.
Scyphozoans	• also called jellyfish • includes *Obelia* and *Aurelia* • spend most of their lives as medusas • use tentacles to trap prey • Toxins of some are strong enough to kill a large animal.
Anthozoans	• includes sea anemones and corals • exist only as polyps • Most contain symbiotic algae that provide food for the polyp in exchange for a place to live. • feed on fish and other organisms that pass close to their tentacles

Talk About It

Research With a partner, choose an organism from one of the three groups of cnidarians. Research this organism to learn about its life cycle, body form, where it lives, and other unique characteristics. Create a poster about your organism and present the poster to the class.

LOOKING CLOSER

4. Identify Which group of cnidarians includes corals?

____

5. Identify Which body form is most common for scyphozoans?

____

Name ______________________ Class ______________ Date ______________

Section 2 Review

SECTION VOCABULARY

cnidocyte a stinging cell of a cnidarian **medusa** a free-swimming, jellyfish-like, and often umbrella-shaped sexual stage in the life cycle of a cnidarian; also a jellyfish or a hydra **nematocyst** in cnidarians, a stinging component of a specialized cell that is used to capture prey or inject prey with a toxin	**planula** the free-swimming, ciliated larva of a cnidarian **polyp** a form of a cnidarian that has a cylindrical, hollow body and that is usually attached to a rock or to another object

1. Identify What is the distinguishing characteristic of cnidarians?

____

2. List What are the three main groups of cnidarians?

____

3. Summarize Complete the process chart below to summarize the life cycle of a cnidarian that has medusa and polyp body forms at different parts of its life cycle.

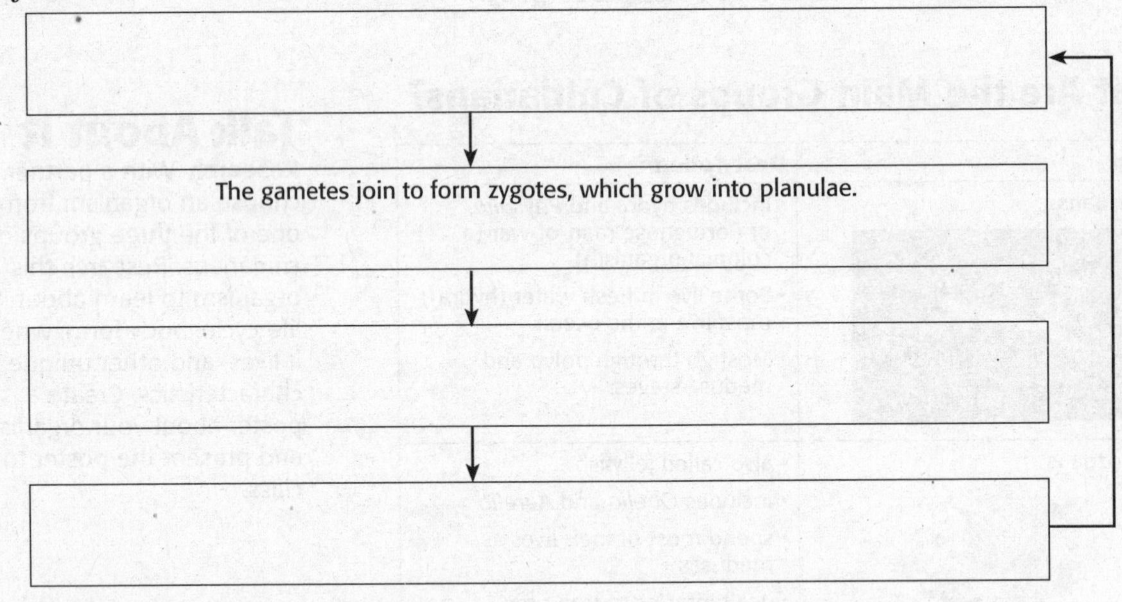

4. Describe What does a radially symmetrical organism look like?

____

____

5. Compare How does the arrangement of cells in a cnidarian's body differ from that of a sponge's body?

____

____

Name ______________________ Class ______________ Date ______________

CHAPTER 27 Simple Invertebrates

SECTION 3

Flatworms

KEY IDEAS

As you read this section, keep these questions in mind:

- What are three important characteristics of flatworms?
- What are three groups of modern flatworms? Is each group free living or parasitic?

What Are Flatworms?

The flatworms are named for their thin, flat bodies, which are typically only a few cell layers thick. The flatworm body is simple. However, it is more complex than the body of a sponge or cnidarian. Unlike sponges and cnidarians, flatworms have:

- bilateral symmetry
- three tissue layers
- *cephalization*, a concentration of nerve tissue at a "head" end ☑

READING TOOLBOX

Summarize Before you read, create a table on a sheet of paper that describes the characteristics of sponges and cnidarians. As you read this section, add a column to your table that lists the characteristics of flatworms. When you read the final section of this chapter, add a fourth column to your table.

1. Define What is cephalization?

____

____

____

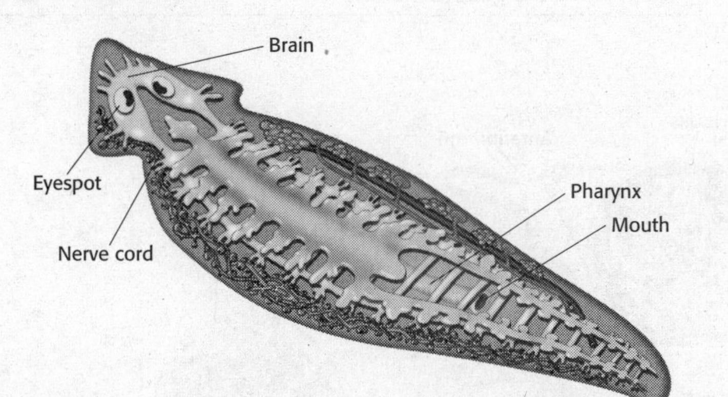

Unlike sponges and cnidarians, flatworms have tissues that are organized into organs.

Bilaterally symmetrical animals such as flatworms have bodies with left and right halves. The two halves are mirror images. Bilateral symmetry allows an animal to have a head end. In general, animals with a head end can move through their environments more easily than less-complex animals can. A flatworm has a group of cells at its head end that functions like a primitive brain. ☑

Flatworms do not have circulatory or respiratory systems. Each cell in a flatworm's body is close to the body surface. Thus, gases can move efficiently through the flatworm's body by diffusion.

2. Describe What does an organism with bilateral symmetry look like?

____

____

____

____

Name ______________________ Class ______________ Date ______________

What Are the Three Groups of Flatworms?

Scientists have discovered about 20,000 species of flatworms. Some flatworms are free-living marine animals that feed on small invertebrates. Some species are less than 1 mm long. Other species may be many meters long. Many flatworms are parasites of humans and other vertebrates. Scientists classify the flatworms that are living today into three main groups.

Group	Characteristics
Turbellarians	• Most are predators; some are herbivores or parasites. • mostly marine • Some can reproduce asexually by fragmentation.
Tapeworms	• parasites of vertebrates, including humans • live in the intestines of hosts • no digestive system; absorb nutrients through their skin
Flukes	• largest group of flatworms • parasites • Some live inside their hosts *(endoparasites)*; others live on their hosts *(ectoparasites)*. • have complex life cycles involving several hosts • reproduce sexually • no digestive system

LOOKING CLOSER

3. Identify Which two groups of flatworms contain only parasites?

____

____

Critical Thinking

4. Hypothesize What do you think are the functions of the hooks and suckers on the head end of a tapeworm?

____

____

____

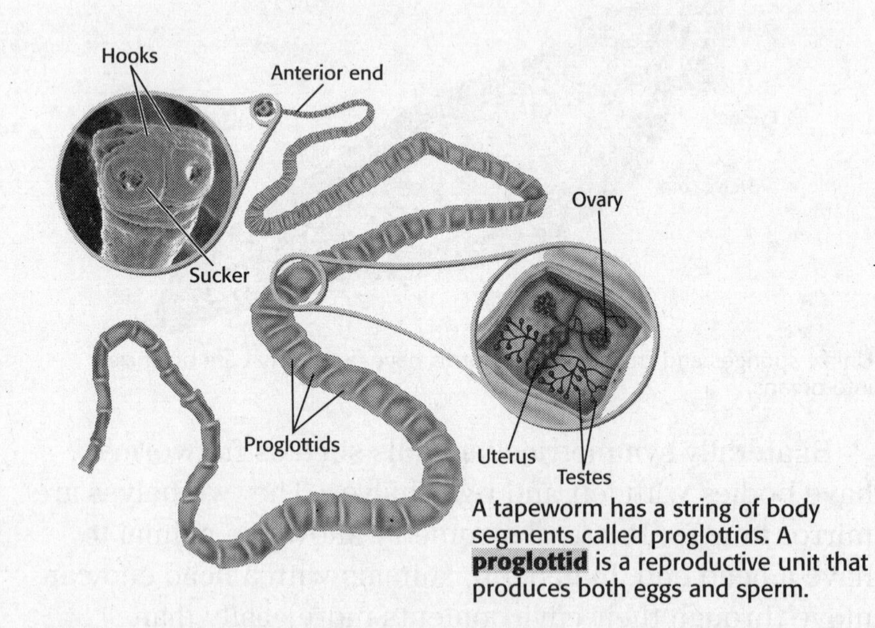

A tapeworm has a string of body segments called proglottids. A **proglottid** is a reproductive unit that produces both eggs and sperm.

Tapeworms are parasites that live in the intestines of their hosts. Mature proglottids with fertilized eggs break off a tapeworm and leave the host's body in feces. Another host may then ingest the eggs.

LOOKING CLOSER

5. Infer What type of reproduction do tapeworms use?

____

Name ______________________ Class ______________ Date ______________

Section 3 Review

SECTION VOCABULARY

proglottid one of the many body sections of a tapeworm; contains reproductive organs	

1. List What are three characteristics of flatworms that make them more complex than sponges or cnidarians?

____

2. Explain What is the advantage of cephalization?

____

____

3. Explain Why do flatworms not need respiratory systems?

____

____

____

4. Identify What are the three main groups of flatworms?

____

5. Compare Complete the Venn diagram below to compare the three main groups of flatworms.

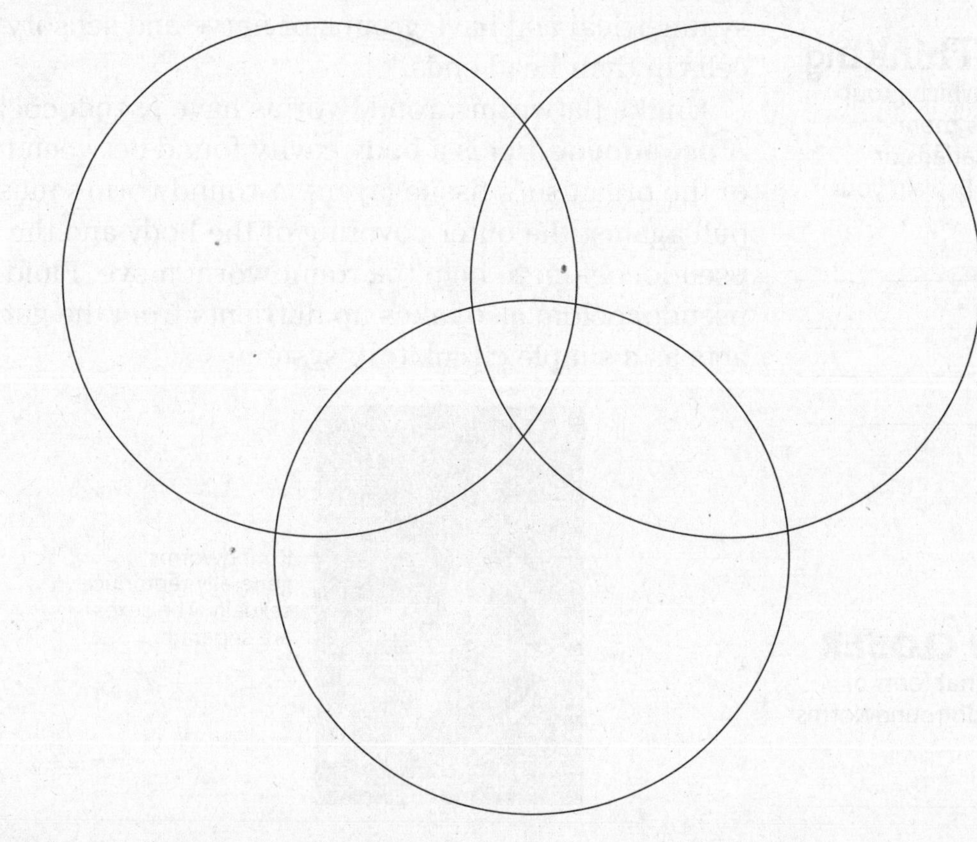

Name ______________________ Class ______________ Date ______________

SECTION 4

Roundworms

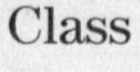

KEY IDEAS

As you read this section, keep these questions in mind:
- What are three key characteristics of roundworms?
- What are four common types of parasitic roundworms?
- What steps can help people avoid roundworms and other parasites?

What Are Roundworms?

Earth is covered with roundworms. Scientists know of more than 15,000 species, but more than half a million species might exist. Roundworms have thin, cylinder-shaped bodies. Some roundworms grow to a foot or more in length, but most species are only a few millimeters long. Thousands of tiny roundworms can live in a handful of soil. Roundworms have three key characteristics:

- three tissue layers
- a pseudocoelom
- a digestive system with separate openings for feeding and getting rid of wastes

Like flatworms, roundworms are bilaterally symmetrical and have groups of nerve and sensory cells in their head ends.

Unlike flatworms, roundworms have pseudocoeloms. A **pseudocoelom** is a body cavity found between two of the organism's tissue layers. A roundworm's muscles pull against the outer covering of the body and the pseudocoelom to help the roundworm move. Fluid in the pseudocoelom also takes up nutrients from the gut and acts as a simple circulatory system.

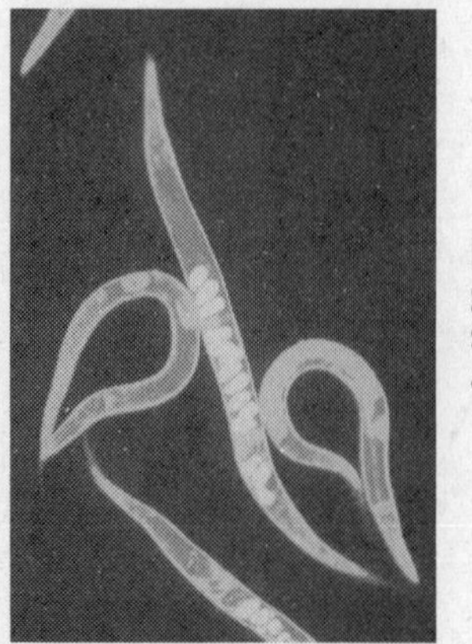

Roundworms generally reproduce sexually. The sexes are separate.

READING TOOLBOX

Summarize After you read, make a four-square diagram with one of the following labels in each square:
- characteristics roundworms have but other simple invertebrates do not
- characteristics roundworms share with at least one other group of simple invertebrates
- examples of roundworms
- habitats of different kinds of roundworms

Critical Thinking

1. Compare Which group of organisms is more complex—cnidarians or roundworms? Explain your answer.

____

____

____

____

LOOKING CLOSER

2. Identify What form of reproduction do roundworms use?

____

What Are Some Common Parasitic Roundworms?

Most roundworms are free living and play important roles in decomposition and nutrient recycling in ecosystems. However, many are parasitic. The table below describes four common parasitic roundworms. ☑

3. Describe What are two important roles of free living roundworms?

____

Group	Characteristics
Pinworms	• live in human intestines • infect as many as 50% of preschool and school-age children • cause itching around anus • Eggs spread through feces of an infected person. • easily treated with medication and washing bedding in hot water
Hookworms	• live in human intestines • infect about one-fifth of the world's population • can cause diarrhea, cramps, and anemia • enter body through feet when people walk barefoot on soil containing the worm's larvae
Filarial worms	• live in the blood or other tissues of vertebrates • example: dog heartworm • In human lymphatic system, can cause severe swelling of body parts • some can be spread by mosquitoes
Ascarids	• live in intestines of pigs, horses, and humans • feed on food that passes through the host's intestines • Fertilized eggs leave a host's body in feces. Eggs enter another host through contaminated food or water.

LOOKING CLOSER

4. Identify Which parasitic roundworms can enter the human body through an individual's feet?

____

5. Identify Members of which group of parasitic roundworms can be carried to new hosts by mosquitoes?

____

How Can Humans Avoid Parasite Infections?

Parasitic worms cause billions of infections around the world. These infections are more common in areas without good sewage systems or clean drinking water. Also, in many areas it is difficult to control organisms that carry diseases. To avoid infection, people who live in or travel to places where parasites are common should ☑

- wash hands frequently
- drink bottled or boiled water
- eat only fully cooked meat
- use insect repellant
- wear protective clothing
- sleep under mosquito netting

6. Identify What are two common conditions in areas with high rates of parasitic infections?

____

____

____

Name ______________________ Class ______________ Date ______________

Section 4 Review

SECTION VOCABULARY

pseudocoelom the type of body cavity, derived from the blastocoel and referred to as a "false body cavity," that forms between the mesoderm and the endoderm in rotifers and roundworms	

1. **List** What are three key characteristics of roundworms?

____

____

2. **Compare** What are two ways roundworms and flatworms are similar? What is one way they are different?

____

____

3. **Explain** What are three functions of the pseudocoelom in roundworms?

____

____

4. **Explain** What are four groups of common parasitic roundworms?

____

____

5. **Infer** Why are people who live in areas with poor sewage systems at a high risk for infections with roundworm parasites? (Hint: How are many roundworm parasites spread?)

____

____

6. **List** What are three things people can do to avoid infection by parasites?

____

____

Name ______________________ Class ______________ Date ______________

CHAPTER 28 Mollusks and Annelids

SECTION 1

Mollusks

KEY IDEAS

As you read this section, keep these questions in mind:

- What are the key characteristics of mollusks?
- What are the three parts of the mollusk body plan?
- What are the similarities and differences between gastropods, bivalves, and cephalopods?

What Are the Key Characteristics of Mollusks?

Snails, oysters, clams, octopuses, and squids all belong to the phylum Mollusca. Despite their varied appearances, mollusks share the following key characteristics:

- a soft body
- a three-part body plan
- bilateral symmetry
- a shell containing calcium carbonate (in most)
- a *coelom*, a body cavity that contains the internal organs

Like a roundworm, a mollusk has a one-way digestive system. However, unlike a roundworm, a mollusk has three major body sections. These three body sections make mollusks more complex than roundworms. ☑

Outline After you read, make an outline to summarize the information in this section. Use the Key Idea questions and the header to help you organize your outline.

READING CHECK

1. Identify What is one way roundworms and mollusks differ?

____

____

____

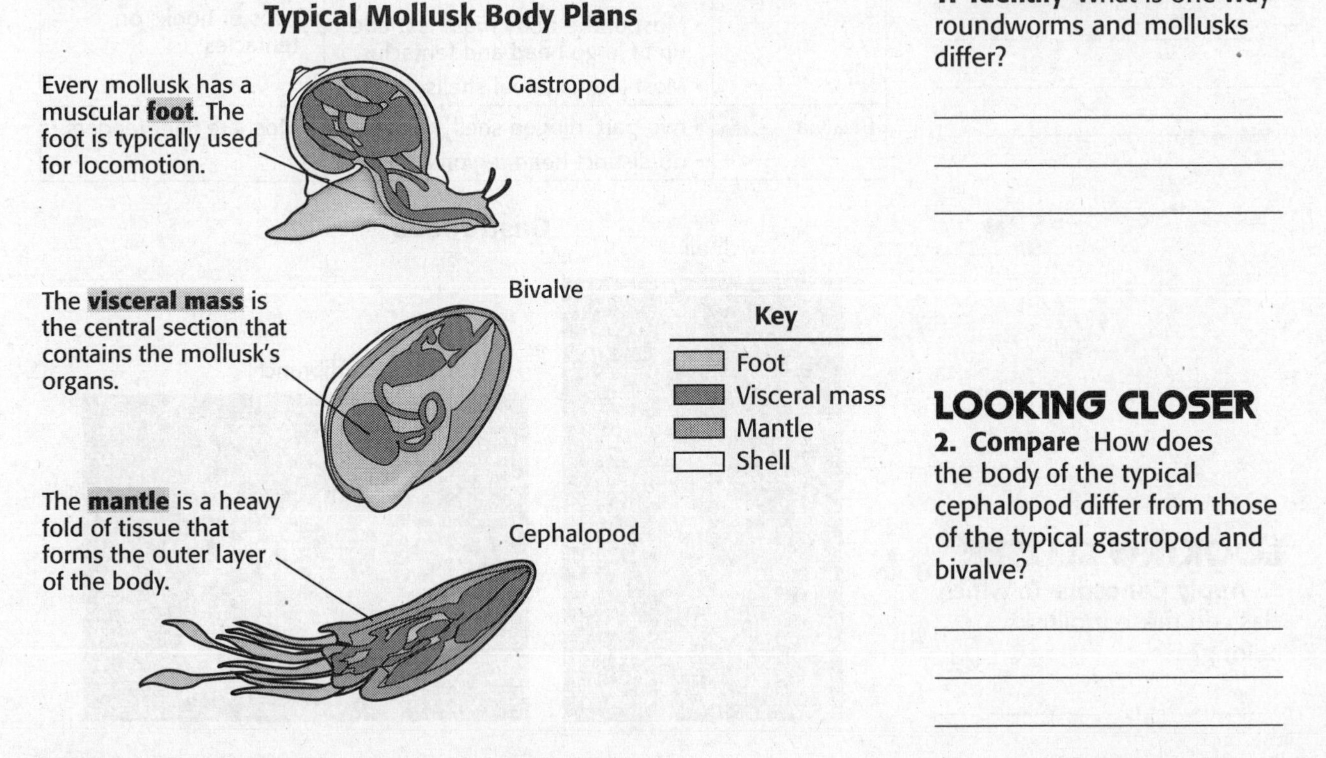

LOOKING CLOSER

2. Compare How does the body of the typical cephalopod differ from those of the typical gastropod and bivalve?

____

____

____

What Are the Three Main Classes of Mollusks?

The three major classes of mollusks are Gastropoda (snails and slugs), Cephalopoda (octopuses and squids) and Bivalvia (clams, oysters, and scallops). Mollusks in these classes share the same basic 3-part body plan and organ systems. However, they differ in feeding strategies and specific body plans. ☑

READING CHECK

3. Identify In what two main ways do different classes of mollusks differ?

____

____

These flame scallops are members of class Bivalvia.

LOOKING CLOSER

4. Compare How do the shells of gastropods differ from those of bivalves?

____

____

____

Class	Body type	Feeding habits
Gastropoda	• Most have a single shell. • no shell in slugs and nudibranchs	• many herbivorous • some predatory
Cephalopoda	• foot divided into tentacles • Most of the body mass is made up of large head and tentacles. • Most lack external shells.	• grab prey with suction cups or hooks on tentacles
Bivalvia	• two-part, hinged shell • no distinct head region or radula	• Most are filter feeders.

Gastropods

Snail

Nudibranch

LOOKING CLOSER

5. Apply Concepts To which class do these mollusks belong?

____

Cephalopods

Octopus

Squid

Nautilus

Critical Thinking

6. Apply Concepts What is one characteristic a nautilus shares with gastropods? What is one characteristic it shares with other cephalopods? Why do you think the nautilus is classified with cephalopods?

MOLLUSK STRUCTURES AND ORGAN SYSTEMS

Mollusks have organ systems for digestion, circulation, respiration, excretion, and reproduction. Most mollusks have open circulatory systems, in which blood does not stay within blood vessels. Octopuses and their relatives have closed circulatory systems. Most mollusks use gills for respiration. ☑

READING CHECK

7. Describe What is an open circulatory system?

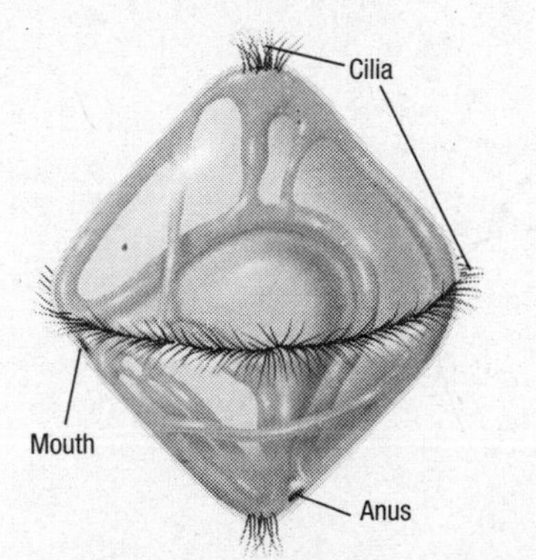

Most mollusks reproduce sexually and many mollusks go through a free-swimming larval stage. The larva is called a **trochophore**.

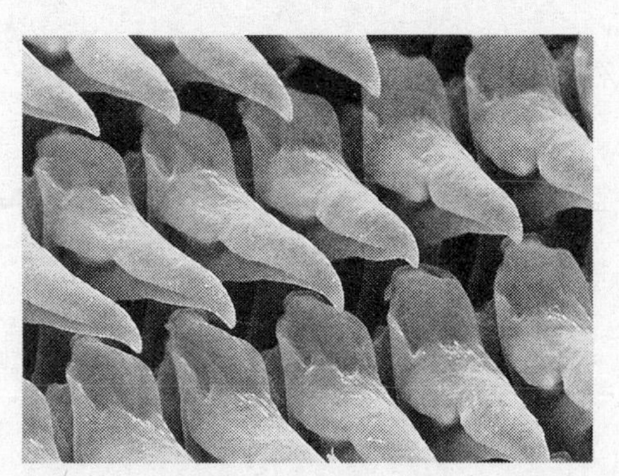

All mollusks except bivalves feed using a radula. A **radula** is a tongue-like organ covered with teeth that a mollusk uses to scrape food from surfaces.

LOOKING CLOSER

8. Identify What is the function of the radula?

Cephalopods and bivalves have siphons. A **siphon** is a hollow tube that a mollusk uses to draw water into the mantle and push water out. Cephalopods use siphons for movement. Bivalves use siphons for feeding and respiration.

Name ______________________ Class ______________ Date ______________

Section 1 Review

SECTION VOCABULARY

foot an appendage that some invertebrates use to move **mantle** in biology, a layer of tissue that covers the body of many invertebrates **radula** a rasping, tonguelike organ that is covered with chitinous teeth and that is used for feeding by many mollusks	**siphon** a hollow tube of bivalves used for sucking in and expelling sea water **trochophore** a free-swimming, ciliated larva of many worms and some mollusks **visceral mass** the central section of a mollusk's body that contains the mollusk's organs

1. List What are five key characteristics of mollusks?

____

____

____

2. Describe In what general way are mollusks more complex than roundworms?

____

3. Identify What are the three body parts of mollusks?

____

4. Compare Fill in the Venn diagram below to compare the characteristics of the three main groups of mollusks.

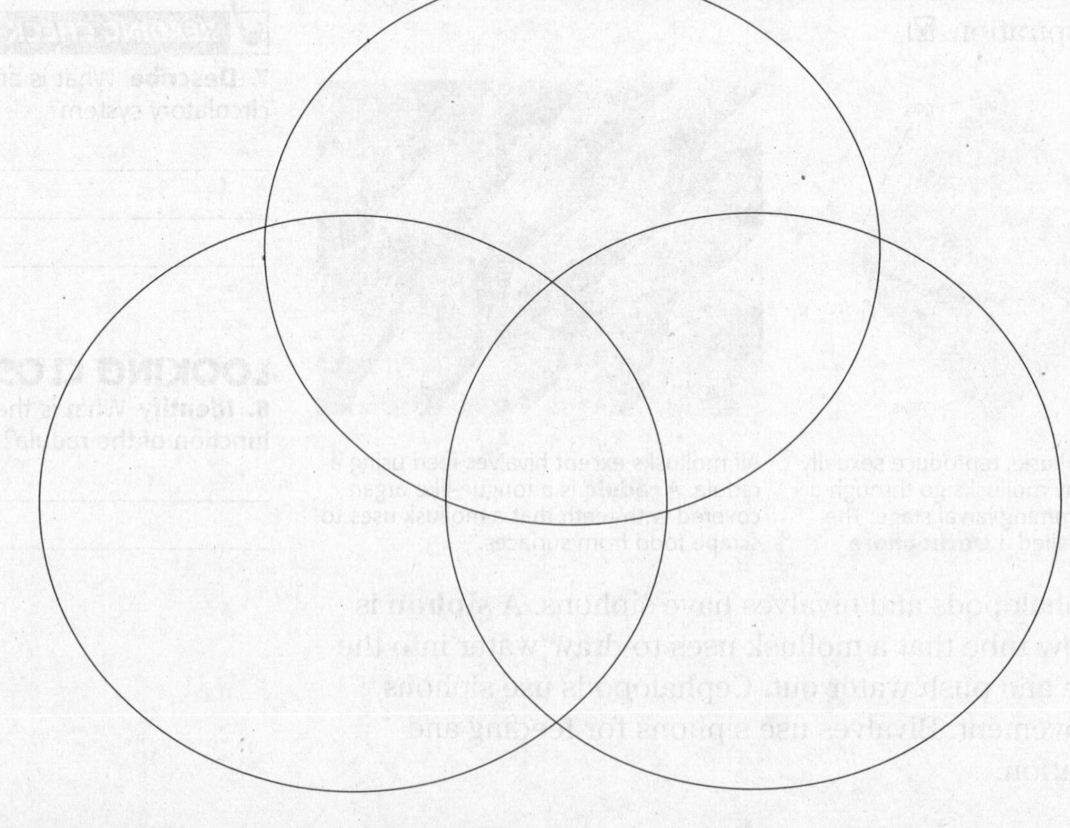

Name ________________ Class ________________ Date ________________

SECTION 2

Annelids

KEY IDEAS

As you read this section, keep these questions in mind:

- What are the key characteristics of annelids?
- Which characteristics are used to classify annelids?

What Are The Key Characteristics of Annelids?

You can easily recognize an annelid by its *segments*, ring-like structures along the length of its body. Segmentation gives an annelid greater body complexity and lets it move more easily than animals without segments. Some other key characteristics of organisms in the phylum Annelida are listed below.

- a coelom
- highly specialized organ systems
- external bristles called **setae** (singular, *seta*) on most
- trochophore larva

The paired bristles, or setae, on each segment help the worm grip a surface as it moves.

Annelids have repeated body segments. Internal body walls called **septa** (singular, *septum*) separate the segments of most annelids.

Most annelids have a primitive brain made up of a pair of nerve clusters called *cerebral ganglia* (singular, **cerebral ganglion**). The ganglia connect to a nerve cord that runs along the underside of the worm's body.

READING TOOLBOX

Organize After you read, make a Venn diagram to describe and compare the three classes of annelids.

Talk About It

Compare With a partner, review the key characteristics of mollusks. Compare these with the key characteristics of annelids. What characteristics do these groups share? How do they differ?

LOOKING CLOSER

1. Identify What is the function of setae?

____

____

____

How Do Scientists Classify Annelids?

Scientists group annelids in different classes based on the number of setae and the presence or absence of parapodia. *Parapodia* are flap-shaped appendages that many annelids use for gas exchange and movements, such as swimming, crawling, or burrowing. ☑

2. Identify What are two main functions of parapodia?

____

____

LOOKING CLOSER

3. Identify Which class of annelids lacks both parapodia and setae?

____

4. Compare What feature do leeches have that marine worms and earthworms do not?

____

Critical Thinking

5. Define Use a dictionary to find the meanings of the following roots: *poly-*, *oligo-*, and *–chaeta*. How do the meanings of these roots apply to organisms in the classes Polychaeta and Oligochaeta?

____

____

____

____

____

____

____

Classes of Annelids

Class	Key characteristics
Polychaeta (marine worms)	• parapodia present on most segments • many setae on each segment • well-developed head with eyes and other sensory structures • mostly marine • Some trap food particles from water. Others are active predators that feed on small animals.
Oligochaeta (earthworms)	• lack parapodia • only a few setae on each segment • lack a distinctive head and eyes • found on land and in fresh water • Most are scavengers.
Hirudinea (leeches)	• lack parapodia and setae • no internal separation between segments • have muscular suckers at both ends of the body • Most live in fresh water, but some live on land. • Some are parasites. Most are predators or scavengers.

Name ______________________ Class ____________ Date ____________

Section 2 Review

SECTION VOCABULARY

cerebral ganglion one of a pair of nerve-cell clusters that serve as a primitive brain at the anterior end of some invertebrates, such as annelids	**septum** a dividing wall, or partition, such as the wall between adjacent cells in a fungal hypha, the internal wall between adjacent segments of an annelid, and the thick wall between the right and left chambers of the heart **seta** one of the external bristles or spines that project from the body of an annelid

1. Explain How would you determine if a worm-like organism was an annelid?

____

____

2. Identify Relationships What is the relationship between segments and septa?

____

____

3. Identify How do scientists group annelids into different classes?

____

____

4. Identify What are two advantages of segmentation?

____

____

5. Describe Describe the nervous system of an annelid.

____

____

____

6. Apply Concepts You recently discovered a new species of annelid. It has visible external segments, but it does not have internally separated segments. With which group of annelids does this new species belong? What other characteristics could you look for to support your identification?

____

____

____

Name ______________________ Class ______________ Date ______________

CHAPTER 29 Arthropods and Echinoderms

SECTION 1

Arthropods

KEY IDEAS

As you read this section, keep these questions in mind:

- What are the distinguishing features of arthropods?
- How is molting an important feature of the arthropod life cycle?
- What are the four main types of arthropods?

READING TOOLBOX

Organize As you read this section, make a chart that describes the characteristics of arthropods.

What Are Characteristics of Arthropods?

Arthropods make up a diverse phylum of species that are found in almost every habitat on Earth. Although they are diverse, arthropods share many internal and external features. They are characterized by a segmented body, jointed appendages, and a hard external skeleton.

SEGMENTED BODY

Young arthropods in the larval stage of development, such as caterpillars, often have many tiny body segments. As arthropods become adults, body segments fuse to form three distinct regions. These regions are the head, **thorax** (mid-body), and abdomen. In some arthropods, such as crabs, the head is fused with the thorax. This forms a body region called the **cephalothorax**. ☑

1. Describe How do the three main body regions of adult arthropods form?

____

____

____

An adult dragonfly has a segmented body with three main regions. It also has jointed legs.

Critical Thinking

2. Infer What do you think is the reason that many arthropods have jointed legs? (Hint: Imagine walking without bending your legs.)

____

____

JOINTED APPENDAGES

An **appendage** is a structure that extends from an arthropod's body wall. As shown above, arthropod appendages have joints that bend. The phylum name *Arthropoda* means "joint footed." A variety of jointed appendages are found in arthropods, including legs, sensory antennae, and several kinds of mouthparts.

COMPOUND EYES

Many arthropods have compound eyes. A **compound eye** is made up of thousands of visual units. The brain interprets the information from all of the units in order to produce an image. Compound eyes are good at detecting movement. ☑

3. Describe What are compound eyes made up of?

____

____

____

EXOSKELETON AND MOLTING

The rigid outer layer of the arthropod body is called an *exoskeleton*. It is composed primarily of the carbohydrate chitin. The exoskeleton provides protection against predators and helps prevent water loss. However, the exoskeleton does not grow as the arthropod grows. ☑

To grow larger, every arthropod must shed its exoskeleton and grow a new, bigger one. Arthropods shed and discard their exoskeletons in a process called **molting**. Molting is triggered by the release of certain hormones. Just before molting, a new exoskeleton forms beneath the old one. In an arthropod life cycle, most arthropods molt several times before they become adults.

4. List Name two advantages of an exoskeleton to arthropods.

____

____

____

CIRCULATION AND RESPIRATION

Most arthropods have an open circulatory system. This means that their blood is not always contained in blood vessels. Instead, it flows to and from the heart through the body cavity. It bathes organs in the body cavity.

Many land arthropods, such as insects, breathe through a network of fine tubes. Each tube is called a **trachea** (plural, *tracheae*). Tracheae deliver oxygen to the body. Air enters a trachea through an opening in an arthropod's body called a **spiracle**. Most aquatic arthropods breathe through gills instead of tracheae.

Talk About It

Discuss With a partner or in a small group, talk about how circulation and respiration in arthropods and humans compare.

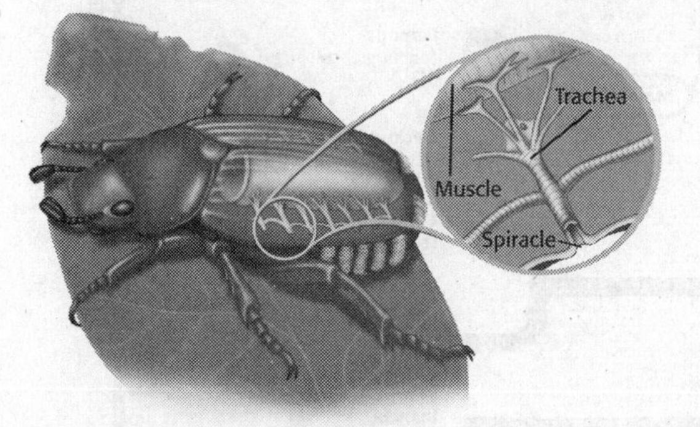

Tracheae run throughout the body of many land arthropods. They deliver oxygen to the arthropod's body.

LOOKING CLOSER

5. Identify How does air enter a trachea?

____

Name ______________________ Class ______________ Date ____________

Critical Thinking

6. Infer How are land arthropods able to survive long periods without rain?

____

____

EXCRETION

The excretory system in land arthropods is composed of Malpighian tubules. **Malpighian tubules** are narrow tubes that extend from the lower intestinal tract and are bathed in blood. Wastes pass from the blood, through the tubules, and to the gut for excretion. Water is retained in the body.

How Are Arthropods Classified?

Scientists group arthropods based on the mouthparts they use for feeding. *Chelicerates* are arthropods that have fangs or pincers. Chelicerates belong to the subphylum Chelicerata. *Mandibulates* are arthropods that have jaws for chewing. Scientists further divide mandibulates into three main subphyla: Hexapoda, Myriapoda, and Crustacea. The arthropods within these subphyla are shown below. ☑

7. Define What are mandibulates?

____

____

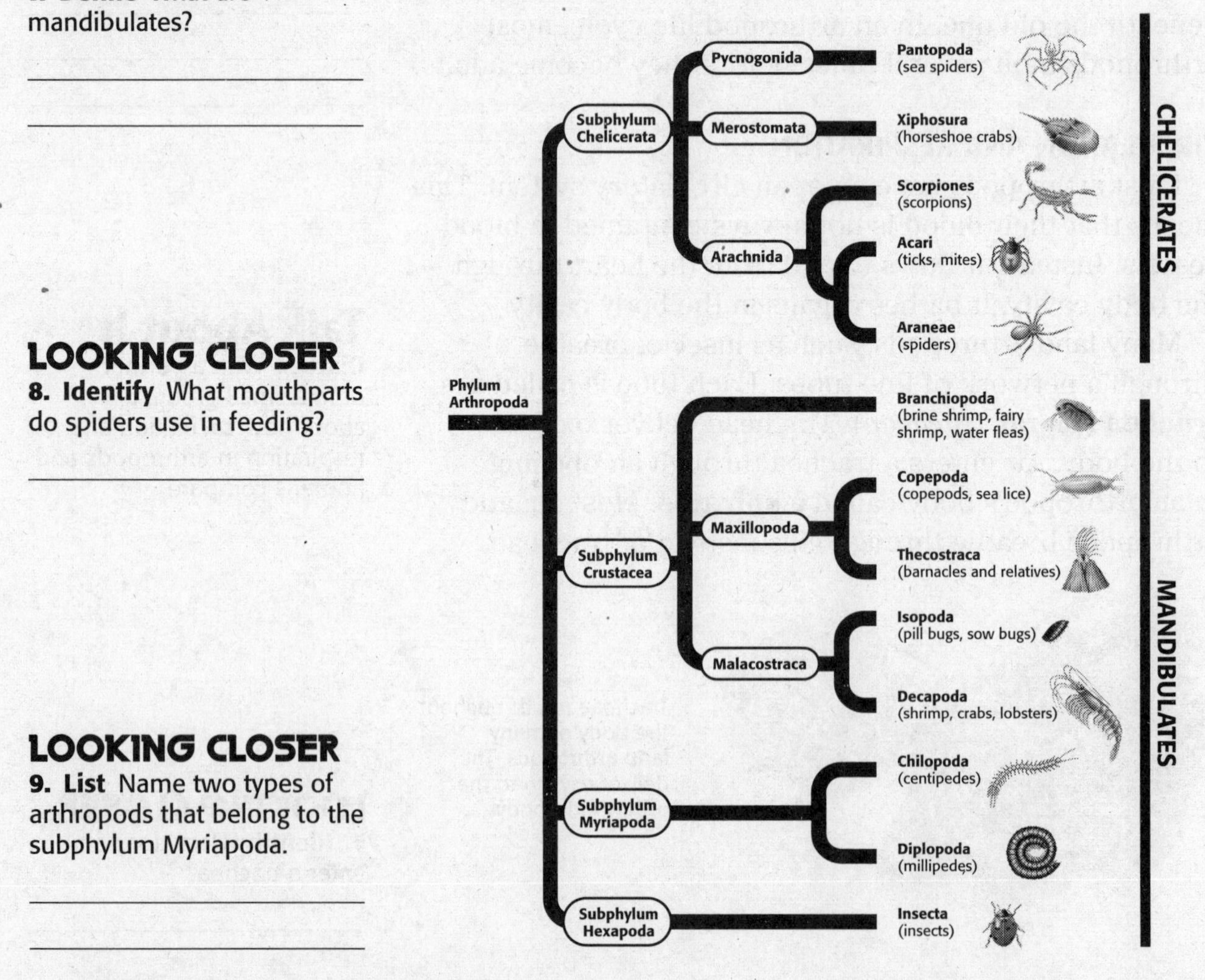

LOOKING CLOSER

8. Identify What mouthparts do spiders use in feeding?

____

LOOKING CLOSER

9. List Name two types of arthropods that belong to the subphylum Myriapoda.

____

____

Name ____________ Class ____________ Date ____________

Section 1 Review

SECTION VOCABULARY

appendage a structure that extends from the main body, such as a limb, tentacle, fin, or wing

cephalothorax in arachnids and some crustaceans, the body part made up of the head and the thorax

compound eye an eye composed of many light detectors separated by pigment cells

Malpighian tubule an excretory tube that opens into the back part of the intestine of most insects and certain arthropods

molting the shedding of an exoskeleton, skin, feathers, or hair to be replaced by new parts

spiracle an external opening in an insect or arthropod, used in respiration

thorax in higher vertebrates, the part of the body between the neck and the abdomen; in other animals, the body region behind the head; in arthropods, the mid-body region

trachea in insects, myriapods, and spiders, one of a network of air tubes; in vertebrates, the tube that connects the larynx to the lungs

1. **Summarize** Indicate whether each feature below can be found in the subphyla of arthropods in the table.

Feature	Hexapoda	Myriapoda	Crustacea	Chelicerata
Wings	yes	no	no	no
Chewing mouthparts				
Fangs or pincers				
Exoskeleton				
Segmented body				
Jointed appendages				

2. **Describe** What process must arthropods go through to grow? Describe this process.

____

____

3. **Classify** What subphylum of arthropods do insects belong to?

____

4. **Describe** How do most land arthropods deliver oxygen from the air to the body?

____

____

5. **Identify** What three body regions do most adult arthropods have?

____

6. **Predict** What would happen to the life cycle of arthropods if they could not molt?

____

____

Name ______________________ Class ______________ Date ____________

CHAPTER 29 Arthropods and Echinoderms

SECTION 2

Arachnids and Crustaceans

KEY IDEAS

As you read this section, keep these questions in mind:

- What adaptations have evolved in arachnids?
- What adaptations have evolved in crustaceans?

READING TOOLBOX

Compare As you read this section, make a table comparing adaptations in arachnids and crustaceans.

What Adaptations Evolved in Arachnids?

Arachnids are land arthropods with many appendages. Their first pair of appendages, called **chelicerae** (singular *chelicera*), are adapted for feeding. Chelicerae are fangs or pincers. **Pedipalps** are the second pair of appendages. Pedipalps are used mostly to catch and handle prey.☑

READING CHECK

1. Explain What are the first pair of appendages in an arachnid adapted for?

____

Arachnids do not have jaws and eat only liquid food. They inject enzymes into prey to turn the prey's tissues to liquid. Then they suck the liquid food into their stomach.

Arachnids also have four pairs of appendages called *walking legs*, but they lack antennae. Arachnids include spiders, scorpions, mites, and ticks, described below.

Arachnid	Features
Spiders	Spiders have glands that secrete toxins through fangs to kill or paralyze prey. Most have appendages at the end of the abdomen, called **spinnerets**, that secrete sticky strands of silk used to make webs and cocoons.
Scorpions	Scorpions have long, segmented abdomens that end in stingers used to stun prey. Scorpions have large pedipalps used in grasping prey and in mating.
Mites and Ticks	The head, thorax and abdomen of mites and ticks are fused into a single, unsegmented body.

LOOKING CLOSER

2. Describe How do scorpions grasp their prey?

____

____

What Adaptations Evolved in Crustaceans?

Crustaceans are a group of arthropods that include organisms such as pillbugs, water fleas, copepods, barnacles, and crabs. Almost all crustaceans are aquatic and breathe using gills. They have appendages for walking, swimming, feeding, or reproduction. Crustaceans such as shrimps, crayfish, crabs, and lobsters have five pairs of legs and are often called *decapods*. Almost all crustaceans have a larval form called a *nauplius*.

Crustaceans have an abdomen and a cephalothorax that is hardened into a *carapace*. Unlike arachnids, they have jaws that are adapted for feeding. They also have two pairs of antennae that act as sensors.

Critical Thinking

3. Infer What is the function of a carapace in a crustacean?

____

____

Name ______________________ Class ______________ Date ____________

Section 2 Review

SECTION VOCABULARY

chelicera in arachnids, either of a pair of appendages used to attack prey **pedipalp** in certain arthropods, one of the second pair of appendages	**spinneret** an organ that spiders and certain insect larvae use to produce silky threads for webs and cocoons

1. Describe What is the name of the first pair of appendages in an arachnid, and what is their function?

____

____

2. Describe What is the name of the second pair of appendages in an arachnid, and what is their function?

____

____

3. List Name four different types of arachnids.

____

4. Describe What is the function of spinnerets?

____

____

5. Explain How are spiders able to eat food when they do not have jaws to chew their prey?

____

____

6. Compare Name two features that crustaceans have but arachnids do not have.

____

7. List Name four organisms that are crustaceans.

____

8. Infer Do crustaceans digest their food inside or outside of their bodies? Explain your answer.

____

____

____

Name ______________ Class ______________ Date ______________

CHAPTER 29 Arthropods and Echinoderms

SECTION 3

Insects

KEY IDEAS

As you read this section, keep these questions in mind:

- What are common insect characteristics?
- How are insects adapted to flight?
- How is insect development unique among arthropods?
- What are the characteristics of social insects?
- Which arthropods are known as myriapods?

READING TOOLBOX

Outline As you read, make an outline of this section. Use the header questions to help you organize the main ideas in your outline.

What Are Common Insect Characteristics?

Insects live mostly on land. Most insects have the same general body plan, which includes a head, thorax, and abdomen. The thorax of insects is composed of three fused segments with three pairs of attached walking legs.

Most insects also have specialized mouthparts for feeding and wings for flying. Adult insects usually have one or two pairs of wings attached to their thorax. Some insects, such as fleas and lice, do not have wings. The life cycle of all insects is unique from other arthropods. ☑

1. Identify What region of an insect's body do wings attach to?

____

ADAPTATIONS FOR FEEDING

Insect mouthparts that are specialized for eating are called **mandibles**. Some insects, like the mosquito below, have mandibles that are adapted to pierce skin and suck blood. Mandibles in other insects are adapted for chewing materials, like wood or leaves, or sponging up liquid. ☑

2. Define What is a mandible?

____

____

____

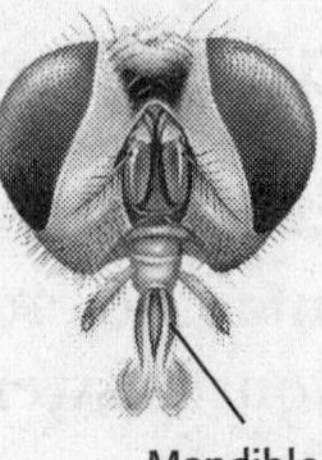

The mouthparts of different insect species are adapted for different ways of feeding.

LOOKING CLOSER

3. Explain Why are the shapes of the mandibles in the figure different?

____

____

____

ADAPTATIONS FOR FLIGHT

Insects are adapted for flight by having wings, a lightweight body, and strong muscles to power flight. Insects were the first animals to have wings. The evolution of wings enabled insects to reach new food sources and to escape quickly from danger. ☑

READING CHECK

4. Identify What are two advantages of flight to insects?

How Do Insects Develop?

Most insects have complex life cycles. During development, a young insect undergoes metamorphosis. **Metamorphosis** is a process of physical change. It can be complete or incomplete.

COMPLETE METAMORPHOSIS

Most insects undergo complete metamorphosis. Complete metamorphosis includes four stages: egg, larva, pupa, and adult. A wingless larva emerges from an egg and grows by molting. The larva then encloses itself in a protective capsule, called a **chrysalis** in some species. Inside a chrysalis, a larva becomes a pupa. A **pupa** is resistant to cold and dry conditions and does not feed. A pupa emerges from a chrysalis when it becomes an adult. ☑

READING CHECK

5. Identify What does a larva become before it emerges as an adult insect?

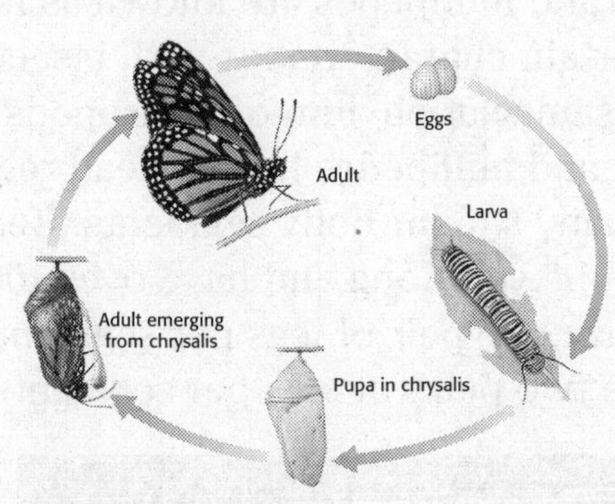

Complete metamorphosis includes a pupa stage. In some insects, such as butterflies, the pupa stage takes place inside a chrysalis.

INCOMPLETE METAMORPHOSIS

A few insect species undergo incomplete metamorphosis. During incomplete metamorphosis, an egg hatches into a juvenile, or *nymph*, that looks like a small, wingless adult. Wings may be acquired in a later stage. After several molts, the nymph develops into a sexually mature adult. A pupa stage does not occur.

Critical Thinking

6. Apply Concepts What does a grasshopper nymph look like?

What Are Characteristics of Social Insects?

Social insects live in highly organized groups of related individuals. These groups are called *colonies*. Colonies have a social system for carrying out work, parental care, and communication. The role that an individual plays in a colony is called a **caste**. Heredity, diet, hormones, and pheromones determine caste. *Pheromones* are chemicals that are used for communication. ☑

7. List Name three things that determine the role an insect plays in a colony.

____

____

____

HONEYBEES

A honeybee hive contains a queen, workers, and drone males. The honeybee queen usually is the only reproductive female in the hive. The workers care for the eggs, the larvae, the queen, and the drones. Workers also get food and maintain and defend the hive.

TERMITES

Termite colonies have kings and queens. Only the king and queen reproduce. Workers gather the food, raise the young, and make tunnels through wood. Termites called *soldiers* use their large jaws to defend the colony.

Critical Thinking

8. Predict What could happen to a termite colony without soldiers?

____

____

Are Centipedes and Millipedes Insects?

Centipedes and millipedes are known as myriapods. They share certain characteristics with insects but do not belong to the same subphylum of arthropods as insects.

Centipedes and millipedes have a head region that is followed by many similar body segments. Centipedes and millipedes can be very long and have over 100 segments. Centipedes have one pair of legs per segment. Millipedes generally have two pairs of legs per segment.

LOOKING CLOSER

9. Identify Is the myriapod in this picture a centipede or a millipede? Explain your answer.

____

____

____

Myriapods are not considered insects.

Name ______________________ Class ______________ Date ______________

Section 3 Review

SECTION VOCABULARY

caste a group of insects in a colony that have a specific function

chrysalis the hard-shelled pupa of certain insects, such as butterflies

mandible a type of mouthpart found in some arthropods and used to pierce and suck food; the lower part of the jaw

metamorphosis a phase in the life cycle of many animals during which a rapid change from the immature organism to the adult takes place; an example is the change from larva to adult in insects

pupa the immobile, nonfeeding stage between the larva and the adult of insects that undergoes complete metamorphosis; as a pupa, the organism is usually enclosed in a cocoon or chrysalis and undergoes important anatomical changes

1. Identify What insect mouthpart is specialized for feeding?

____

2. Identify Which two types of arthropods are known as myriapods?

____

3. Summarize Fill in the blank spaces in the chart below to show the four stages of complete metamorphosis.

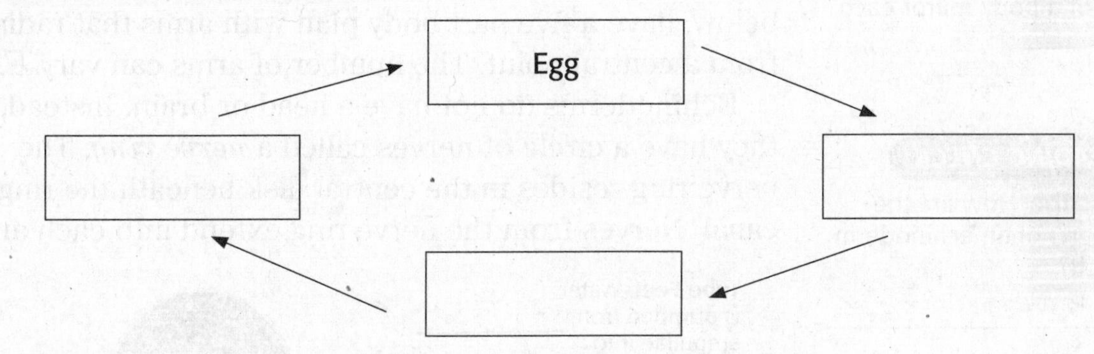

4. List What are three adaptations that allow insects to fly?

____

____

5. Describe What is the role of workers in a honeybee colony?

____

____

6. Compare How are juvenile insects that go through complete metamorphosis different from those that go through incomplete metamorphosis?

____

____

Name ______________________ Class ______________ Date ______________

CHAPTER 29 Arthropods and Echinoderms

SECTION 4

Echinoderms

KEY IDEAS

As you read this section, keep these questions in mind:

- What characteristics do echinoderms share?
- What are the different classes of echinoderms?

READING TOOLBOX

Summarize in Pairs Read this section quietly to yourself. Then, talk about what you read with a partner. Together, try to figure out the parts that you didn't understand.

What Characteristics Do Echinoderms Share?

Echinoderms make up a diverse phylum of species. However, the classes of echinoderms share four basic characteristics. All adult echinoderms have an internal skeleton, five-part radial symmetry, a water-vascular system, and the ability to breathe through their skin.

FIVE-PART RADIAL SYMMETRY

As larvae, all echinoderms have bilateral symmetry. As the larvae grow into adults, they develop five-part symmetry. All adult echinoderms, such as the sea star below, have a five part body plan with arms that radiate from a central point. The number of arms can vary. ☑

Background

Recall that *bilateral symmetry* is when equal halves of a body mirror each other.

Echinoderms do not have a head or brain. Instead, they have a circle of nerves called a *nerve ring*. The nerve ring resides in the central disk beneath the ring canal. Nerves from the nerve ring extend into each arm.

READING CHECK

1. Describe How are the body parts of an echinoderm arranged?

____

____

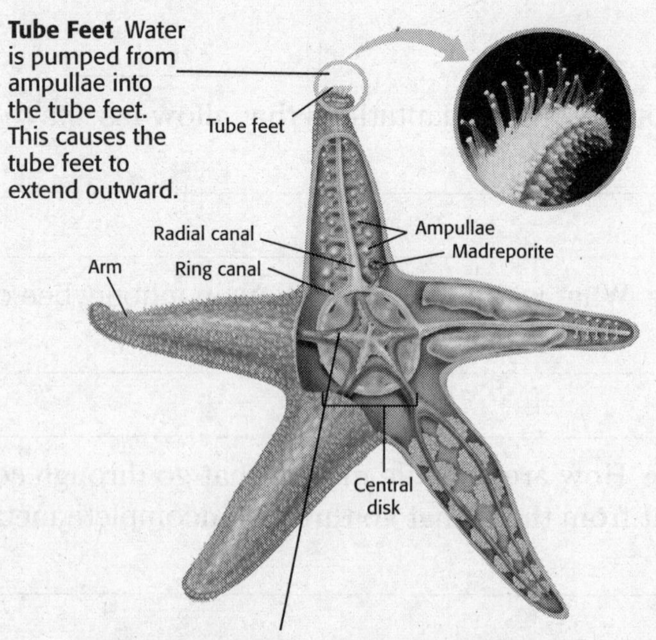

Tube Feet Water is pumped from ampullae into the tube feet. This causes the tube feet to extend outward.

Central Disk Nerves extend into each arm from a nerve ring in the central disk beneath the ring canal. The arms function independently.

LOOKING CLOSER

2. Identify What kind of symmetry does this adult sea star have?

____

____

WATER-VASCULAR SYSTEM

Echinoderms have a water-filled system of canals that make up a **water-vascular system**. *Radial canals* branch into the arms from a *ring canal* in the central disk. Water enters the system though a structure called a *madreporite.*

Tube feet, shown on the previous page, are tiny legs that can extend to move or grip surfaces. They are attached to canals of the water-vascular system. An *ampulla* contracts and forces water into a tube foot. This causes the foot to extend. Gas exchange and waste removal also take place through the tube feet. ☑

READING CHECK

3. Describe How does a tube foot extend?

____

____

____

ENDOSKELETON

Echinoderms have a calcium-rich internal skeleton called an endoskeleton. The endoskeleton is composed of individual plates called **ossicles**. Proteins and minerals make the endoskeleton flexible. The ossicles of adult echinoderms are covered by a thin layer of skin. In most echinoderms, the endoskeleton is covered in spines.

Talk About It

Discuss With a partner or in a small group, discuss how the skeleton of echinoderms is different from the skeleton of arthropods.

CIRCULATION AND RESPIRATION

Particles and gases move freely throughout the fluid-filled body cavity of echinoderms. All echinoderms breathe through their skin. Many have skin gills that aid respiration. **Skin gills** are small, fingerlike structures that grow among an echinoderm's spines. They create a large surface area for the exchange of respiratory gases.

What Kinds of Animals Are Echinoderms?

The table below describes the features of the living classes of echinoderms.

Class of Echinoderms	Features
Sea stars	Commonly called *starfish*. Most often have five arms that do not branch off.
Brittle and basket stars	Similar to sea stars, but their arms are narrower and may be branched.
Sea lilies and feather stars	Adults do not move around, but larvae can swim. This allows them to disperse.
Sea urchins and sand dollars	Do not have arms. Sea urchins have spines that protect them from predators.
Sea cucumbers	Have a shape like a slug. Lack arms or spines and look different from most echinoderms.

Critical Thinking

4. Apply Concepts How do sea cucumbers breathe?

____

____

Name ______________________ Class ______________ Date ______________

Section 4 Review

SECTION VOCABULARY

ossicle one of the small, calcium carbonate plates that make up the endoskeleton of an echinoderm

skin gill a transparent structure that projects from the surface of a sea star and that enables respiration

tube foot one of many small, flexible, fluid-filled tubes that project from the body of an echinoderm and that are used in locomotion, feeding, gas exchange, and excretion

water-vascular system in echinoderms, a system of canals filled with a watery fluid

1. List What are the four major characteristics of echinoderms?

____

____

____

____

2. Describe How do sea stars use their water-vascular system to move?

____

____

3. Explain What is the function of skin gills?

____

____

4. Identify What structures make up the endoskeleton of an echinoderm?

____

5. Identify What types of echinoderms do not move around but have larvae that can swim?

____

6. Compare How is the body symmetry of echinoderms different in larvae and in adults?

____

____

7. List Give four functions of tube feet.

____

____

Name _______________ Class _______________ Date _______________

CHAPTER 30 Fishes and Amphibians

SECTION 1

The Fish Body

KEY IDEAS

As you read this section, keep these questions in mind:

- What are the main characteristics of fishes?
- What structures do fishes use to swim and sense their environment?
- How do fishes obtain oxygen from the environment?
- How do fishes maintain their salt and water balance?
- How do fishes reproduce?

What Are Characteristics of Fishes?

Fish species can be found in almost every watery habitat on Earth. Fishes have a variety of adaptations to these habitats. Despite this variation, all fishes share certain characteristics: gills, endoskeletons, closed-loop circulation, and kidneys.

READING TOOLBOX

Outline As you read, make an outline of this section. Use the header questions to help you organize the main ideas in your outline.

How Do Fishes Swim?

Fishes have many structures that help them swim. These structures include their endoskeletons, fins, and swim bladders. In addition, a fish's shape and muscular tail allow it to move quickly in the water. ☑

1. List Name three structures that help fishes swim.

____

____

____

FINS AND SWIM BLADDER

Fins, shown below, propel fishes forward and keep them facing upright as they swim. Some fishes use paired fins to help them move, turn, dive, or rise rapidly. Many fishes use a gas-filled sac, called a **swim bladder** to adjust their depth in the water. Gas moves in and out of the swim bladder to help fishes move up and down in the water. ☑

2. Describe What is a swim bladder and what is it used for?

____

____

____

Many different fins help this goldfish swim.

ENDOSKELETON

All fishes have an endoskeleton, or internal skeleton made of either cartilage or bone. Muscles attach to the endoskeleton. These muscles allow fishes to make strong movements and swim through the water. ☑

READING CHECK

3. Identify What attaches to the endoskeleton of a fish?

____

How Do Fishes Sense Their Environment?

Fishes have a variety of organs that allow them to sense light, smells, tastes, sounds, and vibrations. Fishes sense light through their eyes. They sense odors using one or two nostrils. Fishes taste using taste buds in their mouths, and on their lips, fins, and skin. They hear sounds with their inner ears.

Talk About It

Discuss With a partner or in a small group, discuss different reasons why it is important for fishes to sense their environment.

Fishes also have a unique sense organ called the lateral line, shown below. The **lateral line** is a system of small canals in the skin. The canals are lined with sensory cells. These sensory cells detect vibrations in the water caused by currents or waves. The lateral line also connects to nerves that send information from the sensory cells to the brain. Fishes use this sensory information to direct their movements as they swim. ☑

READING CHECK

4. Describe What is the function of the lateral line?

____

____

Lateral line

Lateral line The lateral line runs the length of a fish's body and helps the fish sense vibrations in the water.

A catfish's mouth, skin, fins, and these whisker-like organs contain taste buds.

Lateral line canal

Nerve

Opening to exterior

Sensory cells

LOOKING CLOSER

5. Explain Why is the lateral line connected to nerves?

____

____

____

How Do Fishes Get Oxygen?

Fishes obtain oxygen from water. The major respiratory organ of a fish is the **gill**. Gills are made up of rows of filaments through which gases enter and leave the blood. Gills are located between a fish's mouth and cheeks.

COUNTERCURRENT FLOW

As a fish swims, it opens and closes its mouth to pump water over its gills. Water passes over the gills in one direction while blood flows through them in the opposite direction. This movement of water and blood is called *countercurrent flow*. Countercurrent flow allows oxygen from water to move into blood. Water then exits the fish through an opening in the cheek called a **gill slit**. ☑

SINGLE-LOOP BLOOD CIRCULATION

Blood makes a single loop through a fish's body. When blood leaves the gills, it is oxygen-rich. It moves through vessels to deliver oxygen to the body. Once oxygen is delivered, the blood becomes oxygen-poor. Oxygen-poor blood from the body travels to the top portion, or *atrium*, of the heart. It moves to the bottom portion, or *ventricle*, where it is pumped back to the gills for more oxygen. ☑

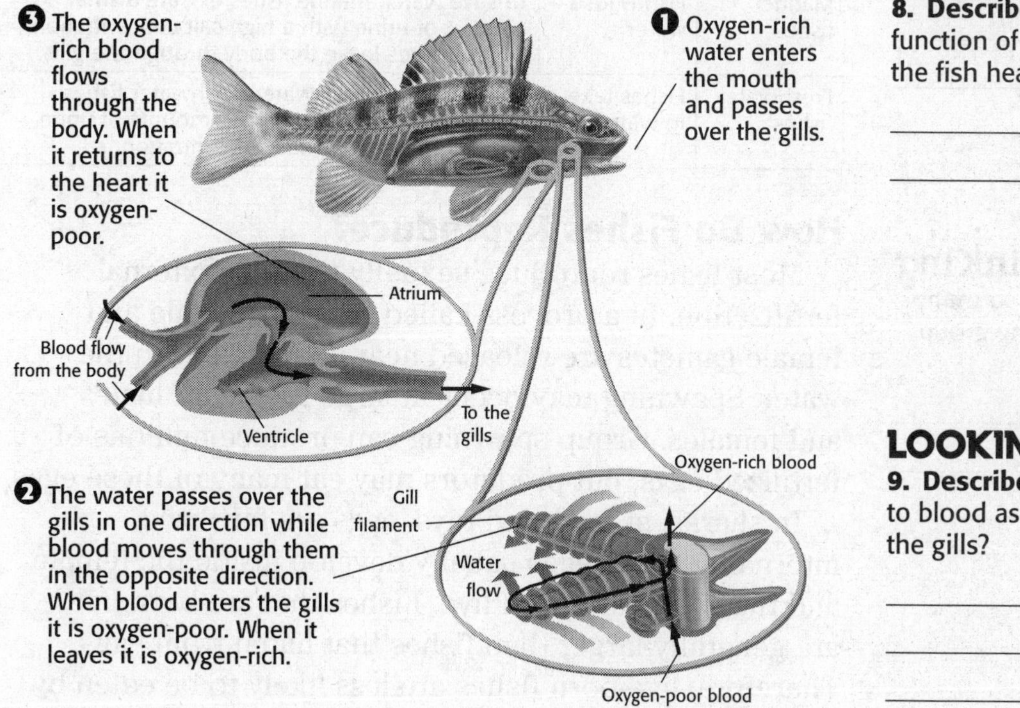

Critical Thinking

6. Apply Concepts Why can't fishes live on land?

____

____

____

READING CHECK

7. Explain Why does a fish open and close its mouth as it swims?

____

____

READING CHECK

8. Describe What is the function of the ventricle in the fish heart?

____

____

LOOKING CLOSER

9. Describe What happens to blood as it moves through the gills?

____

____

____

How Do Fishes Maintain Salt and Water Balance?

Even though fishes live in water, their bodies can lose water by osmosis. Recall that osmosis is a net movement of water toward regions of higher ion concentration.

The concentration of salt ions in ocean water is higher than the concentration in most fishes. As a result, most marine fishes lose water to the environment by osmosis. To make up for the lost water, the fishes drink ocean water and pump the salt from it out through their gills. ☑

10. Explain Why do marine fishes tend to lose water to their environment by osmosis?

Fishes that live in freshwater tend to take in water by osmosis because their bodies contain more salt than the surrounding water. This extra water decreases the concentration of their body salts. To help regain salt, freshwater fishes take in salts from the environment.

KIDNEYS

Fishes also use kidneys to maintain salt and water balance. A **kidney** is an organ that removes wastes from the blood. Excess water and wastes leave the kidneys as fluid called *urine*. Urine is excreted from the body.

LOOKING CLOSER

11. Compare How is the amount of urine excreted by freshwater fishes different from marine fishes?

Type of Fishes	Result of Osmosis	How Kidneys Help Maintain Salt and Water Balance
Marine fishes	Fishes lose water	To save water, marine fishes excrete a small amount of urine with a high salt concentration. Other wastes leave the body through the gills.
Freshwater fishes	Fishes take in water	To eliminate excess water, freshwater fishes excrete their wastes in large amounts of urine. The urine has a low salt concentration.

How Do Fishes Reproduce?

Most fishes reproduce sexually through external fertilization. In a process called spawning, male and female gametes are released near one another in the water. Spawning may occur in large groups of males and females. Group spawning can produce millions of fertilized eggs, but predators may eat many of these eggs.

Critical Thinking

12. Infer Why are so many eggs released during group spawning?

In sharks, skates, and rays, eggs are fertilized internally. These eggs usually develop inside the female and the young are born live. Fishes that are born live are generally larger than fishes that hatch from eggs. Therefore, live-born fishes are less likely to be eaten by predators.

Name ______________________ Class ______________ Date ____________

Section 1 Review

SECTION VOCABULARY

gill in aquatic animals, a respiratory structure that consists of many blood vessels surrounded by a membrane that allows for gas exchange

gill slit a perforation between two gill arches through which water taken in through the mouth of a fish passes over the gills and out of the fish's body

kidney one of the organs that filter water and wastes from the blood, excrete products as urine, and regulate the concentration of certain substances in the blood

lateral line a faint line visible on both sides of a fish's body that runs the length of the body and marks the location of sense organs that detect vibrations in water

swim bladder in bony fishes, a gas-filled sac that is used to control buoyancy

1. List Name four characteristics that all fishes share.

____

2. Describe What are three ways a fish could sense that a predator is nearby?

____

____

3. Infer Why is blood circulation in fishes called closed-loop?

____

____

4. Summarize Fill in the blank spaces in the chart below to show how blood circulates between structures in a fish.

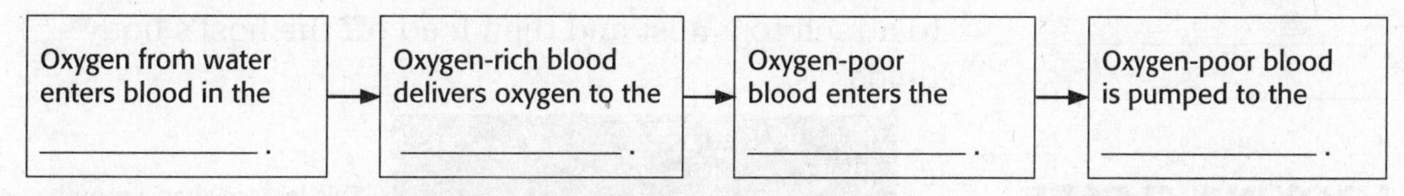

5. Explain How do marine fishes maintain their salt and water balance? Include two different methods in your answer.

____

____

____

6. Compare How is fertilization in sharks different from fertilization in most fishes?

____

____

Name ______________________ Class ______________ Date ____________

CHAPTER 30 Fishes and Amphibians

SECTION 2

Groups of Fishes

KEY IDEAS

As you read this section, keep these questions in mind:

- What are the characteristics of the jawless fishes?
- What are the main traits of cartilaginous fishes?
- Why have bony fishes been so successful compared to the other groups of fishes?

READING TOOLBOX

Compare As you read this section, make a table comparing characteristics of jawless fishes, cartilaginous fishes, and bony fishes.

How Do Scientists Group Fishes?

Scientists divide fishes into three general groups: jawless fishes, cartilaginous fishes, and bony fishes.

What Traits Do Jawless Fishes Share?

Jawless fishes do not have jaws. They have endoskeletons made of cartilage instead of bone. Cartilage is a strong connective tissue. Jawless fishes also have a *notochord* instead of a backbone. They are the only living vertebrates without a backbone, or vertebral column. ☑

1. List Name three characteristics that jawless fishes share.

____

____

____

Jawless fishes include hagfishes and lampreys. Hagfishes are scavengers and predators that live at great depths on the ocean floor. They feed off dead fishes and small prey. Lampreys are parasites. They use their mouth to attach to a host and then feed off the host's body fluids.

This lamprey has a mouth with spines and a rough tongue, but it does not have jaws. The mouth acts like a suction cup to attach the lamprey to a host.

LOOKING CLOSER

2. Explain How can a lamprey eat without jaws?

____

____

____

What Traits Do Cartilaginous Fishes Share?

Cartilaginous fishes include sharks, skates, rays, and ratfishes. All cartilaginous fishes have jaws and paired fins. They also have a backbone and endoskeletons made of cartilage strengthened by calcium carbonate. Calcium carbonate forms a thin layer that reinforces the cartilage. The result is a very light, yet strong, skeleton. ☑

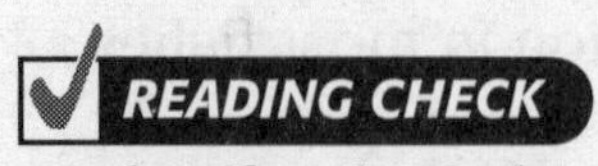

3. Identify What is the endoskeleton of cartilaginous fishes made of?

____

____

What Makes Bony Fishes So Successful?

Together, there are about 1,000 species of jawless and cartilaginous fishes. In contrast, there are about 24,000 species of bony fishes.

Bony fishes have been successful because they have strong endoskeletons made of bone. They also have structural adaptations, such as lateral lines, opercula, swim bladders, and paired fins, described below.

Structure	Adaptation for Success
Well-developed lateral line	As moving water presses against bony fishes, nerve impulses from sensory cells go to the brain. The lateral line enables bony fishes to detect their own position and movement. It also allows them to detect objects by the movement of water around the object.
Opercula (singular, *operculum*)	**Opercula** are hard plates that cover the gills in most bony fishes. Movements of the opercula draw oxygen-rich water over the gills. Bony fishes do not have to swim forward with their mouths open to take in oxygen.
Swim bladder	Bony fishes do not have to swim to keep from sinking. Instead, they use their swim bladders to control their depth in the water. This saves energy. As the swim bladder fills with gas, the fishes rise. As it empties, the fishes sink.
Paired fins	Paired fins enable bony fishes to make sharp turns and paddle backward.

Critical Thinking

4. Apply Concepts Can bony fishes take in oxygen without swimming? Explain your answer.

____

____

____

LOOKING CLOSER

5. Identify What structure helps keep bony fishes from sinking?

____

RAY-FINNED FISHES

Most bony fishes are ray-finned fishes. Ray-finned fishes have fins supported by bony structures called *rays*. **Teleosts** are a type of ray-finned fish. Teleosts have movable fins, thin scales, and symmetrical tails. About 95% of all fishes are teleosts. One reason for the success of teleosts is their ability to suck food toward their mouth. They can also stick out their upper jaw to grasp food. ☑

READING CHECK

6. Explain How does the upper jaw of teleosts help them in feeding?

____

____

____

LOBE-FINNED FISHES

A small number of bony fishes are lobe-finned fishes. Lobe-finned fishes have fins called lobe fins that are fleshy, muscular, and supported by bones.

The bones that support lobe fins are connected by joints, like the joints in human fingers. Rays are found only at the tips of each lobe fin. Muscles within each lobe fin can move the rays independently of one another. A lobe-finned fish is the most likely ancestor of amphibians and all other land vertebrates.

Name ______________________ Class ______________ Date ______________

Section 2 Review

SECTION VOCABULARY

operculum in fish, a hard plate that is attached to each side of the head, that covers gills, and that is open at the rear	**teleost** a group of ray-finned fishes that have a caudal fin, scales, and a swim bladder; the largest group of bony fishes

1. **Identify** Name two types of jawless fishes.

2. **Compare** What are two traits that cartilaginous fishes have but jawless fishes do not have?

3. **Explain** What is the advantage of a skeleton made of cartilage and reinforced by calcium carbonate?

4. **Explain** How does a swim bladder allow bony fishes to save energy?

5. **List** In addition to the swim bladder, name three other structures that have contributed to the success of bony fishes.

6. **Explain** How do fishes without opercula take in oxygen?

7. **Evaluate Conclusions** Why are lobe-finned fishes the most likely ancestors of amphibians and all other land vertebrates?

8. **Identify** What type of bony fishes are teleosts?

Name ______________________ Class ______________ Date ______________

CHAPTER 30 Fishes and Amphibians

SECTION 3

The Amphibian Body

KEY IDEAS

As you read this section, keep these questions in mind:

- Which characteristics do most amphibians share?
- How do amphibians sense their environment?
- Which amphibian body structures work together to provide oxygen to body tissues?
- How does an amphibian circulatory system differ from those of most fishes?

What Characteristics Do Amphibians Share?

Amphibians were the first vertebrates to live on land. They include organisms such as frogs and salamanders. Most amphibians share five characteristics: legs, lungs, double-loop circulation, a partially divided heart, and respiration through the skin. Although amphibians live on land, they need to reproduce in a wet area. Therefore, most amphibians live in moist habitats. ☑

How Do Amphibians Sense Their Environment?

Most amphibians have well-developed senses of sight and sound. Their main sensory organs are the eyes and ears. An amphibian's eyes are covered and protected by a thin, movable layer called a *nictitating membrane*. Sight is important to amphibians in hunting and avoiding danger.

The inner ear of an amphibian detects sound. Sounds first strike the **tympanic membrane**, or eardrum, shown below, and cause it to vibrate. The tympanic membrane sends sound vibrations to the inner ear. In the inner ear, sensitive hair cells change sound vibrations into nerve impulses that are sent to the brain. ☑

The eye is covered by a nictitating membrane.

The tympanic membrane transmits sound to the inner ear.

READING TOOLBOX

Outline As you read, make an outline of this section. Use the header questions to help you organize the main ideas in your outline.

READING CHECK

1. Explain Why do most amphibians live in moist habitats?

____

____

READING CHECK

2. Describe What happens to sounds in the inner ear and where do they go?

____

____

____

How Do Amphibians Get Oxygen?

In amphibians, the lungs, double-loop circulation, a partially divided heart, and skin work together to bring oxygen from the air to the body tissues.

LUNGS

Although amphibians have gills as larvae, most adult amphibians breathe with lungs. A **lung** is an internal, baglike organ. It allows oxygen and carbon dioxide to be exchanged between the air and the bloodstream.

An amphibian breathes oxygen-rich air into its lungs. In the lungs, oxygen is transferred to the blood to be circulated through the body.

Talk About It

Discuss With a partner or in a small group, discuss how lungs and gills are the same and how they are different.

DOUBLE-LOOP CIRCULATION

Recall that fishes move blood through their body in a single loop. The fish heart pumps blood through the gills before it reaches the body tissues and returns to the heart. Blood flow slows as it moves through the gills. ☑

In contrast, amphibians have a double-loop circulatory system. One circulatory loop connects the heart and lungs. This loop contains pulmonary veins, which are not found in fishes. **Pulmonary veins** are vessels that carry oxygen-rich blood from the lungs to the heart.

When oxygen-rich blood enters the heart, it is pumped directly to the body tissues in the second circulatory loop. This loop connects the heart and body. It allows blood and oxygen to be delivered to the amphibian body quickly. Fish and amphibian circulation are compared below. ☑

3. Describe In fishes, what happens to the flow of blood between the heart and the body tissues?

____

____

4. Explain In amphibians, why does oxygen-rich blood from the lungs enter the heart?

____

____

LOOKING CLOSER

5. Identify What two structures do the pulmonary veins connect?

____

____

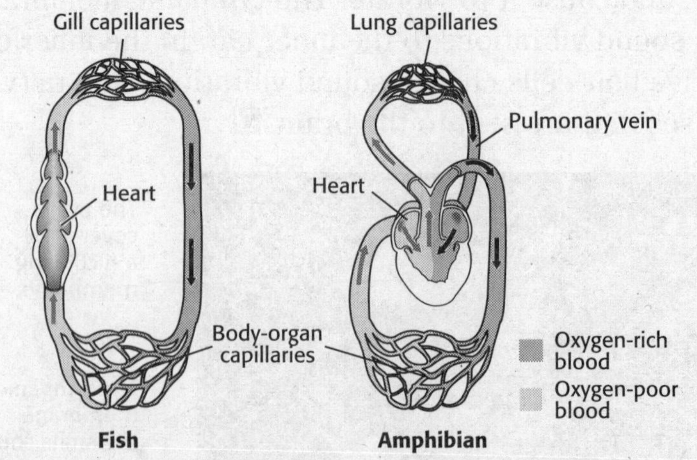

Most fishes have single-loop circulation while amphibians have double-loop circulation.

PARTIALLY DIVIDED HEART

The amphibian circulatory system includes a partially divided heart. The top of the heart is divided into left and right sides by a wall called a **septum**. Each chamber in the top of the heart is called an *atrium*. The bottom chamber of the heart, called the *ventricle*, is not divided. ☑

READING CHECK

6. Explain What makes the amphibian heart partially divided?

____

As shown below, oxygen-poor blood from the body enters the right atrium of the heart. Oxygen-rich blood from the lungs enters the left atrium of the heart. Both streams of blood empty into the ventricle of the heart. Since the ventricle is not divided by a septum, some mixing of oxygen-rich and oxygen-poor blood occurs.

However, the shape of the ventricle tends to keep the two streams of blood separate. When the ventricle contracts, the blood is pushed into vessels. Most oxygen-rich blood is pumped to the body, while most oxygen-poor blood is pumped to the lungs. However, some oxygen-poor blood does get delivered to the body tissues.

Critical Thinking

7. Infer What could prevent oxygen-poor blood from being delivered to the body?

____

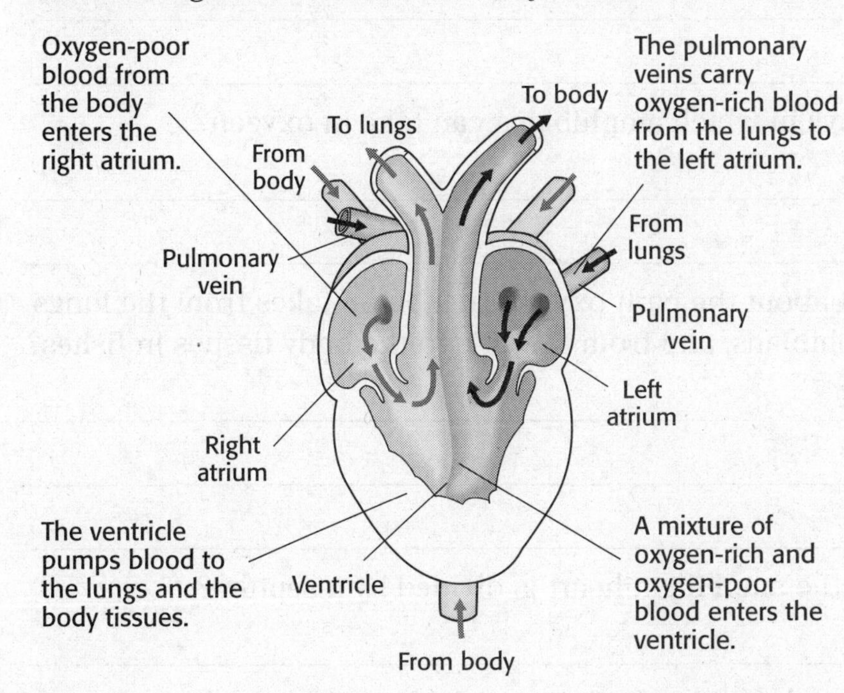

LOOKING CLOSER

8. Describe What is the function of the ventricle?

____

SKIN

In addition to using their lungs for respiration, many amphibians can take in oxygen through their skin. This process is called *cutaneous respiration*. In order for oxygen to be taken in by cutaneous respiration, the skin must be moist. Therefore, amphibians have glands in their skin that secrete mucus to keep their skin moist. ☑

READING CHECK

9. Identify What substance do amphibians secrete to keep their skin moist?

____

Name _______________ Class _______________ Date _______________

Section 3 Review

SECTION VOCABULARY

lung the central organ of the respiratory system in which oxygen from the air is exchanged with carbon dioxide from the blood **pulmonary vein** the vein that carries oxygenated blood from the lungs to the heart	**septum** a dividing wall, or partition, such as the wall between adjacent cells in a fungal hypha, the internal wall between adjacent segments of an annelid, and the thick wall between the right and left chambers of the heart **tympanic membrane** the eardrum

1. List Name five characteristics that most amphibians share.

____

____

2. Describe What is the function of the tympanic membrane?

____

____

3. Explain Why is a well-developed sense of sight important to amphibians?

____

____

4. Describe What are two ways in which amphibians can take in oxygen?

____

____

5. Compare What is different about the path oxygen-rich blood takes from the lungs to the body tissues in amphibians, and from the gills to the body tissues in fishes?

____

____

____

6. Identify What chamber in the amphibian heart is divided by a septum?

____

7. Compare Does blood flow to body tissues faster in fishes or in amphibians? Explain your answer.

____

____

____

____

Name ______________________ Class ______________ Date ______________

CHAPTER 30 Fishes and Amphibians

SECTION 4

Groups of Amphibians

KEY IDEAS

As you read this section, keep these questions in mind:

- What are the main characteristics of salamanders?
- What are the key traits of caecilians?
- What are the kinds of environments in which frogs and toads are adapted to live?

How Do Scientists Group Amphibians?

Scientists divide modern amphibians into three main groups: salamanders, caecilians, and frogs and toads. Organisms in these three groups are shown below.

READING TOOLBOX

Organize As you read this section, make a chart that lists key traits of the three main groups of amphibians.

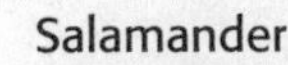

Salamander

Caecilian

Frog

Toad

LOOKING CLOSER

1. Identify Which type of amphibian does not have legs?

____

What Characteristics Do Salamanders Share?

There are about 400 species of salamanders. All salamanders have long bodies, long tails, and smooth, moist skin. Most salamanders must have frequent contact with water to keep their skin moist. However, a few salamander species can go without water for long periods by being inactive during the day. ☑

Salamanders lay their eggs in water or in moist places. Fertilization is usually external. A few species of salamanders have a type of internal fertilization. The female picks up a sperm packet from a male and places it inside her body. Young salamanders look like small versions of adults, except that they usually have gills.

READING CHECK

2. Describe What is the skin of a salamander like?

____

____

What Characteristics Do Caecilians Share?

Caecilians are legless amphibians with small, bony scales in their skin. Caecilians look like worms and are found in tropical swamps. Most species of caecilians burrow in the soil, but some species live in the water.

Most caecilians are blind because they have small eyes that are located beneath their skin or under bone. All caecilians have teeth that help them catch and eat prey. A caecilian uses a tentacle on the side of its head to sense chemicals given off by its prey. ☑

3. Explain How can a caecilian that cannot see detect its prey?

____

____

____

During mating, a male caecilian deposits sperm into a female. Some species of caecilians lay eggs, which the female guards. In a few species, the young are born live.

Where Can Frogs and Toads Live?

Frogs and toads are known as *anurans*. There are about 4,000 species of anurans. They can live in a wide variety of environments such as deserts, rain forests, valleys, mountains, and ponds. However, like most amphibians, anurans need water to complete their life cycle.

Critical Thinking

4. Apply Concepts How does breathing differ in adult frogs and in tadpoles?

____

____

____

In frogs, the female releases her eggs into the water. They are fertilized externally by sperm released from a male. As shown below, the fertilized eggs hatch into swimming, fishlike larvae called **tadpoles**. Tadpoles breathe with gills and have tails. As a tadpole becomes an adult frog, legs appear and its tail and gills disappear.

LOOKING CLOSER

5. Describe What physical change do tadpoles first undergo as they develop into adult frogs?

____

____

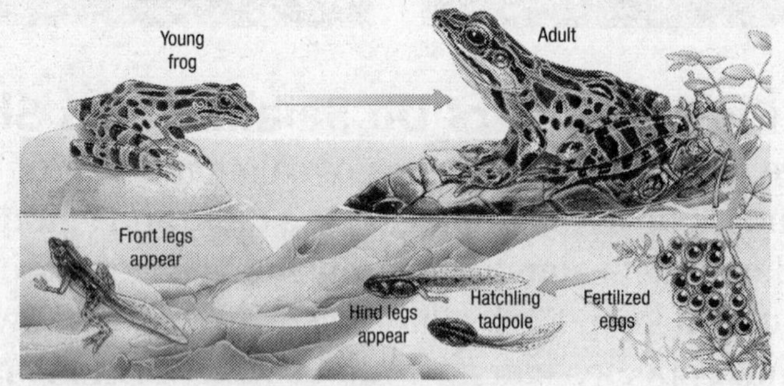

A tadpole becomes an adult frog through a process of physical changes called *metamorphosis*.

Adult frogs catch small prey by quickly extending a long, sticky tongue. The frog body is adapted for jumping with long muscular legs. Toads are very similar to frogs but have squat bodies with shorter legs. A frog's skin is smooth, but a toad's skin is covered with bumps.

Name ______________________ Class ______________ Date ______________

Section 4 Review

SECTION VOCABULARY

tadpole the aquatic, fishlike larva of a frog or toad	

1. List Name three characteristics that salamanders share.

____

____

2. Compare How is reproduction in caecilians different from reproduction in most salamanders and anurans?

____

____

3. Compare Describe one way in which frog and salamander larvae are the same and one way in which they are different.

____

____

____

____

4. Summarize Fill in the blanks in the chart below that describes the process of metamorphosis in frogs.

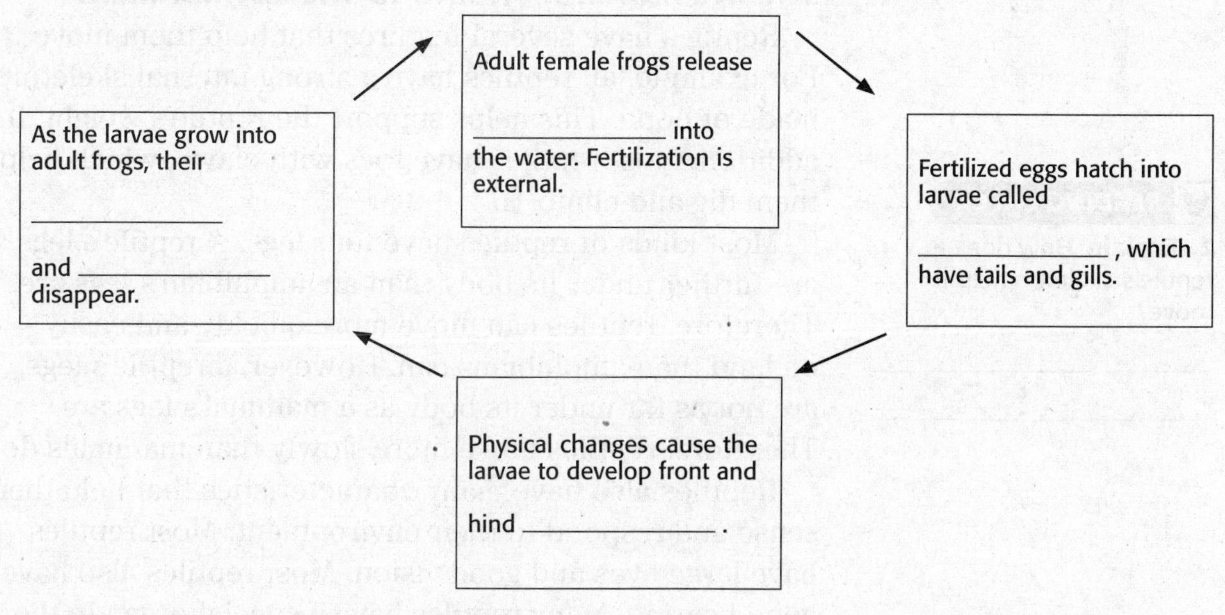

5. Identify Although anurans can live in a variety of environments, what do they need to complete their life cycle?

____

Name ______________________ Class ______________ Date ______________

CHAPTER 31 Reptiles and Birds

SECTION 1

The Reptile Body

KEY IDEAS

As you read this section, keep these questions in mind:

- What are the key characteristics of reptiles?
- What characteristics allow reptiles to move through and sense their environment?
- What makes a reptile's heart and lungs more efficient than an amphibian's?
- What structure allows reptiles to live successfully on land?

READING TOOLBOX

Summarize After you read this section, make a Spider Map describing the characteristics of reptiles.

What Are the Key Characteristics of Reptiles?

Snakes, lizards, turtles, and dinosaurs are all examples of reptiles. Although there are many kinds of reptiles, all reptiles share some features.

Characteristic	Description
Skin	All reptiles have dry, scaly, almost waterproof skin, with no feathers or hair.
Skeleton	All reptiles have a strong internal skeleton. Most have four legs and toes with claws.
Metabolism	All reptiles are **ectothermic**. That is, they cannot control their body temperature using their metabolisms.

LOOKING CLOSER

1. Describe What is a reptile's skin like?

____

____

SENSING AND RESPONDING TO THE ENVIRONMENT

Reptiles have several features that help them move. For example, all reptiles have a strong internal skeleton made of bone. This helps support the reptile's weight. In addition, most reptiles have toes with claws, which help them dig and climb. ☑

READING CHECK

2. Explain How does a reptile's skeleton help it move?

____

____

Most kinds of reptiles have four legs. A reptile's legs are further under its body than an amphibian's legs are. Therefore, reptiles can move more quickly and easily on land than amphibians can. However, a reptile's legs are not as far under its body as a mammal's legs are. Therefore, reptiles move more slowly than mammals do.

Reptiles also have many characteristics that help them sense and respond to their environment. Most reptiles have large eyes and good vision. Most reptiles also have good hearing. Many reptiles have a special organ in the roof of the mouth, the **Jacobson's organ**, which helps them sense odors.

Name ______________________ Class ______________ Date ______________

How Do a Reptile's Heart and Lungs Work?

Reptiles have more efficient respiratory and circulatory systems than amphibians do. This is important because, unlike an amphibian, a reptile cannot breathe through its skin.

LUNGS

The inside of a reptile's lung contains many folds. This increases the amount of surface area inside the lung. The large surface area allows the lung to exchange more oxygen and carbon dioxide with the air.

HEART

Remember that an amphibian's heart has only one *ventricle*, or chamber that pumps blood to the rest of the body. Within that ventricle, oxygen-rich blood from the lungs and oxygen-poor blood from the body mix together.

In contrast, a reptile's ventricle is almost completely divided in half by a structure called a *septum*. The septum reduces the mixing of oxygen-rich and oxygen-poor blood. As a result, the blood that reaches a reptile's body is more oxygen-rich. ☑

A Reptile's Heart

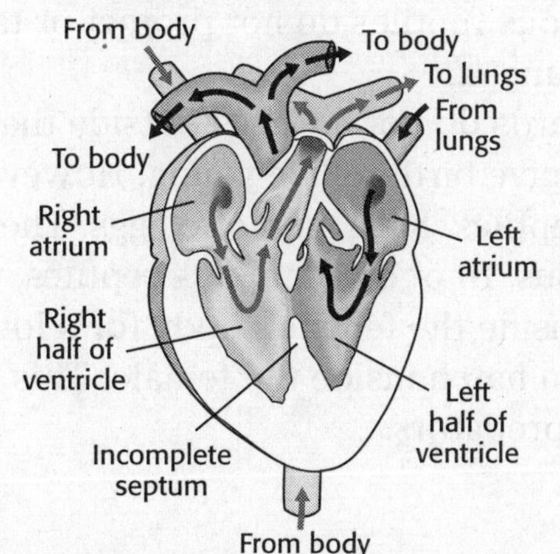

The septum in a reptile's ventricle reduces the mixing between oxygen-rich and oxygen-poor blood in the heart.

Critical Thinking

3. Infer What do you think is the reason that reptiles can't breathe through their skin? (Hint: What kind of skin do reptiles have?)

____

____

____

____

LOOKING CLOSER

4. Describe How does the structure of a reptile's lung allow it to exchange more gases with the air?

____

____

____

5. Explain How does the septum in a reptile's heart allow more oxygen to reach the reptile's body?

____

____

____

____

How Can Reptiles Survive and Reproduce on Land?

Unlike amphibians, reptiles do not require water to breed. Reptiles have two important adaptations that allow them to reproduce and live their lives entirely on land. First, fertilization in reptiles occurs inside the female's body. This keeps the gametes from drying out. Second, reptiles lay amniotic eggs. ☑

6. Explain How does internal fertilization help reptiles reproduce on land?

An *amniotic egg* contains a water supply, a food supply, and a shell to protect the developing organism. Amniotic eggs allow reptiles to reproduce far from water. Therefore, amniotic eggs have helped reptiles live successfully on land. The figure below shows the structure of an amniotic egg.

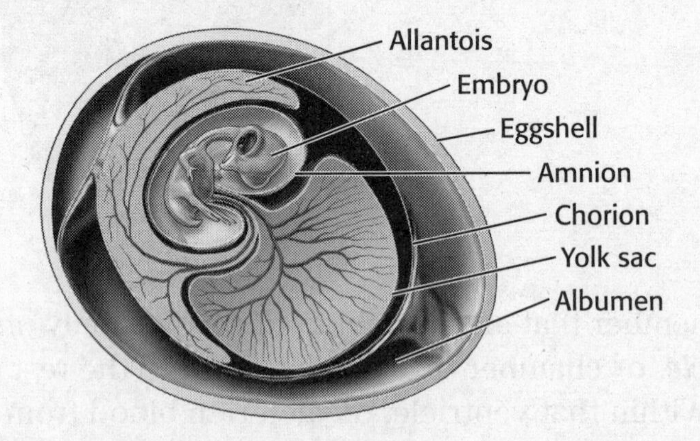

Each part of an amniotic egg has a specific function. The shell and albumen cushion and protect the embryo. The albumen and yolk sac supply food for the embryo. The amnion maintains a watery environment for the embryo. The allantois stores the waste that the embryo produces. The allantois and the chorion allow the embryo to exchange oxygen and carbon dioxide with its environment.

LOOKING CLOSER

7. Identify Which two parts of an amniotic egg provide food for the embryo?

Most reptiles are **oviparous**. In other words, the female lays eggs outside her body. The young hatch from these eggs. Most oviparous reptiles do not protect or take care of their eggs or young. ☑

8. Define What does oviparous mean?

Some snakes and lizards do not lay eggs outside their bodies. They appear to give birth to live young. However, these reptiles, like all reptiles, have amniotic eggs. These reptiles are ovoviviparous. In **ovoviviparous** reptiles, the fertilized eggs remain inside the female's body for a long time. The eggs may even hatch inside the female. This protects the eggs from predators.

Name ______________________ Class ______________ Date ______________

Section 1 Review

SECTION VOCABULARY

ectothermic describes the ability of an organism to maintain its body temperature by gaining heat from the environment

Jacobson's organ an olfactory sac that opens into the mouth and is highly developed in reptiles

oviparous describes organisms that produce eggs that develop and hatch outside the body of the mother

ovoviviparous describes organisms that produce eggs that develop and hatch inside the body of the mother

1. **Identify** Give three characteristics of reptiles.

____

____

____

2. **Explain** Why can reptiles move more quickly than amphibians, but not as quickly as mammals, on land?

____

____

3. **Identify** Give three characteristics that allow reptiles to sense and respond to their environment.

____

____

____

4. **Compare** How is a reptile's heart different from an amphibian's heart?

____

____

5. **Explain** How has the amniotic egg allowed reptiles to live successfully on land?

____

____

6. **Compare** What is the difference between oviparous reptiles and ovoviviparous reptiles?

____

____

____

Name ______________________ Class ______________ Date ______________

CHAPTER 31 Reptiles and Birds

SECTION 2

Groups of Reptiles

KEY IDEAS

As you read this section, keep these questions in mind:
- Which physical characteristics make turtles and tortoises unique?
- How are tuataras different from other reptiles?
- Why are crocodilian young more likely to survive than the young of other reptiles?
- How are snakes and lizards similar?

READING TOOLBOX

Describe After you read this section, make a chart describing the features of each of the four main groups of reptiles.

What Are the Four Main Groups of Reptiles?

There are many different species of reptiles. Scientists classify reptiles into four main groups:

- turtles and tortoises
- tuataras
- crocodilians
- lizards and snakes

How Are Turtles and Tortoises Unique?

Unlike other kinds of reptiles, turtles and tortoises have hard shells that protect their bodies. Most turtles and tortoises can pull their legs and heads into their shells for protection. A turtle or tortoise's spine is *fused*, or attached, to its shell. ☑

READING CHECK

1. Compare How are turtles and tortoises different from other reptiles?

____

____

____

The **carapace** is the upper part of a turtle's shell. The **plastron** is the lower part.

Turtles and tortoises do not have teeth. Instead, their jaws have sharp plates that they use to cut their food.

Tortoises live on land. Most of them have domed shells. In contrast, most turtles live in water. Their shells are streamlined to help them swim more easily.

How Do Tuataras Differ From Other Reptiles?

Tuataras look like lizards, but they are not lizards. Tuataras have existed for about 150 million years. There are only two species alive today.

Unlike most other reptiles, tuataras are more active at low temperatures. They burrow or lie in the sun during the day. They feed on insects, worms, and other small animals at night.

Infer Tuataras are sometimes called "living fossils." What do you think is the reason for this? Talk about your thoughts with a partner or a small group.

How Are Crocodilians Unique?

Crocodilians include crocodiles, alligators, caimans, and gavials. Unlike most other reptiles, crocodilians take care of their young. For example, an American alligator builds a nest for her eggs. After the eggs hatch, the mother may tear open the nest to free the hatchlings. She may protect the young alligators for up to a year after they hatch.

Crocodilians are carnivores. They usually capture their prey by ambushing them. For example, a crocodilian may float just below the water's surface, near the shore. When an animal comes to drink, the crocodilian moves quickly out of the water and seizes its prey.

Critical Thinking

2. Explain What do you think is the reason that crocodilian young are more likely to survive than the young of other reptiles?

____

____

____

____

Crocodilians are carnivores with very sharp teeth. Their sharp teeth help them tear apart, rather than chew, their prey.

LOOKING CLOSER

3. Describe How do crocodilians kill and eat their prey?

____

____

How Are Snakes and Lizards Similar?

Because snakes and lizards look so different, many people think they are not closely related. However, snakes and lizards are closely related. They evolved millions of years ago from a common ancestor with legs.

CHARACTERISTICS OF SNAKES AND LIZARDS

Because lizards and snakes have a common ancestor, they have many features in common. For example, both snakes and lizards regularly *molt*, or shed their skin. In addition, the jaws of snakes and lizards are only loosely attached to their skulls. This allows their mouths to open wide enough to eat large prey.

Snakes and lizards evolved from a common ancestor. Therefore, they have many features in common.

LOOKING CLOSER

4. Explain Why do snakes and lizards share many characteristics?

____

____

CHARACTERISTICS OF LIZARDS

Common types of lizards include iguanas, geckos, anoles, and horned lizards. A few species of lizards are herbivores, but most are carnivores. Most lizards live in tropical forests or deserts. Some are fast runners. Others, such as the chameleon, are good climbers. Some lizards are legless, like snakes. However, unlike snakes, lizards have external ears and eyelids. ☑

5. Identify Where do most lizards live?

____

____

CHARACTERISTICS OF SNAKES

Snakes are carnivores. Snakes eat their prey whole because their teeth are not useful for cutting or chewing. Because their jaws are so flexible, snakes can eat very large prey.

Snakes kill their prey in different ways. Some snakes, such as boas and pythons, are constrictors. **Constrictors** wrap their bodies around their prey. They slowly squeeze the prey to death before eating it. Some snakes, such as vipers and cobras, use *venom*, or poison, to kill their prey.

Name ______________________ Class ______________ Date ______________

Section 2 Review

SECTION VOCABULARY

carapace in some crustaceans, a shieldlike plate that covers the body; in turtles and tortoises, the upper shell **constrictor** a snake that kills its prey by crushing and suffocating it	**plastron** the bottom, or ventral, portion of a turtle's shell

1. Draw In the space below, draw a sketch of a turtle's shell. Label the carapace and the plastron.

2. Compare How are turtles and tortoises different?

____

____

3. Compare How are tuataras different from other reptiles?

____

____

4. Identify What are four kinds of crocodilians?

____

____

____

____

5. Describe How are crocodilians different from other reptiles?

____

____

6. Identify What are two characteristics that snakes and lizards have in common?

____

____

7. Describe What are two ways that snakes kill their prey?

____

____

Name ______________________ Class ______________________ Date ______________________

SECTION 3

The Bird Body

KEY IDEAS

As you read this section, keep these questions in mind:

- What are the key characteristics of modern birds?
- How is a bird's body adapted for flight?
- How do birds meet their need for a large amount of oxygen?
- How does bird reproduction differ from reptilian reproduction?

READING TOOLBOX

Summarize After you read this section, make a chart showing the similarities and differences between birds and reptiles.

What Are the Key Characteristics of Birds?

Modern birds and reptiles look very different. However, the ancestors of birds were reptiles. Birds evolved from carnivorous dinosaurs. Therefore, birds and reptiles are closely related.

Because birds evolved from reptiles, they share some common features. For example, birds lay amniotic eggs similar to those of reptiles. In addition, birds' feet and legs are covered with scales. ☑

1. Identify Give two ways that birds and reptiles are similar.

____

____

____

____

Birds also have many characteristics that make them different from reptiles. The key characteristics of modern birds include:

- feathers and wings
- a lightweight skeleton with hollow bones
- an endothermic, or warm-blooded, metabolism
- lungs that contain air sacs
- a beak

Some people think that all birds fly. However, some birds, such as the penguin and the ostrich, cannot fly.

What Is an Endothermic Metabolism?

Birds are **endothermic**. In other words, their metabolisms generate enough heat to maintain high body temperatures. Birds' body temperatures may range from 40°C to 44°C (104°F to 111°F). Birds can maintain their body temperatures even in very cold environments.

2. Explain Why can birds obtain energy from food quickly?

____

____

Birds need a great deal of energy for flight. They can obtain energy from their food very quickly because their digestive systems are very efficient. They use most of the energy for flight, but some of it is converted to heat. This is why their body temperatures are so high. ☑

How Are Birds Adapted for Flight?

Birds have many adaptations that allow them to fly. Two of the most important adaptations are feathers and a lightweight skeleton.

FEATHERS

Birds have two main types of feathers: contour feathers and down feathers. **Contour feathers** cover an adult bird's body. Specialized contour feathers, called *flight feathers*, are found on a bird's wings and tail. These feathers help provide lift for flight.

Down feathers cover the body of young birds and are found beneath adult birds' contour feathers. The fluffy down feathers trap warm air. This helps the birds stay warm.

Critical Thinking

3. Compare How is the function of flight feathers different from the function of down feathers?

____

____

____

____

LIGHTWEIGHT SKELETON

The bones of a bird's skeleton are thin and hollow. The low weight of the skeleton makes it easier for the bird to fly. In addition, many of the bones are fused. Therefore, a bird's skeleton is stiffer and lighter than that of a reptile. The fused bones form a sturdy frame that anchors muscles during flight.

Flight muscles stretch from the wing to the breastbone. The breastbone is very large. It extends away from the bird's ribs to form a large *keel*. The flight muscles attach to the keel and to the bird's collarbones. ☑

4. Identify To which bones do a bird's flight muscles attach?

____

____

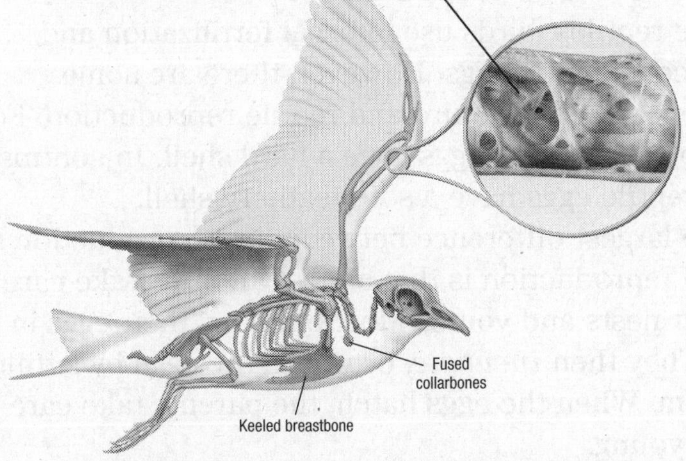

A bird's skeleton is made of hollow, lightweight bones.

LOOKING CLOSER

5. Explain How can a bird's bones be both strong and lightweight?

____

____

____

____

How Do Birds Get Enough Oxygen to Fly?

Birds need a large amount of oxygen to fly. Therefore, their circulatory and respiratory systems are much more efficient than those of reptiles.

Talk About It

Discuss Why is a four-chambered heart more efficient at getting oxygen-rich blood to the body than a three-chambered heart? In a small group, talk about how each type of heart pumps oxygen-rich and oxygen-poor blood.

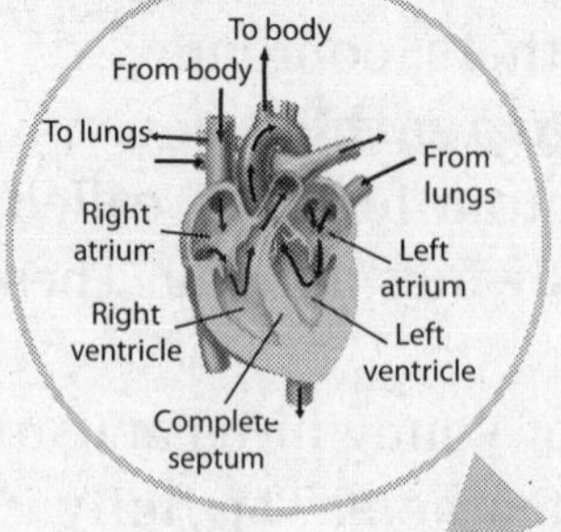

A bird's heart has four chambers. The separate chambers prevent oxygen-rich and oxygen-poor blood from mixing. A bird's heart generally beats very quickly to supply the bird's body with enough oxygen for flight.

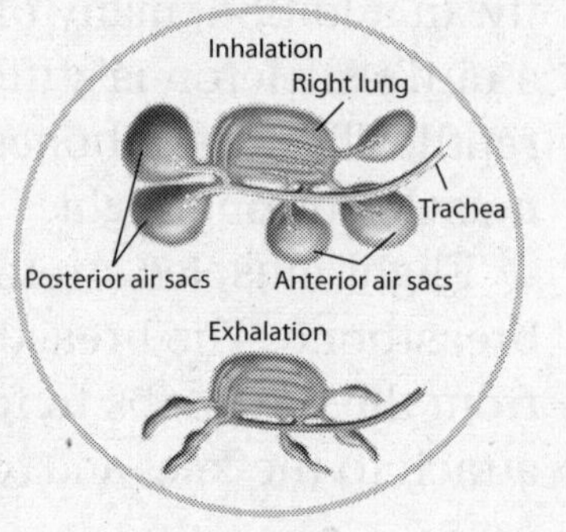

A bird's lungs have special structures called *air sacs*. When the bird breathes in, the fresh air flows into the *posterior*, or back, air sacs. Stale air flows into the *anterior*, or front, air sacs. When the bird breathes out, the fresh air flows into the lungs. The stale air flows back into the environment.

LOOKING CLOSER

6. Color In the figure, color the air sacs that contain fresh air red. Color the air sacs that contain stale air blue.

How Do Birds Reproduce?

Like reptiles, birds use internal fertilization and produce amniotic eggs. However, there are some differences between bird and reptile reproduction. For example, most bird eggs have a hard shell. In contrast, most reptile eggs have a soft, leathery shell.

The largest difference between bird reproduction and reptile reproduction is that almost all birds take care of their nests and young. Most birds lay their eggs in a nest. They then *incubate*, or warm, the eggs by sitting on them. When the eggs hatch, the parents take care of the young.

Name ______________________ Class ______________ Date ______________

Section 3 Review

SECTION VOCABULARY

contour feather one of the most external feathers that cover a bird and that help determine its shape **down feather** a soft feather that covers the body of young birds and provides insulation to adult birds	**endothermic** describes the ability of a living thing to keep a constant body temperature by using the heat produced from metabolism

1. Identify Give four characteristics of modern birds.

2. Explain Why are birds' body temperatures so high?

3. Identify Describe two adaptations that help birds fly.

4. Explain Why is it important that birds' circulatory and respiratory systems are very efficient?

5. Compare Give two similarities and two differences between bird reproduction and reptile reproduction.

6. Apply Concepts Why can birds live in colder climates than reptiles?

Name ______________________ Class ______________ Date ______________

CHAPTER 31 Reptiles and Birds

SECTION 4

Groups of Birds

KEY IDEAS

As you read this section, keep these questions in mind:

- How are the bodies of terrestrial birds related to their lifestyles?
- What physical characteristics do aquatic birds have?

READING TOOLBOX

Define As you read, underline words you don't know. When you figure out what they mean, write the words and their definitions in your notebook.

What Characteristics Do Land Birds Have?

Many birds are *terrestrial*, which means that they live mainly on dry land. There are three main kinds of terrestrial birds: perching birds, birds of prey, and flightless birds. Each type of bird has different characteristics that help it survive.

Group	Characteristics
Perching birds, such as finches, bluebirds, and woodpeckers	A perching bird's feet have one toe that points backward. The other toes point forward. This helps them grasp their perches. The beaks of perching birds are related to the food they eat. For example, birds that eat seeds have thick, strong beaks for cracking the seeds open.
Birds of prey, such as owls and falcons	Most birds of prey are hunters. They have good vision to help them locate prey. They also have **talons**, or claws, on their toes and sharp, hooked beaks for tearing prey.
Flightless birds, such as ostriches	Flightless birds have small wings, but they have strong legs that allow them to run on land.

LOOKING CLOSER

1. Explain How do a perching bird's feet relate to its lifestyle?

____

____

____

____

What Characteristics Do Aquatic Birds Have?

Some birds are *aquatic*, which means that they live mostly in water. There are three main groups of aquatic birds: diving birds, water birds, and wading birds. Like terrestrial birds, each kind of aquatic bird has characteristics that help it survive.

Group	Characteristics
Diving birds, such as penguins	The wings, feet, and body of an aquatic bird are adapted for swimming. Therefore, most diving birds are flightless.
Water birds, such as swans, geese, and ducks	Water birds swim on or near the surface of the water. They have large, webbed feet that help them paddle through the water. They also have long, flat beaks that allow them to eat many kinds of food.
Wading birds, such as storks, herons, and flamingos	Wading birds have long, slender legs that allow them to wade in deep water. The shapes of their beaks allow them to stab fish or filter organisms out of the water for food.

Critical Thinking

2. Infer Most water birds can fly. Therefore, their bodies are adapted to both flight and swimming. Do you think water birds are better or worse at swimming than most diving birds? Explain your answer.

____

____

____

____

____

____

Name ______________________ Class ______________ Date ______________

Section 4 Review

SECTION VOCABULARY

talon claw of a bird of prey	

1. Identify What are the three main kinds of terrestrial birds?

____

____

____

2. Describe Give two examples of how a bird of prey's characteristics are related to its lifestyle.

____

____

3. Compare Fill in the blank spaces in the Spider Map below to describe the different kinds of aquatic birds.

Aquatic Birds

- ______________
  - ______________
  - beaks for stabbing fish or filtering food out of water
- ______________
  - bodies are adapted for swimming
  - most are flightless
- Water birds
  - long, flat beaks
  - ______________

4. Explain Are all flightless birds terrestrial birds? Explain your answer.

____

____

____

Name ______________________ Class ______________ Date ______________

CHAPTER 32 Mammals

SECTION 1

Characteristics of Mammals

KEY IDEAS

As you read this section, keep these questions in mind:

- What are the key characteristics of mammals?
- How are the respiratory and circulatory systems of mammals adapted for endothermy?
- What kinds of teeth do mammals have?
- How do mammals differ from other vertebrates in terms of parental care?
- In what ways do mammals move?

READING TOOLBOX

Summarize As you read this section, underline the main ideas. When you finish reading, make an outline of the section using the underlined ideas.

What Are the Key Characteristics of Mammals?

Some of the animals we are most familiar with are mammals. Lions, mice, whales, and humans are all mammals. Obviously, mammals vary in shape and size. So, what makes a mammal a mammal? All mammals share four characteristics:

- hair or fur
- *endothermy*, or a warm-blooded metabolism
- specialized teeth
- ability of females to produce milk to feed their young

Critical Thinking

1. Compare Name one characteristic that both birds and mammals have.

____

How Does a Mammal's Body Stay Warm?

Like birds, mammals are *endothermic*. That is, their metabolisms generate heat, which helps their bodies maintain consistent internal temperatures. Therefore, like birds, mammals can live in very cold climates. They can also be more active than reptiles and amphibians. ☑

2. Explain Why can mammals live in colder climates than reptiles or amphibians?

____

____

However, moving quickly and maintaining a high body temperature require a great deal of energy. Mammals get this energy from the food they eat. Because it requires more energy, a mammal needs to eat more food than a reptile or amphibian that is a similar size.

Mammals use mainly aerobic respiration to get energy from food. Remember that *aerobic respiration* requires oxygen. Therefore, in order to support their endothermic metabolisms, mammals require a great deal of oxygen. A mammal's respiratory and circulatory systems provide this oxygen to the mammal's body.

RESPIRATORY SYSTEM

A mammal's lungs have more surface area than a reptile's or an amphibian's lungs. As a result, a mammal's lungs can take in more oxygen than a reptile's or an amphibian's lungs can. The large surface area also allows mammals to release the large amounts of carbon dioxide that their bodies produce during aerobic respiration. ☑

3. Explain How does the structure of a mammal's lung help it survive?

CIRCULATORY SYSTEM

Like birds, mammals have a four-chambered heart. The two *atria* (singular, *atrium*) receive blood from the rest of the body. The atria pump blood to the ventricles. The *ventricles* pump blood away from the heart. One of the ventricles pumps oxygen-poor blood to the lungs. The other ventricle pumps oxygen-rich blood to the body.

A wall called a *septum* separates the two ventricles. The septum prevents oxygen-rich and oxygen-poor blood from mixing. As a result, only oxygen-rich blood reaches the mammal's tissues.

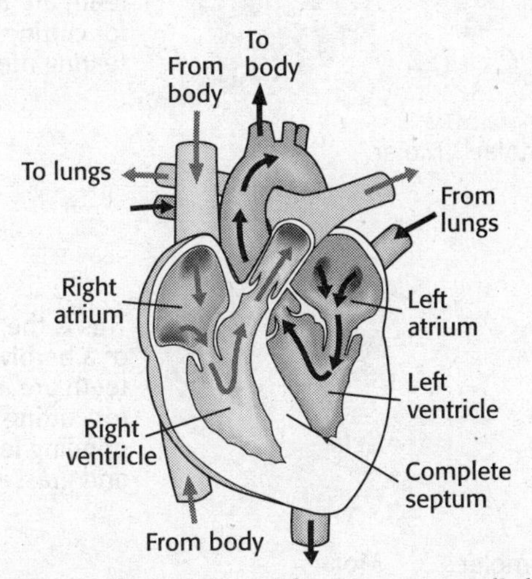

A septum separates the two ventricles in a mammal's heart. Therefore, oxygen-poor blood does not mix with oxygen-rich blood in the heart.

Critical Thinking

4. Apply Concepts Color the ventricle that pumps oxygen-rich blood red. Color the ventricle that pumps oxygen-poor blood blue.

What Types of Teeth Do Mammals Have?

In general, all of the teeth in a non-mammal's mouth look similar. In addition, the teeth may fall out and grow back many times during the animal's life. In contrast, a mammal's teeth typically fall out and grow back only once in its life. In addition, most mammals have four different kinds of teeth: incisors, canines, premolars, and molars.

FUNCTIONS OF TEETH

Each type of tooth in a mammal's mouth has a different function. In other words, a mammal's teeth are *specialized*. *Incisors*, the front teeth, are used for biting and cutting. Behind the incisors are the *canines*, which are used for stabbing and holding. The *premolars* and *molars* are located farther back in the jaw. They crush and grind food. ☑

5. Describe What is the function of the incisors?

____

____

Mammals eat many types of foods. Some mammals, such as zebras and elephants, are herbivores. Others, such as tigers and killer whales, are carnivores. Still other mammals, such as raccoons and bears, are omnivores. The shape and size of a mammal's teeth are related to the types of food it eats. Therefore, one can learn a lot about what a mammal eats by looking at its teeth.

Background

Recall that a *herbivore* is an animal that eats only plants. A *carnivore* is an animal that eats only other animals. An *omnivore* is an animal that eats both plants and other animals.

Coyote

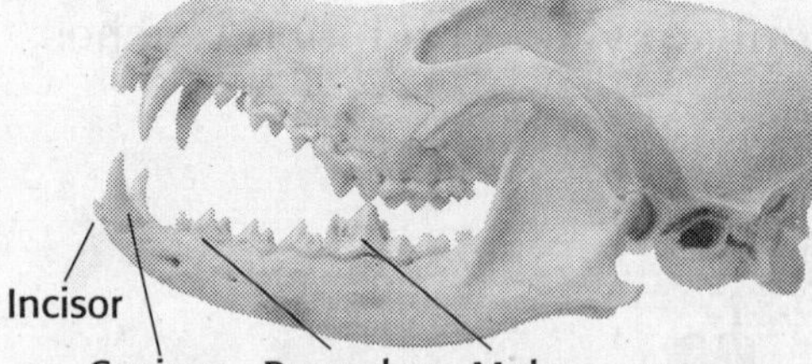

This is the skull of a carnivore. Its teeth are adapted for cutting and tearing meat.

Deer

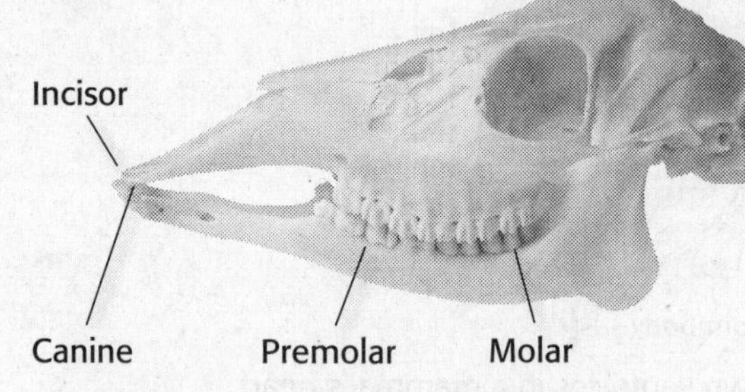

This is the skull of a herbivore. Its teeth are adapted for cutting and grinding leaves and grasses.

LOOKING CLOSER

6. Describe What characteristics of the carnivore's teeth make them good for cutting or tearing meat?

____

____

How Do Mammals Care for Their Young?

Unlike the young of most other vertebrates, young mammals depend on their mothers for a relatively long period of time. Mammal mothers provide food, protection, and shelter for their young. Although adult mammals eat different kinds of food, all baby mammals drink milk that their mothers produce. A female mammal's milk is produced by specialized glands called **mammary glands**. They are located on the female's chest or abdomen.

HOW MAMMALS DEVELOP

Like reptiles and birds, mammals use internal fertilization. However, the fertilized eggs of different groups of mammals develop in different ways. Scientists divide mammals into three main groups based on how their eggs develop.

Group	Examples	How their eggs develop
Monotremes	platypus, echidna	Monotremes lay eggs. When the eggs hatch, the mother stays with and nurses the young for several months.
Marsupials	kangaroo, koala	Marsupials give birth to live young only a few days or weeks after fertilization. The time between fertilization and birth is called the **gestation period**. After birth, the young attach to their mother's nipple. They nurse for many weeks or months as they continue to develop.
Placental mammals	dolphin, cheetah, human	Placental mammals have longer gestation periods than marsupials do. Therefore, the young of placental mammals are more developed at birth than the young of marsupials are. While the young are developing inside the mother, they receive food through a structure called the **placenta**.

LOOKING CLOSER

7. Compare How are monotremes different from other mammals?

____

____

How Do Mammals Move In and Sense Their Environment?

Mammals can move in many different ways. They may run, walk, jump, swim, climb, burrow, and even fly. Every mammal has adaptations that allow it to move in specific ways in its environment. For example, a mountain lion has strong leg muscles and bones that allow it to run and jump. In contrast, a bat has lightweight bones and wings that allow it to fly.

Mammals also have many different adaptations that allow them to sense and respond to their environments. For example, dolphins and bats use sound to help them locate food. They produce clicks or high-pitched squeaks that travel through the water or air. When the sounds strike an object, they bounce back to the animal. The dolphin or bat can use these echoes to "see" the objects around them. This process is called **echolocation**.

Talk About It

Relate In a small group, brainstorm examples of two or three different mammals. Discuss how each animal shows the characteristics of mammals that are described in this section.

Name ______________________ Class ______________ Date ______________

Section 1 Review

SECTION VOCABULARY

echolocation the process of using reflected sound waves to find objects; used by animals such as bats **gestation period** in mammals, the length of time between fertilization and birth	**mammary gland** a gland that is located in the chest of a female mammal and that secretes milk **placenta** the structure that attaches a developing fetus to the uterus and that enables the exchange of nutrients, wastes, and gases between the mother and the fetus

1. List Give four characteristics of mammals.

____

____

____

2. Explain How do a mammal's circulatory and respiratory systems help it maintain its metabolism?

____

____

____

3. Apply Concepts A scientist finds the skull of an organism. All of the teeth in the organism's mouth look the same. Was the organism a mammal? Explain your answer.

____

____

4. Identify What are the three main groups of mammals?

____

____

____

5. Describe Give an example of one mammal that can fly, one mammal that can swim, and one mammal that can jump.

____

____

____

Name ______________________ Class ______________ Date ______________

SECTION 2
Groups of Mammals

KEY IDEAS

As you read this section, keep these questions in mind:

- How are monotremes different from all other mammals?
- What are the key characteristics of marsupials?
- How are placental mammals different from monotremes and marsupials?

What Are Monotremes?

Remember that the earliest mammals evolved from a group of reptiles called *therapsids*. Today, most mammals are very different from reptiles. However, one group of mammals, the **monotremes**, share more characteristics with reptiles than other mammals do.

Like reptiles, monotremes lay eggs. In addition, a monotreme's legs are not as far under its body as other mammals' legs are. Instead, they are spread out to the sides, like the legs of a reptile. Both reptiles and monotremes have a *cloaca*, a single opening for the urinary, digestive, and reproductive systems. ☑

Although monotremes are similar to reptiles in many ways, they are mammals because they share the characteristics of mammals. Like all mammals, monotremes are endothermic and have fur and specialized teeth. Female monotremes also produce milk to feed their young.

Monotremes are not very common today. Platypuses and echidnas are the only living groups of monotremes. They are found only in Australia and New Guinea.

This short-beaked echidna is an example of a monotreme.

READING TOOLBOX

Organize As you read this section, make a Spider Map describing the traits of the three main groups of mammals.

READING CHECK

1. Describe What are three characteristics that reptiles and monotremes share?

____

____

____

Critical Thinking

2. Apply Concepts Where is the short-beaked echidna probably found?

____

What Are Marsupials?

Marsupials include kangaroos, wombats, koalas, and opossums. The young of marsupials develop inside the mother for only a few days or weeks. When they are born, the young are generally very small and helpless. They continue to grow and develop as they nurse. ☑

3. Identify Name three mammals that are marsupials.

____

____

____

The females of most marsupials have a pouch. The young of marsupials spend most of their time developing inside this pouch while they nurse and grow.

Like most other marsupials, this baby wallaby grows and develops inside its mother's pouch. It spends much of that time nursing.

LOOKING CLOSER

4. Describe Where does the baby wallaby get its food?

____

What Are Placental Mammals?

Cats, dogs, whales, horses, and humans are all placental mammals. In fact, nearly 95% of all mammal species are placental mammals. Unlike the young of monotremes and marsupials, the young of placental mammals fully develop inside the female's uterus.

The name *placental mammal* is based on the word *placenta*. Remember that a *placenta* is an organ that connects a developing mammal to its mother. A young placental mammal receives nourishment from its mother's blood through the placenta.

Background

Recall that the *gestation period* is the time between fertilization and birth.

Placental mammals have longer gestation periods than marsupials do. Therefore, the young of most placental mammals are more developed at birth than the young of marsupials are.

Name ______________________ Class ______________ Date ______________

TYPES OF PLACENTAL MAMMALS

There are many different kinds of placental mammals. Scientists group placental mammals into about 18 different orders, 12 of which are described below.

Order	Examples	Characteristics
Artiodactyla	pig, camel, cow	have hooves with an even number of toes
Perissodactyla	zebra, horse	have hooves with an odd number of toes
Cetacea	whale, dolphin	• live in the water • have smooth, streamlined bodies and powerful tails called *flukes*
Primates	human, ape, lemur, monkey	• have excellent eyesight • have long arms and legs • have hands and feet that can grasp objects
Rodentia	mouse, rat, beaver	• have teeth that are specialized for gnawing • most common type of placental mammal
Chiroptera	bat	• the only mammals that are able to fly • Most are carnivores that use echolocation to locate prey. • Some are herbivores.
Xenarthra	anteater, sloth, armadillo	• have no teeth or only simple teeth • Most eat plants or insects.
Lagomorpha	rabbit, hare	• have no tail or only a short tail • have large front teeth
Insectivora	shrew, hedgehog, mole	• small • eat mainly insects • Many have adaptations for burrowing.
Proboscidea	elephant	• have long, flexible trunks • Many have large front teeth called *tusks.*
Carnivora	cat, dog, bear, seal	• have teeth that are specialized for tearing • Many are carnivores. • Some are omnivores or herbivores.
Sirenia	dugong, manatee	• related to elephants • have flipper-like front limbs • have flattened tails that are used for swimming

LOOKING CLOSER

5. Identify Into which mammal order are humans classified?

____

6. Identify Which order contains the only mammals that can fly?

____

Critical Thinking

7. Apply Concepts A biologist discovers a placental mammal that is tiny and mostly eats insects. It has large front feet that allow it to dig through the ground. In which order does this mammal probably belong?

____

Name ______________ Class ______________ Date ______________

Section 2 Review

SECTION VOCABULARY

monotreme a mammal that lays eggs	

1. **Explain** Why are monotremes classified as mammals if they share so many characteristics with reptiles?

____

____

2. **Compare** Fill in the blank spaces in the Venn diagram to show how marsupials and placental mammals are different.

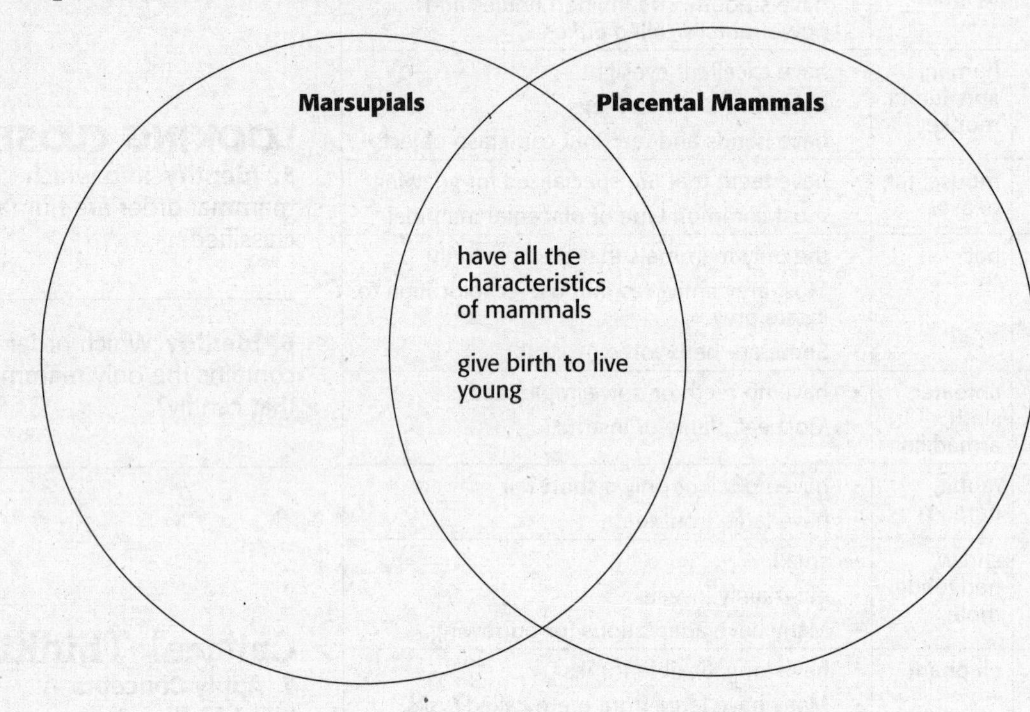

3. **Identify** What is the most common group of mammals?

____

4. **Apply Concepts** A mammal is a member of order Lagomorpha. Is the mammal a monotreme, a marsupial, or a placental mammal? Explain your answer.

____

____

5. **Compare** Give one similarity and one difference between mammals in the order Artiodactyla and mammals in the order Perissodactyla.

____

____

CHAPTER 32 Mammals

SECTION 3

Evolution of Primates

KEY IDEAS

As you read this section, keep these questions in mind:
- What are two unique features of primates?
- What are the three groups of modern primates?
- How are hominids different from other primates?
- What does the hominid fossil record tell us?
- Where and when did modern humans evolve?

What Unique Features Do Primates Have?

A **primate** is a member of order Primates. The first primates evolved more than 50 million years ago. Two characteristics helped primates become successful: grasping hands and binocular vision.

All primates have hands that can grasp objects. Most primates also have feet that can grasp objects. Their hands and feet generally have flat nails instead of claws. This makes it easier for them to grab objects.

In most mammals, the eyes are located on either side of the head. In contrast, a primate's eyes are located at the front of its head. This gives primates *binocular vision.* Binocular vision allows primates to see depth.

READING TOOLBOX

Answer Questions Before you read this section, write the five Key Ideas questions in your notebook. After you read, write answers to the questions in your notebook. Write your answers in your own words.

Critical Thinking

1. Infer Many kinds of animals have binocular vision. Why are they not all considered primates?

____

____

____

What Are the Groups of Modern Primates?

The table below describes the three groups of primates that are alive today.

Group	Characteristics
Lemurs and their relatives	These primates are small. They live in trees and are most active at night. Primates in this group probably most closely resemble the earliest primates.
Tarsiers	These primates are also small and are active at night. They live mainly in Southeast Asia. Scientists used to think that tarsiers were close relatives of lemurs. However, new evidence has shown that tarsiers are more closely related to monkeys than to lemurs.
Monkeys, apes, and humans	Monkeys, apes, and humans are most active during the day. They have opposable thumbs that can bend inward toward their fingers. *Monkeys* are the smallest members of this group. Some monkeys have flexible tails that can grab objects. *Apes* include gibbons, orangutans, gorillas, chimpanzees, and bonobos. Apes have relatively larger brains than monkeys. Humans are different from apes and monkeys in several ways.

LOOKING CLOSER

2. Identify Members of which group of primates are most active during the day?

____

____

How Are Hominids Unique?

Hominids include humans and their ancestors. Unlike other primates, hominids walk on two legs. Based on the fossil record, scientists think hominids evolved about 7 million years ago. The figure below shows how hominids are different from other primates.

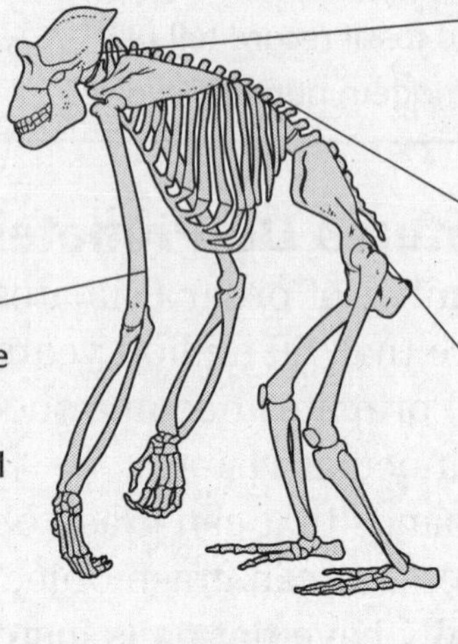

In most primates, the spinal cord comes out the back of the skull.

Most primates have a C-shaped spine.

Most primates have longer arms than legs. This allows them to walk on all four limbs.

Most primates have tall, narrow pelvises.

Gorilla

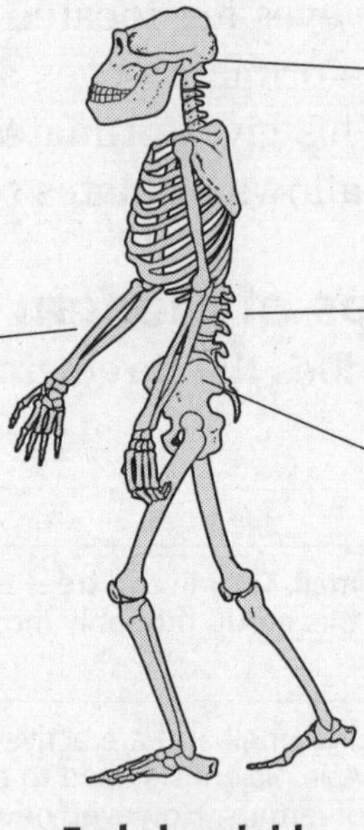

A hominid's spinal cord comes out the bottom of the skull.

Hominids have an S-shaped spine.

A hominid's arms are shorter than its legs. It walks upright, using only its legs.

A hominid's pelvis is bowl-shaped.

Early hominid

Scientists are not sure how hominids evolved. Some scientists think that a change in climate may have played a role in hominid evolution. About 15 million years ago, Earth's climate began to cool. Forests became smaller, and grasslands became larger. Some scientists think that hominids were better adapted to living in grasslands. This allowed them to survive better than other primates.

Talk About It

Research and Share Learn more about one of the characteristics of hominids that is described in the figure. Share what you learn with a small group.

LOOKING CLOSER

3. Compare How is a hominid's spine different from the spines of other primates?

____

____

____

What Does the Hominid Fossil Record Tell Us?

Based on the fossil record, scientists know that many different hominid species have lived in the past 7 million years. Until about 30,000 years ago, more than one species of hominid existed on Earth at the same time. Except for humans, all of these hominid species are now extinct.

Scientists do not always agree on exactly how to classify ancient hominid fossils. The table below describes how most scientists today classify hominids.

Group	Characteristics
Earliest hominids	These species had some hominid traits. They also had some apelike traits. They lived between about 7 million and about 4.4 million years ago. Some scientists do not think some of these species are true hominids.
Australopiths	These hominids were part of the genus *Australopithecus*. Their legs, arms, and teeth were more humanlike than earlier hominids. Their bodies were small, with small brains. They lived from about 4.4 million to about 2 million years ago. Modern humans may have evolved from an australopith species.
Paranthropus	This genus of hominids lived more recently and were larger than most of the australopiths. They had heavy jaws and skulls and relatively small brains. They lived from about 2.5 million to about 1 million years ago. Modern humans probably did not evolve from members of the genus *Paranthropus*.
Homo habilis	This was probably the first species in the human genus, *Homo*. They lived from about 2.5 to about 1.5 million years ago. In English, *Homo habilis* means "handy man." This species got its name because fossils of the species were found with tools.
Homo ergaster and *Homo erectus*	At least 1.8 million years ago, the species *Homo ergaster* began to become more dominant than *Homo habilis*. *Homo ergaster* had a much larger brain than *Homo habilis*. However, *Homo ergaster* was probably not descended from *Homo habilis*. Most scientists think that *Homo ergaster* or a similar species, *Homo erectus*, was the direct ancestor of modern humans.
Neanderthals	Neanderthals, members of the species *Homo neanderthalensis*, lived in Europe and Asia from about 230,000 years ago to about 30,000 years ago. They may have lived at the same time as some members of the modern human species, *Homo sapiens*. They were short and powerfully built. The average Neanderthal brain was slightly larger than that of a modern human.

Talk About It

Summarize In a small group, create a timeline of hominid evolution using the information in the table.

LOOKING CLOSER

4. Identify Name two groups of hominids that were alive about 2.5 million years ago.

______

______

5. Explain Where did *Homo habilis* get its name?

______

______

______

______

Where and When Did Modern Humans Evolve?

The oldest known fossils of primitive *Homo sapiens*, our own species, are about 500,000 years old. These hominids were slightly different from modern humans, but they were still members of our species.

By studying the genes of humans today and the fossils of ancient humans, scientists can estimate when modern humans evolved. Scientists think modern humans first evolved about 160,000 years ago in Africa. These humans would have looked much like humans today do. ☑

6. Describe How have scientists been able to estimate when modern humans evolved?

______

______

______

Why Have Humans Been So Successful?

After they evolved in Africa, modern humans probably migrated to Europe and Asia. They may have reached North America as early as 15,000 years ago. Modern humans replaced other hominid species as they populated Earth.

Homo sapiens have several qualities that other hominids probably did not have. These characteristics have helped humans survive. Some of the characteristics that have helped humans survive are:

- the ability to think abstractly (to apply existing knowledge to new situations)
- the ability to plan for future events
- the ability to make and use tools
- spoken and written language, which allows communication between people

Talk About It

Discuss What are some other unique characteristics that humans have? In a small group, talk about how humans' characteristics may have helped them survive. Which of these characteristics do you think are most important for humans today?

Homo sapiens can make tools, such as this spear.

Name ______________________ Class ______________ Date ______________

Section 3 Review

SECTION VOCABULARY

hominid a member of the family Hominidae of the order Primates; characterized by bipedalism, relatively long lower limbs, and lack of a tail; examples include humans and their ancestors	**primate** a member of the order Primates, the group of mammals that includes humans, apes, monkeys, and prosimians; typically distinguished by a highly developed brain, forward-directed eyes and binocular vision, opposable thumbs, and varied locomotion

1. Identify What are two unique features that all primates have?

____

____

2. Describe Which two groups of primates are active mainly at night?

____

____

3. Compare Describe three differences between the bodies of hominids and the bodies of other primates.

____

____

____

4. Identify Based on the fossil record, when did the first hominids probably evolve?

____

5. Describe From which earlier hominid genus did humans probably evolve?

____

6. Identify How old are the oldest primitive *Homo sapiens* fossils?

____

7. Describe Where and when do most scientists think modern *Homo sapiens* evolved?

____

____

8. List Give four characteristics of *Homo sapiens* that have helped us to survive.

____

____

____

____

Name ______________________ Class ______________ Date ______________

CHAPTER 33 Animal Behavior

SECTION 1

The Nature of Behavior

KEY IDEAS

As you read this section, keep these questions in mind:
- What questions help scientists study behavior?
- What factors influence behavior?
- How does evolution shape behavior?
- What factors cause innate behavior?
- What are examples of learned behaviors?

READING TOOLBOX

Underline As you read this section, underline the answers to the Key Ideas questions. With a partner, compare the parts of the text that you underlined.

What Is Behavior?

Has a sudden loud sound ever caused you to jump? The armadillo shown below is having a similar experience. Like the armadillo, we constantly interact with our surroundings and change our behavior depending on the situation.

A **stimulus** (plural, *stimuli*) is something in the environment that an organism might respond to, such as a smell or a sound. An organism's reaction to a stimulus is its **response**. Animals generally respond to stimuli with behaviors. A **behavior** is an action or series of actions an organism performs in response to a stimulus. ☑

READING CHECK

1. Identify Relationships What is the relationship between a response and a behavior?

____

____

____

This armadillo is jumping in response to a stimulus. A behavior such as jumping is a type of response.

Scientists studying behavior ask two kinds of questions: "how" questions and "why" questions. "How" questions ask how a behavior is triggered, controlled, and performed. For example, we might ask how a squirrel chooses which nuts to bury. "Why" questions address the evolution of a behavior. For example, we might ask why burying nuts helps a squirrel survive and reproduce. ☑

READING CHECK

2. Describe In the study of behavior, what do "why" questions address?

____

____

What Factors Influence Behavior?

Genetic and environmental factors interact to control an animal's behaviors. Genes may increase the likelihood that an individual will display a particular behavior. However, the environment determines whether and how well the animal performs the behavior.

How Do Behaviors Evolve?

One or a few male lions control a group, or pride, of lions. When a new male takes over a pride, he often kills the cubs of the other males. Why would such a behavior evolve?

Background

Recall that *natural selection* favors traits that allow an individual to survive and reproduce more successfully than other individuals. Over time, traits that provide an advantage become more common in a population.

A male lion generally does not harm his own cubs.

Male lions often kill the cubs of other male lions.

Like other traits, some behaviors can make an individual more likely than others to survive and reproduce. A behavior that allows one individual to have more offspring than another individual is an advantage. When a male lion kills the cubs of other males, he can father new cubs in the pride. Thus, he has greater reproductive success than his rivals.

Talk About It

Hypothesize After a male lion kills cubs, the female lions can soon become pregnant again. How do you think the cub-killing behavior evolved if it causes fewer of a female's offspring to survive? In a small group, propose a hypothesis to explain.

What Are Innate Behaviors?

To survive, most animals need to perform behaviors that they do not have time to learn. For example, a newborn mammal must be able to suckle without learning how to do so. Without this ability, the infant would starve. An **innate behavior** is a natural response to a stimulus that does not develop through experience. Genetic factors are the main cause of innate behaviors. Innate behaviors are also called *instinctive behaviors*.

Critical Thinking

3. Infer Why do you think animals with short life spans, such as many insects, depend mainly on innate behaviors for survival?

____

____

____

LOOKING CLOSER

4. Explain Does a spider such as this one learn to build its web? Explain your answer.

______

______

______

______

Fixed action patterns are innate behaviors that always happen the same way. They are triggered by a stimulus in the environment. Fixed action patterns, such as this web-building behavior, do not stop once the behavior has begun.

What Are Learned Behaviors?

The development of behaviors through experience is called **learning**. Learning may happen through habituation, problem solving, associative learning, and imprinting. ☑

READING CHECK

5. Identify In learning, how do behaviors develop?

______

HABITUATION

An animal's environment is full of stimuli, including scents, sounds, and other species. In *habituation*, an animal learns not to respond to a frequent, harmless, or unimportant stimulus. For example, chimpanzees can learn to ignore the researchers that study them. ☑

READING CHECK

6. Describe What happens during the process of habituation?

______

______

______

______

PROBLEM SOLVING

Drawing a conclusion from facts or an assumption is called **reasoning**. The raven shown below uses reasoning to solve the problem of getting the food on the end of the string.

With experience, this raven learned to use its beak to reach the food.

CONDITIONING

In **conditioning**, an animal learns to associate two factors. The two main kinds of conditioning are classical and operant. In *classical conditioning*, an animal learns to associate an unrelated response with a stimulus. Ivan Pavlov conditioned dogs to salivate when he rang a bell.

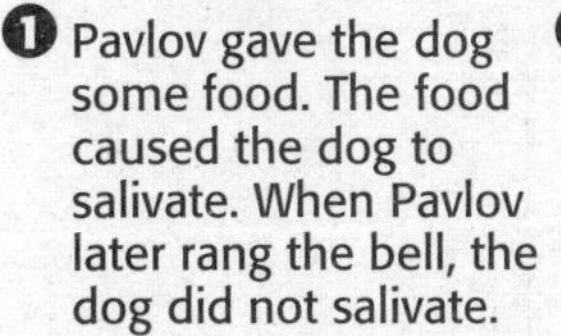

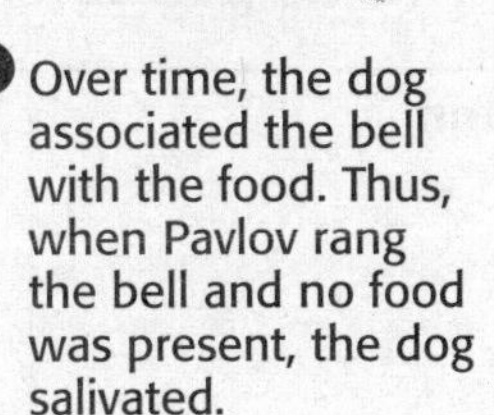

❶ Pavlov gave the dog some food. The food caused the dog to salivate. When Pavlov later rang the bell, the dog did not salivate.

❷ Then, Pavlov gave the dog food and rang the bell at the same time. The dog salivated.

❸ Over time, the dog associated the bell with the food. Thus, when Pavlov rang the bell and no food was present, the dog salivated.

LOOKING CLOSER

7. Infer In Pavlov's work with dogs, what was the original stimulus? What was the conditioned stimulus?

____

____

____

____

Many animals, including humans, can learn from their mistakes. Learning from your mistakes is a form of trial and error. For example, rats can learn by trial and error that they will receive food if they push a lever. Learning by trial and error is called *operant conditioning*.

IMPRINTING

Some behaviors develop only during a short period of an animal's life. This process is called **imprinting**. For example, baby ducks and geese will follow the first moving object they see soon after they hatch.

Critical Thinking

8. Infer How do you think the imprinting behavior of ducks and geese evolved?

____

____

____

____

____

____

____

Typically, the first moving object young cranes see is their mother. However, these young cranes imprinted on a researcher.

Name ______________________ Class ______________ Date ____________

Section 1 Review

SECTION VOCABULARY

behavior an action that an individual carries out in response to a stimulus or to the environment **conditioning** the process of learning by association **fixed action pattern** a highly stereotyped pattern of innate behavior that is triggered by a simple sensory cue **imprinting** learning that occurs early and quickly in a young animal's life and that cannot be changed once learned	**innate behavior** an inherited behavior that does not depend on the environment or experience **learning** the development of behaviors through experience or practice **reasoning** the act of drawing a conclusion from facts or assumptions **response** any biological reaction or behavior resulting from the application of a stimulus **stimulus** anything that causes a reaction or change in an organism or any part of an organism

1. **Organize** Complete the four-square diagram below to describe learning. Use as many of the vocabulary terms as possible. Include other terms as necessary.

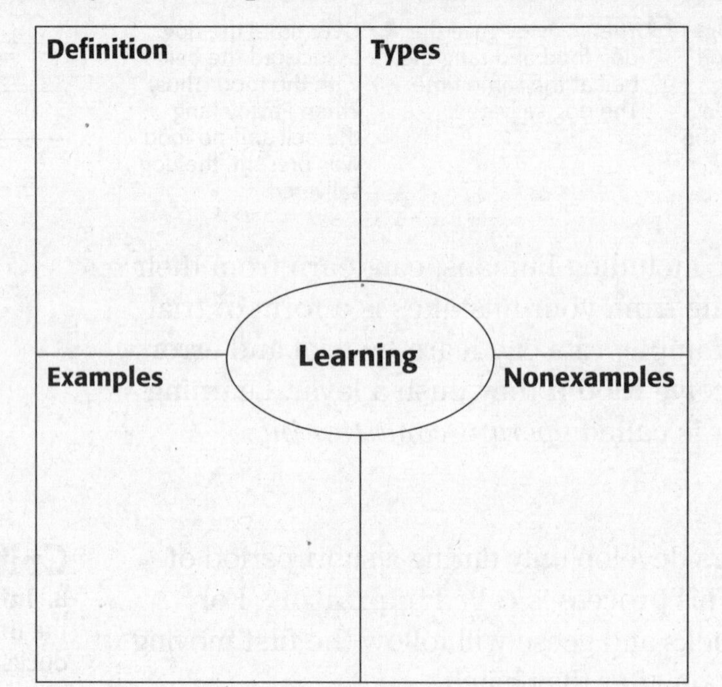

2. **Explain** How do behaviors evolve?

____

____

____

3. **Explain** How do genetic and environmental factors interact to determine an animal's behaviors?

____

____

Name ______________________ Class ______________ Date ______________

CHAPTER 33 Animal Behavior

SECTION 2

Classes of Behavior

KEY IDEAS

As you read this section, keep these questions in mind:
- What behaviors are essential for survival?
- How do animals communicate with each other?
- How do animals maximize reproductive success?

What Are Some Survival Behaviors?

Natural selection favors individuals that survive long enough to reproduce successfully. To survive, an individual must avoid predators and find resources such as food. ☑

Organize After you read, make two Spider Maps. One should describe the different modes of communication that animals use. The other should describe the strategies animals use to increase their reproductive success.

Animals use many behaviors called **foraging** to find, capture, and consume food. Animals can be divided into two broad groups based on the range of foods they eat.

Group	Description	Examples
Specialists	eat one or very few kinds of food	monarch butterflies, pandas
Generalists	eat many kinds of food	black bears, humans, rats

1. Identify What are the two components of survival for an individual?

____

____

Almost every animal must avoid becoming a meal for a predator. Some of the defenses against predators that animals use are listed below:

- using physical defenses, such as a porcupine's spines
- using chemical defenses, such as a skunk's spray
- playing dead
- running away
- forming groups

CYCLIC BEHAVIORS

Many species have behaviors that repeat daily or seasonally. For example, many species move to different areas throughout the year to look for food, to find mates, or to give birth. These seasonal movements are called **migration**.

Daily cycles, called **circadian rhythms**, include sleep patterns and activity levels. For example, some animals are *nocturnal*, which means they feed at night and sleep during the day. Many owls are nocturnal animals.

Critical Thinking

2. Infer *Diurnal* is the opposite of nocturnal. Describe the behavior pattern of a diurnal animal.

____

____

____

How Do Animals Communicate?

Any behavior that contains information and involves a sender and a receiver is known as **communication**. Animals send and receive communication signals through all the senses. The figure below shows examples of modes of communication among animals.

Chemical Chemical signals can last longer in the environment then other signals and can move over long distances. These ants are using chemicals to mark their paths. Other animals use chemicals to mark their territories or to attract mates.

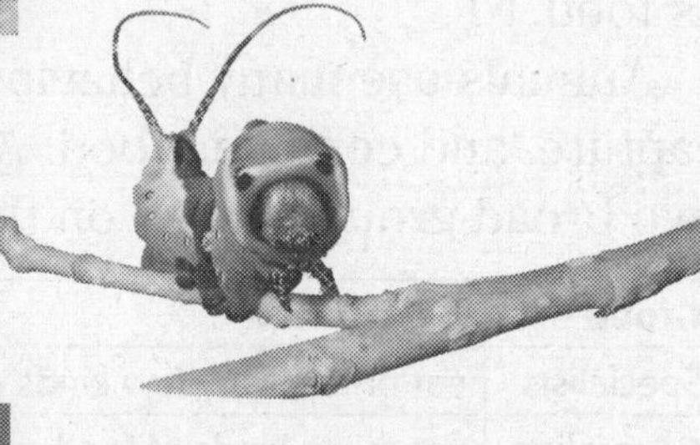

Sight Many animals use visual displays to seem threatening. This puss moth caterpillar displays its false face to warn off predators.

Touch Many species, including these prairie dogs, use touch to build social bonds and to reassure members of their groups.

Sound Sound is better than visual signals for getting attention or for communicating over long distances. Animals may use sound to identify themselves, to tell others that food or predators are present, or to indicate their moods.

Language is a mode of communication that uses symbols to express abstract concepts. Humans can teach other primates such as chimpanzees and gorillas to recognize and use language. However, only humans can combine elements of language, such as words or hand gestures, in new ways. ☑

Talk About It

Research Choose an animal species and research the types of communication it uses. Create a poster or a computer slide presentation and present to the class what you have learned. Be sure to include how you think the communication behaviors of this species help individuals survive and reproduce.

LOOKING CLOSER

3. Identify What are two ways animals may use chemical signals?

____

____

4. Identify Which two types of signals are useful over relatively large distances?

____

____

5. Define What is language?

____

____

____

____

What Are Some Reproductive Strategies?

Animals may use a variety of mating and parenting behaviors that help them reproduce and raise offspring. Any interaction between individuals is known as *social behavior*.

Behavior	Description	Function
Territorial behavior	An animal defends part of a habitat against other members of its species.	A territory gives an individual access to resources such as food or mates.
Courtship	a behavior ritual that leads to mating • **Sexual selection**: Females of some species prefer to mate with males that have certain traits. • Competition: Males fight or display certain traits to get the attention of the females.	• Some courtship behaviors help members of a species recognize one another. • In many cases, an individual displays traits that indicate the individual's quality.
Parental care	Some species provide food, shelter, and care for young. Other species provide little or no care to their young.	Increased parental care generally helps more offspring survive. However, parental care requires a great deal of energy from the parent.
Cooperative behaviors	Two or more individuals interact to help one another.	Teamwork helps individuals perform tasks, such as hunting for large prey, that they could not do alone.

LOOKING CLOSER

6. Explain How does territorial behavior help an individual reproduce successfully?

____

____

____

7. Identify What is a disadvantage of parental care?

____

____

____

Competition

Courtship

Parental care

Talk About It

Hypothesize Mammals tend to show a great deal of parental care, while amphibians tend to show little parental care. In a small group, discuss why amphibians and mammals differ in the amount of parental care they give their young. Consider how many offspring individuals in each group produce. How does the number of offspring affect the amount of parental care? Form a hypothesis to explain.

Name ______________________ Class ____________ Date ____________

Section 2 Review

SECTION VOCABULARY

circadian rhythm a biological daily cycle

communication a transfer of a signal or message from one animal to another that results in some type of response

courtship behavior that leads to mating and the rearing of young

foraging behavior associated with seeking, obtaining, and consuming food

migration in general, any movement of individuals or populations from one location to another; specifically, a periodic group movement that is characteristic of a given population or species

sexual selection an evolutionary mechanism by which traits that increase the ability of individuals to attract or acquire mates appear with increasing frequency in a population; selection in which a mate is chosen on the basis of a particular trait or traits

territorial behavior behavior exhibited by an animal in defending its living space

1. **List** What are five modes of communication that animals use?

____

____

2. **Compare** How does the range of foods eaten by generalists and specialists differ?

____

____

3. **Hypothesize** The long tail of a male peacock can make it hard for the bird to fly. This difficulty may affect a male's survival. Why do you think the long tail trait still exists in peacock populations?

____

____

____

4. **Predict** A monkey can smell an intruder in its territory, but it cannot see him through the trees. What mode of communication will the monkey use to warn the intruder? Explain your answer.

____

____

____

____

Name ________________ Class ________________ Date ________________

SECTION 1

Body Organization

KEY IDEAS

As you read this section, keep these questions in mind:
- What two properties make stem cells different from other body cells?
- What four types of tissues can be found in the human body?
- How are tissues, organs, and organ systems related?
- How does the body maintain homeostasis?

What Are Stem Cells?

Cells are the basic building blocks of all organisms. An adult human body contains many different types of cells. All of those different types of cells started out as a single cell that grew, divided and became specialized to perform specific functions.

Stem cells are cells that can develop into many different types of cells and can divide many times. Embryonic stem cells can become any type of cell, are easy to grow in the lab, and can make millions of cells. But an embryo is destroyed when embryonic stem cells are collected. Adult stem cells may only become a few types of cells, are rare in the body, and cannot be grown easily. But collecting adult stem cells does not destroy an embryo, and adult stem cells from a patient's own body would not be rejected by the patient's immune system. ☑

READING TOOLBOX

Ask Questions As you read this section, write down questions you have about the material. Discuss your questions with a partner. Together, try to figure out the answers to your questions.

1. Define What is a stem cell?

What Kinds of Tissues Does the Human Body Contain?

Similar cells that work together make up a *tissue*. The human body contains four main types of tissue: epithelial tissue, nervous tissue, connective tissue, and muscle tissue.

Tissue	Function
Epithelial tissue	Lines the surfaces of the body; protects the body from damage and dehydration
Nervous tissue	Transmits and interprets information within the body
Connective tissue	Connects and supports other tissues in the body
Muscle tissue	Produces movement by contracting and relaxing

LOOKING CLOSER

2. Identify What are the four main kinds of tissue in the human body?

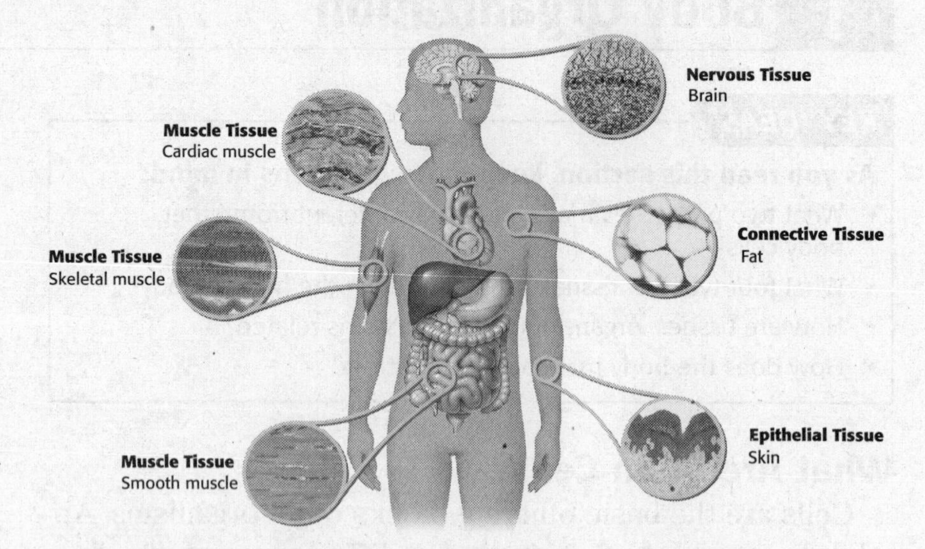

The human body contains four main kinds of tissue: muscle tissue, nervous tissue, connective tissue, and epithelial tissue. There are three kinds of muscle tissue.

LOOKING CLOSER

3. Identify Name one place where nervous tissue is found.

____

4. Identify Name one place where epithelial tissue is found.

____

How Is the Body Organized?

Cells can work together to form a tissue. In a similar way, two or more kinds of tissue can work together to form an *organ*. Each organ belongs to at least one *organ system*, or group of organs that perform specific processes for the body. In other words, cells make up tissues, tissues make up organs, and organs make up organ systems.

Critical Thinking

5. Apply Concepts A blood vessel contains muscle tissue, epithelial tissue, and connective tissue. Blood vessels work together with the heart to transport materials throughout the body. Is a blood vessel a tissue, an organ, or an organ system? Explain your answer.

____

____

____

____

____

____

How Does the Body Maintain Homeostasis?

Remember that *homeostasis* is the steady internal conditions an organism maintains despite changes in the external environment. To maintain homeostasis, the human body senses changes in internal conditions. Then, the body responds to these changes.

For example, imagine walking outside on a cold day without a jacket on. What happens? You may start to shiver. This happens because your body is trying to maintain homeostasis. When you walk outside, your body temperature could drop. You shiver because your body is trying to maintain its internal temperature.

When you shiver, your muscles contract and relax. This produces heat. As a result, your body temperature increases. Therefore, shivering helps your body maintain homeostasis when you are cold.

Name ______________________ Class ______________ Date ______________

Section 1 Review

SECTION VOCABULARY

connective tissue a tissue that has a lot of intracellular substance and that connects and supports other tissues

epithelial tissue tissue that covers a body surface or lines a body cavity

muscle tissue the tissue made of cells that can contract and relax to produce movement

nervous tissue tissue of the nervous system, including neurons and their supporting cells

stem cell a cell that can divide repeatedly and can differentiate into specialized cell types

1. Compare Give two differences between stem cells and other kinds of body cells.

____

____

2. Define What is a tissue?

____

____

3. Describe What is the function of nervous tissue?

____

____

4. Infer What kind of tissue lines the stomach and intestines?

____

____

5. Describe Relationships Fill in the blank spaces in the diagram below to show how organ systems, cells, organs, and tissues are related.

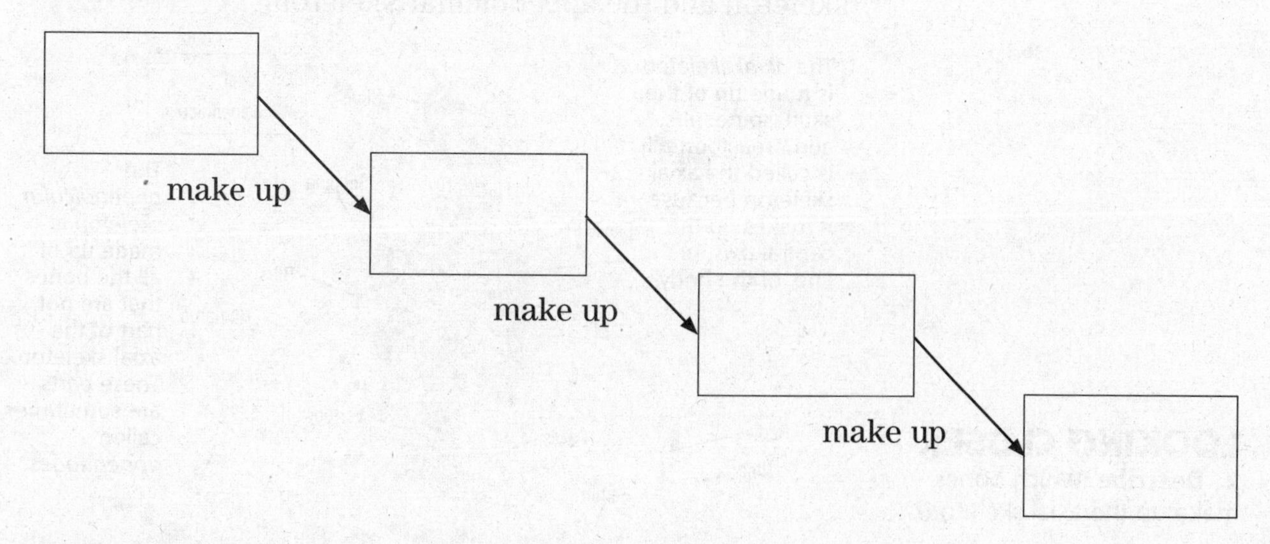

6. Explain How does the body maintain homeostasis?

____

Name ______________________ Class ______________ Date ______________

CHAPTER 34 Skeletal, Muscular, and Integumentary Systems

SECTION 2

The Skeletal System

KEY IDEAS

As you read this section, keep these questions in mind:

- What are five important functions of the skeletal system?
- What are the four layers that make up a bone?
- What structures make up movable joints?

READING TOOLBOX

Describe Relationships After you read this section, make a Concept Map that includes the terms *skeleton, bones, joints, movement, support, ligament, cartilage, immovable*, and *movable*.

What Are the Functions of the Skeletal System?

Your *skeletal system* is made up of your bones and the structures that connect them. The skeletal system has five main functions, as shown below.

Function	Description
Support	Your bones support your body. They give your body its shape and structure.
Protection	Many of your bones protect your internal organs. For example, the bones in your skull protect your brain.
Movement	The joints between your bones allow your body to move in many different ways.
Mineral storage	Your bones store important minerals, such as calcium and phosphorus. These minerals help your body function.
Blood cell production	Most of the blood cells in your body are made in your bones.

LOOKING CLOSER

1. Identify Where are most blood cells made?

____

THE TWO PARTS OF THE SKELETON

Your skeleton can be divided into two parts: the axial skeleton and the appendicular skeleton.

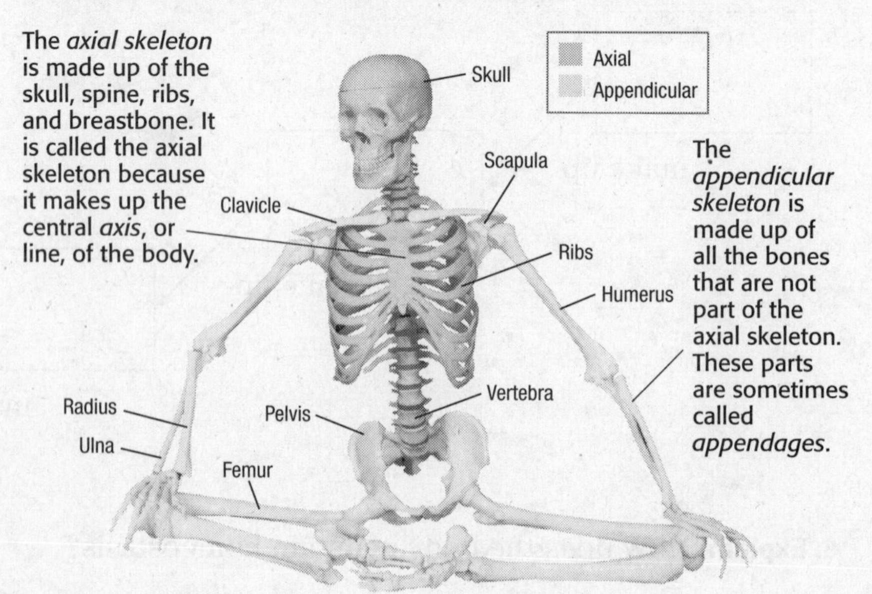

LOOKING CLOSER

2. Describe Which bones make up the axial skeleton?

____

____

What Is the Structure of a Bone?

Although there are many kinds of bones, most bones have similar structures. A typical bone is made up of four main layers: the periosteum, compact bone, spongy bone, and bone marrow, as shown below.

The spaces inside some bones contain soft tissue called **bone marrow**. There are two types of bone marrow. Red bone marrow produces blood cells. Yellow bone marrow stores energy in the form of fat.

Inside the compact bone is a layer of *spongy bone*. The cells in spongy bone are less tightly packed than the cells in compact bone. Bone marrow fills some of the spaces in spongy bone.

Blood vessels

Bones are covered by a tough membrane called the *periosteum*.

Beneath the periosteum is a layer of *compact bone*. Compact bone is made of mature bone cells called **osteocytes** that are packed closely together.

Talk About It

Learn Word Roots Look up the prefix *peri-* and the root *osteo* in the dictionary. Then, explain to the rest of the class why the membrane that covers bone is called the *periosteum*.

Critical Thinking

3. Apply Concepts What do you think may happen to a person whose red bone marrow does not function properly?

____

____

____

BONE GROWTH

When you were born, most of your skeleton was not made of bone. It was made of a type of connective tissue called *cartilage*. As you got older, bone cells called *osteoblasts* deposited calcium and other minerals in the cartilage. These minerals hardened the cartilage and turned it into bone. ☑

By the time you are an adult, almost all of the cartilage will have been replaced by bone. In adults, cartilage is only found in a few places, such as the nose and the spaces between some bones.

4. Describe What do osteoblasts do?

____

____

____

BONE INJURIES AND DISEASES

The most common bone injury is a fracture. In a *fracture*, a bone breaks or cracks. Most fractures heal with time.

Two diseases that affect bone are osteoporosis and leukemia. *Osteoporosis* is a disease in which bones become brittle because they have lost calcium and other minerals. This causes the bones to break more easily. ☑

5. Describe What happens to bones in a person with osteoporosis?

____

____

____

Leukemia is a type of cancer that affects the tissues that produce blood cells. It causes these tissues to produce large numbers of immature white blood cells. The immature cells prevent other blood cells from functioning properly.

How Can Bones Move?

The places where two or more bones meet are called **joints**. There are three main kinds of joints: immovable joints, slightly movable joints, and freely movable joints.

Bones cannot move along *immovable joints*. These joints are found mainly between the bones of the skull. Bones can move a small amount along *slightly movable joints*. These joints are found in the spine and the rib cage. Bones can move a great deal along *freely movable joints*. These joints are found in the appendicular skeleton. ☑

6. Identify Where are immovable joints found?

____

____

Movable joints contain bones, cartilage, and ligaments. A **ligament** is a strong band of connective tissue that holds joints together.

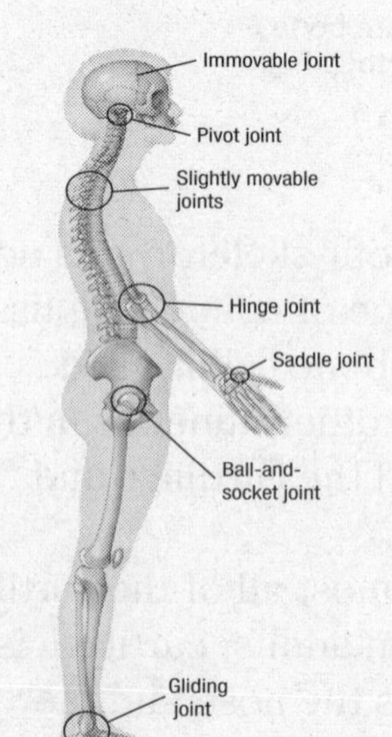

Pivot joints, hinge joints, saddle joints, ball-and-socket joints, and gliding joints are different kinds of freely movable joints. The name of each joint describes how the bones move around the joint.

LOOKING CLOSER

7. Identify Circle two freely movable joints in the figure.

Name _______________ Class _______________ Date _______________

Section 2 Review

SECTION VOCABULARY

bone marrow soft tissue inside bones that either produces blood cells or stores fat **joint** a place where two or more bones meet **leukemia** a progressive, malignant disease of the blood-forming organs	**ligament** a type of connective tissue that holds together the bones in a joint **osteocyte** a mature bone cell that maintains bone tissue

1. List What are the five main functions of the skeletal system?

____

2. Compare How is compact bone different from spongy bone?

____

3. Identify What are the functions of the two types of bone marrow?

____

4. Explain How is a joint different from a bone?

____

5. Compare How is a slightly movable joint different from a freely movable joint?

____

6. Explain How are ligaments related to joints?

____

Name ______________________ Class ______________ Date ______________

SECTION 3

The Muscular System

KEY IDEAS

As you read this section, keep these questions in mind:

- What three types of muscles are found in the human body?
- How do muscles produce energy for movement?
- What are the structures found in skeletal muscle?
- How do actin and myosin interact to cause muscle contraction?
- How can muscles be affected by exercise?

READING TOOLBOX

Summarize As you read this section, underline the main ideas. When you finish reading, write a short summary of the section using the ideas you underlined.

LOOKING CLOSER

1. Compare How are smooth muscle tissue and cardiac muscle tissue similar?

____

____

____

____

Critical Thinking

2. Apply Concepts Muscles called the quadriceps in your upper leg cause your knee to straighten. Muscles called the hamstrings in your upper leg cause your knee to bend. Are the quadriceps extensors or flexors? Explain your answer.

____

____

____

What Are the Three Types of Muscle Tissue?

Remember that muscle tissue is one of the four main kinds of tissue in the body. There are three main kinds of muscle tissue, as shown below.

Type of muscle tissue	Description	Locations
Skeletal	Skeletal muscles are *voluntary*, which means that you can control them. They help move the body.	attached to bones
Smooth	Smooth muscles are *involuntary*, which means that you cannot control them. They help materials move through the body.	blood vessels, digestive system, bladder, uterus
Cardiac	Cardiac muscle is involuntary. Its powerful contractions pump blood to the rest of the body.	heart

How Do Muscles Cause Bones to Move?

Skeletal muscles are attached to bones by tendons. **Tendons** are strips of very strong, flexible connective tissue.

Generally, pairs of muscles cause bones to move. One muscle in the pair pulls the bone in one direction. The other muscle pulls the bone in the opposite direction. When one muscle contracts, the other relaxes. This allows bones to move.

In the arms and legs, the muscles that cause movement are either flexors or extensors. A **flexor** is a muscle that causes a joint to bend. For example, the biceps muscle is a flexor that causes the arm to bend at the elbow. An **extensor** is a muscle that causes a joint to straighten. The triceps is an extensor that straightens the arm.

Name ______________________ Class ______________ Date ______________

How Do Muscles Get the Energy They Need?

Muscles cause movement by contracting and relaxing. To contract, muscles need energy. Recall that cells use ATP as their main energy source. Muscles switch between two processes to produce ATP. The availability of oxygen and the level of exercise determine which process is used.

Process	Description	When it is used
Aerobic respiration	Cells use oxygen to release energy from glucose. Aerobic respiration produces a great deal of ATP, but requires a great deal of oxygen.	when oxygen is available; during normal, light exercise
Anaerobic respiration	Cells use a type of fermentation to produce ATP from glucose. Compared to aerobic respiration, anaerobic respiration produces very little ATP and can only occur for a short time. However, anaerobic respiration is faster than aerobic respiration.	when little oxygen is available; during vigorous exercise

Background
Recall that *fermentation* is a process in which cells produce ATP without using oxygen.

LOOKING CLOSER
3. Compare How is aerobic respiration different from anaerobic respiration?

____

____

What Is the Structure of a Skeletal Muscle?

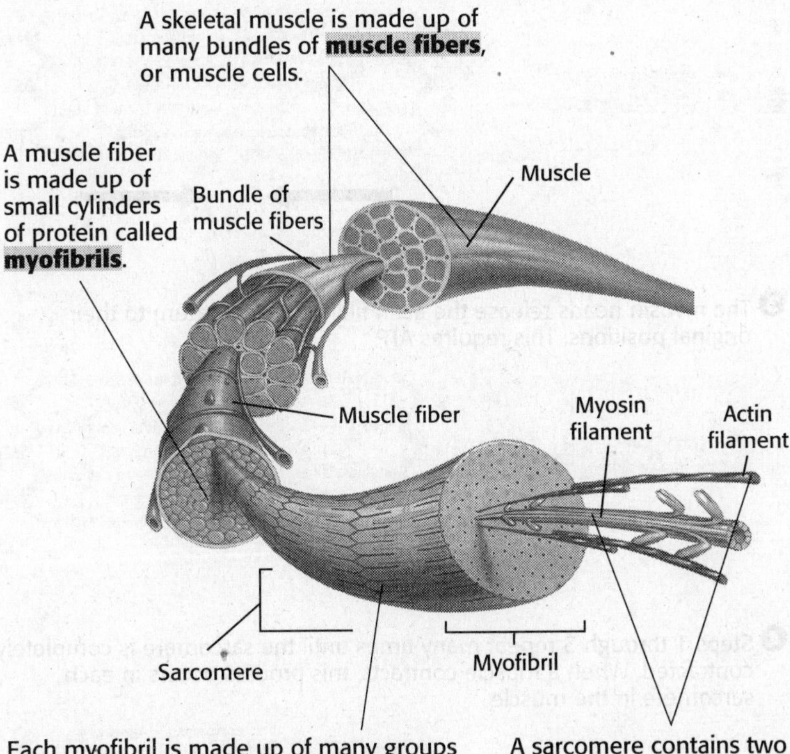

LOOKING CLOSER
4. Define What is a muscle fiber?

____

5. Identify What are myofibrils made up of?

____

____

____

How Do Skeletal Muscles Contract?

The actin and myosin filaments in sarcomeres interact to cause muscles to contract. Most muscle contractions begin when a muscle fiber receives a signal from a nerve cell. The figure below shows how actin and myosin interact to produce a muscle contraction. ☑

6. Identify What causes most muscle contractions to begin?

____

____

How Muscle Contraction Occurs

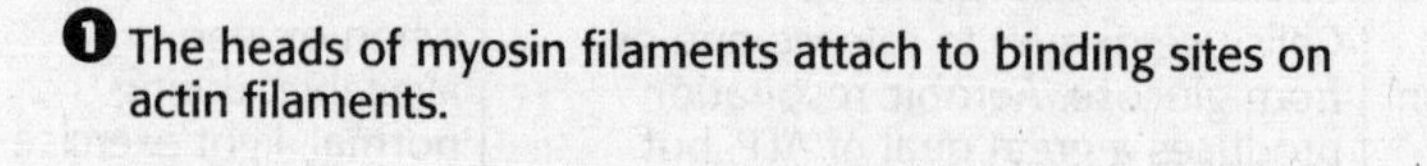

❶ The heads of myosin filaments attach to binding sites on actin filaments.

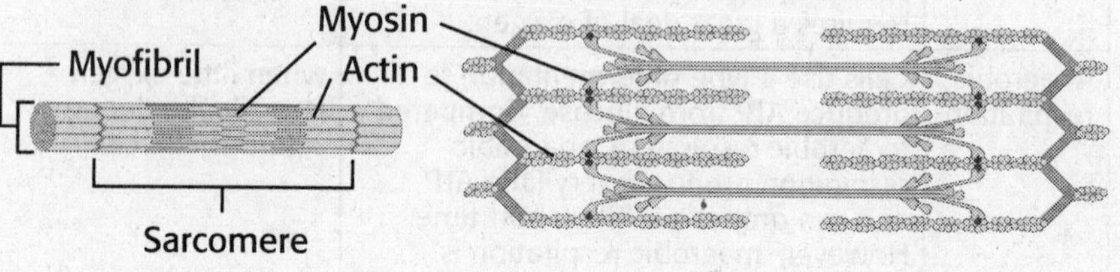

❷ The myosin filament heads rotate. This pulls the actin filaments closer together. The sarcomere gets shorter.

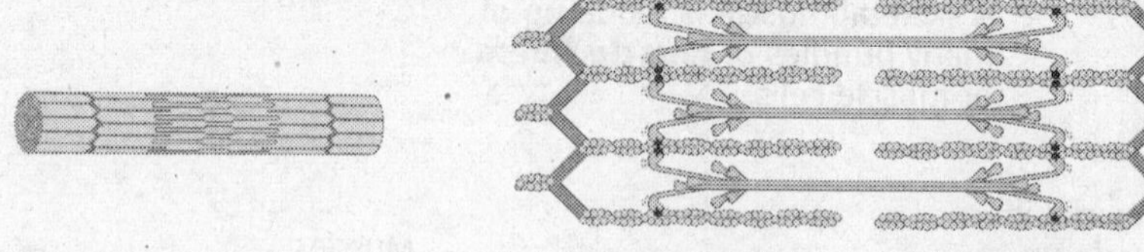

❸ The myosin heads release the actin filaments and return to their original positions. This requires ATP.

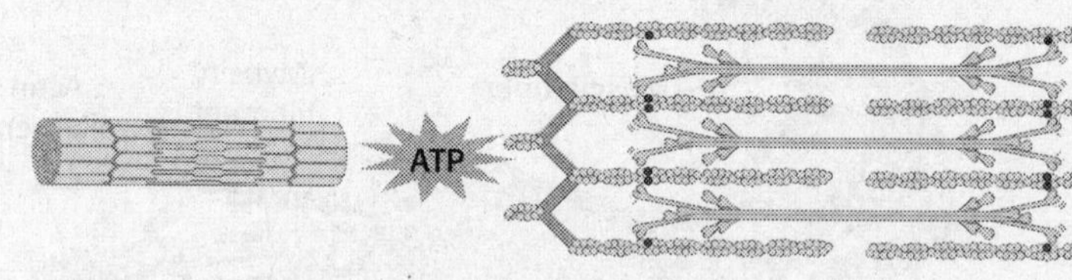

❹ Steps 1 through 3 repeat many times until the sarcomere is completely contracted. When a muscle contracts, this process occurs in each sarcomere in the muscle.

LOOKING CLOSER

7. Identify Where does the head of a myosin filament bind to?

____

____

8. Explain What causes a sarcomere to shorten?

____

____

____

____

____

____

How Can Exercise Affect Muscles?

Exercise can help you increase your strength, speed, and endurance. However, too much exercise can cause muscle fatigue or injuries.

SLOW-TWITCH AND FAST-TWITCH MUSCLE FIBERS

All skeletal muscles contain muscle fibers, but not all muscle fibers are the same. There are two main kinds of muscle fibers: slow-twitch fibers and fast-twitch fibers. Most muscles contain both types of muscle fibers. ☑

9. Identify What are the two main kinds of muscle fiber?

____

____

Slow-twitch fibers use mainly aerobic respiration to produce ATP. They produce a small amount of force, but can produce the force for a long period of time. Slow-twitch fibers give you endurance for long-term exercise, such as a marathon.

Fast-twitch fibers use mainly anaerobic respiration to produce ATP. They produce a great deal of force, but cannot produce the force for very long. Fast-twitch fibers give you strength and speed for short-term exercise, such as weight lifting or sprinting.

Anaerobic exercise, such as weight lifting, can increase the strength of fast-twitch muscle fibers.

LOOKING CLOSER

10. Infer What type of respiration are the muscles in this man's arm probably using?

____

FATIGUE, INJURY, AND ATROPHY

If you exercise too hard, your muscles may use up all their available ATP and glucose. When this occurs, the muscles can no longer contract. This is called *muscle fatigue*. Muscle fatigue eventually goes away as muscle cells generate more ATP. ☑

READING CHECK

11. Define What is muscle fatigue?

____

____

____

Muscles can tear if they stretch too much during exercise. They may also become *inflamed*, or swollen, if they are overused.

Atrophy occurs when the mass of a muscle decreases. This can happen if a person does not get enough exercise. It can also happen as a result of a disease or an injury.

Name ______________________ Class ______________ Date ______________

Section 3 Review

SECTION VOCABULARY

actin a protein responsible for the contraction and relaxation of muscle

extensor a muscle that extends a joint

flexor a muscle that bends a limb or other body part

muscle fiber a multinucleate muscle cell, especially of skeletal or cardiac muscle tissue

myofibril a fiber that is found in striated muscle cells and that is responsible for muscle contraction

myosin the most abundant protein in muscle tissue and the main constituent of the thick filaments of muscle fibers

sarcomere the basic unit of contraction in skeletal and cardiac muscle

tendon a tough connective tissue that attaches a muscle to a bone or to another body part

1. **Identify** What are the three kinds of muscle tissue?

2. **Compare** Give one similarity and one difference between flexors and extensors.

3. **Describe** What process do muscles use to produce ATP during light activity?

4. **Identify Relationships** How are muscle fibers, myofibrils, sarcomeres, actin, and myosin related?

5. **Explain** How is ATP involved in muscle contraction?

6. **Describe** Give one positive effect and one negative effect of exercise.

7. **Define** What is muscle atrophy?

Name ______________________ Class ______________ Date ______________

CHAPTER 34 Skeletal, Muscular, and Integumentary Systems

SECTION 4

The Integumentary System

KEY IDEAS

As you read this section, keep these questions in mind:

- What is the structure of the skin?
- What are four important functions of the skin?
- How do hair and nails form?
- What are three possible causes of skin diseases and disorders?

What Is the Skin Made Up Of?

Your skin is the largest organ in your body. In fact, it makes up about 7% of your total body weight. Your skin, hair, fingernails, and toenails make up your *integumentary system.*

The skin consists of three layers. The outer layer is called the **epidermis**. It is about as thin as a piece of paper. The epidermis is made of epithelial tissue. It is covered by a thin layer of flattened, dead cells. The dead cells protect the epidermis from water and other materials.

The **dermis** is the layer under the epidermis. The dermis contains blood vessels and structures that produce sweat, oil, and hair. The dermis also contains nerve cells that detect heat, cold, pain, pressure, and touch.

The **subcutaneous tissue** is located below the dermis. It is made mostly of fat. It helps keep the body warm. It also protects the body by absorbing energy from objects that hit it. The subcutaneous tissue connects the skin to the body.

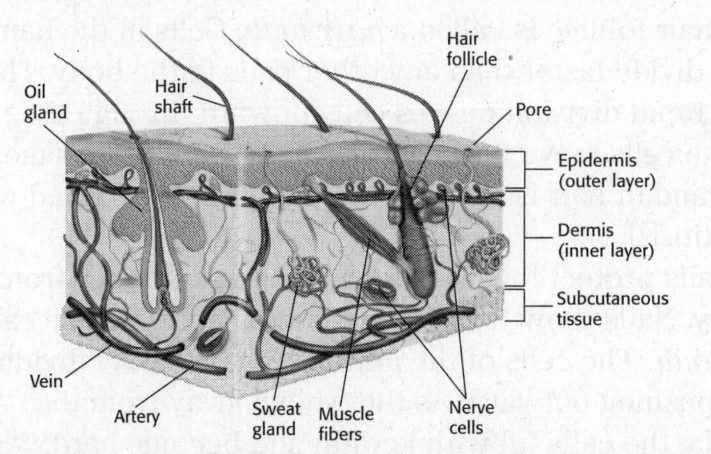

The skin contains many different structures. For example, *hair follicles* produce hair. Tiny muscles attached to hair follicles cause your hair to stand up if you are cold. This produces "goose bumps."

READING TOOLBOX

Summarize After you read this section, make a Concept Map using the highlighted vocabulary words as well as the words *skin*, *hair*, *nails*, and *integumentary system*.

Talk About It

Learn Word Roots Look up the prefixes *epi-* and *sub-* and the root *cutaneous* in a dictionary. With a partner, discuss the meanings of the word parts and why they are used to describe the epidermis and the subcutaneous tissue.

LOOKING CLOSER

1. Identify Name three structures found in the skin.

____

____

____

What Are the Functions of the Skin?

Your skin performs many important functions for your body. The table below describes four of these functions.

Function	Description
Protection	Your skin helps protect the other organs in your body from physical injury. It also contains cells that produce the pigment **melanin**. Melanin absorbs ultraviolet (UV) radiation in sunlight. UV radiation can damage DNA and cause cancer. Therefore, skin helps protect your body from damage by UV radiation.
Disease prevention	Your epidermis helps to prevent bacteria, viruses, and other pathogens from entering your body. If your epidermis is cut, these pathogens can enter your body. This is why cuts and scrapes become infected more easily than intact skin.
Temperature control	The hair on your skin and the fat in your skin help keep your body warm. In addition, your skin contains many blood vessels and sweat glands. These structures help keep your body cool. When you are too hot, the blood vessels expand and you start to sweat. The expanding blood vessels allow heat from the blood to move into the environment. The evaporating sweat absorbs heat from your body.
Waterproofing	Your skin contains a hard protein called **keratin**. This protein helps make skin tough and waterproof. In addition, special glands in your skin produce an oily substance called **sebum**. Sebum helps prevent the skin from losing or absorbing water.

Background
Recall that a *pigment* is a chemical that absorbs light.

Background
Recall that a *pathogen* is something that causes disease.

Critical Thinking
2. Explain Severe burns can destroy the epidermis and the dermis. People with severe burns are more likely to get infections or to become dehydrated. What do you think is the reason for this?

____

____

____

____

____

How Do Hair and Nails Form?

Hair and nails are formed by cells in the skin. These cells contain a great deal of keratin. This protein makes hair and nails strong.

Recall that the dermis contains hair follicles. The base of a hair follicle is called a *hair bulb*. Cells in the hair bulb divide faster than any other cells in the body. This very rapid division pushes cells upward through the skin. As the cells move farther from the hair bulb, they die. A strand of hair is made of dead cells that are filled with keratin. ☑

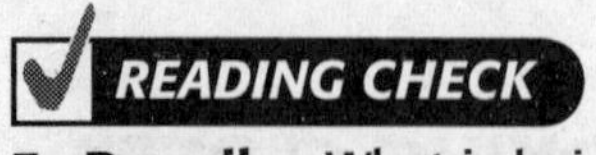

3. Describe What is hair made of?

____

____

Nails protect the tips of your fingers and toes from injury. Nails grow from a curved area at their base called a *lunula*. The cells of the lunula are constantly dividing and pushing outward. As they move away from the lunula, the cells fill with keratin and become hard.

What Causes Skin Problems?

There are many kinds of skin problems. Some are caused by genetic factors. Others are caused by infections or parasites. Some are caused by changes in the skin that happen over time. ☑

4. Identify What are three things that can cause skin problems?

____

____

____

Eczema is an example of a skin problem that has a genetic cause. *Eczema* is a red, itchy rash on the skin. The rash can occur during hot, humid weather. It can also occur when the skin is irritated or when the body's immune system is stressed.

Acne is an example of a skin problem that is caused by bacteria. It develops when bacteria clog and infect pores in the skin. In many cases, acne can be prevented by washing the skin with soap and water to remove bacteria. In serious cases, an antibiotic may be needed to kill the bacteria.

Skin cancer is an example of a skin disease that is caused by changes in the skin over time. Remember that UV radiation can damage DNA. This can cause cancer in skin cells. The most common types of skin cancer are *carcinomas*. These cancers develop in cells that do not produce melanin. ☑

5. Explain What causes skin cancer?

____

____

____

Cancers that occur in melanin-producing cells are called *melanomas*. A melanoma can grow very quickly and spread to other parts of the body. These *malignant melanomas* account for about 80% of deaths from skin cancer. However, if this cancer is detected before it starts spreading, it can be treated and cured. In fact, melanoma is one of the most treatable cancers. Avoiding UV radiation can help reduce the risk of developing melanoma.

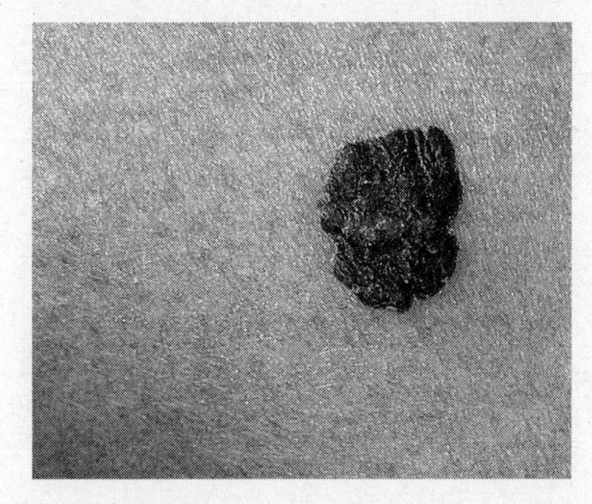

Melanoma is a type of skin cancer. Most cases of melanoma are caused by exposure to UV radiation.

Name ______________________ Class ______________ Date ____________

Section 4 Review

SECTION VOCABULARY

dermis the layer of skin below the epidermis

epidermis the outer surface layer of cells of a plant or animal

keratin a hard protein that forms hair, bird feathers, nails, and horns

melanin a pigment that helps determine the color of skin, hair, eyes, fur, feathers, and scales

sebum the oily secretion of the sebaceous glands

subcutaneous tissue the layer of cells that lies beneath the skin

1. **Identify** Name three functions of the subcutaneous tissue.

2. **Describe** How does your skin protect your body? Give two ways.

3. **Explain** Why is it important to keep cuts and scrapes clean?

4. **Identify** Name two substances your skin produces that prevent your skin from losing too much water.

5. **Explain** How does your skin help your body maintain its temperature? Give two ways.

6. **Compare** How are hair and nails similar?

7. **Identify** What are two kinds of skin cancer?

SECTION 1

The Cardiovascular System

KEY IDEAS

As you read this section, keep these questions in mind:

- What does the cardiovascular system do?
- How is the structure of the heart related to its function?
- How are the structures of arteries, veins, and capillaries related to their functions?
- What are the functions of the main components of human blood?
- How does the lymphatic system work with the cardiovascular system?

What Is the Cardiovascular System?

The **cardiovascular system** consists of the heart, blood vessels, and blood. The cardiovascular system helps to maintain homeostasis by transporting nutrients, oxygen, hormones, and wastes through the body.

The cardiovascular system also moves heat through the body. This helps the body maintain a constant internal temperature. The diagrams below show two examples of how the cardiovascular system can affect body temperature.

READING TOOLBOX

Answer Questions Before you read this section, write the questions in the Key Ideas box in your notebook. Leave several spaces after each question. As you read this section, underline the answers to the questions. Then, write the answers in your notebook in your own words.

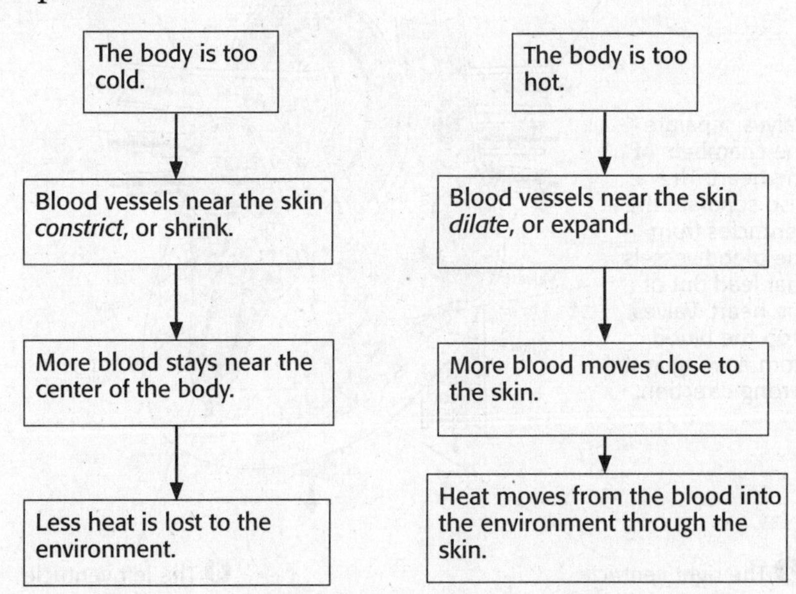

Critical Thinking

1. Infer What do you think is the reason that a light-skinned person's face may turn red when the person is too hot?

____

What Is the Structure of the Heart?

The heart is mostly made up of cardiac muscle tissue. This tissue can contract to pump blood to every part of the body. However, the thickness of the tissue is not the same everywhere in the heart.

ATRIA AND VENTRICLES

The heart contains four chambers. The two lower chambers are called ventricles. The **ventricles** pump blood out of the heart. The two upper chambers are called atria (singular, **atrium**). The atria receive blood returning to the heart and pump it into the ventricles. A wall called the *septum* divides the heart into left and right sides. ☑

2. Identify What is the function of the ventricles?

____

____

The atria pump blood only to the ventricles, so they do not need to pump very hard. As a result, atria have thin walls that do not contain very much cardiac muscle. In contrast, the ventricles must pump blood to the rest of the body. Therefore, they have to pump hard. As a result, ventricles have thick walls that contain a great deal of cardiac muscle.

❶ The right atrium receives oxygen-poor blood from the body. It pumps this blood into the right ventricle.

❸ The left atrium receives oxygen-rich blood from the lungs. It pumps this blood into the left ventricle.

Valves separate the chambers of the heart. They also separate the ventricles from the blood vessels that lead out of the heart. Valves stop the blood from flowing in the wrong direction.

Valve

Valve

Valve

Valve

❷ The right ventricle pumps oxygen-poor blood to the lungs.

❹ The left ventricle pumps oxygen-rich blood to the rest of the body.

LOOKING CLOSER

3. Explain How does oxygen-poor blood get from the body to the lungs?

____

____

____

____

____

Talk About It

Demonstrate Do you know how to take your pulse? In a small group, talk about different places that you can feel a pulse through your skin. How does your pulse change when you exercise? How does it change if you lie very still?

Each time the left ventricle contracts, it pumps blood through blood vessels. The blood vessels stretch as they fill with blood. This stretching of the blood vessels due to the beating of the heart is called a **pulse**.

How Does Blood Flow Through the Body?

Blood flows through the body in a network of organs called blood vessels. There are three main kinds of blood vessels: arteries, capillaries, and veins. The structure of each kind of blood vessel is related to its function. ☑

4. Identify What are the three main kinds of blood vessels?

____

Arteries carry blood away from the heart. Blood that is pumped out of the heart produces a great deal of force on the arteries. Therefore, arteries have thick, muscular walls to help them to withstand the force of the blood moving through them. Farther from the heart, the arteries narrow into smaller vessels called *arterioles*. Within tissues, arterioles narrow even further into capillaries.

Capillaries are tiny blood vessels that allow molecules to move between the blood and the fluid around other cells. The walls of a capillary are only one cell thick. This allows molecules to move through them easily. Capillaries branch throughout the different tissues in the body. In fact, every cell in your body is close to a capillary. ☑

5. Explain Why is it important that the walls of capillaries are so thin?

____

From the capillaries, blood flows into larger vessels called *venules*. Closer to the heart, venules become larger vessels called veins. **Veins** are blood vessels that carry blood to the heart.

The blood in veins does not produce very much force because it is not pumped directly by the heart. Small muscle contractions in the arms and legs move blood through veins. Therefore, the walls of veins are thinner than those of arteries. In addition, veins contain valves that prevent blood from flowing backward.

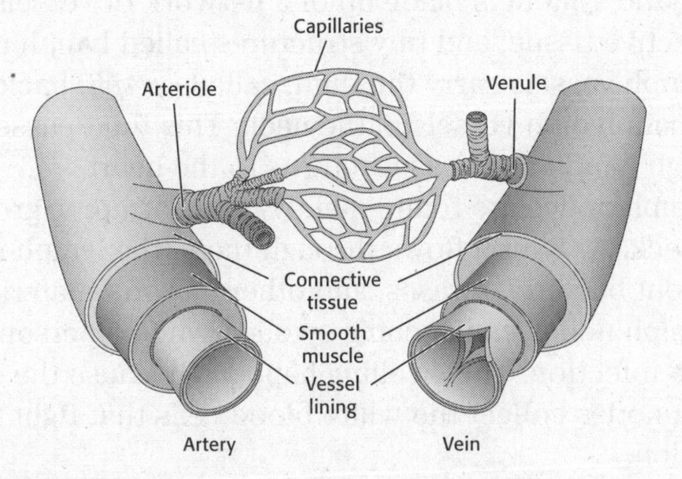

Blood flows from the heart through arteries, arterioles, capillaries, venules, veins, and back to the heart.

LOOKING CLOSER

6. Compare Give one difference between the structure of an artery and the structure of a vein.

____

What Does the Blood Contain?

Blood is a connective tissue. It contains four main components: plasma, red blood cells, white blood cells, and platelets.

Blood component	Description
Plasma	the liquid portion of the blood; mostly water; transports nutrients, wastes, proteins, and salts
Red blood cells	cells without nuclei that carry oxygen
White blood cells	cells with nuclei that defend the body against disease; larger than red blood cells
Platelets	cell fragments that help blood clot

Background
Recall that *connective tissue* connects and supports other tissues in the body.

LOOKING CLOSER
7. Identify What is the function of red blood cells?

______

BLOOD TYPES

Red blood cells have compounds called *antigens* on their surfaces. Different people have different combinations of these antigens on their red blood cells. The antigen combination a person has determines the person's blood type, as shown below.

Antigen(s) present	Blood type
A only	A^-
A and Rh	A^+
B only	B^-
B and Rh	B^+

Antigen(s) present	Blood type
A and B	AB^-
A, B, and Rh	AB^+
Rh only	O^+
none	O^-

LOOKING CLOSER
8. Describe A person's red blood cells contain A and B antigens. What is the person's blood type?

______

What Is the Lymphatic System?

Capillaries have very thin walls. Therefore, fluid can leak through them into the spaces between cells. The **lymphatic system** returns this fluid to the heart. The lymphatic system is made up of a network of vessels, connective tissue, and tiny structures called lymph nodes.

Lymph vessels carry the fluid, called *lymph*, back to two main lymph vessels in the neck. This fluid passes through lymph nodes as it returns to the heart.

Lymph nodes are found mainly in the armpits, groin, and neck. As lymph flows through them, the lymph nodes filter out bacteria, viruses, and other harmful materials.

Lymph nodes can become swollen when a person has an infection. The swelling happens because the lymph nodes collect the white blood cells that fight the infection.

Critical Thinking
9. Describe How is the lymphatic system related to the cardiovascular system?

______

Name ______________________ Class ______________ Date ______________

Section 1 Review

SECTION VOCABULARY

artery a blood vessel that carries blood away from the heart to the body's organs

atrium a chamber that receives blood that is returning to the heart

capillary a tiny blood vessel that allows an exchange between blood and cells in tissue

cardiovascular system a collection of organs that transport blood throughout the body; the organs in this system include the heart, the arteries, and the veins

lymphatic system a collection of organs whose primary function is to collect extracellular fluid and return it to the blood; the organs in this system include the lymph nodes and the lymphatic vessels

plasma in biology, the liquid component of blood

platelet a fragment of a cell that is needed to form blood clots

pulse the rhythmic pressure of the blood against the walls of a vessel, particularly an artery

red blood cell a disc-shaped cell that has no nucleus, that contains hemoglobin, and that transports oxygen in the circulatory system

vein in biology, a vessel that carries blood to the heart

ventricle one of the two large muscular chambers that pump blood out of the heart

white blood cell a type of cell in the blood that destroys bacteria, viruses, and toxic proteins and helps the body develop immunities

1. **Explain** How does the cardiovascular system help the body maintain homeostasis? Give one way.

____

____

2. **Infer** A person's ventricles have thinner walls than normal. What may happen to the person? Explain your answer.

____

____

____

____

3. **Compare** Give one difference between the function of an artery and the function of a vein.

____

____

4. **Identify** What is the function of white blood cells?

____

5. **Explain** Why may lymph nodes become swollen when a person has an infection?

____

____

Name ______________________ Class ______________ Date ______________

CHAPTER 35 Circulatory and Respiratory Systems

SECTION 2

Cardiovascular Health

KEY IDEAS

As you read this section, keep these questions in mind:

- What are the four main cardiovascular diseases that affect Americans?
- What are the most important things people can do to prevent cardiovascular disease?

READING TOOLBOX

Describe Relationships After you read this section, write a short paragraph describing the relationship between blood pressure, arteriosclerosis, heart attacks, and strokes.

What Are Common Cardiovascular Diseases?

Cardiovascular diseases kill more Americans each year than all other diseases combined. The table below describes the four most common cardiovascular diseases.

Disease	Description
High blood pressure (hypertension)	**Blood pressure** is the force that blood produces on blood vessels. If blood pressure is too high, the heart has to work harder to pump blood. This can weaken the heart over time. High blood pressure can also damage arteries.
Arteriosclerosis	Fats and other materials can collect on the inside walls of arteries. This makes the artery walls harder, so they cannot stretch as easily. It also makes the arteries narrower. *Arteriosclerosis* happens when arteries become narrower and harder. Arteriosclerosis can cause high blood pressure and decrease the amount of oxygen that body tissues receive. The fats that collect on the artery walls can cause blood clots, which can block other arteries.
Heart attack	A **heart attack** happens when the blood supply to part of the heart muscle is greatly reduced. This happens when one or more of the arteries that carry blood to the heart becomes blocked.
Stroke	A **stroke** happens when the blood supply to part of the brain is greatly reduced. This can happen if an artery in the brain becomes blocked or breaks.

Critical Thinking

1. Explain How can arteriosclerosis cause high blood pressure? (Hint: The blood pressure in an artery decreases when the artery stretches.)

____

____

____

____

How Can Cardiovascular Diseases Be Prevented?

Some cardiovascular diseases have a genetic cause. However, most cardiovascular diseases are caused by a person's lifestyle. The best ways to prevent cardiovascular disease are to maintain a healthy diet, exercise regularly, and avoid using alcohol and tobacco. It is also important to have regular medical checkups. They can help detect cardiovascular disease early, when it is easier to treat.

Talk About It

Identify In a small group, talk about ways you can reduce your risk for cardiovascular diseases.

Name ______________________ Class ______________ Date ______________

Section 2 Review

SECTION VOCABULARY

blood pressure the force that blood exerts on the walls of the arteries **heart attack** the death of heart tissues due to a blockage of their blood supply	**stroke** a sudden loss of consciousness or paralysis that occurs when the blood flow to the brain is interrupted

1. Identify What are the four most common cardiovascular diseases?

____

____

____

____

2. Compare Give one similarity and one difference between heart attacks and strokes.

____

____

____

____

3. Describe How can high blood pressure affect the heart?

____

____

4. Infer Heart attacks and strokes cause tissues in the heart or brain to die. What do you think is the reason the tissues die? (Hint: What is the function of blood?)

____

____

____

____

5. Identify Give four things that a person can do to prevent cardiovascular diseases.

____

____

____

____

Name ______________________ Class ______________ Date ____________

CHAPTER 35 Circulatory and Respiratory Systems

SECTION 3

The Respiratory System

KEY IDEAS

As you read this section, keep these questions in mind:

- What is the path that air takes from the environment into the lungs?
- How do the diaphragm and rib muscles work together in the process of breathing?
- How does the transport of oxygen differ from the transport of carbon dioxide?
- What are six diseases that affect the respiratory system?

READING TOOLBOX

Define As you read this section, circle the highlighted vocabulary terms. Write these terms in your notebook. Then, write a definition for each term in your own words.

What Does the Respiratory System Do?

The function of the respiratory system is to bring oxygen into the body and eliminate carbon dioxide from the body. The figure below shows the path that air takes when it moves from the environment into your lungs.

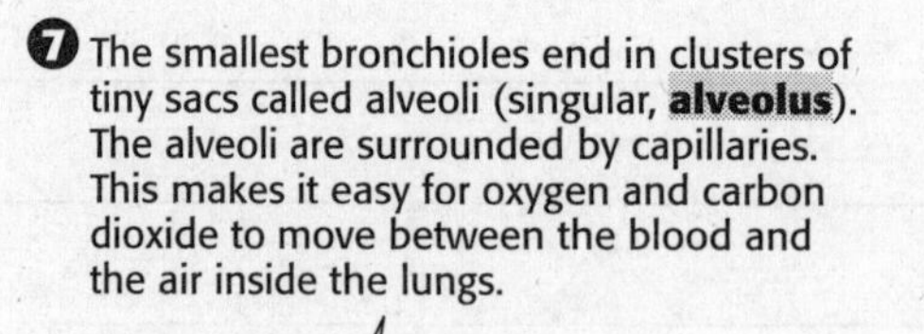

LOOKING CLOSER

1. Draw On the figure, draw blue arrows showing the path that air takes when it moves from the environment into your lungs.

Critical Thinking

2. Infer On the figure, draw red arrows showing the path that air takes when it moves from your lungs into the environment.

BREATHING

Your lungs do not contain any muscles, so they cannot expand or contract on their own. Instead, your diaphragm and rib muscles work together to move air into and out of your lungs. The **diaphragm** is a band of muscle that is located just below your lungs. The figure below shows how your diaphragm and rib muscles cause air to move into and out of your lungs. ☑

READING CHECK

3. Identify What muscles cause air to move into and out of your lungs?

____

Inhalation: breathing in

Exhalation: breathing out

Rib muscles contract (rib cage expands)

Rib muscles relax (rib cage contracts)

Ribs

Diaphragm

Diaphragm contracts (diaphragm moves down)

Diaphragm relaxes (diaphragm moves up)

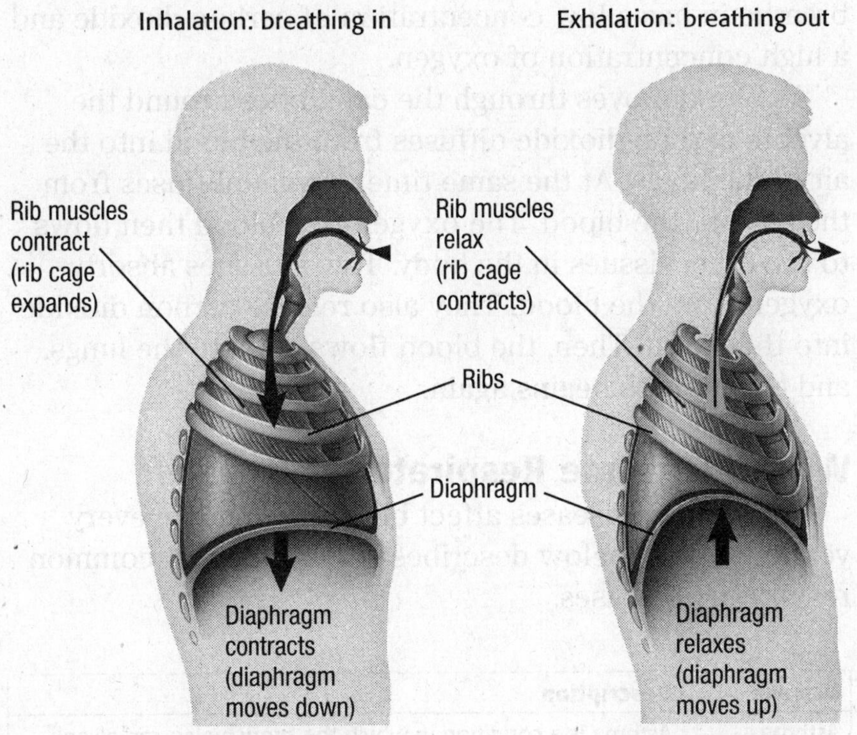

When you breathe in, your diaphragm and rib muscles contract. This makes your chest larger. As a result, air moves into your lungs.

When you breathe out, your diaphragm and rib muscles relax. This makes your chest smaller. As a result, air moves out of your lungs.

LOOKING CLOSER

4. Explain What causes air to move into your lungs when you breathe in?

____

____

____

____

How Does Blood Carry Oxygen and Carbon Dioxide?

Blood carries both oxygen and carbon dioxide. However, blood carries these gases in different ways. Most oxygen in the blood is bound to a compound called *hemoglobin* in red blood cells. In contrast, most carbon dioxide dissolves in blood plasma to form ions called *bicarbonate ions*.

How Do Oxygen and Carbon Dioxide Move Between the Lungs and the Environment?

Both oxygen and carbon dioxide move between the lungs and the environment by diffusion. Remember that *diffusion* happens when a substance moves from an area of high concentration to an area of low concentration. ☑

5. Identify How do oxygen and carbon dioxide move between the lungs and the environment?

____

The blood that enters the lungs has come from the body. It has a high concentration of carbon dioxide and a low concentration of oxygen. In contrast, the air you breathe in has a low concentration of carbon dioxide and a high concentration of oxygen.

As blood moves through the capillaries around the alveoli, carbon dioxide diffuses from the blood into the air in the lungs. At the same time, oxygen diffuses from the air into the blood. The oxygen-rich blood then flows to the other tissues in the body. These tissues absorb oxygen from the blood. They also release carbon dioxide into the blood. Then, the blood flows back to the lungs, and the process begins again.

Critical Thinking

6. Infer What would happen in the lungs if the concentration of carbon dioxide in the air was higher than the concentration of carbon dioxide in the blood?

____

____

____

What Are Some Respiratory Diseases?

Respiratory diseases affect billions of people every year. The table below describes six of the most common respiratory diseases.

Disease	Description
Asthma	Asthma is a condition in which the bronchioles and alveoli are easily irritated. Exercise or other triggers can cause the bronchioles to swell and produce too much mucus. This makes breathing difficult.
Bronchitis	Bronchitis occurs when the bronchioles become swollen. This causes the cells in the lungs to produce too much mucus, making breathing difficult.
Pneumonia	Pneumonia occurs when the alveoli become swollen. Most kinds of pneumonia are caused by infections.
Tuberculosis	Tuberculosis occurs when bacteria destroy the tissues in the lungs.
Emphysema	Emphysema occurs when the alveoli become less flexible. This makes breathing difficult. Most cases of emphysema are caused by smoking.
Lung cancer	Lung cancer occurs when cells in the lungs divide too often. They can invade and destroy healthy lung tissue. Most cases of lung cancer are caused by smoking.

LOOKING CLOSER

7. Identify What are two respiratory diseases that can be caused by smoking?

____

____

Name ______________________ Class ______________ Date ____________

Section 3 Review

SECTION VOCABULARY

alveolus any of the tiny air sacs of the lungs where oxygen and carbon dioxide are exchanged **bronchus** one of the two tubes that connect the lungs with the trachea **diaphragm** a dome-shaped muscle that is attached to the lower ribs and that functions as the main muscle in respiration	**larynx** the area of the throat that contains the vocal cords and produces vocal sounds **pharynx** in flatworms, the muscular tube that leads from the mouth to the gastrovascular cavity; animals with a digestive tract, the passage from the mouth to the larynx and esophagus **trachea** in insects, myriapods, and spiders, one of a network of air tubes; in vertebrates, the tube that connects the larynx to the lungs

1. **Describe Processes** Fill in the blank spaces in the flowchart below to describe the path that air takes from the environment into the alveoli.

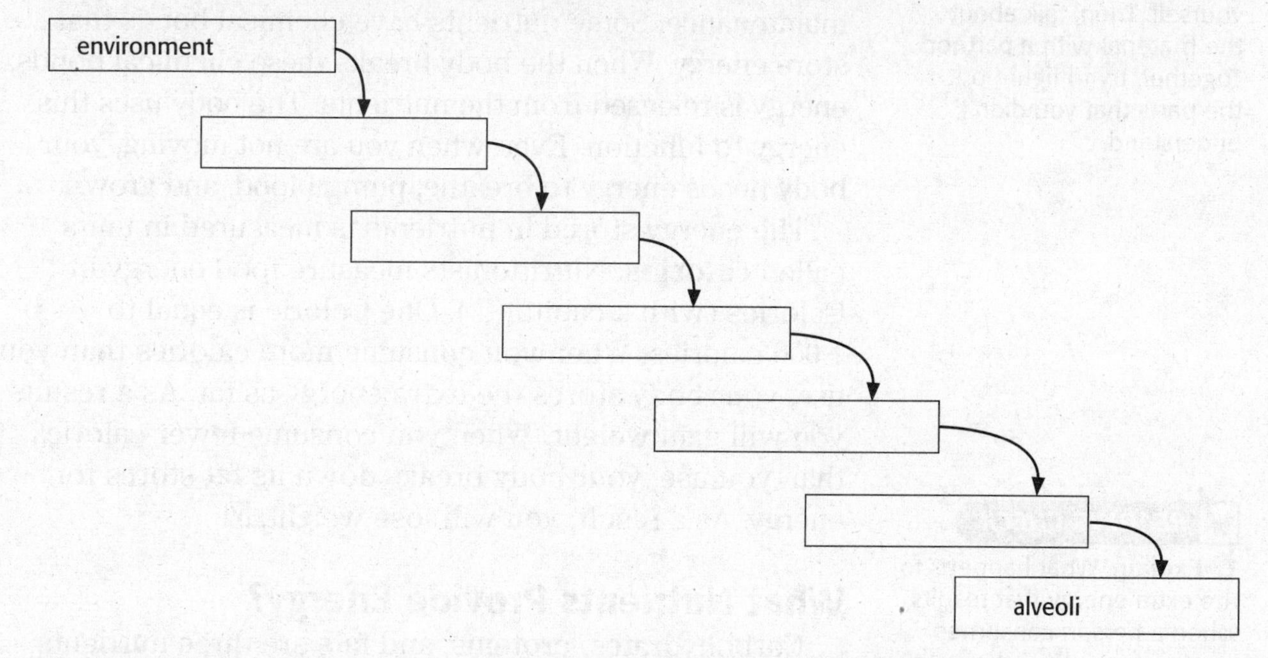

2. **Explain** Why does air move out of your lungs when you breathe out?

____

____

3. **Compare** Give one difference between how the blood carries oxygen and how the blood carries carbon dioxide.

____

____

4. **Identify** What are two common respiratory diseases?

____

____

CHAPTER 36 Digestive and Excretory Systems

SECTION 1

Nutrition

KEY IDEAS

As you read this section, keep these questions in mind:
- How do our bodies use energy from food?
- What nutrients provide energy for cellular activity?
- What other types of nutrients are required in our diets?
- Why is it important to be physically active?

READING TOOLBOX

Summarize in Pairs Read this section quietly to yourself. Then, talk about the material with a partner. Together, try to figure out the parts that you didn't understand.

How Do Foods Supply Energy?

Foods contain nutrients. A **nutrient** is a substance that the body requires for energy, growth, repair, and maintenance. Some nutrients have chemical bonds that store energy. When the body breaks these chemical bonds, energy is released from the nutrients. The body uses this energy to function. Even when you are not moving, your body needs energy to breathe, pump blood, and grow.

The energy stored in nutrients is measured in units called **calories**. Nutritionists measure food energy in Calories (with a capital *C*). One Calorie is equal to 1,000 calories. When you consume more calories than you use, your body stores the extra energy as fat. As a result, you will gain weight. When you consume fewer calories than you use, your body breaks down its fat stores for energy. As a result, you will lose weight. ☑

READING CHECK

1. Explain What happens to the extra energy that results when a person consumes more calories than they use?

____

What Nutrients Provide Energy?

Carbohydrates, proteins, and fats are three nutrients that the body requires in large amounts. These nutrients, described below, contain many chemical bonds that can be broken to release energy. They supply most of the energy the body needs. They also provide the body with building materials for growth, repair, and maintenance.

Talk About It

Compare With a partner or in a small group, talk about how carbohydrates and fats are the same and how they are different.

Nutrient	Functions	Food sources
Carbohydrates (made of sugars)	used for energy	honey, potatoes, breads, cereal grains
Proteins (made of amino acids)	used as enzymes and antibodies, make up muscles	eggs, milk, fish, poultry, and beef
Fats (made of fatty acids)	store energy, provide insulation, make cell membranes, dissolve certain vitamins	butter, cream, oils

What Other Nutrients Does the Body Require?

The body also requires nutrients that do not provide energy. These nutrients include water, vitamins, and minerals. They help the body function. The body requires smaller amounts of vitamins and minerals than of carbohydrates, proteins, fats, and water. ☑

READING CHECK

2. List What are three nutrients the body requires that do not provide energy?

____

____

____

WATER

You can survive longer without food than without water. The body uses water to regulate temperature and transport substances such as gases, nutrients, and wastes.

VITAMINS

Vitamins are organic substances that are found in many foods. There are many different kinds of vitamins. Each vitamin plays a different role in metabolism. For example, vitamin D helps the body absorb calcium.

Vitamins are classified into two groups: fat soluble and water soluble. Vitamins A, D, E, and K dissolve in fats. They are stored in body fat and are toxic in excess amounts. Vitamins B and C dissolve in water. Therefore, excess amounts of these vitamins are excreted.

Background

Recall that *metabolism* is the sum of all chemical processes that occur in an organism.

MINERALS

A **mineral** is an inorganic compound that must be supplied in the diet. A few common minerals and their functions are described in the table below.

Mineral	Function	Food sources
Sodium	maintains water balance, helps nerves function	table salt, processed foods
Potassium	maintains water balance, helps nerves and muscles function	meats, fruits, vegetables, beans
Calcium	helps form healthy bones and teeth, helps blood clot	milk, dark-green leafy vegetables
Iron	helps in bone growth, transports oxygen in blood	red meat, whole grains, peas, eggs
Iodine	helps regulate thyroid hormone	iodized salt, seafood

Critical Thinking

3. Predict What would happen if there were no iron in the blood?

____

____

Why Is Physical Activity Important?

Good nutrition must be balanced with regular physical activity to maintain a healthy body. Physical activity can help the body maintain a healthy amount of body fat. Excess body fat can increase a person's risk for many diseases, such as heart disease and Type II diabetes.

Name ______________________ Class ______________ Date ______________

Section 1 Review

SECTION VOCABULARY

calorie the amount of energy needed to raise the temperature of 1 g of water 1 °C; the Calorie used to indicate the energy content of food is a kilocalorie **mineral** a class of nutrients that are chemical elements that are needed for certain body processes	**nutrient** a substance or compound that provides nourishment (or food) or raw materials needed for life processes **vitamin** an organic compound that participates in biochemical reactions and that builds various molecules in the body; some vitamins are called *coenzymes* and activate specific enzymes

1. List What are four roles of nutrients in the body?

____

____

2. Identify What three nutrients provide most of the energy the body needs?

____

3. Explain How is energy released from nutrients?

____

____

4. Describe What are two ways that the body uses water?

____

____

5. Explain Which vitamins are not stored in body fat and why?

____

____

6. Describe What two things must be balanced to maintain a healthy body?

____

____

7. Explain When does a person's body store fat?

____

____

8. Describe Why is excess body fat unhealthy?

____

____

Name ______________________ Class ______________ Date ______________

CHAPTER 36 Digestive and Excretory Systems

SECTION 2

Digestion

KEY IDEAS

As you read this section, keep these questions in mind:

- How is food broken down into a form that the body can use?
- Where does digestion begin?
- How does the body absorb nutrients?
- What happens to the material that the body cannot use?

How Does the Body Break Down Food?

The process of breaking down foods into molecules that the body can use is called **digestion**. As shown below, the digestive system consists of a long, winding tube that food passes through from the mouth to the esophagus, stomach, small intestine, and large intestine.

The digestive system also includes the liver and pancreas. Food does not pass through these organs. Instead, they aid digestion by delivering fluids to the digestive tract through tubes called *ducts*. ☑

Organize As you read this section, make a chart that describes the function of each part of the digestive system.

1. Explain How do the liver and pancreas aid in digestion?

____

____

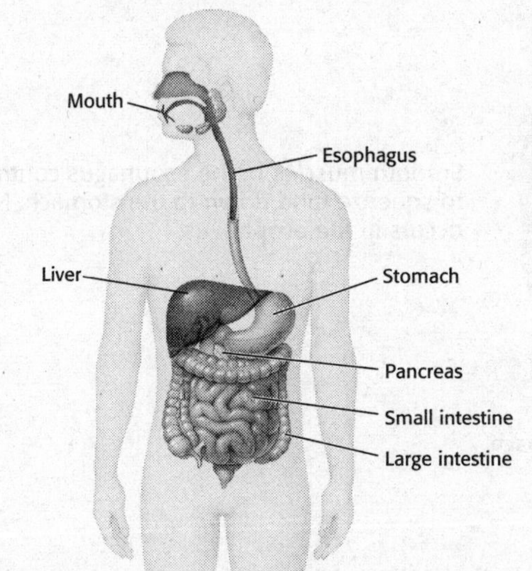

The digestive system breaks down food into individual molecules that can be absorbed in the bloodstream.

LOOKING CLOSER

2. Identify What structure does food pass through from the mouth to the stomach?

____

MECHANICAL DIGESTION

In *mechanical digestion*, food is physically broken into smaller pieces, but the molecules of food do not change. This digestion includes chewing food with the mouth and churning food in the stomach and small intestine.

CHEMICAL DIGESTION

The process by which chemical bonds in food are broken is called *chemical digestion*. Chemical digestion uses enzymes to produce new molecules that the body can use. Carbohydrates are broken down into simple sugars, proteins into amino acids, and fats into fatty acids. ☑

READING CHECK

3. Describe What does chemical digestion of food produce?

____

____

____

What Are the Steps in Digestion?

Both mechanical digestion and chemical digestion start in the mouth. Teeth break food into smaller pieces. The tongue mixes the food with a watery solution called *saliva*. Saliva contains *amylases*, which are enzymes that begin the chemical digestion of starches.

When the food is swallowed, it passes from the mouth into the esophagus. The **esophagus** is a long tube that connects the back of the mouth to the stomach. As shown below, smooth muscles in the lower portion of the esophagus contract in waves called **peristalsis**. Peristalsis helps move food through the digestive tract.

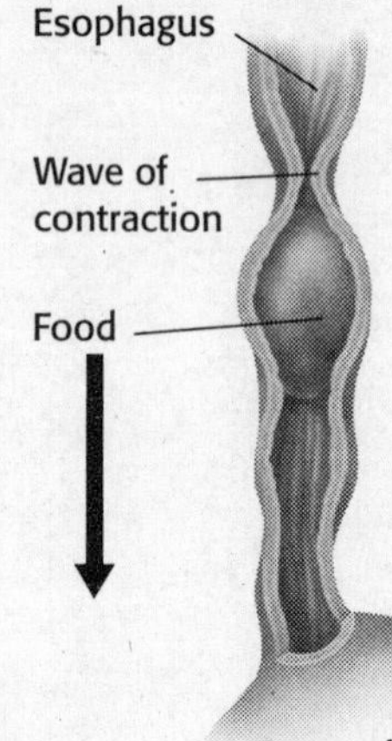

Smooth muscles in the esophagus contract in waves to squeeze food down to the stomach. No digestion occurs in the esophagus.

LOOKING CLOSER

4. Explain What does peristalsis in the esophagus do?

____

____

STOMACH

Mechanical digestion of food continues in the stomach. The stomach is a muscular, saclike organ that churns food to break it into smaller pieces. The stomach also begins the chemical digestion of proteins. ☑

READING CHECK

5. Describe How does mechanical digestion occur in the stomach?

____

____

____

Cells of the stomach lining secrete gastric juice, which contains hydrochloric acid and an enzyme called **pepsin**. Pepsin breaks down proteins into smaller chains of amino acids. It works only in an acidic environment. A mucous coating protects the lining of the stomach from the acid.

SMALL INTESTINE

Partially digested food passes from the stomach into the first portion of the small intestine, the *duodenum*. In the duodenum, digestive enzymes, shown below, complete the breakdown of nutrients into molecules that are small enough for the body to absorb.

Enzyme	Substrate	Digested products
Amylase	starch	disaccharides
Trypsin	proteins	peptides
Lipase	fat	fatty acids, glycerol
Maltase, sucrase, lactase	disaccharides	monosaccharides
Peptidase	peptides	amino acids

LIVER AND PANCREAS

The liver and the pancreas play important roles in the digestive system and in other body systems. The pancreas secretes several enzymes into the small intestine. The liver secretes bile. Bile is a greenish fluid that is stored in the gallbladder. A duct carries bile from the gallbladder to the small intestine. Bile breaks down fat into tiny droplets that can be digested by enzymes called *lipases*. ☑

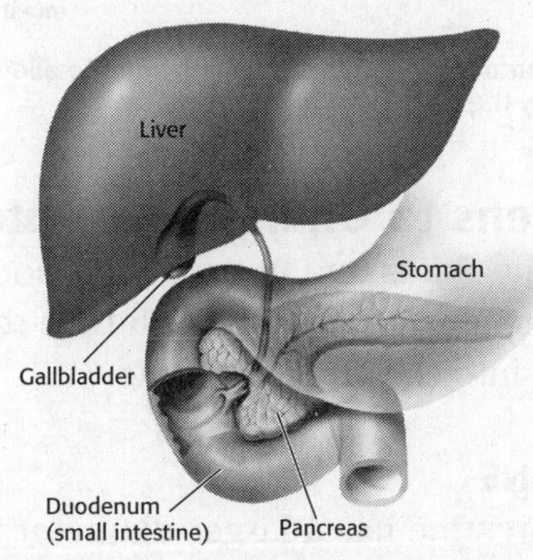

The liver and pancreas contribute to the complete digestion of nutrients in the duodenum of the small intestine.

How Does the Body Absorb Nutrients?

The body absorbs nutrients after digestion is complete. Absorption of nutrients takes place mainly in the small intestine after the duodenum. The small intestine is a very long, coiled organ. The lining of the small intestine is covered in structures that allow nutrients to pass into the bloodstream.

Critical Thinking

6. Apply Concepts What type of digestion occurs in the small intestine?

____

7. Describe What is the function of bile?

____

____

LOOKING CLOSER

8. Identify Where do digestive enzymes from the pancreas go?

____

____

VILLI

Villi (singular, *villus*) are fingerlike extensions that cover the lining of the small intestine. Each villus is covered with smaller extensions called *microvilli*. Together, the villi and microvilli greatly increase the surface area available for the absorption of nutrients. ☑

9. Identify What structures cover villi?

____

Sugars and amino acids enter the bloodstream through capillaries in the villi. Fatty acids and glycerol are absorbed by lymphatic vessels in the villi and eventually enter the bloodstream. Blood carries these digested nutrients to cells throughout the body.

LOOKING CLOSER

10. Identify Name two structures that are located inside villi.

____

____

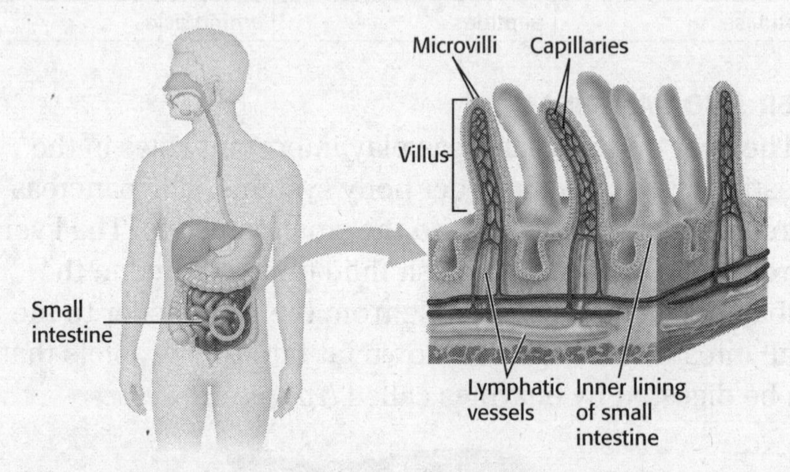

Villi expand the surface area of the small intestine to allow more nutrients to be absorbed by the blood.

What Happens to Undigested Materials?

Almost all the fluids and nutrients in food are absorbed by the small intestine. Materials that are not absorbed pass into the large intestine.

LARGE INTESTINE

The large intestine has a larger diameter than the small intestine and is not coiled. Many bacteria live in a region of the large intestine called the colon. These bacteria make vitamins that are not easily obtained from foods. They also help change undigested materials into solid waste, or feces. Peristalsis moves feces to the final section of the large intestine, called the rectum. Feces exit the body through the anus. ☑

READING CHECK

11. Describe What are two functions of bacteria that live in the large intestine?

____

____

____

The large intestine absorbs minerals and water. Failure of the large intestine to balance water absorption can lead to diarrhea (watery feces) or constipation (hard feces).

Name _______________ Class _______________ Date _______________

Section 2 Review

SECTION VOCABULARY

digestion the breaking down of food into chemical substances that can be used for energy **esophagus** a long, straight tube that connects the pharynx to the stomach **pepsin** an enzyme that is found in gastric juices and that helps break down proteins into smaller molecules	**peristalsis** the series of rhythmic muscular contractions that move food through the digestive tract **villus** one of the many tiny projections from the cells in the lining of the small intestine; increases the surface area of the lining for absorption

1. Explain What is the purpose of the digestive system?

2. Describe How does mechanical digestion occur in the mouth?

3. Describe How does saliva contribute to digestion?

4. Identify What are the components of gastric juice and how do they function?

5. Explain How do amino acids from digested proteins enter the bloodstream?

6. Identify What enters the large intestine from the small intestine?

7. Predict How would a person be affected if the large intestine absorbed too much water from undigested materials?

Name ______________________ Class ______________ Date ______________

CHAPTER 36 Digestive and Excretory Systems

SECTION 3

Excretion

KEY IDEAS

As you read this section, keep these questions in mind:

- Why is excretion important?
- What do the kidneys do?
- How are metabolic wastes removed?
- How does kidney damage affect the body?

READING TOOLBOX

Organize As you read this section, create a chart that describes what happens inside the kidneys.

What Is Excretion?

Our bodies must get rid of wastes to remain healthy. **Excretion** is the process of removing wastes that are produced by metabolic reactions.

Some metabolic reactions produce toxic nitrogen-containing wastes, such as **urea**. Urea is produced during the metabolism of proteins. Excess amounts of carbon dioxide and water are produced during cellular respiration. Excretion of these wastes enables the body to maintain proper water balance and pH.

Background

Recall that *metabolic reactions* are the chemical processes that occur in an organism.

EXCRETORY ORGANS

The organs involved in excretion are shown below. Your skin excretes water, salts, and some nitrogen wastes when you sweat. Your lungs excrete carbon dioxide when you breathe. The kidneys are the main organs of excretion. They sort and excrete cellular wastes in your blood. ☑

READING CHECK

1. Identify What are three things that the skin excretes in sweat?

____

____

____

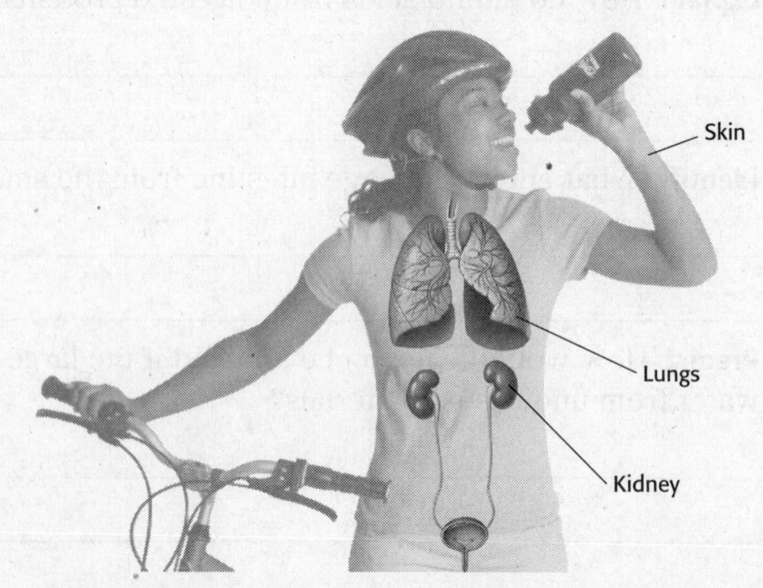

The lungs, kidneys, and the skin all function as excretory organs.

LOOKING CLOSER

2. Identify How many kidneys does a person have?

____

What Do the Kidneys Do?

The kidneys are a pair of bean-shaped organs. They filter wastes out of the blood and keep molecules at the correct levels. Each kidney contains millions of blood-filtering units called **nephrons**. A nephron, shown below, has tiny tubes surrounded by capillaries. ☑

3. Describe What is the function of a nephron?

____

____

FILTRATION

Blood enters the kidney and flows to a bed of capillaries in a nephron, called the *glomerulus*. In the glomerulus, blood undergoes a process called *filtration*. Filtration occurs when fluid and small molecules from the blood pass into Bowman's capsule. Bowman's capsule is a structure that surrounds the glomerulus.

The fluid that enters Bowman's capsule from the blood is called *filtrate*. Filtrate is composed of water, salt, glucose, amino acids, and urea.

REABSORPTION AND SECRETION

The filtrate passes from Bowman's capsule into the renal tubule. Capillaries wrap around the tubule. Useful molecules that were removed from the blood during filtration reenter the blood through these capillaries. This process is called *reabsorption*.

Urea, some salts, and some water remain in the filtrate. Additional wastes are secreted into the filtrate as it passes through the renal tubule into the collecting duct.

Critical Thinking

4. Apply Concepts What molecules in filtrate are reabsorbed by the blood?

____

____

____

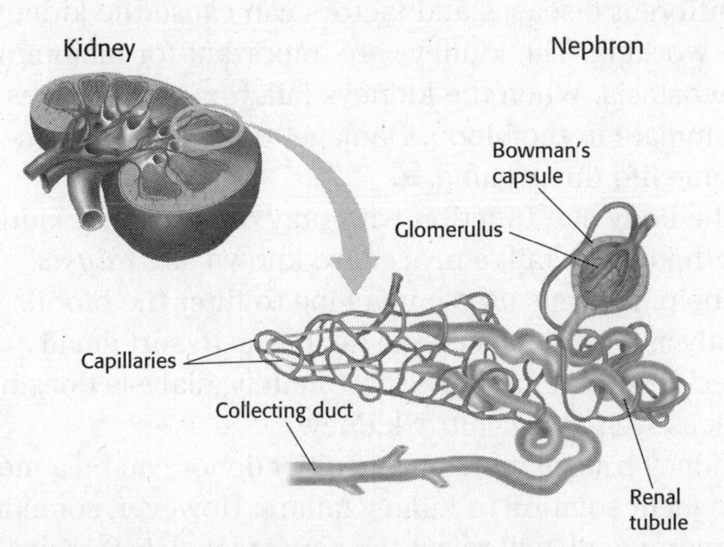

Unfiltered blood enters the kidney (left). Nephrons (right) clean the blood as it moves through the kidney. Wastes from the blood are collected and emptied through the collecting duct. Filtered blood returns to the body.

LOOKING CLOSER

5. Identify Through what structure does filtrate from the blood enter the renal tubule?

____

How Is Urine Excreted?

After filtration, reabsorption, and secretion, the remaining salt, urea, and water form **urine**. Most metabolic wastes are removed from the body through the formation and excretion of urine. ☑

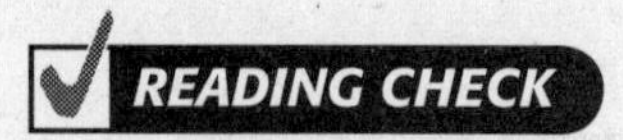

READING CHECK

6. Identify In what fluid are most metabolic wastes removed from the body?

____

Collecting ducts from nephrons empty into a ureter. A **ureter** is a tube of smooth muscle that carries urine from a kidney to the urinary bladder. The **urinary bladder** is a hollow, muscular sac that stores urine. Urine passes from the bladder through the **urethra** to exit the body.

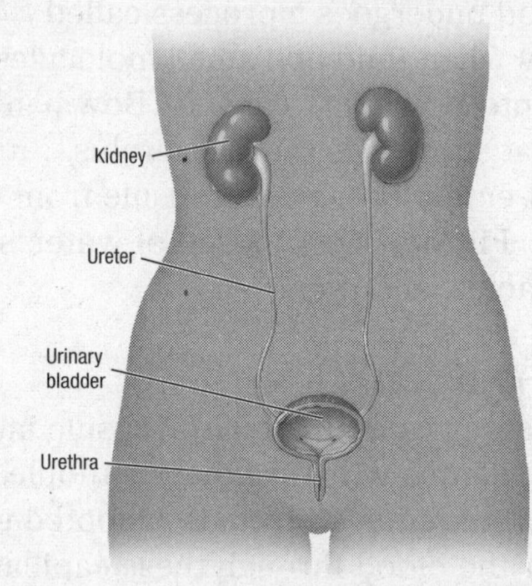

During excretion, urine passes from the kidneys to the urinary bladder through a ureter. It exits the body through the urethra.

LOOKING CLOSER

7. Identify What structure connects a kidney to the urinary bladder?

____

What Happens When the Kidneys Fail?

Different diseases and factors can cause the kidneys to stop working. The kidneys are important for maintaining homeostasis. When the kidneys fail, toxic substances accumulate in the blood. Damage to the kidneys can become life threatening. ☑

READING CHECK

8. Explain What happens to the blood when both kidneys fail?

____

____

The body can function with only one working kidney. If both kidneys fail, a procedure known as *dialysis* can help. Dialysis uses a machine to filter the blood. A dialysis machine acts like nephrons to sort small molecules in the blood. Unfortunately, dialysis does not work as well as a healthy kidney.

Kidney transplant from a healthy donor can be a more permanent solution to kidney failure. However, sometimes a person's body will reject the new organ. Doctors use drugs to help reduce the chances of rejection.

Name ______________________ Class ______________ Date ______________

Section 3 Review

SECTION VOCABULARY

excretion the process of eliminating metabolic wastes

nephron the functional unit of the kidney

urea the principal nitrogenous product of the metabolism of proteins that forms in the liver from amino acids and from compounds of ammonia and that is found in urine and other body fluids

ureter one of the two narrow tubes that carry urine from the kidneys to the urinary bladder

urethra the tube that carries urine from the urinary bladder to the outside of the body

urinary bladder a hollow, muscular organ that stores urine

urine the liquid excreted by the kidneys, stored in the bladder, and passed through the urethra to the outside of the body

1. **Identify** What waste product is excreted by the lungs?

____

2. **Compare** How does the blood that enters the kidney differ from the blood that leaves the kidney?

____

____

____

3. **Identify** What process returns filtered nutrients to the blood in the nephron?

____

4. **Summarize** Fill in the following chart to trace the path of urine from the kidneys out of the body. Use words from the vocabulary list.

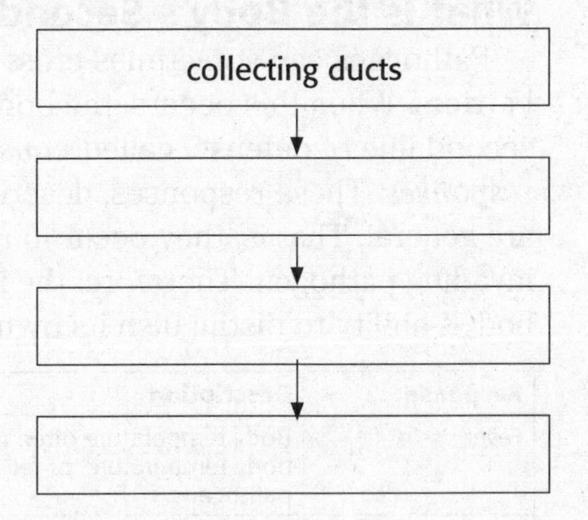

5. **Explain** What does a dialysis machine do?

____

____

Name ______________________ Class ______________ Date ______________

CHAPTER 37 The Body's Defenses

SECTION 1

Protecting Against Disease

KEY IDEAS

As you read this section, keep these questions in mind:
- What physical barriers protect the human body?
- What are three general defense mechanisms that the body uses to fight pathogens?
- How does the body respond to pathogens that have infected a cell?

READING TOOLBOX

Outline As you read this section, create an outline of the information. Use the header question to help you organize the main ideas in your outline.

What Is the Body's First Line of Defense?

A **pathogen** is a microorganism, virus, or protein that can cause a disease. The body's first defense against pathogens is two physical barriers that prevent pathogens from entering the body: the skin and mucous membranes.

The skin is the first barrier. Oil makes the skin's surface acidic and inhibits the growth of many pathogens. Sweat contains enzymes that kill bacteria.

Mucous membranes are a second barrier. They cover internal body surfaces, such as the digestive, respiratory, and reproductive tracts. Mucous membranes produce a thick, sticky fluid, called *mucus*. Mucus traps pathogens before they can cause infections. ☑

READING CHECK

1. Describe What is one way mucous membranes prevent infections?

____

____

____

____

What Is the Body's Second Line of Defense?

Pathogens can sometimes cross the body's physical barriers. When this occurs, the body responds with a second line of defense, called *nonspecific immune responses*. These responses, described in the table below, are general. That is, they occur in response to any type of invading pathogen. Therefore, the responses depend on the body's ability to distinguish its own cells from invaders.

Response	Description
Fever	Body temperature often rises to fight a pathogen. High body temperature, or *fever*, is harmful to many bacterial pathogens.
Protein Activation	The body also produces proteins that attack pathogens. *Complement proteins* create holes in bacterial cell membranes. Proteins called *interferons* prevent viruses from functioning.
Inflammation	An injury or infection in the body causes **inflammation**. During inflammation, chemicals and cells gather at the site of infection to destroy pathogens. The diagram on the next page shows this response.

LOOKING CLOSER

2. Explain Does fever only result from a bacterial infection? Explain your answer.

____

____

____

____

Inflammation

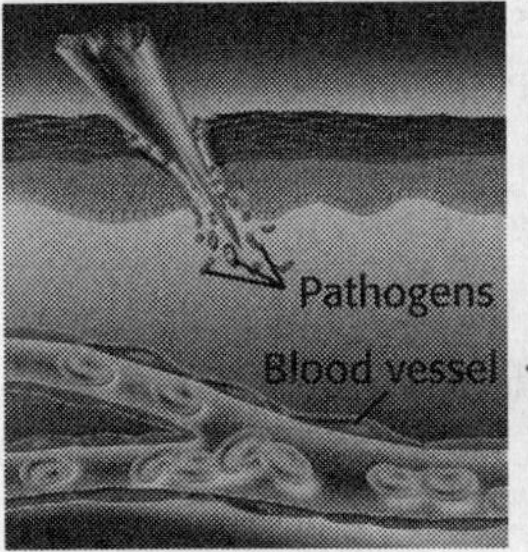

When skin is damaged, such as from a puncture wound, pathogens can enter the body.

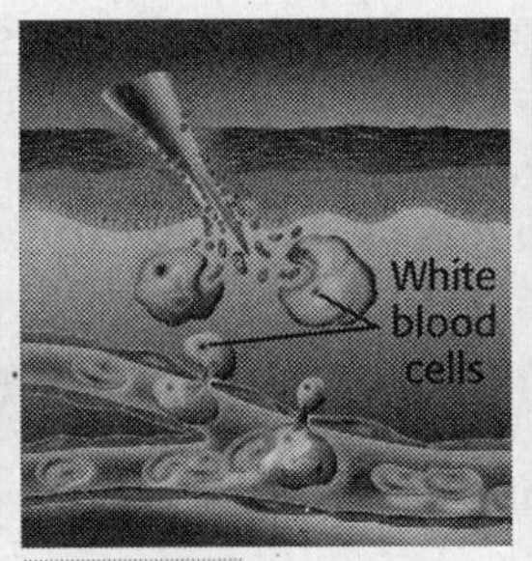

Histamine is released from infected cells. Histamine causes local blood vessels to dilate. This increases blood flow to the infected area and causes warmth, swelling, and redness.

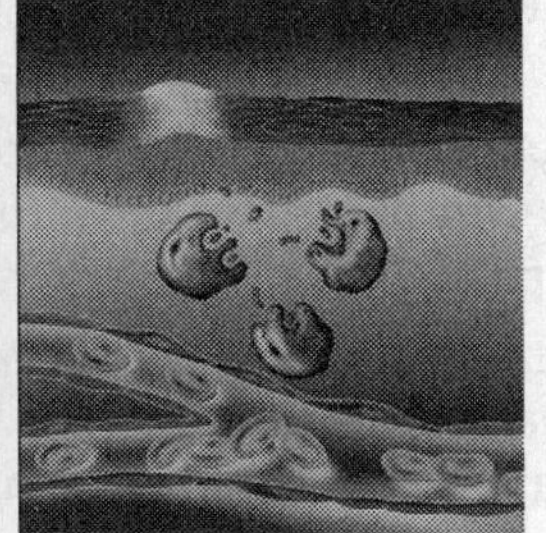

White blood cells attack and destroy the pathogens. Pus is a whitish liquid with white blood cells and dead pathogens.

Talk About It

Discuss With a partner or in a small group, talk about any experiences you have had with inflammation. What did inflammation look and feel like and why?

What Is the Body's Third Line of Defense?

Pathogens have unique proteins, called **antigens**, on their surfaces. Antigens help the body identify pathogens as invaders. A **macrophage** is a white blood cell that ingests and destroys general pathogens. After a macrophage destroys a pathogen, it displays the pathogen's antigens on its surface.

This display alerts the immune system to an invader and activates the *specific immune response*. This response occurs when general responses fail and when a pathogen infects a cell. It involves white blood cells, or immune cells, that target particular pathogens.

Immune cells have receptors that only recognize certain antigens. The shape of these receptors exactly matches the shape of specific antigens. As shown below, these receptors bind to antigens. Such binding produces many more specific white blood cells to fight the infection.

Critical Thinking

3. Infer Why do people with infections often have a higher than normal number of white blood cells?

____

____

____

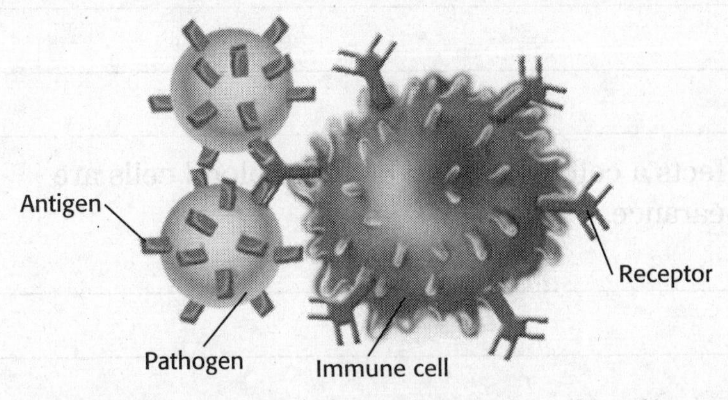

In a specific immune response, receptors on the surface of immune cells bind to specific antigens on pathogens. More immune cells are then produced to destroy the remaining pathogens.

Name ______________________ Class ______________ Date ______________

Section 1 Review

SECTION VOCABULARY

antigen a substance that stimulates an immune response

histamine a chemical that stimulates the autonomous nervous system, secretion of gastric juices, and dilation of capillaries

inflammation a protective response of tissues affected by disease or injury; characterized by pain, swelling, redness, and heat

macrophage an immune system cell that engulfs pathogens and other materials

mucous membrane the layer of epithelial tissue that covers internal surfaces of the body and that secretes mucus

pathogen a microorganism, another organism, a virus, or a protein that causes disease; an infectious agent

1. **Identify** What two physical barriers make up the first line of defense against pathogens?

____

2. **Identify** What three defenses occur when a person breathes in a virus that crosses the mucous membranes in the respiratory tract?

____

3. **Describe** What role does histamine play in inflammation and what symptoms does it cause?

____

____

____

4. **Describe** What does a macrophage do after it ingests a pathogen?

____

____

5. **Compare** How are the nonspecific immune responses different from the specific immune response?

____

____

____

6. **Describe** When a pathogen infects a cell, what kind of white blood cells are activated? Describe their appearance.

____

____

____

Name ______________________ Class ______________ Date ______________

CHAPTER 37 The Body's Defenses

SECTION 2

Eliminating Invaders

KEY IDEAS

As you read this section, keep these questions in mind:

- How is the specific immune response activated?
- How does the body eliminate pathogens inside body cells?
- How does the body eliminate pathogens outside body cells?
- How does the immune system protect the body against repeated infection by the same pathogen?

How Is the Specific Immune Response Activated?

Recall that white blood cells called macrophages ingest and destroy general pathogens. They display antigens from these pathogens on their surface. This display activates specific immune cells called helper T cells.

Helper T cells are white blood cells that activate the specific immune response. They have receptors on their surface that bind to specific antigens. Such binding causes helper T cells to grow and divide. This produces more helper T cells with the same receptors. An example of the activation of helper T cells is shown below. ☑

READING TOOLBOX

Organize As you read this section, create a flow chart that describes the specific immune response. Include the activation of helper T cells, the T cell response, and the B cell response.

1. Identify What type of cells activate the specific immune response?

____

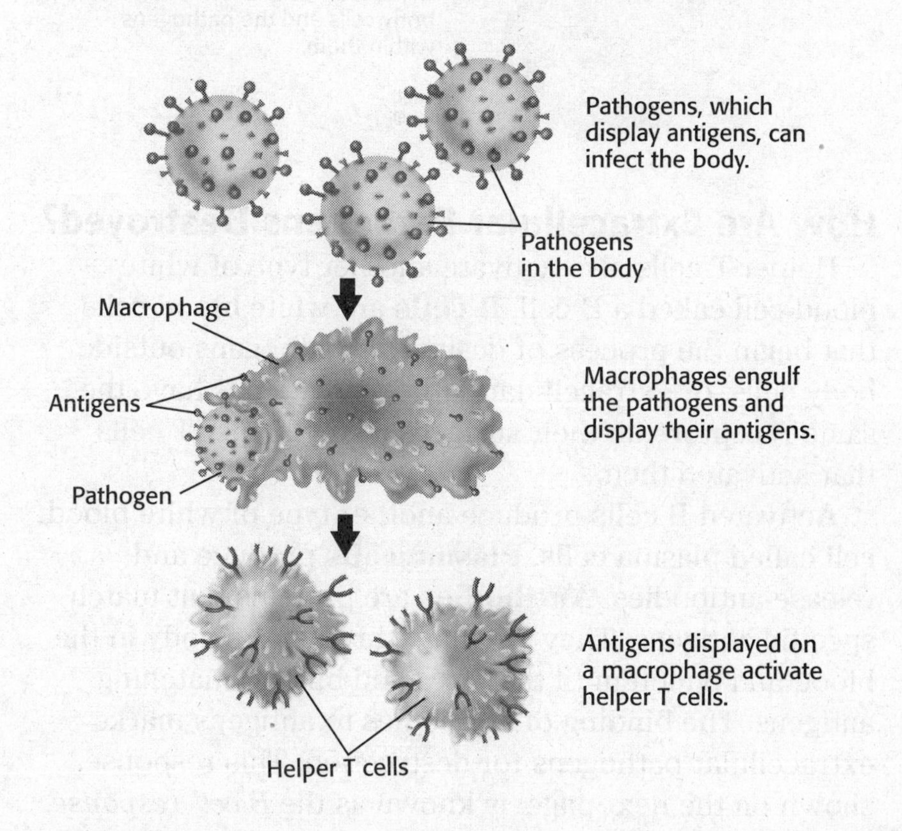

LOOKING CLOSER

2. Describe What does the shape of T cell receptors allow them to do?

____

____

How Are Intracellular Pathogens Destroyed?

Helper T cells regulate the function of other cells in the immune system. When pathogens infect a body cell, the cell displays the pathogen's antigens on its surface. These antigens activate helper T cells with matching receptors. These helper T cells release chemical signals to activate a second type of T cell, called a cytotoxic T cell. ☑

3. Explain How does the immune system recognize body cells that have been infected by a pathogen?

____

____

____

Cytotoxic T cells are white blood cells that destroy pathogens inside body cells, or intracellular pathogens. Cytotoxic T cells have the same receptors as the helper T cells that activated them. They bind to infected body cells and destroy the cell and its pathogens. This response, shown below, is known as the *T cell response*.

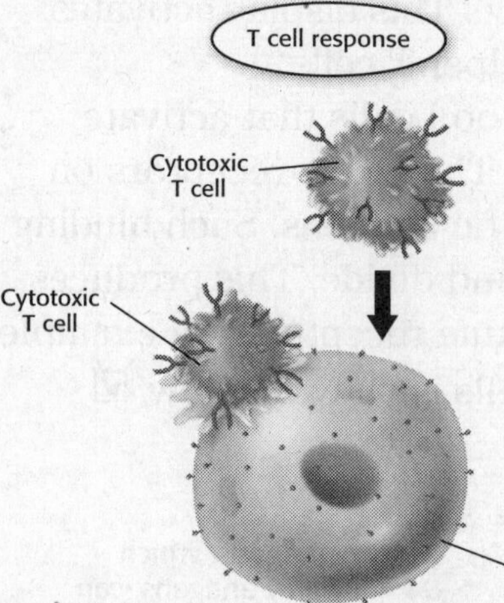

LOOKING CLOSER

4. Identify What kind of pathogens do cytotoxic T cells destroy?

____

____

How Are Extracellular Pathogens Destroyed?

Helper T cells also activate another type of white blood cell called a B cell. **B cells** are white blood cells that begin the process of destroying pathogens outside body cells, or extracellular pathogens. B cells have the same receptors on their surfaces as the helper T cells that activated them.

Activated B cells produce another type of white blood cell called plasma cells. **Plasma cells** produce and release antibodies. **Antibodies** are proteins that match specific antigens. They circulate through the body in the blood and lymph until they find and bind to matching antigens. The binding of antibodies to antigens marks extracellular pathogens for destruction. This response, shown on the next page, is known as the *B cell response*.

Critical Thinking

5. Apply Concepts What does it suggest if a person has a high level of antibodies in his or her bloodstream?

____

____

____

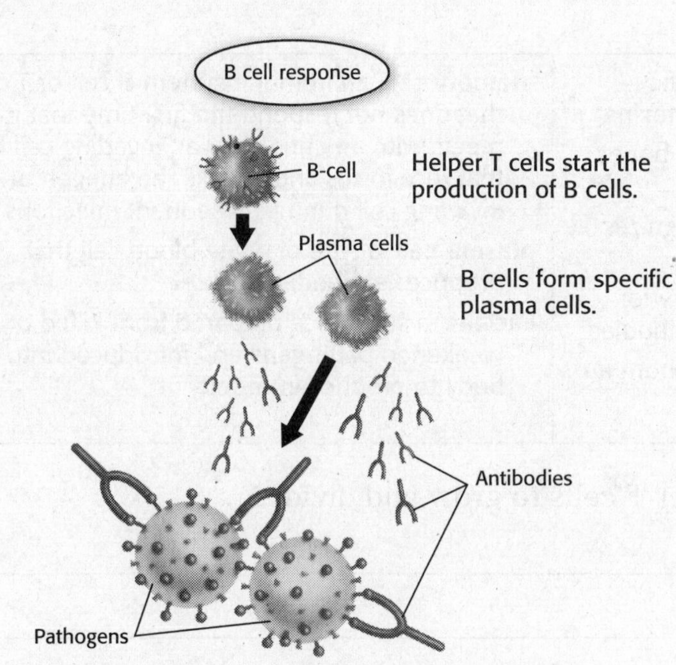

Plasma cells make and release antibodies that bind to matching antigens on the pathogen. This action tags pathogens outside cells in the body for destruction.

LOOKING CLOSER

6. Describe How do antibodies prevent pathogens from invading body cells?

____

What Is Long-Term Protection?

In addition to plasma cells, activated B cells also produce memory cells. **Memory cells** are white blood cells that have receptors for specific antigens. They circulate through the body after a pathogen has been destroyed. If the same pathogen invades the body again, the immune system is prepared. ☑

7. Explain Are memory cells produced the first or second time the body encounters a pathogen?

____

When memory cells encounter a pathogen that had previously infected the body, they start a rapid immune response. They produce helper T cells, cytotoxic T cells, and plasma cells. Together, these cells attack the pathogen before it can cause harm. This long-term ability to resist an infectious disease is called **immunity**.

VACCINATION

The body can also develop immunity with the help of a vaccine. A **vaccine** is usually an injection that contains dead or weakened pathogens. Because the pathogens are dead or weakened, they cannot cause illness.

However, the pathogens in the vaccine carry surface antigens that trigger an immune response. This response includes the production of memory cells. If the actual pathogen entered the body after a vaccination, the immune system would be prepared to destroy the invaders before they could cause harm.

Talk About It

Discuss With a partner, or in a small group, talk about diseases in people and animals that doctors can prevent by vaccination.

Name ______________________ Class ______________ Date ______________

Section 2 Review

SECTION VOCABULARY

antibody a protein that reacts to a specific antigen or that inactivates or destroys toxins

B cell a white blood cell that matures in bones and makes antibodies

cytotoxic T cell a type of T cell that recognizes and destroys cells infected by a virus

helper T cell a white blood cell necessary for B cells to develop normal levels of antibodies

immunity the ability to resist or recover from an infectious disease

memory cell an immune system B cell or T cell that does not respond the first time that it meets with an antigen or an invading cell but that recognizes and attacks the antigen or invading cell during subsequent infections

plasma cell a type of white blood cell that produces antibodies

vaccine a substance prepared from killed or weakened pathogens and introduced into a body to produce immunity

1. Describe What stimulates helper T cells to grow and divide?

____

____

2. Explain How does the T cell response destroy intracellular pathogens?

____

____

____

3. Summarize Complete the following Process Chart to describe how the immune system destroys extracellular pathogens.

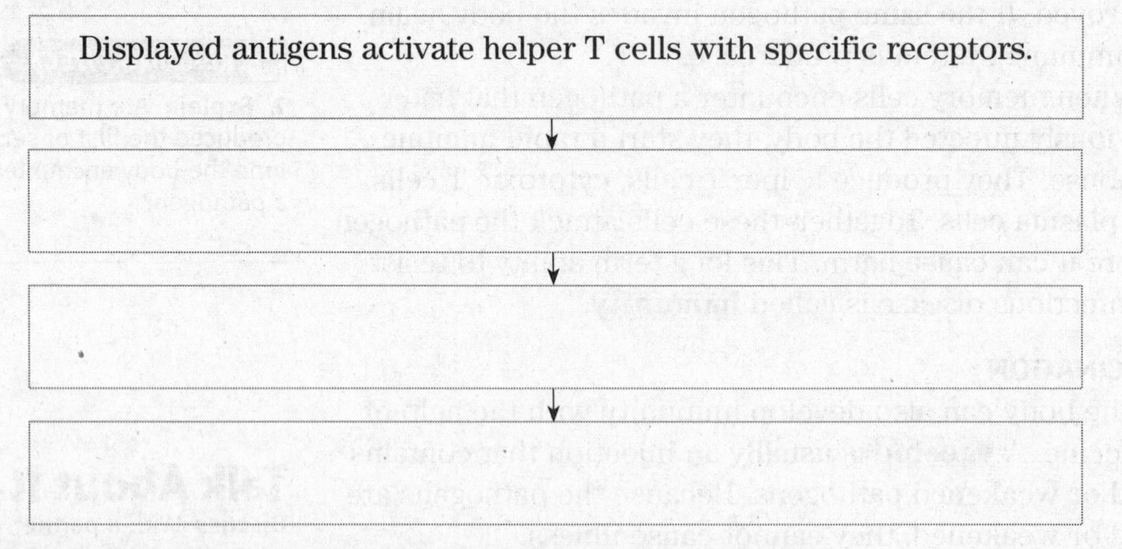

4. Identify What type of cells start the process of immunity?

____

CHAPTER 37 The Body's Defenses

SECTION 3

Immune System Dysfunctions

KEY IDEAS

As you read this section, keep these questions in mind:
- What causes an allergic reaction?
- What are autoimmune diseases?
- What happens when the immune system is deficient?

What Is an Allergy?

Many people have allergies. An **allergy** is an immune response to an antigen that is weak or harmless. Such antigens are called **allergens**. Allergens do not cause an immune response in every person. Common allergens include particles in the air, such as pollen and dust. They also include certain foods, insect stings, and chemicals.

An allergic reaction is an immune response that includes histamine release. Recall that histamine causes the redness and swelling of inflammation. Asthma is an inflammation of the respiratory tract often caused by allergens in the air. Most allergy medicines contain antihistamines to prevent the action of histamine. ☑

READING TOOLBOX

Summarize After you read this section, write a short paragraph explaining what goes wrong with the immune system in allergies, autoimmune diseases, and immune deficiencies.

1. Explain Why does the respiratory tract swell during an asthma attack?

____

____

What Is an Autoimmune Disease?

The immune system can normally distinguish body cells from pathogens, and attack only invading pathogens. However, sometimes the immune system attacks certain body cells as if they were pathogens. This causes a condition called an **autoimmune disease**. The table below describes some common autoimmune diseases.

Disease	Area affected	Symptoms
Type I diabetes	pancreas	increased thirst and urination, weight loss
Multiple sclerosis	nerve coverings	numbness, weakness, paralysis in limbs
Graves' disease	thyroid gland	weakness, weight loss, heat intolerance, sweating
Lupus	connective tissue, joints, kidneys	skin rash, painful joints, fatigue, fever, weight loss
Rheumatoid arthritis	joints	severe pain, fatigue, inflammation of joints
Psoriasis	skin	dry, scaly, red patches
Crohn's disease	digestive system	abdominal pain, nausea, vomiting, weight loss

LOOKING CLOSER

2. Describe How is Crohn's disease caused?

____

____

____

What Is Immune Deficiency?

3. Define What is an opportunistic infection?

In some people, the immune system does not properly fight infections because it is deficient. Immune deficiency means that part of the immune system is missing or not working. People with immune deficiencies get infections by pathogens that healthy immune systems eliminate before they cause harm. These infections are called *opportunistic infections*. ☑

Immune deficiency can be inherited. In a rare disease called *severe combined immunodeficiency* (SCID), babies are born without any functioning B cells or T cells. As a result, they can get life-threatening infections.

Immune deficiency can also be caused by medications. Some cancer medications cause immune deficiency as a side effect. This is called immune suppression. Other medications intentionally cause immune suppression to prevent the body from attacking a transplanted organ.

AIDS

Critical Thinking

4. Infer Why does the number of helper T cells in a person with AIDS make getting the flu dangerous?

Immune deficiency can also be caused by infection. **AIDS**, or acquired immune deficiency syndrome, is caused by a virus that kills helper T cells. This virus is called the human immunodeficiency virus, or **HIV**.

When the body is first infected with HIV, it produces antibodies against the virus. However, as time passes, fewer antibodies are made. This is because the number of viral particles increases and the number of helper T cells decreases. HIV infection eventually progresses to AIDS. HIV can be passed between people in body fluids.

5. Reading Graphs According to the graph, about how long after infection is the number of T cells half as many as at the time of infection?

Course of HIV Infection

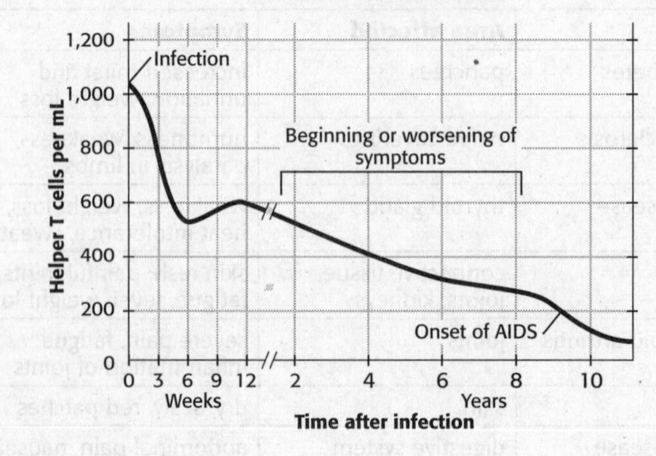

Name ______________________ Class ______________ Date ______________

Section 3 Review

SECTION VOCABULARY

AIDS acquired immune deficiency syndrome, a disease caused by HIV, an infection that results in an ineffective immune system

allergen a substance that causes an allergic reaction

allergy a physical response to an antigen, which can be a common substance that produces little or no response in the general population

autoimmune disease a disease in which the immune system attacks the organism's own cells

HIV human immunodeficiency virus, the virus that causes AIDS

1. **Describe** What name is given to substances that cause allergic reactions?

2. **Explain** Why is asthma considered an allergy?

3. **Apply Concepts** Would a person with type I diabetes be able to activate an immune response against a flu virus? Explain your answer.

4. **Compare** What is one difference between an immune system response that causes an allergic reaction and one that causes an autoimmune disease?

5. **Identify** List three different causes of immune deficiency.

6. **Describe** How does the HIV virus make the immune system deficient?

7. **Explain** Why would a person take medication that causes immune deficiency?

CHAPTER 38 Nervous System

SECTION 1

Structures of the Nervous System

KEY IDEAS

As you read this section, keep these questions in mind:
- What is the function of the central nervous system?
- What are the two components of the peripheral nervous system?
- How is a spinal reflex generated?

READING TOOLBOX

Learn New Words As you read this section, underline words you don't know. When you figure out what they mean, write the words and their definitions in your notebook.

What Is the Central Nervous System?

Your *nervous system* consists of your brain, spinal cord, and nerves. These structures are made of nervous tissue, which contains specialized cells called neurons. A **neuron** is a cell that receives and transmits electrical signals.

There are two main parts of your nervous system: the central nervous system and the peripheral nervous system. The **central nervous system** includes the brain and the spinal cord. It receives, interprets, and responds to internal and external information. ☑

1. Identify Which two structures make up the central nervous system?

____

____

STRUCTURE OF THE BRAIN AND SPINAL CORD

Your **brain** is the organ that interprets information from the rest of your body. Your brain also sends out signals that control the rest of your body. The brain has several different parts.

The **cerebrum** is the largest part of the brain. It interprets information from the rest of the body. It also controls most movements. The left side of the cerebrum controls the right side of the body. The right side of the cerebrum controls the left side of the body.

The **cerebellum** controls balance, posture, and coordination. For example, it interprets information from your body to help you maintain your balance while you walk.

The **brainstem** is located at the bottom of the brain. It helps the body maintain homeostasis. For example, it controls heart rate and breathing rate.

The **spinal cord** is a thick column of neurons that runs through the spine. It connects the brain to most of the rest of the body.

LOOKING CLOSER

2. Describe What is the function of the brainstem?

____

____

What Is the Peripheral Nervous System?

The **peripheral nervous system** consists of sensory neurons and motor neurons. *Sensory neurons* transmit signals from sensory organs, such as the eyes and skin, to the central nervous system. These signals are called *stimuli* (singular, *stimulus*). ☑

Motor neurons transmit messages from the central nervous system to muscles and other organs. There are two main parts of the peripheral nervous system that control motor neurons: the autonomic nervous system and the somatic nervous system.

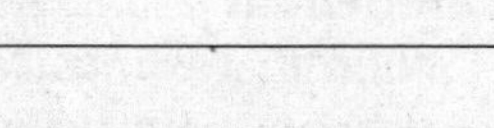

3. Define What is a stimulus?

____

____

System	Functions
Autonomic nervous system	controls cardiac and smooth (involuntary) muscles; helps maintain homeostasis
Somatic nervous system	controls skeletal (voluntary) muscles; responds to signals from outside the body

Background

Recall that a *voluntary muscle* is a muscle that you can control. An *involuntary muscle* is a muscle you cannot control.

What Is a Reflex?

Have you ever touched something hot, and had your hand jerk away quickly, without your even thinking about it? This is an example of a reflex. A **reflex** is an involuntary, very fast muscle contraction that is caused by a stimulus. Spinal reflexes involve the peripheral nervous system and the spinal cord, but not the brain. Spinal reflexes protect parts of the body from being harmed. The flowchart below describes an example of how a spinal reflex occurs.

Critical Thinking

4. Infer Reflexes occur more quickly than responses a person controls. What do you think is the reason for this? (Hint: Which type of signal has to travel farther?)

____

____

____

____

____

____

____

____

Your hand touches a hot object. This produces a signal in the sensory neurons in your hand.

↓

The signal travels from the sensory neurons to your spinal cord.

↓

Your spinal cord produces a signal that travels through motor neurons to your hand.

↓

The signal in the motor neurons causes muscles in your arm to contract. Your hand jerks away from the hot object.

Name ____________ Class ____________ Date ____________

Section 1 Review

SECTION VOCABULARY

brain the mass of nerve tissue that is the main control center of the nervous system

brainstem the stemlike portion of the brain that connects the cerebral hemispheres with the spinal cord and that maintains the necessary functions of the body, such as breathing and circulation

central nervous system the brain and the spinal cord; its main function is to control the flow of information in the body

cerebellum a posterior portion of the brain that coordinates muscle movement and controls subconscious activities and some balance functions

cerebrum the upper part of the brain that receives sensation and controls movement

neuron a nerve cell that is specialized to receive and conduct electrical impulses

peripheral nervous system all of the parts of the nervous system except for the brain and the spinal cord (the central nervous system); includes the cranial nerves and nerves of the neck, chest, lower back, and pelvis

reflex an involuntary and almost immediate movement in response to a stimulus

spinal cord a column of nerve tissue running from the base of the brain through the vertebral column

1. **Describe** What is the function of the central nervous system?

2. **Apply Concepts** The right side of a person's cerebrum is damaged. What effect could this have on the person? Explain your answer.

3. **Infer** What might happen to a person whose cerebellum is damaged? Explain your answer.

4. **Identify** What are two functions of the autonomic nervous system?

5. **Explain** How might reflexes help protect parts of the body?

Name ______________________ Class ______________ Date ______________

CHAPTER 38 Nervous System

SECTION 2

Neurons and Nerve Impulses

KEY IDEAS

As you read this section, keep these questions in mind:
- What path do impulses follow when they move through a neuron?
- How is a nerve impulse generated?
- How do impulses travel through the nervous system?
- How do neurons communicate with each other?

What Is the Structure of a Neuron?

Recall that a *neuron* is a cell that is specialized for conducting *impulses*, or electrical signals. Each part of a neuron has a different function, as shown below.

READING TOOLBOX

Summarize As you read this section, sketch each figure in your notebook. In your own words, summarize the main ideas of each figure in your sketches.

The Structure of a Neuron

Nucleus

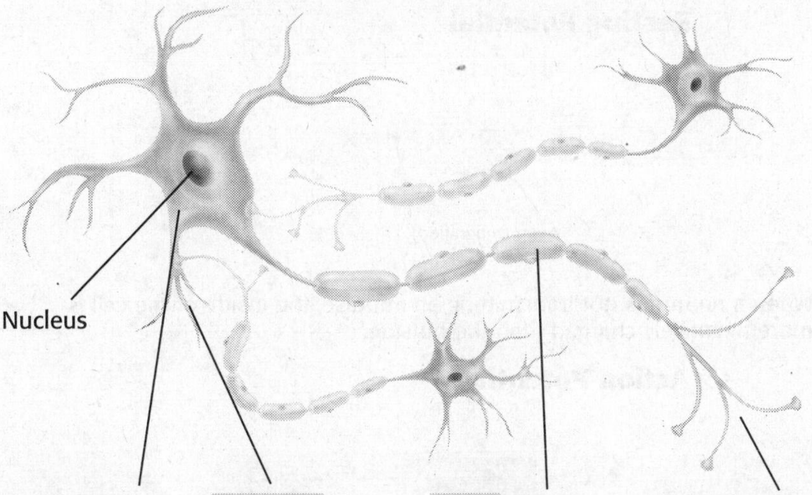

The *cell body* of the neuron contains the nucleus and most of the organelles. The cell body receives impulses from the dendrites, processes them, and passes them on to the axons.

Dendrites extend from the cell body. They receive impulses from other cells.

Axons also extend from the cell body. They carry impulses away from the cell body, toward other cells. Bundles of axons are called **nerves**.

The ends of an axon are called *axon terminals*.

LOOKING CLOSER

1. Identify What does the cell body of a neuron do?

____

Critical Thinking

2. Compare Give one similarity and one difference between axons and dendrites.

____

How Do Impulses Travel Through a Neuron?

A signal from another neuron or the environment can generate an impulse in a neuron. The impulse travels through the neuron as a result of the movement of ions across the neuron's cell membrane. ☑

3. Explain How is a nerve impulse generated?

____

____

A cell has an electric charge on the inner surface of its membrane. This charge is different from the charge of the fluid outside the cell. The difference in electric charge between the inside and outside of a cell is called a **membrane potential**. Changes in a neuron's membrane potential allow the neuron to conduct electrical impulses.

When a neuron is not conducting an impulse, its membrane potential is called the *resting potential*. When a neuron receives a signal, its membrane potential changes. Sometimes, this change in membrane potential produces a nerve impulse, called an **action potential**.

Talk About It

Discuss Relationships How are membrane potential, resting potential, and action potential related? With a partner, discuss the similarities and differences between them. Together, think of a method to help you remember what they are.

Resting Potential

Axon (magnified)

When a neuron is not transmitting an impulse, the inside of the cell is more negatively charged than the outside.

Action Potential

When a neuron receives a signal, ions move across the cell membrane. Sometimes this causes part of the inside of the cell to become more positively charged than the outside. This change in membrane potential is called an action potential. It moves down the axon very quickly.

4. Describe What happens during an action potential?

____

____

____

____

You may think that a strong stimulus produces a stronger action potential than a weak stimulus. However, this is not the case. Every action potential is the same strength.

How Do Neurons Communicate?

Neurons communicate with one another and with other cells at synapses. A **synapse** is a place where a neuron meets another cell. The other cell may be a muscle cell, a gland, or another neuron. ☑

5. Define What is a synapse?

A neuron does not touch the cells it communicates with. Instead, chemicals called **neurotransmitters** carry signals across synapses. The figure below shows how this happens.

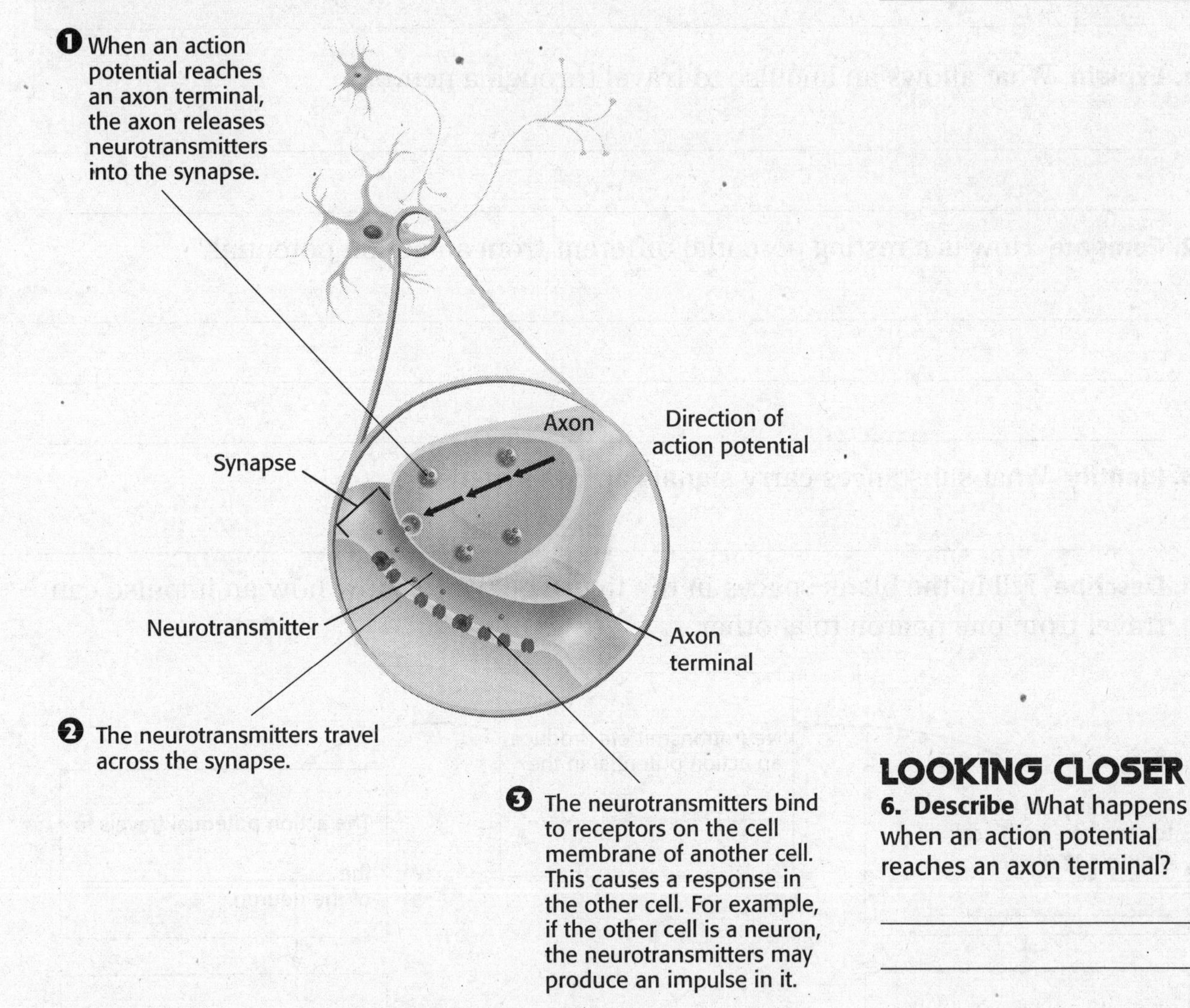

LOOKING CLOSER

6. Describe What happens when an action potential reaches an axon terminal?

There are many types of neurotransmitters. Neurotransmitters do not cause changes themselves. They bind to receptors, and influence which ions will flow across the cell membrane.

The effects of neurotransmitters do not last very long. Cells reabsorb most neurotransmitters soon after they are released. Enzymes break down other neurotransmitters.

Name ______________________ Class ______________ Date ______________

Section 2 Review

SECTION VOCABULARY

action potential a sudden change in the polarity of the membrane of a neuron, gland cell, or muscle fiber that facilitates the transmission of electrical impulses

axon an elongated extension of a neuron that carries impulses away from the cell body

dendrite a cytoplasmic extension of a neuron that receives stimuli

membrane potential the difference in electric charge between the two sides of a cell membrane

nerve a collection of nerve fibers through which impulses travel between the central nervous system and other parts of the body

neurotransmitter a chemical substance that transmits nerve impulses across a synapse

synapse the junction at which the end of the axon of a neuron meets the end of a dendrite or the cell body of another neuron or meets another cell

1. Explain What allows an impulse to travel through a neuron?

____

____

2. Compare How is a resting potential different from an action potential?

____

____

____

3. Identify What substances carry signals across synapses?

____

4. Describe Fill in the blank spaces in the figure below to show how an impulse can travel from one neuron to another.

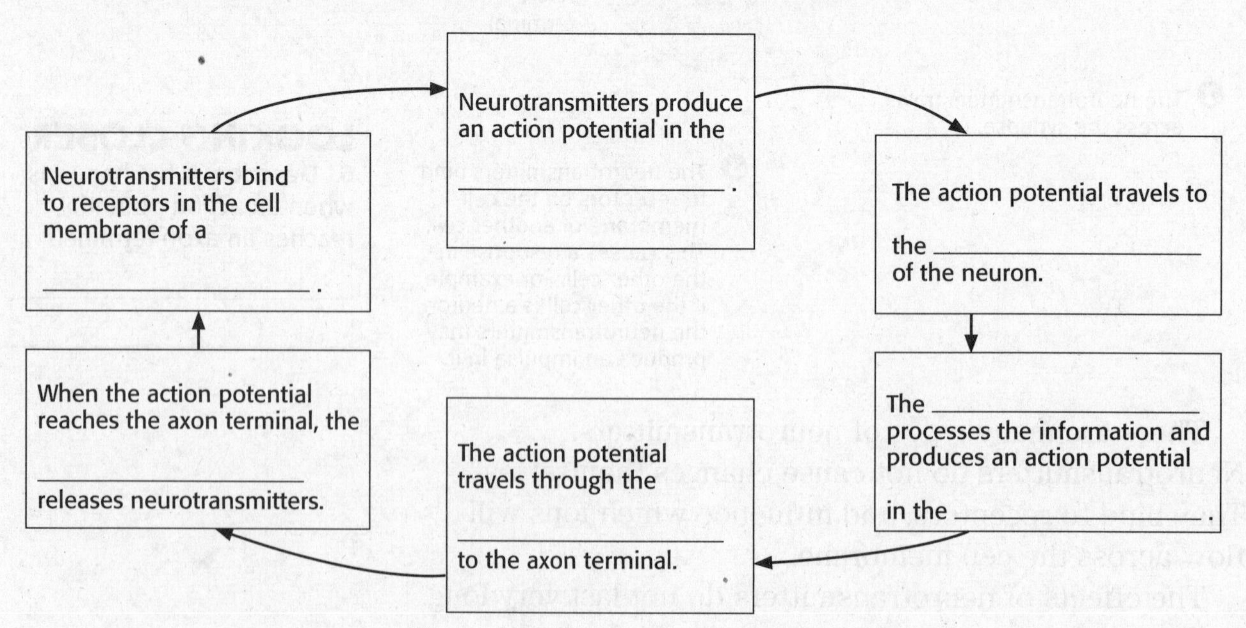

Name ______________________ Class ______________ Date ______________

CHAPTER 38 Nervous System

SECTION 3

Sensory Systems

KEY IDEAS

As you read this section, keep these questions in mind:

- How is sensory information detected?
- What are the five types of sensory receptors?
- Where is sensory information processed in the brain?

How Do You Detect Stimuli?

Stimuli, such as light, sound, and chemicals, are all around you. Specialized neurons called **sensory receptors** detect these stimuli and produce impulses, which travel to the brain. The brain interprets the impulses as images, sounds, tastes, or other sensations.

There are five types of sensory receptors: photoreceptors, chemoreceptors, mechanoreceptors, pain receptors, and thermoreceptors.

READING TOOLBOX

Summarize After you read this section, make a Concept Map using the terms *sensory receptor*, *mechanoreceptor*, *chemicals*, *light*, *chemoreceptor*, *photoreceptor*, *vibrations*, *images*, *sounds*, and *tastes*.

Critical Thinking

1. Predict What do you think thermoreceptors respond to? Explain your answer.

____

____

____

____

PHOTORECEPTORS

Photoreceptors respond to light. They are located in the **retina**, which is a layer of cells that lines the inner surface of the eye. Light that enters your eyes strikes photoreceptors on your retina. The photoreceptors produce electrical signals that your brain interprets as images.

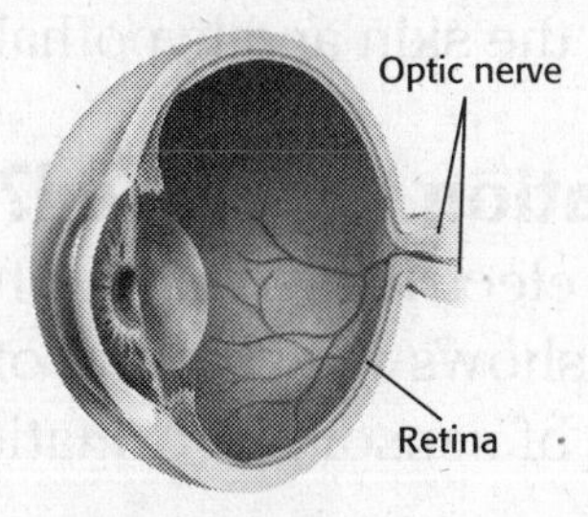

Photoreceptors in the retina detect light. They produce electrical signals, which travel along the optic nerve to the brain.

LOOKING CLOSER

2. Identify What type of stimulus do photoreceptors respond to?

____

CHEMORECEPTORS

Chemoreceptors respond to chemicals. They are found mainly on your tongue and in your nose. The chemoreceptors on your tongue are found in **taste buds**. They respond to chemicals in food and produce electrical impulses that your brain interprets as tastes. The chemoreceptors in your nose respond to chemicals in the air. They produce electrical impulses that your brain interprets as smells.

MECHANORECEPTORS

Mechanoreceptors detect motion and pressure. Your ears contain two kinds of mechanoreceptors. One kind is located in your cochlea. Your **cochlea** is a fluid-filled chamber in your inner ear. The mechanoreceptors in your cochlea respond to some kinds of vibrations. They produce electrical signals that your brain interprets as sounds. ☑

3. Identify What do the mechanoreceptors in your cochlea respond to?

Another kind of mechanoreceptor is found in your semicircular canals. The **semicircular canals** are several small, fluid-filled chambers in your inner ear. The mechanoreceptors in your semicircular canals detect motion. They help you keep your balance.

Your skin also contains many mechanoreceptors. They respond to pressure, tension, and other similar stimuli. The signals they produce give you your sense of touch.

Critical Thinking

4. Describe What type of sensory receptor allows you to feel the paper in this book?

PAIN RECEPTORS

Pain receptors respond to stimuli that could hurt you, such as extreme heat or cold. These receptors are found mainly in the skin.

THERMORECEPTORS

Thermoreceptors respond to changes in temperature. They can signal your brain when you are too hot or too cold, and play an important role in maintaining homeostasis. They are found in the skin and hypothalamus.

How Is Sensory Information Processed?

Sensory receptors produce electrical signals, which travel to the brain. The figure shows which parts of the brain interpret different kinds of sensory information.

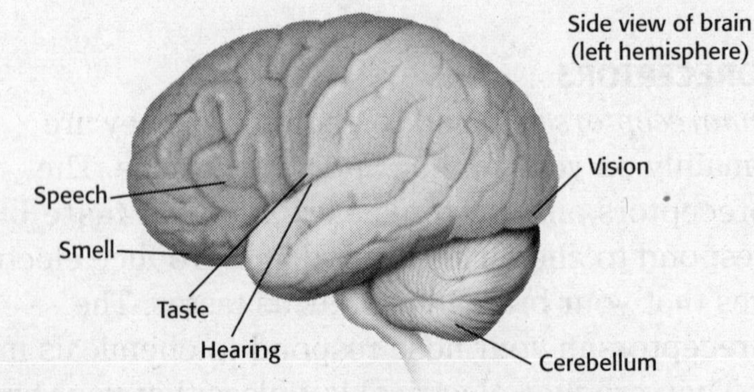

Different parts of the brain process information from different sensory receptors.

LOOKING CLOSER

5. Identify Circle the part of the brain that interprets signals from photoreceptors.

Name ______________________ Class ______________ Date ____________

Section 3 Review

SECTION VOCABULARY

cochlea a coiled tube that is found in the inner ear and that is essential to hearing

retina the light-sensitive inner layer of the eye, which receives images formed by the lens and transmits them through the optic nerve to the brain

semicircular canal one of three fluid-filled canals in the inner ear that helps maintain balance and coordinate movements

sensory receptor a specialized structure that contains the ends of sensory neurons and that responds to specific types of stimuli

taste bud one of many oval concentrations of sensory nerve endings on the tongue, palate, and pharynx

1. **Identify** What do sensory receptors do?

2. **Describe** Where are photoreceptors located?

3. **Apply Concepts** A person is born without chemoreceptors. Which two senses will the person not have?

4. **Identify** Name three functions of mechanoreceptors.

5. **Explain** How can thermoreceptors help the body maintain homeostasis?

6. **Apply Concepts** Why may being hit on the back of the head cause blindness?

7. **Describe** Explain what must happen in order for you to see a candle.

Name ______________________ Class ______________ Date ______________

CHAPTER 38 Nervous System

SECTION 4

Nervous System Dysfunction

KEY IDEAS

As you read this section, keep these questions in mind:
- Why are psychoactive drugs dangerous?
- What neural changes cause drug addiction?
- How can the nervous system be damaged?

READING TOOLBOX

Ask Questions As you read this section, write down questions you have about the material. When you finish reading, discuss your questions with a partner. Together, try to figure out the answers to your questions.

What Are Psychoactive Drugs?

The nervous system interacts with all other systems of the body. As a result, damage to the nervous system can affect these other systems.

One way that damage to the nervous system can occur is through the use of psychoactive drugs. A **psychoactive drug** changes how the central nervous system functions. Psychoactive drugs are dangerous because they can harm the body and cause addiction. There are several kinds of psychoactive drugs, as shown below.

LOOKING CLOSER

1. Describe What do stimulants do?

____

____

____

Type of drug	Effects	Examples
Depressants	decrease the activity of the central nervous system; can cause brain damage, coma, or death	sedatives (such as sleeping pills), alcohol
Stimulants	increase the activity of the central nervous system; can cause high blood pressure, brain damage, heart attack, or death	cocaine, nicotine, amphetamines
Inhalants	cause confusion; can damage the brain, liver, kidneys, or lungs; can cause death	nitrous oxide, ether, glues, paint thinners
Hallucinogens	cause hallucinations; can cause depression, anxiety, or dangerous behavior	LSD, PCP, Ecstasy (MDMA)
THC	can cause short-term memory loss, poor judgment, and loss of motivation	marijuana, hashish
Narcotics	highly addictive; can cause drowsiness, numbness, coma, or death	heroin, morphine, codeine, opium

Talk About It

Review and Discuss In a small group, review the effects of different kinds of psychoactive drugs. Discuss why each may be harmful. What other effects may these drugs have?

What Causes Drug Addiction?

Many psychoactive drugs produce pleasant feelings. A person may use a drug to produce these feelings. Over time, the person's nervous system may become *dependent* on, or used to, a certain amount of the drug. Then, the person must use larger amounts of the drug to produce the same pleasant feelings. **Tolerance** occurs when larger and larger amounts of a drug are needed to produce the same effect. ☑

A person who is dependent on a drug is said to be addicted to the drug. **Addiction** is a psychological or physical dependence on a drug. Addiction occurs when repeated use of a drug changes how neurons function. When the drug is not present in the body, the altered neurons cannot function properly. This causes **withdrawal**, which produces negative physical and emotional symptoms.

READING CHECK

2. Identify What causes tolerance?

____

____

____

____

What Are Some Common Nervous System Disorders?

In addition to psychoactive drugs, diseases and injuries can damage the nervous system. The table below describes some common causes of nervous system damage.

Condition	Description
Meningitis	• inflammation of the membranes surrounding the brain and spinal cord • most cases caused by bacteria or viruses • causes severe fever, stiff neck, and headache • bacterial form is fatal in 40% of cases, but can be prevented with a vaccine
Multiple sclerosis	• destruction of the insulating material around axons in the central nervous system • exact cause unknown, but thought to be mainly genetic • causes weakness, fatigue, and problems with balance, coordination, and thought processes
Injury	• physical damage to the brain or spinal cord • most caused by automobile accidents or sports injuries • can cause permanent paralysis, seizures, loss of coordination, blindness, or headache • most can be prevented by wearing safety helmets or car seat belts

Critical Thinking

3. Infer Meningitis spreads more easily in crowded areas, such as dormitories and cafeterias, than in less crowded areas. What do you think is the reason for this?

____

____

____

____

____

Name ________________________ Class ________________ Date ____________

Section 4 Review

SECTION VOCABULARY

addiction a physiological or psychological dependence on a substance, such as alcohol or drugs

depressant a drug that reduces functional activity and produces muscular relaxation

psychoactive drug a substance that has a significant effect on the mind or on behavior

stimulant a drug that increases the activity of the body or the activity of some part of the body

tolerance the condition of drug addiction in which greater amounts of a drug are needed to achieve the desired effect

withdrawal the set of symptoms associated with the removal of an addictive drug from the body

1. Explain Why are psychoactive drugs dangerous?

____

____

2. Identify Name four kinds of psychoactive drugs.

____

____

____

____

3. Describe What causes drug addiction?

____

____

____

4. Explain What causes withdrawal?

____

____

____

5. Identify What are the two most common causes of injuries that damage the nervous system?

____

____

6. Explain How can you prevent most injuries to the nervous system?

____

____

Name ________________________ Class ______________ Date ______________

CHAPTER 39 Endocrine System

SECTION 1

Hormones

KEY IDEAS

As you read this section, keep these questions in mind:

- What are the major functions of the endocrine system?
- Which structures produce and release hormones?
- Which cells can be affected by hormones?
- What are two ways that hormones cause changes inside a cell?
- How are hormone levels in the blood regulated?

What Is the Endocrine System?

Like the nervous system, the endocrine system helps to regulate and control other systems in your body. Remember that signals from the nervous system travel along neurons. They move very quickly. In contrast, signals from the endocrine system travel more slowly. In general, endocrine signals travel in the form of chemicals in the blood. They control changes that happen in the body over relatively long periods of time. ☑

READING TOOLBOX

Summarize As you read this section, underline the main ideas. When you finish reading, write an outline of the section using the ideas you underlined.

READING CHECK

1. Compare Give two differences between endocrine signals and signals from the nervous system.

____

____

____

____

The endocrine system has four main functions:

- regulate metabolism
- maintain salt, water, and nutrient balance in the blood
- control the body's responses to stress
- regulate growth, development, and reproduction

What Carries Endocrine Signals?

Hormones carry most signals from the endocrine system. **Hormones** are substances produced in one part of the body that cause changes in another part of the body. These changes generally help the body maintain homeostasis.

Background

Recall that *homeostasis* is the consistent internal conditions that your body maintains.

As these bicyclists sweat, they lose water and salt. In response, their endocrine systems produce hormones that help their bodies retain water and salt. This helps them maintain homeostasis.

LOOKING CLOSER

2. Explain How does the endocrine system help maintain homeostasis when a person sweats?

____

____

____

Where Are Hormones Made?

Not all cells can make hormones. Only cells that are part of endocrine glands or endocrine tissues can produce and *secrete*, or give off, hormones.

A *gland* is a structure that secretes hormones or other substances. There are two main kinds of glands: endocrine glands and exocrine glands. **Endocrine glands** release hormones directly into the blood or the fluid around cells. The main functions of endocrine glands are to produce and secrete hormones. The figure below shows the main endocrine glands. ☑

3. Identify What are the main functions of endocrine glands?

____

____

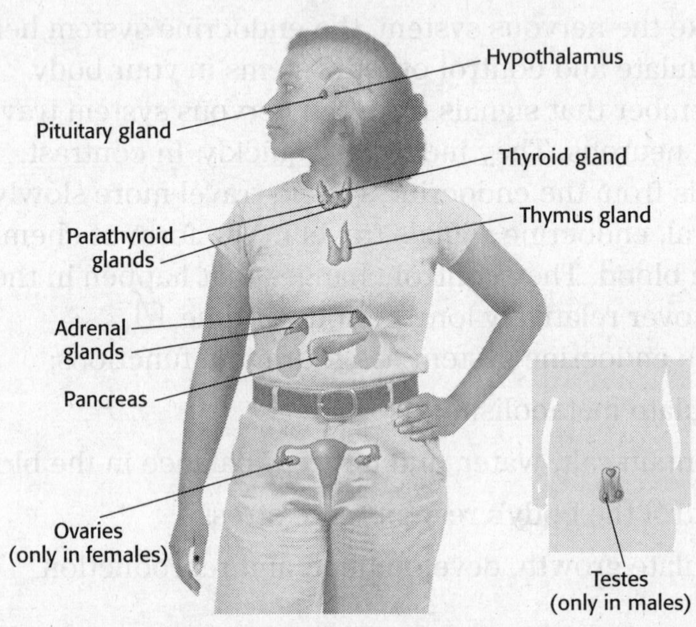

There are many endocrine glands in the human body. The hormones that endocrine glands secrete have many different functions.

LOOKING CLOSER

4. List Name four endocrine glands that are found in both males and females.

____

____

____

____

Exocrine glands do not produce or secrete hormones. They secrete nonhormonal substances, such as enzymes, through tubelike structures called *ducts*. Unlike exocrine glands, endocrine glands do not have ducts.

Some organs are both endocrine glands and exocrine glands. For example, the pancreas acts as an exocrine gland when it secretes digestive enzymes to the small intestine. However, the pancreas acts as an endocrine gland when it secretes hormones into the bloodstream.

Some organs, such as the brain, stomach, kidneys, and liver, contain cells that release hormones. These organs are not considered endocrine glands because their main function is not to secrete hormones. The cells in these organs that secrete hormones are called *endocrine tissues*.

Critical Thinking

5. Compare Give two differences between endocrine glands and exocrine glands.

____

____

____

____

____

How Do Hormones Affect Cells?

Recall that hormones travel through the bloodstream. As a result, they come into contact with most cells of the body. However, a hormone affects only certain cells. The cells that are affected by a hormone are called **target cells**.

Target cells have specific *receptor proteins* that recognize and bind to a specific hormone. These receptor proteins can be on the cell membrane or inside the cell.

There are two main types of hormones: amino-based hormones and cholesterol-based hormones. Amino-based hormones cannot pass through cell membranes. Cholesterol-based hormones can. Because of this difference, the two types of hormones affect cells in different ways.

Type of hormone	How it works
Amino-based hormones	Amino-based hormones bind to receptor proteins on the surfaces of target cells. The proteins then cause enzymes inside the cell to produce molecules called **second messengers**. Second messengers activate other enzymes within the cell.
Cholesterol-based hormones	Cholesterol-based hormones bind to receptor proteins inside target cells. When the hormone is bound to the receptor protein, it can directly activate or inactivate genes.

Amino-based hormones and cholesterol-based hormones can produce the same effect through different processes. For example, *glucagon* is an amino-based hormone. *Cortisol* is a cholesterol-based hormone. Both hormones can increase the amount of glucose in the bloodstream. However, they produce this effect in different ways.

Glucagon, like most amino-based hormones, binds to proteins on the outsides of target cells. The protein activates an enzyme, which produces a second messenger called *cAMP*. The cAMP molecules activate other enzymes, which break a compound called *glycogen* down into glucose. The glucose is then released into the blood.

In contrast, cortisol passes through cell membranes and binds to receptor proteins inside target cells. The proteins then activate genes. The genes produce proteins that break down fats and proteins into glucose. The glucose is then released into the blood.

LOOKING CLOSER

6. Compare How is the location of receptor proteins that bind to amino-based hormones different from that of receptor proteins that bind to cholesterol-based hormones?

____

____

____

____

Talk About It

Summarize After you read this page, make a diagram showing the similarities and differences between glucagon and cortisol. Share your diagram with a small group. Explain how your diagram describes the two hormones.

What Controls the Production of Hormones?

The body has to have a way of controlling how much of a hormone is in the blood at a given time. For example, imagine what would happen if the amount of glucagon or cortisol in the blood never changed. The body would keep producing glucose. Eventually, the amount of glucose in the blood would get too high, and the person would die.

The body uses feedback mechanisms and antagonistic hormones to control hormone levels in the blood. In a **feedback mechanism**, one step in a series of events controls a previous step in the series. **Antagonistic hormones** are pairs of hormones that have opposite effects on the body. ☑

7. Identify What are two ways the body controls hormone levels?

____

____

FEEDBACK MECHANISMS

There are two main kinds of feedback mechanisms in the body: positive feedback and negative feedback. Most hormone systems in the body use negative feedback.

Type of feedback	Description	Example
Positive	A change in the body causes more change in the same direction.	A hormone controls the release of eggs in women. A small amount of the hormone causes more of the hormone to be made, until an egg is released.
Negative	A change in the body prevents more change in the same direction.	The thyroid gland produces several hormones. The presence of these hormones in the blood causes the thyroid to stop making and releasing them.

Talk About It

Apply Concepts In a small group, brainstorm examples of positive and negative feedback that you may see in everyday life. For example, a thermostat that controls the temperature of a room is an example of a negative feedback mechanism. Share your examples with the rest of the class. Explain why each is an example of a feedback mechanism.

ANTAGONISTIC HORMONES

Antagonistic hormones work in pairs to control body systems. For example, remember that glucagon causes the amount of glucose in the blood to increase. A hormone called *insulin* is an antagonistic hormone to glucagon. Insulin causes the amount of glucose in the blood to decrease.

These two hormones act to control the level of glucose in the blood. When glucose levels are high, the body secretes insulin, which lowers glucose levels. When glucose levels are low, the body secretes glucagon, which increases glucose levels.

Critical Thinking

8. Explain Why are insulin and glucagon antagonistic hormones?

____

____

Name ______________________ Class ______________ Date ______________

Section 1 Review

SECTION VOCABULARY

antagonistic hormone a hormone that counteracts the effect of another hormone

endocrine gland a ductless gland that secretes hormones into the blood

feedback mechanism a cycle of events in which information from one step controls or affects a previous step

hormone a substance that is made in one cell or tissue and that causes a change in another cell or tissue located in a different part of the body

second messenger a molecule that is generated when a specific substance attaches to a receptor on the outside of a cell membrane, which produces a change in cellular function

target cell a specific cell to which a hormone is directed to produce a specific effect

1. Identify What are the four major functions of the endocrine system?

____

____

____

____

2. Describe Which cells can produce and secrete hormones?

____

3. Explain Hormones move in the blood, so they come into contact with many different cells. Why don't they affect every cell they come into contact with?

____

____

4. Describe Fill in the blank spaces in the flowchart below to describe how amino-based hormones affect cells.

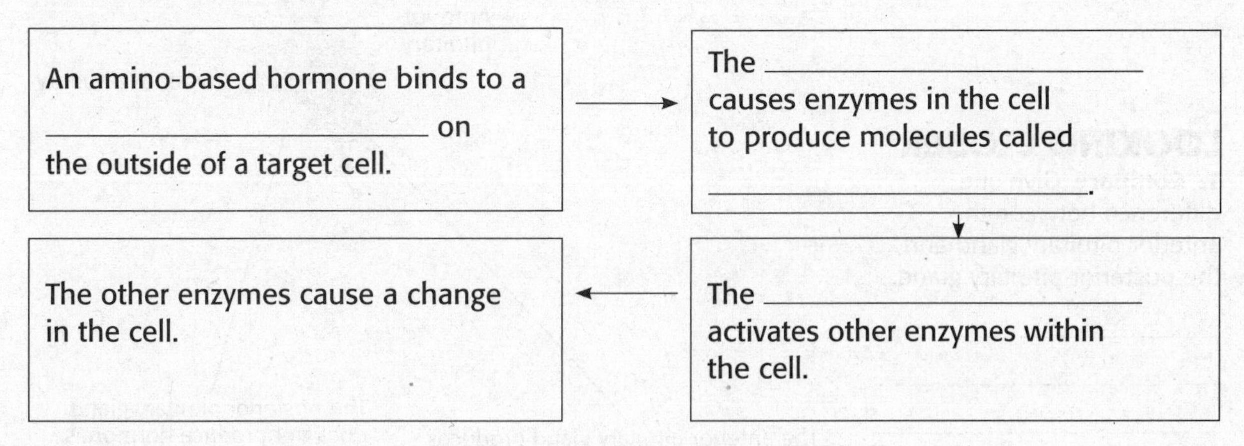

5. Compare How is positive feedback different from negative feedback?

____

____

Name ______________________ Class ______________ Date ____________

CHAPTER 39 Endocrine System

SECTION 2

Major Endocrine Glands

KEY IDEAS

As you read this section, keep these questions in mind:
- Which two glands control the endocrine system?
- Which glands regulate metabolism?
- How is the adrenal gland involved in responding to stress?
- Which glands and hormones regulate reproduction?

READING TOOLBOX

Define As you read this section, underline words you don't know. When you figure out what the words mean, write the words and their definitions in your notebook.

What Controls the Endocrine System?

Remember that endocrine glands produce and secrete hormones. Two of these glands—the hypothalamus and the pituitary gland—work with the nervous system to control the endocrine system. Both the hypothalamus and the pituitary gland are located in the brain.

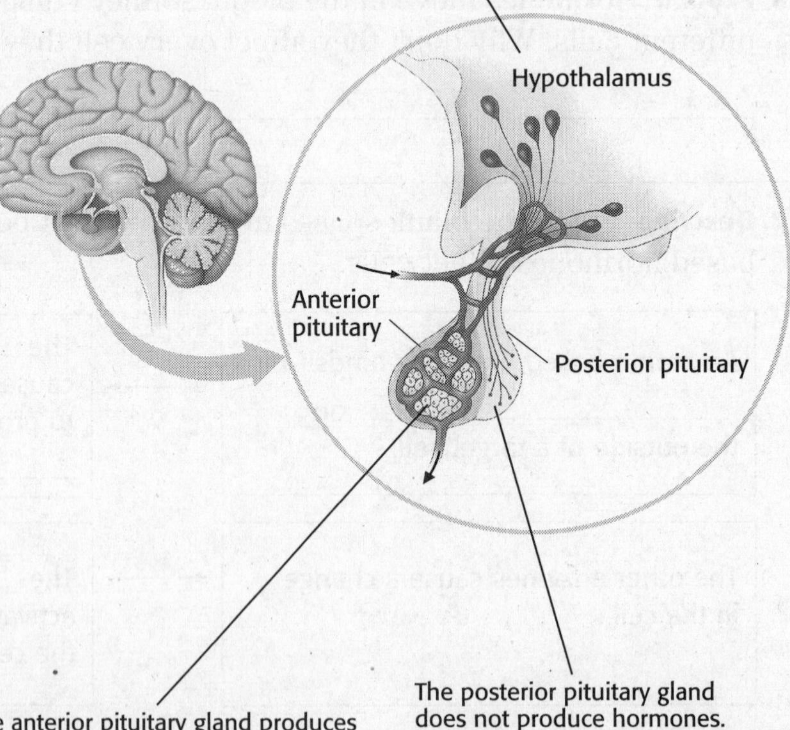

The hypothalamus affects both the nervous system and the endocrine system. It controls feelings of hunger and thirst. It also produces hormones that affect the pituitary gland and other parts of the body.

The anterior pituitary gland produces several important hormones. Some of them, called *tropins*, control hormone production in other glands. The others affect body processes, such as cell growth and division.

The posterior pituitary gland does not produce hormones. However, it does store and release hormones that are made by the hypothalamus. These hormones affect other parts of the body, such as the kidneys.

LOOKING CLOSER

1. Compare Give one difference between the anterior pituitary gland and the posterior pituitary gland.

____

____

____

____

____

____

Which Glands Regulate Metabolism?

Remember that *metabolism* is all of the chemical reactions that occur in the body. The thyroid gland, parathyroid glands, pancreas, and pineal gland control metabolism. Each has a different function.

Gland	Location	Role
Thyroid	throat	produces hormones that control metabolic rate, protein production, growth, development, and reproduction
Parathyroid glands	throat, below the thyroid	produce a hormone that increases the amount of calcium in the blood
Pancreas	abdomen	produces hormones that control the level of sugar in the blood
Pineal gland	brain	produces the hormone that controls the sleep cycle

Critical Thinking

2. Infer A person has Type I diabetes. His body cannot control the amount of sugar in his blood. Which gland do you think Type I diabetes affects? Explain your answer.

____

____

____

____

How Does the Endocrine System Respond to Stress?

Think about how you feel when someone scares you. Your heart beats faster. You may breathe harder. Your hands may start to sweat or shake. These are all reactions to stress. Two glands above your kidneys, the *adrenal glands*, control responses like these. ☑

Each adrenal gland has two parts: the adrenal medulla and the adrenal cortex. The *adrenal medulla* controls short-term responses to stress, which generally occur quickly and do not last very long. The *adrenal cortex* controls long-term responses to stress, which generally happen slowly and last a longer time.

3. Identify Which glands control the body's responses to stress?

____

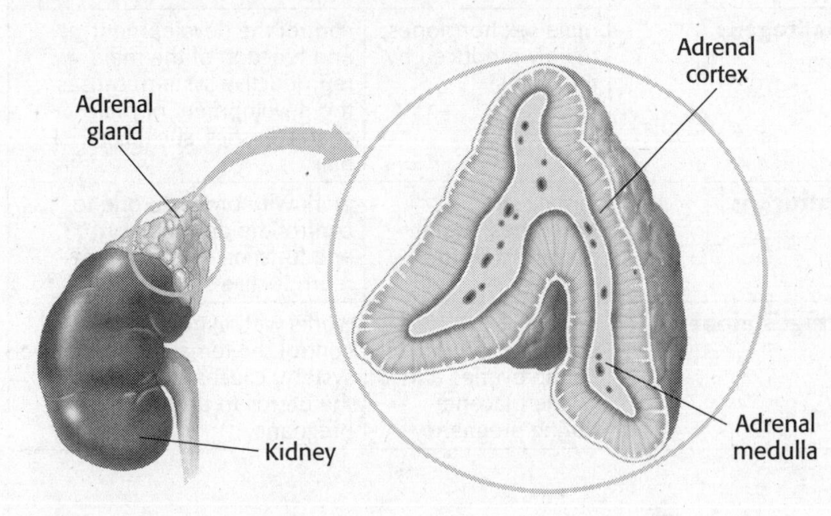

LOOKING CLOSER

4. Label On the figure, label the functions of the adrenal cortex and the adrenal medulla.

HORMONES PRODUCED BY ADRENAL GLANDS

The adrenal medulla produces epinephrine and norepinephrine. **Epinephrine** increases heart rate and blood flow to the muscles and brain. It also causes the liver to produce more glucose so that the muscles have more energy available. **Norepinephrine** increases blood pressure to make sure muscles get enough oxygen and nutrients. This results in the "fight-or-flight" response humans feel when they are under sudden stress. ☑

5. Describe What does epinephrine do?

____

____

____

The adrenal cortex produces several different hormones called *corticosteroids*. These hormones increase blood pressure and glucose levels. This helps a person's body respond to severe or long-term stress. However, if the stress lasts too long, corticosteroids can make the person more likely to get sick.

What Hormones Control Reproduction?

There are two main types of hormones that control reproduction: gonadotropins and sex hormones. *Gonadotropins* are produced by the pituitary gland. They control the functions of the *gonads*—the ovaries and the testes. They cause the gonads to mature during puberty. They also cause the gonads to produce sperm and egg cells.

Sex hormones are produced by the gonads. There are three types of sex hormones: androgens, estrogens, and progesterone.

Critical Thinking

6. Compare Give one similarity and one difference between gonadotropins and sex hormones.

____

____

____

____

____

Type of hormone	Description	Effects
Androgens	male sex hormones; mainly produced by the testes	control the development and function of the male reproductive system; causes the development of male characteristics, such as facial hair
Estrogens	female sex hormones; mainly produced by the ovaries	work with progesterone to control the development and function of the female reproductive system
Progesterone	female sex hormone; produced by the ovaries and by the placenta during pregnancy	works with estrogens to control the female reproductive system; causes changes in the uterus to prepare it for pregnancy

Name ______________________ Class ____________ Date ____________

Section 2 Review

SECTION VOCABULARY

androgen a type of hormone that regulates the sexual development of males and that stimulates development of secondary sex characteristics in males

epinephrine a hormone that is released by the adrenal medulla and that rapidly stimulates the metabolism in emergencies, decreases insulin secretion, and stimulates pulse and blood pressure; also called *adrenaline*

estrogen a hormone that regulates the sexual development and reproductive function of females

norepinephrine a chemical that is both a neurotransmitter produced by the sympathetic nerve endings in the autonomic nervous system and a hormone secreted by the adrenal medulla to stimulate the functions of the circulatory and respiratory systems (abbreviation, NE)

progesterone a steroid hormone that is secreted by the corpus luteum of the ovary, that stimulates changes in the uterus to prepare for the implantation of a fertilized egg, and that is produced by the placenta during pregnancy

1. Identify Which two glands control the endocrine system?

____

____

2. Describe What are four functions of the thyroid gland?

____

____

____

____

3. Compare Give one similarity and one difference between epinephrine and norepinephrine.

____

____

____

4. Explain How can corticosteroids be both helpful and harmful to a person?

____

____

____

5. Describe What do androgens do?

____

____

Name ______________________ Class ______________ Date ______________

CHAPTER 40 Reproduction and Development

SECTION 1

The Male Reproductive System

KEY IDEAS

As you read this section, keep these questions in mind:

- Where are male gametes produced?
- What path do sperm take to exit the body?
- What occurs as sperm move into the urethra?
- What happens to sperm after they exit the body?

READING TOOLBOX

Outline As you read, make an outline of this section. Use the header questions to help you organize the main ideas in your outline.

How Are Sperm Produced?

Reproductive organs called **testes** produce *sperm*, the male gametes. They also make the hormone testosterone. Two testes (singular, *testis*) are located inside a *scrotum*, a sac that hangs outside the body. The inside of the scrotum is about 3°C cooler than normal body temperature. This cooler temperature is ideal for sperm production. ☑

READING CHECK

1. Explain Why does the scrotum hang outside the body?

____

____

____

Sperm are produced through meiosis in tightly coiled tubes within the testes called **seminiferous tubules**. These sperm cannot yet fertilize an egg. They mature in the epididymis. The **epididymis** is a long, coiled tube attached to each testis. Mature sperm are stored in the epididymis.

STRUCTURE OF MATURE SPERM

As shown below, a mature sperm consists of a head, a midpiece, and a long tail. Enzymes in the head enable a sperm to penetrate an egg. Mitochondria in the midpiece power movement of the tail and enable sperm to swim.

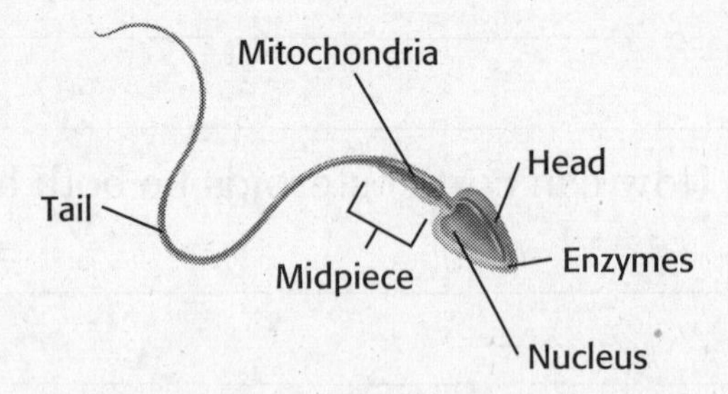

What Path Do Sperm Take to Exit the Body?

Sperm travel from the epididymis to another long tube called the **vas deferens**. The vas deferens leads to the urethra. As shown in the diagram on the next page, sperm exit the body through the *urethra*, which passes through the penis. Urine also exits the body through the urethra. ☑

READING CHECK

2. Identify What two tubes does the vas deferens connect?

____

____

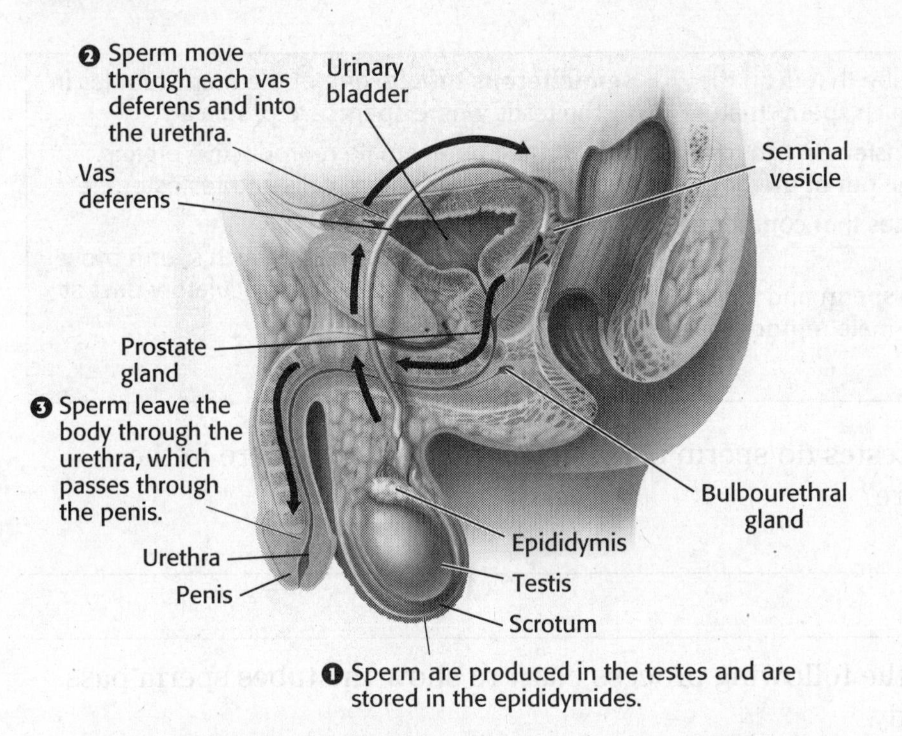

The arrows show the path that sperm take to exit the body. Both urine and sperm exit the body through the urethra. A valve prevents urine from entering the urethra when sperm are in it.

LOOKING CLOSER

3. Identify What organ does the urethra pass through?

____

What Happens to Sperm in the Urethra?

As sperm move into the urethra, they mix with fluids secreted by the seminal vesicles, the prostate gland, and the bulbourethral glands. These glands are shown above.

The *seminal vesicles* produce a fluid rich in sugars that the sperm use for energy. The **prostate gland** secretes an alkaline fluid that helps to balance the acidic pH in the female reproductive tract. Fluid from the *bulbourethral glands* lubricates the path as sperm leave the body. The mixture of these fluids and sperm is called **semen**.

Critical Thinking

4. Infer What would happen to sperm without fluid from the seminal vesicles?

____

____

What Happens to Sperm in the Female Reproductive System?

The **penis** is the male organ that deposits sperm into the female reproductive system. During sexual arousal, blood flows to the penis and makes it erect. Muscles around the vas deferens then move sperm into the urethra. The movement of semen out of the penis is called *ejaculation*.

After semen is deposited in the female reproductive system, sperm swim until they reach an egg or until they die. About 300–400 million sperm are present in an ejaculation. Many of these sperm die in the acidic environment of the female reproductive system before they reach an egg.

Critical Thinking

5. Apply Concepts Why are there so many sperm in an ejaculation?

____

____

____

Name ______________ Class ______________ Date ______________

Section 1 Review

SECTION VOCABULARY

epididymis the long, coiled tube that is on the surface of a testis and in which sperm mature

penis the male organ that transfers sperm to a female and that carries urine out of the body

prostate gland a gland in males that contributes to the seminal fluid

semen the fluid that contains sperm and various secretions produced by the male reproductive organs

seminiferous tubule one of the many tubules in the testis where sperm are produced

testes the primary male reproductive organs, which produce sperm cells and testosterone (singular, *testis*)

vas deferens a duct through which sperm move from the epididymis to the ejaculatory duct at the base of the penis

1. **Identify** Where in the testes do sperm begin development, and where in the scrotum do they mature?

____

____

2. **Summarize** Complete the following process chart to show the tubes sperm pass through to exit the body.

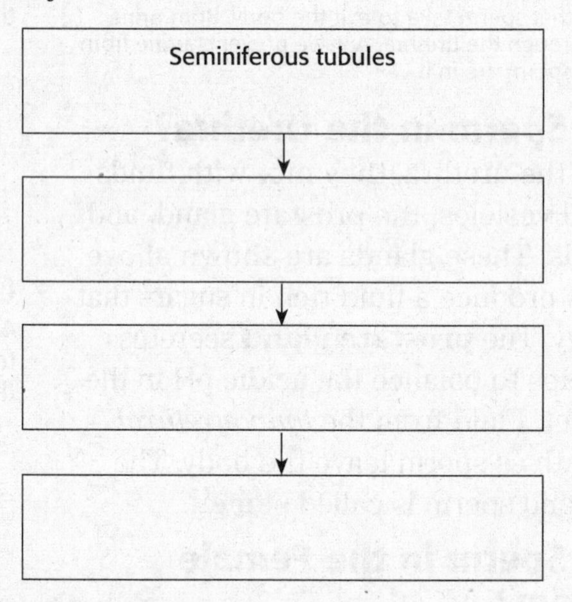

3. **Describe** What are two functions of the fluids in semen?

____

____

____

4. **Explain** What happens to sperm that are deposited in the female reproductive system?

____

____

Name ______________________ Class ______________ Date ______________

CHAPTER 40 Reproduction and Development

SECTION 2

The Female Reproductive System

KEY IDEAS

As you read this section, keep these questions in mind:

- What are the functions of the ovaries?
- How does the female body prepare for pregnancy?
- What changes occur in the female's body when an ovum is not fertilized?

How Are Eggs Produced?

Female gametes, or egg cells, are produced in organs called **ovaries**. Two ovaries are found within a female's abdomen. Before a female baby is born, her ovaries begin to produce egg cells by meiosis. However, these egg cells do not complete meiosis until the female reaches puberty.

The ovaries also produce the female sex hormones, estrogen and progesterone. The level of these hormones rises at puberty. This increase in hormones allows the egg cells to complete meiosis, or mature. However, typically only one egg cell matures inside an ovary each month. ☑

READING TOOLBOX

Summarize in Pairs Read this section quietly to yourself. Then talk about the material with a partner. Together, try to figure out the parts that you didn't understand.

READING CHECK

1. Identify What two hormones do the ovaries produce?

____

____

THE EGG'S PATH

A mature egg cell is called an **ovum** (plural, *ova*). About once a month, one of the ovaries releases an ovum. Once the ovum is released, it is swept by cilia into a **fallopian tube**. Muscular contractions in the fallopian tube move the ovum to the uterus. The **uterus** is a hollow, muscular organ. The opening at the bottom of the uterus is called the *cervix*.

Front View of the Female Reproductive System

Fallopian tube

Uterus

Ovary

Cervix

LOOKING CLOSER

2. Identify What structure does an ovum travel through from an ovary to the uterus?

____

Critical Thinking

3. Describe What path does a baby take to leave the mother's body during childbirth?

____

____

____

____

FEMALE REPRODUCTIVE SYSTEM

The external structures of the female reproductive system are called the *vulva*. The vulva includes the *labia*, which are folds of skin that cover and protect the opening of the vagina. The **vagina** is a muscular tube that leads from the vulva to the uterus.

During sexual intercourse, sperm are deposited inside the vagina. They swim through the uterus to the fallopian tubes, where they may fertilize an ovum. If fertilization occurs in a fallopian tube, the ovum travels to the uterus to develop into a baby. This process is called *pregnancy*.

LOOKING CLOSER

4. Identify What structure must sperm in the vagina travel through to reach an egg in a fallopian tube?

____

Side View of the Female Reproductive System

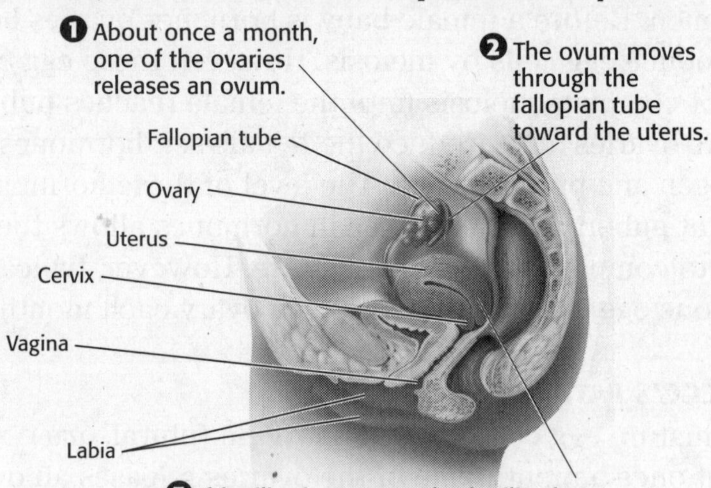

How Does the Female Body Prepare for Pregnancy?

Throughout a female's reproductive years, two cycles prepare her body for pregnancy. The ovarian cycle prepares an egg for fertilization. It includes a follicular phase, ovulation, and a luteal phase. At the same time, the **menstrual cycle** prepares the uterus for pregnancy. Both cycles are regulated by hormones and last about 28 days.

OVARIAN CYCLE–FOLLICULAR PHASE

In an ovary, egg cells mature within follicles. A *follicle* is a cluster of cells that surround and nourish an immature egg. The egg begins to mature inside the follicle in response to follicle-stimulating hormone (FSH) from the pituitary gland in the brain. As the level of FSH rises, the ovary begins to secrete estrogen. Estrogen aids in the growth of the follicle and causes the egg cell to mature into an ovum. ☑

5. Describe What is a follicle?

____

____

____

OVARIAN CYCLE–OVULATION

The release of an ovum from an ovary is called **ovulation**. During ovulation, the ovum bursts out of the follicle and is swept into a fallopian tube. Ovulation occurs about halfway through the ovarian cycle.

OVARIAN CYCLE–LUTEAL PHASE

After ovulation, luteinizing hormone from the pituitary gland causes the cells of the ruptured follicle to grow. The cells fill the empty follicle and form a structure called the *corpus luteum*. The corpus luteum secretes estrogen and progesterone. ☑

The luteal phase lasts about 14 days. If the egg has been fertilized in the fallopian tube, it will embed in the uterus. A high level of progesterone will prevent another egg from maturing within a follicle.

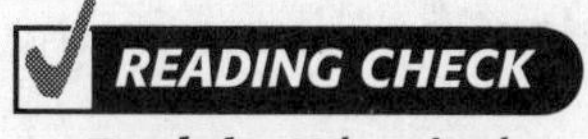

6. Explain What is the function of the corpus luteum?

____

____

MENSTRUAL CYCLE

The menstrual cycle is driven by the changes in estrogen and progesterone during the ovarian cycle. Before ovulation, increasing levels of estrogen cause the lining of the uterus to thicken with blood vessels. This prepares the uterus to receive and nourish a fertilized ovum. High levels of both estrogen and progesterone maintain the lining of the uterus during pregnancy.

If pregnancy does not occur, the levels of estrogen and progesterone drop. This decrease causes the lining of the uterus to be shed in a process called **menstruation**. Menstruation usually begins about 14 days after ovulation.

Critical Thinking

7. Infer Why doesn't a pregnant woman experience menstruation?

____

____

____

____

Ovarian and Menstrual Cycles

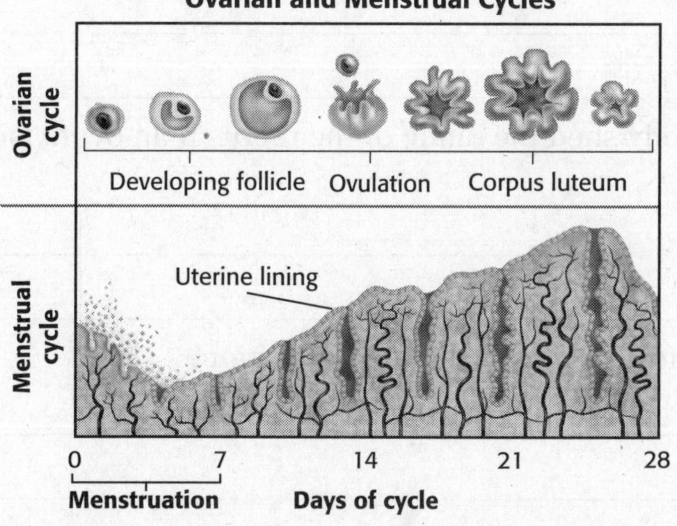

8. Describe What happens to the lining of the uterus after menstruation?

____

Name ______________________ Class ______________ Date ______________

Section 2 Review

SECTION VOCABULARY

fallopian tube a tube through which eggs move from the ovary to the uterus

menstrual cycle the female reproductive cycle, characterized by a monthly change of the lining of the uterus and the discharge of blood

menstruation the discharge of blood and discarded tissue from the uterus during the menstrual cycle

ovary in the female reproductive system of animals, an organ that produces eggs

ovulation the release of an ovum from a follicle of the ovary

ovum a mature egg cell

uterus in female placental mammals, the hollow, muscular organ in which an embryo embeds itself and develops into a fetus

vagina the female reproductive organ that connects the outside of the body to the uterus and that receives sperm during reproduction

1. Identify Where in the female reproductive system are egg cells produced?

____

2. Calculate Women are born with about 2 million immature eggs in their ovaries. Throughout a woman's lifetime only about 400 of these eggs will mature. Approximately what percent of a woman's eggs will mature in her lifetime?

3. Describe What happens to an egg cell during ovulation?

____

____

4. Identify What hormone causes an egg to begin to develop inside a follicle?

____

5. Explain What does estrogen released during the follicular phase of the ovarian cycle do to the lining of the uterus?

____

____

6. Explain Why does the female body shed the lining of the uterus if an ovum is not fertilized?

____

____

7. Identify What change in hormone levels brings on menstruation?

____

____

Name ________________ Class ____________ Date __________

CHAPTER 40 Reproduction and Development

SECTION 3

Human Development

KEY IDEAS

As you read this section, keep these questions in mind:
- How does fertilization occur?
- What important events occur in the first trimester of pregnancy?
- What important event occurs at the end of the third trimester of pregnancy?

How Does Fertilization Occur?

If sperm are present in a fallopian tube after ovulation, fertilization may occur. During fertilization, the sperm's head releases enzymes that break down the jelly-like layers around an ovum. The head of the sperm then enters the ovum. The nuclei of the sperm and ovum fuse together. This produces a diploid cell called a *zygote*.

On the way to the uterus in a fallopian tube, the zygote undergoes a series of mitotic divisions, called *cleavage*. The first cleavage produces two small cells. These cells divide to produce four cells, then eight cells, and so on. The clump of cells that results is called an **embryo**. ☑

By the time the embryo reaches the uterus, it is a hollow ball of cells called a *blastocyst*. The blastocyst embeds itself into the thickened lining of the uterus in an event called **implantation**.

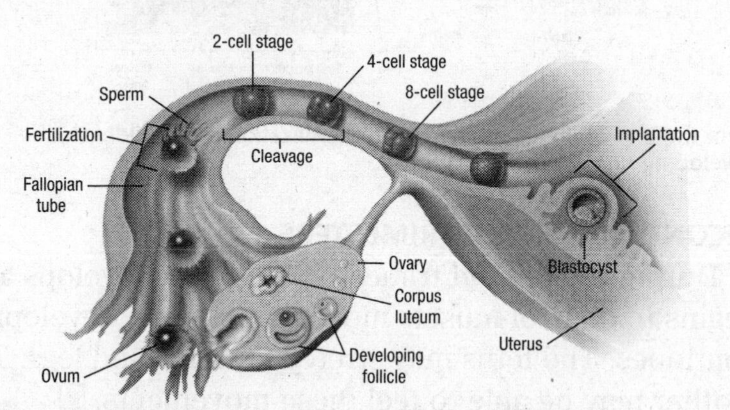

Fertilization, cleavage, and implantation may occur after ovulation.

What Happens During Pregnancy?

Human development takes about nine months. This time period is called *gestation*, or pregnancy. The nine months are usually divided into three-month periods called *trimesters*.

Organize As you read this section, make a three-column table that summarizes the major events during each trimester of pregnancy.

Background

Recall that a *diploid* human cell contains two haploid sets of 23 chromosomes, for a total of 46 chromosomes.

1. Explain What is cleavage and what does it produce?

____

____

____

2. Predict What could happen if two ova are released while sperm are in the fallopian tubes?

____

____

____

FIRST TRIMESTER

The most important events of development occur during the first trimester. During this time, all of the embryo's organ systems develop. By the end of the third week of pregnancy, the embryo's circulatory and digestive systems begin to develop. The heart begins to beat by the end of the fourth week.

Membranes that protect and feed the embryo also develop during the first trimester. A membrane called the *amnion* encloses and protects the embryo. Another membrane called the *chorion* interacts with the uterus to form the placenta. The *placenta* is the structure through which the mother feeds the embryo. The *umbilical cord* connects the placenta to the embryo. ☑

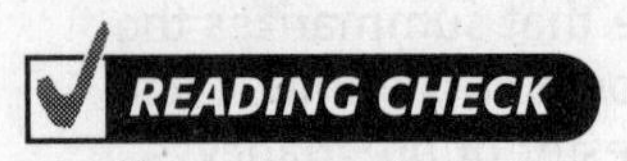

3. List Name three membranes that protect or feed the developing embryo.

____

____

____

Blood vessels in the umbilical cord transport nutrients and wastes between the mother and the embryo. The mother's blood does not mix with the embryo's blood. Instead, substances in the mother's blood pass to the embryo through the placenta. Any harmful substances in the mother's blood can damage the developing embryo.

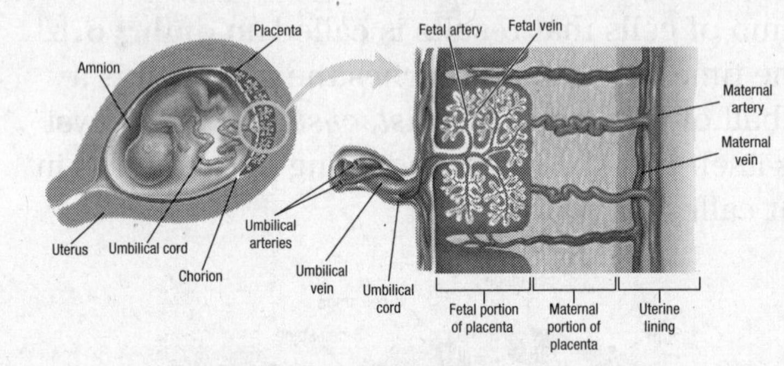

From the end of the eighth week after fertilization until childbirth, the developing human is called a **fetus**.

LOOKING CLOSER

4. Infer What must happen to the amnion before a baby is born?

____

SECOND AND THIRD TRIMESTERS

During the second trimester, the brain develops and begins to control muscle movements. Bone development continues. The fetus may stretch its arms and legs. The mother may be able to feel these movements. ☑

5. Explain Why doesn't a mother feel a baby kick before the second trimester?

____

____

____

During the third trimester, the fetus can hear, smell, and see light. Its lungs mature. It moves to position its head near the vagina. By the end of the third trimester, the fetus can live outside its mother's body. It leaves the mother's body through the vagina in a process called labor. During labor, the uterine walls contract to move the baby out.

Name ______________________ Class ____________ Date ____________

Section 3 Review

SECTION VOCABULARY

embryo in humans, a developing individual from first cleavage through the next eight weeks **fetus** a developing human from the end of the eighth week after fertilization until birth	**implantation** the process by which a blastocyst embeds itself in the lining of the uterus; occurs about six days after fertilization

1. Describe How is a sperm able to enter an ovum?

____

____

2. Identify Where does fertilization occur?

____

3. Summarize Fill in the blank spaces in the process chart to show what happens after fertilization.

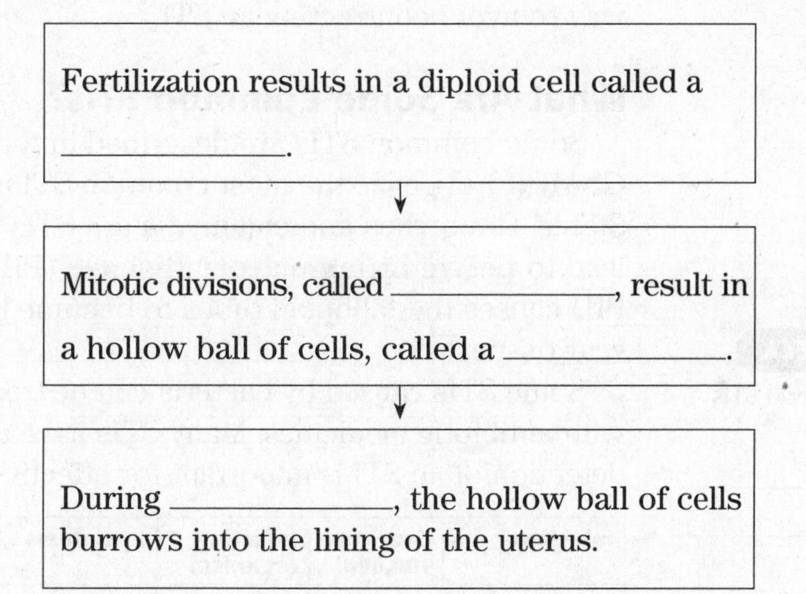

4. Identify What develops within the embryo during the first trimester of pregnancy?

____

5. Describe How does a mother feed an embryo during pregnancy?

____

____

____

6. Explain When does labor occur, and what happens to the uterus during labor?

____

____

Name ______________________ Class ______________ Date ______________

CHAPTER 40 Reproduction and Development

SECTION 4

Sexually Transmitted Infections

KEY IDEAS

As you read this section, keep these questions in mind:

- How can you avoid getting an STI?
- What are some common STIs in the United States?

Graph Create a bar graph to show the incidence of the common STIs per 100,000 individuals.

What Is an STI?

Disease-causing infections that are spread by sexual contact are called sexually transmitted infections (STIs). The pathogens that cause STIs include both bacteria and viruses. They can be passed from one person to another during sexual contact in body fluids, such as semen. Abstinence, or a lack of sexual contact, is the only sure way to avoid contracting an STI.

What Are Some Common STIs?

Some common STIs are described in the table below. **Genital herpes** is the most common STI in the United States. Gonorrhea and chlamydia are STIs that can lead to **pelvic inflammatory disease** (PID) in women. PID causes the fallopian tubes to become blocked with scar tissue. ☑

Some STIs caused by bacteria can be treated and cured with antibiotic medicines. Many STIs have no cure. Early detection of an STI is important for effective treatment.

READING CHECK

1. Identfiy What two STIs can lead to PID?

____

____

Infection	Cases per 100,000	Infecting organism	Symptoms
Genital herpes	22,300	virus	painful blisters around genital region; flulike symptoms
Genital HPV	6,700	virus	often no symptoms; sometimes warts on genital region
Trichomoniasis	1,700	protist	often no symptoms in males; vaginal discharge in females
Chlamydia	1,300	bacteria	painful urination in males; discharge
AIDS	350	virus	immune-system failure; infections
Gonorrhea	250	bacteria	painful urination in males; discharge
Hepatitis B	250	virus	yellowing of skin; flulike symptoms
Syphilis	25	bacteria	sore on genitals; fever and rash

LOOKING CLOSER

2. Apply Concepts Why can a person have genital HPV and not know it?

____

____

Name ______________________ Class ______________ Date ______________

Section 4 Review

SECTION VOCABULARY

genital herpes a sexually transmitted infection that is caused by a herpes simplex virus	**pelvic inflammatory disease** a sexually transmitted infection of the upper female reproductive system, including the uterus, ovaries, and fallopian tubes

1. **Describe** What is the best way to avoid being infected with an STI?

____

2. **Identify** Name four common STIs that are caused by a virus.

____

____

3. **Infer** Name three common STIs that can be treated with antibiotics.

____

____

4. **Describe** What happens to women with pelvic inflammatory disease?

____

____

5. **Calculate** If there are 22,300 cases of genital herpes in 100,000 people, what percentage of these people have the STI? Show your work.

6. **Explain** Why can a person still be at risk of contracting an STI if they have sexual contact with a person who does not have symptoms of an STI?

____

____

7. **Predict** What can happen when gonorrhea and chlamydia go untreated?

____

____

8. **Describe** What is the cause of a trichomoniasis infection, and what are the symptoms of this STI in females?

____

____

Name ______________________ Class ______________ Date ______________

CHAPTER 41 Forensic Science

SECTION 1

Introduction to Forensics

KEY IDEAS

As you read this section, keep these questions in mind:

- What are the two major duties of forensic scientists?
- What types of tools are used by forensic scientists?

READING TOOLBOX

Summarize As you read this section, underline the main ideas. When you finish reading, write a short summary of the section using the underlined ideas.

What Is Forensic Science?

Most criminals try not to leave any evidence at a crime scene. However, no matter how careful they are, criminals almost always leave some kind of evidence behind. In some cases, the evidence is very obvious, like bloodstains or footprints. In other cases, the evidence is harder to see, like hairs or fingerprints. However, whatever the evidence is, forensic scientists try to find and interpret it.

Forensic science is the use of science to investigate legal matters. People use forensic science to investigate many different things. ☑

READING CHECK

1. Define What is forensic science?

____

____

____

Forensic scientists have two main jobs: analyzing evidence and testifying in court. Forensic scientists generally want to learn two things about the evidence they analyze: what it is and whose it is. When they have learned about the evidence, they may be asked to discuss what they have learned in court.

BEYOND THE CRIME SCENE

Forensic scientists do more than just investigate crime scenes. The table below describes some other things that forensic scientists may study.

Area of study	Description
Accidents and disasters	Forensic scientists may be involved in investigating accidents and natural disasters. For example, they may help determine the cause of a plane crash. They may also help identify victims of accidents or natural disasters.
Forgeries	Some forensic scientists work to detect *forgeries*, or fakes. For example, forensic scientists may study documents, money, or passports to determine whether they are real.
Computer crimes	Today, many crimes are committed using computers and other technology. Some forensic scientists specialize in studying such computer crimes. For example, they may work to stop criminals from spreading computer viruses.

LOOKING CLOSER

2. Explain What may forensic scientists help with after a natural disaster?

____

____

What Tools Do Forensic Scientists Use?

Forensic scientists rely on many tools to help them analyze evidence. One of the most important tools of forensic science is a good education. Forensic scientists must have college degrees in either forensic science, chemistry, biology, or another related field. Because they may testify in court, forensic scientists must also have good communication skills.

In addition to education and communication skills, forensic scientists use many other tools. These tools include chemistry, chromatographs, spectrometers, microscopes, and computers.

Forensic scientists may use special chemicals to help them identify evidence. For example, some chemicals make blood, gunpowder, or fingerprints glow under special lights. Forensic scientists may also use chemistry to identify drugs, poisons, and explosives.

Forensic scientists may use devices such as chromatographs and spectrometers to identify chemicals. A **chromatograph** is a device that separates chemicals based on their physical properties, such as boiling point. A **spectrometer** records how a substance interacts with different kinds of light.

In many cases, the evidence left at a crime scene is very tiny. Therefore, forensic scientists often use microscopes to examine evidence.

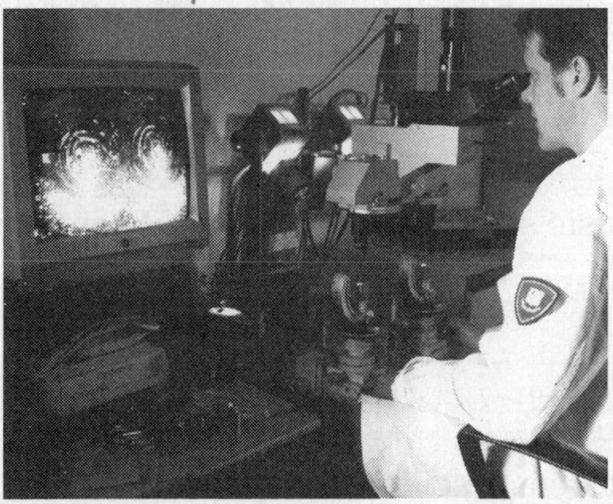

This forensic scientist is using a microscope to study the marks on two bullets.

One of the most important tools that forensic scientists use today is the computer. Computers control many other devices, such as spectrometers. They also help forensic scientists store, compare, and share data.

Talk About It

Discuss Aside from those listed here, what are some other fields that a person might study in order to become a forensic scientist? Think of two or three other fields. Then, explain your choices to a small group.

Critical Thinking

3. Compare What is the difference between a chromatograph and a spectrometer?

____

____

____

____

____

LOOKING CLOSER

4. Explain Why are microscopes important tools for many forensic scientists?

____

____

____

Name ______________________ Class ______________ Date ______________

Section 1 Review

SECTION VOCABULARY

chromatograph an instrument that separates components of a chemical mixture based on physical properties as the mixture flows through a stationary medium	**forensic science** the application of scientific knowledge to questions of civil and criminal law **spectrometer** an instrument that measures wavelengths and intensity of visible light or other electromagnetic radiation

1. Identify A forensic scientist is studying a mixture of three different chemicals. Each chemical has a different boiling point. Should the forensic scientist use a spectrometer or a chromatograph to separate the three chemicals?

____

2. Describe What are the two main jobs of forensic scientists?

____

____

3. Identify When a forensic scientist examines evidence, what two things is the scientist trying to learn?

____

____

4. List Name two things that forensic scientists may investigate besides crime scenes.

____

____

5. Explain Name two ways that computers are helpful for forensic scientists.

____

____

6. Explain Why is it important for forensic scientists to have good communication skills?

____

____

7. Describe What are two ways that a forensic scientist may use the science of chemistry?

____

____

CHAPTER 41 Forensic Science

SECTION 2

Inside a Crime Lab

KEY IDEAS

As you read this section, keep these questions in mind:
- Which two unique characteristics can be used to identify a person?
- What are the five major types of trace evidence?
- What are the duties of firearms and toolmarks specialists?
- What kinds of information do toxicologists look for?
- What does a forensic pathologist do?
- How are anthropology and entomology related to forensic science?

How Can Forensic Scientists Identify a Person?

Many forensic scientists work to identify the person or people involved in a crime. There are two characteristics that forensic scientists often use to identify people: friction ridges and DNA.

The ridges on the skin of your hands and feet are called *friction ridges*. No two people—not even identical twins—have exactly the same pattern of friction ridges on their bodies. Therefore, forensic scientists can use friction ridge patterns, such as those in fingerprints, palm prints, and footprints, to identify a person. ☑

Forensic scientists may use special chemicals or tools to make friction ridge prints more visible. Then, they analyze and identify the prints by comparing them to databases of prints from different people.

Except for identical twins, no two people have exactly the same DNA. Therefore, forensic scientists can also use a DNA profile to identify a person.

Forensic scientists can generate DNA profiles, such as this one, from tiny samples of skin or other body cells.

READING TOOLBOX

Define As you read this section, underline the words you don't know. When you figure out what they mean, write the words and their definitions in your notebook.

READING CHECK

1. Explain Why can forensic scientists use friction ridges to identify a person?

____

____

____

Talk About It

Brainstorm With a small group, try to think of four other types of trace evidence that forensic scientists could use.

What Is Trace Evidence?

Forensic scientists can use *trace evidence*—including hair, fibers, glass, paint, soil, and pollen—to link a person to a crime scene.

Type of trace evidence	Description
Hairs and fibers	Forensic scientists can identify where a hair or fiber came from by examining its color, texture, length, and composition.
Glass	If a person breaks a piece of glass, tiny pieces of the glass may stick to the person's clothing. If fragments on a suspect's clothing match glass from a crime scene, the suspect may have been at the crime scene.
Paint	Forensic scientists can use samples of paint to identify the make, model, and year of a car involved in a crime.
Soil	Soils from different places contain different materials. Forensic scientists can use the characteristics of a soil sample to determine where it came from.
Pollen	Pollen grains on clothing or other objects can indicate where a suspect or victim has been.

LOOKING CLOSER

2. Explain Why can forensic scientists use the characteristics of a soil sample to learn where it came from?

____

____

____

How Can Forensic Scientists Identify the Tools Used in a Crime?

Many crimes involve guns, tools, or other objects that leave distinctive marks. Forensic scientists may use these marks to identify the object that was used to commit a crime. For example, when a bullet is fired from a gun, the gun leaves unique marks on the bullet. *Firearms specialists* can use the marks to match a bullet from a crime scene to a bullet fired from a suspect's gun. ☑

3. Describe What is one way that forensic scientists can identify the object used to commit a crime?

____

____

Some forensic scientists deal with ballistics. **Ballistics** is the study of how bullets, missiles, and bombs move through the air and strike other objects. Ballistics experts may be able to figure out where a gun was fired from and what objects it struck.

Forensic scientists called *toolmarks specialists* study the marks left by pliers, saws, knives, or other objects. They may be able to use these marks to identify the type of tool that was used in a crime. They may also locate serial numbers or other identifying marks on an object. This can help them determine whom the object belongs to.

What Do Forensic Toxicologists Do?

Guns and knives are not the only objects that can hurt or kill people. Chemicals, such as drugs and poisons, can also be involved in crimes. **Toxicology** is the study of toxins and their effects on the body. A *toxin* is any substance that can physically harm an organism. ☑

4. Define What is toxicology?

Toxicologists may work with victims that are living or dead. For example, they may test blood or urine samples from a living patient. The results of the tests can tell the toxicologist whether the patient has taken any drugs or has been poisoned. Toxicologists may also study blood or tissue samples from dead bodies.

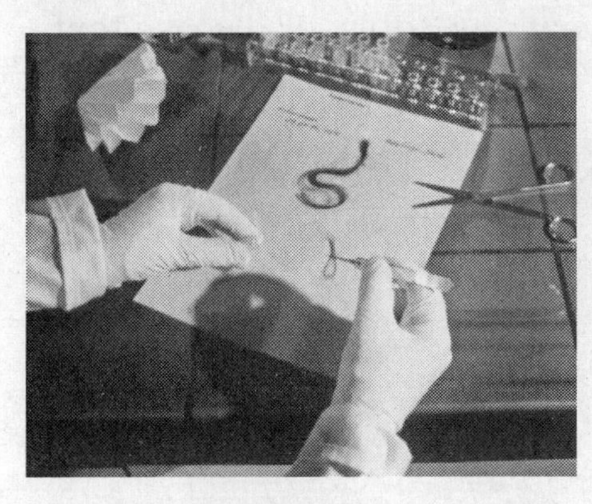

This toxicologist is studying hair samples from a victim of a crime. As hair grows, it can absorb chemicals that are in the body. These chemicals include drugs and poisons. Therefore, toxicologists can test hair samples for chemicals to learn whether drugs or poisons were present in a person's body.

LOOKING CLOSER

5. Explain Why can toxicologists use hair to determine whether a person has been using drugs?

Forensic toxicologists may help police identify substances that they suspect are illegal drugs. They may also analyze blood or urine samples to determine whether a person has been drinking alcohol.

What Is Pathology?

Pathology is the study of changes to the body that are caused by disease or injury. Forensic pathologists may perform autopsies to determine how and when a person died. An **autopsy** is an examination of a dead body. Autopsies include both external and internal examination of the body.

Critical Thinking

6. Infer What do you think is the reason that forensic pathologists look for unusual marks on a dead body?

During an autopsy, a pathologist examines the outside of the body for wounds and unusual marks, such as tattoos. The pathologist also cuts the body open to examine the internal organs. The pathologist may take samples of the organs for a toxicologist to study.

How Can Anthropology Help Forensic Scientists?

Anthropology is the study of humans and human culture. Forensic anthropologists can help identify decomposed remains of bodies. For example, a forensic anthropologist may examine the skeleton of a victim of a crime. They may be able to determine a victim's gender and approximate height and age from the skeleton. This can help police identify the victim. ☑

READING CHECK

7. Explain What are three things about a person that a forensic anthropologist can determine by examining a skeleton?

____

____

____

Some forensic anthropologists do facial reconstructions. They can model what a person's face may have looked like based on skull features. They also study bones for signs of weapons, tools, or disease that caused injury or death.

LOOKING CLOSER

8. Describe How can a forensic anthropologist help in a criminal investigation?

____

____

____

By studying this person's skull, this forensic anthropologist may be able to determine how the person died.

How Can Forensic Scientists Use Insects in Investigations?

Entomology is the study of insects. Forensic entomologists use their knowledge of insects to investigate legal issues. For example, a forensic entomologist may examine damaged buildings to determine whether insects caused the damage. They may also examine food that has been contaminated by insects.

Forensic entomologists may also help determine when a person died. After a person dies, different insects are attracted to the body. However, not all kinds of insects arrive at the body at the same time. Forensic entomologists may examine the types and ages of insects on a body. They can use this information to estimate how long the body has been dead. ☑

READING CHECK

9. Explain How can a forensic entomologist determine how long a body has been dead?

____

____

____

Name ______________________ Class ______________ Date ____________

Section 2 Review

SECTION VOCABULARY

autopsy an examination of a body after death, usually to determine the cause of death **ballistics** the science that deals with the motion and impact of projectiles	**pathology** the scientific study of disease **toxicology** the study of toxic substances, including their nature, effects, detection, methods of treatment, and exposure control

1. Identify What are two characteristics that forensic scientists can use to identify a person?

____

____

2. Describe Fill in the blank spaces in the table below.

Type of forensic scientist	What this type of scientist studies	How this type of scientist can help in a criminal investigation
Ballistics expert	studies how bullets, missiles, bombs, and other objects move through the air and strike other objects	
	studies changes in a body due to injury or disease	
Forensic toxicologist		may be able to figure out whether a person was poisoned or was using drugs or alcohol; may help police identify illegal drugs
Forensic anthropologist	studies humans, human remains, and human culture	
	studies insects	

3. Identify List five kinds of trace evidence.

____

____

____

____

Name ______________________ Class ______________ Date ______________

CHAPTER 41 Forensic Science

SECTION 3

Forensic Science in Action

KEY IDEAS

As you read this section, keep these questions in mind:

- What are the steps of an investigation at a crime scene?
- What information is used to estimate the time of death?
- What three components describe how a person was killed?
- Which two identities must be determined in a homicide investigation?

READING TOOLBOX

Summarize After you read this section, make a flowchart showing the steps that investigators follow at a crime scene.

What Happens in a Crime Scene Investigation?

When forensic scientists investigate a crime scene, they follow a set of specific rules. The rules help prevent evidence from being overlooked. They also help make sure that evidence is not altered or contaminated before it can be examined.

The first step in a crime scene investigation is to keep out people who are not supposed to be there. Investigators may put up tape, string, or fences to keep people out of the area. This is called *securing the scene.* Securing the scene prevents people from accidentally damaging or destroying evidence. ☑

READING CHECK

1. Explain Why do investigators try to keep people out of a crime scene?

____

____

Once the area has been secured, investigators begin to collect evidence. This may involve interviewing witnesses or other people nearby. The figure below shows another example of how evidence is collected.

This investigator is marking the locations of pieces of evidence using numbered tags. After the evidence is marked, a photographer will take pictures of each piece.

Critical Thinking

2. Infer What do you think is the reason that investigators record where and when each piece of evidence was found?

____

____

____

____

____

____

Investigators are careful to record exactly where and when they found every piece of evidence. Once the evidence has been identified, investigators begin to analyze it. Many pieces of evidence are analyzed in a lab, but some can be analyzed only at the crime scene.

How Can Forensic Scientists Determine the Time of Death?

Forensic scientists cannot calculate the exact time of death. However, they can make good estimates by studying the four indicators shown in the table below.

Indicator	Description
Rigor mortis	**Rigor mortis** is the process in which the muscles in the body stiffen after death. The muscles begin to stiffen within a few hours of death. After about 12 hours, the muscles are completely stiff. After about 24 hours, the muscles begin to loosen again. By about 36 hours after death, the body is completely loose.
Livor mortis	**Livor mortis**, or *lividity*, is the process in which blood settles to parts of the body that are closest to the ground. It happens because gravity pulls the blood toward the ground. This generally starts to happen within about 30 minutes after a person dies. It starts as light red patches on the lower parts of the body. After about 10 hours, the lowest parts of the body are dark purple. After this time, the lividity is *fixed*. It will not change if the body is moved.
Algor mortis	**Algor mortis** is the cooling of a body after death. Generally, a body cools by about 1.5°F per hour for the first 24 hours after death. However, many factors can affect how fast a body cools. For example, a body in a warm room will cool more slowly than a body outside on a cold day. After about 24 hours, chemical reactions within the body cause it to warm up again.
Decomposition	After about 24 hours, chemical reactions within the body cause it to start to decompose. The skin on some parts of the body, such as the abdomen, begins to turn green. After about 48 hours, enzymes that break down blood cause the blood to look black. At the same time, bacteria within the digestive system are breaking down the body and releasing gases. This causes the body to become bloated by about 72 hours after death.

How Can Forensic Scientists Describe How a Person Died?

Forensic scientists try to determine three things about a person's death: cause, mechanism, and manner. The *cause of death* is the event that started the process that resulted in the person's death. For example, a gunshot wound may be a cause of death.

LOOKING CLOSER

3. Explain Why does livor mortis happen?

______

______

4. Describe If a body has fixed lividity, how long ago did the person die?

______

______

5. Explain Why can't body temperature be used to estimate the time of death of a person who has been dead for more than 24 hours?

______

______

______

Critical Thinking

6. Compare What is the difference between the cause of death and the mechanism of death?

____

____

____

____

____

____

MECHANISM AND MANNER OF DEATH

The *mechanism of death* is the actual process that caused the person to die. It describes what happened in the body that caused it to stop functioning. For example, if the cause of death is a gunshot wound, the mechanism of death may be loss of blood.

The *manner of death* describes what the intent was behind the cause of death. Manner of death falls into one of five categories: homicide, suicide, accident, natural, or undetermined.

How Do Forensic Scientists Determine Who Was Involved in a Homicide?

A homicide investigation generally focuses on identifying the victim and the perpetrator. The *perpetrator* is the person who killed the victim. In many cases, a victim can be identified from personal items, such as a driver's license. However, sometimes forensic scientists must rely on other methods to identify a victim. For example, they may use fingerprints, DNA, or dental records to identify a victim.

LOOKING CLOSER

7. Infer Why might a forensic scientist need to make clay models to learn what a person looked like?

____

____

____

____

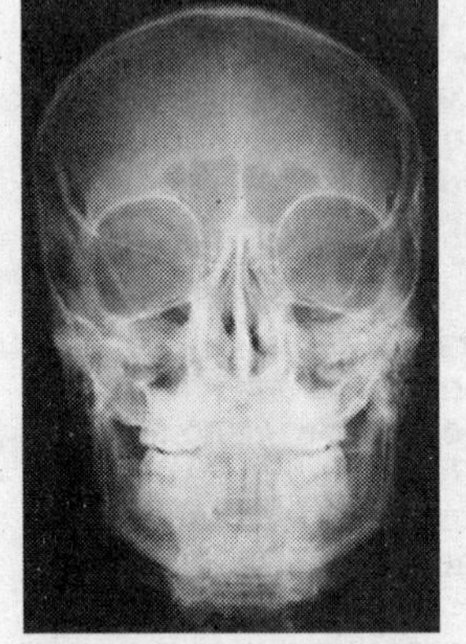

An X ray of a skull can show the structure of the bones in the skull.

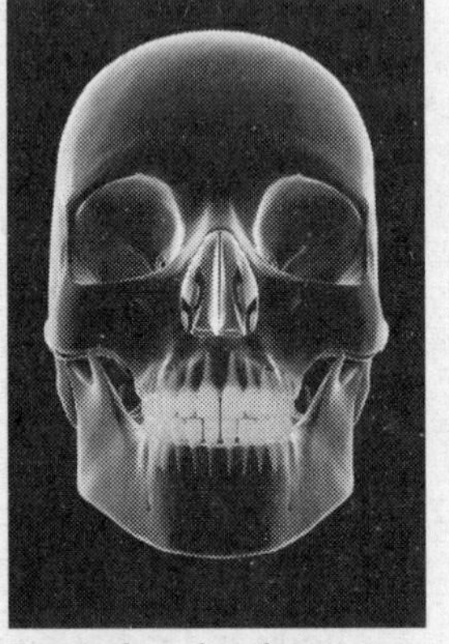

Forensic scientists may use computer models of skulls to study them in more detail.

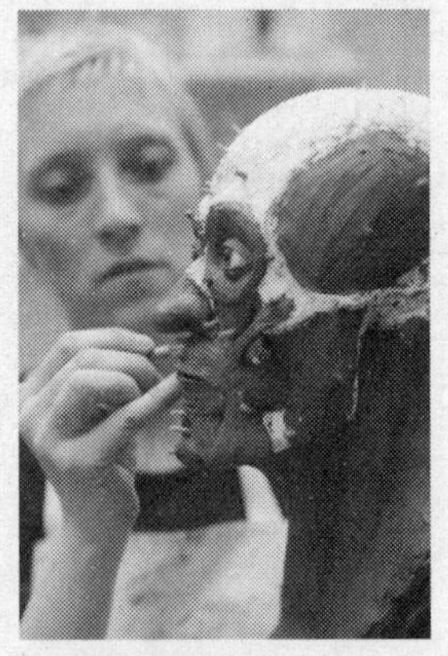

In some cases, scientists make clay models of a person's face based on the skull.

Much of the evidence gathered at a crime scene is used to try to identify the perpetrator. Evidence such as fingerprints and trace evidence can show that a person was present at a crime scene. This can help investigators prove that a particular suspect carried out the murder.

Name ______________________ Class ______________ Date ______________

Section 3 Review

SECTION VOCABULARY

algor mortis the cooling of the body following death **livor mortis** after death, the settling of the blood to the lowest point in the body, which causes a red to purple discoloration of the skin; also called hypostasis	**rigor mortis** temporary stiffness of muscles after death

1. **Describe** What is the first thing that investigators do at a crime scene?

____

____

2. **Compare** What is the difference between algor mortis and livor mortis?

____

____

3. **Apply Concepts** A forensic scientist is examining a dead body. She observes that the muscles in the body are completely stiff, that lividity is fixed, and that the body has cooled by about 18°F. The body shows no visible signs of decomposition. About how long ago did the person probably die? Explain your answer.

____

____

____

____

4. **Infer** A forensic pathologist examines a dead body. He determines that the cause of death was several stab wounds to the person's chest. What is the most likely manner of death for the person? Explain your answer.

____

____

____

____

5. **Identify** What are the two things that a homicide investigation generally focuses on?

____

____

Photography Credits

Abbreviations used: (t) top, (b), bottom, (c) center, (l) left, (r) right, (bkgd) background

Page 2 Deep Light Productions/Photo Researchers; **3** Victoria Smith/HRW; **16** Peter Menzel/Photo Researchers; **18** Mark Maio/King-Holmes/Photo Researchers; **20** Mike Johnson; **21** Andrew Dunn; **35** ER Degginger/Color-Pic; **40** (b) Jason Brindel Photography/Alamy Photos; (t) Brian Wheeler/VIREO; (c) D. Robert & Lorri Franz/CORBIS; **46** ABPL/Daryl Balfour/Animals Animals/Earth Scenes; **56** Lester Lefkowitz/CORBIS; **65** Richard Price/Getty Images; **76** (tl) Lawrence Naylor/Photo Researchers; (tr) Eddy Marissen/Foto Natura/Minden Pictures; (br) IT Stock International/Jupiter Images; (bl) Age FotoStock/SuperStock; **77** (tl) Dr. George Chapman/Visuals Unlimited; (cl) Clouds Hill Imaging/CORBIS; (cr) Photo Insolite Realite/SPL/Photo Researchers; **83** (c,l,r) Dr. David M. Phillips/Visuals Unlimited; **88** Michael Newman/PhotoEdit; **116** (tc,tl,tr) PhotoDisc/Getty Images; (cl) Jason Burns/Ace/Phototake; (c) Yorgos Nikas/Tony Stone/Getty Images; (cr) David M. Phillips/Visuals Unlimited; **121** (bl) Christian Grzimek/Okapia/Photo Researchers; (br) Barry Runk/Grant Heilman Photography; **129** (tl) Dan Guravich/Photo Researchers; (tr) Tom Walker/Tony Stone/Getty Images; **136** Dr. Gopal Murti/SPL/Photo Researchers; **138** Louie Psihoyos/CORBIS; **165** (l) David Hosking/Alamy; (c) Images & Stories/Alamy; (r) Adrienne Gibson/Animals Animals/Earth Scenes; **185** (l) Norbert Wu; (c) WorldSat; (r) Doug Perrine/SeaPics; **188** (wolf) Maresa Pryor/Animals Animals/Earth Scenes; (cheetah) Winfried Wisniewski/Foto Natura/Minden Pictures; (teen) Simon Marcus/CORBIS; (shark) Masa Ushioda/Seapics; (sponge) Doug Perrine/Seapics; (paramecium) Dr. Dennis Kunkel/Visuals Unlimited; (leopard) Angela Scott/Nature Picture Library; (lion) Martin Harvey/NHPA; **190** (r) Michael & Patricia Fogden/Minden Pictures; (cr) Roger Harris/Photo Researchers; (c) John Erlach/Animals Animals/Earth Scenes; (cl) James Watt/Animals Animals/Earth Scenes; (l) James Robinson/Animals Animals/Earth Scenes; **204** Spike Walker/Getty Images; **208** Dr. Dennis Kunkel/Phototake; **215** CNRI/Science Photo Library/Photo Researchers; **223** (br) Dennis Kunkel/Phototake; (tr) Linda Sims/Visuals Unlimited; (l) Gregory G. Dimijian, M.D./Photo Researchers; **224** (tl) Dr. Stanley Flegler/Visuals Unlimited; (bl) Kent Wood; (br) Dennis Kunkel/Phototake; **238** (b) Victoria Smith/HRW; **255** (bl) Brand X Pictures; (br) Paul Hein/Unicorn; **258** Larry Mellichamp/Visuals Unlimited; **259** Runk/Shoenberger/Grant Heilman Photography; **261** (l) R. Calentine/Visuals Unlimited; (c) Dwight Kuhn; (r) Herb Charles Ohlmeyer; **262** (cl) Runk/Schoenberger/Grant Heilman Photography; (cr) Royalty Free/CORBIS; (r) Runk/Schoenberger/Grant Heilman Photography; (l) PhotoDisc/Getty Images; **266** Robert P. Comport/Animals Animals/Earth Scenes; **268** National Geographic Image Collection/Bianca Lavies; **273** (tl) Cathlyn Melloan/Getty Images; (bl) Ed Reschke/Peter Arnold; (br) Joel Arrington/Visuals Unlimited; **274** (bl) Barry Rice/Visuals Unlimited; (br) D. Heuclin/Peter Arnold; **278** (t) Norbert Wu/Minden Pictures; (c) Art Wolfe/Tony Stone Images; (b) Fabio Liverani/Nature Picture Library; **283** (l) Joyce and Frank Burek/Animals Animals/Earth Scenes; (c) Purestock/SuperStock; (r) Michael and Patricia Fogden/Minden Pictures; **288** (c) Mike Parry/Minden Pictures; **289** Zigmund Leszczynski/Animals Animals/Earth Scenes; **290** S. Nielsen/DRK Photo; **291** Frans Lanting/Minden Pictures; **302** James King-Holmes/Photo Researchers; **306** (bl) Meul/Arco/Nature Picture Library; (br) Fred Bavendam/Minden Pictures; (t) Rod Clarke/John Downer Productions/Nature Picture Library; **307** (br) Andrew Syred, Science Source/Photo Researchers; (tl) David Shale/Nature Picture Library; (tr) Stephen Frink/CORBIS; (tc) Norbert Wu/Minden Pictures; **309** Age Fotostock/SuperStock; **310** (tl) Chris Newbert/Minden Pictures; (b) Bill Beatty/Animals Animals/Earth Scenes; (tr) Kim Taylor/Nature Picture Library; **312** Leroy Simon/Visuals Unlimited; **320** John Mitchell/Jupiter Images; **325** Breck P. Kent/Animals Animals/Earth Scenes; **330** Breck P. Kent/Animals Animals/Earth Scenes; **333** Chris Mattison; Frank Lane Picture Agency/CORBIS; **337** (tl) Joseph T. Collins/Photo Researchers; (tr) Juan Manuel Renjifo/Animals Animals/Earth Scenes; (bl) Joe McDonald/CORBIS; (br) Adam Jones/Photo Researchers; **344** A. Witte/C. Mahaney/Stone/Getty Images; **345** Jonathan Blair/CORBIS; **346** (l) Dr. E. R. Degginger/Color-Pic; (r) Art Wolfe/Photo Researchers; **356** (b,t) Sergio Purtell/Foca/HRW; **359** (b) Tom McHugh/Photo Researchers; **366** Erich Lessing/Art Resource; **369** (r) George Schaller; (l) Davis/Lynn Images; (c) Theo Allofs/Visuals Unlimited; **370** (t) Ken M. Highfill/Photo Researchers; (b) Dr. Bernd Heinrich; **371** Ray-Operation Migration; **374** (tr) Darlyne A. Murawski/National Geographic; (tl) Mark Moffett/Minden Pictures; (bl) David Kjaer/Nature Picture Library; (br) Creatas/SuperStock; **375** (tl) Theo Allofs/CORBIS; (r) Don Enger/Animals Animals/Earth Scenes; (bl) Frans Lanting/Minden Pictures; **378** (cardiac) Eric V. Grave/Photo Researchers; (skeletal) Dr. John D. Cunningham/Visuals Unlimited; (smooth) Carolina Biological Supply/Phototake; (nervous) John D. Cunningham/Visuals Unlimited; (connective) Ed Reschke/Peter Arnold; (epithelial) G. W. Willis/Stone/Getty Images; **387** Lucille Khornak/Index Stock Imagery; **391** Dr. P. Marazzi/SS/Photo Researchers; **439** Bob Daemmrich/The Image Works; **461** Muaro Fermariello/Photo Researchers; **463** (b) Richard T. Nowitz/CORBIS; **465** (c) Dr. Jurgen Scriba/Photo Researchers; **466** Karen Kasmauski/CORBIS; **468** AP Photo/Mary Altaffer; **470** (l) Silvia Otte/Photonica/Getty Images; (c) 3D4Medicalcom/Getty Images; (r) Michael Donne, University of Manchester/Photo Researchers